SOCIOLOGY

SOCIOLOGY

Traditional and Radical Perspectives

SECOND EDITION

Howard J. Sherman
University of California, Riverside

James L. Wood
San Diego State University

1817

HARPER & ROW, PUBLISHERS, NEW YORK
Cambridge, Philadelphia, St. Louis, San Francisco,
London, Singapore, Sydney, Tokyo

Chapters 9 and 10 have been adapted from Barbara Sinclair Deckard's *The Women's Movement: Political, Socioeconomic, and Psychological Issues,* Third Edition (New York: Harper & Row, 1983). Copyright © 1983 by Harper & Row, Publishers, Inc. Reprinted by permission of Harper & Row.

Portions of lyrics from songs by Bob Dylan appear on page 104 as follows:

Like a Rolling Stone © 1965 Warner Bros. Inc. All rights reserved.

The Times They Are A-Changin' © 1963 Warner Bros. Inc. All rights reserved. Used by permission.

Sponsoring Editor: Alan McClare
Project Editor: Jo-Ann Goldfarb
Cover Design: Katherine Urban
Text Art: ComCom Division of Haddon Craftsmen, Inc.
Production Manager: Jeanie Berke
Production Assistant: Paula Roppolo
Compositor: David E. Seham Associates, Inc.
Printer and Binder: R. R. Donnelley & Sons Company
Cover Printer: Lynn Art Offset Corporation

Sociology: Traditional and Radical Perspectives, Second Edition

Library of Congress Cataloging in Publication Data

Sherman, Howard J.
    Sociology, traditional and radical perspectives / Howard J.
Sherman, James L. Wood.—2nd Ed.
        p.   cm.
    Includes bibliographies and indexes.
    ISBN 0-06-046111-X
    1. Sociology. 2. Radicalism. 3. Sociology—United States.
I. Wood. James L., 1941– . II. Title.
    HM51.S518   1989   88-25961
    301—dc19   CIP

88 89 90 91 9 8 7 6 5 4 3 2 1

Dedicated with love to
Lisa and Paul Sherman
and
Maxine, Jay, and David Wood

Contents

CONTENTS

Part Five
SOCIAL EVOLUTION   359

Preface

This book offers an introduction to radical sociology, as well as an introduction to and critique of traditional sociology. *Radical sociology* attempts to view social arrangements from the perspective of oppressed groups—such as the poor, the unemployed, blue-collar workers, blacks and other minorities, and women. From this view it carefully analyzes the major institutions of our society. It asks how these institutions—social, political, and economic—evolved into their present forms. It asks who benefits from these institutions and if a major change in our society is possible and necessary. Finally, radical sociology considers possible alternatives to the present social organization.

Traditional sociology, in contrast, tends to view social arrangements from the perspective of established society, though often from a liberal standpoint. It tends to portray existing arrangements as fair and just, peaceful and harmonious. In addition, traditional sociology often assumes that it is difficult to make fundamental changes in the status quo. Thus, traditional sociology often supports—implicitly or explicitly—the dominant role in our society of large corporations with their allies in government. When traditional sociology deals with change, it usually focuses on limited reforms, such as the lessening of poverty, the reduction of prejudice against minorities, and the securing of voting rights for all Americans. Rarely does it emphasize the need for broad social change. Traditional sociology remains dominant in most universities, although it has lately been challenged by a more radical or critical approach to the discipline, as detailed in Part One.

A UNIFIED SOCIAL SCIENCE

Traditional sociologists ignore some important issues because they have a narrow view of the subject matter of their discipline and rigidly categorize the social sciences into fields that never overlap. For example, some traditional sociological studies are based on surveys of the attitudes of a particular social group—such as the unemployed, whites, youths, males, females, drug addicts, police, or criminals—and do not go beyond an analysis of these attitudes, which makes the studies incomplete.

When traditional sociologists examine the attitudes of the unemployed, they seldom look at other crucially related aspects of unemployment. The causes of unemployment are left to economists, while the political impact and the mechanisms of political struggles surrounding unemployment are left to political scientists; the periodic pattern of unemployment in the history of the United States is left to historians. As we shall see, this prevents traditional social science disciplines from looking at social problems as a whole. It also means that problems that fall between the different, narrowly defined disciplines are hardly investigated at all.

Radicals emphasize the need for a unified social science. For this reason, although we treat many of the same problems that traditional sociologists do, this book considers them more broadly. Radicals do not hesitate to follow problems such as those of race, sex, or class into areas usually defined as political science, economics, anthropology, psychology, or history. There is no way to understand the full implications of a subject like race without examining all these aspects.

Of course, it is perfectly legitimate—and often necessary—for a single research study to concentrate on only one aspect of a problem such as the economics or psychology of an issue. *But* it is usually illegitimate to draw public policy conclusions from such a limited study. One should integrate a particular factual study into a unified social science framework in order to investigate all its relevant aspects before drawing policy conclusions. We hope to show how to undertake such an investigation in this book.

PLAN OF THE BOOK

This book has a different organization from the first edition, being divided into five sections instead of three. The new organization is aimed at further clarifying the ideas underlying specific topics of the book. Part One introduces the basic concepts of traditional and radical sociology and shows how these perspectives lead to differing analyses of social organization, poverty, and social class. In Part Two, the contrasting traditional and radical approaches are used to analyze several social institutions and processes, such as modern industry and work alienation, the family, and the socialization of males and females into adult roles. Part Three examines several consequences of social institutions, including sexism, racism, and economic exploitation. Part Four focuses on political institutions and political movements. The role of social class in politics is examined, as are the movements of less powerful groups to organize politically to attain a greater share of society's resources. Finally, Part Five focuses on broad patterns of social change, in which several sequences of social evolution are discussed. To sum up, the contrasting perspectives of traditional and radical sociology are applied to the understanding of social institutions and processes, to the consequences of these institutions, to political movements aimed at redressing inequities arising from them, and to large-scale social changes throughout history that have periodically benefited oppressed and subordinated groups.

Along with the new book organization, a new Chapter 6, on culture, has been added to amplify comparisons of traditional and radical sociology in areas familiar to many readers, such as popular music and American values. Chapter 6 also aims at presenting several key topics of traditional sociology—such as norms, values, and sanctions—more directly than in the first edition. In addition to up-dating the book in terms of recent studies and ideas, other new topics have been included, such as an appendix to Chapter 15 on theories of the state in capitalist society and a new discussion in Chapter 9 on changing male-female relationships.

A decade has produced changes in both traditional and radical sociology. These perspectives—much like other aspects of the world during this period—have not remained static. Yet basic differences between them persist, and these differences will be the focus of our attention throughout the book.

ACKNOWLEDGMENTS

This book would not have been written without the initial suggestion by Harold Levinson. We are grateful to Shirlee Pigeon, who did an excellent job of prelim-inary editing of parts of the book. We also wish to thank all those who did such a superior job typing different parts of the manuscript: Mary Kaufman, Shirlee Pigeon, Madeleine Scott, and Andrea Valentine. Betty Lovejoy did an outstanding job of proofreading the book. Alan McClare and Jo-Ann Goldfarb did outstanding editorial work for the book; their efforts are greatly appreciated.

Barbara Sinclair is coauthor of Chapters 8–11. Chapters 9 and 10, on so-cialization and on marriage, have been adapted from her book, Barbara Sinclair Deckard, *The Women's Movement*, 3d ed. (New York: Harper & Row, 1983). Her work also provides the basis for much of the material on the origin of the family and on sex discrimination.

Robert Blauner deserves special thanks for his participation in this project. He read two early drafts of our manuscript and commented on them extensively. His constructive suggestions and lucid, thoughtful comments have been of great value.

Since this book covers many subjects, we were fortunate to receive useful criticisms from specialists in various fields: from professors of sociology Pat Allen, Edna Bonacich, Robert Blauner, Paul Crook, G. William Domhoff, Gary T. Marx, Samuel Oliner, Irwin Sperber, Diana Tumminid, Norma Wikler, and Elena Yu; from professors of economics William Darity, Jr., Robert Heilbroner, E. K. Hunt, Clinton Jencks, and Howard Wachtel; from professors of political science Michael Harrington, Michael Levin, Max Nieman, Bertell Ollman, and Barbara Sinclair; from a professor of history, Irwin Wall; from a professor of anthropology, Pauline Kolenda; and from five graduate students, Alan Baron, William Harnett, Barney Hope, Robert Kneisel, and Patrick Blake, who also assisted in research on Chapter 13. Various academic reviewers made many thoughtful comments for which we thank:

Roger Cook, *SUNY-Buffalo*
Ted Goertzel, *Rutgers University*
Donald Hayes, *Sam Houston State University*
R. George Kirkpatrick, *San Diego State University*
Donald McQuarie, *Bowling Green State University*
Fred Pincus, *University of Maryland Baltimore County*
Robert Wood, *Rutgers University*

Additional useful comments were given by Patricia A. Wood, Ann M. Wood, and Jeffrey J. Wood. Many of these colleagues saw only early drafts of the manuscript and disagreed with us on various issues. We are very grateful to all of them for their comments; yet only the authors bear final responsibility for the analysis of this book.

Howard J. Sherman
James L. Wood

A Note on Traditional and Radical Sociology Over the Past Decade

This discussion is especially addressed to those who were familiar with the first edition of this book, published in 1979 (or at least familiar with the main trends in sociology up to 1979), as well as with the trends in sociology after 1979. For the most part, professional sociologists are the principal audience for this commentary on the changes and continuities in the discipline as they pertain to the major themes of the book.

In the decade since *Sociology: Traditional and Radical Perspectives* first appeared, there have been both convergence and divergence in the two sociological approaches discussed here. Traditional sociology has become somewhat more flexible, occasionally including radical analyses in its main journals and book publications. The two most prestigious journals of traditional sociology, *American Sociological Review* and *American Journal of Sociology,* have both published lead articles by radical sociologists (Burawoy and Lukács, 1985; Burawoy, 1984). Other radical sociologists have likewise on occasion contributed to prestigious journals such as these or have been published by major book publishers (Offe, 1984; Bluestone and Harrison, 1982; Griffen, Devine, and Wallace, 1982; Katznelson, 1981; Wright and Perrone, 1977). The *Annual Review of Sociology* has similarly included some topics of interest to radical sociology as well as some authors from that perspective (Block, 1981; Jaret, 1983; Glasberg and Schwartz, 1983). At times, critical and insightful works, such as those of Erving Goffman and Gary Marx, emerge from the academy (see Chapter 6).

In addition, discussions about the social or political impact of the class system may appear in the publications of traditional sociology (Useem and Karabel, 1986; Rubin, 1986; Ricketts, 1987). Similarly, topics such as oppression or deprivation based on race, gender, and age have appeared in traditionalist publications (Bridges, Crutchfield, and Simpson, 1987; Tienda, Smith, and Ortiz, 1987; Johnson, O'Brien, and Hudson, 1985).

Radical sociology has, to a degree, moderated its class analysis. In several discussions of political democracy in capitalist society, the state is portrayed as at least partly independent of the capitalist class (Carnoy, 1984; Levin, 1988; Bowles and Gintis, 1986; Block, 1977). Few radical thinkers currently argue that the government is simply the "executive committee of the capitalist class" or that only corporate executives run the government (Block, 1977). Some radical thinkers have attempted to show how family relations, love, and community cohesiveness can develop in today's society (Lerner, 1986; Bowles and Gintis, 1986). There has been some rethinking of the most appropriate role that progressive movements from the 1960s could play in the 1980s and 1990s (Lerner, 1986, 1988).

For the most part, however, traditional and radical sociology remain distinct in their aims and analyzes. Radical sociology continues to focus on oppressed or subordinated groups, such as ethnic minorities, the aged, and women, and it particularly analyzes the effects of unequal social class position on these groups (Reich, 1981; Katsiaficas and Kirkpatrick, 1987; Omvedt, 1986). The notion of *applied sociology* often means solving organizational or practical problems for traditional sociology, whereas it means ending oppression and subordination for radical sociology (ASA *Footnotes,* 1975–1987; Katsiaficas and Kirkpatrick, 1987; Flacks and Turkel, 1978). Traditional sociology remains more detached, or "value neutral," in its analysis of social issues generally, and in its own discussions of subordinated groups (Kaufman, 1986; Fitzpatrick and Logan, 1985; de Vaus and McAllister, 1987). This detachment can legitimize the study of social problems because the investigator appears to be using only scientific criteria—not his or her personal value judgments—to understand conditions like poverty or unemployment. However, this detachment can also, at least implicitly, support the status quo of existing inequalities, since changing inequalities and oppressive social conditions are not emphasized in such discussions.

The analyses of traditional sociology can point to needed social reforms (Dreeben and Gamoran, 1986). Yet traditional sociology often deemphasizes the impact of social class position on less privileged groups, thereby omitting a major obstacle less privileged groups face in improving their circumstances (Fossett, Galle, and Kelly, 1986; Curtis, 1986; Atchley, 1982). Studies of educational achievement, for example, that do not stress financial and other difficulties posed by a lower (or even middle) social class background on obtaining an outstanding higher education are omitting an important obstacle that many face in getting this kind of education. Similarly, traditional sociology deemphasizes the importance of social class on distribution of political power, thereby omitting a major obstacle to significant democratization of society (Orum, 1978; Domhoff, 1983). Studies of power distribution in the United States that do not stress the influence of wealth on obtaining political power, for example, are omitting an important obstacle to shaping public policy that most citizens face. More generally, traditional sociology includes several topics that tend to deemphasize the role of social class, such as the effects of sibling birth order on achievement, self-concept, and gender differences in religion (Blake, 1985; Gecas, 1982; de Vaus and McAllister, 1987). Traditional sociology has even occasionally argued *for* the negative effects on privileged groups of improvements for less privileged groups (Glazer, 1975; Wharton and Baron, 1987).

Traditional and radical sociology thus continue, to a significant degree, to go their separate ways. This second edition shows continued divergence, as well as occasional convergence, of these two perspectives in its examination of social institutions such as the family, education, politics, and the economy, and in its examination of social processes such as socialization, protests, and social change.

Convergence between the two perspectives is especially reflected in discussions where less sharp distinctions between the approaches are drawn, as in some analyses of aging, protests, and culture. Convergence also occurs where radical sociology has somewhat deemphasized its class analysis, as in recent theories of the state, or where traditional sociology has incorporated more radical themes, as in its analysis of deprivation based on gender.

Yet, divergence of the two perspectives is apparent throughout the book. Contrasting analyses are presented for numerous topics, including poverty, stratification, race relations, social change, education, and power distribution. While cross-fertilization of ideas among scholars from different viewpoints has occurred during the past decade, important differences between traditional and radical sociology remain. These differences constitute the analytical framework of this book.

REFERENCES

ASA *Footnotes.* 1975–1987. Newsletter of the American Sociological Association.

Atchley, Robert C. 1982. "Retirement as a Social Institution." *Annual Review of Sociology* 8:263–287.

Blake, Judith. 1985. "Number of Siblings and Educational Mobility." *American Sociological Review* 50 (February):84–94.

Block, Fred. 1981. "The Fiscal Crisis of the Capitalist State." *Annual Review of Sociology* 7:1–27.

Block, Fred. 1977. "The Ruling Class Does Not Rule: Notes on the Marxist Theory of the State." *Socialist Revolution* 7:6–28.

Bluestone, Barry, and Bennett Harrison. 1982. *The Deindustrialization of America.* New York: Basic Books.

Bowles, Samuel, and Herbert Gintis. 1986. *Democracy and Capitalism.* New York: Basic Books.

Bridges, George S., Robert D. Crutchfield, and Edith E. Simpson. 1987. "Crime, Social Structure and Criminal Punishment: White and Nonwhite Rates of Imprisonment." *Social Problems* 34 (October):345–361.

Burawoy, Michael. 1984. "Karl Marx and the Satanic Mills: Factory Politics under Early Capitalism in England, the United States, and Russia." *American Journal of Sociology* 90 (September):274–282.

———, and János Lukács. 1985. "Mythologies of Work: A Comparison of Firms in State Socialism and Advanced Capitalism." *American Sociological Review* 50 (December):723–737.

Carnoy, Martin. 1984. *The State and Political Theory.* Princeton, NJ: Princeton University Press.

Curtis, Richard F. 1986. "Household and Family in Theory on Inequality." *American Sociological Review* 51 (April):168–183.

de Vaus, David, and Ian McAllister. 1987. "Gender Differences in Religion: A Test of the Structural Location Theory." *American Sociological Review* 52 (August):472–481.

Domhoff, G. William. 1983. *Who Rules America Now? A View for the '80s*. Englewood Cliffs, NJ: Prentice-Hall.

Dreeben, Robert, and Adam Gamoran. 1986. "Race, Instruction, and Learning." *American Sociological Review* 51 (October):660–669.

Fitzpatrick, Kevin M., and John R. Logan. 1985. "The Aging of the Suburbs, 1960–1980." *American Sociological Review* 50 (February):106–117.

Flacks, Richard, and Gerald Turkel. 1978. "Radical Sociology: The Emergence of Neo-Marxian Perspectives in U.S. Sociology." *Annual Review of Sociology* 4:193–238.

Fossett, Mark A., Omer R. Galle, and William R. Kelly. 1986. "Racial Occupational Inequality, 1940–1980: National and Regional Trends." *American Sociological Review* 51 (June):421–429.

Gecas, Viktor. 1982. "The Self-Concept." *Annual Review of Sociology* 8:1–33.

Glasberg, Davita Silfen, and Michael Schwartz. 1983. "Ownership and Control of Corporations." *Annual Review of Sociology* 9:311–332.

Glazer, Nathan. 1975. *Affirmative Discrimination*. New York: Basic Books.

Griffin, Larry J., Joel A. Devine, and Michael Wallace. 1982. "Monopoly Capital, Organized Labor, and Military Expenditures in the United States, 1949–1976." In Michael Burawoy and Theda Skocpol, eds., *Marxist Inquiries*. Supplement to the *American Journal of Sociology* 88:113–153. Chicago: University of Chicago Press.

Jaret, Charles. 1983. "Recent Neo-Marxist Urban Analysis." *Annual Review of Sociology* 9:499–525.

Johnson, Tanya F., James G. O'Brien, and Margaret F. Hudson, eds. 1985. *Elder Neglect and Abuse*. Westport, CT: Greenwood.

Katsiaficas, George N., and R. George Kirkpatrick. 1987. *Introduction to Critical Sociology*. New York: Irvington Publishers.

Katznelson, Ira. 1981. *City Trenches: Urban Politics and the Patterning of Class in the United States*. New York: Pantheon.

Kaufman, Robert L. 1986. "The Impact of Industrial and Occupational Structure on Black-White Employment Allocation." *American Sociological Review* 51 (June):310–323.

Lerner, Michael. 1986. *Surplus Powerlessness*. Oakland, CA: Institute for Labor and Mental Health.

———. 1988. "The Legacy of the Sixties for the Politics of the Nineties." *TIKKUN* 3, no. 1 (January–February):44–48, 87–91.

Levin, Michael. 1988. *Marx, Engels and Liberal Democracy*. London and Basingstoke: Macmillan.

Offe, Claus. 1984. *Contradictions of the Welfare State*. Cambridge, MA: MIT Press; London: Hutchinson.

Omvedt, Gail. 1986. " 'Patriarchy': The Analysis of Women's Oppression." *The Insurgent Sociologist* 13:30–50.

Orum, Anthony M. 1978. *Introduction to Political Sociology*. Englewood Cliffs, NJ: Prentice-Hall.

Reich, Michael. 1981. *Racial Inequality: A Political-Economic Analysis*. Princeton, NJ: Princeton University Press.

Ricketts, Erol. 1987. "U.S. Investment and Immigration from the Caribbean." *Social Problems* 34 (October):374–387.

Rubin, Beth A. 1986. "Class Struggle American Style: Unions, Strikes and Wages." *American Sociological Review* 51 (October):618–633.

Tienda, Marta, Shelly A. Smith, and Vilma Ortiz. 1987. "Industrial Restructuring, Gender Segregation, and Sex Differences in Earnings." *American Sociological Review* 52 (April):195–210.

Useem, Michael, and Jerome Karabel. 1986. "Pathways to Top Corporate Management." *American Sociological Review* 51 (April):184–200.

Wharton, Amy S., and James N. Baron. 1987. "So Happy Together? The Impact of Gender Segregation on Men at Work." *American Sociological Review* 52 (October):574–587.

Wright, Erik Olin, and Luca Perrone. 1977. "Marxist Class Categories and Income Inequality." *American Sociological Review* 42:32–55.

SOCIOLOGY

one

INTRODUCTION

chapter 1

Alternative Approaches to Sociology

Sociology is the study of human relationships in society. Some important questions in sociology are: Why do prejudice and discrimination exist against minority groups? What are the relationships between the rulers and the ruled, and between the oppressors and the oppressed, in various societies? What are the roles of the family, education, the media, and other institutions in various societies? How do human relationships evolve in one social system as compared to another?

Sociologists do *not* agree on the answers to these questions. They hold many different views both of the answers and even of the proper questions to ask. In political terms, a few sociologists are right-wing conservatives, *most* sociologists are liberals, and some are left-wing radicals. These political outlooks affect their approaches to sociology. As we shall see, the political outlook of sociologists has changed according to the historical period and society in which they have lived, and so have their sociological approaches.

THE CONSERVATIVE OUTLOOK IN MEDIEVAL SOCIETY

According to the dominant ideology in feudal Europe, kings and nobles were divinely ordained to rule by the will of God. Serfs were divinely ordained to work and produce for themselves and for the nobility, while God gave the nobility the duty to give protection, justice, and Christian charity to the serfs. From this viewpoint, social relations were (1) designed by supernatural beings, (2) were ultimately harmonious, and (3) would last forever without change. This is the basis of the conservative outlook—and some elements of it still float beneath the surface of the social sciences, though almost all social scientists explicitly disown such views today.

THE LIBERAL PERSPECTIVE OF MODERN SOCIOLOGISTS

Most modern mainstream sociologists—called *traditional* sociologists in this book—have a liberal perspective of society. Their viewpoint reflects our modern industrialized capitalist society. Our society is characterized by the domination of a relatively small number of enormously wealthy and powerful corporations, as well as by many millions of workers who do the labor in our society and receive wages for their work. Even in our rich society, millions of American families live below the poverty level, due to low wages, unemployment, or inflation. (Unless explicitly stated otherwise, the term American is used in this book to describe citizens of the United States. It is used here for convenience even though it is not accurate, because it ignores the millions of Central or South Americans as well as the Canadians and the citizens of Mexico.)

Most traditional sociologists recognize difficult problems, such as poverty and unemployment. Many suggest the need for more welfare legislation to ameliorate the suffering of the poorest of the working class. These sociologists support the modern liberal view that government has a duty to intervene to reduce poverty and unemployment. This is obviously different from the older view (sometimes called classical liberalism) that argued for a policy of complete laissez faire—that is, noninterference by government in the capitalist economy. Thus, the need for liberal reforms by government is a widespread assumption among many traditional sociologists at the present time.

It is impossible to give a history of traditional sociology in a short space. We shall only mention here two traditional sociologists whose work will come up time and again in this book: Max Weber and Talcott Parsons. Max Weber (1864–1920) was one of the most famous founders of modern liberal sociology, and Talcott Parsons (1902–1979) is perhaps the most famous modern sociologist. Both remain influential in sociology (Sciulli and Gerstein, 1985; Alexander, 1983a, 1983b, 1985).

Weber criticized the remnants of traditional aristocracy in Germany, but he felt that capitalism was basically a rational system. He studied bureaucracy in the capitalist corporation and in the government. He attacked bureaucratic rigidity and narrowness, but felt that it was an inevitable development in all industrial societies. He argued that such bureaucracies are necessary to increase political and economic efficiency by their centralization of power and authority. Although Weber criticized capitalist bureaucracy, he felt bureaucratic rigidity would be even worse under socialism. Thus Weber's works have a two-edged impact, since they expose the inhuman bureaucratic workings of corporations and governments but also accept them as inevitable. Weber also contributed important studies of the origins of modern capitalist forms of organization, as well as pioneering studies of class stratification under capitalism. Both of these contributions will be discussed later in Chapters 4 and 15.

Parsons is the most important proponent of an approach called *functionalism*, which means the investigation of how each social institution—such as the family, religion, and government—operates in relation to the survival of the whole society. Parsons's theory has the liberal implication that those with authority should strive to reform institutions to make the society work more smoothly and efficiently. But he also assumes that society tries to maintain its present structure when faced with possible changes, so some sociologists have seen in it a bias against fundamental change. Parsons's work—and the recent approach of *neofunctionalism*—is discussed in detail in later chapters.

In addition to Parsons, the traditional, or liberal, perspective on sociology—which predominates in American universities—has a diversity of viewpoints within it. Yet most traditional sociologists do have some broad characteristics in common (beside their basic outlook of liberal reform within the capitalist system).

First, many traditional sociologists sharply distinguish sociology from economics, political science, and psychology, each of which has a separate department in most universities. Theoretically, all sociologists would admit the need to work with other related fields and to study problems that overlap several fields. In practice, however, most sociologists tend to leave economics to economists, politics to political scientists, and psychology to psychologists. This leaves some major social problems unexamined because they fall between fields or overlap several fields.

To separate sociology from history is particularly questionable. Many modern mainstream sociologists have largely given up the classical attempt to examine the overall evolution of society. As a result, they in turn often ignore history.

A second feature of traditional sociology is the tendency to analyze how the society reaches a harmonious equilibrium, or how the society functions to maintain its stability. Traditional social scientists do not deny conflict in the abstract (for example, conflict between socioeconomic classes), but they deemphasize it in practice. Many deemphasize major historical changes and revolutions. The conflicts that are acknowledged are usually seen as resolvable by liberal reforms, such as regulations against pollution and dangerous working conditions.

The third feature of traditional, liberal sociology is the notion that all social science should be neutral in terms of political policies. But it is difficult for traditional sociology to be neutral when much of its work has political implications. Most sociologists do believe in the political neutrality of their scientific work even though important sociological conclusions are not usually neutral, as shall be documented in later chapters.

THE OUTLOOK OF RADICAL SOCIOLOGY

Radical sociology attempts to view society from the position of oppressed groups in society, such as the poor, the unemployed, blue-collar workers, blacks and other minorities, and women. From this view it carefully analyzes all of the present institutions of our society. It asks how these institutions—social, political, and economic—evolved into their present forms. It asks who is benefited by the present institutions. It asks if a major change in our society is both possible and necessary. And, finally, radical sociology asks, What are the possible alternatives to our present society?

In the 1960s many sociology students and faculty members participated in the civil rights movement against racial discrimination. Many more sociologists were involved in the movement against the Vietnam War in the middle to late 1960s and early 1970s. From these experiences, as well as from much reading and discussion, they became sensitized to the fact that discrimination and imperialism are traceable to some extent to the basic structure of our capitalist society. This led them toward a radical approach to sociology. Most were influenced by the theories of Karl Marx.

Karl Marx (1818–1883) was the first great radical sociologist. With his friend and collaborator, Frederick Engels (1820–1895), he established a unified radical paradigm for all of the social sciences. Marx's writings, in the period 1840–1880, reflected the misery of the urban working class in the industrial revolution, their increasing numbers in capitalist industry, and their increasing attempts to organize.

Present-day radical sociologists draw their inspiration from Marx, but do not treat his words as sacred dogma. Not only have radicals learned more since Marx wrote, but there are always new conditions and new problems. Therefore, radical sociologists must think for themselves, although it is true that much of the basic radical approach ultimately derives from Marx. Most radical sociologists believe that Marx asked many of the right questions and had a useful method of approach to sociology. On the other hand, Marx was *not* perfect; he did *not* ask every important question in sociology, and he did *not* give all the answers. Radical sociologists reject *any* great man or dogma as a final authority or an ultimate truth.

Radicals who are not Marxists include radical feminists, black nationalists, and anarchists. They are all radicals in the sense that they agree that some basic part of the present socioeconomic system must be changed. But they do not tend to focus on the capitalist system as the primary source of oppression. Instead they focus on sexism, racism, and the government as sources of oppression. Marxist radicals tend to focus on capitalism as the source of various oppressions and inequalities. Moreover, within the Marxist tradition, there are also many very different interpretations of Marx, and of the world, that can be strongly opposed to one another (Vaillancourt, 1986).

In spite of these widely divergent views among radical sociologists, their approach is characterized by some common features. First, radicals emphasize the need for a unified social science. For this reason, although they treat some of the same problems as traditional sociologists, radicals treat them in a much broader way. Radicals do not hesitate to follow problems such as race, sex, or social class into areas usually defined as political science, economics, anthropology, psychology, or history. There is no other way to understand the full origins and implications of such subjects as race or sex without examining all these aspects. Since this book covers the radical approach, there is a much stronger emphasis on historical and economic aspects of society than is common in basic sociology texts. On the other hand, since space is limited, we have been forced to neglect some other usual sociological topics, such as the behavior of small groups (which we believe is less crucial than some other issues) or health-care problems and urban housing (which we would have liked to include).

Second, instead of mainly analyzing harmony and equilibrium in a society, radicals also analyze conflict and change, as well as their causes and results. Thus radicals discuss conflicts among socioeconomic classes, racial conflicts, and conflicts between male and female. They examine how socioeconomic conditions can lead to conflicts that can cause changes in ideology and consciousness, as well as eventual change in the socioeconomic conditions themselves.

Third, radical sociologists recognize that sociology is not neutral in analyzing conflicts between classes, races, or sexes. They attempt to design research questions to examine relevant problems in ways that will aid an exploited or oppressed class, race, or sex. Radicals believe that honest sociological research, which asks the right questions, will aid the most oppressed groups by revealing the true situation in the society.

Within this general outlook, radical sociological analysis tends to have a particular framework. It often concentrates on the relations between ideas about society and actual socioeconomic institutions. It emphasizes that ideas and values do not emerge from nowhere, but arise from the actual living conditions and relations of human beings. It stresses that revolutionary thoughts come from situations of tensions within a society. Thus, in the American Revolution, the views of people like Tom Paine or Thomas Jefferson reflected the oppression keenly felt by the American colonists. In turn, those views helped lead other Americans to a consciously revolutionary outlook. This radical framework of analysis will be examined in detail in Chapter 2.

SUMMARY

In this first chapter we have sketched some differences between radical and traditional sociology. We have seen that radical sociology often focuses on issues that are not central to traditional sociology. Radical sociology is especially concerned with conditions of inequality and oppression and how to change them. Traditional sociology also may discuss these topics, but it does not emphasize them.

Three main points of difference between radical and traditional sociologists are as follows. First, most traditional sociologists view sociology more narrowly and keep it distinct from other social sciences. Radical sociologists attempt to build a unified social science including political, economic, and historical aspects.

Second, many traditional sociologists—such as Talcott Parsons—view the main task of sociology as the explanation of how our present social system maintains its stability, particularly which institutions promote harmony and cohesiveness. Radical sociologists stress that conflicts within society (such as the conflict between slaves and slave owners) can lead to changes, sometimes even to revolutionary changes that result in entirely new societies.

Third, although most traditional sociologists advocate liberal reforms, many claim that their sociology is politically neutral and value-free. Radical sociologists believe that it is difficult, if not impossible, to have a neutral sociology. They therefore assert that their own sociological research will center on questions that are relevant to the interests of oppressed groups such as the majority of workers, minorities, and women.

It must be stressed that this brief discussion does not do full justice to either traditional or radical sociology. Both contain many different positions on any given point, with wide disagreements *within* each school. Later chapters will spell out and compare some of the most important positions in detail.

APPENDIX: Disputes About Approaches

What is a scientific method? It is the way a sociologist systematically investigates and discovers the facts and ideas of sociology. In feudal Europe the medieval scholars believed that all knowledge of society came from revelations from God. Their arguments were all based on "authorities"—the Bible, St. Augustine, or St. Thomas Aquinas—who in turn had been granted revealed knowledge by God.

Toward the end of the feudal period, with the beginnings of capitalist industry and commerce, concrete technological knowledge became increasingly important. In this context, natural scientists like Galileo rejected all these authorities and decided to examine the actual world around them. Rather than accept the word of various authorities on how fast two objects would drop, Galileo experimented by actually dropping two objects. The medieval establishment—particularly the Church—objected to this scientific mode of investigation. In contrast, in the last few centuries of capitalist society, except under the most dictatorial governments, the natural sciences have mostly been allowed to base themselves on real-world observation and experiments.

ABSTRACT THEORY VERSUS EMPIRICISM

In the eighteenth century, some people maintained that it was not necessary to gather any facts, that pure rational speculation was sufficient to understand the social world. Writers such as Jean Jacques Rousseau created imaginative—but fanciful—schemas of social evolution with little factual basis.

Rousseau's theory was very progressive in its inception because it claimed that human beings could think out any problem for themselves, without being bound by the God-given revelations of previous authorities. The medieval authorities proclaimed that kings were chosen by God and ruled by divine right. Rousseau thought about the issue and decided instead that it was the natural right of every man to be equal in political decision making (but Rousseau did *not* think that women were naturally equal).

The nineteenth century saw many elaborate schemas of the evolution of society, such as that of Herbert Spencer, often based more on theoretical speculation than systematic empirical investigation. Since then, as we shall see, many social scientists have swung to the opposite extreme. There remain only a few sociologists who continue to develop abstract and elaborate "grand theory." The late Talcott Parsons is the best-known such thinker in the modern period. Though it may contain many insights, the problem with such grand theorizing in sociology is its tendency to obscure many of the most important—and unpleasant—facts of the real world, such as exploitation and racist oppression.

Most practicing sociologists have deemphasized grand theories because they have found that these abstract theories have little to say about concrete issues. Indeed, many sociologists tend toward an empiricist view that sociological research should emphasize empirical investigations and the analysis of facts.

The "facts" are defined as all those items of knowledge that the sociologist has discovered. The facts may be discovered, for example, through interviews with people or examination of historical data. These facts relate to what is chosen as the sociological issue under investigation. A few traditional sociologists even go as far as to view all theories as, at best, a sort of summary of the facts and, at worst, useless conceptualizing.

Most traditional sociology texts recognize the need for both theory and facts. In practice, however, many traditional sociologists are data gatherers, accumulating facts with less attention to broader theoretical issues. "Sticking to the facts" means that they tend to investigate narrower problems while ignoring the big, controversial ones (for example, the causes of sexism or the Vietnam War). Empirical analyses of narrower topics are often publishable in sociology journals—and such publication leads to promotions in universities. The process by which sociologists narrow down their analyses to a limited focus is usually not conscious because this view is often taken for granted by senior professors and colleagues.

Radicals criticize *both* the grand theories *and* the narrow empirical studies for the same tendency to deemphasize major historical conflicts and changes. Marx's materialist method directs sociologists to derive their knowledge from observation, experiment, and participation in the real material and social world. Marx and Engels note: "The premises from which we begin are not arbitrary ones, not dogmas, but real premises from which abstraction can only be made in the imagination" (Marx and Engels, 1847, pp. 6–7). By real premises he clearly refers to our knowledge about live human beings in the context of their actual life and work situations. Marx and Engels go on to conclude, "These premises can thus be verified in a purely empirical way" (ibid., p. 7).

Yet Marx also rejects simplistic empiricism (separation of facts from theory) and wraps his facts together in a tight theoretical framework. Marxists and radicals have always criticized empiricism just as much as they have criticized grand abstract theorizing. Empiricism is criticized on two grounds. First, one cannot choose problems, collect facts, or interpret facts without a theoretical framework. Contrary to the empiricists, theory and fact are inseparable parts of one continuing scientific process. We cannot do without theory in empirical research, and if a sociologist claims to collect facts with no theory, then he or she is likely just using a theory implicitly and unconsciously instead of explicitly and consciously. Furthermore, the implicit theory is usually influenced by the dominant social ideology or set of social myths. Second, in the practice of sociological research, this often means not only unconscious acceptance of the dominant ideology, but also concentration on easily quantifiable smaller problems and neglect of the larger controversial problems. Radicals urge the need to examine facts, but always in a clear theoretical framework.

In sociology, it is often difficult to conduct experiments. We usually cannot hold all the important factors but one constant, while allowing only one social factor to vary. Therefore, sociologists must use the tool of abstraction. At first, we seem to face a huge mass of unrelated facts. By using our theoretical scalpel, we can cut away or ignore the many irrelevant facts in the study. We *abstract* as facts only those items of knowledge that seem relevant to the social issue under investigation. Then we arrange our ideas about the facts into a tighter and tighter theory. By abstracting from irrelevancies, our theory (or model of society) becomes more general and more applicable to a wide range of real problems. In this way, a well-balanced sociology tries to combine broad theories with careful factual studies.

SCIENTIFIC FACTS AND HUMANIST ETHICAL VALUES

Traditional sociologists have tried to separate empirical facts from ethical values in a manner that has caused much confusion. When this distinction was first made, it constituted a major advance in scientific method. In the Middle Ages, science and theology were inseparable. In economics, for example, the normal price wasn't just average, but it was "good" according to Aquinas. In politics, monarchy wasn't just useful, but it was divinely ordained. In religion, criminals were not merely bad for society, but they were direct agents of the Devil.

The philosopher David Hume first emphasized the view that ethics should be separated from science. He argued that no accumulation of facts can lead to an ethical value judgment and that no value judgment tells us anything about actual relationships. Thus scientists should keep their values separate from science. This positivist view, emphasizing the independence of scientific facts, did help liberate science from theology.

Now, however, the logical distinction between fact and value has been extended to a portrayal of traditional sociology as objective and value-free. Various traditional sociologists feel that their research should be essentially free of ethical values.

It is true that facts and values can logically be separated, but the problem is what sociologists do in *practice*. In actual practice there is usually an intimate relationship between the ethical values of most sociologists and what they do in their sociological research.

In practice, any sociologist *must* make decisions involving ethical judgments and preferences at every step of research. First, some particular material must be selected for study, while other material is ignored. For example, does the sociologist investigate styles of dress in the nineteenth century *or* the current problem that black unemployment rates are twice as high as white unemployment rates? Both the focus and the policy results are quite different; yet the selection depends on one's ethical judgment of what is important to study. Second, which facts does the sociologist choose to collect from the infinite available ones? Again, this means that the sociologist does indeed have preferences about the selection of certain facts to study, since he or she will ignore other facts. Third, the sociologist must determine which facts are fully supported and which are merely false interpretations; thus one's preferences again are given much room to influence decisions. Fourth, having picked an array of "hard facts," the sociologist must still decide which are relevant and what model is to be used to interpret them. In choosing a theoretical model or framework of interpretation, the sociologist's choice will usually depend in part upon ethical judgments. Fifth, even in the statement of supposed scientific conclusions, policy evaluations and suggestions will often be implied. Thus, if one describes misery on a slave plantation, it is hardly necessary to explicitly recommend abolition of slavery. Conversely, if the plantation is described as a joyous place of happy slaves, the opposite implication can be drawn. Thus ethical preferences and preconceptions do condition the way that facts are selected and interpreted in the social sciences.

One example of sexist preconception by a traditional social psychologist, in a paper by David Campbell called "The Clash Between Beautiful Women and Science" (1971), was presented at the American Psychological Association meetings in 1968. His thesis is that beauty and scientific ability are mutually exclusive in women. Campbell used a questionnaire asking women their interests. From his many statistical correlations he found that women Ph.D. chemists and Ph.D. mathematicians are less interested in being actresses, artists, dancers, or "the first to wear the very latest fashions" than are top fashion models, airline stewardesses, or TV entertainers. Big surprise! Campbell says "the correlational relationship is clear—scientific interests and beauty in women are antagonistic. . . ." (1971, p. 129). One reason women scientists are ugly and dull, according to him, is that training for a scientific career "may dampen one's livelier instincts." Another reason, he asserts, is that all the pretty women students get married, leaving only the ugly ones to go for a Ph.D. More "evidence" he gives is: "Of the last 78 Playmates (in *Playboy*) only three of these spectacularly displayed women have expressed any interest in scientific activities" (1971, p. 139). Here is the *form* of objective, value-free social psychology, but the *content* is dominated by a pronounced sexist bias.

Similarly, the social historian T. Harry Williams describes the abolitionist movement against slavery with all the popular biased terms used by the apologists of slavery. He claims that the abolitionists were "radical . . . zealous . . . fiery, scornful, revolutionary . . . spirit of fanaticism . . . hasty Jacobins, aggressive, vindictive, narrowly sectional . . . bitter, sputtering, fanatical, impractical . . . extreme" (quoted in Zinn, 1978, p. 130). This is *not* a value-free description.

In the radical or Marxist view, sociology must be based on a materialist scientific method *and* must be guided by humanist ethics—that is, values supporting oppressed groups. A sociologist without humanist ethics is incomplete. At the same time, humanist ethical values without sociological analysis cannot help us understand—or change—the world. Radicals incorporate humanist values into science. They select problems according to criteria of social relevancy and interpret the problems in terms of appropriate social theory, solidly grounded in humanist ethical values.

In the process of sociological research, radicals begin with certain ethical values, as well as previous facts and theories. Then they do research and experience the world, thereby learning new facts and modifying theories. If we are open-minded and willing to learn, this experience will also modify, deepen, and extend our ethical values. Viewed as a process, both ethical values and scientific knowledge evolve together.

In our present social reality, the main value judgment is, Which side are you on? Is the sociologist on the side of the ruler and oppressor, such as the capitalist class, the white majority, and dominant males? Or is the sociologist on the side of the ruled and the oppressed, such as the working class, blacks and Chicanos, and women? Unfortunately, many sociologists have mainly operated in the interests of the rulers. Yet there are also radical or critical sociologists opposing these ruling interests.

The social class approach makes all political issues concrete. There is neither an abstract right of revolution nor an abstract right to defend the government. The government in each society mainly represents the dominant social class, which will defend it and resist fundamental change. Other classes may find that the government oppresses them and as a result may fight for revolutionary change, as the slaves fought against slavery. Radical morality thus derives from the interests of the poor, the oppressed and the working class. In sociology this means investigating oppression and class conflicts, as well as dispelling inaccurate social myths.

To champion the interests of the oppressed does *not* mean that radicals either try to perpetuate social divisions or narrowly favor the short-term interests of one class or group. In the reality of class conflict, radicals support the oppressed, but with the eventual goal of an equalitarian society and the end of group oppression.

DETERMINISM VERSUS FREE WILL

Many religions of the world have considered the path of history to be predetermined by God or fate. On this basis many followers of these religions conclude that what will happen will happen—they accept their existence with *fatalism*. The philosophy of fatalism strongly inhibits any political action, and for centuries, in fact, religious fatalism stood as a barrier to any serious attempts to improve the world in which people lived.

Implicit elements of predeterminism or fatalism are included in some sociological theories. For example, a major social issue today is the question of why so many young workers are alienated and angry about their specialized jobs, their dealings with corporate bureaucrats, and their dealings with government bureaucrats. Some sociologists argue that *any* technologically advanced society *must* inevitably produce highly specialized and boring jobs, a faceless hierarchy of economic bureaucrats to deal with economic complexity, and an equally faceless hierarchy of government bureaucrats to deal with political complexity. Such sociologists accept the problem as predetermined, with no way out—except possibly to improve the functioning of the bureaucrats. They do not consider the possibility that a different type of society, such as one in which workers' cooperatives run the factories, might eliminate much of the problem.

This debate has immediate implications for sociological research. A fatalist in sociology will only explore "inevitable" trends in social structures, neglecting the role of conscious human beings. On the contrary, radical sociologists—and most other sociologists—investigate human beings and their decisions among the factors that may cause any social event. Human beings are active factors in the shaping of society, not merely passive pawns in a game fully determined by biological inheritance, culture, or social structure.

John Stuart Mill attacks one of the most persistent variations of the fatalist argument: the notion that you can't change human nature. This argument has been used against many proposals to improve society, and even to deny that major social changes could have ever taken place or will ever take place (except for those somehow predetermined by human nature). Mill argued that "human nature can no longer be regarded as the final and most general cause of historical progress; if it is constant, then it cannot explain the extremely changeable course of history; if it is changeable, then obviously its changes are themselves determined by historical progress" (Mill, 1959, p. 164).

Radical sociologists deny that human conduct is predetermined by God, economics, or any other given factor. They certainly consider that human conduct is what makes history. Yet, radical sociologists also believe that *if* certain conditions exist, then we can predict that many people will act in specified ways determined by those conditions.

The idea of behavior determined by free will developed in reaction to previous theological fatalism. The free-will viewpoint was dominant in the early eighteenth century, when it was thought that there was no determined course of history. Rather, the free-will view contended that human beings can do whatever they want. The concept of free will is rooted in a moralistic view that wishes to condemn certain individual actions. Given this view, history is not determined in any way and is not predictable even in the long run.

On the contrary, social scientists like John Stuart Mill and Karl Marx have pointed out that one can discover regularities in human behavior—that, on the average, people do behave in certain predictable ways. The ways in which we behave also change systematically, with predictable trends, in association with changes in our technological and social environments. For example, the regularities of human behavior appear in the fairly constant annual numbers of suicides and divorces. If people did not, on the average, behave in fairly predictable ways, not only sociologists but also insurance companies would long ago have gone out of business. Any given individual may make any particular choice, but if the social composition of a group is known, sociology can predict, on the average, what they will do. Thus, on the average, most large owners of corporate stock will vote in favor of ending taxes on corporate profits, and most farmers will favor payment of government subsidies to farmers.

Radicals accept neither the predeterminist viewpoint *nor* the free-will viewpoint. Predeterminism claims that man is a puppet of fate, God, or economic forces and leads to the position of fatalism. The free-will position claims that history is accidental and that there are no laws—which leads to social and political voluntarism, the argument that humans can do anything they wish.

Radicals accept a scientific determinist position, which asserts that everything—not only natural events but also social and psychological events—is explicable on the basis of observed relationships. In this view, humans make their own history; that is, humans can make their own decisions on the basis of their own psychologies, but under given natural and social constraints.

> Scientific determinism is the view that every event occurs in some system of laws . . . *if* we knew [all] these laws and the state of the universe at any given time, then we could explain the past and predict the future. This frame of reference includes, as it consistently must, human actions which, therefore, can be the object of scientific study. (Brodbeck, 1968, p. 669)

Of course, we are limited at any given time by the following:

1. The limited extent of known facts
2. The limited analytic theories available (including our limited mathematical knowledge)
3. Our limited reasoning power
4. Limited time to research the problem
5. The fact that we are part of the social process and therefore have "limited" or biased views of it

So we know *something* about social laws at any given time, but not everything.

Social events are determined by human behavior. It is also true, however, that human behavior is determined by the entire set of existing conditions. These conditions include:

1. Our present technology and capital
2. Our present resources and natural environment
3. Our present social-economic-political institutions
4. Our present ideas, including each individual's own psychology

Human beings are free, for example, to make or not to make a revolution. Yet our actual behavior is partly predictable because of a knowledge of present and past conditions that are likely to produce or inhibit revolutionary activities. "To say that the revolution is inevitable is simply (in Marx's scheme) to say that it will occur. And it will occur . . . not in spite of any choices we might make, but because of the choices we will make" (Addis, 1968, p. 335). Marx's prediction of socialist revolution must be expressed, however, in terms of a likelihood rather than a certainty because of our present limited knowledge of the impact of social conditions.

DIALECTIC METHOD VERSUS STATIC APPROACHES

Marx used the dialectic method to examine conflict and change. What exactly are the rules suggested by Marx's dialectic method?

1. Interconnection The approach to problems should be relational; never try to treat something in isolation. Always ask, What are the interconnections of this problem to other aspects of society? Do not assume that a particular social phenomenon—such as drug pushing, suicide, the Vietnam War, Watergate, or the Iran-Contra scandal—is accidental or isolated; ask how it is related to the entire social-political-economic environment surrounding it. Although one may analytically separate a single phenomenon from the whole for study, no complete scientific nor valid policy conclusions can be drawn until the possible relations to the rest of the social system are also studied.

As an example of the nondialectical approach of traditional sociology, we find many sociologists who look at alcoholics, delinquents, drug users, and the poor as isolated groups or individuals, separate from each other and separate from the rest of society. Thus each one is seen as a unique problem. The poor, it is said, have little money because they lack socially favorable attitudes or backgrounds—that is, they lack skills, social amenities, or motivation. Similarly, drug users or alcoholics are said to be frustrated or alienated types because they could not measure up to social requirements. Thus various (though not all) traditional sociologists "understand social problems as relatively independent and haphazard happenings, and try to solve them one at a time" [Ollman, 1973, p. 504].

The radical orientation, on the contrary, sees all problems interconnected in a social whole. In this view: capitalist society functions in such a way as to create poverty; poverty helps keep cheap and willing labor available; and so poverty helps maintain capitalism. Moreover, it is the relationships of capitalism—and *not* the isolated characteristics of victimized individuals—that create the widespread frustration and alienation leading to excessive alcoholism, drug use, and delinquency.

2.   Conflict   The radical sociologist should *ask* (not assume): What are the opposing sides in any social process? How are they related? What kinds of conflict exist, and in what direction are they moving? Specifically, what are the opposing interests of different classes? What holds the opposing classes together in the relative unity of the present system? Which classes are growing in numbers or power, and which are declining?

The radical, dialectic approach does not merely ask about random interconnections, but asks if they are structured into conflicting polar opposites. Examples of such interconnected opposites are debtors and creditors, slaves and slave owners, and workers and capitalists.

One of the most interesting applications of the dialectic method of seeking interconnections among apparent "opposites" has been in the method of sociological research itself. Traditional sociologists engage in many disputes based on rather rigid dichotomies between sociological categories. For example, we have noted the dichotomy between narrow, quantitative research and speculative "grand theory." There is also the dispute between a free-will approach to events and the fatalist approach of predeterminism. Another classic dispute is between the proponents of value-free, factual sociology versus the proponents of ethical values as the basis of sociology.

Each of these opposites is merely a different, one-sided aspect of the ongoing process of scientific research in sociology. When we understand this process through a dialectic approach to sociological research, then the apparent opposites become false dilemmas of method posed by a nondialectic approach. These false dichotomies can be understood, overcome, and corrected.

3.   Change   The radical sociologist should *ask* (not assume): Is the social system changing? Specifically, what changes are going on in its ideas, institutions, productive relations, or productive forces? What are the specific features of this historical period? What kind of society preceded this one, and how did this one evolve from it? Radical sociologists are never content with a static picture, though that may be a necessary first approximation. They try to achieve a dynamic, historical view of each social process. For example, they are not content with a statement of what the women's movement is like right now. Radicals ask questions about where it came from and where it is going from here. They do *not* limit their research by the inaccurate view that human nature never changes.

4. Quantitative and Qualitative Changes When a social process shows a discontinuity or qualitative jump, ask what continuous evolution led it to that point. When a social process shows only continuous quantitative change for a long period, ask what discontinuities or qualitative leaps in society may occur in the future. More concretely, the radical sociologist should *ask* (not assume): What are the present quantitative trends in ideologies, institutions, classes, and productive forces? Will these trends eventually create a sufficient level of class conflict to cause a revolutionary change? In what direction is that change likely to be? Will it be positive or negative from the viewpoint of the oppressed class?

The Cuban Revolution was an example of a qualitative change. Radical sociologists have investigated the questions: Why did it occur at that time? What quantitative trends led up to it? Since that big jump, what trends have developed in Cuba?

These suggestions of dialectic method for ways of approaching sociology are all grounded in past empirical research and scientific practice. Yet these suggestions do not presume to make statements about sociology, but they are intended only to direct the sociologist to ask certain questions. A question is neither true nor false; only answers are. Therefore, our method cannot be a dogma and cannot be true or false. The test of any method is whether it leads sociologists in fruitful or useful directions of research.

SUMMARY

The first part of this appendix reviewed a split in traditional sociology. On one side are those who develop abstract or grand theories that deemphasize empirical research. On the other side are the majority who do narrower empirical studies that deemphasize broader theoretical issues. Radicals emphasize the need for empirical investigations to fit within a broader theoretical framework.

The second part of this appendix noted the dominant view of traditional sociology that factual studies can—and should—be done independently of ethical values. Radicals argue that this separation is impossible, so scientific sociology should always be combined with a humanist ethical view.

The third part of this appendix contrasted those sociologists who think social events are predetermined (fatalists) with those who think humans have free will and can do anything they want (voluntarists). Radicals take the position that human beings do make history by their own choices and actions, but that human behavior and ideas are influenced by prior and existing conditions. These conditions include our existing psychology as well as the natural and social environment.

The fourth part of this appendix explored the dialectic method as a series of questions that are useful to ask in any analysis of society. These include questions about (1) social interconnections, (2) social conflicts among opposing classes or groups, (3) social changes, and (4) revolutionary, as well as evolutionary, changes in human society.

SUGGESTED READINGS

All of the topics covered in this book are discussed in one of the main journals of radical sociology, *The Insurgent Sociologist* (new title: *Critical Sociology*), (address: Department of Sociology, University of Oregon, Eugene, OR 97403). Similarly, articles in the *Berkeley*

Journal of Sociology: A Critical Review should be consulted. For a critical evaluation of sociology, the best place to start is C. Wright Mills, *The Sociological Imagination* (New York: Oxford University Press, 1959). Then look at David Horowitz, ed., *Radical Sociology* (San Francisco: Harper & Row (Canfield Press), 1971), and J. David Colfax and Jack Roach, eds., *Radical Sociology* (New York: Basic Books, 1972). An excellent—and controversial—history of early American sociology is Herman and Julia Schwendinger, *Sociologists of the Chair: A Radical Analysis of the Formative Years of North American Sociology, 1883–1922* (New York: Basic Books, 1974). In an excellent synthesis of methodological issues, *When Marxists Do Research* (New York: Greenwood Press, 1986), Pauline Marie Vaillancourt discusses many important topics and debates of special interest to radical sociologists.

An excellent discussion of the radical method in sociology is Michael Harrington's *The Twilight of Capitalism* (New York: Simon & Schuster, 1976), Part I. Marx's views on sociological method are presented in lengthy excerpts from his writings in Howard Selsam and Harry Martel, *Reader in Marxist Philosophy* (New York: International Publishers, 1963). A very interesting and sophisticated but difficult book on method is Lucio Colletti's *From Rousseau to Lenin* (New York: Monthly Review Press, 1972). For a good introduction to traditional methods in sociology, see Earl R. Babbie, *The Practice of Social Research* (Belmont, CA: Wadsworth, 1973, 1983). A good introduction to the use of social statistics is Herman J. Loether and Donald G. McTavish, *Descriptive and Inferential Statistics: An Introduction*, 3rd ed. (Boston: Allyn & Bacon, 1988). A more advanced discussion of the topic is Hubert M. Blalock's *Social Statistics,* 2d ed. (New York: McGraw-Hill, 1972). For a good introduction to an advanced statistical method, see Willem Saris and Henk Stronkhorst, *Causal Modelling in Nonexperimental Research: An Introduction to the LISREL Approach* (Amsterdam: Sociometric Research Foundation, 1984). Concerning dialectics, see Howard Sherman, "Dialectics as a Method," *The Insurgent Sociologist* 4 (Summer 1976): 57–64. Also see Howard Wachtel, "Capitalism and Poverty in America"; Barry Bluestone, "A Discussion of Capitalism and Poverty in America"; and David Gordon, "American Poverty"—all in the *Monthly Review* 24 (June 1972): 49–79. Also see Pradeep Bandyopadhyay, "One Sociology or Many," *Science and Society* 35 (Spring 1971): 1–26.

REFERENCES

Addis, Laird. 1968. "The Individual and the Marxist Philosophy of History." In May Brodbeck, ed., *Readings in Philosophy of the Social Sciences*. New York: Macmillan.

Alexander, Jeffrey C. 1983a. *Theoretical Logic in Sociology,* Vol. 3: *The Classical Attempt at Theoretical Synthesis: Max Weber*. Berkeley: University of California Press.

———. 1983b. *Theoretical Logic in Sociology,* Vol. 4: *The Modern Reconstruction of Classical Thought: Talcott Parsons*. Berkeley: University of California Press.

———., ed. 1985. *Neofunctionalism*. Beverly Hills, CA: Sage.

Brodbeck, May, ed. 1968. *Readings in Philosophy of the Social Sciences*. New York: Macmillan.

Campbell, David. 1971. "The Clash Between Beautiful Women and Society." In Athena Theodore, ed., *The Professional Woman*. Cambridge, MA: Schenkman.

Marx, Karl, and Frederick Engels. 1847. *The German Ideology*. New York: International Publishers.

Mill, John Stuart. 1959. "Elucidations of the Science of History." In Patrick Gardiner, *Theories of History*. New York: Free Press.

Ollman, Bertell. 1973. "Marxism and Political Science." *Politics and Society* 3 (Summer).
Sciulli, David, and Dean Gernstein. 1985. "Social Theory and Talcott Parsons in the 1980s." *Annual Review of Sociology* 11:369–387.
Vaillancourt, Pauline Marie. 1986. *When Marxists Do Research*. New York: Greenwood Press.
Zinn, Howard. 1978. *The Politics of History*. Boston: Beacon Press.

chapter *2*

Structure of Society

A fundamental question is, How does a given society survive? That is, how do all the parts of society hang together rather than fall apart? We shall begin with the traditional approach, which calls this the "problem of order." Specifically, we shall consider the functionalist view which is still influential, though it has been seriously criticized by many sociologists; and the recently developed neofunctionalism. Then we shall look at the radical approach to the structure of society, beginning with Marx's conception.

FUNCTIONALISM

Conservatives used to explain all social phenomena in terms of God, physical nature, or unchanging human nature. By contrast, many modern liberals in sociology explain social phenomena by the functional approach. *Functionalism* is a major advance insofar as it tries to explain social ideologies and institutions, such as religion or prejudice, in terms of the role they play within a given society— rather than by eternally given divine or natural factors. One functionalist says that functionalism "seeks to do no more than assay the place of a particular element of culture or societal institutions in relation to other elements. The question may then be posed as to whether an institution leads to or assists in the perpetuation of the social entity in which it appears" (Spencer, 1965, p. 1). In this innocuous form, it would seem that few modern social scientists could disagree with functionalism.

The most famous functional analyst in the United States, and the Western world, was Talcott Parsons. In writings spanning over half a century, Parsons has clearly left his mark on the discipline (Alexander, 1985). Probably his major contribution has been his insistence that sociological analysis focus on the whole social system. This focus helps sociologists avoid isolated emphases on such specific issues as juvenile delinquency, family problems, or even poverty. Parsons's analysis suggests that each of these issues—and many others—must be examined in the context of the functioning of the entire social system.

This focus on the larger system is actually quite similar to Marx's focus on the system of entire societies. Marx felt it was necessary to examine each institution in terms of its contribution to the stability or change of entire societies. These two thinkers diverge considerably on many issues, such as their appraisal of the role of social classes in modern society. But they do share a system focus.

Because of the significance of Parsons's analysis in sociology—and the controversies it has raised—we feel it appropriate to specially focus on his version of functionalism. In particular, we will look at various elements of his analysis in comparison with radical, or Marxist, analysis.

Functionalists who follow the lead of Parsons make social stability the ultimate goal of sociological analysis (see Demerath and Peterson, 1967). This means that these functionalists focus primarily on conditions leading to harmonious social relations and on the smooth integration of the many separate parts of society into a coherent whole (Parsons, 1951). In many of his writings, Parsons, as it were, stands back and examines the great diversity in a society like the United States, with its diverse ethnic groups (whites, blacks, Asians, Chicanos), different income groups (well-off, middle class, and poor), and different age groups (elderly, middle-aged, and young). He then addresses the problem of order noted above: How do all these divergent groups come together into a relatively harmonious whole, instead of going their separate ways and coming into serious conflict?

Much of Parsons's work on specific institutions, such as the family, the economy, the government, and religion, could be viewed as his attempt to show how each of these institutions contributes to social stability (Parsons, 1964, pp. 359–370). For example, in his analysis of the family, Parsons explicitly wishes to see how the family contributes to the stability of American society (Parsons and Bales, 1955, chap. 1). Parsons argues that the modern "nuclear family," comprised of parents and children only, has two main functions: socialization of the children into the larger society, and the stabilization of adult personalities. By performing both of these functions, Parsons sees the family contributing to social stability.

In a very complex analysis, Parsons shows the mechanisms whereby the family teaches its children social values, expectations, and activities, in order that the children may fit into society as it exists and thereby contribute to that society. The family teaches boys they will need to become educated and eventually get jobs, and it teaches girls they must develop nurturing skills, such as "giving care" to others, so that later they will be able to run their own families (ibid., pp. 14–17, 84, 187–257). By training children in this fashion, the family contributes to social stability by preparing the next generation of workers and mothers. Thus society will have the needed personnel in the near future.

Parsons is quite insightful on his second—and less discussed—family function, the stabilization of adult personalities. He views the family as part of a much larger social system that includes the occupational system and many other adult relationships. He correctly assumes that occupational and other relationships outside the family can be difficult and stress-creating for the adult members of the nuclear family. In a world where individuals often work with those who have no particular loyalty based on long-standing social contacts, family ties, or neighborhood backgrounds, the chances for tension are high. Parsons argues that a main function of the modern family is to ease this tension from outside sources and hence to stabilize the adult personality. In turn, this personality stabilization permits the adults to perform their various activities in the larger society and thereby contributes to the maintenance of the society.

CRITIQUES OF FUNCTIONALISM

From its inception, functionalism has been the focus of criticism (Mills, 1959). Such criticism has continued (Giddens, 1977, 1979; Elster, 1982).

The emphasis on harmony and stability has been seen to lead to a conservative bias in the theory. That is, functional theory committed primarily to explaining harmonious relations can imply that what is functional for the preservation of the present society (and, ultimately, its ruling class) is beneficial for the large majority of that society. This is, at best, a questionable assumption that requires supportive evidence. If religion helped perpetuate a slave society, for example, it would be easy to document how the slave owners benefited, but it would be impossible to document that the slaves benefited from the continuance of slavery.

At points, Parsons's functional analysis of society is self-consciously opposed to that of Karl Marx. Although Marx analyzed the parts of society in great detail, he always kept his eye on the overall conflict of the major social classes in society as a whole. Parsons, on the contrary, breaks society down into smaller parts that can obscure the larger economic conflict. Parsons writes:

> Marx . . . tended to treat the socioeconomic structure of capitalist enterprise as a single indivisible entity rather than breaking it down analytically into a set of the distinct variables involved in it. It is this analytic breakdown which is for present purposes the most distinctive feature of modern sociological analysis. (1954, p. 324)

Parsons emphasizes that this analysis of a particular system of variables—which, as he says, is a distinctive feature of modern traditional sociology—not only modifies or obscures the Marxist view of class, but turns our attention to entirely different social divisions and different systems of relationships. Instead of focusing on the conflict between capitalist corporations and the working class, Parsons examines the system of roles within the society. These roles include teacher, pupil, husband, wife, plumber, dentist, and other occupational categories. Parsons says that in the functionalist view:

> The primary structural emphasis no longer falls on the orientation of capitalist enterprises to profit and the theory of exploitation, but rather the structure of occupational roles within the system of industrial society. (1954, p. 324)

Yet, Parsons's focus on occupational roles leads to a lack of attention to the structure of class divisions or class interests.

Furthermore, Parsons appears to argue merely in favor of a more efficient order for any society, with no particular stake in the present one. If this view is examined more carefully, however, it becomes apparent, as Gouldner argues: "To seek order is to seek a reduction of social conflict, and thus it is to seek a moratorium on such social changes as are sought through conflict or which may engender it" (Gouldner, 1970, p. 251).

In addition, Parsons and other functionalists have praised institutions preserving the status quo. For example, they say that "Christianity provided the underpinning for the distinctive western economy, science, intellectual autonomy" (Gouldner, 1970, p. 254) and other implied positive attributes in the present society. They often do not seem to distinguish between description of a function and evaluation of its worth. They point out the function of religion in preserving the present society—and then assume that preserving the present society is good for the majority of people in this society. Since Parsons deemphasizes class conflict, he usually does not consider that preservation of our present society could be useful only for a minority, but negative for the interests of a majority.

Parsons often stresses American ideals of liberty, equality, and fair play, arguing that these ideals are institutionalized in the American system of government. He thus argues that the government is not class dominated and serves collective goals. Also, he assumes that everyone is equal in voting power in the United States. He thus deemphasizes the enormous political power of wealth and property (Bendix and Lipset, 1966, pp. 240–265). In fact:

> There is no fixed unambiguous class system in the United States. . . . hardly any development of an hereditary upper class, no clear-cut hierarchy of prestige, considerable mobility between groups . . . it looks very much as though the traditional "bottom" of the occupational pyramid was in the course of almost disappearing. (Parsons, quoted in Gouldner, 1970)

Because of automation, says Parsons, most Americans can have good jobs and upward mobility, based on education, and how much education is obtained depends largely on ambition.

Besides the functionalist deemphasis of conflict, there is a second major area of difference between radical and functionalist sociologists—and that is their view of social change. Functionalists concentrate on stable and relatively unchanging forms of society. Radicals emphasize the history of major changes in society. The lesser interest in a theory of change among various functionalists is partly a result of their emphasis on functions or activities that are said to be universally present in every society. Every society, for example, rears children, provides food to eat, and protects it citizens. A concentration on these universals can detract from an analysis of change.

Many functionalists believe that certain functional relations are found in every society. One functionalist writes:

> In this work we have adopted . . . the conceptualization developed by Parsons. He and his associates have postulated that any social system has four functional requisites:

(1) pattern maintenance and tension management, (2) goal attainment, (3) adaptation, and (4) integration. [Holt, 1965, p. 92]

These functional needs refer to problems that all social systems must solve in order to maintain their stability. For example, for a family to maintain its stability, it must coordinate the various activities of the parents with each other and with those of the children. When this coordination is attained, the family as a social system is considered to have solved the integration problem. Without such co-ordination, the family could be disrupted in its functioning, perhaps ending in divorce. Similarly, in the occupational sphere, it is necessary for both workers and managers to agree on the basic value of producing goods. When there is this kind of agreement, the problems of pattern maintenance and tension management are said to be solved. Without a basic value agreement, the work process might be halted.

Parsons argues that these four functional systems problems apply to all social systems—to those as diverse as the family, the economy, politics, small groups, the military, bureaucratic organizations, and the entire society. Although it is useful to have general classifications, the difficulty with this framework is that it is exceedingly vague and ambiguous; and it *must be* vague and ambiguous if it is to apply to *any* social system.

In addition, functionalists argue that roles played by individuals in given social structures solve these four functional problems. For example, workers "solve" the problem of goal attainment by their role in making products like cars in factories. Also, mothers are seen to solve the integration problem in families by coordinating family members. Yet given social structures appear in some so-cieties, but not in others, because social systems are often very different from each other. There are no universal structures to perform these functions, as is sometimes implied by functionalists. For example, our society has prisons in which to lock some people away from society, but many primitive societies have no prisons and would think the whole idea of this type of structure to be very strange. Also we have financial markets that function to exchange goods at certain rates of value between individuals, a structure whose very concept would be unknown or unappealing in some societies.

Thus, Parsons, wishes "to assert what is presumably true of *all* social action, *all* societies, *all* social systems" (Gouldner, 1970, p. 207). The trouble with this and other such formulations is that, in order to present something as universal, they often come up with functions and structures so broadly and vaguely defined that they avoid concrete social issues. When the complex definitions are specified, the concepts frequently tell us little in particular about any given society and little about how to approach the problems of any given society. Thus there is an apparent lack of substantive content in such broadly defined concepts.

Actually, some content does enter into these concepts. Although they are stated as universals, the description often seems to be—in a very abstract way—of our present society. Many of the categories relating to political systems—such as democratic voting procedures—are quite irrelevant in many primitive societies that do not have our type of political structure. One doubtful aspect of focusing too much attention on these universal statements of "order" and "pattern maintenance" is that it allows dissenters to be discredited because they disrupt the present social order. A good example is the position taken by Elton Mayo, an American management sociologist, "who argued that shop stewards in industry who were seen as non-cooperative by management were in some way ill" (Coulson and Riddell, 1970, p. 48).

Furthermore, since the institutional structure and its functions are seen as given, the institutions should *not* be adjusted to individuals. On the contrary, many functionalists imply that people who are deviant or who dissent must be adjusted to social institutions to fill their social role. For example, the shop stewards of trade unions in industry might be taught to see their role as one of cooperation with management. If a male teacher wears a beard or a female an unfeminine suit, and if either is perceived as disruptive by the principal or school board, then the teacher must be *adjusted* to his or her proper role.

Like other traditional sociologists, many functionalists claim to practice value-free social science. This seems unlikely since they often ask—as a matter of basic approach—how institutions or people can best serve the status quo. They do not perceive their approach as biased, because these structures and functions are seen as necessary and operating for the benefit of the whole society.

To see how all these general principles of functionalism affect the practices of sociology, consider a couple of important applications. In the area of male and female relationships, functionalists such as Parsons, describe how women's function in the family is to be kind, sensitive, and emotionally supportive, while men function as aggressive leaders. Since these functions are seen as necessary for society, they must be properly performed. When applied to actual families, this view would permanently keep women home-oriented and men work-oriented.

Perhaps the most controversial use of functionalism has been to defend inequality. Two functionalists, Kingsley Davis and Wilbert Moore, defined socioeconomic inequality as "an unconsciously evolved device by which societies insure that the most important positions are conscientiously filled by the most qualified persons" (Davis and Moore, 1945, p. 243). They claim that it is functionally necessary to have great extremes of wealth and prestige because this is the only way to tempt highly qualified people to take the top jobs. For example, if a Rockefeller or a Du Pont were not paid millions of dollars a year, he would refuse to run a big corporation. They claim that every society *needs* the mechanism of inequality in order to function efficiently; therefore, there is no way to get rid of it.

This functionalist approach to inequality is very misleading because the highest incomes go to members of families like the Rockefellers and Du Ponts, who inherited their wealth and do very little direct and useful economic work at present. Most of them spend more time in other activities, such as politics, philanthropy, or sports, and a few do nothing, but still get large incomes. On the contrary, the lowest incomes go to people who spend very long hours at the dreariest and hardest jobs. Thus, as we shall see in detail in later chapters, our present income structure is not functionally useful for all of society, though it is functionally useful for the wealthy.

NEOFUNCTIONALISM

A recent approach called *neofunctionalism* has emerged (Alexander, 1985). Neofunctionalism is derived from Parsons's functionalism and has stirred interest among social theorists. Influenced by the work of Alexander, Münch, and others (Sciulli and Gerstein, 1985), a revision of functionalism is now under way. As indicated by several articles in Alexander (1985), neofunctionalism includes many topics that have been discussed in traditional functional analysis. While there may be a tendency away from discussions of social stability to an increased focus on social conflict and change, neofunctionalism nevertheless shares with functionalism an interest in topics such as the relative importance for social organization of values and material interests, value conflicts and economic inequality among diverse social groups, increasing social complexity (differentiation), the state (or government), advanced technology and science, social crisis, and social cohesion. All of these issues have implications for the functioning of the larger social system.

It appears that some of the controversies surrounding functionalism, such as its conservative bias, may be receding for neofunctionalism. Even leftist scholars like Jürgen Habermas have been seen as contributing to neofunctionalism (Sciulli, 1985). Yet, "[No] one knows where such developments will lead, whether a neofunctionalist school actually will emerge, or whether, instead, neofunctionalism will shape contemporary sociology in less conspicuous ways" (Alexander, 1985, p. 16). The question if neofunctionalism is "simply old wine in new bottles, or a new brew, is something history will decide" (Alexander, 1985, p. 16). For now, it suffices to say that issues of functional analysis continue to be debated in sociology.

THE FRAMEWORK OF RADICAL ANALYSIS

The radical framework divides society into various levels of analysis: (1) ideas and ideology, (2) social-political institutions, (3) human relations in the economy (called relations of production), and (4) the technology-labor base of the economy (called forces of production). This framework is used to describe and explain how society is organized, as well as to show how and why society changes. It is often in contrast to the functional approach.

1. Ideas   Ideas refer to various mental conceptions, from individual human psychologies and attitudes to general social ideologies. By an ideology we mean a set of beliefs that is held as a matter of faith by a significant part of society—for example, the idea that private ownership is the only way to run an economy, or that some races are superior to others, or that one sex is superior to the other.

2. Institutions   Institutions are organized patterns of group behavior. There are a wide range of social-political institutions, such as the family, the news media (television, newspapers, radio), the government or state apparatus (President, Congress, courts, police, prisons, army), the churches, and the educational system. Each of these institutions, such as the media, tend to control and shape our thoughts and ideas. Ideas are shaped by the whole environment of these social-political institutions.

3.   Economic relations   The economy is concerned with how people work and make a living. Groups of human beings have certain relationships within the economy. For example, one group may be slaves to another group, as were blacks in the U.S. South before the Civil War. For example, workers are subordinate to owners of companies in our economy and produce profit for the owners. Those who own the capital (money, factories, and machinery) are called capitalists—so our system is called capitalism. These types of relationships are what Marx called *relations of production*.

4.   Technology-labor base   The material basis for our society consists of the labor force (including its degree of training and education), the means of production (factories, machinery, and natural resources), and technology. Marx called this technology-labor base the *forces of production*.

Each of these four levels influences the others. Ideologies are shaped by the news media, the churches and schools, and the family. But who determines what the news media say? The most important power in the news media is their owners. In the South before the Civil War, the media, as well as the churches and schools, were all controlled by the slave owners. Not surprisingly, they spread ideologies claiming that slavery was ordained by God and that blacks were inferior to whites. Today, the media, schools, and churches are mostly owned, controlled, or financed by a predominantly white, male, capitalist class of owners of business. Not surprisingly, these institutions usually support the ideology that capitalism is good, but some also tend to support racism and sexism. Thus our dominant ideologies are mostly shaped by those who are dominant in our economic relations. Furthermore, it is just as clear that these ideas or ideologies have enormous power to affect behavior. Ideology may be the most important single source of reinforcing the relations between groups of people in the economy.

THE ECONOMIC BASE

The human relation to nature, our economic activity, is a foundation or basis for human society. On the other hand, by definition, the economic base (sometimes called the mode of production) includes *not only* the relations of humans to nature, *but also* the relations of humans to other humans in the work process. A definition of the economic base that included only our technical relations to nature would be too restrictive to be a useful tool of social science.

The economic base of society has two basic elements. As has been previously discussed, one is the "forces of production," which are all the human beings and all the natural resources necessary to the productive process. Adam Smith separated them into land, labor, and capital. Marx spoke of human labor, technology, and the "means of production"—where they include the raw materials extracted from nature plus the human-made plant and equipment.

The second element in the economic base is the "relations of production."

The relations of production are the human relationships of class to class in the productive process. For example, under slavery the main productive relationship is the relation of the slave-owning class to the slaves. The forces of production relate humans to nature; the relations of production relate humans to humans. Thus, by definition,

Economic base = forces of production + relations of production

The whole economic base is pictured in Figure 2.1.

Let us examine the forces of production in more detail. First, there is the labor force—that is, all the workers able to work at a given level of skill. Workers may be slaves or serfs or "free" workers hired by capitalists, but in every case they are the main productive force. Second, there are the means of production. These are all the elements, such as land and raw materials, that are transformed from nature by the productive process. The means of production also include all those instruments, from machines to factory buildings, that are utilized by labor in the productive process. Finally, there is technology. Technology is the level of sophistication of machinery and the knowledge of how to train labor, how to improve machinery, and how to combine labor and the means of production most efficiently. Therefore,

Forces of production = labor + means of production + technology

Now let us examine the human relations in more detail. The human relations of production are the most crucial element to grasp from the radical view. Except

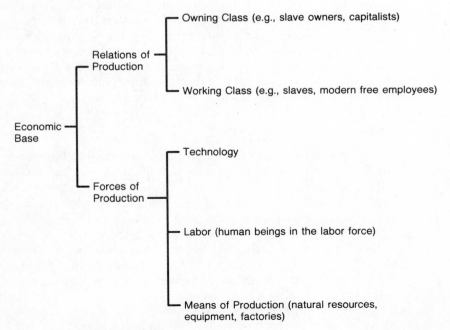

Figure 2.1 The economic base.

in a primitive classless society, these relations describe the interconnections of classes of humans in the production process. The relationship of the working class to capitalist employers is a part of the human relations of production. The productive relations may be summed up in the answers to two questions: (1) Which class does the work of society? All manual labor was done in a slave system by the slaves, in feudalism by the serfs, and in capitalism by the workers. (2) Which class owns the means of production and the product? Both the means of production and the final product are owned in a slave system by the slave owners, in feudalism by the noble lords, and in capitalism by the capitalists.

Of course, different class societies are very different in their relations. Under slavery the slave is also owned by the slaveowner. Under feudalism, the serf is not owned directly but is bound to the land. Most serfs also own some instruments of production and have the right to possess and use some land for themselves. The serf also has the duty to work on the lord's land for a specified number of days per year (often 200 or more). The worker under capitalism is not bound to one job, but is free to look for a job anywhere, free to take a job at any wage, free to be unemployed, and free to be fired. On the other hand, slave owners, feudal lords, and capitalists constitute dominant classes that control those subordinate classes that do the work. The dominant class owns or controls the means of production and owns the final product of the productive process. To sum up the human relations very generally,

Relations of production = working class + owning class

In the rest of this book, these relations figure quite prominently. In Chapter 3, we shall examine the known facts about classes in the United States, including how many people live in poverty and the incomes of different groups. In Chapter 4, we shall examine how different classes come into conflict with each other and what divisions occur within classes. In Chapter 5, we examine the *feelings* of American workers and employers toward each other and within the group during the productive process in industry. In Chapter 14, we examine the objective relation between workers and employers, including the degree of exploitation of American workers, the extent of monopoly power, the spread of U.S. corporations overseas, and the nature of the world system of capitalism. Finally, in Chapter 21, we describe the broad sweep of historical evolution from primitive productive relations among early humans to slave civilizations (such as Rome or Egypt) to modern capitalist and socialist relationships.

DEFINITION OF SOCIAL SUPERSTRUCTURE

Using the economy as a base or foundation of society, Marx spoke metaphorically of building upon it "society's superstructure" of ideas and sociopolitical institutions. In another metaphor, the mode of production is the heart or core of society; the other institutions and the ideas of people are the rest of the body, equally necessary for its functioning.

What institutions are included in the social superstructure? Some major superstructural institutions are the media, religious organizations, and the educational system (discussed in Chapter 7). Of similar importance are the institutions of marriage and the family (discussed in Chapters 8–10). Other key institutions of the superstructure are the government (legislature, courts, army, prisons, and police), the legal system, and political parties. All of these political institutions are discussed as regards the United States in Chapters 15 and 16 and as regards the so-called socialist countries in Chapter 19. The way in which social institutions evolve is discussed in Chapters 20 and 21.

The ideas that people have are also a powerful force in society. Ideas include religious views, opinions on social issues, deeply rooted personal psychologies, cultural values (see Chapter 6), prejudices related to race, sex, and age (see Chapters 11–13), and political ideas in support of the status quo, as well as the views of various protest movements (see Chapters 17 and 18).

The entire social superstructure thus consists of ideas, such as racial prejudice, as well as institutions, such as marriage and the family.

$$\text{Social superstructure} = \text{ideas} + \text{institutions}$$

The social superstructure is pictured in Figure 2.2.

STRUCTURE OF SOCIETY

We must stress that the economic base and social superstructure are intimately related in a reciprocal connection at every point. Thus it is impossible to say that any phenomenon is *completely* in the base or the superstructure because they interact. For example, is science in the economic base (a force of production) or is science a set of ideas in the social superstructure? Society is a unified whole consisting of the social superstructure as well as the economic base of society.

$$\text{Society} = \text{economic base} + \text{social superstructure}$$

The above framework, like all sets of concepts, is tentative. These concepts are clearly important for sociological investigation, but they are always subject to change and modification in degree and emphasis as our knowledge increases.

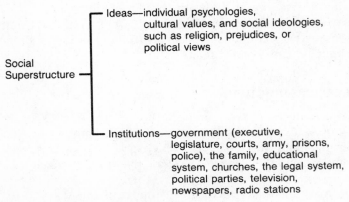

Figure 2.2 The social superstructure.

The definitions of the concepts used here derive from those found most useful by radicals in their studies of relevant problems. Next, we ask the question, What is the relation of the economic base to the social superstructure? We examine both traditional and radical views.

PSYCHOLOGICAL DETERMINISM: A TRADITIONAL VIEW

Many early-nineteenth-century theorists believed that human society is determined by ideas, whether the ideas of great men, the ideas expressed by eternal "human nature," or the ideas that reflect innate psychological instincts. Most of these theories have—fortunately, in our opinion—vanished from modern sociology. Yet there are still those few sociologists who see society as primarily determined by psychological instincts. These psychological instincts are, in turn, either left unexplained or explained as inherited in our biology and transmitted by our genes. For example, some writers explain wars in terms of human instincts of aggression. But where do these aggressive instincts have their origin? Why are people so aggressive as to have wars at certain times and places but not at others? What is the relation of these aggressive instincts to the socioeconomic structure in which we live?

Although few sociologists accept such extreme psychological determinism (Rabow, 1983), it exists as an important popular mythology. And it frequently comes to the surface in a widespread ideological fad, as when the popular media repeat the ideas of a handful of academics who push "psychohistory," the explanation of history by the psychological characteristics of a few great leaders. The media also report on those few academics who declare in favor of "sociobiology," the explanation of society by biological instincts. Among the few sociologists so arguing are those who explain rising crime rates as the result of an increased number of "sociopaths," defined as psychologically sick people who attack society. On the contrary, most sociologists (including radicals) explain trends in crime, divorce, or suicide rates by changes in our socioeconomic conditions, relations, or structure.

In the tradition of psychological determinism, Lewis Feuer, a well-known social scientist, attributes many social conflicts and historical events to the parricidal instinct of members of student movements to destroy their fathers. (See Feuer, 1969, criticized by Zinn, 1970, pp. 162–166; also see Wood, 1974, pp. 65–81.) He finds student movements responsible for:

1. World War I, because a student assassinated Archduke Ferdinand (his chapter title is "The Bosnian Student Movement Blindly Provokes the First World War").
2. Hitlerism, because a student assassinated a right-wing dramatist in 1819, which led to a repression and a heritage "transmitted to the Nazis."
3. The Bolshevik revolution, because a student assassinated liberal Tsar Alexander II when he "was about to give a constitution" (Zinn, 1970, p.163).
4. Stalinism, because students assassinated Stalin's friend Kirov in 1934.

5. World War II, because student pacifism in the 1930s reduced resistance to Hitler.
6. The Chinese Communist revolution, because "Mao's conflict with his father and its primacy as a motivation for his political ideas were typical of the Chinese students who emerged with him" [Zinn, 1970, p. 164].
7. The Cuban revolution, because for the student Castro "the United States became a surrogate father to be blamed" (1970, p. 164).
8. Espionage and treason in America, because Ethel and Julius Rosenberg (who were executed for espionage) had a "reason-blinding passion of generational hatred [that] begot a corrupted idealism which led to treason" (1970, p. 164).

Feuer claims that students rebel because they have "intense, unresolved Oedipal feelings, a tremendous attachment to their mothers, and a violent hostility to their fathers" (1970, p. 165).

Among the psychological determinists are two cultural anthropologists who claim that most Russians have revolutionary urges because of the Russian custom of tightly wrapping and swaddling infants, which leads to psychological traumas and rebellious children (Gorer and Rickman, 1949, p. 211). It must be emphasized that many sociologists and anthropologists reject such theories and consider them weak because they neglect the wider social and economic environment. Nevertheless, a much more subdued and sophisticated form of psychological determinist theory of social events does surface in some mainstream sociology. As one critic put it rather strongly: "The value of Feuer's book is that, by carrying to absurdity what other social scientists do with more sophistication, it may awaken us to their methodological inanity. . . ." (Zinn, 1970, pp. 164–165). Notice that *any* event can be explained by *some* alleged psychological instinct of human nature, that the psychological determinist theory ignores or denies class conflicts, and that it allows for little social change.

CULTURAL DETERMINISM: A SECOND TRADITIONAL VIEW

Another approach in sociology argues that society is primarily determined by the values shared by the majority (Spates, 1983, pp. 30–33). Thus American society is seen to have a capitalist economic organization because the majority of Americans are said to believe in buying and selling for profit, in the ability of each person to freely negotiate a salary on the job, and in employers' freedom to hire and fire workers at will. In other words, it is said that Americans believe in the principles of capitalism. We practice capitalism because we believe in capitalism, just as we get married because we believe in marriage. The problem with this approach is that the origin of these values is often not examined.

Why do some societies value ambition and private gain very highly, while others do not? Why do some societies believe each individual should stay in his or her "proper place," while others believe that the individual should try to "get ahead"? Why do some societies value a lifelong relationship between one man and woman, while others do not? Why do some societies regard one race as superior, while others do not? Many of these cultural values can be at least partly explained by the socioeconomic institutions of society. These and other issues about culture are discussed in Chapter 6.

ECONOMIC DETERMINISM: A THIRD TRADITIONAL VIEW

A few sociologists analyze behavior in a purely economic-determinist manner. In the view called *economic determinism,* economics and technology determine society, and ideas play little of an active role.

Economic determinism asserts that people act in voting, for example, exactly according to their economic interests—and that we can ignore the importance of ideas and human psychological emotions (rational or irrational). Economic determinists ignore the fact that people can be persuaded, for example, to vote against their own economic interests by ideologies such as racial prejudice or even religious ideas (such as ideas on abortion)—and that many people are unaware of exactly how different political policies affect their own economic interests.

As another example, economic determinism asserts that crime is caused by economic conditions alone. Yet there are also crimes of passion—though, of course, passions may be conditioned by a given socioeconomic system. Still, why don't *all* poor people commit crimes if economic motives are automatic?

According to the theory of economic determinism, in the 1984 election President Reagan represented the capitalist class and attempted to gain more power so as to preserve the rule of that class. But, in those simplistic terms, why have some capitalist groups opposed Reagan? How and why does Congress, which the economic determinists also assert is simply a tool of the capitalist class, often oppose Reagan? Certainly, Reagan is tied to some sections of big business—as the millions of dollars of corporate contributions prove—but the full explanation is much more complex, involving factional fights within the capitalist class and different ideological positions of capitalists. Human ideas, though they arise from and are conditioned by the socioeconomic base of society, do play an active and partially independent role and must be included in any complete sociological analysis.

While a few traditional sociologists still hold to a psychological or cultural determinist approach—beginning with ideas and psychological instincts to explain society—there is one school of sociologists and cultural anthropologists that has reached far in the direction of economic determinism. This is the school headed by Leslie White (Harris, 1968, chaps. 22 and 23). Although they differ in emphasis, all of the members of this school emphasize a research strategy in which a social scientist stresses technoeconomic variables rather than psychological or cultural variables. For an extreme example, one technological determinist has argued that the sacredness of the cow in India depends more on the need for fertilizer than on religious values.

Although several followers of White's approach have produced superb sociological studies, at least some of them have overemphasized economic factors and have had a narrowly technological view of these economic factors. Leslie White himself states the following as a major law: "Other factors remaining constant, culture evolves as the amount of energy harnessed per capita per year is increased. . . ." [Harris, 1968, p. 637]. Such technological determinism ignores the reciprocal impact of ideology on technological conditions. For example, the United States is right now engaged in a serious ideological debate over energy—with different ideologies expressed by conservative Republicans, liberal Democrats, and socialists. The laws enacted as a result of this debate—as well as the political and economic power of the participants—will help determine Leslie White's "amount of energy." The energy level, in turn, will affect the evolution of our culture, but not in the one-to-one fashion White assumes.

At any rate, traditional sociology contains tendencies toward psychological or cultural determinism, as well as toward economic determinism. Radical sociologists try to avoid both types of errors through an historical materialist approach. The three views may be pictured as in Figure 2.3.

HISTORICAL MATERIALISM: THE TWO-WAY INTERACTION OF BASE AND SUPERSTRUCTURE

Radical, or Marxist, sociology does *not* deny the historical role of the ideas and institutions in the superstructure (Aronowitz, 1981; see also Giddens, 1981). It emphasizes how these affect the economic base; however, it also explains that ideas do not arise in a vacuum, but within an historically specific social environment on a particular economic base. Marx's critiques of psychological and cultural determinism stress that people's ideas are shaped by their way of living and their experiences in life. Marx wrote:

> In the social production which men carry on they enter into definite relations that are indispensable and independent of their will; these relations of production correspond to a definite stage of development of their material powers of production. The totality of these relations of production constitutes the economic structure of society—the real foundation, on which legal and political superstructures arise and to which definite forms of social consciousness correspond. The mode of production of material life determines the general character of the social, political and intellectual processes of life. It is not the consciousness of men that determines their being, but, on the contrary, their social being determines their consciousness. (Marx, 1859, 1904)

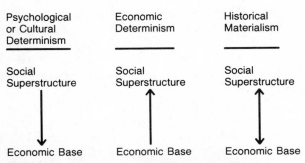

Figure 2.3 Three views of social interconnections.

For example, if an unemployed woman steals a loaf of bread, Marx argues that her consciousness is shaped by the fact that she is unemployed and that she and her children are consequently hungry. Of course, Marx recognized that her consciousness then got her to steal the loaf of bread.

How Conditions Shape Ideas: The Change in Male-Female Attitudes

Women were employed in large numbers in World War II. After the war, however, women were often replaced by men, so that the percentage of women with jobs dropped somewhat. In the conservative postwar period, it was asserted that women would find happiness in raising large numbers of children in neat suburban homes filled with the latest shining gadgets. Women were said not to need jobs since a good husband could provide for them. Thus it was alright to pay much less to women who did work than to men who did the same work. This ideology suited the capitalist employers of women because they made much higher profits from the cheap wages of women—and because unions were weakened by the prejudice and tension between women workers and men workers.

By the end of the 1960s, there was a large women's movement that called for, and won to some extent, laws forbidding unequal pay and other unequal treatment. Moreover, many men's and women's basic attitudes were changing. Consequently, fewer women were satisfied to remain only housewives, and more women were overcoming the barriers to enter law, medicine, and other professions. What caused this enormous change of viewpoint?

A psychological or cultural determinist explanation might begin with a few outstanding women protagonists. For example, Betty Friedan's writing and organizing in the mid-1960s undoubtedly had a strong impact on many women. This was particularly the case with the impact of Friedan's most famous book, *The Feminine Mystique,* written in 1963. But a materialist will ask two further questions: (1) *Why* did Friedan have these ideas at that time? (2) *Why* did her ideas find such a warm welcome at that time?

On an individual level, one would have to examine Friedan's own life experiences to explain her ideas. This would include her education (she studied psychology), her own work experience, her family and marital background, and so forth. To understand the *form* of expression of her ideas, we would have to look at all the previous psychological and sociological writing on women. Any writer, whether Marx, Talcott Parsons, or Friedan, is shaped to some extent by preceding ideas in the same area. For example, Friedan's writing reflects some of the Freudian psychological terminology of the 1950s, though she is very critical of it, and reaches different conclusions.

In addition to her personal biography and the previous ideas on the subject, Friedan and the nascent women's movement were influenced by some fundamental changes that were occurring in the economic base of American society in the 1950s and 1960s. It was these fundamental trends that made many American women so receptive to the ideas of women's liberation at that time.

The most basic change (relevant to women) that occurred in the American economic base in this period was the increasing number of women with jobs other than, or in addition to, their work in the home. In 1940, before World War II, only 29 percent of all women 16 years of age and over had paid jobs. During the war this percentage increased significantly to 38 percent in 1945. After the war many women were fired, but by 1950, 34 percent were still paid workers. By 1960, in spite of a contrary ideology, the percentage of women working at outside jobs rose back to 38 percent. By 1972, 44 percent of all women 16 years of age and over were working outside the home. By 1985, a *majority*, 52 percent, were working outside the home.

The social reality in the 1960s was thus changing very rapidly. Yet a social myth, reflected in women's consciousness (a "false consciousness" in this regard), continued to be propagated by the media, the educational system, the church, and other institutions. The myth asserted that a woman's natural and proper place always has been, and always will be, exclusively in the home. This mythology was what Betty Friedan called the feminine mystique.

It was the increasing gap between the myth and the reality that led to an expanding consciousness of the social and economic oppression of women. This consciousness is reflected both in the books and speeches of women leaders *and* in the quick acceptance of their views by millions of women—in spite of the continued propaganda for the old myth by very powerful interests on the other side.

How Class Relations Affect the Law

Law is affected by changes in (1) ideology, (2) class relations, and (3) productive forces. The *forms* of legal change are also affected, however, through the internal evolution of the legal profession. It is certainly true that lawyers and courts develop the verbal forms of the law along the lines that have a basis in previous precedents. Thus the previous history of the law does influence current legal decisions. The main substance of those decisions, however, depends on prevailing ideology, which in turn roughly coincides with the existing balance of forces among economic classes. Thus the legal institutions and the results of these institutions have significant connections to class relations in society (Spitzer, 1983).

Criminal laws enforce capitalist policies supporting private property or contract rights. If a man living under the American private property system steals a loaf of bread, he is guilty of theft regardless of his need or that of his family.

The laws necessary to protect the many privileges of private property are so pervasive that the President's Commission on Law Enforcement estimated that 91 percent of the American people have committed crimes for which they could have received prison sentences (1968, p. 87). This raises the important question of which laws are enforced and against whom they are enforced. The commission report concluded that "the poor are arrested more often, convicted more frequently, sentenced more harshly, rehabilitated less successfully than the rest of society" (1968, p. 151).

Crimes by the poor are usually given much stiffer sentences than crimes by white-collar or more affluent citizens. For example, a man named Jack Greenberg stole $15 from the post office and got six months in jail; but a clerk named Howard Lazell "misapplied," or embezzled, $150,000 from the bank and was simply put on probation (both in May 1972 in the same courthouse). This difference in sentences is a general rule according to U.S. Attorney Whitney Seymour, Jr.:

> There's a traditional difference in sentences for different types of crime, and it tends to discriminate against the uneducated, unloved social reject. . . . The guy who steals packages . . . is going to get four years, and the guy who steals $45,000 is going to get three months. (Quoted in Oelsner, 1972, p. B1).

Stiffer sentences are given not only to the poor rather than to the rich, but also to blacks as compared to whites. For example, for income tax evasion, the average white was jailed for 12.8 months and the average black for 28.6 months. For the use, sale, or possession of drugs, the average white was jailed for 61.1 months and the average black for 81.1 months. This reflects the fact that whites have considerably more political and economic power, as well as more lawyers and judges, than blacks in American society.

The effects of the socioeconomic structure thus stand out very clearly in law enforcement practices and in procedures of both civil and criminal courts. Yet a paradox exists: inequality of treatment is concealed in the concept of formal legal equality. Both a Rockefeller family member and an unemployed black worker have the same formal rights in court and with the police, but they are treated quite differently. As Anatole France put it: "In its majesty the law of the French Republic allows neither the millionaire Rothschild nor the Paris *clochard* [beggar] to sleep under the bridges of the Seine" (quoted in Deutscher, 1971, p. 97).

Aside from the social deference to the one and the prejudice against the other, there is also the enormous difference that the millionaire can employ the best possible lawyer, whereas the poor with legal problems often must accept an overworked public defender. The wealthy can keep even an open-and-shut case against them stalled in the courts for several years, while the poor lose many cases against them—whether brought by the police, the landlord, or the bill collector—even when they are totally in the right under the existing laws, simply because they have no money with which to fight the case. Consequently, the President's Commission on Law Enforcement reported that white-collar or upper-class "criminals are only rarely dealt with through the full force of criminal sanctions" (1968, p. 156). Even when convicted—as in the case of several of the politically powerful criminals in the Watergate bugging conspiracy—the white-collar criminal is often sent to a more pleasant prison farm, quite unlike the usual brutalizing prison for lower-income working-class offenders.

The large majority of lower-income people lack the financial resources to hold out for a trial, and most are forced to plead guilty in order to avoid lengthy detention before their case comes to trial. "It may surprise most people that there are almost no criminal trials in the United States; but since seventy percent (over ninety percent in some states) of all defendants plead guilty, the need for most trials is eliminated" (Lefcourt, 1971, p. 27). Moreover, in the pretrial period, the rich are usually able to get out on bail, while the poor are often unable to raise the required bail, which is more likely to be set higher because they are not "respectable" citizens. Thus, at every stage in the process of criminal "justice," individuals from the poor and the working class are not given truly equal treatment with members of the affluent, capitalist class.

INTERPRETATIONS OF MARX'S VIEWS

The main point of the radical, or Marxist, orientation is to focus the sociologist's attention on the *two-way relationship* of economic base and social superstructure (and other two-way relationships within each of these). Nevertheless, many critics of Marxism still think that Marx believed in a one-way relation wherein economics determines ideas, but ideas do not affect the economy (Danto, 1965, p. 269). Since Marx stressed the two-way interconnection of base and superstructure, it is hard to see how the critics could find in Marx such a one-sided view of social processes.

Two mainstream American sociologists, Berger and Luckman, acknowledge that this two-way view is probably the correct interpretation of Marx, thus doing away with most of the criticism of Marx's alleged economic determinism (or one-way causation by the economic base). They write: "It is safe to say that much of the great 'struggle with Marx' that characterized not only the beginnings of the sociology of knowledge but the 'classical age' of sociology in general . . . was really a struggle with a faulty interpretation of Marx." (1966, p. 6). They explain that Marx did not believe in any one-way determinism, but in a dialectic interaction of activity and ideas. "What concerned Marx was that human thought is founded in human activity ('labor' in the widest sense of the word) and in social relations brought about by this activity" (1966, p. 6).

In other words, Marx's materialism means that ideas do not emerge from nowhere, and that ideas and the other important aspects of human society are conditioned by our productive activity. *But* his materialist method also insists that the investigator should consider all the relevant cultural and ideological feedbacks as part of the social totality. Human activity and conditions determine human thinking, but human thinking at any given time also reciprocally determines the conditions and activity.

Human activity forms the conditions under which human ideas come into being, but once these ideas exist, they constitute an important force. For example, socioeconomic conflicts in France before the French Revolution of 1789 led to the ideas of liberty, equality, and fraternity. These ideas then became a mighty force for revolutionary changes in economic relationships after the French Revolution.

Some confusion has been expressed over how base and superstructure can affect each other at the same time. In the natural sciences there are many such simultaneous and reciprocal relations. For example, the moon's motion is a mathematical function of the earth's position and motion, while the earth's motion is a function of the moon's position and motion (all other things being constant). Similarly, under capitalism a person's income is partly a function of their education, while their education is partly a function of their family's income. So, too, there is a functional relationship (not necessarily harmonious) of the economic base and the sociopolitical superstructure; each affects the other at the same time, though in very different ways.

The point of Marx's historical materialism is not a magic formula to decide all things by economics, but a directive to sociologists to spell out in detail the significant relations between base and superstructure in a specific historical situation. How does a specific economic base affect the ideology and social institutions of a society? How do the ideology and social institutions affect the economic base of a society?

Marx himself clarified this relation in response to a critic who admitted that Marx's theory was true in the capitalist phase of history, but claimed that it was false if applied to the medieval period, when religion was supreme, or to ancient Rome, where politics was supreme. Marx commented: "This much is clear, that the Middle Ages could not live on Catholicism, nor the Ancient World on politics. On the contrary, it is the mode in which they gained their livelihood that explains why their politics and their Catholicism played the chief part" (Marx, 1859, p. 54). So the Marxist theory does not deny the role of politics or religion, but *explains* their importance within a given economic base.

SUMMARY

The traditional formulation of functionalist sociology emphasizes that social institutions tend to operate, most of the time, in ways designed to make their society survive. When phrased this way, most sociologists can agree on the observation. The trouble is that many functionalists go further, to assume that it is generally beneficial to those living in a society to have their society survive in its present form. This has the conservative implication that sociologists should find ways to make existing institutions function more efficiently in order to preserve the status quo (though liberals may also support reforms to make the system function better). The radical critique of functionalism points out that the subordinate class in a society, such as slaves or serfs, may *not* be interested in preserving the society, and may want a different type of society.

The radical, or Marxist formulation (sometimes called historical materialism) sees society as comprised of an economic base and a derived superstructure consisting of ideas and institutions. An economic determinist position sees other institutions and ideologies as being greatly influenced by the economic base—with little or no feedback involved. Radicals argue, on the contrary, that the correct position of radical sociology sees a two-day relationship between base and superstructure. For example, at various points in history, religion may have a great effect on the economic functioning of a society, even if in the long run the economic structure may influence and change religious patterns. The best strategy is to examine the roles of both the economic base and the elements of the superstructure of specific societies at given points in time. It will then be possible to see the importance of different social institutions, such as politics, education, or religion, as they affect the stability of a given society, or as they contribute to changes within the society or even the downfall of that society.

Although the Marxist approach of radical sociologists argues against economic determinism, it also argues against psychological or cultural determinism. If the economic determinists derive ideas and institutions from the economic system, the psychological or cultural determinists derive institutions—including economic institutions—from personality dispositions or from the basic values in a society. We have shown the limits of these approaches by pointing to the impact of socioeconomic institutions on, say, religious values. The radical position should not be distorted, however, to argue that values are directly and simply derived from economics, with no reciprocal effect. Rather, there is an interaction between cultural values and the economic base, and the exact nature of this relationship must be examined case by case, society by society. Thus, the radical approach is different from both the economic determinism of some sociologists and the psychological or cultural determinism of some other sociologists.

SUGGESTED READINGS

The best, most sophisticated, and well-written presentation of Marx's theory of society is found in the first half of Michael Harrington's *Twilight of Capitalism* (New York: Simon & Schuster, 1977). A good explanation and critique of Parsons's functionalism may be found in Alvin Gouldner, *The Coming Crisis of Western Sociology* (New York: Basic Books, 1970). Another critique is Anthony Giddens, "Functionalism: après la lutte," on pp. 96–134 of his *Studies in Social and Political Theory* (New York: Basic Books, 1977). An explicit attempt to reinvigorate the perspective is Jeffrey C. Alexander, ed., *Neofunctionlism* (Beverly Hills, CA: Sage, 1985). An excellent discussion of the basics of radical sociology is presented in a too little-known British book by Margaret Coulson and David Riddell, *Approaching Sociology* (London: Routledge & Kegan Paul, 1970). The best single source for Parsons's version of functionalism is Talcott Parsons, *The Social System* (New York: Free Press, 1951).

A radical view, with a different emphasis from ours and relying heavily on the insights of Freudian psychoanalysis, is presented very clearly and interestingly in Bruce Brown, *Marx, Freud, and the Critique of Everyday Life* (New York: Monthly Review Press, 1973). In contrast, a radical criticism of Freudian psychoanalysis is argued challengingly in Keith Brooks, "Freudianism Is Not a Basis for Marxist Psychology," in Phil Brown, *Radical Psychology* (New York: Harper & Row, 1973). A comprehensive evaluation of the two approaches is found in Richard Lichtman's three-part "Marx and Freud," *Socialist Review* 30 (Dec. 1976), 33 (June 1977), and 36 (Dec. 1977). For additional discussions of related topics, see Jerome Rabow, "Psychoanalysis and Sociology," *Annual Review of Sociology* 9 (1983): 555–578.

Some of the material in this chapter is adapted, with permission, from Howard Sherman, "Technology Vis-à-vis Institutions: A Marxist Commentary," *The Journal of Economic Issues* 13 (March 1979): 175–193.

REFERENCES

Alexander, Jeffrey C., ed. 1985. *Neofunctionalism*. Beverly Hills, CA: Sage.
Aronowitz, Stanley. 1981. *The Crisis in Historical Materialism*. New York: Praeger.
Bendix, Reinhard, and Seymour Martin Lipset, eds. 1966. *Class, Status, and Power*. 2d ed. New York: Free Press.

Berger, Peter, and Thomas Luckman. 1966. *The Social Construction of Reality*. Garden City, NY: Doubleday.

Coulson, Margaret, and David Riddell. 1970. *Approaching Sociology*. London: Routledge & Kegan Paul.

Danto, Arthur. 1965. *Analytical Philosophy of History*. New York: Cambridge University Press.

Davis, Kingsley, and Wilbert Moore. 1945. "Some Principles of Stratification." *American Sociological Review* 10 (April).

Demerath III, N. J., and Richard A. Peterson, eds. 1967. *System, Change, and Conflict*. New York: Free Press.

Deutscher, Isaac. 1971. *Marxism in Our Time*. Berkeley, CA: Ramparts Press.

Elster, Jon. 1982. "Marxism, Functionalism, and Game Theory." *Theory and Society* 11:453–492.

Feuer, Lewis. 1969. *The Conflict of Generations*. New York: Basic Books.

Giddens, Anthony. 1977. "Functionalism: après la lutte." In Giddens, *Studies in Social and Political Theory*, pp. 96–134. New York: Basic Books.

———. 1979. *Central Problems in Social Theory*. Berkeley: University of California Press.

———. 1981. *A Contemporary Critique of Historical Materialism*. Berkeley: University of California Press.

Gorer, G., and J. Rickman. 1949. *The People of Great Russia*. London: Cresset.

Gouldner, Alvin. 1970. *The Coming Crisis of Western Sociology*. New York: Basic Books.

Harris, Marvin. 1968. *The Rise of Anthropological Theory*. New York: Crowell.

Holt, Robert. 1965. "A Proposed Structural-Functional Framework for Political Science." In Don Martindale, ed., *Functionalism in the Social Sciences*. Philadelphia: American Academy of Political and Social Sciences.

Lefcourt, Robert. 1971. "Law Against the People." In Robert Lefcourt, ed., *Law Against the People*. New York: Vintage Books.

Marx, Karl. 1859, 1904. Preface to *A Contribution to the Critique of Political Economy*. Chicago: Charles Kerr.

———. 1867. *Capital*. Vol. I. London: Allen & Unwin.

Mills, C. Wright. 1959. *The Sociological Imagination*. New York: Grove Press.

Oelsner, Leslie. 1972. "Scales of Justice." *Riverside Daily Enterprise* (September 28).

Parsons, Talcott. 1954. *Essays on Sociological Theory*. New York: Free Press.

———. 1964. *Social Structure and Personality*. New York: Free Press.

———. 1951. *The Social System*. New York: Free Press.

———. 1966. "On the Concept of Political Power." In Reinhard Bendix and Seymour Martin Lipset, eds., *Class, Status, and Power*. 2d ed. New York: Free Press.

———, and Robert F. Bales. 1955. *Family, Socialization and Interaction Process*. New York: Free Press.

President's Commission on Law Enforcement and the Administration of Justice. 1968. *The Challenge of Crime in a Free Society*. New York: Avon.

Rabow, Jerome. 1983. "Psychoanalysis and Sociology." *Annual Review of Sociology* 9:555–578.

Schevitz, Jeffrey M. 1968. "The Shadow Knows: A Synthetic Review of Domhoff's *Who Rules America?* and Parsons' "On the Concept of Political Power." *Berkeley Journal of Sociology* 13:82–96.

Sciulli, David. 1985. "The Practical Groundwork of Critical Theory: Bringing Parsons to Habermas (and vice versa)." In Jeffrey C. Alexander, ed. *Neofunctionalism*. Beverly Hills, CA: Sage.

————, and Dean Gerstein. 1985. "Social Theory and Talcott Parsons in the 1980s." *Annual Review of Sociology* 11:369–387.

Spates, James L. 1983. "The Sociology of Values." *Annual Review of Sociology* 9:27–49.

Spencer, Robert. 1965. "Nature and Value of Functionalism in Anthropology." In Don Martindale, ed., *Functionalism in the Social Sciences*. Philadelphia: American Academy of Political and Social Sciences.

Spitzer, Steven. 1983. "Marxist Perspectives in the Sociology of Law." *Annual Review of Sociology* 9:103–124.

Wood, James L. 1974. *The Sources of American Student Activism*. Lexington, MA: Lexington Books, Heath.

Zinn, Howard. 1970. *The Politics of History*. Boston: Beacon Press.

chapter *3*

Poverty and Social Class

Many people realize that much of the world lives in poverty, but it may come as a shock to learn that there is a vast amount of poverty in the richest country in the world, the United States. Before President Reagan began his first term in office, in 1980, there were 29 million Americans (or 13 percent) living in poverty. By 1983, as a result of a recession that the President allowed to intensify, there were 36 million Americans (or 15.3 percent) living in poverty (U.S. Bureau of the Census, 1986, p. 457; see also Rothschild, 1988).

Yet the official definition of poverty appears to be set much too low by contemporary American standards. It is based on what the government describes as "an economy diet . . . meant for emergency or temporary use when funds are low—in other words a diet which over long periods of time does not meet minimum nutritional requirements" (Light, 1969, p. 2). Other aspects of the official poverty-income level are estimated in proportion to this "economy diet." This means that the 36 million Americans under the poverty line did not have enough nutritional foods to eat, that many of them lived in slum neighborhoods, and that they could not afford to give their children a good higher education. The number of homeless people rose during the first Reagan administration from 250,000 in 1980 to 350,000 in 1984 (MacDougall, 1984, p. 29). By 1987, estimates pointed to a further dramatic increase to between 750,000 and 5 million people! (*Newsweek,* 1987; CNN, 1987). This alarming new homeless population has taken on the proportions of a national scandal; some of the homeless are called "bag people" since they literally carry around their few belongings in shopping bags.

Table 3.1   INEQUALITY OF UNITED STATES DISTRIBUTION, 1984

Income group of family	Income range	Percent of total income received by group
Top 20%	$45,300 and over	43
Upper middle 20%	31,501–45,299	24
Middle 20%	21,710–31,500	17
Lower middle 20%	12,490–21,709	11
Bottom 20%	12,489 and under	5

Source: U. S. Census Bureau, Department of Commerce, *Statistical Abstract of the United States, 1986* (Washington, DC: Government Printing Office, 1986), p. 452.

INCOME INEQUALITY

Let use examine the full range of income in the United States, from very poor to very rich. This is clearly portrayed in Table 3.1. The poorest 20 percent of Americans had only 5 percent of all U.S. income in 1984; their incomes were under $12,500 a year. By contrast, the top 20 percent of Americans had 43 percent of all income; their incomes were over $45,300 a year. So some Americans had many times the income of other Americans—and the gap increased during the Reagan administration. By 1983, the top 20 percent of U.S. families had an average of 9 times the income of the bottom 20 percent of U.S. families. The top 2 percent alone had as much income as the bottom 40 percent.

TRENDS IN INCOME DISTRIBUTION

Has there been any reduction in the inequality of income distribution in the United States in the last 70 years? The answer is shown in Table 3.2. The most noticeable change is a *fall* from 8 percent down to 5 percent in the share of income of the poorest 20 percent of Americans—a fall of almost half. On the other hand, the share of the richest 20 percent of Americans has fluctuated in a narrow range, rising from 46 percent in 1910 to 51 percent in 1929, and then falling to 43 percent by 1984. Therefore, we conclude that in spite of all the outcry about income inequality and all the government promises and programs to reduce it, there has been little change and certainly no improvement in equality since 1910.

TRENDS IN ABSOLUTE LEVEL OF INCOME

There is one important qualification to this argument. In general, most categories of Americans are now better off than the corresponding categories of Americans in 1910. This is primarily because of increases in American production, most of which were stimulated by victories in World War I and World War II (and by the demand for American goods in the devastated countries of Europe). By and large, the United States emerged from these wars as the main victor, which permitted the continued expansion of American industry and American profits. These profits,

Table 3.2 **HISTORY OF INEQUALITY OF UNITED STATES PERSONAL INCOME, 1910–1984**
Percentages of U.S. personal income, before taxes, received by richest 20 percent and poorest 20 percent of U.S. families

Year	Richest 20 percent	Poorest 20 percent
1910	46%	8%
1918	47	7
1929	51	5
1937	49	4
1947	43	5
1957	42	5
1965	41	5
1974	41	5
1984	43	5

Source: U.S. Department of Commerce, Bureau of the Census, *Statistical Abstract of the United States, 1986* (Washington, DC: Government Printing Office, 1986).

which added to the wealth of the American nation, were greatly augmented by American imperial expansion and world domination in the 1950s and 1960s.

After the American victory in World War I and especially after the victory in World War II, the economic "pie" for the United States got larger and larger because, for several years after each war, American corporations had no strong competitors in international markets. There were literally more millions and billions of dollars for Americans to share. One of the crucial results was the development of a relatively large middle-income group. Especially after World War II, even manual laborers could aspire to middle-level incomes. Attaining a middle-level income became possible for such diverse groups of workers as high school teachers, plumbers, electricians, truck drivers, middle-level managers, and college professors. However, because so much additional money has come into American society since the end of World War I, it has *not* been necessary for the ruling class to *redistribute* income significantly between the richer and poorer population groups. The rich, as it were, can have their cake (or "pie") and eat it too.

TYPES OF INCOME

Income is not randomly distributed among all individuals. On the contrary, *distribution* of income is closely related to *type* of income. Does most of a person's income come from labor (wages), or does it come from property (rent, interest, or profits)? If this fact is known, a good prediction can be made about his or her income bracket.

Almost all the bottom 40 percent of families in 1984 were working-class families, and most of their income came from wages and salaries earned by their labor. But most of the income of the top 2 percent came from ownership of property in the form of rent, interest, or profit—in short, the income of the capitalist class. Thus in 1976, according to the federal income tax returns, 88 percent of income under $30,000 was wages and salaries, whereas 88 percent of income over $1,000,000 was property income (U.S. Internal Revenue Service, 1979). Moreover, the super-rich elite (less than one-tenth of 1 percent of all taxpayers) collects 23 percent of all dividends and 37 percent of all capital gains.

Furthermore, wealth (what people own) is even more concentrated than income (what people earn each year). Data on wealth used to be very limited, but new government studies now afford plentiful and relatively reliable data. (One error in one study was widely discussed by conservatives, but the corrected data make the same point; the two studies are in close agreement, though they were done independently.) One study for 1983 (updating a 1962 study) was by the Federal Reserve System with the cooperation of six other government agencies, while the other study, for 1984, was by the Bureau of the Census. Fortunately, an excellent article by Andrew Winnick (forthcoming) puts these two massive studies, as well as the previous data on income distribution, into one comparable framework, so his summary of the findings will be used here.

The Bureau of the Census found that the families designated by it as poor and low-income, that is, with incomes of from $0 to $25,000 per year, included 56 percent of all families, but that these families had only 39 percent of net worth (wealth). In fact, the median net worth of the poor families (less than $11,200 yearly income) was only $5,623, *including homes;* the median net worth of the low-income families ($11,200 to $25,000 per year) was only $25,534, similarly including homes. The middle-income families ($25,001 to $50,000 per year) included 31 percent of all families and had 32 percent of all net worth, with a median net worth of $48,427. Finally, high-income families (over $50,000 income per year) were just 12 percent of all families, but had 38 percent of all net worth, with a median net worth of $127,919.

Similarly, the Federal Reserve study (reported in Winnick) found that the top 10 percent of families have 34 percent of all net worth (including homes), 64 percent of all financial assets, 85 percent of all publicly owned corporate stocks, and 92 percent of all municipal bonds. Moreover, if we look at the super rich with the most capitalist income, this top 0.5 percent of families by income held 19 percent of all net worth (including homes), 31 percent of all financial assets, 43 percent of all publicly owned corporate stocks, and 56 percent of all municipial bonds!

Furthermore, comparison of the 1962 and 1983 Federal Reserve studies (after statistical corrections were made for sake of comparability) shows that the rich (0.5 percent of all families) increased their share of the wealth by two percentage points in this period, while the share of the middle-income, low-income, and poor families, which comprise the bottom 90 percent of families, decreased by three percentage points. Finally, at the very top, a survey by *Forbes* magazine (see Winnick, forthcoming) found that in 1983 the wealthiest 400 individuals had over $150 million each and the wealthiest 82 families over $200 million each—with a total ownership of $166 billion of assets and direct or indirect control of $2.2 trillion of business assets!

Notice the cumulative and self-reinforcing nature of the concentration of wealth and income. High concentration of stock ownership leads to a high concentration of income from profits. This income from profits, in turn, is sufficiently high that it puts its recipients in the highest income brackets. But it is only in these highest income brackets that people are willing and able to save significant amounts of money for investments. Therefore, they are the ones who make large investments, thus increasing their stock ownership. In other words, large ownership of stock leads to high income in the form of profits, and high income leads to more stock ownership and further profits. This might be called the "Matthew Effect" in economics, a concept invented by Robert K. Merton (1968) and refers to the biblical notion: he who has, gets.

The process of wealth and income concentration is self-reinforcing in other ways. For example, one vital prerequisite of upward mobility—improving one's social and economic position—is education. But many studies have revealed that often "the father's income rather than the boy's brains determines who shall be college trained" (Mills, 1959, p. 257). If you are poor, it is hard to support yourself through college even if you are of above-average intelligence. If you are rich, but not bright enough to get into a top university, you can always find some private university that is willing to accept you for the money it costs.

Even with an education, though, the poor person can attempt to work his or her way up in business only from the point at which he or she is hired. The rich heir to a business might have little education and less intelligence but could still step into his or her parents' shoes if they control enough stock in the corporation. "It is very difficult to climb to the top. . . . It is easier and much safer to be born there" (Mills, 1959, p. 115). In their study of top corporate managers, Useem and Karabel (1986) substantiated this conclusion. In fact, many of the wealthy today merely inherited a great deal of stock. From 1900 to 1950 some 70 percent of the fathers of very rich men were big businessmen (Mills, 1959, p. 105). It is true that most of the very rich have worked as big business executives; nevertheless, completely at leisure "coupon clippers"—nonworking, absentee owners receiving stock income—increased from 14 percent of the very rich in 1900 to 26 percent by 1950 (Mills, 1959, p. 108). The overall conclusion is that Horatio Alger stories of poor boys rising into great wealth are largely myths. There is a certain amount of mobility from poor to middle-income status, but very little upward mobility from low-income or middle-income status into the richest elite groups. (Blau and Duncan, 1967, pp. 90–113).

CLASSES IN AMERICAN CAPITALISM

The United States is a capitalist system. *Capitalism* is defined as a system in which

1. Products are sold on the market for a private profit.
2. There is a class called capitalists, which owns the capital—that is, the factories and machines—and also the final products of work performed, as well as the profits from that work.

3. There is a class called workers, which owns no capital, but does own its labor power (and which is free to work if jobs can be found).

The previous section showed that American workers do indeed have low incomes relative to capitalists, as well as little wealth or savings for investment, while a small number of capitalists do own significant amounts of corporate stock and other kinds of wealth.

In addition to the capitalist class and the working class, there are also various middle, or intermediate, classes in the United States. The history of class composition in the United States, as far as it is revealed in official government data, is shown in Figure 3.1. The largest single class in the United States is the working class. The working class consists of all those people who work for others and derive most of their income from wages or salaries paid for their labor. Some salaries paid to higher-level professionals, such as top medical personnel, top sports people, or top movie actors, are very high. Most wage earners, however, have significantly lower incomes. Many, especially minorities or women, have particularly low incomes or are unemployed. American welfare and tax reforms are inadequate and leave a mass of poor at the bottom of the social ladder. "Millions of American families continue . . . to have such low incomes that they must be classified as poverty-stricken, and our tax structure does little to diminish the vast inequalities that exist in before-tax income." [Reagan, 1963, p. 36.] According to radicals, the main reason for the poverty and low incomes of many working-class people is the exploitation of workers—that is, appropriation of part of each worker's product by capitalists. This appropriation constitutes the profits of the capitalist class.

At the beginning of American history, most people were farmers. It is estimated that in 1780 wage-earning and salaried workers were only 20 percent of all active participants in the American economy (Reich, 1978, pp. 174–183). (Slaves are not part of these calculations since that class is no longer in existence.) By 1880, wage and salaried workers were 62 percent of all active participants in the economy. By 1974, wage and salaried workers were 83 percent of all active participants in the economy. This 83 percent included manual and intellectual workers, industrial, agricultural, service, and technical workers of all kinds. These are the people who produce almost all our national product. Thus Marx's prediction of an increasing working class has certainly been fulfilled in the United States.

The working class, as defined here, is comprised not only of manual workers, but also of intellectual workers—what may be called "educated labor." Although these two branches of the working class are usually distinguished in traditional sociology, both manual and intellectual laborers share important characteristics in capitalist society. They all work for other people instead of owning the means of economic production; thus they all depend on employers to pay their salaries and can be fired for anything from having a "bad" personality to having "bad" political views, as well as performing poorly on the job (according to the criteria of job performance set by the employers).

There is also a middle class of self-employed entrepreneurs in the United States. This category in the census includes some capitalist businesspeople who hire workers. Most of this category, however, does *not* hire other people, nor does it work for other people. This class produces goods owned by itself; it includes farmers, self-employed professionals (*not* those who work for others), independent artisans and craftspeople, small business entrepreneurs, and other property owners. In 1780 this middle class constituted 80 percent of the population, mostly farmers (Reich, 1978, pp. 174–183). By 1880 the self-employed had declined to 37 percent of the active economic population. By 1974 the self-employed had declined to 8 percent of the active economic participants—and their percentage

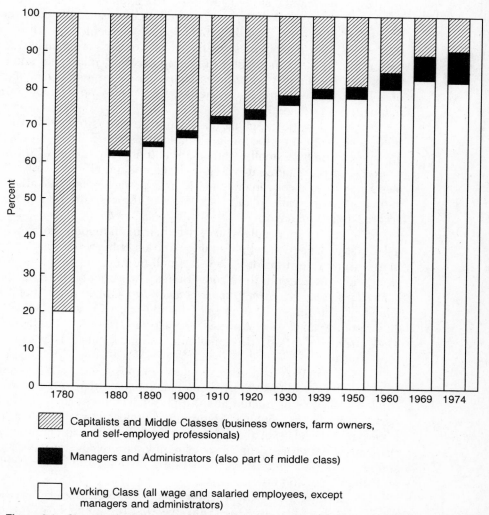

Figure 3.1 Class composition in the United States, 1780–1974 (as percent active participants in the economy). Adapted from Michael Reich, "The Development of the Wage-Labor Force," in R. Edwards et al., *The Capitalist System,* 2d ed. (Englewood Cliffs, NJ: Prentice-Hall, 1978), p. 180. Copyright © by Michael Reich.

continues to decline. Of that 8 percent, some 2 percent are self-employed farmers, 3 percent are self-employed professionals and artisans, and 3 percent are self-employed businesspeople. Thus Marx's prediction of a rapidly declining middle class has been fulfilled, according to this definition of middle class.

The third category listed in government data is salaried managers and administrators. Theoretically, all of these are simply workers who are highly paid for doing managerial labor. In practice, they fall within a spectrum from very highly paid (over a million dollars a year for some executives) to only average pay. Most *are* in fact just well-paid workers. A small number at the top, however, are part of the capitalist class. In 1780 the managerial class was negligible. By 1880 they were listed as 1 percent of the active participants in the economy of the United States. By 1974 they had risen to 9 percent. Again, it must be stressed that, realistically, most of these managers and officials are merely well-paid *workers* with a middle-class mentality. Furthermore, most managers and officials, even low-paid ones, identify with the capitalist class—an instance of "false consciousness" for these workers. Nevertheless, we classify most middle- and lower-level managers as middle class.

How big is the capitalist class? Its true size is hidden in the categories of self-employed businesspeople and managers. Of the 3 percent classified as businesspeople, only a small number are actually capitalists who hire and exploit workers. Of the 9 percent who are managers and officials, only a small percent own large amounts of corporate stock, have profit or interest as their main income, and can thus be called capitalists. Most of the rest are a "new middle class" of organizational managers.

Capitalists are people who derive their main income from ownership of capital—that is, legal control of factories and machinery (or "plant and equipment" in government terminology). A very small number of capitalists own *most* of the plant and equipment in the United States. *Only about 1 percent of all Americans derive large incomes from property ownership.* Only 9 percent of Americans hold any stock and just 420,000 people (or one-half of 1 percent) own 43 percent of all corporate stock (see Winnick, forthcoming). As C. Wright Mills showed in *The Power Elite* (1956), this small number of capitalists is a very politically powerful group.

To summarize the present class composition in the United States: The working class is at least 83 percent of all active participants in the economy. The capitalist class is estimated at from one-half percent to 2 percent of all active participants in the economy. Assuming capitalists are estimated at 1 percent, that leaves a middle class of about 16 percent of all participants in the economy. That middle-class category includes all self-employed professionals and artisans; smaller self-employed businesspeople; most farm owners; and most middle- and lower-level managers and officials.

In his day, Marx saw a whole spectrum of classes. He predicted *correctly* a polarization of classes. One critic says that the greatest "distortion of the facts is seen in Marx's polarization theory. It may even be true that the number of classes has become smaller, but modern society has certainly not been reduced to two classes" (Dupre, 1966, p. 211). No Marxist claims there are only two classes in modern capitalism. There is a very small—but powerful—capitalist class. At the same time, there are many remnants of old classes, such as farmers, independent professionals, and small businesspeople, who constitute a rapidly shrinking old middle class. There is also a new middle class of managers and officials, but it will likely remain a relatively small segment of the class structure of the United States. Last, there is a very large and still growing working class (whose internal composition is considered in the next section).

Since the middle classes—as defined here—are small and declining in numbers and power, they may sometimes be omitted from a very abstract analysis, but must be considered in any concrete study. Because of the objective polarization of workers versus capitalists, important political issues in the United States—such as unemployment or inflation—are often also polarized around a capitalist position versus a workers' position. Issues involving farmers or small business entrepreneurs exist, but are more peripheral, and may be seen as one of many secondary conflicts in society.

Thus, our position is that America is largely a *working-class* society with a small but powerful capitalist class at the top. This position is clearly distinguished from traditional sociology's position that American society is basically *middle class*. We do not deny that the cultural lifestyle of many American workers is middle class (that is, two children, suburban home, various luxuries such as color TV sets and campers). Nevertheless, most Americans are employed by others and thus depend on others for their material existence; hence they can be legitimately considered workers.

STRATIFICATION OF THE WORKING CLASS

While the working class has grown in the United States, its composition has certainly not remained the same. Moreover, it is not a homogeneous class, but has many different racial, religious, sexual, and ethnic groups within it, and it consists of many different strata by income level, education, or occupation.

In the early United States, one could have described the working class (aside from slaves) as mainly Anglo-Saxon, white, Protestant, and male. Their occupations were mainly agricultural and manual industrial labor. Since that time the working class has changed and differentiated in many ways.

First, millions of new immigrants came from southern, western, and eastern Europe: Irish, Italians, Germans, Poles, and so forth (including many Catholics and Jews). Then came immigrants from China—many imported to build railroads—and Japan. Millions of Chicanos became American citizens when the American Southwest was occupied by conquest. Puerto Ricans were also incorporated by conquest. During and after World War II, blacks moved to urban areas, to become a significant part of the industrial work force. In 1985, women workers comprised 44 percent of the work force. Therefore, it is possible for the working class to be divided by nationalist, religious, racist, and sexist prejudices.

These prejudices do exist and serve to blur or deemphasize the common interests of all workers. Moreover, such prejudices have often been encouraged by the dominant institutions and the capitalists who control them. Capitalist employers can and do pay lower wages to all groups of workers when workers are split and weakened by nationalist, racist, or sexist prejudices. *Both* male and female workers, and *both* black and white workers end up being hurt by prejudice. As the sociologist Edna Bonacich observes: "White capitalists would gladly dispense with and undercut white working-class brethren if they could, and have done so whenever they had the opportunity" (1972, p. 547).

The working class has also changed in terms of occupational categories. Workers in agriculture have been a steadily declining percentage, while technical and service workers have increased. Thus, from 1910 to 1980, farmers, farm managers, and farm workers declined from 31 to 3 percent of the labor force (Reich, 1978, p. 178; U.S. Bureau of the Census, 1986, p. 400). Manual, or blue-collar, industrial workers (craftspeople and supervisors, semiskilled and unskilled) declined in the same period from 38 to 31 percent of the work force. On the contrary, white-collar workers (clerical, sales, professional, and technical) rose from 15 to 42 percent of the work force in those same years. Service workers (such as waitresses or barbers) rose from 10 to 13 percent of the work force in the same period. Finally, the managers, proprietors, and officials rose from 7 to 11 percent of the total force.

Agricultural and blue-collar workers are usually considered the older kind of working class, while white-collar and service workers are the "new" working class. Yet all of the various strata of the working class are exploited and produce profit for their employers. Nevertheless, there are many obvious differences among the strata. For example, in 1970, the family income of farm workers averaged $4672, but the average family income of professional-technical workers was $14,135 (Anderson, 1974, p. 106).

In addition, the social prestige, or status, of professional-technical workers is much higher than that of manual workers or farm workers. As a result, each of these strata tends to have different cultural patterns, different attitudes toward unions, and a different working-class self-consciousness. For example, many professional-technical workers consider themselves middle class rather than working class. The different strata also have very different political attitudes on various issues. The divisions and stratification of the working class are thus considerable barriers to its unity versus the capitalist class and provide considerable complications in any class analysis. In Chapters 8 through 13 we shall examine differences between low- and middle-income workers, black and white workers, male and female workers, and younger and older workers.

TWO EXPLANATIONS OF POVERTY AND WEALTH

Why is there poverty? Why is there a large degree of inequality between groups? In Chapter 14 we shall see that two quite different explanations have been advanced to explain unequal income distribution.

One, promoted by conservatives, is called the theory of *mariginal productivity*. It asserts that each component factor of production (such as human labor power) is compensated (e.g., by paying wages) according to the last, additional or marginal product produced by that factor. So, in this view, people receive different incomes—for different work or for providing different capital—because the labor (or the machine) has different productivity. Stated bluntly, this view contends that people get paid according to what they produce, so that a person with inferior productivity gets a lower wage.

The second theory, usually espoused by radicals, is called the theory of *surplus value*. According to this theory, all the value of commodities is produced by human labor—either by present human labor or by past human labor embodied in machines. This human labor produces valuable products that are owned, under our present capitalist institutions, by the capitalist owner of the enterprise. After paying out money for raw materials and wages, the capitalist owns the surplus product, derived from human labor, above the costs of wages and material. This surplus is what we call a profit. The workers' wages are set by supply and demand, approximately at a level equal to the workers' socially expected necessities of life. As workers become more and more productive, their wages rise only relatively, so that profits keep growing.

This is only a brief sketch of these two complex theories, which will be discussed in more detail in Chapter 14.

SUMMARY

We began this chapter with a look at various economic facts of American society. In 1983, for example, 36 million people lived in poverty. At the other extreme of this unequal income distribution, about 2000 people make over $1 million a year. In terms of social classes, most people in the United States are workers (over 83 percent of the active economic participants). There is a relatively small number (16 percent) of middle-class people: owners of small businesses and farms, independent professionals, and lower-level managers. There is a tiny capitalist class (1 to 2 percent) of those who own industries and make profits. Victory in two world wars, along with the production stimulated by military spending in war and peace, has increased the total economic "pie" of the Unites States; yet there has been no significant income redistribution since 1910. The conservative theory asserts that this unequal income distribution merely reflects unequal productive contributions. The radical theory asserts that high income profits result from exploitation of human labor, leaving some workers in poverty (from low wages, unemployment, or discrimination). The economic facts discussed in this chapter have significant social, cultural, and political consequences that will be analyzed throughout the book.

SUGGESTED READINGS

The best single source of data—as well as some important sociological controversies—on the economy is the collection of articles edited by Maurice Zeitlin, *American Society, Inc.: Studies of the Social Structure and Political Economy of the United States*, 2d ed. (Chicago: Rand McNally, 1977). The most comprehensive radical introduction to this subject is E. K. Hunt and Howard Sherman, *Economics: An Introduction to Traditional and Radical Views*, 5th ed. (New York: Harper & Row, 1985). Two other excellent and useful books are Erik Olin Wright, *Classes* (New York: Schocken Books, 1986), and Paul Blumberg, *Inequality in an Age of Decline* (New York: Oxford University Press, 1980). For an outstanding detailed discussion of how the Reagan presidency has benefited the wealthy, hurt the poor, and been contradictory regarding its conservative economic philosophy and actual economic policies, see Emma Rothschild, "The Real Reagan Economy," *New York Review of Books* 35 (11): 46–53.

REFERENCES

Anderson, Charles. 1974. *Toward a New Sociology*. Homewood, IL: Dorsey Press.

Blau, Peter M., and Otis D. Duncan. 1967. *The American Occupational Structure*. New York: Wiley.

Bonacich, Edna. 1972. "A Theory of Ethnic Antagonism: The Split Labor Market." *American Sociological Review* 3 (October):547–559.

CNN. 1987. Broadcast of Cable News Network.

Dupre, Louis. 1966. *The Philosophical Foundations of Marxism*. New York: Harcourt Brace Jovanovich.

Joint Economic Committee, U.S. Congress. 1986. *The Concentration of Wealth in the United States*. Washington, DC: U.S. Government Printing Office.

Light, Donald. 1969. "Income Distribution." *Occasional Papers of the Union for Radical Political Economics* (December).

MacDougall, A. Kent. 1984. "Rich-Poor Gap in U.S. Widens During Decade." *Los Angeles Times* (October 25).

Merton, Robert K. 1968. "The Matthew Effect in Science." In Norman W. Storer, ed., *The Sociology of Science: Theoretical and Empirical Investigations,* pp. 439–459. Chicago: University of Chicago Press.

Mills, C. Wright. 1959. *The Power Elite*. New York: Oxford University Press.

Newsweek. 1987. "Forcing the Mentally Ill to Get Help." Nov. 9, pp. 47–48.

Reagan, Michael. 1963. *The Managed Economy*. New York: Oxford University Press.

Reich, Michael. 1978. "The Evolution of the Labor Force." In Richard Edwards, Michael Reich, and Thomas Weisskopf, eds., *The Capitalist System*. 2d ed. Englewood Cliffs, NJ: Prentice-Hall.

Rothschild, Emma. 1988. "The Real Reagan Economy." *New York Review of Books* 35 (11):46–53.

U.S. Bureau of the Census, Department of Commerce. 1986. *Statistical Abstract of the United States, 1986*. Washington, DC: Government Printing Office.

U.S. Internal Revenue Service. 1979. *Statistics of Income—1976: Individual Income Returns*. Washington, DC: Government Printing Office.

Useem, Michael, and Jerome Karabel. 1986. "Pathways to Top Corporate Management." *American Sociological Review* 51 (April):184–200.

Winnick, Andrew. Forthcoming. "The Changing Distribution of Income and Wealth in the U.S., 1960–1985: An Examination of the Movement Toward Two Societies, Separate and Unequal." In Patricia Voydanoff and Linda Majka, *Families and Economic Distress*. Beverly Hills, CA: Sage.

chapter 4

Stratification and Class Conflict

Some traditional functionalists acknowledge the existence of class divisions. However, they also tend to see a harmonious social organism, in which even class divisions and routine class conflicts play a useful, functional role. Class differences in income are held to be necessary to give the poor the incentive to work harder. In the political arena, class conflicts between the poor and the propertied (and between many other groups according to traditional political sociologists) result in a process of give and take that ends in a consensus for the good of the majority. We may conclude that "functional theory commonly predisposes analysis to those equilibrating forces which make for cooperation and harmony. . . . The stress of functional theories on goal-maintenance markedly reduces their capacity for dealing with conflict-ridden systems" (Krupp, in Martindale, 1965, pp. 65, 78).

In other words, if traditional functionalist sociologists examine the exploitation of workers, the oppression of blacks, or the oppression of women, they tend to ask what mechanisms exist for *adjusting* these conflicts. They seldom ask what are the basic structural reasons for the existence of such conflicts.

After Parsons's basic writings appeared, there were many attempts by functionalists to deal more directly with conflict. One sophisticated writer on conflict within the functionalist framework is Neil J. Smelser, whose analysis of conflict is stated in detail in his *Theory of Collective Behavior* (1963).

Within a functionalist perspective—but a different version from that of Parsons—Smelser explains a series of conflicts ranging from riots to reform and revolutionary movements. He shows that when a society is in a state of disorganization, these types of conflict are likely to occur. Smelser argues that when six necessary and sufficient conditions are present, certain types of collective behavior will occur. *Collective behavior* refers to a variety of unconventional group actions such as fads, crazes, riots, and social movements. For example, when a revolutionary movement is likely to develop there are:

1. Social arrangements that permit protests
2. Radical beliefs
3. Many social problems and inequities
4. Incidents that provide a catalyst
5. Attempts to mobilize the masses
6. A breakdown of social control

Smelser uses many illustrations and engages in a complex analysis of these issues. In doing so, he attempts to show that functionalism can explain conflict. In fact, one major contribution Smelser makes to the traditional literature on protests is that he introduces a multiple-variable model of protest, focusing on the six conditions noted above, that goes beyond the usual, single-factor explanations of protest that stress only one or two of these conditions. These ideas will be developed further in Chapter 17.

THE TRADITIONAL VIEW OF CLASS

The functionalist approach is reflected in the traditional sociologists' description of classes. They do *not* see a deep division between two opposed classes, one of which exploits the other (as in the radical view of workers and capitalists). On the contrary, most empirical research uses a framework that assumes a continuum in which each class has only somewhat less income, prestige, or status than the next class. One example of such class categories is lower lower, upper lower, lower middle, middle middle, upper middle, lower upper, and upper upper. This is a continuous scale. Moreover, this view implies that there are few major barriers to upward movement and that everyone has the same chance to climb the social and economic pyramid (see Colfax and Roach, 1973, p. 62).

The most famous and interesting discussion of class and stratification of society within traditional sociology is that of Max Weber. *Stratification* refers to the differences in ranking between social groups in terms of income, prestige, and other factors. Marx viewed the stratifiction of society as based primarily on class. Weber based it on class, status, and power. Yet many modern interpretations of Weber tend to overemphasize his differences from Marx. Their approach to class was similar. Weber defined a class as a number of people with a similar economic opportunity in life and with similar economic interests in income, products, and the labor movement (See Weber, 1968). Therefore, Weber finds that "property [and] lack of property [are the] basic categories of all class situations" (p. 927). Weber also agrees with Marx that the factor that creates "class" is unambiguously economic interest (p. 928).

Weber specifies three kind of classes, of which the first and most important is the "property class," a concept similar to that of Marx. Each property class has different holdings of property. Weber talks about a "positively provileged" class (like Marx's bourgeoisie or capitalist class), which has a *monopoly* over interest and profit income, savings and investment, luxury consumer goods, the best educations, and executive positions in corporations. Weber also discusses a "negatively privileged" property class (like Marx's proletariat or working class), which owns no property, but whose own labor power is bought and sold on the labor market. In addition, he discusses an intermediate, or middle, class living off both property and labor.

Second, Weber considers "acquisition classes," which differ according to occupation (which is the basis for acquisition of property). In this case, the positively privileged acquisition class includes people such as bankers, financiers, and industrial entrepreneurs. The negatively privileged includes the working class. This second concept of class thus overlaps and merges with the first concept.

Weber's third concept of class is the "social class." The social class results from, or is based on, the acquisition of property by a set of persons who then commonly associate with each other. Weber's social class is thus the natural result of his property classes. He discusses four different social classes: the privileged classes, the intelligentsia, the lower middle classes, and the working class.

Social stratification for Weber is also based on "social status," which is defined in terms of the prestige derived from a family's style of life, its inherited prestige, or the occupation of its members. Hence social status is primarily based on a family's *consumption* of goods, not on its production of goods or acquisition of property. Yet consumption itself is based on control of income or property. Therefore, as Weber himself emphasizes, "Property classes often constitute the nucleus of a (social) stratum" (1968, p. 429). Thus social status is itself determined largely by class.

Finally, Weber's third basis of stratification is power. Weber defines power as "the chance of man or a number of men to realize their own will in a social action even against the resistance of others who are participating in the action" (1968, p. 926). He notes that some people want power for its own sake, while some want it to gain further economic advantage. He also shows that power may exist in its economic forms, such as the power of General Motors over the hiring and firing of people and over the setting of prices. But he says power may also exist in political forms, as through political parties. One interpreter of Weber points out, however, that Weber clearly recognized that "property classes represent the most dominant underpinnings of political parties, together with the influences of acquisition classes . . . In other words, the most important single seat of power is class, i.e., economic power" (Anderson, 1974, p. 120).

In this interpretation, Weber's social status and power are clearly derivative from economic class—so we are left with a view of class and stratification very similar to Marx's, though with a different emphasis, whereas most traditional sociologists have interpreted Weber as being more opposed to Marx. The most complete modern attempt to reconstruct Weber's view of stratification is Milton Gordon's *Social Class in American Society* (1958), which veiws class, status, and power as quite independent facets of stratification. Most modern empirical studies of stratification have likewise seen the strata of American society as a continuum of individuals differing in many different ways along Weber's dimensions of class, status, and power. This is how they come to define strata, or classes, from "lower

lower" to "upper upper." Radical sociologists, as we shall see, tend to see more sharply differentiated groups (capitalists, workers, and middle class), based primarily on economic class, with social status and power as derivatives of economic class.

Some traditional sociologists have gone much further, to claim that the usual classes and class conflicts have mostly disappeared from the American scene. Therefore, they say that identifications of groups and strata should be based not on occupation or property, but only on social status as individuals see it themselves. For example, Harvard sociologist Daniel Bell (1970, p. 22) says that "as the traditional class structure dissolves, more and more individuals want to be identified, not by their occupational base (in the Marxist sense), but by their cultural tastes and lifestyles."

Bell has been criticized on various grounds. First, classes still exist in the United States and there is no evidence that the class structure is disappearing. Second, cultural tastes and lifestyles are clearly influenced by class position. Third, sociologists cannot rely merely on how people self-identify their social position, because many people have a false consciousness of their own class position and class interests; hence, more objective criteria are needed to indicate a person's class position.

CLASSES IN A RADICAL PERSPECTIVE

The radical perspective is as follows. As noted in Chapter 3, the working class now accounts for about 83 percent of all American economic participants. There, the working class is defined as all of those whose main source of income is labor for others, whether received as wages, salaries, bonuses, or any other form of labor income. (Other radical thinkers, such as Erik Olin Wright [1986, 1979], have focused more on manual workers and thus point to a lower percent of working class, which is closer to the percent for manual workers presented in Chapter 3.) On the other hand, capitalists are defined as people who own factories, machinery, land, and money capital—and who get most of their income by exploiting the labor of workers. They hire workers, who need jobs, but also make profits through the workers' labor power. The capitalist class, so defined, is estimated at from one-half to 2 percent of the work force, as shown in Chapter 3.

Chapter 3 also discussed people who are neither workers nor capitalists. For example, a farmer or businessperson may own a business that is too small to hire any workers. Such persons do not exploit anyone else, nor are they directly exploited by capitalists (unless they must pay interest to them). A professional artist or a doctor who employs no one else, and sells his or her product directly to the consumer is likewise neither a worker nor a capitalist. All of these may be called middle class, which is, by this definition, about 14 percent in American society. It includes the middle level of management (though the top level of management may be capitalists and the bottom level workers).

Radicals do *not* use income to define class. They believe that property ownership or nonownership is more basic. If a person owns corporate stock, that person derives income from it. If a person works for a living, then he or she receives a certain amount of wage income. If people with the same income obtain that income in different ways, they may have very different views and behavior. For example, a small businessperson may have the same low income as a factory worker, yet the businessperson's political outlook may be very different from the worker's because of the difference between ownership and labor.

Similarly, in the United States a person's prestige, or status, largely depends on income and class position. Therefore, status should not be considered an additional factor determining class. Obviously, one's income and status *are* important sociological facts. The point is only that they are not independent facts; for the most part, they *reflect* class.

Self-identification of class means the specification of one's class position according to the respondent's own opinion given in a questionnaire. In addition to the errors in identifying one's social class noted above, the wording of the question can influence one's choice. For example, suppose Americans are asked, Do you belong to the lower, middle, or upper class? Then a large majority may say middle class. But suppose Americans are asked, Do you belong to the working class or the capitalist class? Then a similar majority may say working class. So, much depends on how the question is asked.

Moreover, all of us are subjected to messages from the media designed to make us identify with a vaguely defined, but comfortable, average American middle class. So perceptions of our own class position depend to some extent on how society has conditioned us to see ourselves. Obviously, the views held by most Americans *are* real facts of great importance to sociologists. The point is only that for analysis and understanding, radicals stress that these ideas about class *reflect* (1) actual class position *and* (2) the propaganda and conditioning relating to social classes that are dominant in the society. Thus, the fact that someone *thinks* he or she is middle class may be of immediate importance, but it may be even more important to his or her long-run behavior and life chances that the person really is a worker and is exploited by an employer.

Finally, in Chapter 3 it has also been shown that each class is divided into different *strata* according to income, status, occupation, race, sex, and other factors. In particular, the American working class is not one homogeneous, unified group, but consists of strata that are different in many of their characteristics. Thus, the situation of poorly paid farm workers, who may be mostly ethnic minority groups, is very different from that of highly paid white, male engineers—though both groups are part of what we call the working class. They have in common that both groups earn their living by labor and are exploited to produce profits. But they are very different both in objective circumstances and in ways of thinking. Thus their self-identification, income, status in society, and political behavior will be very different.

The distinction among different types of workers is reflected in the popular concept of blue-collar workers and white-collar workers. Blue-collar workers do manual jobs and are paid by the hour or by the piece; white-collar workers do nonmanual jobs requiring educational skills and are usually paid monthly.

TYPES OF SOCIAL CONTRADICTIONS

A radical sociological analysis of any society begins with an examination of the economic base and the contradictions within it. Radicals use the term *contradiction* to refer to conflict inherent in the social structure. It does not refer to logical inconsistencies; instead it indicates that there are some conflicts that may not be resolved within the present system.

If our leading ideologies and economic relations mutually support one another (through the mechanism of compliant social and political institutions), how can anything ever change? The answer is that beneath the outer shell of apparent harmony in society there are many kinds of conflicts that can lead to change. We divide these conflicts, again somewhat arbitrarily, into four levels that generally correspond to the four levels of analysis previously discussed.

1. Conflicting Ideas   While the ideas of competition and capitalism are dominant in our society, there is also the opposing idea of alternative societies built on social cooperation. Big business may sponsor conservative ideological views, but there are opposing liberal or radical views pushed by labor unions, small farmers, and by many liberal or radical organizations. Some of the media still portray stereotyped roles for blacks or women, but opposing ideas of tolerance and equality are pushed by the civil rights movement and by the women's movement.

2. Conflicts Within Institutions   While most of the media are controlled by big business, there are also competing liberal and radical media. Most school systems are dominated by local businesspersons, and many of the regents or trustees of universities are from big business. Thus conservative ideas are usually favored by these groups. Yet liberal and even radical ideas are introduced into the schools and universities by some teachers and professors and by some student organizations. Even within the churches there are sharp disagreements over racism or sexism.

3. Conflicts Within Economic Relations   The economic or productive relations of our society have always been the scene of major confrontations. In Appalachia the miners confront the mine owners to ask for decent wages and better safety conditions (many miners develop black lung disease from the poor safety conditions). In Detroit the auto workers strike against the auto companies. In California the farm workers—who work with bent backs in hot fields for low wages—organize against the farm owners (mostly large corporations in California). Such conflicts at the level of productive relations spill over into conflicts within institutions. For example, representatives of the farm workers fight representatives of the owners within the California state legislature over laws on agricultural labor relations. Conflicts also spill over into the realm of ideas, so that most of the California newspapers support the farm owners, but some support the farm workers. Similarly, where blacks, chicanos, or women are subordinate to white, Anglo males within economic relations, there arise conflicts not only at the purely economic level, but also at the legislative, institutional level and at the level of rival ideologies concerning race, gender, and economics.

4. Tensions Between Economic Relations and Technology   All of the human conflicts discussed above reflect to some degree the fact that there are structural tensions in our society that are unresolved. The most important structural tension is between our frozen economic or property relations and our rapidly improving technological potential. Property relations tend to be frozen because the wealthy and the powerful have a strong vested interest in preserving our present economic relationships. On the other hand, one of the things that the capitalist system does very well is to encourage the development of new technological inventions and improvements.

Our capitalist productive system is a cornucopia—a veritable horn of plenty—that *could* pour out vast quantities of every kind of good. Its *potential* increases by leaps and bounds every year. Unfortunately, however, we have frequent recessions or depressions, with continuing unemployment of labor, while many factories run at half speed. The reason is that our economic relations, or arrangements between capitalists and workers in the economy, constitute a barrier to full employment. Specifically, we shall see that workers' wages are held down, but this results in a lack of purchasing power. Yet, in a capitalist system, if there is a lack of purchasing power, then products cannot be sold at a profit. If products cannot be sold at a profit, then they are not produced—so unemployment results.

All of these conflicts can generate change in our society. Thus the struggles of the labor movement in the Great Depression of the 1930s resulted in laws to allow unions to organize, as well as to provide unemployment compensation. The struggles of the civil rights movement in the 1950s and 1960s produced civil rights laws making racial discrimination unlawful, particularly guaranteeing the right to vote (though blacks and chicanos still suffer much economic inequality). The struggles of the women's movement in the 1960s and 1970s have brought many laws against sex discrimination (though women still suffer much economic discrimination). The struggles of the antiwar movement helped force President Nixon to end the Vietnam War.

In addition to these short-run reforms, there are sometimes revolutionary changes in society, such as the American Revolution of 1776 or the Russian Revolution of 1917. These revolutionary changes occur when the four types of tensions and conflicts reach such a white-hot intensity that they can no longer be contained within the old society. The old society bursts asunder. New classes come to the fore, resolving some of the old conflicts, though sometimes eventually creating new ones. The hope of all radicals is that some day a society will be created in which all of these conflicts are eliminated and freedom, equality, and human dignity are realized for everyone. Radicals study conflicts in order to learn how to eliminate them. They believe that there could be a society (usually called a democratic socialist society) in which people would live together cooperatively with a high degree of equality, with no class of owners and no subordinate groups, but with everyone joining together democratically to control the economy and society.

TECHNOLOGICAL CHANGE AND RESISTANCE BY VESTED INTERESTS

Technological change makes some people uncomfortable, eliminates the jobs of some workers, puts out of business capitalists producing obsolete products, and brings vast gains to others. Technological change may bring misery to displaced peasants or even to feudal lords and knights who become obsolete, while it may bring joy to a rising merchant class or, more recently, to computer manufacturers.

According to radical sociologists, the most fundamental level of contradiction in capitalist society is the tension between the changing technological forces of production and the unchanging human relations of production. The growing forces of production—new technology, more capital, and more skilled labor—produce a rapidly increasing potential for abundance *and* increasingly require social co-operation of millions of workers in many industries and continents. On the contrary, the relations of production consist of frozen class relationships of ownership by a relatively few capitalists, poverty and unemployment for some workers, and economic insecurity even for many employed workers. These are relationships of competition rather than cooperation, so that each individual—and class of individuals—is out for his or her own maximum gain. Any change in class relations implies one group gaining and another losing; consequently, any change in productive relations may be strongly resisted. The technology of production is rapidly changing and requires new human relationships to work smoothly. Yet the class relations of production resist change, and so a strong tension or contradiction is created.

The first social scientist to state the problem in this way was Karl Marx, who on the basis of his extensive historical research observed:

> At a certain stage of their development, the material forces of production in society come in conflict with the existing relations of production, or—what is but a legal expression for the same thing—with the property relations within which they had been at work before. From forms of development of the forces of production these relations turn into their fetters. Then comes the period of social revolution. With the change of the economic foundation the entire immense superstructure is more or less rapidly transformed. . . . (Marx, 1859, 1904, p. 12)

Marx added that this situation of unchanging class relations in conflict with new productive forces is *not* an eternal conflict, but will be ended with the end of capitalism:

> The bourgeois relations of production are the last antagonistic form of the social process of production—antagonistic not in the sense of individual antagonism, but of one arising from conditions surrounding the life of individuals in society; at the same time the productive forces developing in the womb of bourgeois society create the material conditions for the solution of that antagonism. This social formation constitutes, therefore, the closing chapter of the prehistoric stage of human society (Marx, 1859, 1904 p. 12).

Many traditional sociologists think that the notion of a contradiction between forces and relations of production is a strange Marxist aberration. Yet radicals argue that it is a very practical concept helping us to understand much that is otherwise mysterious. For example, many politicians and traditional sociologists thought that the outwardly subdued life of the black ghettos of the 1950s would continue indefinitely. They were bewildered when the ghettos exploded in the mid-1960s. Radical sociological analyses since then have investigated the contradiction between the frozen economic relations of blacks to whites and the increasing productive abundance that blacks could observe in the surrounding society. Changes in productive forces also led to a more and more concentrated black population in the urban areas, which hastened their growing organization and consciousness, which in turn led to more attacks on existing class relations.

The classic example given by Marx explains the recurring phenomena of economic depression in the midst of abundance. Basically, capitalist production in an expansion rapidly improves the forces of technology and productivity, leading to a flood of new goods on the market. Yet capitalist class relations impose limits on the income available to purchase these goods. Workers' wages are usually held down as far as capitalists can hold them, so that consumer demand due to lower wages falls behind the flood of available consumer goods. Capitalists have a surplus of money from profits, but they are already consuming more than they need. Capitalists are afraid to increase the production of new goods because the outlook for selling more products is deteriorating. Thus depressions often result from the expanding productive forces meeting the barrier of frozen class relations (see Sherman, 1983).

ECONOMIC CLASS CONFLICT

Within the productive process, there are—in the radical view—several modes of class struggle. As discussed in Chapter 3, capitalists exploit workers, where *exploitation* means the extraction of profits from the products created by the workers' toil. Workers resist this exploitation by individual slowdowns, by tossing "monkey wrenches" into the productive process, and by organized activity such as collective bargaining and strikes. In most industries the collective arm of the workers, their unions, meet head-on against the collective arm of capital, whether a single monopolistic corporation or a business association. The strength on either side determines the split between wages and profits, the length of the working day, and the general working conditions. These class conflicts are neither random nor accidental; they are internal to the normal functioning of the capitalist productive process.

Class conflicts are partly reflected in and partly intensified by workers' alienation. Chapter 5 will examine the radical view that workers are objectively alienated, or separated, from their product by capitalists who own it and sell it at a profit, thus exploiting the workers. Subjectively, many workers are psychologically alienated from their work. This is especially the case when the worker does only a small, routinized part of the whole job. Subjectively, workers can also become alienated, not only from capitalists, but from each other as the result of competition against each other in the labor market.

Some New Left radicals in the 1960s stressed that subjective psychological alienation is a *more important* basis of class struggle than the objective alienation of product and jobs caused by capitalist exploitation. Workers are usually aware of subjective alienation caused by competitive pressures and the existence of authorities over them. But many workers are also conscious of objective alienation through exploitation and unemployment. Therefore, radicals emphasize that *both* subjective and objective types of alienation should be analyzed for most jobs under capitalism.

It should be noted that the *degree* of economic class conflict is largely determined in the long run by the amount of contradiction between developing productive forces and static class relations. For example, in the late feudal period, the growth of productive forces in industry and commerce greatly increased the economic wealth of capitalists and merchants, but the old feudal class relations, in which landlords held political power and restricted many industrial activities, persisted. This led to a high level of tension and, eventually, to revolution in England and France.

SOCIOPOLITICAL CLASS CONFLICT

The class struggle at the productive level is mirrored in and modified by the class struggle within all social and political institutions. The direct political struggle is illustrated by the fights in Congress over budgetary spending and taxes. For example, President Reagan's proposals to cut the taxes of the rich, while reducing spending for the poor, were supported by almost every business group and opposed by almost every labor group. In his reelection campaign, Reagan was supported by most capitalists and opposed by most union workers. When Reagan cut corporate taxes, capitalists agreed, but blue collar workers opposed it. When Reagan cut school lunch programs, the rich agreed, but the poor were opposed.

This third type of contradiction includes all of the political and social conflicts between economic classes. Briefly, capitalist and working-class interests and perspectives clash within the mass media, the churches, the educational system, the legal system and the courts, and the legislative and executive branches of government. In all of these institutions, capitalist interests dominate, though there is some pressure from and expression of working-class interests in spite of capitalist domination.

As we shall see in Chapter 15, radicals argue that there are innumerable ways in which the economic power of big business is translated into political power. Perhaps least important is the direct bribery and corruption of politicians and political parties. Even the use of large sums of money in political and general advertising by businesses and business-oriented political parties is not of overwhelming importance. Most important is the general milieu created by big business influence, as it controls most of the channels of communication, from the media to the churches to the universities. In spite of our formal guarantees of free speech, over 95 percent of American cities have only one newspaper or two newspapers owned by the same corporation. In the words of one political scientist: "Formal guarantees of free expression may not have much practical effect when the instruments of communication are concentrated in the hands of one interest and access to the media depends primarily upon wealth" (Michael Reagan, 1963, p. 46). Or, as the well-known economist John Kenneth Galbraith concludes: "there can no longer . . . be any separation by economists [or sociologists] between economics and politics. When the modern corporation acquires power over markets, power in the community, power over the state, power over belief, it is a political instrument" (1973, p. 6).

The very real power of corporations and the capitalist class over all social and political institutions in American society does *not* mean that capitalists have *all* the power, or that the United States government is only a puppet on a string. Workers have the power of their numbers *to the extent they are organized* and can sometimes win important reforms through the formal democratic processes of American and West European capitalism. The capitalist class remains politically dominant, but it does not win every battle. For example, in the Great Depression of the 1930s, American workers won many new rights through pressure on the New Deal government. Under *some* circumstances and to *some* extent, universal suffrage and free elections can represent working-class views against those of the propertied class. To put it another way, if there is no formal democracy with universal suffrage, then working-class views will *not* be represented. For example, in Hitler's Germany there was no formal democracy, no free elections, repression of dissent, and *no* representation of the working class. Thus, universal suffrage and representative democracy are a necessary condition—that is, a requirement—of political democracy for the masses of people.

Another necessary condition of a truly high level of political democracy, in the radical view, is a high degree of equality in income as well as public ownership of productive property (in short, socialism). With universal suffrage, but with a continued concentration of wealth and power in a relatively few capitalist hands, there can be only a limited amount of democratic influence by the masses of workers. In the United States, democracy exists *to some limited degree*. There are "democratic" struggles among factions of the capitalist classes—as represented by the disputes between upper-echelon Republicans and upper-echelon Democrats. There is, however, also a small amount of "outside" pressure exerted by farmers or industrial and professional workers (as we shall see in detail in Chapter 15).

Radicals also critically analyze many so-called socialist countries, however, because public ownership does *not* automatically mean a high level of democracy. If there are *no* formal democratic institutions, or if the universal vote is only allowed for the purpose of endorsing a single party, then the degree of democracy for the working class is also very low. According to radicals, a much higher degree of democracy is now possible than the levels existing in either the United States or in the Soviet Union. The necessary conditions are *both* a formal democratic political process and democratic control of the whole economy (by the public representatives, rather than a few capitalists). Only with democratic political *and* economic institutions, and a high level of political consciousness, do radicals expect a high degree of equality of power.

IDEOLOGICAL CLASS CONFLICT

The fourth type of social contradiction, according to the radical perspective, is the reflection of class struggles in clashing ideologies. There are very real conflicts between ideologies. For example, there is the ideological battle between the defenders of the quality of the environment of the United States and the growth-at-any-cost school. Moreover, each of these ideologies can develop with increasing sophistication and elegance. The path of development of each opposing idea is partly determined by the battle with its opposite. Yet these internal developments of ideologies are influenced by social class relations and are influential on the pattern of class relations. Thus the fact that prevention of pollution could cause loss of profits for powerful capitalists has had a great deal to do with the creation of ideologies favoring economic growth and deemphasizing pollution. On the other side, the surge of interest in ecological protection against pollution was related to the involvement of intellectuals in the 1960s civil rights and antiwar movements, both of which challenged the social order of advanced capitalism.

Ideologies make use of social myths. In the radical view, it is a myth—pushed by Ronald Reagan—that any American has an equal chance to be president. Then there is the myth that most women are happy housewives—a myth that contrasts with the reality that the majority of women work outside the home. It is also a myth that workers and capitalists willingly cooperate for the good of all; in reality, there is constant struggle. Similarly, it is a myth that everyone can go to college and that this educational opportunity promotes equality; the reality is that the percentage attending college drops rapidly as family income drops. Thus colleges can reproduce inequality (as shown in detail in Chapter 7). Last, it is a myth that everyone can be a capitalist; actually, most capitalists are born into affluent capitalist homes (Mills, 1956; Useem, 1984).

SOCIAL HARMONY VERSUS CLASS CONFLICT

Some traditional sociologists primarily see harmony in social relations; some economic determinists primarily see conflict in social relations. Few such extreme cases exist. Radical sociologists try to examine each social system in detail to determine the type and degree of social harmony or social conflict, without presuming either conflict or harmony in advance. Marx himself emphasized the findings of class conflicts in capitalist, feudal, and slave societies; but Marx also emphasized that there was *no* class conflict in very primitive societies, and that there will be *no* class conflict in the future communist society.

Even within capitalism there is actually a mixture of harmony and conflict in the productive process. As long as capitalism exists, workers *need* capitalists to give them jobs. Bankruptcy for the capitalist means unemployment for the worker. Yet, while a capitalist business continues to exist and has a certain revenue, there is an objective conflict over how much of that revenue goes to wages and how much to profits.

Joseph Schumpeter, who recognized that capitalism does contain class conflict, argued that some Marxists exaggerate the antagonism between capitalists and workers: "To any mind not warped by the habit of fingering the Marxian rosary, it should be obvious that their relation is, in normal times, primarily one of cooperation and that any theory to the contrary must draw largely on pathological cases for verification" (Schumpeter, 1950, p. 19). In normal times, in the subjective view of most workers, he is correct. There are even cases of great affection of workers for a boss; a secretary may identify with her boss even when he exploits her. Few believe that the majority of the American working class is now in a revolutionary mood. In normal times, as Marx emphasized, the majority of the working class *believes* this is the best—or only—possible system. That was true of the masses for most of the period of the Roman Empire, for most of the period of feudalism, and is equally true for most of the period of capitalism. In normal times, the ideology of the ruling class is clearly dominant. Only in revolutionary, transitional periods is there a mass response to revolutionary ideas; only then do class conflicts become widely recognized.

The class struggle that Marx asserted in normal times is not usually a conscious or subjectively felt conflict, but a conflict of objective interests between the exploiters and the exploited. It was not in the interests of slave owners to give up their slave property; it is not in the interests of capitalists to give up their corporate property. But it was in the interests of slaves to end slavery, and it is in the interests of American workers to change or end capitalism.

"HUMAN NATURE" VERSUS CLASS RELATIONS

It is one of the oldest social myths that social relations are determined by human nature. Aristotle wrote:

> It is thus clear that there are *by nature* free men and slaves, and that servitude is agreeable and just for the latter. . . . Equally, the relation of the male and the female is *by nature* such that one is better and the other inferior, one dominates and the other is dominated. (Aristotle, 1986)

Radicals argue that this view is incorrect and must be refuted before any real social science is possible.

In the first place, the physical nature of humans—our level of physical evolution—changes much too slowly to explain social evolution. Societies change in a hundred or a thousand years; significant changes in human physical makeup, *including our brain capacity,* take at least a hundred thousand years (see Childe, 1951).

In the second place, our psychological characteristics and behavior—what is usually meant by human nature—often change as a *result* of socioeconomic changes. Humans are each born into a functioning society and are shaped psychologically to a large extent by that society—though, of course, we are born with a certain physical brain capacity. Once our ideas are shaped, they certainly play an important role in future social development. Thus, modern human nature is very different from that of the ancient Egyptians, even though there has been no perceptible evolution in our physical and mental capacities.

Children in each society are conditioned by their social environment, as shown dramatically by Margaret Mead's several graphic books on growing up in New Guinea and Samoa. In the United States, when a child born in the slums has been orphaned and brought up from birth in an affluent family, the child shows all the cultural habits and aptitudes of the affluent. Even the geographical location of a society changes that society's view of human nature:

> In desert societies—including the American Southwest—water is so precious that it is money. People connive and fight and die over it; governments covet it; marriages are even made and broken over it. If one were to talk to a person who has known only that desert and tell him that in the city there are public water fountains and that children are even sometimes allowed to turn on the fire hydrants in the summer and to frolic in the water, he would be sure one were crazy. For he knows, with an existential certitude, that it is human nature to fight over water. (Harrington, 1970, p. 373)

The notion that there is an eternal human nature, that it cannot be changed, and that it shapes society is largely supported by a variety of myths. Why do these myths have so much life in them? The answer is that they play an important functional role as an ideology helping to support the status quo. "If it is 'human nature' that determines the historical process, and if this 'human nature' is unalterable, then all attempts to achieve a radical transformation of the human character and of the foundations of the social order are necessarily doomed to failure" (Baran, 1960, p. 6). Radical sociology rejects all such pessimistic assumptions.

SUMMARY

Max Weber emphasized power and status as well as class.

Karl Marx emphasized class, with power and status being largely derivative from class. He saw four kinds of conflicts in class societies: (1) Technology changes, but prior vested interests resist change; (2) the exploiters and the exploited struggle over the distribution of profits from the product of labor; (3) political conflicts reflect those economic class conflicts; and (4) the battle of ideas—in the media and elsewhere—reflects those political and economic struggles.

Some deemphasize conflict and see primarily harmony. This view is refuted by the four types of conflict noted. Others say that human nature causes inequality and conflict, so that no changes in social structure can ever reduce inequality or conflict. This is refuted by the argument that changes in circumstances *do* change people. Changes in social or economic conditions can alter the attitudes, behavior, and life chances of the people affected by these changes, and the reduction in inequality can ultimately reduce conflict.

SUGGESTED READINGS

The best single book on class relations in the United States is Charles Anderson, *The Political Economy of Social Class* (Englewood Cliffs, NJ: Prentice-Hall, 1974), which is good on both theory and American empirical data. A very thorough study using British data is John Westergaard and Henrietta Resler, *Class in a Capitalist Society: A Study of Contemporary Britain* (New York: Basic Books, 1975). A fascinating work on the evolution of class structure in the United States is Harry Braverman, *Labor and Monopoly Capital* (New York: Monthly Review Press, 1974). For an article portraying specific changes in American society, see Albert Szymanski, "Trends in the American Class Structure," *Socialist Revolution* 2 (July–August 1972). A useful discussion of the subjective, conscious aspects of class is Richard Sennett and Jonathan Cobb, *The Hidden Injuries of Class* [New York: Random House (Vintage Books), 1973]. An important functionalist view of conflict appears in Robert K. Merton, *Social Theory and Social Structure,* rev. ed. (London: Free Press of Glencoe, 1957; originally published in 1949). Radicals have written on almost every important aspect of society from a class perspective. Following are some excellent books in particular areas written from a radical point of view: on class and sex discrimination, Barbara Sinclair Deckard, *The Women's Movement,* 3d ed. (New York: Harper & Row, 1983); on class and racial discrimination, Victor Perlo, *Economics of Racism, USA* (New York: International Publishers, 1976); on class and the labor movement, Richard Boyer and Herbert Morais, *Labor's Untold Story* (New York: United Electrical, Radio, and Machine Workers, 11 East 51st Street, New York, 1971); on class and education, Samuel Bowles and Herbert Gintis, *Schooling in Capitalist America* (New York: Basic Books, 1976); on class and law, Ann Fagan Ginger, *The Law, the Supreme Court, and the People's Rights,* 2d ed. (New York: Barron's Educational Series, 1977), and Michael Tigar and Madeline Levy, *Law and the Rise of Capitalism* (New York: Monthly Review Press, 1977); on class and government, Albert Szymanski, *The Capitalist State and the Politics of Class* (Cambridge, MA: Winthrop, 1978); on class and health care, "The Political Economy of Health," entire issue of *Review of Radical Political Economics* 9 (Spring 1977); on class and political attitudes, Robert F. Hamilton, *Class and Politics in the United States* (New York: Wiley, 1972); and on class and intelligence, Jeffrey M. Blum, *Pseudoscience and Mental Ability* (New York: Monthly Review Press, 1978).

REFERENCES

Anderson, Charles. 1974. *The Political Economy of Social Class.* Englewood Cliffs, NJ: Prentice-Hall.

Aristotle. 1986. *Politics.* Grinnell, IA: Peripatetic Press.

Baran, Paul. 1960. *Marxism and Psychoanalysis.* New York: Monthly Review Press.

Bell, Daniel. 1970. "The Cultural Contradictions of Capitalism." *The Public Interest* 21 (Fall).

Childe, V. Gordon. 1951. *Social Evolution.* London: Watts.

Colfax, J. David, and Jack L. Roach, eds. 1973. *Radical Sociology.* New York: Basic Books.

Galbraith, J. K. 1973. "Power and the Useful Economist." *American Economic Review* 63 (March).

Gordon, Milton. 1958. *Social Class in American Sociology.* Durham, NC: Duke University Press.

Harrington, Michael. 1970. *Socialism.* New York: Saturday Review Press.

Krupp, Sherman. 1965. "Equilibrium Theory in Economics." In Don Martindale, *Functionalism in the Social Sciences.* Philadelphia: American Academy of Political and Social Science.

Marx, Karl. 1859, 1904. *Contribution to the Critique of Political Economy.* Chicago: Charles Kerr.

Mills, C. Wright. 1956. *The Power Elite.* New York: Oxford University Press.

Reagan, Michael. 1963. *The Managed Economy.* New York: Oxford University Press.

Schumpeter, Joseph. 1950. *Capitalism, Socialism and Democracy*. 3d ed. New York: Harper & Row.

Sherman, Howard. 1983. *Stagflation, An Introduction to Traditional and Radical Macroeconomics*, 2d ed. New York: Harper & Row.

Smelser, Neil J. 1963. *Theory of Collective Behavior*. New York: Free Press of Glencoe.

Useem, Michael. 1984. *The Inner Circle*. New York: Oxford University Press.

Weber, Max. 1968. *Economy and Society*. Vol. I. New York: Bedminster Press.

Wright, Erik Olin. 1986. *Classes*. New York: Schocken Books.

————. 1979. *Class Structure and Income Determination*. New York: Academic Press.

two

SOCIAL INSTITUTIONS AND PROCESSES

chapter 5

Industrial Sociology

Industrial sociology is concerned with the role of economic production in the larger society. Many issues discussed so far in this book have concerned the social consequences of producing economic goods. This chapter continues the topic and sharpens the focus on certain specific effects of industrial manufacturing, such as work alienation, viewed historically and currently.

This chapter first examines the development of the traditional version of industrial sociology; then it discusses the radical version.

INDUSTRIAL SOCIOLOGY: THE TRADITIONAL PERSPECTIVE

Industrial sociology began with the work of Frederick W. Taylor. Taylor was not a sociologist; he was the very first "scientific manager" (his concept). Yet the general ideas he pioneered were later developed by traditional sociologists. Taylorism—named after its creator—was the application of supposedly scientific principles to problems of industrial management and organization. Taylor wrote in the early part of the twentieth century, when large-scale American capitalism was relatively new. Taylor felt that factories were not being run efficiently enough and, as a result, were not maximizing their profits. This would be corrected, he argued, if factories and businesses would apply his scientific methods to their operations.

What were these "scientific" methods that would create greater efficiency and productivity for American capitalism? One incisive review states that "the specifics of the Taylor system were a grab-bag of new and made-over practices" (Merkle, 1968, p. 59). These included using a stopwatch to time workers at their tasks, and a payment system rewarding fast workers and docking slower workers. Less controversial aspects of Taylorism were the use of a cost accounting system for systematically keeping tabs on business expenses, the regular procurement of supplies, and the use of mathematics as part of efficient management. A favorite Taylor theme was the familiar slogan: "A place for everything, and everything in its place" (Merkle, 1968, p. 59).

At present, Taylorism is "dead" as a particular strategy for managing workers. Any mention of this strategy to an experienced unionist would undoubtedly generate heated discussion. Connotations of speedup, exploitation, and increased power for management would immediately come to mind. Taylorism has nevertheless remained influential in shaping modern work organization in two primary ways.

On the one hand, many of Taylor's less controversial efficiency practices have crept into modern business. Cost accounting, the use of systematic management, and the goal of efficiency itself are all part of the modern commercial world, and they are not particularly challenged even by labor unions. On the other hand, Taylor's basic idea of using science—including social science—to aid capitalism produced a host of traditional sociologists who wished to be similarly "useful" to capitalist management.

A number of well-known traditional sociologists, following in Taylor's footsteps, created the "human relations" school of industrial sociology. (See Etzioni, 1961.) In partial contrast to Taylor, the human relations school did not manipulate workers as obviously and directly. Nevertheless, these men were clearly sociologists allied with management in attempting to manipulate workers to work more efficiently and to be less interested in organizing trade unions.

These issues come out forcefully in an essay by the late C. Wright Mills, a pioneer in radical sociology. Mills (1970) notes that an earlier generation of American sociologists was concerned mainly with social problems, such as unassimilated immigrants, juvenile delinquency, and crime. But, after World War II, a very different trend was emerging, as some American sociologists were now being invited to participate in the operations of modern capitalist industry (and, we might add, also in the government and military establishments). These sociologists attempted to develop efficiency and "sound morale" among workers, regardless of whether working conditions were negative and conducive to low efficiency and low morale. In particular, C. Wright Mills (1970, pp. 15—16) shows that business managers looked to sociologists

> to lower production costs, ease tensions inside their plants, as revealed by high turnover, expensive absenteeism, and unsound disgruntlement, and find new symbols of justification for the concentrated power which they exercise in . . . modern society.

One of the chief findings of the human relations school was the importance of small work groups in the functioning of businesses. Smaller, intimate groups of workers were seen to be potentially disruptive to the organization. This was especially the case when these informal work groups were very disapproving of rate busters (those who produced significantly more than the other workers), chiselers, and squealers. That is, these groups of workers were negative toward individuals who would further company and management interests. As Mills notes, sociologists who reported these types of findings to management were often looked on by workers as a new (though more respectable) type of labor spy.

On the other hand, the human relations sociologists offered something more positive than merely spying on workers. They suggested that human relations "experts," such as themselves, should train company managers and supervisors how to relate to informal group networks of workers. If the trained managers would intelligently talk with workers, they could find out, for example, what bothered them. Then the managers could try to manipulate the workers' feelings in favor of management. If workers felt (correctly or incorrectly) that management was interested in their problems, then the workers would identify more with the company and improve their efficiency and productivity. When various workers felt this way, even the informal work groups could be used to increase rather than decrease efficiency, loyalty, productivity, and ultimately company profits.

This trend of recruiting sociologists into the business and organizational worlds has continued to the present—though with some modifications. A decade or so after the famous studies by the early human relations writers, various other sociologists were writing and consulting in the area of industrial and/or organizational sociology. Although the school of human relations was not so explicitly central to this next group of sociologists (as there had been serious critiques of the human relations school), the newer sociologists remained concerned with such organizational problems as hierarchy and authority patterns in organizations, staff-line conflicts, management-union relations, the "corruption" of authority, and policy changes in organizations. (See Etzioni, 1961.) All of these issues, even when studied academically and phrased abstractly, were of practical concern to industrial managers. In fact, industrial relations institutes spread throughout the country in order to explain these academic findings to members of the business community who attended meetings and seminars at these sociological institutes or read the institutes' publications.

More recently, other sociologists have wished to be as useful to present-day businesses and organizations as were their predecessors. Paralleling previous studies, there have also been studies of worker attachment to the organization (Bielby and Baron, 1983); "quit rates," or worker resignations (Burdett, 1978); and patterns of employee lateness and absence from the job (Clegg, 1983). In addition, at least two very different trends have emerged in recent years: one similar to the older human relations approach and the other tied to "hard science." The T-group movement is sensitivity training aimed at sensitizing people to one another's needs. It is parallel to the human relations approach. The T-group movement has focused on the use of sociologists to get managers and workers to discuss their problems, philosophies, and even prejudices in small groups. The idea is that sociologists can improve the functioning of organizations by helping managers and workers better understand themselves, which will permit better interactions with others—again, ultimately, to facilitate efficiency, productivity, and profits.

The other group of recent sociologists has attempted to study broad structural characteristics of organizations in mathematical terms. They have tried to give mathematical formulations to organizational size, administrator-worker ratios, and organizational change. (See Scott, 1975.) These recent organizational analysts clearly wish to be as useful as other traditional sociologists. But their approach to organizational relations is often extremely abstract and usually does not deal with specific interpersonal relations, as did the earlier sociologists' approach. Also, the broad structural characteristics they study may not be as appropriate for organizational intervention as the small groups of the human relations school. Thus their "message" to management may often be unclear and shrouded in the obscurantism of mathematical formulas. At least human relations people had ideas that could be translated into organizational policy.

The problem of much traditional industrial sociology—from its beginnings in Taylorism to its recent mathematized form—is that sociology is often subservient to industrial and organizational needs. Radicals argue that an improved industrial sociology should not consciously serve capitalism, but instead should serve the working class and others affected by capitalism. As Mills says, workers would rather have sociology study "inhuman relations in industry" instead of "human relations" (Mills, 1970, p. 17).

In fact, around the 1950s a beginning in the direction of studying *in*human relations did occur within the field of sociology. Some liberal-minded traditional sociologists investigated the alienating and dissatisfying aspects of modern industrial work (Chinoy, 1955; on industrial democracy, see Lipset et al., 1956). Although an explicit critique of capitalism was usually not developed, they were later joined in their efforts by other sociologists who did focus on serious drawbacks of working in modern capitalist industry.

INDUSTRIAL SOCIOLOGY: THE RADICAL PERSPECTIVE

Radicals distinguish between the work situation in precapitalist societies and in capitalist societies.

In very primitive societies, the social and economic unit is an extend family of 30–40 people. Since each person is related to all of these people and grows up among them, one has a very strong sense of community. Moreover, all of the women gather fruits and vegetables together, sharing the result collectively. All of the men hunt together, also sharing the product collectively. The work experience therefore reinforces the close community spirit. Exile from the group is usually viewed as the harshest form of punishment.

In the feudal society of Western Europe immediately preceding capitalism, there was still a very strong sense of community. People remained in the same tiny farming villages for many generations; everyone around was a friend or acquaintance and a neighbor. Most people never traveled further than 5–10 miles in their life. The villagers used many things in common, such as the land for grazing animals or the forest for cutting wood. When the villagers, who were serfs governed by the same feudal lord, were obliged to work on the lord's land or to do construction work for the lord, they generally did this work collectively. Many villagers in other parts of the world (such as Russia or Peru) shared a collective responsibility for services or taxes to the landlords. In Russia the village elders frequently reassigned possession of land to maintain equality among the serfs. The experiences of equality, close ties with neighbors, communal use of some lands, and collective responsibilities all led to a high level of community feeling among feudal serfs.

Neither primitive nor feudal societies were idyllic. There was disease, hard work, poverty, and danger—all leading to short life spans. The sense of community noted previously was often a necessity of survival.

Under capitalism this sense of community is replaced by loneliness and social alienation for various people. Some move from city to city; many do not know their neighbors; many work at unappealing jobs among strangers strictly for money; and the employer is often a large-scale corporation making profit from the employees' labor. Two radical critics, Paul Baran and Paul Sweezy (1966, p. 281) characterize many people living under American capitalism as filled with a sense of apathy, futility, and malaise (note that President Carter also used the term "malaise" to describe the situation): "The malaise deprives work of meaning and purpose; turns leisure into joyless, debilitating laziness; fatally impairs the education system and the conditions of healthy growth in the young; transforms religion and church into commercialized vehicles of 'togetherness'; and destroys the very foundation of bourgeois society, the family."

There have recently been many stories about unhappy or alienated workers. One anecdote may help to dramatize the issue. The story has been told—and it was said to be a true story—about a millionaire who bought a new Cadillac and was highly annoyed because it seemed to have a rattle in it. He took it to many mechanics and finally back to the dealer, who took apart the whole motor, but could find no rattle. Yet, whenever he drove the car, he could hear a distinct rattle. Finally, at a small gas station in the mountains of California, the gas station attendant said to him, "You know, mister, I heard a rattle in your car when you drove up." The millionaire said, bitterly, "Yes." The attendant then said, "I think it's in your door." The millionaire, who was very stingy, said, "You can take apart the door, but I won't pay you anything unless you find the rattle." The attendant, however, was sure he had heard a rattle in the door, so he took the risk and pulled apart the door. Inside the door was an old beer can, undoubtedly put there by a worker at the Cadillac plant. Inside the beer can was a note: "So you finally found it, you rich son of a bitch." Now that is work alienation!

A recent emphasis on work alienation involves the personal consequences of industrial plants closing down and moving to other states or other countries. In the depression era of the 1930s, this was (colorfully) called a "runaway shop," whereby machinery and other industrial assets were loaded "onto flatcars or moving vans and [the owners] set up essentially the same operation elsewhere" (Bluestone and Harrison, 1982, p. 7–8). In their important study, *The Deindustrialization of America,* Barry Bluestone and Bennett Harrison show that plant closings and the abandonment of American communities by major industries characterize the current situation as they did the depression era of the 1930s.

They show, for example, that during the 1970s, between 450,000 and 650,000 jobs were lost in the private sector due to runaway shops. However, when these figures are added to job losses due to plant, store, and office *shutdowns* during the 1970s, between 32 and 38 million jobs were lost! A significant proportion of these jobs were re-created by corporations reinvesting the money elsewhere. (See Bluestone and Harrison, 1982, p. 25–26, 29–31.) But the laid-off workers frequently did not even have the opportunity to obtain these new jobs (p. 12).

The personal consequences of such plant closings are many and serious: depression, anxiety, high or increased blood pressure and cholesterol (which are related to heart disease), loss of confidence, feelings of uselessness, aggressiveness, and mental illness. In addition, these workers often lose pension benefits and health insurance, and some even have to give up their homes or apartments (pp. 61–66). Clearly this form of work alienation has a multitude of negative effects.

MARX'S VIEW OF ALIENATION

Traditional and radical sociologists agree on the existence of alienation, though they disagree on the intensity of the problem and its source. For example, a recent presidential address of the American Sociological Association was entitled "On Work and Alienation" (Erikson, 1985). Traditional sociology has actually shown more interest in Marx's concept of alienation than in his related concept of exploitation. Traditional sociologists believe that the problem of alienation exists in any industrialized society. Radicals agree that some alienation will exist in any industrialized society, but they stress that capitalist class relationships with their competitive emphasis and atmosphere of impersonal forces directing the individual cause significantly more alienation than industrialization alone.

Marx described capitalist industrial production as a locus of conflict in which capitalists make profits by exploiting workers. He used the concept of alienation to describe the separation of workers from (1) the work process (i.e., their jobs), (2) the products they produce, (3) their fellow workers, (4) "species-life," and (5) even themselves (Marx, 1844).

Marx's concept of alienation thus refers to several forms of separation experienced by workers in capitalist industry. Alienation from the work process refers to workers' feelings of being psychologically separated from their work. For example, as has been illustrated above, auto workers have often been found to feel that their assembly-line work is "only a job"—only something they need to do to earn money. Assembly-line work is not stimulating, rewarding, or interesting. It is not a task with which the workers personally identify; they do not feel this work is what they want to do.

Although Marx also used the term self-alienation as if it were different from alienation from the work process, the two types of alienation actually overlap considerably. This is because Marx felt that a person's work was intimately tied into the person's identity. For Marx, a person was greatly influenced by what he or she did occupationally. A capitalist was not just a capitalist eight or ten hours a day; this occupational status influenced the rest of his or her existence. The same could be said for workers. Their occupational status highly influenced their political views, family life, cultural tastes, and so forth. As a result, when a person is alienated from the work process, the person will be alienated from a major part of his or her own life, thus lowering one's self-esteem.

Alienation from the work product is at the very heart of capitalism. This means that as soon as the workers finish the final product—say, an automobile—this product immediately becomes the legal property of the capitalist. The final product thus becomes instantly separated from the people—that is, the workers—who made it. If a worker decided—and acted on the idea—that the car he or she helped produce was his or her personal property (or the joint property of all workers who made it), the worker would be jailed. This form of separation is an important aspect of Marx's concept of exploitation.

The next form of alienation, alienation from "species-life," gets at the distinction between human beings and animals. Under capitalism, Marx felt, humans are debased to an animal level of existence, and are only concerned with such functions as eating, sleeping, and procreation. Higher-level human functions such as creativity and intellectuality are all but eliminated from the lives of industrial workers. Rather than engaging in these human functions, each worker feels that he or she is doing only one small, overspecialized, routinized, and dull task that is meaningless to the worker for its own sake and done only to earn money to stay alive. Hence, Marx felt that workers are separated—or alienated—from their uniquely human functions, and hence alienated from species-life.

The last form of alienation is social alienation. On the one hand, Marx felt capitalism produced the separation of one social class, the capitalists, from other social classes, such as workers. The nature of capitalism itself causes employers and workers to be distinguished from and antagonistic to each other. In addition, Marx felt that things like competition for jobs cause workers to become separated emotionally from other workers. The result is social alienation between workers.

This alienation between workers is the least discussed aspect of alienation in Marx's analysis. In fact, in his later book, *Capital,* he drops the idea and instead focuses on workers coming together in factories to fight the capitalist class. Nevertheless, there is a tendency for capitalism to separate workers from one another. Given the large amount of unemployment, workers are forced to compete against each other to be hired or promoted. One worker can obtain a job at the expense of another worker, and this competition in fact produces social alienation.

FROMM'S VIEW OF ALIENATION

Erich Fromm, the psychoanalyst, social philosopher, and author, argues that the most important single cause of alienation is the fact that the individual feels no sense of participation in the forces that determine social policy (Fromm, 1965, p. 125). Individuals see these forces as anonymous and totally beyond their ability to influence.

Fromm believes that conditions of employment alienate workers. Their livelihoods depend on whether capitalists and managers are able to make a profit by hiring them, and thus workers are viewed only as means, never as ends. The individual worker is "an economic atom that dances to the tune of atomistic management. [Managers] strip the worker of his right to think and move freely. Life is being denied; need to control, creativeness, curiosity, and independent thought are being balked, and the result, the inevitable result, is flight or fight on the part of the worker, apathy or destructiveness, psychic regression" (Fromm, 1965, p. 115). The worker feels that the capitalist controls his or her whole life; both workers and consumers (and voters) feel weak and insignificant compared to the great power of the corporations over working conditions, prices, and even government policy.

Yet Fromm argues that the "role of the manager is also one of alienation," for managers, too, are coerced by the relentless forces of capitalism and have very little freedom. They must deal "with impersonal giants; with the giant competitive enterprise; with giant impersonal markets; with giant unions; and the giant government" (Fromm, 1965, pp. 115–116). Their position, status, and income—in short, their very social existence—all depend on ever-increasing levels of profits. Yet managers must do this in a world in which they have little personal influence on the giants surrounding them.

Fromm also maintains that the process of consumption in a capitalist society "is as alienated as the process of production." Those who have money are subjected to a constant barrage of propaganda designed to create consuming automatons:

> The act of buying and consuming has become a compulsive, irrational aim . . . with little relation to the use or pleasure in the things bought and consumed. To buy the latest gadget, the latest model of anything that is on the market, is a dream of everybody in comparison to which the real pleasure in use is quite secondary. (Fromm, 1965, p. 123)

Finally, the most severe alienation is that of a person from his or her self. A person's worth in a capitalist market economy is determined in the same way as the worth of anything else: by sales in the marketplace. Because of this situation, Fromm states:

> His sense of self does not stem from his activity as a loving and thinking individual, but from his socio-economic role. . . . If you ask a man "Who are you?," he answers "I am a manufacturer," "I am a clerk," "I am a doctor." That is the way he experiences himself, not as a man, with love, fear, convictions, doubts, but as that abstraction, alienated from his real nature, which fulfills a certain function in the social system. His sense of value depends on his success. (1965, p. 129)

Thus, radical critics argue that the impersonal competition of the capitalist market dominates human relationships. It makes profit and loss the ultimate and pervasive evaluative criteria of a worker's worth.

EVIDENCE OF WORK ALIENATION

There is ample evidence of work alienation in capitalist industry. One study, for example, found that most of the industrial workers studied around 1956 would have preferred to spend their time doing activities other than work (Dubin, 1956, pp. 131–142). When asked their preferences, these workers said they would rather spend time with their family, friends, or associates in other institutions, such as lodges, bowling clubs, and recreational groups. Only a minority of these workers (about 25 percent) preferred to spend their time at work instead of other places.

There is also more recent evidence of work alienation. A fascinating study of the varieties of modern work, as narrated to the interviewer by workers themselves, documents various instances of alienation (Terkel, 1972). A farm worker bluntly stated:

> I walked out of the fields two years ago. I saw a need to change the California feudal system, to change the lives of farm workers, to make these huge corporations feel they're not above anybody. (p. 7)

Not surprisingly, this worker turned his feeling of work alienation into active political organizing for Cesar Chavez's union, the United Farm Workers of America.

Similarly, a strip miner stated:

> You get up between three-thirty and four in the morning (and) start to work about six. . . . We usually got out around maybe dark or seven or eight, nine o'clock . . . I just got short-winded and just couldn't walk across the street . . . My heart got bad to where I couldn't get enough oxygen . . . My hearin' . . . it coulda been affected with so much noise. (p. 16)

The interview continues like this, depressingly illustrating Marx's notion that capitalism can push human beings to the animal level of existence—Marx's alienation from species-life.

A prostitute in a big city illustrates a near total estrangement from her "work process," which, for Marx, means she is totally alienated from herself. Having been "demoted" from high-priced call girl to streetwalker, she noted:

> As a streetwalker, I didn't have to act. I let myself show the contempt I felt for the tricks. They weren't paying enough to make it worth performing for them. As a call girl, I pretended I enjoyed it sexually. You have to act as if you had an orgasm. As a streetwalker, I didn't. I used to lie there with my hands behind my head and do mathematic equations in my head or memorize the keyboard typewriter. (p. 62)

Marx could not have given a better example of a person completely separated from her work role.

A more subtle form of alienation occurred for a businesswoman in the same study. With the advent of women's liberation, it is possible to find women in positions of greater power than men and who command higher incomes than male coworkers. This also can mean a form of social estrangement of women from their male coworkers. As this woman noted: "I'm probably one of the ten highest paid people in the agency. It would cause tremendous hard feelings if, say, I work with a man who's paid less" (p. 67). Furthermore, she reports that it's difficult for men to find a "place" for her, since women in higher positions are still relatively unusual. As a result, the men try to categorize her and seem to feel relieved if they can put her in *some* category—such as married woman, boss's mistress, compulsive castrator, women's libber, or even lesbian (pp. 67–68). As a result of these male-female work problems, this businesswoman feels, "It's the thin, good nigger line that I have to toe" (p. 67).

Finally, many workers in this study felt they were exploited—that is, deprived of the profits of the work they do. A college-educated receptionist, who could not get a better job, said: "I don't think they'd even hire a male receptionist. They'd have to pay him more . . . You can't pay someone who does what I do very much. It isn't economically feasible. (Laughs.)" (p. 29). Others, like the strip miner and the farm worker, similarly felt that the product of their work was going to the employers, not to them.

In an overview study compiled by the government, *Worker Alienation, 1972,* a considerable amount of alienation was discovered (Committee on Labor and Public Welfare, 1972). For example, in 1969 about one-third of a national sample reported job problems with health and safety hazards, unpleasant physical working conditions, inadequate fringe benefits, inadequate transportation to and from work, and inconvenient or excessive hours at work. In 1975 there were 98 million workers in the labor force; this means that about 32 million workers suffered these serious problems. In addition, somewhat lesser percentages (10–26 percent) said that they experienced problems with inadequate income, work-related illness or injury, and unsteady employment.

It is important to recognize the significance of these problems to the workers. A relatively high percentage of workers reported these problems to be "sizable or great" among those who felt a problem existed in the first place. For example, 51 percent of them felt that health and safety hazards were sizable or great problems on their job. Similarly, 43 percent felt that inadequate fringe benefits were a large problem, 62 percent felt this way about inadequate income, and around 38 percent felt the same way about poor transportation to and from work, unpleasant physical working conditions, and inconvenient or excessive hours on the job.

These are major job issues. It is clear that a large minority of workers feel that genuine problems exist with some of the most basic aspects of their jobs: physical working conditions, health and safety hazards, wages and fringe benefits, hours at work, getting to and from work, and regularity of employment.

In addition, there is evidence of alienation from the content of the job itself—that is, alienation from the work process. When asked if they would choose similar work again, urban university professors top the list, with 93 percent saying that they would (Committee on Labor and Public Welfare, 1972). Other professionals who work for corporations in highly paid, creative jobs, such as mathematicians, physicists, and lawyers, report similarly high levels of desire to remain in their occupations. This high percentage noticeably drops to 43 percent for nonprofessional white-collar workers.

Dropping to an even lower percentage on this scale are blue-collar workers, only 24 percent of whom would remain in the same job. Only 21 percent of unskilled steelworkers and 16 percent of unskilled auto workers would remain in their jobs if they could get out of them. Somewhat higher percentages of more skilled laborers would stay at their jobs, though in only one category—skilled printers—would a majority (52 percent) stay at their jobs. Thus we see many workers indicating a desire to get out of their present occupations, and do something else, something less alienating.

Of course, workers want to be able to change jobs voluntarily, but do not want to be suddenly without a job for no fault of their own. Most workers who are fired—in some industries this can be 10,000 at one time—get one or two days notice, or even a few hours notice. There are few things more alienating than to suddenly lose a job because of the failure of the company due either to its own inefficiency or to general economic conditions. In spring 1988, Congress passed a bill mandating 60 days notice to workers before being fired. Big business opposed the bill, and President Reagan originally vetoed it (later, under intense pressure by Republicans who had to stand for election, he permitted it to become law without his signature).

WHITE-COLLAR ALIENATION

One of the areas of work that presumably should be nonalienating consists of the white-collar occupations, including teachers, accountants, salespersons, engineers, secretaries, and clerks. These occupations presumably require greater training than manual labor and, it has often been argued, employees can use their acquired skills on the job. Hence they should find their work more interesting, have more control over it, and identify with it more than manual laborers do.

Various studies have, in fact, reported lower levels of alienation for white-collar than blue-collar workers. (See Wilensky, 1966, pp. 117–166.) For example, university professors have often been found to be very low on the scale of work alienation because they are seen to control significant parts of their work situation. They prepare and give lectures, grade papers and examinations based on their assignments, and generally choose the type of research in which they wish to engage. This type of work situation would be seen as the opposite of the assembly-line worker, who does repetitive work, is controlled by impersonal machines and supervisors, and who often does not see—let alone own—the end product of his or her work.

This near truism—that white-collar work is inherently less alienating than blue-collar work—has been challenged. One theory says that white-collar workers constitute a new working class. This new working-class theory has argued that white-collar workers are often alienated in a similar manner to blue-collar workers (Gintis, 1970). This theory sees both types of work as part of capitalist production. For example, several studies have documented how clerical workers are increasingly treated as small cogs in a big machine—such as just being known as typist X in the typing pool (Braverman, 1974, chap. 15).

Moreover, white-collar workers are controlled by bureaucracies that are tied to capitalism directly, as in large corporations, or indirectly, as in the cases of universities or public agencies. White-collar workers are told what to do in order to further the purposes of the system, and if they refuse, they face firing. For example, antiwar scientists face particular dilemmas when they work on defense projects. If they refuse to build better weapons, their jobs could end; if they build such weapons, they are highly alienated from the work process.

In addition, the new working-class theory correctly points to the growth of trade unionism among various white-collar groups, such as teachers, clerks, and government employees. This union movement is seen as a response to an alienated work situation that is increasingly controlled by external administrators and threatened by job losses. This work situation finds the white-collar worker increasingly dependent on the goodwill of others, so that the white-collar worker must constantly fight to perform the tasks as he or she sees fit.

The new working-class theory is a useful tool to help analyze discontent among groups previously felt to be part of the "establishment." This theory helps us understand the development of radical caucuses in many professional associations in recent years—not just in sociology and economics, but also in medicine and law. Even English professors have inquired how to make the study of English more relevant. And students—quiet in the 1940s and 1950s—erupted into a large protest movement in the 1960s, which stirred again in the mid to late 1980s.

In contrast to those who feel that the work situation of advanced capitalism is improving, Harry Braverman argues that there are an increasing number of alienated jobs. The subtitle of his book *Labor and Monopoly Capital* is *The Degradation of Work in the Twentieth Century,* another way of saying alienation from work. The book is complex, but one issue is central to our concerns: Braverman convincingly argues that many jobs in capitalist society require less skill than in previous periods, a conclusion differing from common knowledge and traditional sociology (Braverman, 1974, chap. 20).

Instead of work actually becoming more "upgraded" over time, Braverman argues that this may simply be an artificial result of incorrect classification of some jobs in the category of skilled workers. For example, white-collar jobs—no matter how menial—are incorrectly classified as always more skilled than any kind of manual work. Braverman argues that many errors have thus crept into traditional occupational analysis.

For example, Braverman uses data from the Department of Labor's *Occupational Outlook Handbook* to describe how limited are the skills of so-called semiskilled workers. He points out that even in the official description, semiskilled workers are "told exactly what to do and how to do it, and their work is supervised closely. They often repeat the same motions or the same jobs throughout the working day" (Braverman, 1974, p. 431). He shows that most so-called semiskilled jobs can be learned in a day and the most difficult take only a few months to learn. Yet with no experience and brief training, they are expected to "work at a standard, fast, and steady pace. Frequently, good eyesight and good coordination are required" (p. 431). It is apparent from this description that very little upgrading from unskilled labor is involved, although the newer classification of semiskilled labor (created in the 1930s) clearly implies this illusory upgrading.

Farming is another example of the false assumption about unskilled labor (pp. 428–429). Braverman notes that farm laborers are always on the bottom of occupational skill scales; yet these people may have owned their own farms but lost them, and at any rate they had to acquire many specific skills such as "knowledge of land, fertilizer, animals, tools, farm machinery, construction skills, etc. . . ." (p. 434). Thus the decline of farm laborers may mean a loss of skilled jobs instead of a decline in unskilled jobs, as is usually argued.

In addition, Braverman notes that clerical jobs have been increasing. If these are assumed to be more skilled positions than any jobs classified as manual labor (as traditional sociology and the Census Bureau assume), then such clerical jobs should be upgraded. But again, Braverman questions this view. In particular, he shows that many clerical jobs are increasingly routinized, monotonous, rigid, bureaucratic, and controlled. Thus alienated secretaries, record keepers, and file clerks now abound in offices of capitalist bureaucracies. Moreover, office mechanization usually means speedup: "As work has been simplified, routinized, and measured, the drive for speed has come to the fore" (p. 335). As one white-collar operator said: "This job is not different from a factory job except that I don't get paid as much" (p. 336). Hence the common assumption of a general upgrading of the level of skills—and level of interest—of modern capitalist work is seriously challenged by Braverman. He sees much of the labor force working at alienating jobs.

EVIDENCE AGAINST WORK ALIENATION

One of the most specific attempts at negatively appraising Marx's ideas with the use of modern sociological methods has been made by Harold Wilensky (1966). Wilensky attempts to determine the absolute level of alienation among workers in his study. He operationalizes the concept of work alienation by examining the discrepancy (or lack of discrepancy) between a worker's "prized self-image" and the personal image the worker is obliged to assume on the job. When a person's prized self-image is consistent with the kind of person he or she is obliged to be at work, the person is considered *not* alienated (p. 148). However, when there is a discrepancy between a person's prized self-image and his or her image associated with work, the person is considered alienated.

Wilensky has examined six areas in which alienation might exist and has combined his results into an overall index of work alienation. The areas focus upon whether or not the respondent is (1) sociable (talks sociably on the job), (2) intelligent (uses own judgment), (3) conscientious in the sense of doing the job well, (4) conscientious in the sense of using skills on the job, (5) independent (does job own way), and (6) ambitious (tries to get ahead.) For example, if a person wishes to be sociable on the job, but is prevented from being sociable by job restrictions, he is considered alienated. If he has the opportunity to be sociable, and he views himself as sociable—and this is important to him—he is not considered alienated. When Wilensky collected his data, he found that only a small percentage of the respondents were alienated:

> Only 177 of our 1156 employed men score "alienated" on even one of the six possible attributes of the work situation; only 51 are alienated on two or more attributes, eleven on three or more. (p. 142)

Wilensky says that most workers may not be highly attached to their jobs, but neither is their work "an intense threat to their identity" (p. 148). Although he found more workers to be indifferent to work than either alienated or attached, these findings could be taken generally to refute—or at least strongly modify—

Marx's notion that widespread and intense alienation from work existed for industrial capitalist workers.

So, do we now simply reject Marx's insights about work alienation in capitalist society? The answer is no. There is a crucial methodological flaw in Wilensky's approach to measuring work alienation that renders his findings ambiguous rather than definitive. Wilensky is measuring the discrepancy between a person's prized self-image and the image he must assume at work. The problem with this conception is that it overlooks the impact of capitalist work on reducing a person's prized self-image. Marx argued that the capitalist division of labor generated alienation for those who worked in highly detailed, routine jobs.

For Marx, workers were powerless to control their own destiny under capitalism, which instituted such practices as an extremely detailed division of labor, designed to increase profits. Under circumstances where workers have little control over specialized, dull, meaningless, and even dangerous work, there is no reason to believe that workers will develop such positive attributes as conscientiousness, ambition, independence, or intelligence. Workers might, however, turn to sociability on the job to avoid some of the other alienating characteristics.

Wilensky looks only for discrepancies between prized self-image and a negative image at work. He thus ignores the fact that for many workers such a discrepancy will not exist simply because their jobs prevent the development of positive self-images in the first place. Wilensky probably would have done better simply to locate the existence and extent of the negative self-images and call them examples of work alienation. In doing so, he probably would have found higher levels of work alienation in his investigation.

In addition to interviews with alienated workers, Studs Terkel's previously mentioned investigation (1972, chap. 1) contains interviews with many other workers who are only somewhat alienated from their jobs, as well as still others who are not alienated at all. It appears from these many interviews that workers who feel they accomplish something worthwhile or difficult are the ones likely to be positive about their jobs. This seems to be the case for occupations as varied as an independent farmer, a waitress, a policeman, and an industrial spy! As the farmer says: "When you get a good crop, that's more or less your reward. If you weren't proud of your work, you wouldn't have no place on the farm." The policeman apparently enjoys being like a "stern father" to people (especially wayward youth) on his beat. The particular waitress interviewed enjoys the varied social exchanges she adroitly handles at work. Finally, the industrial spy enjoys the challenges of work and the related excitement. As he says:

> Undercover guys are the greatest actors in the world. You make a mistake and you're not allowed to come home. (Laughs.) If they knew I was undercover there, they woulda thrown me out the window. (Terkel, 1972, pp. 143–144)

He concludes: "It's a fast growing field of employment. . . . There's a definite need for it [because department stores are losing] three billion dollars a year. . . ."

Furthermore, there are studies indicating rather high levels of general job satisfaction. Gallup Poll data indicate a decline in job satisfaction from a high of 90 percent in 1963 to 83 percent in 1971 (Committee on Labor and Public Welfare,

p. 80). Still, this is a very high proportion of people reporting general job satisfaction. Similarly, another study of blue-collar workers reports only 19 percent who say that their current job is not very much like the kind they wanted (Committee on Labor and Public Welfare, 1972, p. 304). These data indicate a higher level of general job satisfaction than our earlier data might have predicted. Why is this the case?

First, some people may sound more satisfied with their jobs than they feel because there is a cultural bias toward indicating satisfaction (Blauner, 1960, pp. 354–356). Second, such results can indicate resignation to bad conditions and rather minimal levels of expectations about what constitutes satisfaction on the job. Finally, experts on polling agree that the results are sensitive to exactly how such questions are phrased. For example: "Are you moderately satisfied with your job?" might get a yes; but the response to "Are work conditions bad?" might also be yes; and likewise for "Would you prefer to do something else with your life?" Sociology students should always inquire exactly how questions are asked. For example, results may be very different if you ask people "Are you for desegregated education?" or "Are you for forced busing?" Similarly imagine the different poll results between "Are you for the right of women to choose when to have children?" or "Are you for killing unborn children at the whim of their mothers?"

The reliance on too broad a Gallup Poll type of measure of job satisfaction thus might falsely suggest that almost everyone is content with his or her work despite clear evidence to the contrary (such as studies in the 1980s showing that many workers feel there is little relation between hard work and how much they get paid). We suggest that data on general work satisfaction—particularly when high levels are reported—should be supplemented by the various other, more specific, indicators of work alienation discussed here. Only then would it be possible to see just how alienating work is for literally millions of people, even if others manage to escape.

RELATIVE LEVELS OF WORK ALIENATION

In recent years another type of alienation study has emerged. This type of study examines, not just the absolute level of work alienation as we've seen above, but the relative amount of work alienation. In a pioneering study, *Alienation and Freedom* (1964), Robert Blauner asked, What are the conditions under which work alienation varies? For example, type of job is a very significant condition under which job alienation varies. Jobs that are dull, repetitive, highly specialized, controlled, and where the workers tend to be powerless, generate higher levels of work alienation than jobs with the opposite characteristics.

Blauner's complex set of conditions for work alienation overlap Marx's, but also include other elements. The elements in Blauner's classification of alienation include the dimensions of powerlessness, meaninglessness, social alienation, self-estrangement, and normlessness. (See Seeman, 1959 and 1975.) Blauner discusses—and empirically demonstrates—variations in types and degrees of alienation between four different kinds of industries: an automobile assembly line, a textile mill in the South, a printing shop, and an automated chemical plant.

In general, Blauner found that the various types of alienation were strongest under the conditions of (1) a high level of specialization, (2) dull and repetitive work, (3) highly supervised and controlled work, and (4) lack of cohesive social groups among workers. Blauner found that a high division of labor was associated with feelings of meaninglessness, whereas the lack of cohesive social groups on the job was associated with feelings of social alienation. His study could be seen as a modification of Marx's original formulation. Whereas Marx felt that all jobs under capitalism generated high levels of all types of alienation, Blauner finds that only some forms of capitalist work are associated with high levels of alienation. Other kinds of work under capitalism produce much lower levels of work alienation.

Recent studies have focused on other similar conditions that have reduced work alienation or increased worker commitment. Halaby (1986) argues that workers who perceive management as legitimate are more attached to their workplace than those who do not. This legitimacy tends to be based on the employer being perceived as treating employees fairly, using universal standards to measure accomplishments instead of practicing favoritism. In addition, Lincoln and Kalleberg (1985, p. 757) show that some aspects of the Japanese "corporatist" work organization increase worker commitment. They show that "decentralized and participatory decision-making . . . do contribute to commitment in both [Japan and the United States]."

Blauner's type of study is useful for political organizing. If a political organizer assumes that all workers are equally alienated, serious mistakes about a potential political constituency could be made. However, if the organizer could empirically determine which groups of workers were most likely alienated—and then concentrate on them—this strategy could prove to be very successful. For example, typists working in an enormous and dull typing pool would probably be more likely candidates for recruitment than private secretaries working in one-to-one relations with an employer.

Finally, some research has shown skilled workers to be more politically active than unskilled workers. On the other hand, skilled workers are usually less alienated than unskilled workers. Here the political organizer should also be responding to the better education and sophistication of the skilled workers in addition to their level of alienation. Thus the relationship between alienation and political response is complex. But the greater knowledge the organizer has about the level of alienation of a group of workers, the more successful he or she will be.

More generally, all of the studies discussed seem to agree that those whose jobs more closely resemble the dull, monotonous, and specialized jobs described by Marx in the 1840s still tend to generate alienation and dissatisfaction. In an interesting comparison of military and civilian jobs, Fredland and Little (1983) showed that the lower level of military job satisfaction could be explained by factors similar to these. Military jobs with fewer positive characteristics, such as a "chance to do [one's] best" and "pleasant surroundings," lowered work satisfaction. But the point made emphatically by Braverman is that millions of these types of jobs still exist throughout modern capitalist society in both the civilian and military sectors. Although there is variation in type and level of alienation between jobs, even jobs once considered nonalienating—especially certain white-collar jobs—are now shown to be alienating. As a result, various white-collar workers—such as social workers, teachers without job security, and even some doctors—have been involved in recent protest movements and can be considered likely recruits for future protests. Modern capitalism does not alienate all workers equally. But the structure of capitalist work has been shown to be painfully difficult for millions who neither control nor significantly influence the course of their economic existence.

A REDUCTION IN ALIENATION?

In the 1960s considerable attention was paid to the phenomenon of alienation. Along with analyzing its causes and consequences, there was much interest in discovering how to reduce or avoid it. Often fundamental economic changes were seen as the main way to accomplish this goal. In a useful summary of social and economic experiments over the last two decades, "Alternatives to Bureaucracy: Democratic Participation in the Economy" (1986), Rothschild and Russell discuss various attempts at overcoming different forms of work alienation.

There have been several strategies to reorganize conventional work arrangements devised by employees and employers alike. About one-third of the businesses in the Fortune 500 list have instituted Quality of Work Life (QWL) projects, whereby smaller work groups report directly to the top of the corporation. By 1985 over 6,000 American corporations instituted Employee Stock Ownership Plans (ESOPs), whereby employees own company stock—though only 500 of these involve employee ownership of the majority of stock. In the 1970s from 5,000 to 10,000 food cooperatives, 1,300 alternative schools, and various alternative health clinics were formed. Also some smaller-size work groups have been created for employees to directly influence the work process.

The actual results of these work experiments have been mixed. Some did show increased worker satisfaction with the new arrangements; however, others did not (for example, some worker-owners of businesses exhibited high levels of stress). In the United States, work experimentation occurs within the existing economic system. The question for future research is whether or not the constraints of the existing economic system preclude the widespread reduction in work alienation. This should be of concern to both employees and employers as well as to academic researchers.

SUMMARY

Along with describing how capitalism exploits workers, Marx argued that capitalism also alienates workers. An entire tradition in sociology has been concerned with examining the extent of work alienation under capitalism. A recent focus has been on the impact of plant closings in the United States.

There are some who argue that capitalism is not nearly as alienating as once presumed. This is seen to be especially the case for white-collar workers, although it is also said to be true for many blue-collar workers. Another group of sociologists has argued that under certain conditions capitalism is alienating, but not under improved circumstances, such as greater autonomy on the job and increased skill level of the job. A third group argues that capitalism is highly alienating, a position consistent with Marx's initial ideas.

An examination of much data on work alienation indicates that workers are alienated, but to very different degrees on different jobs. That is, the data indicate, on the one hand, that certain jobs, especially the more skilled, are less alienating and for many workers not alienating at all. On the other hand, more routine, monotonous, and even dangerous jobs can be highly alienating. The importance of the development of a theory of a new working class is that it points to many new degrading jobs in capitalist society (including white-collar jobs) that affect millions more people than previously assumed by those who felt that capitalism had solved the problem of alienation. Finally, there have been several work experiments to reduce alienation. These have produced mixed results, which suggests the need for research to determine if the constraints of capitalism preclude a large-scale reduction in alienation.

SUGGESTED READINGS

Robert Blauner's *Alienation and Freedom* (The University of Chicago Press, 1964) was the major analysis of work alienation in the 1960s. It inspired much research and theorizing about the nature of work alienation in capitalist society. The *Annual Review of Sociology* 3 (1977) discusses much of the research that has followed from Blauner's thesis, as well as the other developments in the field.

Bertell Ollman's *Alienation* (New York: Cambridge University Press, 1971) is an excellent theoretical synthesis of Marx's ideas about work alienation. A provocative analysis of powerlessness and alienation in the modern working class is Michael Lerner, *Surplus Powerlessness* (Oakland, CA: Institute for Labor and Mental Health, 1986). For another view of alienation analyses, see Melvin Seeman, "Alienation Studies," *Annual Review of Sociology* 1(1975): 91–123. A major discussion about how capitalism generates alienation in many occupations is presented in the well-written and provocative book by Harry Braverman, *Labor and Monopoly Capital: The Degradation of Work in the Twentieth Century* (New York: Monthly Review Press, 1974). Barry Bluestone and Bennett Harrison, *The Deindustrializing of America* (New York: Basic Books, 1982), is a recent major discussion of alienation related to plant closings in the United States. Finally, Joyce Rothschild and Raymond Russell, "Alternatives to Bureaucracy: Democratic Participation in the Economy," *Annual Review of Sociology* 12(1986): 307–328, discuss several strategies, and their actual accomplishments, toward reducing work alienation.

REFERENCES

Baran, Paul, and Paul Sweezy. 1966. *Monopoly Capital.* New York: Monthly Review Press.

Bielby, William T., and James N. Baron. 1983. "Organizations, Technology, and Worker Attachment to the Firm." In Robert Robinson, ed., *Research in Social Stratification and Mobility*, p. 77–113. Greenwich, CT: JAI Press.

Blauner, Robert. 1960. "Work Satisfaction and Industrial Trends in Modern Society." In Walter Galenson and Seymour M. Lipset, eds., *Labor and Trade Unionism.* New York: Wiley.

————. 1964. *Alienation and Freedom*. Chicago: University of Chicago Press.

Bluestone, Barry, and Bennett Harrison. 1982. *The Deindustrializing of America*. New York: Basic Books.

Braverman, Harry. 1974. *Labor and Monopoly Capital: The Degradation of Work in the Twentieth Century*. New York: Monthly Review Press.

Burdett, Kenneth. 1978. "A Theory of Employee Search and Quit Rates." *American Economic Review* 68: 212–220.

Chinoy, Eli. 1955. *Automobile Workers and the American Dream*. New York: Random House.

Clegg, Chris W. 1983. "Psychology of Employee Lateness, Absence, and Turnover: A Methodological Critique and Empirical Study." *Journal of Applied Psychology* 68: 88–101.

Committee on Labor and Public Welfare, U.S. Senate. 1972. *Worker Alienation, 1972*. Washington, DC: Government Printing Office.

Dubin, Robert, 1956. "Industrial Workers' Worlds: A Case Study of the 'Central Life Interests' of Industrial Workers." *Social Problems* 3:131–142.

Erikson, Kai. 1986. "On Work and Alienation." *American Sociological Review* 51 (February): 1–8.

Etzioni, Amitai. 1961. *Complex Organizations*. New York: Holt, Rinehart and Winston.

Fredland, J. Eric, and Roger D. Little. 1983. "Job Satisfaction Determinants: Differences Between Servicemen and Civilians." *Journal of Political and Military Sociology* 11 (Fall): 265–280.

Fromm, Erich. 1965. *The Sane Society*. New York: Fawcet & World Library, Premier Books.

Gintis, Herbert. 1970. "The New Working Class and Revolutionary Youth." *Continuum* 8 (Spring–Summer): 151–174.

Halaby, Charles N. 1986. "Worker Attachment and Workplace Authority." *American Sociological Review* 51 (October): 634–649.

Lincoln, James R., and Arne L. Kalleberg. 1985. "Work Organization and Workforce Commitment: A Study of Plants and Employees in the U.S. and Japan." *American Sociological Review* 50 (December): 738–760.

Lipset, Seymour M.; Martin Trow; and James Coleman. 1956. *Union Democracy*. Garden City, NY: Doubleday.

Marx, Karl. 1844. *Economic and Philosophical Manuscripts of 1844*. Trans. T. B. Bottomore. In Erich Fromm, *Marx's Concept of Man*. New York: Ungar, 1963.

Merkle, Judith. 1968. "The Taylor Strategy." *Berkeley Journal of Sociology* 13: 59–81.

Mills, C. Wright. 1970. "The Contribution of Sociology to Studies of Industrial Relations." *Berkeley Journal of Sociology* 15: 11–32.

Rothschild, Joyce, and Raymond Russell. 1986. "Alternatives to Bureaucracy: Democratic Participation in the Economy." *Annual Review of Sociology* 12: 307–328.

Scott, W. Richard. 1975. "Organizational Structure." *Annual Review of Sociology* 1: 1–20.

Seeman, Melvin. 1959. "On the Meaning of Alienation." *American Sociological Review* 24: 783–791.

————. 1975. "Alienation Studies." *Annual Review of Sociology* 1: 91–123.

Terkel, Studs. 1972. *Working*. New York: Pantheon Books.

Wilensky, Harold. 1966. "Work as a Social Problem." In Howard Becker, *Social Problems*. New York: Wiley.

chapter 6

Culture

A society is often characterized by the set of beliefs it holds, symbols it expresses, norms governing it, and values it pursues. This collection of beliefs, symbols, norms, and values is usually referred to as the culture of that society. Culture helps organize social life. It delineates issues of concern to a society, creates goals for society to achieve, and points to the acceptable means to achieve these goals. Yet culture also helps mask over unpleasant social realities. Concepts such as "false consciousness" describe this aspect of culture.

The mass media have attempted to characterize broad American cultural patterns in recent decades by referring to the "Me Generation" of the 1970s, which emphasized personal ambition and importance of self; the "Summer of Love" of 1967 in the Haight-Ashbury district of San Francisco, which extolled the virtues of communal living, sexual liberation, and drugs; the Protestant-ethic values of hard work and family commitment that persisted in the middle American suburbs during the 1960s and 1970s; and the Yuppie (Young Urban Professional) values of material acquisition and rapid upward mobility of the 1980s. Another trend appeared in the 1960s, declined in the 1970s, and reemerged in the mid-1980s: the critical evaluation of widely accepted cultural values and behavior.

This chapter will discuss the basic elements of culture, compare radical and traditional sociology approaches to culture, and examine some examples of unmasking cultural illusions in recent U.S. history. Finally, there will be an examination of the implications for cultural conflict as regards the revelations of Oliver North and the Iran-Contra scandal.

ELEMENTS OF CULTURE

There is probably a greater difference between sociologists and anthropologists on the basic meaning of culture than between traditional and radical sociologists. Anthropologists classically defined culture in terms of entire societies. British culture, for example, was seen as distinguished from French culture, Chinese culture, and primitive culture. Thus British society as a whole was seen as having differing characteristics, such as religion, economy, and educational system, from other societies.

The well-known anthropologist Edward B. Tylor equated culture with civilization in his famous study, *Primitive Culture* (1889, p. 1). He sought to delineate the main elements of primitive culture in contrast with more advanced civilizations. Similarly, the important anthropologist Ruth Benedict refers to culture in terms of entire societies. In her seminal work, *Patterns of Culture* (1959, p. 54), Benedict states: "All the [social] behavior directed toward getting a living, mating, warring, and worshipping the gods . . . [constitute] the culture." So culture equals society in the classical anthropological discussions.

Sociologists of both traditional and radical viewpoints have usually narrowed the focus of the term culture to refer primarily to the main ideas of a society. These main ideas include the previously mentioned beliefs, symbols, norms, and values of a society. Many sociologists, as well as many modern anthropologists, often distinguish between cultural ideas and social organization, which refers to the main institutions, roles, and class arrangements of the society. Thus the economy, educational system, and the family would be part of social organization, whereas Catholic religious beliefs, the Protestant work ethic, and the value of equal educational opportunity would be part of culture (Peterson, 1979; Parsons, 1951; Kroeber and Parsons, 1958).

From the radical standpoint, Karl Marx often distinguished between the economic base of society and the ideologies that arose from it in the superstructure of society. For Marx the superstructure includes both cultural ideas and cultural institutions, such as education or religion. Cultural ideas and institutions, such as religion and the church, are strongly influenced by the economic base. In a frequently quoted passage, Marx notes that religious ideas derive from harsh economic conditions and function to alleviate the suffering as well as to depoliticize the sufferers. He says:

> *Religious* suffering is at the same time an *expression* of real suffering and a *protest* against real suffering. Religion is the sigh of the oppressed creature, the sentiment of a heartless world, and the soul of soulless conditions. It is the *opium* of the people. (Marx, 1973)

Thus both Marx and Parsons distinguish ideas from institutions or organization, but Marx distinguishes ideas *and* noneconomic institutions, including culture, from economic institutions. We first examine the traditional view of culture as ideas.

TRADITIONAL VIEW OF CULTURE

What are cultural beliefs, norms, and values? A *belief* is a conviction about the validity of a principle or fact. Belief in the Christian religion, for example, refers to the conviction that the basic principles of Christianity are correct. *Norms* are rules that govern behavior. These rules can be formal, as in a set of laws (e.g., the laws of the state of California); or informal, as in unwritten expectations that nevertheless guide social interaction (e.g., expectations when greeting a friend). *Values* are conceptions of what is desirable. These are broad sentiments about what is right and proper in the larger scheme of things. Ideas such as individualism, democracy, freedom, and justice are basic values widely shared by Americans (Bellah et al., 1985; Rokeach, 1973, 1979; Myrdal, 1944).

Two concepts that are often discussed in conjunction with these cultural ideas are deviance and sanctions for deviance. *Deviance* is behavior that differs from, or rejects, the dominant cultural beliefs, norms, or values. Juvenile delinquency and adult crime are examples of deviant behavior since they break laws. In a fundamentalist Christian community, dancing and smoking may be considered deviant behavior if these activities violate the belief that Christians should abstain from them. Denial of voting rights to groups—such as white southerners denying blacks the right to vote—is deviance since it violates democratic values and the voting rights law.

When deviant behavior occurs, sanctions may be applied. *Sanctions* (especially negative sanctions, or social control) are punishments for engaging in a disapproved form of behavior. In any of the above instances of deviance—crime, denial of voting rights, or even dancing—punishments may be given to the deviant. For juvenile delinquency or crime, the government—via the police, courts, and prison—applies the sanctions (e.g., a jail sentence). For denial of voting rights, the government would be similarly involved. However, for fundamentalists who violate prohibitions against dancing and smoking, the church would administer the sanctions (e.g., expulsion from the church). Beliefs, norms, values, and sanctions thus constitute important elements of culture.

In recent years, symbols have been a main focus of cultural analysis. Symbols are signs, or external expressions, that represent something else. Peterson (1979) has identified several roles of symbols discussed in the literature, including: (1) symbols reflecting the organization of the larger society, as in Basil Bernstein's work (1977) on the way different British language styles reflect the British class structure and help maintain class differences; (2) the impact of symbols on behavior and social organization, as in Erickson and Schultz's study (1978) of misunderstandings between racial groups due to differing body language symbols; (3) the use of symbols to perpetuate patterns of domination in society, as in Pierre Bourdieu's work on "cultural capital," whereby dominant groups acquire knowledge of art, museums, science, and literature to differentiate themselves from dominated groups (Bourdieu and Passeron, 1977; Bourdieu, 1984; see also DiMaggio and Useem, 1978).

Consequences of Culture

Many traditional sociologists have argued that cultural ideas have important results. One consequence is the "looking-glass self." Charles Horton Cooley (1922) explained that due to the existence of common cultural ideas and language we are able to look at ourselves as others look at us. Other people's behavior toward us constitutes the "mirror" in which we see ourselves. If others treat us with respect, then we will likely have a positive self-image. In contrast, if others treat us disrespectfully, a negative self-image is more likely to result. Juvenile delinquency has been analyzed in part by this approach. If a young person is treated by the authorities like a delinquent (even if he or she is innocent), then the youth begins to see himself or herself as a delinquent. The youth's self-image begins to reflect the behavior of others toward him or her (Broom and Selznick, 1958, p. 88). This is what Robert K. Merton (1957, chap. XI) has called a "self-fulfilling prophecy": The authorities act toward the youth as a delinquent, who then perceives himself or herself as a delinquent and acts accordingly.

The looking-glass self is one aspect of the larger analysis of the self pioneered by George Herbert Mead (1934) and Herbert Blumer (1969). The self, as analyzed by these members of the Chicago school of sociology, is split into an "I" and a "me." The "I" is the active and more spontaneous aspect of self, initiating actions toward objects in the surrounding environment. The "me" is more passive, taking actions and opinions of others into account before acting. The "I" may wish to initiate highly creative or controversial action, but the "me" often intervenes to indicate the likely level of disapproval to be expected. There is clearly a potential tension between the "I" and the "me," but Mead also saw the tendency toward reconciliation and harmony between these two parts of the self. By way of contrast, Freud (1949) often saw tension and lack of harmony between the id, ego, and superego, with neuroses and psychoses resulting from severe splits between these aspects of personality. Any given individual could be analyzed in terms of the integration or the tension between these personality factors that ultimately originate from the culture.

We shall see that radical sociologists challenge any purely cultural determinations of psychology on the grounds that psychologies and ideas are based on people's material and class circumstances.

Emile Durkheim

Emile Durkheim was one of the sociologists who laid the foundations of the traditional view of culture. We will explore his view of the sociology of suicide in detail as one example of traditional views of culture and its consequences.

In his most famous book, *Suicide,* written in 1897, Durkheim (1951) amassed a huge amount of statistical (and other) data to demonstrate the role of social and cultural factors in influencing suicide rates. These factors were specifically contrasted with prevailing theories of suicide at the end of the nineteenth century, which focused on psychological factors, such as madness, or even physical factors, such as season of the year (the summer's heat was thought to incite some people to suicide). In a highly systematic fashion, outlining major principles of research methodology in the course of his investigation, Durkheim eliminated the alternative explanations of suicide and established his own theory of suicide. By addressing a form of behavior widely thought to be explained by individual psychology, Durkheim was able to show the utility of a uniquely sociological analysis.

In particular, Durkheim tried to demonstrate that underattachment *or* overattachment to cultural norms or values led to increased suicide rates. Durkheim distinguished between attachment to norms and attachment to values as they separately affected suicide rates of different groups (discussed in a series of highly stimulating lectures by Neil Smelser, published in part in Smelser and Warner, 1976, pp. 161–178). In this light, Durkheim analyzed egoistic, anomic, and altruistic types of suicide.

According to Durkheim, *egoistic* suicide is due to the lack of attachment to common values, such as Protestant religious values. *Anomic* suicide is due to the lack of attachment to social norms, such as rules governing marital relations. *Altruistic* suicide is due to a very strong attachment to common values, such as Japanese national values concerning success and failure. Further illustrations of these concepts will be provided later.

Though it is often ignored, there is a fourth type of suicide in Durkheim's scheme: fatalistic suicide (Durkheim, 1951, p. 276, note 25). *Fatalistic* suicide is due to a very strong attachment to social norms, such as to rules governing family relations or sexual activities. A young married person, eager for independence, might feel sufficiently trapped in new family obligations to commit fatalistic suicide.

Egoism is too little integration into values, whereas altruism is too much integration into values. In comparison, anomie is too little integration into norms, whereas fatalism is too much integration into norms. It is possible to think of each dimension of norms and values on a 10-point scale. Egoism would have scores of 1–3 and altruism scores of 8–10 on the values scale; anomie would have scores of 1–3 and fatalism scores of 8–10 on the norms scale. Scores of 4 through 7 would be considered moderate levels of integration into norms or values.

How does this relate to suicide rates of different groups? Durkheim states in his first book, *The Division of Labor in Society* (1893), that happiness is the *golden mean* (1964 ed., p. 237). This phrase asserts that moderation of life circumstances instead of extremes is likely to produce happiness. Thus lower rates of suicide will be expected when people are moderately integrated into society by holding the usual social values and following the usual social norms. If, however, a person is extremely egoistic or extremely altruistic, that person is more likely to commit suicide. Similarly, a person who is extremely fatalistic or extremely subject to anomie will be more likely to commit suicide.

Durkheim also defined a third dimension of integration besides norms and values (as Smelser has noted): *integration into groups*. This type of integration would be illustrated by a person's membership in a family or church. Integration into groups overlaps both integration into norms and values, but it operates the same: Lower suicide rates are expected at moderate levels of group integration, as when a person is moderately attached to his or her family, but not overly dependent nor overly detached from the family. Although Durkheim has been criticized (Whitney Pope, 1976), several studies have supported his analysis of suicide (see Broom and Selznick, 1958, p. 24).

Durkheim felt that businessmen were anomic. He looked at the owners of nineteenth-century industries as operating relatively free of commercial regulation, especially as compared with the more regulated guilds of the Middle Ages. The lack of regulation for businessmen meant that their appetites for profits could soar without limit. They could never be satisfied. This inability for economic satisfaction, Durkheim argued, created a frustrating existence for businessmen, who killed themselves in greater numbers than their much more economically controlled workers.

Among the groups Durkheim saw as fatalistic were young husbands, childless married women, and slaves. Each of these groups were overregulated and felt trapped in their oppressive social existence. They could not see a way out and some committed suicide as a result. In contrast to both anomie and fatalism, Durkheim (1951, pp. 270–272) saw adult married males as moderately integrated into social rules and thus less likely to commit suicide. They were regulated in their sexual passions because they were married, but they also could attain sexual satisfaction within the marriage. Indeed, he felt marriage was a greater protector against suicide for males than for females, who were more socially repressed by the institution of marriage.

Durkheim felt Protestants were egoistic, that they were often not sufficiently attached to their religious values. Protestantism, of course, had broken off from Catholicism and had a greater level of religious freedom from its inception. This greater degree of freedom, Durkheim argued, was responsible for the demonstrated higher rates of suicide for Protestants as compared to Catholics. The nineteenth-century Protestants were not so attached to their religious values as Catholics were, and for Durkheim this lesser attachment was a central example of egoism. Indeed, in this example, nineteenth-century Catholics represented the favored moderate level of integration into their value system, for which they were "rewarded" with a lower suicide rate than Protestants.

Durkheim illustrated the high level of value integration—altruism—by the Japanese ritual of committing suicide if a person behaved unacceptably toward society. Durkheim argued that it was an overly high attachment to Japanese national and cultural values that led to some Japanese taking their lives when they did not meet social expectations, as in showing cowardice in battle. Thus, in terms of value integration, Durkheim saw Protestants at one end of the continuum (egoism) and the Japanese on the other end (altruism), with Catholics in between. In sum, suicide rates were highest at the two extremes of value or norm integration, but lowest at moderate levels of integration.

Shared Values and Class Differences

A major question concerning culture is whether or not people in a given nation share a common culture, or whether there are significant cultural differences between the social classes. From the traditional point of view, Talcott Parsons emphasizes the sharing of common values in many publications. One of the best-known discussions on this topic is his analysis of the "pattern variables," which are sets of opposing value—choices Parsons feels any person must make in order to act.

Parsons (1949, 1951, 1962), following Tönnies (1940), says that one set of pattern variables represents traditional, community choices, while another set represents a modern financially oriented society. He refers to these pattern variable choices as (1) affectivity vs. affective neutrality, (2) collectivity-orientation vs. self-orientation, (3) particularism vs. universalism, (4) ascription vs. achievement, and (5) diffuseness vs. specificity. In traditional societies, he believes people often take pleasure when they can get it (rather than repressing desires), are oriented toward the collective interests of the community (rather than individual interests), act on the basis of kinship or friendship (rather than laws), behave toward people on the basis of status or ethnicity (rather than what they can do), and choose friends on the basis of many years of closeness (rather than specific traits). On the contrary, Parsons claims that in modern societies, people often repress desires, act according to their individual interests, base decisions on rules and regulations, accept people for what they can do, and choose their friends by the roles they perform and statuses they occupy (Wood, 1968). As a result, Parsons sees much sharing of common values in both traditional and modern societies.

While empirical studies have shown that tendencies such as these exist (Williams, 1961, pp. 91–92), radical sociologists are skeptical about such sweeping cultural generalities. People in our society do not all think or behave the same way, but are strongly influenced by their different backgrounds and their different places in the present economic organization of society.

Class Differences in Values

An alternative approach to an emphasis on common values focuses on differing values between social classes. The modern origin of this approach is Karl Marx's analysis of the fact that capitalists support ideologies favorable to the existing system, while many workers support political ideas opposed to the system (Marx and Engels, 1939). Karl Mannheim elaborated on this in his famous book, *Ideology and Utopia* (1936), and we discuss class differences in values and viewpoints here and throughout the book.

In the 1940s and early 1950s there was considerable academic interest in demonstrating empirical differences of values between social classes. Several studies collected by Reinhard Bendix and Seymour Martin Lipset in their path-breaking book *Class, Status and Power* (1953) pointed to differences in values between different classes or strata of society. Empirical studies showed class differences in values regarding political choices, sexual activity, religion, upward occupational mobility, the attainment of a college education, and support for ideals such as equality.

Studies have shown, for example, that from the 1930s to the 1950s the working class supported the Democratic party more than the Republican party (Saenger, 1953), felt sexual relations before marriage were more natural than the middle or upper classes (Kinsey et al., 1953), were less likely to be Protestant than the upper class (Pope, 1953), had less desire for occupational mobility or a college education than the middle or upper class (Hyman, 1953; National Opinion Research Center, 1953), and gave more support for equality than the upper class (Knupfer, 1953).

One of the most interesting of these studies is Richard Centers' "Children of the New Deal: Social Stratification and Adolescent Attitudes" (1953). He presents a "collectivism-individualism" scale of the value of government intervention versus individual initiative to attain goals and solve problems. Some of the problems to be solved or goals to be achieved by the government versus individual effort were the provision of affordable public services such as water and electricity, affordable housing for the poor, financial security and medical care for the elderly, protection against racial or sexual discrimination, and assistance for poverty and unemployment.

As might be expected, adolescents from the upper class had a greater individualist orientation than those from the working class, who had a greater collectivist orientation. However, many adolescents from the middle class and even many from the upper class (42 percent) had a collectivist orientation. As Centers explained:

> *These are the children of the New Deal.* Born in depression, reared in unemployment and insecurity . . . witnessing the dramatic victories of welfare legislation, T.V.A., etc., and probably in numerous instances [they] personally . . . [benefited] from welfare measures . . . (1953, p. 362)

Thus the Great Depression of the 1930s and President Franklin Roosevelt's New Deal led to a greater than expected collectivist orientation in American youth of the 1940s. The upper class was still more individualist than collectivist in orientation. But history intervened to *decrease* the relationship between social class and political values for these adolescents who grew up in the Great Depression.

Radical View of Individualism

In the radical view, much of U.S. culture is a rationalization for the kind of society desired by the upper class. One aspect of the previously discussed individualist orientation is the idea that every individual can be a successful millionaire or president of the United States. So when millions of people are unemployed, it is assumed that they must be lazy and prefer not working. But radicals have shown that the millions of unemployed are *not* individual failures, but are the result of the operation of the capitalist system. Without an ideology that tells us it all depends on the individual, could anyone believe that 10 million people would voluntarily choose to be unemployed at exactly the same time?

Similarly, if we believe the ideology that success depends only on the individual, then all those living in poverty have chosen to be failures. But radicals point out that the capitalist system pushes millions of workers into poverty.

The American ideology says that everyone has an equal vote and anyone can be president. But radicals point out that it takes much wealth to have a political impact—that is, to advertise on TV and radio, to own the media, to hire political workers, to print leaflets, to mail millions of letters, and so forth.

The American ideology says that anyone can be wealthy. But C. Wright Mills (1956) found that most of the rich have wealth because their parents were wealthy.

The American ideology says that ill health is just a personal accident, so we should each pay for health care according to our justly deserved income. But the poor cannot afford health care, whereas a rich person can afford many medical miracles. Radicals believe it is a sick society that allows people to remain ill if they do not have enough money to pay for proper care. Thus the views and interests of poor working-class people are often very different from those of millionaire capitalists.

A RADICAL ANALYSIS OF CULTURE

Bases of Ideas: The Sociology of Knowledge

The metaphor of base and superstructure (discussed in Chapter 2) is insufficient for detailed analysis. Figure 6.1 shows some of the complex relations between the constituent parts of the base and superstructure, each of which must be examined systematically (Aronowitz, 1981; Jay, 1973).

In this view, ideologies and social ideas are determined by the present and past history of (1) ideas themselves, (2) the sociopolitical institutions, (3) the class relations of production, and (4) the forces of production. As an example of ideological development, let us consider—very briefly—the prevailing view of women's proper role in the 1950s and how it changed in the late 1960s.

In the 1950s, American economic and political power was at its height relative to the rest of the world. The economy was expanding, unemployment was very low, and American investments (and military forces) overseas were rapidly increasing. The American political mood was complacent and conservative. Nearly

Figure 6.1   Radical (Marxist) view of social interconnections.

all dissident voices had been silenced by the repression of Senator Joseph McCarthy and the House Un-American Activities Committee.

Large numbers of women, of course, worked in World War II. One study showed only 13 percent of Americans were opposed to married women working in the war year 1942, whereas a few years earlier in the 1930s Depression over 80 percent were opposed (Freeman, 1975, p. 22). After the war, however, various women were replaced by men, so the percentage of women with jobs dropped somewhat. In the conservative postwar period, it was assumed that women should be fulfilled by raising large suburban familes with many household conveniences. The pervasive feeling was that women did not need jobs since solid husbands could provide for them. Thus it was all right to pay much less to women who did work than to men who did the same work. This ideology suited the capitalist employers of women because they made much higher profits by paying women lower wages—and because unions were weakened by the prejudice of male workers against women workers.

The women's movement of the 1960s called for, and won to some extent, laws forbidding unequal pay and other unequal treatment. The basic attitudes of many men and women were also changing. Consequently, fewer women were satisfied to remain only housewives, and more women were overcoming the barriers to enter law, medicine, and other professions. Why the changes?

A few outstanding women might be the focus of a psychological or cultural determinist explanation. For example, Betty Friedan's writing and organizing in the mid-1960s undoubtedly had a strong impact on many women (and men). This was particularly the case with Friedan's most famous book, *The Feminine Mystique,* written in 1963. But a materialist asks two additional questions: (1) *Why* did Friedan entertain these ideas at that time? (2) *Why* did her ideas find such a favorable reception at that time?

To explain her personal ideas, one would have to look at Friedan's own life experiences: her education (she had training in psychology), her own work experience, her family and marital background, and so forth. To understand the *form* of expression of her ideas, we would have to look at the previous psychological and sociological writing on women because any writer is shaped to some extent by preceding ideas. Friedan's writing reflects some Freudian thought of the 1950s, though she is quite critical of it and arrives at different conclusions.

Friedan and the developing women's movement were additionally influenced by important changes in the economic base of American society occurring in the 1950s and 1960s. It was these economic changes that made many American women especially receptive to the ideas of women's liberation at that time. We must stress the timing of this acceptance, because some of these ideas of women's liberation had been around in earlier forms throughout the nineteenth and twentieth centuries, but had not won mass approval. For example, the first American convention to declare itself in favor of equal rights for women took place in 1848 at Seneca Falls, New York.

The increasing number of women with outside employment was the most basic change for women that occurred during this period. Right before World

War II, only 29 percent of all women (16 years and over) had paid jobs. This increased significantly to 38 percent during the war, and by 1950, partly because of the war, 34 percent were still paid workers. This increased to 38 percent by 1960 and to 44 percent by 1972. A *majority* of 52 percent were working outside the home in 1985 (Deckard, 1975, pp. 75, 302, 310; Bergmann, 1986).

Thus conditions were changing fast in the 1960s. Yet the myth persisted that all women were housewives and did not and should not work outside the home, a myth Betty Friedan called the "feminine mystique."

The increasingly untenable separation of the myth and the reality of American women led to an expanding consciousness of the social and economic oppression of women. In spite of continued attachment to and support for the myth, the increasing consciousness of women's actual situation spread to millions of women and men.

Radical analysis not only distinguishes between the economic base of society and the superstructure of ideas and culture, but it argues the base and superstructure *interact*. The experience of the Catholic church is instructive in this regard. The church has previously been seen as supporting the economic system of countries in which it existed. Yet Catholicism in recent years has developed critical—even radical—tendencies: liberation theology and the sanctuary movement.

Liberation theology explicitly feels that the church—including priests and nuns—should *aid* the cause of revolution in Third World countries, as in Latin America. Whereas more conservative church ideology stressed adherence to the status quo, liberation theology sees the status quo as oppressive and works to change it. Pope John Paul II has criticized liberation theology because of its association with radical movements. But liberation theology may have indirectly influenced his recent declarations in favor of the world's poor and against the exploitive conduct of richer nations. So the inequities tied to prior church support of the economic system now lead to a different church ideology, in at least part of the church, against the economic system. This is an example of the economic base and religious aspect of the superstructure interacting.

The sanctuary movement similarly involves the Catholic church in activities contrasting with past policies. Due to American involvement—direct or indirect—in recent Latin American conflicts, as in El Salvador, various Catholics—and Protestants—decided to give sanctuary in the United States to refugees from these countries. It is felt that without U.S. involvement in countries like El Salvador, citizens of these countries would not be physically endangered by war conditions. Thus, American Catholics (and Protestants) have provided shelter to illegal refugees from Latin American countries who fled to the United States to escape the threatening circumstances in their own countries. More generally, the economic system in the United States influenced American foreign policy toward Latin America, which the Catholic church has traditionally supported. However, the conflicts arising from U.S. policy in Latin America have helped create the sanctuary movement in the United States, which is critical of the United States. Once again, the economic base and religious part of the superstructure are seen to interact.

Time Lags in Ideological Changes

An element of a superstructure, such as Christianity, may continute through many economic bases. The critics of Marxism have taken this as an exception to the Marxist theory of a relation between base and superstructure (Russell, 1959, pp. 293–294). But the time lag between base and superstructure in no way destroys the relationship; it merely shows one of the ways in which the relationship is complex. Once an idea has arisen on the basis of some socioeconomic system, it may remain entrenched for an incredibly long time. Christianity first corresponded to the sociological conditions and needs of the Roman slave empire. Certainly, it remained important under feudalism and capitalism. But Christianity has not stayed the same. It has changed greatly and has adapted itself to new economic and social systems, playing an important role in each of them.

For example, during the feudal period, the church's condemnation of usury (interest) played a role in support of the then dominant landlord class. But when capitalism was in its early beginnings, Christianity changed its dogmas as a result of the Reformation, which itself reflected the rise of early capitalism. Not only did later Christianity do away with the theological objection to collecting interest on money loaned, it also provided a very positive boost to capitalist ideology with the fashioning of the Protestant work ethic already described. Thus an element of the superstructure may remain important through several economic bases, but it will most likely undergo changes.

Ruling Ideas and False Consciousness

In most normal periods, the predominant ideas of any society will be those which, ultimately, are most useful to the ruling class of that society. There is a confused notion that Marxism asserts that each class simply learns from its own work conditions and always acts in its own interest. On the contrary: "Marx did not say that everyone's beliefs and attitudes flow from his class position. Marx said that the ruling ideas of an epoch are the ideas of the ruling class" (Horowitz, 1971, p. 9).

If a subordinate class, such as the working class in America today, were truly conscious of its own interests, it would toss out the present rulers and elect representatives to serve its own interests. The American working class, however, is often deceived into a *false consciousness*—that is, a misguided belief contrary to its interests. For example, the majority of the working class voted for Richard Nixon in 1972, thinking that he was the candidate who would best defend their interests. Since then, it has been shown that he worked with big business to do everything possible *against* the interests of the working-class majority.

In other words, in normal times when there is no revolutionary situation, not only the small ruling class but also the majority of the subordinate class in most societies, believes that the society is working for their interests—or, at least, that it is the best possible society at the present time. This ruling ideology is not imposed on the United States working class by any magical means. Rather, it is repeated over and over again through television, newspapers, schools, churches, and government, as well as by corporations on the job. Workers are taught an ideology of harmony to cover the facts of oppression. For example, Henry Ford proclaimed the myth: "An American can be anything he wants to be. He can become president of his country, a successful lawyer, doctor, or merchant. All he needs to do is try. With the will to succeed, he will win" (quoted in Hodges, 1974, p. 217). Is it really true that equal will power will give an equal chance to the son of an unemployed worker and the son or daughter of a millionaire, to someone born black and someone born white, or to a female and a male? Existing data suggest otherwise.

The ideological myths of racism and sexism similarly justify and help continue types of oppression. Thus male and female are conditioned to fit certain stereotypes by both words and treatment in the family and in all the other institutions of society. It is, therefore, not surprising that most males and females do fit the stereotypes, since they have been conditioned to behave that way both by internal motivations (based on previous training) and by external barriers if they try to act otherwise. For example, women who have tried to break the stereotype to get into high-paying ("male only") professions have been met by the barriers of both laws and informal discrimination designed to keep women "in their place." As late as 1874, the U.S. Supreme Court ruled that a state could prevent women from becoming lawyers, because this was an "unladylike" profession. To "protect their purity," women until recently could not become higher-paid bartenders but could become low-paid barmaids.

All of the stereotypes of racism, sexism, and the lazy, ignorant worker are useful for maintaining the power and high profits of the capitalist class. These stereotypes are propagated, as noted above, by all the social institutions controlled by the capitalist class. Contrary to the liberal view that all ideas meet in free competition and everyone makes rational choices, we argue that the working class is manipulated through social myths that cause a false consciousness. We shall see later that these myths are *very seldom* propagated by a conscious conspiracy of the ruling class. Rather, the schools, churches, and news media present this ideology as the normal, natural result of the overall operation or functioning of our present social system.

Some writers, such as Herbert Marcuse in his *One Dimensional Man* (1964), seem to think that this manipulation of mass consciousness into false beliefs can be nearly 100 percent perfect. Marcuse thus reaches the pessimistic conclusion that basic change in the present system is almost impossible. Yet such a pessimistic conclusion does not follow because new experiences can shake people loose from false consciousness and the spell of ruling ideology. In the late 1950s and early 1960s, blacks came alive to their situation and to the possibilities of change, and they acted accordingly through legal actions, civil rights protests, and riots. In the last half of the 1960s, students and youth protested the Vietnam War in enormous demonstrations that did eventually have an effect. In the late 1960s and early 1970s, women became more conscious of their true situation—many through experience in the civil rights and antiwar movements—and were able to win some reform antidiscrimination laws. In fact, Marcuse himself became less pessimistic about change by the late 1960s, as reflected in his books such as *An Essay on Liberation* (1969).

In a similar way, in nonrevolutionary periods most sociologists are conditioned by society to follow the dominant, traditional perspective—without really questioning the basis of their approach. Sociologists do pursue new theoretical analyses for many individual reasons, including the pure love of theoretical analysis, the desire for more money and prestige or job security at a university, and—for some—the desire to change or to preserve society. Most sociological endeavors, however, result in routine analysis, expanding and making the dominant perspective more elegant. It is primarily in very unstable periods that sociological analysis can result in a major reform of the dominant sociological or political perspective. Especially when subordinate groups or classes are already on the march and fighting to improve society, sociologists can actually contribute to an overthrow of older perceptions.

DYLAN (BOB), GOFFMAN (ERVING), AND MARX (GARY)

There have been important recent unmaskers of cultural illusions. Operating in different mediums, Gary Marx, Erving Goffman, and Bob Dylan all addressed social appearances and revealed hidden, usually unpleasant but significant realities. The first two are renowned sociologists, the latter the most politically important cultural spokesman of his era.

From the start, Dylan exposed many establishment illusions. As a 19 year old from Hibbing, Minnesota, Dylan made his way to New York's Greenwich Village in February 1961, playing at folk-singing clubs such as Gerde's Folk City and Cafe Wha? (Shelton, 1986, pp. 91–94). Sensitized by small-town oppressions and worldwide outrages such as the Holocaust, Dylan had a remarkable capacity to cut through appearances and reveal unvarnished realities.

Dylan's themes were highly diverse, but the method was similar: take nothing for granted and understand how things really operate below the surface. This approach was used in Dylan's songs to show the hypocrisy in well-off older men sending younger men to war ("Masters of War"); a fair-weather friend who would like to see you harmed ("Positively 4th Street"); New York City, which enjoys your music at the rate of a dollar a day ("Talkin' New York"); con artists who deceive the poor and gullible ("Talkin' Bear Mountain Picnic Massacre Blues"); the genteel South, which greets outsiders with tear-gas bombs ("Oxford Town"); and the rich, who are even able to kill without severe penalty ("The Lonesome Death of Hattie Carroll"). (See Dylan, 1985.)

Against a cultural backdrop of 1950s acceptance of the status quo, these themes were often startling revelations. Dylan had an insider's capacity to see the actual state of affairs, and an outsider's capacity to report on them. Few thought the entire system had serious flaws, but this is the message he delivered. "Like a Rolling Stone" could be interpreted as a dramatic, surrealistic fall from grace by a young woman of the upper class:

> You've gone to the finest school all right, Miss Lonely
> But you know you only used to get juiced in it

Yet it could also be interpreted as a flawed United States about to lose its preeminent position among nations, but unaware of its fate:

> People'd call, say, "Beware doll, you're bound to fall"
> You thought they were all kiddin' you

His "Blowin' in the Wind" implies that large-scale change is not only possible, but that it will occur when people are sufficiently aware of existing oppressions. Dylan was once quoted as saying this political awareness comes and goes as if blown by the wind. But the required consciousness for change does periodically emerge (Scaduto, 1971, pp. 118–119).

"The Times They Are A-Changin' " states an ominous warning across the generations:

> Come mothers and fathers
> Throughout the land
> And don't criticize
> What you can't understand
> Your sons and your daughters
> Are beyond your command
> Your old road is
> Rapidly agin'.
> Please get out of the new one
> If you can't lend your hand
> For the times they are a-changin'.

The older generation's inability to comprehend the changes occurring toward liberation in racial, political, economic, and cultural relations is paralleled by the younger generation's participation in them. Yet Dylan implicitly invites the older generation to join in the emerging new society, with the proviso that they depart if unable to adjust. By stripping away so many myths, Dylan became the harbinger of 1960s change and a major cultural force for this change.

In *The Presentation of Self in Everyday Life* (1959), Erving Goffman exposes many realities behind ordinary social or cultural appearances. Through his "dramaturgical approach" to analyzing social life, Goffman (p. xi) draws on the language and techniques of the theater to shed light on ways people interact with each other. Going way beyond commonsense understandings of everyday life,

Goffman shows how people put on "performances" for the several "audiences" they daily encounter. His book could be seen as an elaborate documentation of Shakespeare's insight that "all the world's a stage."

Goffman begins with a discussion of Preedy, an Englishman who vacations on the Spanish Coast. Within a short time, Preedy, as he walks up, down, and around the Spanish beach is Kindly Preedy, Ideal Preedy, Methodical and Sensible Preedy, Big-Cat Preedy, Carefree Preedy, and Local Fisherman Preedy. (pp. 4–5). The Englishman is thus giving off several impressions of himself, hoping that his audience will act toward him according to his preconceived vacation plans. Preedy does not exactly try to defraud the people surrounding him, but he is engaged in "impression management" and is controlling the "definition of the situation" to advance his own interests. He is not the innocent beach dweller he appears to be.

Goffman (chap. 1) distinguishes between those who believe in their performances and those who do not. The former are judged as sincere, whereas the latter are judged as cynical. But, Goffman argues, both nevertheless present performances.

Goffman provides scores of illustrations where appearance and reality differ: the radio talk show host who spends hours on a script to make his show appear spontaneous; the student who extensively plays at being attentive in class but misses issues in the lecture as a result; the bright 1950s college women who let boyfriends explain subjects they already understood; waitresses kindly attending to customers who are berated behind closed kitchen doors; and the casual literary style used by some authors that conceals the drudgery of writing their books.

Goffman goes into many variations on this theme: the props that can move with the performance, as in the complicated mobile displays of a royal coronation; team activities where two or more actors collaborate on a performance, such as husband and wife at a dinner party; spies who consciously deceive their audience; and "nonpersons," such as servants, who may observe "backstage" behavior because they are not regarded as legitimate parts of the audience. Each variation is aimed at showing aspects of the frequent discrepancy between outward appearances and underlying social or cultural realities.

In university seminars, Goffman said his type of analysis was not political, that he had no political agenda to advocate (Gary T. Marx, 1984). While this is true with regard to not publicly advocating specific political platforms, his analysis had the effect of demystifying social or cultural practices and institutions, including political ones. This method points to the need for looking behind cultural "masks" and analyzing "what's really going on." Whereas Goffman had no explicit political applications for this approach, his student Gary T. Marx does.

Gary Marx has often gone behind political appearances to show the underlying realities. His study of the "agent provocateur" in social movements is a classic in the literature (Marx, 1974). An agent provocateur is an "authorized scoundrel" who joins social movements at the request of the government or police (Conrad, 1965). He or she tries to influence movement members to engage in extreme or violent activities so as to discredit the movement and provide damaging evidence against them in court trials. As Marx (1974, p. 402) says:

> It is surprisiing that Peter Berger's (1966) advice to introductory sociology students—"the first wisdom of sociology is this . . . things are not what they seem"—has not been taken more seriously by students of social movements.

In particular, he points out that analysts have concentrated on those who are loyal to the movement, but they have paid little or no attention to provocateurs who are actively trying to make a movement look ridiculous or more violent than it is, who are trying to spy on it, or who are actively attempting to split it for ulterior reasons.

Marx details the often nefarious role that agents provocateurs have played in social movements. He shows, for example, that these agents have helped build and test explosive devices for radical students, set fire to campus buildings, urged violence on the part of demonstrators, threw a campus president off stage in a demonstration, arranged for the Ku Klux Klan to bomb Jewish businesses, and put a bag full of time bombs on an army truck. This cataloguing of highly irregular activities reads like a novel; yet Marx shows this is not fiction but, instead, a very real part of the social control apparatus.

Marx's discussion of the agent provocateur is connected to his larger analysis of undercover police activities—again, behavior that is not what it seems. His recent discussions of official deceptions transcend appearances to locate hidden realities. His analysis *Undercover: Police Surveillance in America* (Marx, 1988) provides elaborate documentation of the misuse of new technologies, such as advanced computers, by social control agencies. He presents case after case where the privacy and freedom of ordinary citizens are threatened by these methods, which are ostensibly used to produce a safer society but may have the opposite effect. Indeed, there are dozens of laws that will (or should) be created to deal with the threats to a democratic society uncovered by Marx.

Finally, in "External Effects to Damage or Facilitate Social Movements: Some Patterns, Explanations, Outcomes, and Complications" (1982), Marx interprets the mass of documentary data obtained from government hearings—such as the Select Committee to Study Governmental Operations with Respect to Intelligence—and related data. He systematically analyzes this outpouring of information, much of which would have been unavailable prior to Watergate, and which would have remained descriptive data without Marx's analytical efforts.

This article shows, for example, that FBI agents went to great lengths to disrupt New Left groups, whether or not they committed crimes. The FBI was told to "prepare leaflets designated to discredit student demonstrators"; "send articles . . . which show the depravity of the New Left"; and "use . . . friendly news media and law-enforcement officials to disrupt New Left coffeehouses near military bases." Parallel activities were directed at other groups with which the FBI disagreed politically. Marx clearly shows a decidedly political role of the police and FBI agencies that transcends their supposedly neutral role of law enforcement in society. This neutrality was severely compromised when the social control agencies promoted internal and external conflict in social movements, inhibited the supply of resources to them, engaged in the strategy of "derecruitment" to social movements, and sabotaged movement activities.

The late 1950s and early 1960s saw a significant stripping away of the "emperor's clothes" in a segment of American culture and in some sociological analyses. The thaw of McCarthyism ushered in a more critical appraisal of society, which went behind outward images and official pronouncements to portray relationships as they actually existed. Bob Dylan and Erving Goffman were at the forefront of this societal unmasking—along with poet Allen Ginsberg, comedian Lenny Bruce, and novelist Jack Kerouac. Gary Marx—having absorbed this approach as a graduate student at that time—has significantly applied it to the unmasking of many political and governmental activities in the current era. A final note in this regard: Erving Goffman and Gary Marx are central figures in present-day sociology. Their insights show what the discipline can do when it casts a critical, instead of complacent, eye on society.

TRENDS IN THE 1980S

In the early 1980s various commentators and national surveys of young people by scholars such as Alexander Astin pointed to the development of conservative attitudes in America. The movie *Rambo*—which depicted excessive violence and military adventure—was a big hit, probably because it promoted the use of American force against international foes. Under these circumstances, which combined with American frustration over President Carter's policies regarding Iran and inflation, President Reagan was elected on a conservative platform, and 1960s political activist Abbie Hoffman said he couldn't trust anyone *under* 30 (Wood and Jackson, 1982, p. 135).

The key conservative issues were a demand for prayer in public schools, abolition of abortion rights for women, censorship of books in schools, watering down of affirmative action policies, reduction of government funds for the poor, and the promotion of a large military build-up, especially with "Star Wars," President Reagan's Strategic Defense Initiative (SDI). Politics and culture often intersect with these conservative issues—many of which are political issues involving who will dominate our cultural life and institute particular values. The election of Ronald Reagan can be seen as a partial consequence and partial cause of this political struggle over cultural dominance.

COUNTERTRENDS

By the mid-1980s countertrends had begun. It has been said that the rock music world achieved its "finest hour" when it recorded "We Are the World" in 1985 to aid famine victims in Ethiopia (Breskin, 1985). This was followed by the huge international Live Aid benefit concert for additional famine relief. At the Live Aid concert Bob Dylan proposed assistance to American farmers to help pay their large mortgages to the banks, which resulted in the Farm Aid benefit concerts. Dylan's announcement marked his further reinvolvement in progressive social and political issues, which had begun a few years earlier, in 1982, with his surprise appearance with Joan Baez at "Peace Sunday" in Pasadena (Hilburn, 1982). This reinvolvement was significant since the media had used Dylan's "Born-Again" Christian phase of the late 1970s and early 1980s to discredit the actual commitment of 1960s political activists (Wood, 1982).

Giving widespread publicity to the problems of factory closings and unemployment was Bruce Springsteen, whose *Born In the U.S.A.* was the largest-selling album in the history of Columbia Records. In songs like "My Hometown," Springsteen painted a stark picture of the human consequences "when factories leave but people are left behind." At his spectacularly staged and attended concerts, Springsteen discussed these topics between songs and requested the audience to join him in contributing to local food banks.

Many other similar benefits took place in the mid to late 1980s, including Hands Across America for the homeless and the Amnesty International benefit concerts for victims of political oppression. All of this activity was opposite the self-centered "Me Generation" of the 1970s. The vanished idealism of the "Me Generation" was captured in the movie *The Big Chill* and was thought to characterize many in American society during this period. [However, Fendrich (1977) showed retention of ideals among most 1960s political activists.] If the "Me Generation" was closer to cultural attitudes of the 1950s, the outpouring of altruism in the mid-1980s was closer to cultural attitudes of the 1960s.

CONDITIONS OF CHANGE

What accounts for this recent shift toward increasingly progressive or critical values in America? The broad circumstances for this shift appear to be the strains generated by President Reagan's conservative policies beginning in 1981. The development of Star Wars and the impasse in nuclear-weapons negotiations with the Soviet Union revived the peace movement in the United States and Britain (Cook and Kirk, 1984; Wood et al., 1984; Mitchell and Wood, 1985; Wood and Wood, 1986). Reagan's policy of "constructive engagement" toward South Africa's oppression of blacks led to large-scale antiapartheid protests in America (President Carter's daughter, Amy, was jailed for her participation). The U.S. government's illegal support for the Contras fighting the Nicaragua regime led to protests, even in Congress, against further aid to the Contras. The U.S. invasion of Grenada and bombing of Libya created new concerns about the reinstatement of the military draft. The attacks on affirmative action by President Reagan's attorney general, Edwin Meese, as well as Reagan's appointment of many conservative federal judges, including conservative Supreme Court justices, led to calls by the American Civil Liberties Union (ACLU) to replace Meese, and to the concerted—and successful—effort to deny confirmation of the president's controversial choice for Supreme Court justice, Robert Bork.

All of this amounts to a new cycle of cultural criticism and political protests in the mid to late 1980s, matched by a renewed sense of social altruism, and a reaction against the conservative policies of the early 1980s.

OLIVER NORTH AND CULTURAL CONFLICTS

In the summer of 1987, a riveting set of political and cultural conflicts burst onto American television. A Joint Senate–House of Representatives Congressional Committee investigated the Iran-Contra scandal. The scandal involved high-level U.S. government officials secretly selling arms to Iran and illegally using the profits from the arms sales to support the Contras, the anticommunist Nicaraguan rebels favored by President Reagan. During these Congressional hearings, Lt. Col. Oliver North galvanized the nation. As *Newsweek* (1987, pp. 12, 18) asked, was he a "patriot or petty crook," a "fall guy" or a "national folk hero"? North was on the president's National Security Council, a position from which he conducted many complex clandestine operations to aid the Contras at a time when laws called the Boland Amendments prohibited such activities. North admitted to shredding a huge number of official documents, as well as previously lying to Congress, to cover up these activities. However, key documents that survived the "shredding party" implicated North and several others who participated in this "covert operation."

How did the American public view all of this? As Senate Investigating Committee Chairman Daniel Inouye (who was critical of North) said, America likely has a new hero. Indeed, *Newsweek* (1987, p. 18) reported that 44 percent of the American public saw him as a patriot and hero. Only 20 percent felt he should be indicted and tried on criminal charges, even in spite of his admission of shredding documents and previously lying to Congress.

Not all public opinion was favorable, however. In fact, 48 percent did not think North was a patriot and hero, according to *Newsweek*. Only 28 percent would vote for him for public office, in spite of the Ollie for President bumper stickers. While early reports indicated he gave a great boost to public support for the Contras, a more scientific analysis showed that 51 percent of the American public were still opposed to Contra aid after his testimony, whereas 35 percent were in favor (*New York Times*/CBS News Poll, 1987). These figures indicated that North gave only a modest boost to public support for Contra aid (previously 28 percent were supportive). Finally, only 19 percent felt North was telling the whole truth (*Newsweek,* 1987, p. 18).

These Congressional hearings highlighted a conflict in basic values between the practice of democracy at home versus support for American economic and military interests abroad. Congress was kept completely out of this national decision making by a small group of the power elite operating out of the executive branch of government. The power elite is C. Wright Mills's (1956) concept of a combination of highly placed political, economic, and military personnel making decisions of national (and often inernational) consequence without democratic restraint from institutions like Congress. Such an elite in the Iran-Contra scandal was comprised of men like the president's former national security advisor, Rear Admiral John Poindexter, and Lt. Col. Oliver North, assisted by businessmen Albert Hakim and retired Air Force Major General Richard Secord.

These men felt communist forces from the Sandinista government in Nicaragua threatened U.S. economic and military interests in Central America, even though many others disagreed with this viewpoint. They felt capitalism would be challenged in Central America, possibly extending to Mexico, without the Contras. Thus, secretly and illegally, they aided the war against the Sandinistas.

One reason Congress was so upset—and this included Republicans like Senator Warren Rudman—was the total disregard for the separation of powers guaranteed by the U.S. Constitution (whose bicentennial was ironically being celebrated at the time of the hearings). North stated that he would not have told Congress "one word" about these operations if he had the choice. Instead North and a handful of other powerful men decided the United States would support the Contras regardless of the Congressional ban. Democracy in the United States was, at least implicitly, deemed less important than American interests abroad. This is a political and cultural struggle that could yet erupt into the conflict between a new patriotism supporting armed intervention in Central America versus a renewed commitment to democracy and peaceful solutions to international disputes. The resolution of this conflict will likely influence whether or not United States again gets embroiled in Vietnam-style hostilities in Central America.

SUMMARY

A discussion of the sociology of culture is necessarily broad. We have focused on a variety of otherwise disparate topics, which nevertheless cohere owing to their connection to cultural values. We have discussed the definition and elements of culture, the conditions under which different cultural views emerge, and some consequences of culture. In the process we have seen the traditional and radical approaches to culture, as well as important aspects of how cultural appearances can be unmasked and realities illuminated. Finally, we have examined cultural conflict as revealed in Oliver North's testimony regarding the Iran-Contra scandal.

There is a tendency in the traditional approach to culture to see cultural values determining many patterns of behavior like economic behavior, family behavior, or political behavior. One important position of traditional sociology, for example, sees Protestant ethic religious values influencing the development of capitalist economic behavior.

The radical approach to culture often asks the source of these values, particularly the economic source. Radical scholars have seen capitalism as an important source of Protestant Ethic religious values such as hard work, individualism, and success. Capitalism has been seen to encourage these values because the values are helpful to a capitalist economy. However, the radical approach furthermore points to the importance of the interaction between the economic base of a society and elements of the superstructure like religion, as demonstrated by the discussions of liberation theology and the sanctuary movement.

SUGGESTED READINGS

The concept of culture has been treated somewhat differently in sociology than it has in classical anthropology. The broader focus in anthropology of equating culture with society is found in such works as Edward B. Tylor, *Primitive Culture* (New York: Henry Holt and Company, 1889), and Ruth Benedict, *Patterns of Culture* (New York: New American Library, Mentor Books, 1959; originally published by Houghton Mifflin, 1934). In contrast, the narrower focus of the concept culture stressing ideas such as beliefs, norms, and values is found in Talcott Parsons, *The Social System* (New York: Free Press, 1951), and in his collaboration with a well-known modern anthropologist to present a united front for the narrower definition of culture: A. L. Kroeber and Talcott Parsons, "The Concepts of Culture and of Social System," *American Sociological Review* 23 (October 1958):582–583.

Many sociologists, traditional and radical, have contributed to our understanding of culture. A famous radical critique of culture is Karl Marx and Friedrich Engels, *The German Ideology* (New York: International Publishers, 1939). Karl Mannheim further analyzed the impact of class position on systems of ideas in *Ideology and Utopia*, trans. Louis Wirth and Edward Shils (New York: Harcourt Brace Jovanovich, 1936). More recent radical analyses of culture include: Herbert Marcuse's *One-Dimensional Man* (Boston: Beacon Press, 1964) and *An Essay on Liberation* (Boston: Beacon Press, 1969); Martin Jay, *The Dialectical Imagination* (Boston: Little, Brown, 1973); Stanley Aronowitz, *The Crisis in Historical Materialism: Class, Politics and Culture in Marxist Theory* (New York: Praeger, 1981); and Bertell Ollman, "How to Study Class Consciousness, and Why We Should," *The Insurgent Sociologist* 14 (Winter 1987):57–96.

Traditional sociologists have similarly analyzed culture. Talcott Parsons's analyses of culture were inspired, in part, by the cultural analyses of Emile Durkheim, such as *Suicide*, trans. John A. Spaulding and George Simpson (New York: Free Press, 1951, 1897), and by the works of Max Weber, such as *The Protestant Ethic and the Spirit of Capitalism,* trans. Talcott Parsons (New York: Scribner's, 1958, 1904–1905). Parsons wrote a very interesting preface to the new edition of the latter book. For a different emphasis regarding these thinkers, see Anthony Giddens, *Capitalism and Modern Social Theory: An Analysis of the Writings of Marx, Durkheim and Weber* (New York: Cambridge University Press, 1971). Recent analyses of culture by traditional sociologists include Milton Rokeach, *The Nature of Human Values* (New York: Free Press, 1973) and *Understanding Human Values* (New York: Free Press, 1979); Melvin L. Kohn, *Class and Conformity* (Chicago: University of Chicago Press, 1977); and James L. Spates, "The Sociology of Values," *Annual Review of Sociology* 9 (1983):27–49.

There has been a recent focus on symbols as key aspects of culture. An excellent discussion of this is Richard A. Peterson's "Revitalizing the Culture Concept," *Annual Review of Sociology* 5 (1979): 137–166. In it he discusses important contributions by such theorists as Claude Levi-Strauss, Noam Chomsky, Pierre Bourdieu, Alain Touraine, Michel Foucault, Paul DiMaggio and Michael Useem, and Erving Goffman.

From the late 1950s and early 1960s to the present, there have been important cultural critiques in sociology and in the media. Erving Goffman, in books such as *The Presentation of Self in Everyday Life* [Garden City, NY: Doubleday (Anchor Books), 1959], stripped away many appearances of daily social interaction to locate hidden realities. Bob Dylan, along with Allen Ginsberg, Lenny Bruce, and Jack Kerouac, also stripped away many cultural myths and exposed harsh realities in such works as Bob Dylan, *The Times They Are A-Changin'* (New York: Columbia Records, 1964); *Highway 61 Revisited* (New York: Columbia Records, 1965); *Bob Dylan's Greatest Hits* (New York: Columbia Records, 1967); *Biograph* (New York: Columbia Records, 1985); Allen Ginsberg, *Howl and Other Poems* (San Francisco: City Lights Books, 1985, 1956); Lenny Bruce, *The Essential Lenny Bruce,* compiled and edited by John Cohen (Douglas Books, 1970); and Jack Kerouac, *On the Road* (Penguin Books, 1983; originally published in the United States in 1957). Two very interesting recent discussions of cultural critics in the media are Robert Shelton, *No Direction Home: The Life and Music of Bob Dylan* [New York: Morrow (Beech Tree Books,

1986), and Wayne Hampton, *Guerrilla Minstrels* (Knoxville: University of Tennessee Press, 1986). For an interesting quantitative treatment of some issues in *Guerrilla Minstrels,* see Charles J. Stewart, Craig Allen Smith, and Robert E. Denton, Jr., *Persuasion and Social Movements* (Waveland Press, 1984). Informative and readable syntheses of many of these ideas relating culture to radical politics are found in the essays included in Jerold M. Starr, ed., *Cultural Politics* (New York: Praeger, 1985). For a very interesting, informative, and entertaining book discussing major political and cultural events over the past 30 or 50 years by a participant in them, see Joan Baez, *And a Voice to Sing with: A Memoir* (New York: New American Library, 1987).

Gary T. Marx has continued the tradition of stripping away appearances and exposing important realities. Often focusing on official deceptions, Gary Marx has performed a public service in such scholarly analyses as "Thoughts on a Neglected Category of Social Movement Participant: The Agent Provocateur and the Informant," *American Journal of Sociology* 80(September):402–422; "External Efforts to Damage or Facilitate Social Movements: Some Patterns, Explanations, Outcomes, and Complications," in James L. Wood and Maurice Jackson, *Social Movements: Development, Participation, and Dynamics* (Belmont, CA: Wadsworth, 1982), chap. 12, pp. 181–200; and *Undercover: Police Surveillance in America* (Berkeley: University of California Press, 1988).

The several analyses of culture discussed in this chapter indicate the potential of sociology—and the media—to develop a critical stance toward existing social and cultural arrangements. This critical stance is important in order to inform the public of policies, ideas, and actions that significantly affect it.

REFERENCES

Alexander, Jeffrey C., ed. 1985. *Neofunctionalism.* Beverly Hills, CA: Sage.

Alexander, Jeffrey C. 1983. *Theoretical Logic in Sociology.* Vol. 4: *The Modern Reconstruction of Classical Thought: Talcott Parsons.* Berkeley: University of California Press.

Aronowitz, Stanley. 1981. *The Crisis in Historical Materialism: Class, Politics and Culture in Marxist Theory.* New York: Praeger.

Bellah, Robert N., Richard Madsen, William M. Sullivan, Ann Swidler, and Steven M. Tipton. 1985. *Habits of the Heart: Individualism and Commitment in American Life.* Berkeley: University of California Press.

Bendix, Reinhard, and Seymour Martin Lipset, eds. 1953. *Class, Status and Power: A Reader in Social Stratification.* New York: Free Press of Glencoe.

Benedict, Ruth. 1959. *Pattens of Culture.* New York: New American Library (Mentor); originally published by Houghton Mifflin, 1934.

Berger, Peter. 1966. *Invitation to Sociology.* New York: Doubleday.

Bergmann, Barbara. 1986. *The Economic Emergence of Women.* New York: Basic Books.

Bernstein, Basil. 1977. *Class, Codes and Control.* Boston: Routledge and Kegan Paul.

Blumer, Herbert. 1969. *Symbolic Interactionism: Perspective and Method.* Englewood Cliffs, NJ: Prentice-Hall.

Bourdieu, Pierre. 1984. *Distinction.* Trans. Richard Nice. London: Routledge and Kegan Paul.

———and J. Passeron. 1977. *Reproduction in Education, Society, and Culture.* Beverly Hills, CA: Sage.

Breskin, David. 1985. *We Are The World.* New York: Putnam (Perigee).

Broom, Leonard, and Philip Selznick. 1958. *Sociology: A Text with Adapted Readings.* 2d ed. New York: Harper & Row.

Centers, Richard. 1953. "Children of the New Deal: Social Stratification and Adolescent Attitudes." In Reinhard Bendix and Seymour Martin Lipset, eds., *Class, Status and Power,* pp. 359–370. New York: Free Press of Glencoe.

Conrad, Joseph. 1965. *Secret Agent.* New York: Doubleday.

Cook, Alice, and Gwyn Kirk. 1984. *Greenham Women Everywhere: Dreams, Ideas and Actions from the Women's Peace Movement.* London: Pluto Press. Originally published, 1983.

Cooley, Charles Horton. 1922. *Human Nature and the Social Order,* Rev. ed. New York: Scribner's.

Deckard, Barbara Sinclair. 1975. *The Women's Movement.* New York: Harper & Row.

DiMaggio, Paul, and Michael Useem. 1978. "Social Class and Arts Consumption." *Theory and Society* (5):141–161.

Durkheim, Emile. 1951. *Suicide.* New York: Free Press. Originally published, 1897. Translated by John A. Spaulding and George Simpson.

———. 1964. *The Division of Labor in Society.* New York: Free Press. Originally published in 1893.

Dylan, Bob. 1985. *Lyrics: 1962–1985.* New York: Knopf.

Erickson, F., and J. Schultz. 1978. *Talking to the "Man."* New York: Academic Press.

Fendrich, James M. 1977. "Keeping the Faith or Pursuing the Good Life: A Study of the Consequences of Participation in the Civil Rights Movement." *American Sociological Review* 42 (February): 144–157.

Freeman, Jo. 1975. *The Politics of Women's Liberation.* New York: Longman.

Freud, Sigmund. 1949. *An Outline of Psychoanalysis.* New York: Norton.

Friedan, Betty. 1963. *The Feminine Mystique.* New York: Dell.

Goffman, Erving. 1959. *The Presentation of Self in Everyday Life.* Garden City, NY: Doubleday (Anchor Books).

Hilburn, Robert. 1982. "Rock Music: A Positive Image at 'Peace Sunday' Concert." *Los Angeles Times.* Calendar section, Tuesday, June 8, part IV: 1, 3–4.

Hodges, Harold. 1974. *Conflict and Consensus: An Introduction to Sociology.* New York: Harper & Row.

Horowitz, David. 1971. *Radical Sociology.* San Francisco: Harper & Row (Canfield Press).

Hyman, Herbert H. 1953. "The Values Systems of Different Classes: A Social Psychological Contribution to the Analysis of Stratification." In Bendix and Lipset, op. cit., pp. 426–442.

Jay, Martin. 1973. *The Dialectical Imagination.* Boston: Little, Brown.

Kinsey, Alfred C., Wardell B. Pomeroy, and Clyde E. Martin. 1953. "Social Level and Sexual Outlet." In Bendix and Lipset, op. cit., pp. 300–308.

Knupfer, Genevieve. 1953. "Portrait of the Underdog." In Bendix and Lipset, op. cit., pp. 255–263

Kroeber, A. L., and Talcott Parsons. 1958. "The Concepts of Culture and of Social System." *American Sociological Review* 23 (October): 582–583.

Mannheim, Karl. 1936. *Ideology and Utopia.* Translated by Louis Wirth and Edward Shils. New York: Harcourt Brace Jovanovich.

Marcuse, Herbert. 1964. *One-Dimensional Man.* Boston: Beacon Press.

———. 1969. *An Essay on Liberation.* Boston: Beacon Press.

Marx, Gary T. 1974. "Thoughts on a Neglected Category of Social Movement Participant: The Agent Provocateur and the Informant." *American Journal of Sociology* 80 (September): 402–442.

———. 1982. "External Efforts to Damage or Facilitate Social Movements: Some Patterns, Explanations, Outcomes, and Complications." In James L. Wood and Maurice Jackson, *Social Movements: Development, Participation, and Dynamics,* chap. 12, pp. 181–200. Belmont, CA: Wadsworth.

———. 1984. "Role Models and Role Distince: A Remembrance of Erving Goffman." *Theory and Society* 13:649–662.

———. 1988. *Undercover: Police Surveillance in America.* Berkeley: University of California Press.

Marx, Karl. 1973. "Contribution to a Critique of Hegel's Philosophy of Right." In Neil J. Smelser, ed., *Karl Marx on Society and Social Change,* pp. 13–14. Chicago: University of Chicago Press.

———, and Friedrich Engels. 1939. *The German Ideology.* New York: International Publishers.

Mead, George Herbert. 1934. *Mind, Self and Society.* Chicago: University of Chicago Press.

Merton, Robert K. 1957. "The Self-Fulfilling Prophecy." In his *Social Theory and Social Structure,* chap. 11. Rev. ed. London: Free Press of Glencoe.

Mills, C. Wright. 1956. *The Power Elite.* New York: Oxford University Press.

Mitchell, Robert A., and James L. Wood. 1985. "La Campagne pour le désarmement nucléaire en Grande-Bretagne: ses membres, ses engagements moraux, ses politiques." *Revue Internationale d'Action Communautaire/International Review of Community Development* 13/53 (Printemps): 165–177.

Myrdal, Gunnar. 1944. *An American Dilemma.* New York: Harper & Row.

National Opinion Research Center. 1953. "Jobs and Occupations: A Popular Evaluation." In Bendix and Lipset, op. cit., pp. 411–426.

Newsweek. July 20, 1987.

New York Times/CBS News Poll. 1987. Reported in *The San Diego Union.* "Poindexter says Diversion Would Have Been OK'd." Saturday, July 18: A-1, A-11.

Parsons, Talcott. 1949. *The Structure of Social Action.* New York: Free Press. Originally published in 1937.

———. 1951. *The Social System.* New York: Free Press.

———. 1954. *Essays in Sociological Theory.* Rev. ed. New York: Free Press.

Parsons, Talcott, and Edward A. Shils, eds. 1962. *Toward a General Theory of Action.* New York: Harper Torchbooks. Originally published in 1951.

Peterson, Richard A. 1979. "Revitalizing the Culture Concept." *Annual Review of Sociology* 5: 137–166.

Pope, Liston. 1953. "Religion and the Class Structure." In Bendix and Lipset, op. cit., pp. 316–323.

Pope, Whitney. 1976. *Durkheim's Suicide: A Classic Analyzed.* Chicago: University of Chicago Press.

———. 1979. "Change and Stability in American Value Systems, 1968–1971." In Milton Rokeach, ed., *Understanding Human Values,* pp. 129–147. New York: Free Press.

Rokeach, Milton. 1973. *The Nature of Human Values.* New York: Free Press.

———, ed. 1979. *Understanding Human Values.* New York: Free Press.

Russell, Bertrand. 1959. "Dialectical Materialism." In Patrick Gardiner, *Theories of History.* New York: Free Press.

Saenger, Gerhart H. 1953. "Social Status and Political Behavior." In Bendix and Lipset, *op. cit.,* pp. 348–358.

Scaduto, Anthony. 1971. *Bob Dylan.* New York: Grosset & Dunlap.

Shelton, Robert. 1986. *No Direction Home: The Life and Music of Bob Dylan.* New York: Morrow (Beech Tree Books).

Smelser, Neil J., and R. Stephen Warner. 1976. *Sociological Theory: Historical and Formal.* Morristown, NJ: General Learning Press.

Spates, James L. 1983. "The Sociology of Values." *Annual Review of Sociology* 9:27–49.

Tönnies, Ferdinand. 1940. *Gemeinschaft und Gesellschaft*. New York: American Book Co. Also translated into English as *Community and Society*. Lansing, MI: Michigan State University Press, 1957.

Tylor, Edward B. 1889. *Primitive Culture*. New York: Holt.

Williams, Robin M., Jr. 1961. "The Sociological Theory of Talcott Parsons." In Max Black, ed., *The Social Theories of Talcott Parsons*, pp. 64–99. Englewood Cliffs, NJ: Prentice-Hall.

Wood, James L. 1968. "The Role of Systematic Theory in Parsons' General Theory of Action: The Case of the Pattern Variables." *Berkeley Journal of Sociology: A Critical Review* 13:28–41.

———. 1982. "Bob Dylan: Born-Again Christian or Social Critic?" *Journal of Political and Military Sociology* 10 (Spring): 131–134.

———, and Maurice Jackson. 1982. *Social Movements: Development, Participation, and Dynamics*. Belmont, CA: Wadsworth.

———, Patricia A. Wood, and Robert A. Mitchell. 1984. "Sur la ferme à Maggie: les camps pour la paix en Grande-Bretagne." *Revue Internationale d'Action Communautaire/ International Review of Community Development* 12/52 (Automne): 137–147.

———, and Patricia A. Wood. 1986. "Dilemmas and Opportunities of International Collective Behavior/Social Movements Research: A Case Study." *International Journal of Mass Emergencies and Disasters* 4(2):193–210. Special Issue entitled "Comparative Perspectives and Research on Collective Behavior and Social Movements."

chapter *7*

Sociology of Education

Among all the institutions in society, the educational system has been looked at as the principal hope for equality by liberal academics. The educational system was supposed to be a place where any individual, depending upon his or her intellectual merit, could receive training that would ultimately pay off economically. The son or daughter of a poor family, if he or she did well in school, would be able to secure as good a job and as high an income as the son or daughter of a wealthy family. Conversely, those who did poorly in school would have difficulty securing a good job or income, regardless of their family background. So education was to be an equalizer: according to the plan of the liberal academics, those who did well in school were to be economically rewarded and those who did poorly would not. Thus education would at least promote equality of economic opportunity—whereby all classes, races, and sexes could benefit economically from excellent academic performance.

In recent years this picture of education has been seriously challenged. Instead of education promoting equality, recent studies have shown that it tends to perpetuate existing *inequality* between classes, races, sexes, and other social groupings. It is not denied that a higher education is usually required to obtain a good job and high income. However, it appears that those from better-off families—especially the male children of these families—are often the ones who get superior educations, which can be translated into economic benefits. Others are often still left out of elite educational circles, which is one reason they remain in lower economic positions in adult life.

In this chapter we shall examine who controls the educational system, and for what purposes. Second, we shall examine what sorts of conditioning are effected by the educational system (such as sex stereotyping, discussed in Chapter 11). To put it another way, we shall ask what the educational system teaches. Third, we shall see how education justifies and reproduces the inequalities in the socioeconomic system of advanced capitalism.

WHO RULES THE EDUCATIONAL SYSTEM?

Local boards of education in the United States are mostly elected. However, as will be shown in Chapter 15, elections generally produce those results desired by the ruling capitalist class. Thus, local boards of education are almost always dominated by the local "respectable" citizens, that is, mostly local businesspersons and a few professionals. They are often much more obviously anti-working class than are federal and state government bodies. This is because they are mostly elected in a "nonpartisan" way, which means that the issues are blurred, and people with well-known names have the best chance of election.

The class control of the educational system is even clearer at the university level. Let us examine, for example, the Board of Regents of the University of California [Smith, 1974]. Twenty regents were appointed by the governor. As of 1976, all of the appointed regents were white. For the first time in history, one of the three elected ex officio members of the board was black. All but two regents were male; the two women merely represented the interests of their husbands (one was appointed at the death of her husband). All of the regents were elderly, the median age being 60. "Nor is there any doubt about the economic status of the Regents; some are staggeringly wealthy—at least ten are millionaires—and all are extremely well off" (p. 30). Finally, the 20 appointed regents together sat on the boards of 60 different corporations, including the nation's largest bank holding company, the nation's largest department store chain, the nation's largest single corporation, and the nation's top defense contractor (Lockheed Aircraft). Almost all the regents were conservative Republicans, though a few have been very prominent in the Democratic party. In summary, therefore, most of the regents were white, male, elderly, very rich, and very conservative. (Former Governor Jerry Brown made more innovative appointments not included in this study.)

In his outstanding sociological study of colleges and universities across the country, Smith concluded in 1974:

> The majority of college trustees throughout the nation are financially powerful, politically influential, socially prominent, old, white, male, and Protestant. The trustees and regents of the major universities are even richer, more conservative, and more powerful than their counterparts among the trustees of the lesser colleges, and, because of their greater importance, are more tightly integrated in the military-industrial web of modern capitalism.

Nor is this a new phenomenon. The earliest systematic study of education by a sociologist, in 1917, concluded that "college and university boards are almost completely dominated by merchants, manufacturers, capitalists, corporation officials, bankers, doctors, lawyers, educators, and ministers. These nine occupations contain a total of 1936 persons, nearly four-fifths of the total number of trustees" (Nearing, 1917). He even suggested the necessity of developing a concept of universities that are publicly supported out of taxes, but dominated by business interests.

A sociological study for the years 1934–1935 found that of all college and university trustees in the country, 42 percent were businesspeople (including some of the nation's biggest capitalists); 25 percent were lawyers (most corporate lawyers); 12 percent were other professionals such as doctors (47 percent of the lawyers and other professionals were also on nonuniversity, corporate boards); 7 percent were clergy; 5 percent educators; and 5 percent politicians (Beck, 1947). Only 1.6 percent were housewives, only 1 percent were farmers, *none* were white-collar workers, *none* were blue-collar workers, and *none* were students. Of the 700 trustees studied in this work, they were found to hold 2656 leading business positions, with at least 66 percent of the trustees holding at least one leading business position. In addition, their median age was 59, they were all white, they were 97 percent male, and 87 percent Protestant.

A later study, for the years 1965–1966, of a large sample of all college and university trustees found similar results (Duster, n.d.). The median age of the regents and trustees was 60; their average income was between $50,000 and $75,000; and they were almost all business and professional. In the whole sample, there was only one black and one labor official. There were no white-collar or blue-collar workers. There were only eight clergymen and ten professors. "The remainder were white, in secular and successful business enterprise" (p. 11).

A massive study of 11,000 college trustees (and regents) was conducted in 1968 by Morton Rauh (1969), the vice-president for finance at Antioch College. Although Rauh was not interested in sociological research for its own sake, his results were similar to previous sociological studies. He found two-thirds to be over age 50; 86 percent men; 99 percent white (including black colleges); 75 percent Protestant (including Catholic colleges); and 34 percent to be directors or major executives of corporations listed on the stock exchange (an additional large number were corporate lawyers). Only one percent were labor union officials; *none* were white-collar workers; and *none* were blue-collar workers. The average income was $40,000 a year, but was $50,000 to $100,000 for trustees of the private universities alone. Of the trustees, 58 percent were self-declared Republicans; their most admired politicians were former president Nixon and former governor Rockefeller; and 81 percent agreed that any student found guilty of of disruption by demonstrating or disobeying any rule should be immediately expelled or suspended.

THE FUNCTIONS OF EDUCATION

The preponderance of representatives of the capitalist class on these boards of regents and trustees is not accidental. They are there to ensure the formulation and carrying out of educational policies that support the basic interests of the capitalist class. With this general principle in mind, it is now necessary to ask: what function is education supposed to perform in capitalist society? Let us first see what is the expectation of the businesspeople who control our educational system. It should be noted that their control is exercised not only through dominating boards of education, trustees, and regents, but also through the direct giving of money by big business foundations to schools, colleges, and professors. According to the top management of General Electric, business gets the following for its efforts and its money:

1. *New knowledge* through research and competent teaching
2. An adequate supply of *educated manpower*
3. *An economic, social and political climate* in which companies like GE can survive and continue to progress. [The Council for Aid to Education, 1956]

This fascinating statement does touch on the three most important points concerning the functions of the American educational system; we must look more carefully at each point.

First of all, the educational system is a free source of much new scientific knowledge. Academic researchers and those trained by the universities provide almost all of our new knowledge in biology, chemistry, physics, and other basic sciences. These discoveries are then used by university-trained technicians working for corporations to create new production methods and new products that are the source of large profits. For example, the University of California has invented new agricultural methods and new crops that greatly benefit the huge agribusiness corporations because those corporations have enough capital to immediately utilize the new discoveries. Generally, small farmers cannot make use of such new discoveries because they require too large an initial outlay of capital or too big an area of land.

Second, it is clear that the educational system supplies the educated manpower and womanpower for the corporate enterprises of capitalism. What needs to be stressed is that the educational system in the United States has throughout its history tailored its output of students—as far as possible—to the specific needs of big business. This fact has determined much of this country's educational history. The best sociological study of education to date concludes: "The major characteristics of the educational system in the United States today flow directly from its role in producing a work force able and willing to staff occupational positions in the capitalist system" (Bowles and Gintis, 1976, p. 265). Schools produce able workers by teaching productive skills and knowledge. At the same time, schools produce willing workers, as we shall see, by teaching discipline at work and submission to capitalist expectations as a natural and desirable way of life. By making workers both more productive, and more disciplined and submissive to authority, the educational system greatly increases the profits of big business.

Historical changes in education have been closely correlated with the changing needs of the capitalist socioeconomic system. For example, until the mid-nineteenth century most people did unskilled agricultural labor that did not require a formal education; accordingly, the early United States had no free public educational system (and such a system was labeled communistic when it was proposed). In the last half of the nineteenth century, however, industry spread throughout the United States, and most people eventually became industrial or service workers in urban areas. These people—including foreign immigrants— had to be able to read and write at the least, and many were required to have more advanced skills. Thus, a free public educational system was launched to meet these needs.

At first, the right of women to an education was denied. Eventually, however, it was found much cheaper to employ women than men to be teachers, clerical workers, and nurses. All of these jobs require a formal education. Therefore, women were soon admitted into public elementary schools, into high schools after a little while, and—eventually, after much resistance—into colleges and universities. Their admittance into college-level work increased particularly during the Civil War, when men were not available for teaching or clerical jobs.

Another way the system adjusts to business needs is by setting up several "tracks," whereby many workers do not get much of a liberal arts education, but are shunted into purely technical training for low-level skilled jobs. (It is primarily the black and Spanish-speaking minorities who are pushed into the lower-level tracks, along with whites from poorer families.)

The mid-nineteenth century witnessed the rise of the factory system, a large and permanent class of wage workers, and an increasing gap of inequality between employers and workers—all of which led to more labor militancy. This situation was behind the first wave of educational reform, the so-called common school reforms. The small, local school boards gained a large representation of working people on them in the early 1840s, at least in New England and New York. The reforms, however, produced a change: "Local control was gradually undermined by the formation of centralized school systems, by professionalization of teaching, and the gradual assertion of state government authority over education" (Bowles and Gintis, 1976, p. 229).

By the late nineteenth century, the masses of workers were in schools that strongly emphasized discipline and unquestioning obedience to teachers (and to the economic system). Partly in opposition, the Progressive reformers emphasized the need for individuals with somewhat more initiative, and a greater emphasis on the ideology that any working-class child could rise to the top of a corporation if only he or she were well prepared and hard working.

> The Progressive education movement grew out of the class conflicts associated with the joint rise of organized labor and corporate capital . . . the social unrest and dislocation stemming from the integration of rural labor . . . into the burgeoning corporate wage-labor system. The particular concerns of the Progressives—efficiency, cooperation, internalization of bureaucratic norms, and preparation for variegated adult roles—reflect the changing social organization of production in the giant corporate enterprise (ibid., pp. 234–235)

The statement by General Electric, quoted earlier, stressed in its third point the function of education in establishing the right social, economic and political climate so that "companies like GE can survive and continue to progress." This climate is promoted—as we will see in Chapter 15—by the media, by the family, *and* by the educational system. The educational system reinforces this climate of support for capitalist firms by many means, some obvious and some much more subtle.

The most obvious means are probably not the most important. They include explicit or implicit propaganda for the capitalist system in "civics" courses in elementary and secondary schools, and in economics, sociology, political science, and history courses in the colleges. Until recent decades, the educational system also taught the inherent, genetic superiority of white to black, of male to female; the genetic superiority of capitalists for leading and supervising; and the genetic fitness of workers for subordinate jobs. There is still some of this elitist propaganda—as well as propaganda in support of the system—but there is also growing opposition to it, as we shall see later.

Less obvious, but probably much more important, is the subtle conditioning of every individual who goes through the educational system to accept his or her place in life, whether it be the dominant position of an executive or the subordinate position of a worker. We shall show that this conditioning takes place in most classrooms of most schools in ways that are so routine as to be unnoticed. We shall also find that this conditioning strengthens the socioeconomic inequalities established by family background both before school and after schooling is finished.

HOW INEQUALITY IS REPRODUCED

The second point of General Electric's statement implies that the educational system reproduces inequality by educating the work force for different-level jobs, such as ordinary worker, skilled worker, engineer, white-collar employee, or executive. This is a quite different perspective than that of many reformers—such as John Dewey—who saw education as the royal road to equality. In Dewey's view, everyone would get an equal education and, therefore, everyone would have equal economic opportunity. To show that this is an illusion, we may first look at two contrasting case studies of an imaginary upper middle-class individual and an imaginary working-class individual in the educational system. Then we shall look more systematically at the facts on inequality.

Suppose we ask about the educational experiences of a white, male individual from a family with an upper middle-level income derived from a small to medium business or independent profession. As soon as he is born, this individual begins to have useful learning experiences through interaction with his parents or with people employed to watch and care for the child. The family will have a number of books to read, will normally take some periodicals and newspapers, will have access to cultural events, and will, of course, speak proper English. Moreover, the family assumes that he is going to attend the school system all the way through college and continually impresses him with the importance of education. If there is no good public school, he may be sent to private schools. With such a background, he has a good probability of doing well in the educational system and will usually make it easily through college and perhaps a graduate or professional school. When he gets out of school, his family has the proper connections to get him a good first job, as a manager or professional. He might even fall back on a job in his father's business, especially if it is not too small a business. At any rate, this man is normally quite employable and is usually employed at a decent job.

On the contrary, take the educational perspectives of a black female, born into a poor working-class family in the ghetto. She will meet a series of obstacles before, during, and after her formal educational experience. Because of the obstacles, only a few exceptional individuals of this group can make it to the top. (Somewhat more do get into the middle class.) The first obstacle is family background. The ghetto has its own rich culture, but it is different from the middle-class white culture. Unfortunately for this woman, it is the middle-class white culture that is fundamental to the educational system. Thus when she starts school, this individual may not speak in the approved manner. Her grammar is "incorrect" according to middle-class standards. She has not been exposed to many of the cultural experiences in the arts, in travel, or in conversation on many topics that may be taken for granted in an upper-middle-class home. These types of experiences can be reflected on scores of standardized tests, like IQ tests, that are used to "track" students into different-level classes, classes which may be to the disadvantage of working-class black females.

Moreover, since success in education is still somewhat unusual for the black working-class female (because of the obstacles), it is definitely *not* assumed that she will be successful in school or that she will go on to college. Rather, there are many social as well as economic pressures on her to lose interest in school and to drop out as soon as possible in order to get a job. These include the financial difficulties of all the poor and the special pressures on blacks, as well as the special pressures on women. On all of these counts, she will be counseled to go into the narrow technical track to get some "useful" skill like cooking, typing or word processing, rather than to take a college preparatory course.

If she overcomes the major obstacles to get into college, she must still worry about supporting herself through school, whereas the average middle-income individual is often supported through college. The difference is enormous because college work—and certainly work in a graduate or professional school—requires concentration for many hours a day. If one has a full-time or even part-time job, then one is often too tired to really concentrate in the hours left after work. Suppose, by genuine effort, she does get a professional education, say, as a laywer. She probably has no connections and meets prejudice when she goes job hunting. Until very recently, many women law graduates were frequently insulted by being asked to become legal secretaries rather than lawyers in the major firms. The same major legal firms did not even consider black lawyers.

These are not fantasy cases; they are rather all too typical. Thus, it turns out in our society that economic inequality is reproduced and continued from generation to generation (even without considering the inherited wealth of the capitalist class). This economic inequality is clearly the result of unequal power and property relationships, not primarily the result of the educational system. But it is certainly not true that the educational system decreases this inequality; rather it perpetuates it by pushing each individual, through various kinds of conditioning mechanisms, to remain in the level indicated by his or her family background.

It is true that more education is associated with higher income. Nevertheless, it is also true that differences in education account for only a small part of the differences in income inequality (Bowles and Gintis, 1976, pp. 247–248). In other words, education is only one of the obstacles to a higher income. The other, often more important obstacles, are the socioeconomic background of the family (especially a poverty background) and discrimination by race, sex, or both. Therefore, while increased equality in education would certainly help reduce income equality, it would be a long way from solving the problem of economic inequality.

Traditional sociology has, in part, agreed with this conclusion about education and economic inequality, but has emphasized education more than radical sociology. Different replications (that is, repeated investigations) of the Wisconsin social-psychological model of status attainment are representative of the traditional approach to this issue (*Sociology of Education,* 1983).

Focusing on occupational attainment (*not* income), Jencks, Crouse, and Mueser (1983) showed, for example, that education was the most important single determinant of occupation in three surveys they discussed. Individuals needed greater than average education to get good jobs even if they came from high socioeconomic backgrounds and had high aptitude scores, high grades, and college-bound friends. The authors also note, however, that several studies had overstated the effect of education by not taking these other factors into account. Studies that did not take them into account overstated the significance of education for occupational attainment up to 20 percent.

Thus, to have a good occupation, a person usually needs a good education. But having a good education does not ensure a good job, or a high income, which can also be derived from one's family, gifts, or investments. Education can contribute to the likelihood of getting good jobs and incomes, but the other factors like socioeconomic background are significant in determining one's occupation.

So education does not by itself increase or decrease the amount of economic inequality in the system to a great extent. It does (1) legitimate the existing inequality and (2) tend to reproduce a "preexisting pattern in the process of training and stratifying the work force" (Bowles and Gintis, 1976, p. 265). We saw earlier how the system tends to legitimate inequality by outright propaganda and by more subtle conditioning. For example, education is said to reward merit, just as the economy is said to reward merit. This is one way of justifying the system. In other words, the poor are poor because they are undeserving and the rich are rich because they have much merit. But we have seen that this is not true of the way that people actually get to the top or the bottom of the system—since the final result is mostly determined by an individual's sex, race and family background.

We have noted that the schools tend to classify and to put students into different tracks according to their race, sex, and class background. This happens explicitly by the tracking system, which prepares some students for immediate manual jobs and others to go on to college. What is the basis for selection? Ostensibly, students are chosen according to their performance on IQ and other tests. But one of the things that has been discovered most clearly in recent years is that so-called intelligence (IQ) tests mainly reflect a person's cultural background (ibid., chap. 4). For example, most questions assume an urban background, so rural students do more poorly, not because of some innate difference, but because they often do not know what the questions imply. The same is true for the differences between black and white students, or—more obviously—the differences between English- and Spanish-speaking students on tests given in English. A while ago, a survey of classes for "mentally retarded" students in San Francisco found that many of these students were of average intelligence, but simply spoke Spanish and had little or no knowledge of English.

Tracking of students into lower levels of education, followed by lower levels of jobs, also takes place for entire schools. Schools in affluent districts simply spend more money per pupil than do schools in poor districts. This is one reason why black schools in poor districts are separate but *not* equal. Thus, in Detroit in 1970, public schools teaching first through sixth grade spent only $380 per pupil for teachers' pay in schools that were 90–100 percent black, but in the same year Detroit schools that were only 0–10 percent black spent $432 on teachers per pupil (Michelson, n.d.).

For all students there is considerable evidence that schools tend to reward conformity and obedience rather than substantive knowledge. Examination of a large amount of data for the 1960s shows that school grades were related only slightly to tests of academic achievement (or even IQ tests). Grades were strongly correlated to the teachers' ratings of the students in the categories of "citizenship" and "drive to achieve" (Bowles and Gintis, 1976, pp. 41–42). The meanings of "citizenship" and "drive to achieve" are further suggested by the fact that these students were also ranked as diligent, socially popular, and generally conformed to the teachers' notions of how a good student should behave. Even more fascinating, the students with the highest grades ranked "significantly below average on measures of creativity and mental flexibility." It appears that students are conditioned quite early to accept an authoritarian system and are even penalized for any independent thinking. The same types of traits are probably rewarded and penalized on most jobs. Thus does the educational system condition people to accept the economic system and their places in it.

It is important to emphasize that *none* of this is done by a conscious conspiracy of teachers. It happens in routine ways through the control of boards of education by businesspeople and corporate lawyers; through the appointment of administrators who favor or accept the capitalist system; through the economic needs of students to learn to conform to the economic system if they are to earn a living; and through the structure of schooling.

There are some interesting analogies in the structure of education and in the economic structure. For example, grading is supposed to be by competitive achievement, while wages are also supposed to be given according to competitive achievement. Yet we have shown that this is untrue for blacks, other minorities, and women—and that most capitalists get to the top by inheriting wealth. Moreover, in secondary schools and certainly in colleges, training is highly specialized and fragmented into different narrow disciplines, which is similar to the specialization and fragmentation of jobs.

The conditioning is also somewhat different for students of different class backgrounds, not only in different tracks in a single school but also between schools. High schools provide limited freedom and very close supervision, and those who go no further in the educational system are conditioned for closely supervised unskilled work. State and community colleges have somewhat more freedom and produce skilled workers and lower-level technicians. Universities allow considerably more freedom of individual development (though still restricted) and produce white-collar workers and professionals of all types.

Of course, who gets to go on to college is closely determined by family income level. Specifically,

among those who had graduated from high school in the early 1960s, children of families earning less than $3000 per year were over six times as likely *not* to attend college as were the children of families earning over $15,000. (Bowles and Gintis, 1976, p. 31)

Children from the lower-income families were also less likely to even graduate from high school. If they did graduate from high school, they were not as likely to attend four-year colleges, but were more likely to attend less expensive two-year colleges (Bowles and Gintis, 1976, p. 31).

As another indication of how inequality is passed on and reproduced, it is not surprising that the performance of children on standardized achievement tests is closely correlated with the number of years of schooling of their own parents. Even if we assume the questionable proposition that IQ tests reveal something about inherent ability (or even about acquired ability), how one will perform and how far one will get in school is not related to IQ but to family background. A statistical analysis shows "that even among the children with identical IQ test scores at ages six and eight, those with rich, well-educated, high-status parents could expect a much higher level of schooling than those with less favored origins" (ibid., p. 32).

We saw earlier that less was spent on the schooling of black pupils in Detroit than on white pupils, which is one of the reasons that they achieve less and have fewer years of schooling in the end. In general, across the country, all students receive education according to their family income. Christopher Jencks's important study in 1972 (discussed in Bowles and Gintis, 1976, p. 33) found that children who were lucky enough, as one wit remarked, to "choose" parents in the top 20 percent of the income distribution, generally have twice as much spent on their education by the educational system than children who were unlucky enough to have "chosen" parents in the bottom 20 percent of the income distribution. It is for these reasons that a recent California State Supreme Court decision has called for more equal funding of schools regardless of districts.

Although it is usually admitted that our educational system suffers from great inequality in who attends universities, it is sometimes said that it is improving. It is certainly true that a higher percentage of all groups go to college now than 50 years ago. It is still true, however, that a much larger proportion of the rich do go to college, and that the *proportion* of inequality between rich and poor in attending colleges has *not* changed in a half century (ibid.).

Indeed, the 1980s produced a series of educational reports stressing "excellence" in education—which would seem to be an uncontroversial national goal. In a series of informative articles, Fred Pincus (1983, 1984) has shown otherwise.

The educational reports, such as the highly publicized *A Nation at Risk: The Imperative for Educational Reform* (1983), argue that the United States is falling behind Japan and Western European countries in teaching subjects like math and science. This failure, in turn, is seen to reduce the U.S. economic position in international competition with other capitalist countries (as well as militarily with the Soviet Union). The reports argue that educational mediocrity threatens "our very future as a nation and a people" (Pincus, 1983, p. 350).

What is the cause of this presumed mediocrity in education? The reports feel that the more equalitarian educational policies of the 1960s and 1970s are to blame. Women, minorities, and other groups disadvantaged by the educational system were, according to these reports, too influential on the curriculum at the expense of excellence in education. The curricula of the secondary schools, for example, were "homogenized, diluted, and diffused to the point that they no longer have a central purpose" (cited in Pincus, 1983, p. 350). In particular, the "emphasis on promoting equality of opportunity in the public schools has meant a slighting of its commitment to educational quality" (ibid.).

This is a curious way to blame the victim of previous educational disadvantages. The policies coming out of the 1960s and 1970s, aimed at improving the chances of women, minorities, and the handicapped to be included in higher-level education, were somehow seen as causing mediocre education for all. Worse still, these increased educational opportunities were seen as injuring the economic position of the United States.

The controversial best-selling book by Allan Bloom, *The Closing of the American Mind* (1987), also argues that the inclusion of women and minorities somehow injured American education. Yet Bloom's focus is not on technical expertise, as in many of the reports, but on the supposed decline of liberal education in the United States. He feels it is easier to recover from weakness of technical education (the three R's) than from a decline in liberal education. But how does the inclusion of previously excluded groups into excellent educational programs reduce the entire educational level, let alone the entire U.S. economy? When these excluded groups are included in the existing educational system, they deal with the same educational standards as the other participants.

Indeed, Pincus (1983, p. 352) points out that the actual causes of international economic problems for the United States, such as trade imbalances with Japan, go way beyond educational policies. For example, the U.S. auto industry in the 1970s and 1980s misjudged consumer interest in smaller, fuel-efficient cars that Japan made more cheaply. Similarly, the steel industry's problems are tied to the failure to modernize their plants. Futhermore, the huge U.S. military budget has been shown to take financial resources away from investments in modernized industry; Japan's much lower military budget permits large expenditures on economic modernization (Dumas, 1985). In addition, the issue of union wages in the United States is clearly more political than educational. None of these key economic issues is much related to levels of math or science taught in U.S. schools. Thus, this version of blaming the victim would appear to be greatly overstated. The inclusion of previously excluded groups will likely increase rather than decrease the overall pool of talent in the United States.

Unfortunately, compensatory education and more equal educational achievements for blacks have *not* equalized black and white income. In 1940, blacks had only 38 percent of the median educational level of whites; and, of course, black income was far below white income. By 1972, many blacks had moved from the discrimination and poverty of the South to more liberal and affluent regions; also, various struggles had helped to increase their educational achievements. For young black men aged 25–34 years the gap in years of education in 1972 was only 4 percent below that of similar aged white males. Yet the income level of these young black men was still 30 percent below that of similar aged white men (Bowles and Gintis, 1976, p. 35). Therefore, while an equal education (at least in the number of years of attendance) may be some help to a higher income, the fact of job discrimination—and the greater resources and connections of white families—still produces an enormous amount of income inequality.

Even more obviously, measured in years, women have had, for some time, an equal amount of schooling as men on the average for all workers in the economy. Yet white women's wages were only 64.5 percent of white male wages in 1949 and declined to 58.5 percent in 1975. By 1985, there was some narrowing of the wage gap, yet white women's wages were only 64.1 percent of white men's in 1985 (Winnick, forthcoming). Possibly an increasing level of education and professional training for women has begun to be reflected economically. It is also possible that the wage gap has narrowed due to declining male wages. It is important to know the relative impact of increased education for women and declining wages for men, because the wage gap is still large and workable strategies to further reduce it are necessary.

REFORMING THE EDUCATIONAL SYSTEM

We have noted that most so-called reforms in the past have largely been in the direction of making the educational system conform better to the needs of modern capitalism and our present class relations. Instead of attemping to reduce the male-female or black-white wage gaps, for example, educational reform has often attempted to perpetuate existing differences. The educational reforms of the 1980s discussed above do this. What more thoroughgoing reforms are possible in the educational system of the United States?

First, it must be repeated that, while education reflects the dominance of the capitalist class in its structure and in its teachings, it is not at all a clear and simple dominance. It is rather a contradictory and complex situation which also reflects the strength of the protest movements of workers, minorities, women, and their intellectual allies. It is in part because of the strength of the protest movements—especially the socially critical antiwar movement of the later 1960s and early 1970s—that this book is being used in some universities today. Before that period, there were few radical professors in sociology or in any of the social sciences. Moreover, in the 1950s any radical professor had to keep silent or be threatened with the loss of his or her job. The protest movements on campus increased intellectual freedom of speech and have inhibited administrations from firing all of the new generation of social critics and radicals, though many have been fired when it was possible to do so quietly.

Within the limits of the system, there is a real dilemma posed by reform.

On the one hand, as reflected in all of the progressive reforms of the past and present, the capitalist system would like to train technicians and scientists to have more initiative and independent thinking in order to make new discoveries. This means, however, that there must be a broad education and considerable room for free debate. But these debates cannot be kept out of the humanities and the social sciences as well as the natural sciences. This means that any reforms tending toward freer and more productive scientific thinking (or even initiative in areas such as engineering or business management) also tend to produce controversial thoughts in subjects such as sociology. This dilemma is not unique to the United States, but exists in any exploitative or repressive system, as in the Soviet Union.

Reformers tend to think that education alone can work miracles, but we have seen that most economic inequality is closely related to the class position and wealth of one's parents and/or to one's race or sex—though lack of an equal education has also been one obstacle to equality. The great educator, Horace Mann, wrote:

> Nothing but universal education can counter-work this tendency to the domination of capital and the servility of labor. If one class possesses all of the wealth and the education, while the residue of society is ignorant and poor, . . . the latter in fact and in truth, will be the servile dependents and subjects of the former. (Bowles and Gintis, 1976, p. 24)

Unfortunately, Mann still suffered from some illusions. We now recognize—in all the data cited above—that an equal education is necessary to economic equality. *But* as long as one class possesses much of the wealth and owns the corporations, while other classes are poorer and propertyless, then the latter classes will still be dependent on and subject to the former—even if education is more equalized. So education *alone* is not sufficient for economic equality, though it is a necessary condition. Therefore educational reforms *by themselves* cannot bring about economic equality.

The most important and insightful progressive reformer of all, John Dewey, always argued for a more open, democratic education. Such an education would make people fit to operate and communicate in our democratic society. The problem is that the United States has the forms of political democracy, but our economic system is very undemocratic. A relatively few men control the economic system, making the major decisions on hiring and firing, investment, and production. The masses of workers have no independent say over what is produced, or whether they will have any jobs at all. Almost every enterprise is run for the benefit of its owners, while employees only have to know how to take orders; the system does not care to have the ordinary worker think independently. The system requires workers to be taught certain skills, but it also requires that they be taught discipline and conformity. A radical critic of educational reform argues:

> Big business, in short, is seeking to reconcile two opposites: on the one hand, the need created by the modern process of production for a higher development of human capabilities; and on the other hand, the political need to prevent this development

from leading to an increased autonomy of the individual which would threaten the existing division of social functions and the distribution of power. (Andre Gorz, in Bowles and Gintis, 1976, p. 206)

If educational reforms are to be meaningful in providing a more free and equalitarian society, then they must be part of a wider, radical economic transformation of society. For example, if one wants to have less hierarchical and authoritarian relations in education, then it is also necessary to have more democracy and workers' control of decision making in the economy. Or if it is desirable to abolish grading as an obstacle to an improved learning process, this would only be sensible and feasible in a society in which all work was voluntary and there would be no cutthroat economic competition. As long as the economy is unequal at its base, then no educational reforms can accomplish broad redistribution of wealth and power. If, however, there is a radical economic change to a cooperative and socialist economic system, then this would press toward major educational reforms. Thus, economic democracy will increase educational democracy considerably more than educational democracy will increase economic democracy.

SUMMARY

Many liberal educators sincerely believe that the educational system greatly reduces inequality in the United States. The myth is that everyone has an equal chance to get into higher education, to complete a higher education, and to get an appropriate job on graduation. The reality is, first, that those who are lucky enough to be born into higher-income families are much more likely to get a higher education. Second, whites from higher-income families are much more likely to succeed in higher education than are lower-income whites or minorities because of the way education is linked to the larger society. Last, even if a lower-income white, a minority person, or a woman gets an equal education, this does *not* insure an equal job opportunity. An upper-income white male, on the contrary, is virtually assured a good position in life with the appropriate education.

Studies show that boards of education as well as trustees and regents of university systems are mostly filled with older, white, male businesspeople or lawyers. These directors of the educational system insure that it continues to instill the proper work ethic and discipline in most students as well as to teach the virtues of the existing socioeconomic system.

The 1980s have shown mixed results, at best, for those previously disadvantaged by the educational system. Chapter 12 indicates a decrease in minority participation in higher education in the 1980s. However, there has been some reduction in the large wage gap between males and females, and increased education for females (along with declining male wages) may have had an influence. Yet a number of conservative educational reports purporting to stress "excellence" in education could lead to policies that create renewed disadvantages for minorities, women, and the handicapped. These reports often blame the victims of prior educational disadvantages instead of trying to create excellence in education for all Americans.

SUGGESTED READINGS

A very well-written, readable, and exciting book on those who control the universities—as well as the protests against that control—is David N. Smith, *Who Rules the Universities: An Essay in Class Analysis* (New York: Monthly Review Press, 1974). A radical analysis that is profound, sophisticated, and full of extremely useful facts is Samuel Bowles and Herbert Gintis, *Schooling in Capitalist America: Educational Reform and the Contradictions of Economic Life* (New York: Basic Books, 1976). Martin Carnoy's *Schooling in a Corporate Society* (New York: McKay, 1975) is an excellent collection of articles on the subject. Conservative educational reports such as *A Nation at Risk* (Washington, DC: U.S. Department of Education, 1983) have been thoroughly criticized by Fred L. Pincus in such articles as "Conservative Reports on Educational Problems Are Becoming Part of the Problem," *The Review of Education* 9(4), 1983: 349–355, and "From Equity to Excellence: The Rebirth of Educational Conservatism," *Social Policy* (Winter 1984): 50–56.

REFERENCES

Beck, Hubert. 1947. *Men Who Control Our Universities*. New York: King's Crown Press. Cited in Smith (1974), pp. 38–48.

Bergmann, Barbara. 1986. *The Economic Emergence of Women*. New York: Basic Books.

Bloom, Allan. 1987. *The Closing of the American Mind*. New York: Simon & Schuster.

Bowles, Samuel, and Herbert Gintis. 1976. *Schooling in Capitalist America*. New York: Basic Books.

Council for Aid to Education. 1956. *Aid-to-Education Programs*. Washington, DC.

Dumas, Lloyd. 1985. Speeches to San Diego Economic Conversion Conference (February 8–10).

Duster, Troy. No Date. *The Aims of Higher Learning and the Control of the Universities*. Berkeley: University of California. Cited in Smith (1974), pp. 49–51.

Jencks, Christopher; James Crouse; and Peter Mueser. 1983. "The Wisconsin Model of Status Attainment: A National Replication with Improved Measures of Ability and Aspiration." *Sociology of Education* 56 (January):3–19.

Michelson, Stephen. No Date. "The Political Economy of Public School Finance." Cited in Martin Carnoy, *Schooling in a Corporate Society*. New York: McKay, 1975, p. 225.

National Commission on Excellence in Education. 1983. *A Nation at Risk: The Imperative for Educational Reform*. Washington, DC: U.S. Department of Education.

Nearing, Scott. 1917. "Who's Who Among College Trustees." *School and Society*, no. 6 (Sept. 8). Cited in Smith (1974), p. 38.

Pincus, Fred L. 1983. "Conservative Reports on Educational Problems Are Becoming Part of the Problem." *The Review of Education* 9(4):349–355.

———. 1984 "From Equity to Excellence: The Rebirth of Educational Conservatism." *Social Policy* (Winter):50–56.

Rauh, Morton A. 1969. *The Trusteeship of Colleges and Universities*. New York: McGraw-Hill. Cited in Smith (1974), pp. 52–53.

Smith, David N. 1974. *Who Rules the Universities?* New York: Monthly Review Press.

Sociology of Education. 1983. Editorial comment. (January): 1–2.

Winnick, Andrew. Forthcoming. "The Changing Distribution of Income and Wealth in the United States, 1960–1985." In Patricia Voydanoff and Linda Majka, *Families and Economic Distress*. Beverly Hills, CA: Sage.

chapter 8

The Family

By Barbara Sinclair, Howard J. Sherman, and James L. Wood

There are many different and opposing views among sociologists on the evolution of family relationships. The most conservative tend to maintain that family life has only one form, that it has always been and must always remain unchanged, that women must always play a certain role in the family, and that women cannot and must not play any role outside the family. Radical sociologists dispute every one of these contentions.

The editors of a 1971 collection of articles on the family comment that "in reading through what often seemed like endless piles of books and articles on marriage, the family, and sexuality, we were struck by the uniformity and strenuousness of the efforts to seek out regularity and to deny and rationalize change" (Skolnick, 1971, p. 2). They show that, in the dominant view of traditional sociologists, the nuclear family—defined as a man, a woman, and their children—

> is universally found in every human society, past present, and future. . . . The nuclear family is based on a clear-cut, biologically-structured division of labor between men and women, with the man playing the . . . role of breadwinner . . . and protector, and the woman playing the . . . role of housekeeper and emotional mainstay. (Skolnick, 1971, pp. 7–8)

Many sociologists deny the universality of the nuclear family, but it is still the dominant view. It is a functionalist view that says that men and women each play a specific functional role in the family, and that this will persist indefinitely. Thus, for many functionalists, the very nature of social organization seems to require women to be only in the family but men to play roles outside the family as well. (There are also some traditional sociologists who believe that the family is universal but do not accept the functionalist view of it.)

In this chapter, we shall begin with the views of the family held by traditional (functionalist) sociologists and with related functionalist views in anthropology, political science, and psychology—all of which find the same male-female roles as a universal fact. Next, we examine the liberal, nonfunctionalist view that there are many forms of the family and a wide range of male-female roles, all produced by the social conditioning of different societies. Finally, we present the radical view, which—going further than the liberal position—finds an evolution of different forms of the family and male-female relations, conditioned by the evolution of the socioeconomic base of society.

THE FUNCTIONALIST VIEW OF THE FAMILY

Talcott Parsons's functionalism manifests itself in his view of women as playing the "expressive" role in the family; they are kind, obedient, cheerful, affectionate, and sensitive. Men, on the other hand, must play an "instrumental" role in the family; they are aggressive leaders, creative and original, and bring home the income on which the family economy is built. Parsons describes the American family situation as follows:

> It is perhaps not too much to say that only in very exceptional cases can an adult man be genuinely self-respecting and enjoy a respected status in the eyes of others if he does not "earn a living" in an approved occupational role. . . . In the case of the feminine role the situation is radically different. . . . The woman's fundamental status is that of her husband's wife, the mother of his children. (Parsons, 1954, pp. 223–224)

Not only does he describe these present roles as essential and necessary, but Parsons also warns that any change is fraught with danger:

> It is, of course, possible for the adult woman to follow the masculine pattern and seek a career in fields of occupational achievement in direct competition with men of her own class. It is, however, notable that in spite of the very great progress of the emancipation of women from the traditional domestic pattern, only a very small fraction have gone far in this direction. It is also clear that its generalization would only be possible with profound alterations in the structure of the family. . . . Absolute equality of opportunity is clearly incompatible with any positive solidarity of the family. . . . It is suggested this difference [of roles between men and women] is functionally related to maintaining family solidarity in our class structure. (Parsons, 1954, pp. 174–175)

Parsons does not merely describe the subordinate position of women in our society; he explicitly states that it is functionally necessary to maintain "family solidarity." And family solidarity is functionally necessary to maintain "our class structure." If our class structure is destroyed, then our society is also destroyed. "Thus Parsons finds sexual segregation 'functional' in terms of keeping the social structure as it is, which seems to be the functionlist's primary concern" (Friedan, 1963, p. 97).

Many radical sociologists committed to women's liberation might agree with much of Parsons's description of the present function of women in society. The issue is whether what is functional for the maintenance of the present society (especially for the present ruling class) is positive or negative for most people in the society. Parsons and many other functionalist sociologists draw no distinction between *what is* in the present society and what *should be* in an improved society. Since women's liberation would disturb the present society (and its rules), it is not functional; therefore, it is assumed to be a negative influence.

Parsons's functionalism reigned supreme in the 1940s and 1950s, and carried over to all the popular courses on marriage and family adjustment or life adjustment. Such traditional sociologists told women how to adjust to the present society, since they considered the possibility of adjusting the society to women's needs as unrealistic. Thus, one popular marriage manual, used in many college courses, said:

> The sexes are complementary . . . men and women—together . . . form a functioning unit. . . . When men and women engage in the same occupations or perform common functions, the complementary relationships may break down. . . . To talk about what might be done if tradition and the mores were radically changed . . . may be interesting mental gymnastics, but it does not help the young people of today to adjust to the inevitabilities of life or raise their marriages to a higher plane of satisfaction. (Bowman, 1942, pp. 21–22)

This is clearly a sanctimonious way to tell women to "adjust" to continued subordination and restriction to household duties!

It might be argued that such functionalism was the dominant position in sociology only in the conservative years of the 1950s, but it is not any more. It is true that functionalism has how been less emphasized in sociology. In addition, the women's liberation movement has made most sociologists more cautious in their statements about women's place. Yet some sociologists have, usually unconsciously, joined in the backlash against the women's movement, so that they also attribute various evils to feminist agitation.

We shall see several examples of this tendency in later sections, but here let us take one very mild example from a 1976 textbook on sociology. This text asserts that:

> the sex differences in mental disorders have apparently widened since World War II. This growing distinction coincides with a number of social changes, not the least of which is the new surge of feminist activity. Such activity may have accentuated the sense of dissatisfaction and lack of fulfillment among many women whose consciousness has been raised without a corresponding change in roles or status. (Demerath and Maxwell, 1976, p. 489)

In the view of these functionalists, then, the women's movement contributes to mental disorders. Feminism has this effect, they say, because it makes women feel frustrated in their functional roles in the family. From the radical view this diagnosis turns things upside down. In other words, women's dissatisfaction with their subordinate role in the family—and discrimination in roles outside the family—caused the formation of the modern feminist movement. However, if the movement were removed, the causes of dissatisfaction and frustration would still exist. Women would only understand the causes less well and therefore be less able to change their status.

The same textbook claims that female sex roles and norms of behavior are becoming more like those of males—for example, less passivity and less willingness to be subordinate. Consequently, they say, many traditional sociologists predict that the gradual elimination of the differences in functional roles will lead to a unisex society in which there will be little love or sex. They quote another functionalist text (published in 1973), which states: "Sex will move out of the center of the stage as a source of passion. . . . There will be no Romeos or Juliets because no one will be able to develop a level of passion sufficient to die for either love or sex" (quoted in Demerath and Maxwell, 1976, p. 489).

Will the elimination of the subordination and oppression of women really lead to the end of love and sex? Isn't the opposite more likely? Most participants in the women's movement claim that the effect of the movement to date has been to increase the recognition and pleasure of women's sexual experience. This hardly points to a decrease in the amount of sex or passion. Furthermore, we shall see in Chapter 10 that marriages based on equality are likely to have a greater degree of love than those based on subordination.

THE FUNCTIONALIST ANTHROPOLOGISTS' VIEW OF THE FAMILY

G. P. Murdock, a well-known anthropologist, writes:

> The nuclear family is a universal social grouping. Whether as the sole prevailing form or as the basic unit from which more complex familial forms are compounded, it exists as a distinct and strongly functional group in known society. No exception . . . [exists] in the 250 representative cultures surveyed. . . . (Murdock, 1949, p. 11)

Murdock's definition of the nuclear family is so broad that it can accommodate almost anything. It includes any structure in which a man, a woman, and their children live together, *no matter who else lives with them.* Under this definition, Murdock considers both polygamous and extended families as forms of the nuclear family since in all these forms of the family a man, a woman, and their children live together, even though they also live with many other people. In common usage and in the usage of most social scientists, in term "nuclear family" refers to a separate group composed solely of a man, a woman, and their children; suppose we call this the isolated nuclear family to distinguish it from Murdock's all-encompassing nuclear family. Then, *according to Murdock's own data* (on the 192 societies for which comparable data were found), 42 societies had isolated nuclear families, 53 had families consisting of one husband and several wives, and 92 had some form of extended family (including aunts, uncles, cousins, and/or several generations in one family). Thus, according to his own data, what we commonly mean by a nuclear family system represents the minority.

A recent text on family structures puts it another way: "Most anthropologists today do not go along with the universality of the nuclear family: it is becoming a dead issue in that field. The study of complex systems of kinship . . . is hindered rather than helped by assuming that the nuclear family is the basic unit" (Skolnick, 1971, p. 89). Only a very few conservative anthropologists still claim that the nuclear family is, always has been, and always will be the only form of the family. Clellan Ford, a traditional anthropologist, argues that in every culture men are the more dominant, aggressive, and sexually active, while women are more emotionally expressive, and nurturant. He denies that these family roles can ever change.

> It does not seem likely that changes in technology or conscious striving for an equality of the sexes with respect to the roles they play will make any real fundamental changes in the foreseeable future. . . . The differences arising from their reproductive roles alone impose a basic cleavage between the sexes with respect to the kinds of lives they can live, and there are limits to the modification that can be tolerated if the social group is to survive. If women were somehow persuaded to forsake their basic biologic functions, there would soon be no society. (Ford, 1970, p. 42)

Ford seems to think that the liberation of women is going to "somehow persuade" women not to have sex or babies. Here is functionalism at its weakest.

THE FUNCTIONALIST VIEW OF WOMEN IN POLITICS

Since many functionalists believe that women's function in society is limited to the family, they tend to think that a role for women in the economy or in politics is dysfunctional for our present society. For example, some traditional political scientists claim that the functions of wife and mother necessarily exclude women from major political participation. The argument is based on the functionalist view of the family. Two feminist political scientists show that this argument against women in politics is distorted because it

> involves an assumption that women's present weak political position is necessary and functional. Society rests upon the services provided by women in the social realm. . . . We must tolerate limited participation to assure that we have wives to nurture our leaders and mothers to preserve the race. (Bourque and Grossholtz, 1974, p. 229)

The well-known political scientist, Robert Lane, in his book *Political Life*, claims that women participating in politics (or any interests outside the home) rob their families of the time they use in politics. He writes:

> It is too seldom remembered in the American society that working girls and career women, and women who insistently serve the community in volunteer capacities, and women with extra-curricular interests of an absorbing kind are often borrowing their

time from their children to whom it rightfully belongs. As Kardiner points out, the rise of juvenile delinquency (and, he says, homosexuality) is partly to be attributed to the feminist movement and what it did to the American mother. (Quoted in Bourque and Grossholtz, 1974, p. 238)

Why doesn't Lane complain about the time that men take away from their family for economic or political activity? Clearly, the answer is that he accepts the functionalist's view that women's sole function is in the home, while men also function for society outside the home.

If these functions are disturbed, then—according to Lane, Parsons, or other functionalists—all of society is disturbed. If we add up all of these allegations as well as the earlier-mentioned charges by traditional sociologists, the sins of the women's movement are legion. According to these allegations, women under the influence of the feminist movement have disrupted the family so as to cause:

1. More mental disorders
2. Less love
3. Less sex
4. Less child care
5. More juvenile delinquency
6. More homosexuality

Some traditional sociologists have even attributed rising crime rates to feminism. Dawn Currie (1986) has illuminatingly shown the relationship between feminism and rising crime rates to be a spurious, erroneous relation. This is called "blaming the victim." Many women are the *victims* of mental disorders, lack of love, lack of sex, juvenile delinquency, and crime. The causes of these problems lie, as we shall see, in the present structure of the family and in the present politico-economic structure of capitalist society. It is the women's movement that is trying to change these structures in order to end frustration and oppression in the home and on the job.

Furthermore, the allegation that feminists have disrupted the family by getting women to take outside jobs is distorted. Most women who work outside the home are forced to do so for purely economic reasons, as we shall see in Chapter 11. Thus, women take jobs, not because the women's movement tells them to take jobs, but from economic necessity. Moreover, many women are unhappy because of the structure of traditional marriages. It is true that the women's liberation movement may make them more conscious of their oppression, but it is not the cause of this oppression. It is also true that consciousness of oppression may disrupt society; however, disruption of oppression can be positive for the oppressed.

Many functionalists assume that it is always wrong to disrupt the present order, the apparently peaceful status quo. But if the orderly, peaceful status quo hides a reality of oppression in the home and discrimination on the job, is it wrong to disrupt it?

FREUDIAN PSYCHOLOGY ON WOMEN AND THE FAMILY

In addition to the closely related functionalist views of traditional sociologists, political scientists, and anthropologists, support for the subservient role of women comes from traditional Freudian and neo-Freudian psychologists. According to Freud, the normal woman is passive, masochistic, and narcissistic. Woman's inferiority is anatomically based. A woman is an incomplete—"maimed"—man because she lacks a penis. (See the discussion of Freud in Weisstein [1971] and Hyde and Rosenberg [1976], pp. 32–38.)

Freud sees female development as very different from male development. From her observation of other little girls, the girl learns that she lacks a penis and concludes that she has been castrated. Lacking "the only proper genital organ" (quoted in Bardwick, 1971, p. 9), the girl develops *penis envy*. In normal development, the girl will eventually transfer her desire for a penis into a desire for a child. "The feminine situation is only established . . . if the wish for a penis is replaced by one for a baby. . . . Her happiness is great if later on this wish for a baby finds fulfillment in reality, and quite especially so if the baby is a little boy who brings the longed-for penis with him" (Freud, 1969, p. 24).

This process has a number of effects on female psychology, according to Freud. Women do not develop strong superegos or consciences. "In the absence of fear of castration the chief motive is lacking which leads boys to surmount the Oedipus complex (i.e., the strong emotional attachment to the parent of the opposite sex). Girls remain in it for an indeterminate length of time; they demolish it late and, even so, incompletely. In these circumstances the formation of the super-ego must suffer; it cannot attain the strength and independence which give it its cultural significance. . . ." (Freud, 1969, p.25).

Because penis envy is never entirely sublimated even in normal women, "envy and jealousy play an even greater part in the mental life of women than of men" (Freud, 1969, p. 22). "The fact that women must be regarded as having little sense of justice is no doubt related to the predominance of envy in their mental life" (Freud, 1969. p. 29).

Normal femininity is attained, according to Freud, when the girl represses her own impulses toward activity—that is, when she becomes passive. A woman who is not passive, who wishes to participate in the world outside the home, to pursue an intellectual profession, is neurotic. According to Freud, such desires in a woman are symptoms of penis envy.

In the 1920s and early 1930s a strong tide of women's liberation led many psychologists to downplay Freud's instinct theories and to emphasize his theories of sexual repression. Whereas Freud himself tended to be pessimistic, seeing eternal repression of eternal instincts, those progressive Freudians believed that people could be liberated from this repression by psychoanalysis. In the 1940s and 1950s, on the other hand, a conservative reaction emphasized the impossibility of change in male and female instincts. They stressed Freud's implication that any woman who is not passive, who wishes to pursue an intellectual profession or participate in the world outside the home, is neurotic. Independence in a woman was seen as a symptom of penis envy. Particularly, any militancy in a woman showed penis envy. Two conservative Freudians, Marynia Farnham and Ferdinand Lundberg, claim: "Fesminism, despite the external validity of its political program and most (not all) of its social program, was at its core a deep illness" (1947, p. 142). They particularly stress that education and achievement by women shows neurotic penis envy: "It is not in the capacity of the female organism to attain feelings of well-being by the route of male achievement . . . the more educated the woman is, the greater chance there is of sexual disorder, more or less severe" (1947, p. 143). The conservative conclusion seems to be that women should have less education, strive less for achievement, and do less political activity.

In the 1970s most textbooks were cautious and critical in their approach to Freud. The modern texts discuss not only neo-Freudian theories but many anti- and non-Freudian theories. In spite of the many new theories in various areas, a revealing survey found that many practicing psychologists still accept the Freudian view of women without question. In 1972, 79 clinically trained psychologists, psychiatrists, and social workers were questioned as to the nature of men and women (Braverman et al., 1972, pp. 320–324). According to these "experts," the mature and healthy male is "very aggressive, very independent, not at all emotional, very logical, feelings not easily hurt, can make decisions easily, very self confident." According to these same "experts," the healthy and mature female is "not at all aggressive, not at all independent, very emotional, very illogical, very submissive, very sneaky, feelings easily hurt, has difficulty making decisions, not at all self-confident, very dependent." Their mature and healthy male seems rather cold and unpleasant; but their mature and healthy female is just plain sick! The views of these psychologists not only accord with their biases and vested interests in the status quo, they also stem from acceptance of a paradigm that views human attitudes and behavior as determined by eternal instincts rather than social relations.

The same paradigm also restricts for them the range of possible solutions to psychological problems. Current social relations are taken as given, determined by current individual psychological attitudes. The most conservative of these experts see psychology as determined by eternal instincts; the more liberal will usually add some mixture of social effects on psychology. Many psychologists assume that it is not possible to change an oppressive world. Therefore, they try to adjust their patients to the present oppressive world. If a women who is independent and logical but frustrated by her experiences in a sexist world comes to them for help, they try to adjust her psyche to approach the norm *they* expect— dependent, illogical, and passive—so that she will be "happy."

The viewpoint of traditional psychology, which begins from the given individual psyche, does not allow those trained in that school to see the present social structure as the root of the problem. Conservative (and even liberal) psychologists are thus prohibited from even considering the possibility of radical adjustments or changes in the social structure. In their view, women are designed by nature to be eternally passive and submissive while men are eternally aggressive and dominant. No change is *necessary* because this is the "natural" situation that produces harmonious relations of male and female. No change is *possible* because the fundamental psychological characteristics of men and women are biologically determined and fixed.

LIBERAL VIEWS OF MALE-FEMALE RELATIONS

Today, most traditional sociologists and anthropologists do not accept the strict Freudian view that biologically given innate instincts determine the personalities of men and women. One of the founders of American social anthropology, Franz Boas, stressed social conditioning rather than innate instincts. His student, Margaret Mead, pioneered an exciting study of male and female behavior among primitive peoples. She began by investigating the question, What are the approved personalities of male and female among three primitive peoples in New Guinea? Among the Arapesh, *both* men and women have (and are expected to have) personalities that most Americans would call maternal and feminine. *Both* male and female Arapesh are normally mild, unagressive, and sensitive to the needs of others. On the contrary, in the second society, Mundugumor men and women both behave in ways that most Americans would call masculine. *Both* male and female Mundugumor usually develop into the ruthless, violent, and aggressive individual that is considered ideal in their society.

Among the third group, the Tchambuli, everything is, according to current American notions, unnatural and upside down. "In the third tribe, the Tchambuli, we found a genuine reversal of the sex-attitudes of our own culture, with the woman the dominant, impersonal, managing partner, the man the less responsible and the emotionally dependent person" (Mead, 1971, p. 259). Mead concludes that one primitive society (Arapesh) produces men whose behavior is quite contrary to males in modern Western society, a second (Mundugumor) produces women with contrary behavior, and in a third (Tchambuli) both men and women behave contrary to what Western society considers normal. Therefore, "we no longer have any basis for regarding such aspects of behavior as sex-linked" (p. 259).

Why this variation? Mead found that, contrary to Freudianism, men and women behaved in different ways in each society because they had different social conditioning:

> The material suggests that we may say that many, if not all, of the personality traits which we have called masculine or feminine are as lightly linked to sex as are the clothing, the manners, and the form of head-dress that a society at a given period assigns to either sex. When we consider the behavior of the typical Arapesh man or woman as contrasted with the behavior of the typical Mundugumor man or woman, the evidence is overwhelmingly in favor of the strength of social conditioning. In no other way can we account for the almost complete uniformity with which Arapesh children develop into contented, passive, secure persons, while Mundugumor children develop as characteristically into violent, aggressive, insecure persons. . . . Standardized personality differences between the sexes are . . . cultural creations to which each generation, male and female, is trained to conform. (p. 260)

In other words, the characteristic behaviors of men and women in a given society are determined *not* by genetic inheritance but by social and cultural conditioning. Each child could go in any direction, depending upon the society in which it is reared. Mead concludes, contrary to Freudian instinct psychology, that "the same infant could be developed into a full participant in any one of these three cultures" (pp. 260–261).

RADICAL VIEWS OF THE FAMILY: THE FAMILY AND DIVISION OF LABOR

Family organization and forms of marriage differ drastically in various periods and societies. The nuclear family, with husband, wife, and their children living in a separate household, is not eternal, omnipresent, or "natural." In fact, this small, restricted family is somewhat rare in human history. Much more usual is an extended family that includes various relatives, frequently of several generations. Moreover, most primitive societies are organized into groups or clans, and they, not individuals, are the prime determiners of marriages. "As New Guinea natives put it, the real purpose of getting married is not so much to obtain a wife but to secure brothers-in-law" (Levi-Strauss, 1971, p. 58).

Most clan societies are *patrilineal,* meaning that descent and inheritance are derived from the father. The wife usually goes to live with her husband's family, and in some cases, if the man dies, his brother must support and may marry his widow. All the kin terms relate the husband, wife, and children to the man's clan relatives. Many, but not all, patrilineal societies are also patriarchal, that is, male-dominated.

Yet there are also many clan societies that are *matrilineal,* with descent and inheritance derived from the mother, with kinship related to the mother's clan, so that usually the husband goes to live with the wife's clan, and in some cases, if a man is widowed, he may marry his wife's sister. Matrilineal societies still exist among some American and Canadian Indians, in some areas of Africa, and among the Dravidians of India. In most matrilineal societies the status of women is very high, and in some of them it is similar to the status of men. There is, however, little or no evidence of matriarchy, that is, clear female dominance.

Marriages of one man and many women, called polygyny, are also not uncommon. Polygyny is allowed in most Moslem societies—and was practiced among the Mormons in nineteeth-century Utah. In practice, however, only the very wealthy men could afford many wives, so it has never been a common practice among the lower-income groups. On the other hand, there are a few societies in which one woman marries several men. Among the Todas of India, a woman marries a man and all his brothers, and no importance is attached to identifying the biological father of her children.

There are no undisputed cases of group marriage in primitive societies, but societies differ in their views on sex. Among many Eskimo tribes, the wife would normally offer sexual hospitality to each visitor from afar. Among the 50 people of the Emerillon tribe of French Guiana, "marriages" are so short-lived that almost everybody marries everyone else of the opposite sex at some time. In the Muria tribe in India, all adolescent boys and girls live together in communal huts with a high degree of sexual freedom, although adolescent lovers are not later permitted to marry.

So far it can be observed that the attitudes and status of women and men, as well as the forms of marriage and family, differ drastically in various societies. How and why? We find that the status of women and the form of marriage are closely related to the division of labor between the sexes and the occupational roles of women and men. One anthropologist writes: "The most important clue to woman's status anywhere is her degree of participation in economic life and her control over property and the products she produces" (Leavitt, 1971, p. 396).

Because it is more efficient and aids survival, every known society divides and specializes labor tasks to some degree. In every known society, women and men do somewhat different tasks (though some still unknown, very primitive societies may have no such division of labor). But the division of labor by sex may be totally different in different societies. Whatever one sex does in a given society, the other sex does in some other society.

Less than 15 percent of all American doctors are women, while about 75 percent of all Soviet doctors are women. American men seldom take responsibility for child care, but in the Nambikwara tribe fathers take care of babies and clean them when they soil themselves, while many young Nambikwara women disdain domestic activities and prefer hunting and even war expeditions. Most Americans think it is "natural" for men to do the heavy work in society, but women carry all the heavy burdens in about four times as many societies as men do. Likewise, it may seem "natural" for men to be the providers, but there are many societies, such as the Alorese of Eastern Indonesia or the Otomi Indians of Mexico, in which women do all the heavy labor necessary to earn a living, while their husbands lie in the shade and gossip.

In most primitive societies the group doing the labor and providing the food has a high status, while the opposite is often true in more advanced societies. We saw that among the Tchambuli of New Guinea the women tend to be aggressive and dominant, the men passive and responsive. This is closely related to the fact that Tchambuli women fish and sell their catch in the market; Tchambuli men do the shopping, wear jewelry, and love to dance and paint pictures.

Thus male and female personalities are intimately connected in each society to their economic role. Moreover, just as Mead shows how society conditions each sex to a particular type of personality and status, so she also shows how they are conditioned to accept a certain economic role, a certain part in the division of labor. We shall see in Chapter 11 that this conditioning—called the *socialization process*—is determined by the power relationships of groups and classes in the society so as to defend the status quo.

Hunting and Gathering Societies (Old Stone Age)

For 1 to 2 million years humans lived in societies based on hunting animals and gathering wild food. Available evidence indicates that the men did most of the hunting, while the women gathered fruits, vegetables, and grains. So this first division of labor was along sexual lines. In this very limited sense, biological determinists are correct: It appears that the biological facts of childbirth and nursing did limit women's mobility, so that it made more sense for men to do the wide-ranging hunting.

This does not mean that women played an inferior role. On the contrary, everything indicates that they worked just as long and hard as men, their economic contribution was at least as important and more stable, and their status roughly equal. One should not think of "status" in its complex modern forms. These were small groups, all relatives, of 10 to 30 people. There was little private property, except one's immediate tools or weapons, and really very little wealth or property of any kind. There was no government. People worked as a collective unit and shared collectively by tradition and out of the dire necessity of survival. "The large collective household *was* the community, and within it both sexes worked to produce the goods necessary for livelihood. . . . Women usually furnished a large share—often the major share of the food" (Leacock, 1972, pp. 33–34). Many hunter-gatherers, such as the Bushmen of the Kalahari Desert, depended primarily on the fruits and vegetables that were gathered by women; whereas the meat provided by men was a mere luxury.

When Europeans from capitalist societies first came into contact with some of these primitive hunting-gathering societies, they were both shocked and con-fused by the high status of women and the role of the extended family or collective community. For example, in the seventeenth century, Jesuit missionaries en-countered the Naskapi tribe of Canada. The Jesuits were shocked at the great power women possessed to decide where to live and what projects to undertake; they scolded the men for not being masters in their own homes "as in France." They were particularly worried about the degree of sexual freedom that women enjoyed; men often didn't know who their biological children were. The Naskapi, however, thought this objection was nonsensical, and that the French were im-moral to love only their own children. The Naskapi said: "You French people love only your own children; but we love all the children of our tribe" (quoted in Leacock, 1972, p. 37).

Agricultural Versus Herding Societies (New Stone Age)

For hundreds of thousands of years, women and men slowly improved their tools and weapons without major changes in social structure. Eventually enough prog-ress was made in improving implements and methods of work to affect social conditions. This change from the Old to the New Stone Age is called the Neolithic Revolution. It occurred 10,000 to 12,000 years ago in the Middle East, somewhat later in other areas, and not at all in a few still existing primitive tribes.

Two different "discoveries" occurred in the Neolithic Revolution. One was agriculture—the domestication of plants; the other was herding—the domesti-cation of animals. Most societies discovered or emphasized one or the other long before they could do both. In a majority of cases agriculture probably came first.

What does this have to do with the relations of men and women? Everything. There was no change in human biology, but a major social change depending on which sex discovered what. Since men had been hunters, they were the inventors of systematic herding. Since women had been gathering plants, they were the inventors of systematic agriculture.

> It is generally accepted that owing to her ancient role as the gatherer of vegetable foods, woman was responsible for the invention and development of agriculture. Modern analogies indicate that so long as the ground was prepared by hoeing and not by ploughing woman remained the cultivator. (Hawkes and Wooley, 1963, p. 263)

The business of learning agriculture, selection, planting, weeding, and so forth was an extended process that took place over many hundreds of thousands of years. To accomplish it, women had to invent many other things besides methods of cultivation and better hoes. They learned enough chemistry to make pottery that would hold water and could be cooked in. "It has never been doubted that . . . pottery was both shaped and decorated by women" (Hawkes and Wooley, 1963, p. 331). Women learned enough mechanics to construct looms for spinning textiles, as well as better ways of home building (a purely feminine occupation in some Neolithic tribes). They also learned—and shaped tools for—grinding wheat, constructing ovens, and using the biochemistry of yeast to make bread.

In mainly agricultural societies of the primitive hoe type, women were the most important food providers. The meat provided by male hunters was much less in quantity and more unstable in supply. As a result, women had a very high status in most of these societies. "The earliest Neolithic societies throughout their range in time and space gave women the highest status she had ever known" (p. 264).

Of course, in class-divided societies the fact that a group does a lot of work does not mean that it has high status—quite the contrary. But in Neolithic societies these activities were still communal, carrying out work collectively without rulers or bosses. The group that performed a task made all the decisions concerning it. Therefore, the fact that women were often the main food-providing group meant that they made some of the most important social decisions.

On the other hand, the fact that this was still a collective working society meant that men still did their collective part by hunting. Women did not hold power over men; their high status did not put the women in a position to exploit the men. Thus, matriarchy probably never existed, if by matriarchy one means that women held as much power over men as men have held over women in some later societies. In some cases, such as the Tchambuli, the women have dominant personalities, and in some cases the women were more warlike, such as the women soldiers of Dahomey (where cowards were admonished not to act like men). There have probably been no societies, however, where women have acted as an exploitive ruling group over men.

Just as the high status of women is strongly correlated with primitive agriculture, so too is the existence of matrilineal clans. When the number of people in a tribe grew to 300 or 400, the old unstructured family organization was no longer possible. The denser population that resulted from agricultural productivity required a new form of organization. The primitive family was replaced, at a very early date in many places, by the clan system. Evidence from contemporary primitive tribes indicates that they are composed of groups of clans, while the family is of little or no social importance. Everyone in the clan is supposed to be descended from some mythical ancestor. This ancestor is their symbol, or totem, which may be a plant or animal that is important in the economic life of the tribe.

The clan system lasted through the Neolithic Revolution. The clan, not the family, normally held the land in common. An individual family might be allocated a plot, but only for immediate use, and usually for one year only. Pastures were always held in common by the whole clan. This is still the case in many primitive agricultural societies.

Where a society is almost totally agricultural and women do most of the cultivating, descent and kinship are usually calculated from the female; that is, the clan is matrilineal. Women usually, but not always, have a fairly high status in matrilineal clans. Where a society is primarily based on animal herding and men do most of the herding, descent and kinship are usually calculated from the male; that is, the clan is patrilineal. Men are usually, but not always, strongly dominant in patrilineal herding societies.

Many good examples of matrilineal societies, in which women have a high status, are found among Native American cultures, such as the Navajo and the Hopi. The Hopi technology is similar to the technologies of the New Stone Age, as are their social relations. The Hopi have a matrilineal clan, the leadership of which is mainly in the hands of the older active women. The family group also includes the woman's brothers, but not the women who marry them. The whole clan owns the land together and there is no privileged class. The men collectively own the livestock, but the women own the houses, the furnishings, and all the vegetable food. Since vegetables provide most of the food supply, while livestock constitutes a very small portion, the women are socially and economically secure regardless of whether they are married or not. A woman is always elected clan leader, though her brother leads all ceremonies.

Predominantly livestock-raising tribes were most likely to develop patrilineal clans, since male hunters first tamed animals. Men also invented new weapons and other implements needed for animal herding. In these clans, the family group is organized around and related to an older male. This man is usually, but not always, the dominant personality in the extended family. Yet even where the man is dominant, there is not the demeaning subordination of women found in later class-divided and exploitative societies. So while no Neolithic community shows matriarchy, or all-out female dominance, neither does any Neolithic community show all-out male domination. Each sex continues to do its own important job in its own area; there is no oppression by sex.

In a Neolithic community combining some agriculture and animal herding, the men probably cleared the land, built most of the homes, herded the animals, hunted, and manufactured weapons and some tools. The women did all the other agricultural work on the land, made the clothing and all the pottery, ground the grains, and cooked the food. In such communities, men and women had a rough equality of status.

THE ADVENT OF SLAVERY

The Neolithic life was not idyllic; it was hard for all, but women were not treated like slaves in any Neolithic society. In fact, the Neolithic clan had a collective economy and no slaves. How did all this change in a few thousand years?

Men provided milk and meat from cows, while women hoed the fields. Then great progress was made in lifting the burden of hoeing from women, to be replaced by animal power. "The first step, perhaps, was to make a pair of oxen drag over a field—a variant on the hoe that women had hitherto wielded—a plough" (Childe, 1971, p. 88). Since men had tamed and herded the cattle and oxen, it was the man who followed the plough and thus took over the main agricultural duties. The use of the plough totally changed agriculture from a female to a male occupation. This ended some of the hardest labor for women, but it also ended their control of the main food supply and reduced their socioeconomic status.

Where women's shoulders were the oldest means of transport, they were replaced by animals pulling wheeled vehicles. Along with the animals came male drivers. Besides the wheel for vehicles, men also invented the potter's wheel, and henceforth pottery was made by men. These male inventions helped women live better but reduced their status. When women no longer carried the heaviest burdens, or did most of the agricultural work, or made the pottery, the new situation removed the economic bases of women's equal status. After men took over agriculture, transport, and pottery, as well as cattle raising, most societies became patriarchal. The male dominated the family or household, which included married sons and their families.

Yet even male economic dominance did not automatically mean the total subordination of women—any more than it did in the predominantly herding societies. The subordination of women began with the coming of slavery and/or serfdom, which ended both collective ownership and the matrilineal clan system. The clan system slowly gave way to individual families based on private property, beginning with the cattle owned by the male. The process of replacing the matrilineal clan with the patriarchal family as the basic economic unit was always long and usually painful.

The new inventions, utilizing animal power, greatly increased human productivity. When, in addition, bronze was substituted for wood and stone, a worker could for the first time produce more than his or her own subsistence. This meant that a surplus of food and other wealth could be accumulated. It meant that specialists could concentrate on one task, such as metalworking, while others could produce their food. It meant, above all, that it became profitable to keep slaves or serfs. Prior to the time that a worker could produce a surplus, war prisoners were adopted, killed, or eaten. When these prisoners could produce a surplus, however, they were made into slaves or serfs to be exploited for their master's benefit.

As some men accumulated wealth in goods, cattle, or slaves, they gained the power to oppose the more democratic and collective clan structure. The ancient commune was disrupted by class division, private property became the rule, and internal government and armed forces were formed to support the rule of the wealthy owners over the slaves and serfs. The formerly temporarily elected war chief could consolidate his position as ruler with this new wealth. Moreover, the male chief found ways to give his sons not only his private wealth but also his authority, and this ruling line of wealth and power finally became hereditary.

In such societies, even women of the ruling class came to be treated as property, the same as slaves and serfs, sometimes more valuable and sometimes less so. Woman's value declined both because slaves could do the productive work and because slave women could be used for sexual pleasure. The *double standard* was instituted whereby a husband could have sex with any woman, but the wife was to be strictly monogamous. The reason for the strict control and seclusion of wives was to ensure that only legitimate sons inherited all of the private wealth.

Ancient Slavery

In ancient Greece, slave women sometimes worked in the fields, but most did household drudgery. They were completely the property of the patriarch, who could enjoy them sexually at will. Some of the women were allowed slave husbands, but they were still at the master's pleasure—and their children could be taken and sold at any time. Yet it was a crime for any women of the household to have sex with a stranger. In Homer's *Odyssey*, when Odysseus returns home, he first kills his wife's suitors. Then he discovers that 12 of his servant women have had sex (he was gone 10 years), so he orders his son Telemachus: "Take the women out of the hall . . . and use your long swords on them, till none are left alive to remember their lover and the hours they stole in these young gallants' arms" (quoted in O'Faolain and Martines, 1973, p. 4). Thus, he punishes his property.

Later, in Athenian Greece, 80 percent of all women were slaves—that is, property. The slave owner's wife was to be seen, not heard. She was well-off materially, but even in so-called democratic fifth-century Athens, she was not to leave the house. Women were completely secluded—as in some Islamic countries today—and prohibited from any role in the active political life of the city. She was secluded, not because of romantic love (a modern concept), but to ensure legitimate heirs. In ancient Greece, even in the ruling-class woman's own home, she could not be present at her own dinner parties unless everyone present was a family member. Moreover, she was required to spend most of her day in the *gynaeceum,* an isolated area of the house that was off limits to any stranger.

Woman's place was in the home with children. Demosthenes said: "Mistresses we keep for our pleasure, concubines for daily attendance upon our person, wives to bear us legitimate children and be our faithful housekeepers" (quoted in O'Faolain and Martines, 1973, p. 9). While women were secluded to bear legitimate children, men were free to have sex when they pleased. Euripides had Medea say: "If a man grows tired of the company at home, he can go out, and find a cure for tediousness. We wives are forced to look to one man only" (quoted in O'Faolain and Martines, 1973, p. 15). This was the double standard with a vengeance. For lower-class and slave women, life was very different. Many, often against their will or from dire necessity, were forced to become prostitutes, mistresses, or concubines.

The ruling-class man did not stay at home with his wife. Concern with household matters was considered demeaning. He spent his time in the market, the forum, or the public baths, talking about economics and politics with other men. Women had no political rights in "democratic" Greece. They could not make contracts for more than a bushel of barley. They always had to have a legal guardian, father, or husband or someone else appointed. The guardian could give a woman in marriage and would even will her to someone else at his death. Moreover, a man could easily divorce a wife, provided only that he returned her dowry to her father or other guardian. A woman could get a divorce only on rare occasions under extreme provocation. The husband owned all the property and slaves, and his sons inherited most of it. Ruling-class women usually learned to read and write, but higher education was reserved for boys. Slaves were educated only when necessitated by their job.

FEUDALISM

In Western Europe, slavery was followed by feudalism. Under feudalism, human beings were no longer owned by other human beings; rather, serfdom prevailed. Serfs were slightly better off than slaves as they were not owned, but they were bound to the landlord's land. Serf men and women had to labor a certain number of days a year for the landlord; in return, he was supposed to "protect" them. In the earliest period, serfs did need protection from wandering barbarian tribes, but later they needed protection only from the economic and sexual exploitation of the landlords. The landlords, in turn, held their land at the pleasure of the feudal nobility, to whom they owed military support. The same hierarchy of obligations continued through the lesser nobility, to the greater nobility, and thence to the king, who owed allegiance only to God.

The nobility was divided into the secular and the religious nobles. The Church was the largest single landowner, the holder of most accumulated knowledge, and the greatest power in Europe during this period. The Church had a very low opinion of women. In the first century, St. Paul said: "The head of the woman is the man. . . . For a man . . . is the image and glory of God. . . . I suffer not a woman to teach, nor to usurp authority over the man, but to be in silence." A few hundred years later, St. Augustine repeated the notion: "The woman herself is not the image of God; whereas the man alone is the image of God." Finally, in the thirteenth century, St. Thomas Aquinas could still write: "As regards the individual nature, woman is defective and misbegotten, for the active force in the male seed tends to the production of a perfect likeness in the masculine sex; while the production of woman comes from a defect in the active force." (All quotes are from O'Faolain and Martines, 1973, pp. 128, xi, 131.)

Although the Church stated clearly that women were the weaker and inferior sex, that did not stop either secular or religious landlords from working their serf women in the fields the same as the men. Women did every kind of agricultural labor except heavy plowing. In England, in 1265, a serf's widow had the following obligations to the lord of the manor: "From Michaelmas to the Feast of St. Peter in Chains she must plow half an acre every week. . . . And from the Feast of St. John the Baptist until August she must perform manual service 3 days every week" (quoted in O'Faolain and Martines, 1973, pp. 160–161). One day a week she was also required to transport goods on her back anywhere that the bailiff told her to go. In addition she must find four days in the spring to mow the landlord's meadow, four more days to gather hay for him, and two more days for weeding his land. In some places, female serfs were exempted from work on the lord's land, but that only meant they did most of the work on the serf's own plot.

Female serfs were also used in the lords' homes. Their lot was described by an English Franciscan monk in the thirteenth century. He stated that the domestic serf or chambermaid had to do the heaviest and foulest jobs, was given the poorest food and clothing, had to marry whomever the lord told her to marry, and had to give her children to the lord as serfs. The monk stated matter of factly: "Chambermaids are frequently beaten. . . . they rebel against their masters and mistresses and get out of hand if they are not kept down. . . . Serfs and that sort are kept in place only through fear" (quoted in O'Faolain and Martines, 1973, p. 163).

By the fourteenth and fifteenth centuries, increased urbanization and the spread of commerce and industry had opened up new opportunities for the upper-class women. The wives of some of the powerful lords themselves grasped power when their husbands were frequently away fighting wars. Some of the crafts in the cities were opened to women. However, in most of the guilds, which were a sort of combined monopoly and trade union organization of small craftsmen, women were not admitted to full status—and everywhere women were paid lower wages. Yet in Paris, by 1300, five different crafts were completely dominated by women, some of whom accumulated considerable fortunes. Women monopolized weaving and spinning in most of Europe—hence the name "spinster" for older unmarried women. Women in England were also barbers, apothecaries, armorers, shipwrights, and tailors. By the late medieval period, a few bourgeois women were in business for themselves as wholesale and retail merchants.

As early as the thirteenth century, the rise of embryonic capitalist relations caused some improvements in the lives of well-to-do bourgeois women, due to their greater economic strength. They were still treated, however, as inferiors. There were legal changes that allowed a married woman who was engaged in trade to be considered legally as a *femme sole,* or single woman. In other words, feudal law gave married women no rights, so when women began to go into business they were treated as if they were single. As women went into commerce on a wider scale, both the legal and the social position of women began to rise, although very slowly. Even the nonbusiness woman who was married to a bourgeois husband had a wide range of duties, including acting as a doctor for her family and taking over the family business when necessary. Under these conditions, some increase in respect between husband and wife began to appear.

While women played a greater economic role in the feudal period than stereotypes would grant, they continued to be fettered legally and prohibited from public life as they had under slavery. Married women had no power over property and no power to make contracts. Men managed and had complete power over all the family property. A late sixteenth-century English lawyer wrote:

> Every Feme Covert (married woman) is a sort of infant. . . . It is seldom, almost never that a married woman can have any action to use her wit only in her own name: her husband is her stern, her prime mover, without whom she cannot do much at home, and less abroad. . . . It is a miracle that a wife should commit any suit without her husband. [Quoted in O'Faolain and Martines, 1973, p. 145]

The only exception, even in the late feudal period, was the right of a married woman engaged in trade to make certain binding contracts. Acts making this possible were not passed till the fifteenth century. Only in the seventeenth century did the equity courts of England devise ways for rich women to hold separate property while married. In most areas, in the feudal period, even widows did not usually have ownership of family property, but could use it only in their lifetime as trustees for their male children. The only woman who regained full rights to property and contractual rights was the childless widow.

Among the feudal lords, all marriages were arranged by the parents, often while the children were still in their cradles. The important criteria for a good marriage were the joining of another family's land and military power. Love had nothing to do with it. The feudal lords also generally had the right to decide whom their underlords and ladies should marry. They even had the right to decide whom a widow should marry—though she had to be given a year to herself. The lesser lords, in turn, might decide whom their serfs should marry. In the late feudal period, when bourgeois families first emerged into riches and power, the same custom prevailed. Marriages were arranged on the basis of the relative fortunes of different families. Again, love had nothing to do with it.

Since marriage was not founded on love, even in theory, divorces were never granted for incompatibility, nor in fact were divorces granted for any reason under Church laws. A marriage might be annulled for very specific reasons: fraud in the marriage contract, nonconsummation of marriage, or the parties being too close relatives. A legal separation might be granted for adultery or leprosy, but not much else. Only in very rare cases, in which the woman's family was very powerful, would a legal separation be granted for extreme brutality and cruelty. A "normal" amount of violence against the wife was expected. A writer in late nineteenth-century France said:

> In a number of cases men may be excused for the injuries they inflict on their wives, nor should the law intervene. Provided he neither kills nor maims her, it is legal for a man to beat his wife when she wrongs him—for instance, when she is about to surrender her body to another man, when she contradicts or abuses him, or when she refuses, like a decent woman, to obey his reasonable commands. (Quoted in O'Faolain and Martines, 1973, p. 175)

Her husband was her lord; if she attacked him she was a traitor. She could be burned at the stake if she killed him for any reason; he could kill her for adultery.

THE FAMILY UNDER CAPITALISM

We have noted that women gained a little in status with the increase of commerce and industry and the shift from rural to urban life. At the same time, the conflict between the rising capitalist class and the declining feudal nobility led to revolutions in Western Europe and the United States. These revolutions established a capitalist economy and democratic political processes, dominated by the capitalist class.

The rhetoric of liberty and equality in the French and American revolutions raised the consciousness of millions of women and led some women to demand equality with men. Yet by the middle of the nineteenth century in the United States and Western Europe, women still had very few more rights than under feudalism. Married women in American society were still treated as property of the husband, possessing no separate legal rights. They had no right to make separate contracts, no right to their own wages, no right to their children in case of separation, and certainly no right to vote. Women organized and fought for these rights. They won some contractual rights in the 1850s and 1860s. Women did not win the right to vote till 1920. Other rights of equality before the law were won only very slowly over many decades. Even today there are numerous ways in which women are *not* equal in American law.

Chapter 9 will examine the process by which women are socially conditioned from birth to accept a passive, subordinate role in the political sphere, the economy, and the family. Chapter 10 will discuss the dominant role of men and subordinate role of women in the American family. Chapter 11 will examine sex discrimination against women in the economy. Finally, we will show that it is profitable for capitalists to maintain sex discrimination. We will show that business advertising, the popular news media, the educational system, and other means of social conditioning, all help maintain the system of sexist socialization of men and women.

SUMMARY

Many traditional sociologists (and other social scientists) take a functionalist view of the family. According to this view, the family always has the same form, in which the man is an aggressive leader and breadwinner, while the woman is subordinate and cares for the physical and emotional needs of husband and children. A more liberal view, strongly stated by many social scientists, says that there have been many different forms of the family as well as many different statuses of women (including equality), each conditioned by different social conditions. The radical view accepts these liberal findings, but adds a perspective of society's evolution through certain stages together with the family's evolution through its own stages, which are based on the stages of social and economic evolution. According to this view, the family is likely to evolve new forms in the future.

SUGGESTED READINGS

Much of this chapter is based on Barbara Sinclair Deckard's *The Women's Movement*, 3d ed. (New York: Harper & Row, 1983). On women in primitive societies, see the exciting book edited by Rayna Reiter, *Toward An Anthropology of Women* (New York: Monthly Review Press, 1975). A contemporary discussion of the Marxist approach is found in Eleanor Leacock's introduction to Frederick Engels, *The Origin of the Family, Private Property, and the State* (New York: New World Paperbacks, 1972). The most readable study of sex roles in various societies is Margaret Mead, *Sex and Temperament in Three Primitive Societies* (New York: Dell, 1935, 1971). A good collection of articles on women written by people in each period from ancient times to the nineteenth century is Julia O'Faolain and Laura Martines, eds., *Not in God's Image* (New York: Harper & Row, 1973). One interesting aspect of the capitalist period is described in Linda Gordon's *Woman's Body, Woman's Right: A Social History of Birth Control in America* (New York: Grossman, 1976).

REFERENCES

Bardwick, Judith M. 1971. *Psychology of Women*. New York: Harper & Row.

Bourque, Susan, and Jean Grossholtz. 1974. "Politics An Unnatural Practice: Political Science Looks at Female Participation." In *Politics and Society* 4 (Winter).

Bowman, Henry. 1942. *Marriage for Moderns*. New York: McGraw-Hill.

Braverman, Inge, et al. 1972. "Sex-Role Stereotypes and Clinical Judgments of Mental Health." In Judith Bardwick, ed., *Readings on the Psychology of Women*. New York: Harper & Row.

Childe, V. Gordon. 1971. *What Happened in History*. Baltimore: Penguin Books.

Currie, Dawn H. 1986. "Female Criminality: A Crisis in Feminist Theory." In B. D. MacLean, ed., *The Political Economy of Crime*, pp. 232–246. Scarborough, Canada: Prentice-Hall.

Demerath, N. J., and Gerald Maxwell. 1976. *Sociology*. New York: Harper & Row.

Farnham, Marynia, and Ferdinand Lundberg. 1947. *Modern Woman: The Lost Sex*. New York: Harper & Row.

Ford, Clellan, in Georgene Seward and Robert Williamson. 1970. *Sex Roles in Changing Society*. New York: Random House.

Freud, Sigmund. 1969. "Anatomy Is Destiny." In Betty and Theodore Roszak, eds., *Masculine/Feminine*. New York: Harper & Row.

Friedan, Betty. 1963. *The Feminine Mystique*. New York: Dell.

Hawkes, Jacquetta, and Leonard Wooley. 1963. *Prehistory and the Beginning of Civilization*. New York: Harper & Row.

Hyde, Janet Shibley, and B. G. Rosenberg. 1976. *Half the Human Experience: The Psychology of Women*. Lexington, MA: Heath.

Leacock, Eleanor. 1972. Introduction to Frederick Engels, *The Origin of the Family, Private Property and the State*. New York: New World Paperbacks.

Leavitt, Ruby. 1971. In Vivian Gornick and B. Moran, *Woman in Sexist Society*. New York: Signet.

Levi-Strauss, Claude. 1971. "The Family." In Skolnick, *Family in Transition*.

Mead, Margaret. 1971. *Sex and Temperament in Three Primitive Societies*. New York: Dell.

Murdock, G. P. 1949. "On the Universality of the Nuclear Family." *Social Structure*. New York: Macmillan.

O'Faolain, Julia, and Laura Martines, eds. 1973. *Not in God's Image*. New York: Harper & Row.

Parsons, Talcott. 1954. *Essays on Sociological Theory*. New York: Free Press.

Skolnick, Arlene and Jerome. 1971. *Family in Transition*. Boston: Little, Brown.

Weisstein, Naomi. 1971. "Psychology Constructs the Female, or the Fantasy Life of the Male Psychologist." In Michele Hoffnung Garskof, ed., *Roles Women Play*. Belmont, CA: Brooks/Cole.

chapter *9*

Socialization: How Society Makes Boys and Girls into Men and Women

By Barbara Sinclair, Howard J. Sherman,
and James L. Wood

This chapter discusses how children are brought up, especially in the United States. The first part of the chapter focuses on this socialization process from the 1950s through the early 1970s. Then it focuses on socialization in the last decade or so, when the changes sought by the women's liberation movement had a chance to be implemented. Our question will be: Is contemporary socialization significantly different from before?

SOCIALIZATION AND SOCIETY

When a newborn baby leaves the delivery room, a bracelet with its family name is put around its wrist. If the baby is a girl, the bracelet is pink; if a boy, the bracelet is blue. These different colored bracelets symbolize the importance our society places on sex differences, and this branding is the first act in a sex-role socialization process that will result in adult men and women being almost as different as we think they "naturally" are.

Every society has a set of ideas about what people are supposed to believe and how they should act—about what is natural and right in beliefs and behaviors. Children are taught norms, values, and expectations by parental instruction, in school, and by example. This social learning process is called *socialization*.

While the extent to which this socialization "takes" will vary, most children will grow up to act pretty much as they are expected. The child has internalized society's standard—he or she has come to believe that certain types of behavior are natural and right. Furthermore, behavior at odds with society's standards is costly—at best one is considered deviant, at worse, thrown in jail.

While all societies have expectations of how people are to behave, few expect all their members to behave in the same way. What is considered proper, natural behavior will depend on certain attributes of the person—such as class, age, occupation, or sex. Perhaps because sex is such an obvious differentiating characteristic, one finds sex roles in almost all societies. Women are expected to think and behave differently from men, although the extent varies between different societies.

The societal expectation and belief that women and men are very different tends to be a self-fulfilling prophecy. The socialization process ensures that so long as such beliefs are widely held, girls and boys will grow up to be different from each other in just the ways expected.

EARLY CHILDHOOD

The baby is likely to be taken home wrapped in a blanket of the proper color to a nursery decorated in that color—at least if it is the first child of middle-class parents. While this doesn't make any difference to the baby, it shows the importance the parents attach to its sex. One study of parents' reactions to their newborn infants found that girl babies were described as significantly softer, finer featured, smaller, and more inattentive than boy babies even though there actually were no sex differences in size or weight (Rubin, Provenzano, and Luria, 1974, pp. 512–519). College students' descriptions of a baby were also found to depend on which sex they were told the child was. If told the baby was a girl, the students described it as littler, weaker, or cuddlier. These studies indicate that, to a considerable extent, people see what they expect to see. Sex-role socialization has led us to expect sex differences even in newborns.

These expectations do result in parents treating their male and female children differently. Sex-linked differences in maternal behavior have been observed toward 6-month-old infants. Mothers were found to touch, talk to, and handle their daughters more than they do their sons. Not surprisingly, at 13 months the girls were more dependent on their mothers. They tended to stay closer to their mothers, to talk to them, and touch them more than boys did. Boys tended to show more independence and exploratory behavior, to be more vigorous, and to run and make more noise in their play. The authors of a study of early childhood behavior hypothesize that "in the first year or two, the parents reinforce those behaviors they consider sex-role appropriate and the child learns these sex-role behaviors independent of any internal motives" (Goldberg and Lewis, 1972, pp. 30–33).

The overprotection most little girls receive seems to result in one of the few early intellectual differences between boys and girls. Boys tend to be better at spatial perception, the ability to visualize objects out of context. This is important because it may be related to the sort of analytic thinking required in the sciences. Early independence training, that is, allowing a child to explore and solve problems on its own, is conductive to the development of this ability. Girls are much less likely to receive such training. Overprotected boys also tend to do less well on spatial perception tests.

Reinforcement of sex-role appropriate behavior takes place in a variety of subtle and not so subtle ways. Boys and girls are given different toys from a very young age. Boys' toys are more varied, more likely to encourage activities outside the house, and have a higher "competency-eliciting value." In nursery school, children are strongly encouraged to play with the "appropriate" toys. Girls are more severely reprimanded for noisy and boisterous behavior. Boys are allowed and often encouraged to be aggressive. One study found that a father often takes pride in his son's being a "holy terror" but is worried if his daughter is "bossy" (Aberle and Naegele, 1966, p. 104). Fathers expect their daughters to be nice, sweet, pretty, affectionate, and well-liked.

These middle-class fathers were, however, much more concerned about the behavior of their sons than of their daughters. They worried about "lack of responsibility and initiative, inadequate performance in school, insufficiently aggressive or excessively passive behavior, athletic inadequacies, overconformity, excitability, excessive tearfulness . . . and 'childish' behavior" (p. 103). Such behaviors are considered inappropriate when exhibited by a male child and may be penalized. When they appear in girls, they are not a source of worry and are not discouraged, at least not to the same extent.

Another study of nursery school children found very much the same patterns (Amundsen, 1971, pp. 116–117). Parents valued malleability, cooperativeness, and willingness to take directions, but disapproved of assertiveness and quarrelsomeness in girls. In boys, independence, assertiveness, and inquisitiveness were valued; timidity and fearfulness disapproved. The teachers' attitudes were similar to those of the parents. They encouraged boys to be daring and aggressive, but discouraged girls. Their behavior toward a child having trouble climbing to the top of a jungle gym, for example, varied with the sex of the child. A girl would be told, "Take it easy, dear—we'll help you down"; a boy, "That's the boy! You can make it if you want to!"

Thus, from birth, male and female children are treated differently and are rewarded or punished for displaying differing types of behavior.

By age 3, children can label themselves correctly as boy or girl, although they are not clear about the genital differences underlying that distinction. They do know which jobs are performed by men and which by women, and what they report is the traditional, sex-stereotyped division of labor. By age 5 or 6, children are not only clear that there is a distinction between the male and female role, but they are also aware that the male role is the more highly valued. "Fathers are perceived as more powerful, punitive, aggressive, fearless, instrumentally competent and less nurturant than females. . . . Thus power and prestige appear as one major attribute of children's sex-role stereotypes" (Kohlberg, 1966, p. 99). By age 6, children consistently attribute more social power to the father; they consider him smarter than the mother and the boss of the family.

All small children seem to think their own sex is better and to express preferences for others of the same sex. Psychologists explain these findings on the basis of the child's egotism—"What's like me is best." For boys, the same sex preferences continue throughout childhood. With girls a decline sets in at the time they learn the greater prestige attributed to the male role. Girls, as they get older, become less and less likely than boys to say their own sex is better. Their opinion of boys and boys' abilities grows better with age, while the boys' opinions of girls grow worse. Girls, then, begin to develop a negative self-image at an early age.

In the child's early years the family is the most important socializing agency, but it is not the only one. Children's books and television programs also influence the child's perceptions of what is normal and appropriate. Until very recently both presented a rigidly sex-stereotyped view. Most books for young children are about boys; when girls or women appear, they are restricted to traditional feminine pursuits. One mother reports that when she started reading to her daughter at age 2, the little girl would ask questions like "Why aren't the girls fixing their own bikes?" and "Why isn't the little girl riding the horse?" After a few years of such books, the woman found that her daughter was constantly making derogatory remarks about girls—"Girls can't do anything"; "Girls can only do dumb things."

Children's television programs further reinforce the notion that girls are less important and capable than boys. On the highly acclaimed *Sesame Street*, in the early 1970s, females appeared less than half as often as males and about one-third as often when the appearance involved any dialogue. The women who did appear were almost always wives and mothers. "Virtually all [the programs] emphasized that there is men's work and then there is women's work—that the men's work is outside the home and the women's work in the home" (Jo-ann Gardner, quoted in Hole and Levine, 1971, pp. 250–251). Children are aware of which type of work is valued by society.

GRAMMAR SCHOOL

Grammar school continues the sex-role socialization process. One study found that more than half of the teachers questioned admitted that they consciously behave differently toward boys and girls. Several studies have found that boys receive more attention from the teacher than girls. While teachers tended to direct more supportive remarks to girls and more critical ones to boys, they were much more likely to reward creative behavior in boys than in girls. "The message to girls is that one does best by being good and being conformist; creativity is reserved for boys" (Bardwick, 1971, p. 113).

Having grown up in a sexist society, most teachers—female as well as male—have internalized sexist attitudes, and such attitudes affect their behavior toward their students. Most teachers probably never say girls are inferior to boys; yet they convey their feelings through their behavior. An occasional teacher is more blatant. A young woman recalls a discussion of a story concerning a male chef when she was in grammer school. One student commented that only a "sissy" would cook because that's a woman's job.

The teacher's response surprised us all. She informed us calmly that men make the best cooks just as they make the best dress designers, singers, and laundry workers. "Yes," she said, "anything a woman can do a man can do better." (Howe, 1973, pp. 190–191)

The attitudes of parents, teachers, and peers affect the child's view of what is natural and right. So, also, do the schoolbooks from which he or she learns to read. These provide one of the child's first views of the wider world outside his or her neighborhood. What, then, is "reality" as portrayed by elementary school-books?

An excellent study entitled *Dick and Jane as Victims* (Women on Words and Images, 1972) answers this question. Because the answer is so revealing, the study's results will be presented in detail. One hundred thirty-four elementary school readers being used in three suburban New Jersey towns are examined. Fourteen different national publishers are represented, so these are books used all over the United States.

In the world of elementary readers, there are a lot more boys than girls. There are many more stories about boys. Boys also appear more frequently in illustrations; when girls are shown, they are often just scenery. The ratios speak for themselves (p.6).

Boy-centered stories to girl-centered stories	5:2
Adult male main character to adult female main character	3:1
Male biographies to female biographies	6:1
Male animal stories to female animal stories	2:1
Male folk or fantasy stories to female folk or fantasy stories	4:1

In terms of sheer numbers, these books portray a male-dominated world. The numbers by themselves convey to the child the notion that males are more important and more interesting. The content of the stories leaves no doubt about it.

In stories emphasizing perseverance and initiative, boys outnumber girls by 169 to 47. And what sort of obstacles do girls overcome? In one story a girl wins a tennis match despite a dirty tennis dress.

Bravery and heroism are male traits—143 to 36. Typically boys rescue whole towns and save planes and spaceships; the occasional brave girls rescue younger siblings or small animals.

The acquisition of skills and coming-of-age themes are again found predominantly in stories about boys (151 to 53). In one story a boy kills a grizzly while taking care of the ranch in his father's absence. (We wonder what his frontier mother did before her son was old enough to protect her.) Any grown-up skills a girl learns tend to be domestic ones.

Not only are boys more frequently involved in exploration and adventure stories (216 to 68), but their adventures are a lot more adventuresome. Boys explore in China and meet bears in Yellowstone; girls watch their first snowstorm from inside the house.

When discussing stories on the theme of autonomy and normal assertiveness, the authors comment, "Stories about girls behaving as complete and independent persons are so rare they seem odd" (p. 13). The traits that are considered desirable in our society are depicted in these books as male traits.

When one looks more carefully at how girls are portrayed in these stories, it might be better if there were no stories about girls at all. The traits of passivity, docility, and dependence are displayed by 119 girls and only 19 boys. Girls cry a lot; they depend on boys to help them with things they should be quite capable of doing themselves; they are shown as spectators of life. In both stories and illustrations, girls spend a large part of their lives watching and admiring boys.

A good part of the rest of their lives is spent doing domestic chores—scrubbing floors, washing dishes, baking cookies—and usually enjoying it. "A girl's inborn aptitude for drudgery is presented in the same spirit as a black person's 'natural rhythm.' " A girl who succeeds at anything nondomestic is seen as exceptional. One biographical story insists, "Amelia Earhart was different from the beginning from other girls" (p. 19).

If the image of girls is bad, the portrayal of their mothers is even worse. Mother is not really human at all. She is the perfect servant, "a limited, colorless, mindless creature" (p. 26). When a boy is stuck in a tree, he has to wait for his father to come home to rescue him. Mother is evidently incapable of thinking or bringing the ladder. Not only does mother never do anything undomestic; even in this sphere tasks are strictly sex segregated. Father does all the yard work and is the fixer; mother does all the inside work (p. 27). The notion that tasks might be alternated or even shared appears to be considered heresy. Basically, mother is dull.

Another study (U'Ren, 1971, p. 324), of California school texts, found a woman scientist. She was the only working woman in a series of descriptions of present-day professionals, and the text says twice that she is working on an idea not her own. The men scientists are shown as doing work that requires originality.

According to these books, then, the normal girl is dependent, fearful, and incompetent. Girls are not even shown as excelling in schoolwork, as they actually do in grade school. In some cases, the point that a girl should not be assertive is made in truly gross fashion. In one story an Indian girl who wanted to be tall, brave, and strong like the men is turned into a shadow for her presumption. And what happens when the girl grows up? Not much. She becomes the textbook mother—a household drudge incompetent at anything outside her narrow province. The California study found not one story in which the mother so much as suggests a solution in a family crisis. Textbook mothers don't even drive cars (which, given their IQ, is probably a good thing).

The image of males, while much more positive, does contain some disturbing elements. Ingenuity, independence, creativity, and bravery are presented as admirable male traits, but excessive aggression and even dishonesty are not clearly condemned. Even when the fantasy and animal stories were excluded, almost 100 stories condoning meanness and cruelty as part of the story line were found. The study *Dick and Jane as Victims* concludes that "boys are being given permission to vent a twisted type of aggression and sadism" (Women on Words and Images, 1972, p. 23). As far as dishonesty goes, the authors comment, "There is a blurry line drawn between praiseworthy enterprise and rather shady accomplishment in which a bright lad with a head on his shoulders bends the rules to his needs" (p. 15).

Boys are being taught that overt aggressiveness is at least normal, if not praiseworthy, male behavior and that winning is more important than playing by the rules. They are also taught that displaying emotion is unmasculine. Showing emotions is a feminine trait and one that attests to the female's weakness and foolishness. Under the most extreme circumstances boys must keep calm; in contrast, girls become terrified and cry on the slightest provocation. "Only on the pages of a reader does a girl weep non-stop from morning to night over a broken doll. Only on the pages of a reader does a boy remain impassive while his canoe proceeds out of control through the rapids" (p. 22).

The images the texts present for children to model themselves upon are almost completely negative in the case of girls and contain destructive elements in the case of boys. But do these books really have an effect? They might not have much if these were the only forces pushing children into sex-stereotyped attitudes and behaviors. But in fact the texts present and reinforce society's attitudes toward men and women.

Television carries much the same message as the children's readers. A study of the most frequently watched prime-time shows during the 1973 viewing season found that 61 percent of the major characters were male. On the adventure shows, 85 percent were male. Thus TV, which takes up so many hours of most children's time, portrays a predominantly male world. The women that do appear tend to be stereotyped occupationally—they are housewives, teachers, secretaries and waitresses. Only rarely does a professional woman appear. On the adventure shows particularly, women are depicted as incompetent. Forty-six percent of male behaviors but only 14 percent of female behaviors were classified as displaying competence; in contrast, 3 percent of male but 31 percent of female behaviors displayed incompetence. (All data in this paragraph from Women on Word and Images, 1975, pp. 19–25.)

Sex-role stereotyping thus begins at birth and is conveyed by most of the institutions in our society. Family, school, and the media teach children to think and act in sex-appropriate ways.

In many ways, until adolescence, the pressures are greater on the boy. Girls are allowed and encouraged to be dependent, but this is normal behavior for a small child. From a very young age, boys are told not to cry, not to run to mother, but to fight back, to "be a man," not to "act like a girl."

While allowing a child independence is important for intellectual development, pressing a little boy to be physically aggressive and emotionally impassive is likely to leave scars. The child often knows that he is not really the person his parents expect him to be, even if he outwardly displays the expected behavior. Not surprisingly, many boys grow up with doubts about their masculinity, and many compensate for their doubts through overly "masculine" behavior. A man who values physical strength and aggressiveness above all else, who is convinced that any display of emotion or sensitivity to others' feelings is a feminine characteristic, is likely to find life very difficult. In a complex, industrial society there are actually very few comfortable niches for the John Waynes of the world.

For little boys the male role is frequently defined as the opposite of the female role. Fathers and mothers often tell a boy, when he's doing something of which they disapprove, that he is acting like a girl. This clearly contributes to the virulent antigirl feelings expresed by many little boys. One woman wrote to ask why girls could not be included in the Tonka Toys slogan, which says, "You can't raise boys without Tonka Toys." The company replied that if little boys know that girls also play with a toy, they will not want it.

The idea that males are naturally brave, independent, and resourceful while females are timid and dependent tends to be a self-fulfilling prophecy. Parents base their child-rearing practices on this idea. Thus boys are given more independence at an earlier age than girls. They are allowed to play away from home, to walk to school alone, and to pick their own activities, movies, and books earlier than their sisters. Boys are also given more personal privacy—to pick friends and girlfriends and to come and go as they please without parental consent. Sociologist Mirra Komarovsky concludes, "Parents tend to speed up, most often unwittingly, but also deliberately, the emancipation of the boy from the family, while they retard it in the case of his sister" (1968, p. 261).

That males are physically strong and females weak is another self-fulfilling prophecy. Boys are strongly encouraged and sometimes forced to participate in athletics from a very early age. Being good at sports is an important element of masculinity in our society. A boy who doesn't love baseball and football is considered a sissy, if not an incipient homosexual. A boy learns early that athletic prowess brings prestige with his peers and approval from his parents.

Delicacy and even physical weakness are still components of our notion of femininity. Girls are not encouraged to participate in athletics. Sometimes they are actively discouraged. "Several years ago in California there was a movement trying to say that it's too strenuous for girls to compete in sports," an Indio, California, school principal reports (quoted in Riverside, CA, *Press-Enterprise*, May 27, 1973).

Girls who wish to participate often find little opportunity. The Little League, until recently, admitted only boys, and there was no comparable organization for girls. Although in high school some organized sports are available to girls, the bulk of the money and effort goes into boys' sports. Lucy Komisar reports that not so long ago "the Syracuse school system spent about $90,000 for boys' extracurricular athletics compared to $200 for girls" (Komisar, 1972, p. 32). Until recently, women coaches generally got no coaching pay. Girls' teams did not get special equipment; they had to make do with equipment used in gym classes that was often in poor shape. If the girls wanted new equipment, uniforms, or travel money, they had to raise the funds themselves through bake sales and the like.

The low value put on women's athletics will discourage many girls. They will grow up just about as they are expected to—not delicate or weak, but much less strong and physically fit than their potential.

ADOLESCENCE

When children enter adolescence, they are aware of and have to a large extent internalized society's views of sex-appropriate attitudes and behavior. Good girls are sweet, obedient, and docile; they grow up to be mommies. Good boys are "little men"—daring and aggressive; they grow up to be presidents or at least firemen. Until this point, overt socialization pressures have been directed more at the boy than the girl. After all, turning a child into John Wayne is no easy task. Girls have been allowed and encouraged to remain childish—that is, dependent. They have also been encouraged to be little ladies, but most parents will condone a certain amount of tomboyishness in a preadolescent girl.

At adolescence the situation changes. The pressure on the boy to achieve academically and athletically continues. The pressure on the girl to be feminine increases enormously. Mothers particularly are terribly concerned that their daughters be feminine and popular and may push them into absurdly early dating. Padded bras for 10-years-olds are sold, and it's not the little girls who pay for them. Peer pressures become tremendously important in adolescence. Being popular becomes crucial, and for a girl that means being popular with boys as a female. In grade school, the tomboy or girl clown may be popular, and this sort of popularity may continue. But everyone knows that it's not the right sort of popularity. It doesn't get you dates.

Being popular in high school means living up to boys' expectations of what a girl is supposed to be like. She should be pretty; she should not be too smart or talk in class much; she should be supportive and admiring of the boy she is with. In one study, 40 percent of the girls interviewed admitted to "playing dumb" on dates, at least occasionally (Komarovsky, 1971, p. 60). And of course, not all girls need to play dumb. The really popular, successful high school girl is not a "brain" or even an athlete; she is the cheerleader. She embodies the supportive and admiring role assigned to girls. She is defined in terms of her relationship to boys.

Dating, which for many is a demeaning ritual, intensifies this process. Awakening sexual drives and the societal prohibition against their expression would make American adolescence a difficult time in any case. The dating ritual is clearly painful for many. Because boys and girls have been segregated in play activities, they often find it difficult to talk together, much less be real friends.

The accepted dating procedure reinforces the passive female and aggressive male stereotypes. The boy must call the girl; she must passively sit and wait. The boy who has managed to get by and hide the fact that he is not really John Wayne is now expected to be James Bond. If not enough boys call her, the girl is a failure as a woman. The fact that the boy is expected to pay for both himself and his date not only places a financial burden on him but encourages in both parties the notion of woman as passive object. "I always feel like I'm being rented for the evening," one girl commented. "I have to be nice and charming and do what he wants to do because he's paying" (quoted in Komisar, 1972, p. 39).

The dating ritual reinforces the tendency already instilled in the girl to see herself as passive and to define herself in terms of her relationships with men. It engenders conflicts among girls because they are in competition for the attentions of the same set of boys. The canard that women cannot be true friends contains a grain of truth. Many women do go through life regarding other women as competitors. This is not a healthy sort of competition in which winning depends on the development and expression of skills and abilities. It is, rather, an expression of a slave mentality. Winning depends not on what you can do but on the capricious choice of the master.

The dating ritual also places a tremendous premium on good looks. No girl growing up in America can escape the conclusion that being feminine depends not only on appropriate behavior but also on being pretty. From television, movies, and women's magazines she may well conclude that without beauty happiness is impossible, and her experiences with peers are likely to confirm that conclusion. Boys, too, have been socialized into regarding appearance as a girl's most important characteristic. Dating a plain girl, however interesting she may be, means loss of social prestige.

Who determines the standard of beauty? The media, including Hollywood, decree the ideal. The ideal allows for little variety and individuality and, of course, excludes the vast majority of women. All girls, not just the really plain ones, suffer from this inordinate emphasis on looks. Is there a girl who, during her teen years, was not convinced that some aspect of her looks was just awful? She is too short or too tall, too fat or too thin; her breasts are too small or too big; she has a mole on her face; her nose is too big or crooked; her ears stick out. When beauty becomes the one and only passport to happiness, a morbid sort of self-consciousness results. A girl becomes sure that a flaw so minor that no one notices it completely ruins her looks and thus her life. A pimple becomes a cosmic disaster.

Such a preoccupation with looks, while destructive for the girl, is good for the economy. She is willing to believe the wildest advertising claims and will spend any money she has on clothes and cosmetics. She hopes this product will finally make her look like Brooke Shields or whoever is the latest sex symbol. The girl begins to regard herself as a product that must be adorned and properly displayed so as to command the highest possible price.

The media, of course, encourage such a view. Advertising, with its insistence that you aren't a real woman and will never catch a man unless you use a certain eyeshadow or vaginal spray or whatever, is a major offender. The features in women's magazines are similar. *Seventeen*, which is aimed at high school girls, devotes most of its space to fashions, makeup, and hair styling. The message is clear: Success for a girl means attracting boys, and that requires making the best of your physical resources. (Behavioral tips are also given: Be sweet and charming, a little helpless, and not too smart. And don't be domineering—that is, don't show that you have a mind of your own.)

Given these preoccupations, it's remarkable that girls do as well as they do academically. Throughout grade school, girls are ahead of boys academically. In high school, their grades are on the average as good as boys, and more girls graduate than boys. But girls do begin to slip in some areas—those that are defined as masculine. Thus on college entrance exams the sexes do equally well on the verbal aptitude section, but the boys score significantly higher on math. If the problems are reworded so that they deal with "typically" feminine pursuits (cooking, for example), the girls' performances improve. "It's around the eighth or ninth grade that this kind of thing begins to occur," one teacher said.

Girls don't like to answer in class; they don't volunteer very often. If you call on a girl, she'll much more likely give you a blank stare while boys will try to think of an answer or make one up. Often, even if girls know the answer, they giggle and act stupid. They're always putting themselves down. . . . Even if girls don't have trouble with math, they say they do. They think math is somehow for boys. (Quoted in Komisar, 1972, p. 34)

If an occasional girl does not catch on to all of this, the teacher may well set her straight. A New York high school student explains that although she wanted to be a physics laboratory assistant, her teacher stated that "he was only interested in working with boys" (quoted in Howe, 1973, p. 194).

The expectations of a girl with respect to academic performance are ambivalent. She is aware that achievement is a societal value. Particularly if they are middle class, her parents will expect her to do well at school. At the same time her mother, especially, is likely to warn her not to do too well. "Let him think he's smarter," she'll be told. Not surprisingly, many girls feel resentment. One high school girl complained that her family told her to work hard at school in order to get into a top university. Simultaneously, however, they compared her to her friend next door who was "pretty and sweet" and very popular. So they also hounded her to work on her appearance and have a "successful" social life. "They were overlooking the fact that this carefree friend of mine had little time left for school work and had failed several subjects. It seemed that my family had expected me to become Eve Curie and Hedy Lamar wrapped up in one" (Komarovsky, 1968, p. 59).

Expectations about careers for girls are considerably less ambivalent. Boys are encouraged to think about growing up to be something from a very early age; in high school the pressure seriously to consider career plans intensifies. If the boy is middle class and not obviously mentally deficient, it is assumed that he will go into a profession or into business. Girls may be encouraged to prepare for a job but seldom for a career. They have been taught from earliest childhood that their most important adult role will be that of wife and mother. This is never presented to girls as a matter of choice. You're either normal or not. A girl who did not want to grow up and have babies would be an outcast, if not worse.

Typically it was the mother who impressed the importance of marriage on her daughters. But fathers were in complete agreement. A study of middle-class fathers found that the men interviewed expected their daughters to get married and preferred marriage over a career for them (Aberle and Naegele, 1966, p. 102). Half were willing to accept the *possibility* of a career for their daughters; the rest completely rejected the idea. Only two wanted their daughters to know how to earn a living. Until recently few girls got any push toward career planning from their parents.

Boys are not only encouraged to begin career planning early; they are also provided with a wealth of role models. In textbooks, television, and films and in their everyday life, they see men in a variety of careers. In contrast, the role models to which girls are exposed are very limited (Britton and Lumpkin, 1983). Betty Friedan remarks that, aside from women who were full-time wives and mothers, "the only other kind of women I knew growing up were old-maid, high-school teachers; the librarian; and the one woman doctor in our town, who cut her hair like a man" (quoted in Epstein, 1971, p. 55). A younger woman recalls that at an early age she was already sure she did not want to be like her mother. But the only women she knew who were not full-time mothers were teachers, librarians, secretaries, and waitresses, whom she considered dull (Salper, 1972, p. 14).

Schoolbooks, as we saw earlier, present an even more restricted set of female role models. In one American history text, for example, only 26 of the 643 people mentioned are women. "If we are to accept the view of our society presented by our history text," several girls using the book wrote, "ours is a society without women" (quoted in Hole and Levine, 1971, p. 333). In six richly illustrated high school science texts, Florence Howe reports that she found the only women in illustrations were one doctor, one scientist, one lab assistant, and one author (Howe, 1973, p. 194). A high school text entitled *Representative Men: Heroes of Our Time* featured two women—Elizabeth Taylor and Jacqueline Onassis (ibid., p. 197).

The image of women in the media is largely restricted, stereotyped, and frequently just plain insulting. Television commercials are a major offender with their presentation of women as either housewife-mothers or sex kittens. The former are almost always shallow—their major concern is having the whitest laundry in the neighborhood—and often unintelligent. The latter are always unintelligent and sometimes masochistic. For both, pleasing a man is their primary purpose in life. In response to the great increase in working women, the makers of TV commercials now more frequently dress their models in suits rather than aprons. But the message is still that a woman's life revolves around her man.

Many young girls never see, much less get to know, even one intelligent, dedicated professional woman who could serve as a role model. The role models are important. Daughters of working mothers are more likely to expect to hold a job themselves. They consider working normal rather than extraordinary for a woman (Hartley, 1970, p. 129). One study found that 66 percent of career-oriented college women were daughters of working women (Almquist and Angrist, 1971, p. 301). In contrast, only 22 percent of women not oriented toward careers had working mothers.

The educational system itself encourages girls to live up to sex stereotypes in their career planning or lack of it. Girls are encouraged to take home economics and typing and discouraged from taking shop. Disastrously for their future career prospects, girls are seldom encouraged and too frequently actively discouraged from taking advanced math. Yet a solid math background is a prerequisite for many of the college majors that lead to prestigious occupations. The hard sciences, medicine, computer science, engineering, and architecture all require a solid grounding in math. Yet many girls are disqualified from even attempting such majors by not taking enough math in high school. A 1972 study by sociologist Lucy Sells found that while 57 percent of the entering first-year males at the University of California at Berkeley had the four years of high school math necessary for majoring in science, engineering, and other math-based subjects, only 8 percent of the entering female students did (Weitzman, 1984, p. 210). Replicating her study in 1977 at the University of Maryland, Sells found no change for men but some slight improvement for women: 15 percent of white female students had taken four years of high school math.

Until recently all but one of New York City's special scientific high schools for especially capable students restricted admission to boys. Although, in most cases, laws now make such restrictions illegal, practice often lags far behind the law. A 1983 investigation of New York City's vocational high schools found that rules intended to eliminate sex discrimination were frequently ignored and that practices often perpetuated traditional sex roles:

> Student recruitment tactics . . . perpetuated bias by directing girls to some schools and boys to others. . . . Teacher hiring practices . . . perpetuated the basic problem by assigning males to predominantly male schools and females to predominatly female schools. . . . At Automotive High School, which graduated its first female student in 1979 . . . teachers and administrators . . . said that female students had not enrolled there because they did not want to get their hands dirty. . . . At Aviation High School, there is one restroom for girls and six for boys. At Mabel Dean Bacon Vocational High School, which teaches cosmetology, business education, dental assistance, and health careers, there is no restroom for boys and only one at the school's annex nearby. (Quoted in Weitzman, 1984, p. 185)

The study also cited examples of sexual harassment against the female students in the form of coarse language and sexual comments from their male counterparts and animosity from some of the shop teachers. One teacher, the review said, complained that girls "just take the place that could be filled by another boy" (quoted in Weitzman, 1984, p. 185). As a consequence 11 of New York's 21 vocational schools were still de facto sex segregated—that is, had 95 percent or more single-sex enrollments.

What happens to the young woman who ends her education with high school? She may marry immediately, get a job, or both. In any case, her chance of ever breaking out of the stereotyped female role is slim. Any job she can get will almost certainly be a typical female job—low paid, dull, and dead-end. After a few years at such a job, marriage, motherhood, and full-time housewifery may seem like a welcome change. But when the children are small, she will have little time for self-development; when they enter school, she will probably have to go back to work to help make ends meet. All the bright promises about the fulfillment inherent in being a "real" woman, a wife and mother, do not usually materialize. Often unaware of why she is not content and feeling guilty about it, she will likely try to raise her son to be the aggressive, successful, supermasculine man that her husband probably isn't, and her daughter to be the "real" woman who finds the fulfillment in the traditional role that she herself has never found.

COLLEGE

The young woman who goes to college has another chance to break out of the stereotyped role that society has decreed for her. The college years may be a period of intensified social pressures toward appropriate feminine role behavior, or they may be a period of widening horizons and newly perceived possibilities.

The young woman's college experience may either reinforce or begin to erode previous socialization. A college with a strong sorority system, with its emphasis on football and beauty queens, will act as a reinforcement (Scott, 1965).

Going away to college offers many girls their first taste of independence. As we have seen, girls are kept more dependent on the family than their brothers are. Being away from home when she is at college allows and even forces the young woman to make her own decisions, to develop a certain amount of self-reliance. But sororities act as family surrogates. The social pressures operating within a sorority encourage conformity and discourage independence. Generally they also institutionalize "husband-catching."

This sort of college life—although it is making a comeback—is still less prevalent than in the 1950s. Young college women now have greater freedom from conventional social pressures. Young men and women engage in sexual relations with relatively few restraints and may set up housekeeping together. In many university communities, overt and blatant sexism is no longer socially or legally acceptable.

Beneath the surface, however, the traditional assumptions about males and females often persist. Men are expected to be the leaders in academic and social life. In class, male students are more likely to speak up than women. Men tend to dominate college politics. When male and female students live together, the division of labor again tends to be traditional. She often does the cooking, cleaning, and shopping; he does the yard work if there's any to be done. And what about the image of women as sex objects? Under pressure from the growing women's movement, the present generation of college men may be more likely than their fathers to regard women as people first. But *Playboy* remains popular, and its readership is heavily young, male, and college educated.

During the college years, the results of early sex-role socialization become starkly obvious. Most young women have developed clearly negative self-images. A 1968 study (Hartley, 1970, p. 138) asked college students to rate the typical adult male, the typical adult female, and themselves, on 122 bipolar items describing personal characteristics. Male and female students agreed closely on their descriptions of the typical adult male and female—and both judged the typically male traits as more socially desirable. Furthermore, the women students attributed to themselves the typically feminine but socially less desirable traits. These women saw themselves as not resourceful, intellectual, competent, intelligent, or realistic, but as immature, subjective, submissive, and easily influenced.

Given these negative self-images, it is not surprising that many women lack self-confidence. Numerous studies have found that, on a wide variety of tasks, women's expectations about their performance are lower than men's expectations (Deaux, 1976, pp. 38–39). Generally, in these experiments, a task will be described and the subject will be asked to predict his or her performance. On tasks as widely divergent as solving anagrams, taking tests of verbal intelligence and arithmetic abilities, and a marble-dropping game, males consistently expect to do better than females expect to do. Explicitly labeling the task to be performed as feminine raises women's expectations to approximately the level of the men's.

Women, then, generally do not expect to succeed as well as men. When they do, does this raise their self-confidence and lead to higher expectations in the future? On most of the tasks used in these experiments, men and women perform about the same. Yet men and women explain their performance differently. Women attribute their success to luck, while men attribute their success to ability. Women are more likely to explain their failure as due to lack of ability while men seldom do (Deaux, 1976, p. 41). If success is seen as the result of luck, not of competence, it is unlikely to build self-confidence.

A study by Philip Goldberg further demonstrates the extent to which women have a negative image of women in general (Goldberg, 1971, pp. 167–172). Female college students were asked to evaluate short articles on art history, dietetics, education, city planning, linguistics, and law. Two sets of booklets containing the articles had been prepared, with the only difference being the authors' names. In one set, a given article was attributed to a male author—for example, John T. McKay; in the other set, the same article was attributed to a female author—Joan T. McKay. Each booklet contained articles by three "male" and three "female" authors.

The women students consistently rated "male" authors higher than "female" authors, even in traditionally feminine fields such as elementary school teaching and dietetics. The author concludes that the belief in women's inferiority, particularly in the intellectual and professional sphere, distorted these students' perceptions (p. 168). Facts are interpreted in such a way as to support the belief. The same experiment was run using male students as subjects, and the results were similar. The male students also consistently rated the "male" authors higher (Bem and Bem, 1971, p. 85).

Since many young women have internalized the assumption that women are intellectually inferior to men, it is hardly surprising that relatively few strive for professional achievement. Still, many college women are academically successful, and career opportunities for women are expanding. Given the high premium our society places on achievement, why is the number of women going into the professions not increasing more quickly?

Psychologist Matina Horner has suggested the presence of "the motive to avoid success" as a psychological barrier to success in women. She says that the motive to avoid success

> exists and receives its impetus from the expectancy held by most women that success, especially in competitive achievement situations, will be followed by negative consequences for them. Among these are social rejection and feelings of being unfeminine or inadequate as women. (1971, p. 62)

Horner asked students to write a short story, the first sentence of which was: "At the end of first-term finals Anne/John finds herself/himself at the top of her/his medical school class." From the content of the stories it was determined whether fear-of-success imagery was present. While only 10 percent of the male stories showed fear of success, 65 percent of the female stories did.

Many of the female stories showed fear of social rejection as a result of academic success. In a number of them, Anne is faced with losing her boyfriend; in others she doesn't have one because she's too smart. In another group of stories, Anne's success makes her worry about her normality or femininity. One story says explicitly that Anne is no longer certain about a medical career because she wonders if it's "normal" for a woman to be a doctor. Another account says that Anne starts to feel guilty; and it supplies a classic conclusion: "She will finally have a nervous breakdown and quit med school and marry a successful young doctor" (pp. 111–113). In their stories, some of the women students simply denied the situation in the lead line. One such story claims that Anne doesn't really exist, but that a group of medical students created her as a code name to play a joke on their professors. In another, medical school is taken to mean nursing school. A few stories were truly bizarre. In one, Anne's classmates "jump on her in a body and beat her. She is maimed for life" (p. 114).

In a variant on the basic experiment, students at an outstanding eastern women's college were asked to describe Anne. More than 70 percent said she was unattractive in face, figure, or manners—"Wears long skirts. Not feminine; masculine looking. Has short hair."

Horner's study has been criticized on a number of grounds (Tresemer, 1974). Nevertheless, additional experiments showed that both men and women expected negative consequences when a member of either sex succeeds in a situation that is not considered sex-appropriate (Deaux, 1976, pp. 51–53). Since the occupations that are sex typed as male are more highly valued in our society, women are placed in a no-win situation.

THE COSTS OF SEX-ROLE STEREOTYPING

In this chapter, we have seen how society molds the child along sex-specific lines. That this process is costly for women hardly needs to be argued. But what is its impact on men? Do men benefit? One can argue that a socialization process that largely removes half the population from competition for the best jobs benefits the other half (however, see Chapter 11). Women provide men with a variety of menial and emotional services in the family setting (see Chapter 10). Were women not socialized to believe that doing so is their duty, they would expect a more equal marital relationship. Finaly, the traditional socialization process justifies male power over women. Of course, only a few men have real power, but it is sometimes argued that even the great mass of men benefit by feeling superior to all women.

All of these arguments are highly controversial. Furthermore, there are real costs to men in the sex-role socialization process. The stereotypical masculine male is aggressive, emotionally impassive, self-sufficient, athletic, brave in the face of danger, a natural leader and competent at any task defined as masculine. Living up to this image is expecting much of any human being, and feeling that one should live up to it is likely to produce anxiety and insecurity. Furthermore, in the complex world in which we live, some of these traits are counterproductive. Physical aggressiveness is more likely to lead to jail than to success; a definition of bravery that extends to foolhardiness may get you injured or killed. The male who learns to be emotionally impassive, to hide his feelings from others and often from himself, denies himself a valuable outlet and cuts himself off from an important aspect of human experience.

Sex-role stereotyping limits the options open to men as well as women. The male child is frequently expected to be good at athletics whether or not he has the slightest interest or aptitude. In many families, an interest in music, art, or dance is discouraged if displayed by a boy. A male who desires to enter a "female" field—nursing or kindergarten teaching, for example—is considered even more deviant than a woman in a "male" field.

Not only is the male expected to enter an appropriate field, but he is expected to be a success. Whatever other attributes he may have, he will be largely judged by his career success. While, to many men, women are sex objects, men are frequently success objects to women. Because career success is defined as central to masculinity in our society, men often sacrifice many or all other values in pursuing it.

If masculinity and femininity as defined by our society are detrimental to human individuality, what is the alternative? A reassessment of the value of "feminine" and "masculine" traits and an attempt to inculcate those considered valuable in both boys and girls would seem to be the answer. Studies have found that high-achieving and highly creative children are much less sex stereotyped in behavior than their less outstanding peers (Farrell, 1974). Androgynous people—those who display both masculine and feminine characteristics—have higher self-esteem, achieve more in school, and seem to be more adaptable (Deaux, 1976, pp. 139–140). There *are* alternatives that are better than assigning traits and behaviors on the basis of sex. Society has constructed the feminine female and the masculine male. A superior task would be for society, in the future, to construct the full human being. In fact, this is one of the central goals of the women's liberation movement, which has pioneered significant reforms in areas such as health care, including new birthing practices, and has provided support for women's education, occupational advancement, and political awareness.

HOW MUCH CHANGE?

Most of the studies upon which the preceding discussion of socialization is based are from the 1960s and early 1970s. Has the last decade or so seen significant change? Because socialization is a complex and multifaceted process, a great many studies are required before that question can be answered unequivocally. Such a body of research, however, is under way (Braungart and Braungart, 1986; Aldous, 1977).

Some studies indicate a change in attitudes among parents. Studies of student political activists of the 1960s indicate a retention of their unconventional beliefs as adults in the 1970s and 1980s (Braungart and Braungart, 1986; Fendrich, 1977). The authors of a 1976 study of fathers mostly from the middle class concluded: "Unlike the fathers of the fifties, worried about their sons' careers and wishing some vague sort of marital bliss for their daughters, the fathers in our study were concerned with their daughters' full human potential" (Rivers et al., 1979, pp. 59–60). A number of the fathers were specifically concerned that their daughters not be limited by sex-role stereotypes. The same study found, in contrast to earlier research findings, that parents did *not* show a difference in the ages at which they would grant independence to girls and boys (p. 135). A nationwide survey sample found that women in 1980 were less likely to sex-type household chores than they had been in 1974 (Roper Organization, 1980, p. 68). Women were asked if children of both sexes might be expected to perform certain chores or if only boys or girls should be. In 1974, 54 percent said that both boys and girls could be expected to mow the lawn; by 1980, 70 percent said so. In 1974, only 39 percent said both sexes should be asked to mend their clothes; by 1980, this had increased to 56 percent. In fact, by 1980, a majority of the women saw all of the chores as appropriate to both sexes.

Attitude changes, however, do not always translate into changes in behavior. Psychologist Beverly Fagot completed a study in which she compared parents' attitudes and their behavior toward their 2-year-old children. The parents' attitudes about bringing up their children were nonstereotyped. Fagot says: "These parents would not restrict playmates to one sex, nor would they avoid buying an opposite-sex toy if the child wanted it. They planned to encourage their child to follow up interests, regardless of the sex-appropriateness of the interest, as the child grew older. Eighty percent planned to actively encourage a viewpoint of sex equity. . . ." (quoted in Rivers et al., 1979, p. 101). When Fagot observed the parents' behavior toward their children, however, she found that it often contradicted the attitudes they had expressed. Parents were, for example, likely to react positively when their daughters asked for help and negatively when their sons did. When the girls "manipulated objects," they were given more negative feedback than boys. Thus girls, but not boys, were discouraged from exploring objects and thereby learning about the physical world. Fagot concluded that although there were not a great number of areas in which parents treated girls and boys differently, "the few areas where we do find significant differences have great consequences for the developmental process" (ibid.). Clearly, notions about sex roles are very deeply ingrained; even when people change their attitudes on the conscious or intellectual level, they may unconsciously express older notions in their behavior.

What sort of messages are children receiving from other important forms of socialization? In response to pressure from feminists, schoolbook publishers promised to make changes. The first crop of books that resulted was by and large a disappointment; in it, tokenism was the norm ("Any Change in Sexist Texts?" *Women's Studies Newsletter* 2, p. 3). A major study of children's texts concluded that more females and minorities have lately been included in these texts, but that little or no progress has occurred in terms of realistic and nonstereotyped role models presented (Britton and Lumpkin, 1983). A considerable number of very good nontext children's books are now available. But since parents must seek these out among a mass of traditional works, only the children of upper- or middle-class parents with a feminist bent are likely to be exposed to them.

Systematic studies do not show much change in television (U.S. Commission on Civil Rights, 1979). In its portrayal of women, *Sesame Street* has improved immensely. Commercial television seems to show women in nontraditional roles somewhat more frequently and in really degrading roles somewhat less frequently. Nevertheless, television still presents a stereotyped picture of the sexes. Studies have found that children who watch a lot of TV have more stereotyped perceptions than children who are infrequent viewers. The authors of one recent study said that their data "suggest that heavy television viewing may contribute significantly to children's acquisition of stereotypic perceptions of behavior and psychological characteristics associated with males and females" (McGhee and Frueh, 1980, p. 185).

On the whole, the messages children receive from the media still portray sex roles in a fairly traditional way. Consequently, as a recent study found, "Pre-school children possess pronounced stereotypes about sex differences in emotionality" (Birnbaum et al., 1980, p. 435). The children in the study associated anger with maleness, and happiness, sadness, and fear with females. Children also still tend to sex-type occupations. A recent study of children age 2 1/2 through 8 found that even the youngest classified doctor as a male occupation and secretary as a female occupation (Gettys and Cann, 1981, pp. 301–308). Sex-typing of these and other jobs increased with age. Another study of third through twelfth graders offers somewhat more encouraging findings. The researchers reported that the third graders endorsed a highly sex-typed occupational world, but that the degree of stereotyping decreased with age—more dramatically among girls than among boys. Even so, 44 percent of the twelfth graders said that 7 or more of the 13 occupations asked about should only be performed by either men or women; 55 percent of the twelfth-grade boys and 36 percent of the twelfth-grade girls gave such responses (Cummings and Taebel, 1980, pp. 631–644).

Earlier studies as well as much anecdotal evidence indicate that girls lower their achievement levels at puberty so as to avoid competition with boys. In a 1978 study, fifth, seventh, and ninth graders were given a test described as an intelligence test (Rivers et al., 1979, pp. 157–158). Boys and girls were seated opposite each other. After the first part of the test had been completed, each child was taken aside and told he or she had done better than the opposite-sex child across the table. The children were then sent back to do the second part of the test. Both the male and female fifth graders tended to increase their performance on the second test. Among seventh graders, however, the pattern was radically different. The boys tended to increase their scores, but 80 percent of the girls decreased theirs. About half of the ninth-grade girls decreased their performance. Asked about competing intellectually with the opposite sex, almost all of the seventh-grade girls said they did not like to beat a boy. Several explicitly said, "I'd rather be popular than have good grades or win a game against a boy." Most of the ninth-grade girls responded similarly, but those who did not kept their scores up on the second test.

Nationwide surveys of high school seniors in 1976 and 1977, nevertheless, found that most of the girls expected to work outside the home for most of their adult lives and many expected to work in high-level occupations (Rivers, 1979, p. 171). Asked "What do you think you will be doing 30 years from now?" only 11 percent said they thought they would be full-time homemakers; 44 percent expected to hold professional jobs. Almost as many girls as boys expected work to be central to their lives: 72 percent of the girls and 76 percent of the boys. More than half the girls—56 percent—said it was important that their job be of high prestige.

Recent studies of young adults—mostly college students—also suggest some change. In an experiment similar to the 1968 study referred to earlier, undergraduates were asked to described a socially competent, healthy adult man, a healthy adult woman, or a healthy adult, sex unspecified (Brooks-Gunn and Fisch, 1980, pp. 575—580). The male students described the healthy man as similar to the adult standard and the healthy woman as different. The female students, however, did not perceive the healthy woman as different from the adult standard. This study suggests that current female college students are less likely than their predecessors to attribute negative characteristics to normal women. A recent replication of the Goldberg study of reactions to articles authored by "males" and "females" indicates that female college students are less likely now than they were in the past to derogate work attributed to a woman (Gross and Geffner, 1980, pp. 713–722). However, both student and nonstudent males, as well as older nonstudent females, tended to respond in fairly prejudiced and stereotyped ways. Yet, another study of college students found that neither males nor females subscribed to the traditional belief that success-oriented women were unattractive or unromantic (Micheline et al., 1981, pp. 391–401).

An examination of recent studies thus produces a rather ambiguious picture. Certainly the socialization process has not been revolutionized; sexist messages in the typical child's environment still outnumber nonsexist messages. But the lack of a total transformation should be neither surprising nor discouraging. Because the sex-role socialization process involves all facets of our society, changing it will also. That more options are presented to children and young adults now is encouraging; messages about sex roles are no longer homogeneously traditional. Some children, such as girls from professional families, are probably more likely to receive exposure to nontraditional messages than others. Consequently the impact of changes in sex roles is likely to be spread unevenly across the population for some time to come. Society does not yet construct the full human being, but a significant beginning has been made.

SUMMARY

Despite the effects of the women's movement, in our society men and women are still expected to display different personality characteristics and behavior. Men are expected to be aggressive and unemotional and play the breadwinner role; women are expected to be passive and dependent, and play the supportive role as housewives. Almost from birth, children are taught these expectations by the family, the schools, the media, and other social institutions such as the church.

For women especially, the costs of these sex-role expectations can be high. If a woman does not conform, she is considered deviant by society and, because she is likely to have internalized the standards, also by herself. If she does conform, she is playing a role in the family and in society that is likely to make her discontented because of its lack of intrinsic satisfactions and because society does not highly value it. Yet the women's liberation movement—and other counterforces such as radical sociology—are attempting to reverse these trends. Studies of the last decade or so do indicate some reversal of trends in sex-role expectations and behavior.

SUGGESTED READINGS

A somewhat more extended discussion of the socialization process can be found in Barbara Sinclair Deckard, *The Women's Movement*, 3d ed. (New York: Harper & Row, 1983). For a book length discussion of the socialization process and its results, see Kay Deaux, *The Behavior of Women and Men* (Monterey, CA: Brooks/Cole, 1976). For a discussion emphasizing the cost to men of traditional sex roles, see Warren Farrell, *The Liberated Man* (New York: Random House, 1974). An outstanding discussion of political socialization in different generations is: Richard G. Braungart and Margaret M. Braungart, "Life-Course and Generational Politics," *Annual Review of Sociology* 12 (1986):205–231.

REFERENCES

Aberle, David F., and Kaspar D. Naegele. 1966. "Raising Middle-Class Sons." In Alex Inkeles, ed., *Readings in Modern Sociology*. Englewood Cliffs, NJ: Prentice-Hall.

Aldous, Joan. 1977. "Family Interaction Patterns." *Annual Review of Sociology* 3:105–135.

Almquist, Elizabeth, and Shirley Angrist. 1971. "Role Model Influences on College Women's Career Aspirations." In Athena Theodore, ed., *The Professional Woman*. Cambridge, Mass.: Schenkman.

Amundsen, Kirsten. 1971. *The Silenced Majority*. Englewood Cliffs, NJ: Prentice-Hall.

"Any Change in Sexist Texts?" 1974. *Women's Studies Newsletter* 2(3).

Bardwick, Judith. 1971. *Psychology of Women*. New York: Harper & Row.

Bem, Sandra I., and Daryl J. Bem. 1971. "Training the Woman to Know Her Place: The Power of a Conscious Ideology." In Vivian Gornick and Barbara K. Moran, eds., *Woman in Sexist Society*. New York: New American Library (Signet).

Birmbaum, Dana W.; T. A. Nosanchuk; and W. L. Croll. 1980. "Children's Stereotypes about Sex Differences in Emotionality." *Sex Roles* 6 (June).

Braungart, Richard G., and Margaret M. Braungart. 1986. "Life Course and Generational Politics." *Annual Review of Sociology* 12:205–231.

Britton, Gwyneth, and Margaret Lumpkin. 1983. "Basal Readers: Paltry Progress Pervades." *Interracial Books for Children Bulletin* 14(6):4–7.

Brooks-Gunn, Jeanne, and Melanie Fisch. 1980. "Psychological Androgyny and College Students' Judgments of Mental Health." *Sex Roles* 6 (August).

Corns, Donald. 1973. "Talking About Sex: Notes on First Coitus and the Double Sexual Standard." *Journal of Marriage and the Family* 35 (November).

Cummings, Scott, and Delbert Taebel. 1980. "Sexual Inequality and the Reproduction of Consciousness: An Analysis of Sex-Role Stereotyping Among Children." *Sex Roles* 6 (August).

Deaux, Kay. 1976. *The Behavior of Women and Men*. Monterey, CA: Brooks/Cole.

Epstein, Cynthia. 1971. *Woman's Place*. Berkeley: University of California Press.

Farrell, Warren. 1974. *The Liberated Man*. New York: Random House.

Fendrich, James M. 1977. "Keeping the Faith or Pursuing the Good Life: A Study of the Consequences of Participation in the Civil Rights Movement." *American Sociological Review* 42 (February):144–157.

Flannigan, Joan. 1972. "Women in the Professions." In New York City Commission on Human Rights, *Women's Role in Contemporary Society*. New York: Avon Books.

Gettys, Linda, and Arnie Cann. 1981. "Children's Perceptions of Occupational Sex Stereotypes." *Sex Roles* 7 (March).

Goldberg, Philip. 1971. "Are Women Prejudiced Against Women?" In Athena Theodore, ed., *The Professional Woman*. Cambridge, Mass.: Schenkman.

Goldberg, Susan, and Michael Lewis. 1972. "Play Behavior in the Year-Old Infant: Early Sex Differences." In Judith M. Bardwick, ed., *Readings on the Psychology of Women*. New York: Harper & Row.

Gross, Madeleine M., and Robert A. Geffner. 1980. "Are the Times Changing? An Analysis of Sex Role Prejudice." *Sex Roles* 6 (October).

Hartley, Ruth E. 1970. "American Core Culture: Changes and Continuities." In Georgene Seward and Robert Williamson, eds., *Sex Roles in Changing Society*. New York: Random House.

Hole, Judith, and Ellen Levine. 1971. *Rebirth of Feminism*. New York: Quadrangle.

Horner, Matina. 1971. "Femininity and Successful Achievement: A Basic Inconsistency." In Vivian Gornick and Barbara K. Moran, eds., *Woman in Sexist Society*. New York: New American Library (Signet).

———. 1971. "The Motive to Avoid Success and Changing Aspirations of College Women." In Judith Bardwick, *Readings on the Psychology of Women*. New York: Harper & Row.

Howe, Florence. 1973. "Sexual Stereotypes Start Early." In Marie B. Hecht et al., eds., *The Women, Yes!* New York: Holt, Rinehart and Winston.

Jacoby, Susan. 1973. *Press-Enterprise*. Riverside, CA.

Klemesrud, Judy. 1973. *Press-Enterprise*. Riverside, CA.

Kohlberg, Lawrence. 1966. "A Cognitive-Developmental Analysis of Children's Sex-Role Concepts and Attitudes." In Eleanor Maccoby, ed., *The Development of Sex Differences*. Stanford University Press.

Komarovsky, Mirra. 1968. "Functional Analysis of Sex Roles." In Marvin B. Sussman, ed., *Sourcebook in Marriage and the Family*. Boston: Houghton Mifflin.

———. 1971. "Cultural Contradictions and Sex Roles." In Judith Bardwick, *Readings on the Psychology of Women*. New York: Harper & Row.

Komisar, Lucy. 1972. *The New Feminism*. New York: Warner Paperback Library.

McGhee, Paul E., and Terry Frueh. 1980. "Television Viewing and the Learning of Sex-Role Stereotypes." *Sex Roles* 6 (April).

Micheline, Ronald L.; Donald Eisen; and Stephan R. Snodgrass. 1981. "Success Orientation and the Attractiveness of Competent Males and Females." *Sex Roles* 7 (April).

Rivers, Caryl; Rosalind Barnett; and Grace Baruch. 1979. *Beyond Sugar and Spice*. New York: Putnam.

The Roper Organization. *The 1980 Virginia Slims American Women's Opinion Poll*.

Rubin, Jeffrey; Frank Provenzano; and Zella Luria. 1974. "The Eye of the Beholder: Parents' Views on Sex of Newborns." *American Journal of Orthopsychiatry* 44.

Salper, Roberta. 1972. *Female Liberation*. New York: Knopf.

Scott, John Finley. 1965. "The American College Sorority: Its Role in Class and Ethnic Endogamy." *American Sociological Review* 30 (August):514–527.

Tresemer, David. 1974. "Fear of Success: Popular but Unproven." *Psychology Today* 7 (March).

U.S. Commission on Civil Rights. January 1979. *Window Dressing on the Set: An Update*.

U'Ren, Marjorie B. 1971. "The Image of Woman in Textbooks." In Vivan Gornick and Barbara K. Moran, eds., *Woman in Sexist Society*. New York: New American Library (Signet).

Wallace, Walter L. 1971 "The Perspective of College Women." In Athena Theodore, ed., *The Professional Woman*. Cambridge, MA: Schenkman.

Weitzman, Lenore J. 1984. "Sex-Role Socialization: A Focus on Women." In Jo Freemen, ed., *Women: A Feminist Perspective,* 3d ed. Palo Alto, CA: Mayfield Publishing Co.

Women on Words and Images. 1972. *Dick and Jane as Victims.* P.O. Box 2163, Princeton, NJ 68540.

————. 1975. *Channeling Children.* Princeton, NJ: Women on Words and Images.

chapter 10

Marriage and the Family: Myth Versus Reality

By Barbara Sinclair, Howard J. Sherman,
and James L. Wood

This chapter compares the ideal version of the American marriage and family with the existing realities. Similar to the previous chapter, the discussion will be divided into trends up to the last decade or so and more recent patterns.

While the women's movement has had some impact, female socialization still inculcates the notion that, for women, getting married is supremely important. The typical young woman has been taught that the choice of a marriage partner is the most important decision she will ever make. In marriage she expects to fulfill her true nature as loving wife and mother. This, she has been taught, is the most creative career possible for a woman. She is, in effect, promised instant and complete happiness.

Reality unfortunately is often very different. What marriage is really like depends upon whether the family is white collar or blue collar. White collar refers to the more affluent segment of the working class; most of the husbands in white-collar families have a professional, a managerial, or some other fairly well-paid white-collar occupation. Conversely, blue collar is used to refer to the less affluent segment of the working class; the husbands in these families mostly hold blue-collar jobs—manual labor—although some are found in poorly paid white-collar jobs.

REALITY: THE WHITE-COLLAR VERSION

The white-collar, like the blue-collar, woman is increasingly likely to work until she is pregnant with her first child. During the time she is working outside the home, she finds she has two jobs. She is expected to do most of the housework.

It is, after all, "woman's work." Her husband may help out, but it is usually clearly understood that the inside housework is her responsibility.

Whether she is working or not, the first part of the marriage myth crumbles quickly. Housework is neither interesting nor creative; in the expressive phrase of the women's movement, it is "shit work." For those with the talent and interest, decorating and gourmet cooking are creative and enjoyable. But most housework consists of tasks such as mopping floors, washing dishes, and cleaning toilet bowls. Not only is it boring, it is repetitive and never ending. Housework does not stay done; a chore done today must be done again tomorrow or, at best, next week. Thus it provides no real feeling of accomplishment. Studies have found that doing housework is a perfect job for the feebleminded (Friedan, 1964, p. 244).

When the first baby is born, the young woman may become a full-time housewife and mother. The media tend to present a baby as a wonderful toy— gurgling, smiling, and doing cute things. Babies are wonderful and lovable. But they are also quite demanding. They cry as well as smile. Their needs often must be met instantly. Changing a dirty diaper is *not* a fulfilling experience.

A baby increases the amount of housework that must be done. Even more serious, with the arrival of the child the young woman loses control over her own schedule. As one young mother explained: "Suddenly I had to devote myself to the child totally. I was under the illusion that the baby was going to fit into my life, and I found I had to switch my life and my schedule to fit *him*" (Quoted in Rollin, 1971, p. 351). A baby is not a toy that can be put away when one wishes. The young mother is always on duty. She often cannot take time off to read or rest. When the child becomes mobile, the problem becomes especially acute. A toddler must be watched. The housework must still be done. Neither of these tasks require the woman's full attention, but they require enough of it so that she cannot do anything else.

> In industry the most fatiguing jobs are those which only partially occupy the worker's attention, but at the same time prevent him from concentrating on anything else. Many young wives say that this mental gray-out is what bothers them most in caring for home and children. "After a while, your mind becomes a blank," they say. "You can't concentrate on anything. It's like sleep-walking." (Friedan, 1964, p. 240)

The child also severely restricts the woman's mobility. If she is isolated in her own home in surburbia, she spends most of her time with people under 6 years old. She is progressively cut off from participation in the world outside the home. There is, of course, the television set, but as Myrdal and Klein point out:

> The isolated woman at home may well be kept "in touch" with events, but she feels that the events are not in touch with her, that they happen without her participation. The wealth of information which is brought to her without any effort on her part does not lose its vicariousness. It increases rather than allays her sense of isolation and of being left out. (1968, p. 148)

The lack of adult conversation is a universal complaint among American housewives. In the past, housework was much more physically taxing, but at least the women had other adults around for help and companionship. Philip Slater says:

> The idea of imprisoning each woman alone in a small, self-contained, and architecturally isolated dwelling is a modern invention dependent upon an advanced technology. In Muslim societies, for example, the wife may be a prisoner, but she is at least not in solitary confinement. In our society, the housewife may move about freely, but since she has nowhere in particular to go and is not a part of anything, her prison needs no walls. . . . Most of her social and emotional needs must be satisfied by her children, who are hardly adequate to the task. (Quoted in Bernard, 1973, p. 50)

The young woman's good intentions about staying intellectually or artistically active dissipate. One cannot read a serious book, much less write a novel, in 10-minute snatches. Connected, uninterrupted time is needed, and this she does not have.

Progressively she becomes more and more dependent on her husband as her only link with the outside world. Yet the couple find they have less and less to talk about. Their experiences are too divergent. She becomes boring because her experiences are boring. Small household catastrophes and a few cute stories about the children do not make for stimulating conversation. One of the results is the sort of sex segregation that can be seen at suburban parties—the men in one part of the room discussing business and politics, the woman in the other talking about children and home. Eventually, of course, all the children are in school. For the average American woman this occurs when she is 34 years old (Rubin, 1976, p. 96). If she has previously worked, she is now likely to return to work. For the woman who has been at home rearing children for a number of years, the return to work is not easy. The white-collar woman may well have completed college, but usually she has not been trained for a career. Too often, the only jobs she can get are not commensurate with her education. A clerical job is frequently the best she can get. Many women find that even such jobs are better than staying home. Working at all may provide a feeling of independence as well as social stimulation. The financial costs of holding a job—transportation, new clothes, and especially babysitters—may, however, be similar to or even greater than what she earns. If the husband prefers that she not work, he can use this as an argument.

For the professionally trained woman, the return to work may be even more difficult. Her training is likely to be out of date, and she has probably found it impossible to keep up with the professional literature. In order to become competitive with recent graduates, she will likely have to "retool," and she may fear that she is no longer capable of the analytic thinking and sustained concentration required. Assuming that she survives the retooling process, she will still have difficulty finding a good position. In addition to the prejudice against women, she will face prejudice on the basis of her age. As the prestigious professions require working long hours, she may want a part-time job, but such jobs are often difficult to find and are marginal in pay and prestige.

Some women do manage to develop a full and interesting life of their own without taking a paid job. A few seriously develop an artistic talent; others become deeply involved in community affairs or in politics. Such involvement requires considerable amounts of connected time at regular intervals. Finding this time takes *more* organization and determination for the woman who is "only" a housewife than for the woman holding a paid job. A working woman's family understands that she must go to work regularly. To be sure, in two-job families the woman, not the man, is usually expected to stay home with a sick child. Nevertheless, the family recognizes that the woman will be away from the home during her working hours and should not be disturbed unless a real emergency arises. The woman who does not hold a paid job continuously has to justify and protect her time from encroachments. As she is not getting paid for her efforts, her family is unlikely to take them seriously and thus will expect her to change her schedule to suit them. She will need a great deal of determination and sense of her own rights as an individual if she is seriously to pursue her nonfamily related interests.

Whether she works at a paid job or pursues another interest, the woman is expected to keep it from interfering with her principal functions in the family. Working just because she enjoys doing so is suspect. Women are expected to be service-oriented, not achievement-oriented. A woman who feels that achievement is necessary for her self-realization is considered selfish. A working woman married to a man making a quite large salary often claims she works because the family needs the money. Working in order to help her family is considered legitimate; working because she enjoys it is not.

For the married woman, her husband and children must always come first; her own needs and desires, last. When the children reach school age, they no longer require constant attention. The emotional-expressive function assigned to the woman is still required of her. Called the "stroking function" by sociologist Jessie Bernard, it consists of showing solidarity, raising the status of others, giving help, rewarding, agreeing, concurring, complying, understanding, and passively accepting. The woman is expected to give emotional support and comfort to other family members, to make them feel like good and worthwhile human beings. A man generally expects his wife to center her life around him. She should not need anything but a husband who is a good provider and healthy children to make her happy.

Among better-educated Americans, the ideal is the companionate marriage in which husband and wife are friends. The traditional division of labor in the family along sex lines makes the ideal almost impossible to achieve. Friendship requires common interests. When husband and wife lead very different lives, this can erode any common interests they may have had and does not encourage the development of new ones. Friendship also requires equality. Even if the couple consciously try to attain an egalitarian marriage, so long as the traditional division of labor is maintained, the husband will be "more equal." He is the provider not only of money but of status. Especially if he is successful, society values what he does; she is just a housewife. Their friends are likely to be his friends and coworkers; in their company, she is just his wife. Because his provider function is essential for the family's survival, major family decisions are made in terms of how they affect his career. He need not and usually does not act like the authoritarian *paterfamilias* of the Victorian age. His power and status are derived from his function in the family and are secure so long as the traditional division of labor is maintained. As more and more women enter the labor force, the traditional division of labor is changing. However, since most women work in low-paid, low-status jobs, the balance of power in the family probably has not changed drastically.

REALITY: THE BLUE-COLLAR VERSION

While the white-collar segment of the population pays lip service to the ideal of egalitarian marriage, among blue-collar workers, older more traditional values prevail. In her study of blue-collar families, Lillian Rubin (1976) found that both men and women believe that the man should be the ultimate authority in the family. Thus in discussing something she wanted to do—such as going back to school—the blue-collar wife would frequently conclude, "He won't let me" (Rubin, p. 96). In contrast, white-collar wives do not speak in terms of getting *permission* from their husbands.

The difference may be one of style and language rather than of substance. The blue-collar man simply tells his wife she cannot do certain things; the white-collar husband, with his greater verbal skills, uses a subtler form of coercion. Thus one such husband told his wife that whether or not she got an abortion was her decision. However, if she did, he would never consent to having another child (p. 97).

The differing economic circumstances of white- and blue-collar families also have an effect. The blue-collar families that Rubin interviewed were not poor according to U.S. government standards in the 1970s; their median income was $12,300 (p. 106). Nevertheless, they were economically insecure; for almost all, paying the bills was a continuous struggle. In most families, regardless of class, men have the ultimate decision-making power in important spending decisions (p. 108). In blue-collar families where money is tighter, the husband's power may have a greater effect on the wife's life because harder choices have to be made. Conflicts about spending priorities can seldom be resolved by saying, "Let's buy both."

On housework, a highly traditional division of labor prevailed in these blue-collar families. All agree that housework is the woman's job; her husband may help her, but it is her responsibility. As one man said: "That's just the way life is. It's her job to keep the house and children and my job to earn the money. My wife couldn't do my job and I couldn't be as good a cook and housekeeper as she is. So we just ought to do what we do best" (p. 100).

If the wife works outside the home, as over half the women interviewed do, the burden is especially great. These families lack the money to hire any outside help as white-collar families often can. Asked "Whose life is easier, a man's or a woman's?" the wives often expressed their frustration: "I get mad sometimes and wish I could change places with him. It would be a relief to worry only about one thing. It feels like I drag around such a heavy load" (p. 106).

Despite the double burden these working wives carry, most enjoy holding a job (pp. 168–169). The jobs these women have—sales clerk, waitress, factory jobs—are by no means glamorous, yet they do provide satisfactions not available at home. As a factory worker said: "I really love going to work. I guess it's because it gets me away from the home. It's not that I don't love my home; I do, but you get awfully tired of just keeping house and doing those housewifely things" (p. 170). Another working woman said about her job: "I'm good at it, and I like that feeling. It's good to feel like you're competent" (p. 172).

Thus, while most of these women work out of economic necessity, they do find other satisfactions in holding a job. Getting out of the house, a sense of competence, some feeling of independence are some of these rewards. There are, however, costs involved beyond those of the double burden. In a society in which men so heavily define their masculinity in terms of the provider role, the wife's working may be seen as a threat. As one woman said, "I guess it's a matter of pride with him. It makes him feel bad, like he's not supporting us good enough" (p. 173). A number of the husbands of working women feel that their wives have become too independent, that their authority is threatened: "I'd like to feel like I wear the pants in the family. Once my decision is made, it should be made, and that's it. She should just carry it out. But it doesn't work that way around here. Because she's working and making money, she thinks she can argue back whenever she feels like it" (p. 177).

In her study of blue-collar marriage in the late 1950s, sociologist Mirra Komarovsky found that many of the couples she interviewed did not expect friendship in marriage (1967, p. 112). Men and women were seen as having sufficiently different interests that cross-sex friendship was not really possible. Thus husband and wife had few mutual friends. The wife had female friends whom she saw during the day; the husband, male friends whom he saw on his night or nights out.

Rubin's study indicates that expectations are changing. The wife, especially, does expect marriage to be more than an economic and sexual arrangement. Though she may not express her desires explicitly, she wants communication and companionship. "I keep talking to him about communication, and he says, 'Okay so we're talking, now what do you want?' And I don't know what to say then, but I know it's not what I mean" (p. 120).

The men, not knowing what is expected of them, may feel confused and threatened. The socialization process, which is more sex-stereotyped in blue-collar than in white-collar families (Rubin, pp. 125–127), has produced in the man a "trained incapacity to share" (Komarovsky, p. 156). "The ideal of masculinity into which they were socialized inhibits expressiveness both directly, with its emphasis on reserve, and indirectly by identifying personal exchange with the feminine role" (p. 156). She wants to talk about their inner feelings, to establish a truly intimate relationship. He may try, but he literally does not know how. As one man said: "I sometimes think I'm selfish. She's the support—the moral support— in the family. But she needs support, I just don't give it to her. Maybe it's not just selfishness, it's that I don't know what she wants and I don't know how." (Rubin, 1976, p. 129). Many of the wives, while dissatisfied and yearning for a deeper relationship, for something more out of life, also feel guilty about the new demands they are making on their husbands: "What do I have to complain about? Jim's a steady worker; he doesn't drink; he doesn't hit me" (p. 19). Some even question whether they are normal: "I worry sometimes that maybe there's something the matter with me that I'm not satisfied with what I've got" (p. 132).

Rubin concludes that for most of the couples interviewed, "despite the yearning for more, relations between husband and wife are benumbed, filled with silence; life seems empty and meaningless" (p. 123).

MARRIAGE AND THE FAMILY—IS IT GOOD FOR HUMAN BEINGS?

If the description of the family presented earlier is correct, the traditional American family structure is not good for many human beings. The woman in particular is trapped in a situation that provides little opportunity for intellectual growth or the satisfactions of achievement. The man at least gets a maid.

But surely the picture is overdrawn. Certainly there must be women content with the traditional female role of housewife and mother. Available evidence indicates that the happy housewife may indeed be relatively rare. A number of studies have found that women of all social classes express more dissatisfaction with marriage than men do.

> More wives than husbands report marital frustration and dissatisfaction; more report negative feelings; more wives than husbands consider their marriages unhappy, have considered separation or divorce, have regretted their marriages; and fewer report positive companionship. (Bernard, 1973, p. 28)

Most alarming are the figures on mental health. According to Jessie Bernard, "being a housewife makes women sick" (p. 28). When married men and married women are compared, the men show up much better on various indexes of mental health. "More married women than married men show phobic reactions, depression and passivity; greater than expected frequency of symptoms of psychological distress; and mental-health impairment" (p. 30).

Perhaps women are simply psychologically less stable than men. No, the poorer mental health of married women is not due to a general sex difference. On the same measures, unmarried women show up as mentally healthier than both married women and unmarried men. Unmarried women's mental health compares very favorably with that of unmarried men. "Single women suffer far less than single men from neurotic and antisocial tendencies. More single men than single women are depressed and passive" (p. 33). When unmarried women and married men are compared, little overall mental health difference is found, although the women show a markedly smaller incidence of psychological distress symptoms such as nervousness and insomnia (p. 35).

The data would seem to show that marriage is good for men and bad for women. Perhaps, however, some of these differences are due to selective factors. Men may tend to marry women to whom they can feel superior; women to marry men they can look up to. If women tend to marry up and men to marry down, then "bottom-of-the-barrel" men and "cream-of-the-crop" women are least likely to marry.

The selective process cannot, however, completely explain the poor mental health of wives because almost everyone does eventually get married. Something about the woman's marriage must account for the problem. A comparison between working women, many of whom are married, and housewives is illuminating. Working women, whatever their marital status, are on the average far healthier mentally than housewives (who have no outside job).

> Far fewer than expected of the working women and more than expected of the housewives, for example, had actually had a nervous breakdown. Fewer than expected of the working women and more than expected of the housewives suffered from nervousness, inertia, insomnia, trembling hands, nightmares, perspiring hands, fainting, headaches, dizziness, and heart palpitations. (p. 52)

Clearly being only a housewife is the problem; it literally makes many women sick.

The traditional nuclear family structure, with its strict division of labor along sex lines and the resulting isolation of wives in the home, is not functional for women. For men, the balance between costs and benefits is less clear. In mental health and reported happiness, married men far surpass single men. On the other hand, if there is strict adherence to the traditional division of labor, the husband is solely responsible for the support of his wife and children. This may mean very long working hours, considerable anxiety, and little freedom to change the type of work he does if he should desire to do so. Furthermore, as his wife becomes more and more unhappy with her lot, she is likely to take it out on him.

RECENT TRENDS

The American family has been changing. In 1976, 64.9 percent of all households included a husband and wife; 11 percent included a woman and other individuals—her children, for example—but not a husband; 3.4 percent included a man and other individuals but not a wife; and 20.6 percent were single-person households (Barrett, 1978, Table 2). Thus married-couple households were still the norm, but other forms were far from rare. The supposedly typical family consisting of an employed husband, a wife who does not work, and one or more children under 18 had become distinctly atypical. In 1976 only 19.1 percent of all households fit this description, and as increasing numbers of women have entered the labor force, the proportion has decreased further. Less than 15 percent of all households now conform to this erstwhile ideal.

What has been the effect on family life of this transformation? Careful and up-to-date studies are sparse, but we do know from older research that a working wife has more influence in the family. Certainly attitudes have changed. When a sample of women was asked in 1962 to respond to the statement, "Most of the important decisions in the life of the family should be made by the man of the house," less than one-third disagreed (Institute for Social Research, 1980, p. 3). In 1977, slightly over two-thirds disagreed. We also know that, by and large, working wives tend to be mentally healthier than housewives. Recent studies continue to show that when she takes a job, the wife assumes a double burden.

Husbands have not significantly increased the amount of housework they do. Studies done in 1975 through 1977 found that women do 80–90 percent of the housework (*Los Angeles Times,* July 25, 1980). The full-time homemaker spends eight hours a day, seven days a week, on housework; the wife employed full-time spends five hours a day, seven days a week on housework. Not only was the husband's contribution to household labor minimal even if his wife was employed, but he seldom assumed responsibility for the tasks he did perform. That is, a husband might help his wife by, for example, taking out the garbage or occasionally buying groceries, but reminding him and making the shopping list remained her responsibility. The researcher found that the division of household labor did not vary across classes; white-collar families did not have a more equal division of labor than blue-collar families.

Certainly there are families in which husband and wife have made a real effort to change the traditional division of labor. Such families are, however, still relatively rare. A nationwide survey found only 5 percent of the families questioned had made a conscious effort to do so (ibid.). Furthermore, changing the division of labor is not easy. Because of their upbringing, women are more likely to know how to cook and men how to make repairs; unfortunately for the woman, cooking has to be done every day, while the need for repairs is much less frequent. Sexist attitudes are deeply ingrained; even couples who believe themselves liberated are seldom totally unaffected by traditional notions acquired in childhood. Several studies have found that both men and women exaggerate the husband's actual contribution to housework, with men exaggerating more (ibid.). Such exaggeration is, in part, due to the deepseated notion that housework is basically women's work. A man who has custody of his three children said: "When I was married I thought I was doing fifty percent of the work. Now that I have to do it all, I realize I was doing only about thirty percent" (Rivers, et al., 1979, p. 304).

For women, the combination of traditional and feminist attitudes sometimes leads to the superwoman syndrome. Determined to succeed at a demanding job, she also feels guilty if she does not do all the things a housewife does as wife and mother. She may not feel she is a good mother unless she bakes cookies rather than buys them; when entertaining her husband's colleagues she may feel she must cook a lavish gourmet feast rather than prepare a simple dinner or take them out to a restaurant. This syndrome is clearly a prescription for disaster. But a more realistic approach to married women working need not be.

It *is* possible to combine a demanding and satisfying career with marriage and motherhood. Psychologist Abigail Stewart found that "high role combination"—that is, being wife, mother, and worker—was not a source of psychological distress; on the contrary, it was associated with personal fulfillment (ibid., p. 281). Judith Birnbaum found married professional women to be happy, to have high self-esteem and to feel personally competent and worthwhile (ibid., p. 280). Although these women sometimes worried about whether they spent enough time with their children, they believed themselves to be good mothers.

What will the families of tomorrow be like? Is the truly egalitarian marriage just around the corner? An examination of the attitudes of young people may provide some answers. Surveys of high school seniors indicate marriage is likely to remain the norm: 80 percent said they would eventually marry (Institute for Social Research, 1981, p. 8). The seniors were asked to rate a variety of family/work arrangements as either desirable, acceptable, somewhat acceptable, or not at all acceptable (Institute for Social Research, 1980, pp. 3–5). When no preschool children are involved, the seniors believe the wife should work. Both partners working full time was found unacceptable by only 25 percent of the males and 14 percent of the females; the traditional arrangement was unacceptable to 38 percent of the females and 13 percent of the males. When preschool children are present, however, the seniors endorse more traditional patterns: 41 percent said the husband working and the wife staying home was the most desirable arrangement. A great many—especially of the females—did say it would be acceptable for the wife to work half-time. If both parents work, the seniors believe child care should be equally divided; even when the woman does not work, the seniors endorsed a major child-care role for the husband. Although the high school seniors also thought a working couple should share housework, this belief was not as strongly held as that concerning shared child care, and females favored it more strongly than males.

This study shows that today's young people hold an amalgam of old and new ideas. In some cases, real life will force them to make hard choices. The survey found that many of the girls expected to hold high-prestige professional jobs. They are likely to find that such jobs do not allow for part-time work or an in-and-out employment pattern. Whether the boys' good intentions about sharing child care and housework will be translated into behavior is another big question. The truly egalitarian marriage is not likely to be the norm in the immediate future. Nevertheless, the current generation of high school students enters adulthood with attitudes about marriage very different from those their parents held at that age. Certainly they have a better chance than their parents for devising family arrangements that are good for men, women, and children.

SUMMARY

American girls are brought up to believe in a highly glamorized image of marriage. Reality, however, consists of being burdened with the bulk of the housework and child care, often in addition to paid work outside the home. Moreover, marriage is seldom as satisfying emotionally as young women expect. The companionate marriage requires equality, which is very difficult to achieve in a sexist society. Nevertheless, there are hopeful trends that may, in time, transform marriage.

SUGGESTED READINGS

Further history of the new trends and successes by the women's movement can be found in Barbara Sinclair Deckard, *The Women's Movement*, 3d ed. (New York: Harper & Row, 1983), chaps. 12 and 13, which detail advances in many areas ranging from employment to medical self-help. Lillian Breslow Rubin, *Worlds of Pain* (New York: Basic Books, 1976), is an excellent study of the modern blue-collar family. For a survey of the sociological literature on marriage, see Jessie Bernard, *The Future of Marriage* (New York: Bantam,

1973). A highly publicized, policy-oriented book on the unexpected negative consequences for women and children, and benefits to men, of liberalized divorce policies is Lenore Weitzman's *The Divorce Revolution* (New York: Free Press, 1985). The major conflict over abortion is illuminatingly discussed by Kristin Luker, *Abortion and the Politics of Motherhood* (Berkeley: University of California Press, 1984), and by Rosalind Pollack Petchesky, *Abortion and Woman's Choice: The State, Sexuality, and Reproductive Freedom* (New York: Longman, 1984), both of which are interestingly reviewed by Carole Joffe, "The Meaning of the Abortion Conflict," *Contemporary Sociology* 14 (January 1985):26–29.

REFERENCES

Barrett, Nancy Smith. 1978. "Data Needs for Evaluating the Labor Market Status of Women." Paper prepared for the Census Bureau Conference on Issues in Federal Statistical Needs Relating to Women, April 27–28, table 2.

Bernard, Jessie. 1973. *The Future of Marriage*. New York: Bantam.

Friedan, Betty. 1964. *The Feminine Mystique*. New York: Dell. Originally published in 1963.

Institute for Social Research. 1980. *IRS Newsletter*. Winter.

———. 1981. *IRS Newsletter*. Winter.

Komarovsky, Mirra. 1967. *Blue Collar Marriage*. New York: Vintage Books.

Los Angeles Times. July 25, 1980.

Myrdal, A., and V. Klein. 1968. *Women's Two Roles*. London: Routledge & Kegan Paul.

Rivers, Caryl; Rosalind Barnett; and Grace Baruch. 1979. *Beyond Sugar and Spice*. New York: Putnam.

Rollin, Betty. 1971. "Motherhood: Who Needs It?" In Arlene and Jerome Skolnick, eds., *Family in Transition*. Boston: Little, Brown.

Rubin, Lillian Breslow. 1976. *Worlds of Pain: Life in the Working Class Family*. New York: Basic Books.

three

CONSEQUENCES OF SOCIAL INSTITUTIONS

chapter 11

Sexism

By Barbara Sinclair, Howard J. Sherman, and James L. Wood

Sexism, or the philosophy of male supremacy, is an ideology that serves to justify discrimination against the majority of Americans. Several discussions in Boxer and Quataert (1987) document the long and lamentable history of sexism in the Western world, as well as many attempts to challenge it. Sexism is similar in the pattern of discrimination and in ideology to racism. The black woman is held to be doubly "inferior" and suffers the most discrimination. In the last chapter we examined sexist oppression in the family and social activity. Here we examine sexist discrimination against women in economic activity outside the home.

In the nineteenth century, when most Americans worked on the farm, women not only cooked, washed, and took care of children, but they also did much farm labor, slaughtered and prepared animals, repaired the home, built furniture, and doctored the sick. In the twentieth century, women moved into industry, clerical, and service sectors. There was a slow increase in women working outside the home from 17 percent of the labor force in 1890 to 29 percent in 1940. Then during World War II and during the long economic expansion of the 1950s and 1960s, the participation of women in the labor force rose much more quickly. In 1986, women accounted for 44 percent of the labor force. Well over 52 million women hold paid jobs. Of all American males under 65 years old, 85 percent are in the labor force. Of all American women under 65 years old, 64 percent are in the labor force. Rather than the exception, the working woman has become the norm. More than 90 percent of all women now do paid work at some point in their lives; and, of course, almost all women also do unpaid work in the home. (Unless stated otherwise, all data are from U.S. government publications. See References for a listing.)

Figure 11.1 shows how the pattern of labor force participation by women of different ages has changed over the years. In 1890 most working women were young; after their early twenties, most dropped out of the labor force. By 1940, there were many more women working, but the pattern had not really changed; women still tended to quit working during the child-rearing years and not return. The 1960 pattern is dramatically different; women still left the labor force during their later twenties, but when their children reached school age, many returned. The 1975 curve again shows a major change; the tendency for women to drop out of the labor force during their late twenties and thirties is much less pronounced. Nowadays, fewer women leave the labor force during their child-rearing years, and of those who do, most return. Figures from 1980 show a culmination of this trend. Of women between 20 and 24, 67.7 percent are in the labor force. Of those in the 25 to 34 and the 35 to 44 age categories, slightly more than 65 percent are in the labor force. Thus, the tendency to drop out has almost completely disappeared.

According to the popular stereotype, women work for fun or for "pin money" and can therefore be paid less, hired last, and fired first. Actually women work for the same reason men do—they need the money. In fact, 44.5 percent of working women are single, divorced, separated, or widowed; many of them have children. About one-fifth of working women are married to men who make less than $10,000 a year. Together, these two groups of women who have to work to support their families comprise almost two-thirds of all working women.

Many families are reasonably comfortable financially only because the wife brings in a second income. Two-paycheck families account for 60 percent of all families with incomes over $20,000.

Women nevertheless are paid considerably less than men. In 1985, of all full-time workers, the earnings of white women were only 64 percent of those of white men—which was down from 65 percent in 1949. Black women working full-time earned only 57 percent as much as white men. One result of this income

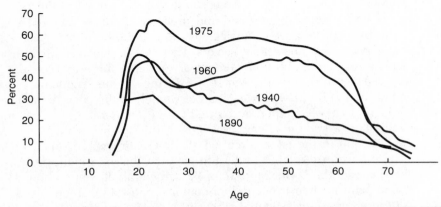

Figure 11.1 Patterns of labor force participation by women of different ages, 1890–1975. *Source:* U.S. Department of Labor, Employment and Training Report of the President, 1976, p. 143.

disparity is much more poverty among women. In 1986, almost half of all families below the poverty level were headed by women—that is, there was no husband present. Of all families headed by black women, 53 percent fell below the poverty level, and 30 percent of those headed by white women did (all data in this paragraph are from Winnick, forthcoming).

Some might assume that women receive lower wages because of less training and education. This is not the case. In spite of discrimination in higher education, the woman worker in 1984 had exactly the same median educational level as the male worker. In 1984, men with four years of high school earned $22,312 a year, while women with four years of high school earned only $14,076 (Bergmann, 1986, p. 67). When we compare income by sex at different levels of schooling, we find that a woman with a four-year high school education gets lower wages than a man with fewer than eight years of elementary school education. A woman with some college education is paid far less than a man with only some high school education. A woman with a college diploma is paid less than a man with a high school diploma.

When we compare men and women with the same education working at similar jobs, we get the same results. Women white-collar workers with four years of high school make only 56.6 percent as much as male white-collar workers with the same education; women managers and administrators with at least a college degree make 59.9 percent of what a man with a comparable job makes. The smallest percentage difference is for professional and technical workers with one to three years of college, and even in that category, women make less than 70 percent of what men do.

A Bureau of Labor Statistics study found that "in each of eight occupations studied for men and women in the same jobs, men always were paid more than women" (Women's Bureau, pp. 145–147). Thus female Class A accounting clerks received on the average 82 percent as much as males doing the same work. Women payroll clerks were paid 77 percent of what male payroll clerks received.

Many economists have long believed that better data on job qualifications would explain the earnings gap. In a study by the Institute for Social Research, however, more precise measures of qualifications were obtained. The study clearly showed the "differences in job qualifications such as education, on-the-job training, and general work experience fail to explain much of the very large wage gap between white men and other workers" (Institute for Social Research Newsletter, Spring 1978, p. 7).

The major cause of the wage gap between men and women is employment segregation. Employer prejudice and women's own internalized sex role socialization keep most women out of better-paying "men's" jobs and channel them into low-paying dead-end "women's" jobs.

Even in the most general classifications used by the Census Bureau, the pattern of segregation is apparent. Men dominate in the better-paying occupations: managers, administrators, and craft workers. Of course, not all male jobs are well paid; nonfarm laborers are mostly men. Clerical work, domestic service, and other service occupations, which are less prestigious and do not pay as well, are predominantly female. Of all women at work, 35 percent are clerical workers.

More detailed occupational classifications show that relatively few occupations are truly mixed in terms of gender, and that women are much more concentrated in proportionately fewer occupations than men are. In 1984, women made up 90 percent or more of the workers in 20 of the 335 occupations identified in government data (Bergmann, 1986, pp. 317–318). Twenty-six percent of all female workers were to be found in these occupations. There were many more predominantly male occupations—104 in which 90 percent of the workers were men and in which almost 40 percent of all men were employed.

In fact, 55 percent of working women are clerical workers, retail sales workers, sewers and stitchers, waitresses, private household workers, nurses, or non-college teachers. These are predominantly female occupations. Women make up more than 70 percent of retail salespersons and of non-college teachers. The other occupations listed here are over 80 percent female.

Although women account for 44.3 percent of what the census calls professional and technical workers, most are concentrated in the lower-paying professions. Thus, women account for 96.5 percent of all nurses, 65 percent of all social workers, 85 percent of all librarians, and 83.7 percent of all elementary school teachers. In the high-paying and high-prestige professions, the situation is very different. In 1980, women made up only 4 percent of engineers, 13 percent of lawyers, 13.4 percent of doctors, 4.3 percent of dentists, and 6.7 percent of architects. Yet these low figures were an improvement over 1960, when only 3.5 percent of lawyers and 6.8 percent of doctors were women. In the academic world the picture is somewhat better, but still points to inequality between the sexes. Women make up 33.9 percent of university and college teachers, but they are found mostly in the less prestigious schools and in the lower-ranking positions.

THEORIES OF DISCRIMINATION: RATIONALIZATIONS FOR SEGREGATION

Segregation in employment is frequently defended as natural; because of supposed biological and psychological differences, some jobs are considered to be obviously women's jobs and others to be just as obviously men's jobs. Yet there is no evidence to support such views. Biological differences may disqualify most women for a very few jobs. Few women are large enough and strong enough to be professional football players—but the same is true of men. About the only jobs for which the sex of the worker is crucial are semen donor and wet nurse.

The sexist defense of segregation, including "explanations" by some sociologists, often rests on the notion that women's jobs are natural extensions of women's family role. But the largest number of employed women are typists (including word processors) whose role at home calls for no typing at all. What women do at home does include cooking and child care, yet men have the top posts in restaurant cooking and in academic child-study projects.

In terms of tasks performed, the argument must be rejected. It is true, however, that in the world of work, as in the home, women are cast in the role of auxiliaries, as support personnel, while men are cast as the decision makers. Thus a good secretary is expected to do more than type and take dictation. She is often expected to take care of domestic-type details—getting coffee, reminding her boss of his appointments, shielding him from people he does not want to see, sometimes even buying birthday presents for members of his family. She is expected to do all this so that he can concentrate on really important tasks. In general, women's jobs are those considered too boring and too unimportant to occupy men. It is the notion that women are naturally subordinate to men that is carried over from the home to the employment world. Only when we realize this can we understand the seeming inconsistency in the sex stereotyping of particular jobs when compared with the tasks performed in the home.

Despite evidence to the contrary, many conservatives deny that there is much, if any, discrimination against women in the job market. Conservatives such as Milton Friedman claim that business would not want to discriminate by sex. Discrimination by business is irrational because business loses profits by it (See Friedman, 1957, pp. 108 ff.). The theory is this: Suppose there are equally qualified male and female workers. Suppose only males are hired because of prejudice. Female workers, because of discrimination against them elsewhere, could be hired more cheaply. Therefore, the capitalist who hires only males must be paying higher wages. Under competition there is no way to pass on this higher cost, so business must pay the price of the irrational exclusion of women. In Friedman's opinion, there is a high degree of competition in most of the U.S. economy; thus, capitalists who discriminate pay for it in much higher costs. He argues that, since capitalists who discriminate lose money, the prejudiced capitalists who are so irrational as not to hire qualified women will be bankrupted by the competition of those who do hire women at lower wages. Therefore, Friedman claims there is very little discrimination now and the little that does remain will disappear in long-run equilibrium under capitalism.

This theory implies that women are paid less because that is all they are worth. Most conservatives would no longer say that this is due to the female's natural inferiority; rather, they blame lower job qualifications and career interruptions. Yet recent studies have shown that neither can explain the wage gap. (See Bianchi and Spain, 1983, p. 24, for a list of such studies.)

Liberal economists, although they concede that there is a great deal of economic discrimination against women, agree with conservatives that capitalists actually lose profits thereby. Such discrimination, they say, means paying men for a job that women could do equally well for less pay. Thus economist Barbara Bergmann writes:

> We come . . . to the allegation, usually made by radicals out to discredit capitalism, that women's subjection is all a capitalist plot. Who benefits financially from maintenance of the *status quo*? The most obvious beneficiaries of prejudice against women are male workers. . . . (1973, p. 14)

So in her view it is not the capitalists but only the male workers who gain from discrimination. The capitalists who actually do the discriminating lose by it. But why do capitalists in business for profits systematically choose to lose money? She says they lose financially but gain psychologically: "It feels so good to have women in their place." Neither she nor anyone else with this view answers the obvious question: If it causes financial losses, why has such discrimination persisted so strongly under capitalism? (It should be noted that Barbara Bergmann's latest book [1986] is a hard-hitting attack on sex discrimination and a powerful critique of conservative economists' apologies for discrimination, but she still traces the discrimination to psychological biases rather than the institutions of capitalism.)

According to radicals, capitalists do *not* merely gain psychologically, and they do *not* incur financial losses from sex discrimination. On the contrary, capitalists gain from sexism both in *power* and in *profits*. Moreover, all workers, male as well as female, lose from sexist attitudes.

THEORIES OF DISCRIMINATION: THE PROFITABILITY OF SEXISM

How do capitalists profit from sexism? Most obviously, they use it as an excuse to pay women lower wages. The average woman worker's wage is only 68 percent of the average male worker's wage, whereas women account for 44 percent of all workers (Bergmann, 1986). On this basis, it may be calculated that if women were paid equal wages with men, it would be necessary to increase labor costs by about 14 percent. Men as well as women are paid less in the mostly female job categories. Take, as an example, the mostly female jobs of elementary school teacher, librarian, and social worker. All require a college education that is well above the average education of the entire work force, so we would expect these jobs to pay above average. Yet the mean annual earnings for men in these jobs was 14 percent—almost $3,000—below the mean for the average male worker. Women, of course, received even less; their mean annual earnings were 32.5 percent below those of the average male worker. Clearly sexism hurts the men in such jobs as well as the women.

Although men are negatively affected by sexism, clearly the consequences of sexism for women are particularly serious. In various chapters we have shown women being denied full access to employment opportunities, equal wages, education, and legal rights. In addition, recent discussions have shown health problems women suffer due to sexism, including unnecessary hysterectomies, mastectomies, and other major surgeries; failure of some male doctors to adequately comprehend female psychological and even physical responses (e.g., related to sex); and problems of obtaining basic medical care for poorer women and their children.

Unions

The existence of sexism makes it harder for the workers in mostly female jobs to unionize, which is one effective way of raising wages. For the entire country, one out of every four male workers but only one out of every seven female workers is unionized. One reason for the lower proportion of women in unions is the hostility or indifference of union men and union leaders toward women, an attitude fostered by their own prejudices. The degree of sexism in unions may be observed by the fact that most union executive boards are exclusively male, even though women do average about 20 percent of all union members. Even in unions such as the International Ladies Garment Workers, where women constitute over three-fourths of the members, only a few token women are on the executive board.

Union men often pay for their prejudices in broken unions and lower wages. In a strike by Standard Oil workers in San Francisco, the union was beaten because of its own prejudices against women. "Women at Standard Oil have the least chance for advancement and decent pay, and the union has done little to fight this. Not surprisingly, women formed the core of the back-to-work move that eventually broke the strike" (McAfee and Wood, 1972, p. 155).

The liberal economist Morris Silver finds that prejudice between black and white workers makes unionization and union activity more difficult and thus may lower the total wage bill. Therefore, "far from being indifferent to the existence of discriminatory attitudes on the part of workers, the capitalist gains from them and may find it profitable to invest in their creation" (Franklin and Resnick, 1973, p. 23). The same conclusion obviously holds for sexist attitudes toward women.

Other Factors

In addition to lower wages and weaker unions, discrimination helps provide a handy but disposable labor force. The process has been well described by Franklin and Resnick in the case of racism. If an employer has 10 black and 10 white workers, and must fire half for a couple of months, which will he fire? "If he is rational and seeks to minimize his labor turnover costs, he will lay off his ten black workers on the assumption that they will be unlikely to get permanent or better jobs elsewhere because of the discriminatory practices of other employers" (p. 20). Women workers are treated the same way by similarly "rational" employers.

Another reason sexism is profitable to capitalists is the closely related factor of savings on fringe benefits. It is now common for employers to keep a permanent crew of skilled white males plus a large number of temporary women (and black) workers. The temporary workers are usually fired in fewer than 90 days. Under most laws this is soon enough to disqualify them for fringe benefits, such as vacation pay, sick leave, extra medical benefits, employer contributions to pension plans, and unemployment insurance—all very important benefits to the workers and all costly to the employers.

Sexism is also profitable because it instills the desire to consume in women. The sexist image of the good woman shows her in her kitchen surrounded by the very latest gadgets, made up with miracle cosmetics, and using the latest laundry detergent, dishwasher soap, and wall cleaner. This image helps business sell billions of dollars of domestic, often unnecessary (or even harmful) goods.

Still another reason sexism is profitable is that women's unpaid work in the home is crucial to the paid labor force. In other words, women raise children to be workers, and they cook, clean for, and take care of adult male workers. These valuable services are unpaid. Such housework is valued at about one-fourth of the GNP, though it is not counted in the official GNP. If business had to pay women *in full* to raise, clean, and cook for the labor force, profits would be much lower.

Women in the family are not only profitable to capitalism because of their unpaid material labor, but perhaps even more for the psychological jobs they perform in the family. The women's role in the traditional family includes keeping the family safe and stable, which sometimes means "adjusting" it to harsh realities. She is expected to train her children to be "good" workers, to be quiet and disciplined, and yet at the same time to be enterprising and competitive with other workers (Morton, 1971, pp. 211–228). As a wife, she is often the one to caution her husband not to involve himself in a strike lest he lose his job. Both his wife's influence and his family responsibilities can combine to reduce the husband's mobility, his resistance to low wages, and his ability to strike. At the same time, wives may act as inadvertent lightning rods for the reactions of men to the system. If he is angered by the boss on the job, a husband can come home and act as a petty dictator to his wife and children. The national attention the media has given to wife battering has increased public awareness of this serious problem.

As a result of their dependent role in the traditional family, women are socialized to be passive, submissive, and docile as workers. Employers can also more easily exploit wives as cheap labor because women are often socialized to believe the myth that they work for pin money or just "supplementary" income. Yet this supplementary income is now massive enough so that many families depend on it.

The last but not the least important way in which capitalism profits from sexism comes in increased support for political stability. Women's psychological role in the traditional family has the same effects politically as it does economically. It tends to make a woman more fearful and conservative; she tends to influence her husband in this direction and to pass it on to her son and especially to her daughter.

In conclusion, sexism yields profits for capitalists by splitting unions and radical organizations, getting cheaper labor from women *and* men, obtaining a flexible reserve army of unemployed workers, saving on fringe benefits, giving an outlet to men's frustrations, providing unpaid maintenance for the labor force, and socializing women to be cautious economically and politically. On the other hand, sexism is costly to society, which loses many of the talents of women. It is frequently detrimental to women themselves, resulting in lower wages and unemployment, the stifling of their creativity and personality, and their subordinate position in the family. It is also frequently detrimental to male workers, as it results in lower wages for some, weaker unions, less political strength, and less satisfactory home lives.

HOW IS SEXISM CREATED AND MAINTAINED?

There is a myth that sexist discrimination is natural and eternal, has always existed and always will, and that men are born with this irrational prejudice. Yet anthropology shows many primitive societies in which men and women are roughly equal. In these societies, a subordinate attitude by women would have been harmful to social survival because women had to be strong and independent. In fact, sexism did not exist in most primitive societies. Sexism seems to have arisen with class-divided societies.

Even in American history, there have been times when this "eternal" prejudice suddenly changed. For example, in World War II women were badly needed by the government and capitalist employers. Suddenly it was discovered that women were perfectly competent to do all sorts of industrial jobs and that it was "natural" for them to do so.

Prejudice is not eternal or innate, but *is learned* through social propaganda, "respected" examples, and social pressures. Men and women are shaped by society to believe in sexism and to conform to sexist roles. The mechanisms of sexist socialization include the family, media, schools, churches, work situation, and even statements by political leaders (as we saw in Chapter 9).

Why is there sexist socialization? The most straightforward answer is that it is functional for those who have social, economic, and political power in our present system. It is functional in the sense that it allows them to maintain and extend their profits and power. This statement must be qualified to note that the sexist ideology originated in and was inherited from slave and feudal societies, where it also had the function of support for the status quo.

How do "the powers that be" control the direction of socialization in our society? The answer is that those male capitalists who benefit from sexism also control the media, jobs, schools, health-care facilities, churches, and political institutions. There are few women in top media positions, top educational positions, and top health positions, and very few women in top corporate or political positions.

This explanation, however, must not be understood in a simplistic fashion. It is often alleged that radicals think sexist oppression is a plot or conspiracy of capitalists. Sexism is not a conspiracy but, rather, the result of the *normal* functioning of our society. Consequently it is hard for most people to even imagine our society operating differently since all the parts fit together. Until recent years, for example, women were routinely excluded from various all-male clubs, such as the Bohemian Club of San Francisco, of which President Reagan has been a member. This exclusion was not questioned until it became apparent that important political and economic decisions were being made, directly or indirectly, in these clubs by men without any input from women. As a result, various court decisions lately have ruled against the all-male policies of such clubs.

However, suppose women suddenly got the top positions in the media, churches, hospitals, politics, and the economy. They would then quickly revolutionize our ideology by ridding it of sexism, or else they would just as quickly be pushed out again by a counterrevolution. Or suppose that somehow, even with males in all power positions, sexist socialization ended and was replaced by an ideology of male-female equality; women would then have to occupy half the top positions, or a revolutionary situation would occur—or else the ideology would revert to sexism. The society's ideology and power structure roughly conform to each other—except in revolutionary situations.

Perhaps the normal operation of our sexist society can best be seen as a circular process that reproduces itself over time. To understand the circular process, we must begin our analysis at an arbitrary point:

1. Children are socialized into sexist views by the family, education, religion, the media (books, radio, TV, magazines, newspapers, advertising), corporations, and politicians.
2. As a result of their sexist upbringing (and further sexist discrimination):
   a. Most women accept or are forced into subordinate positions in the family, economy, churches, schools, media, and politics.
   b. Most women pass on the sexist ideology to their children.
3. As a result of their sexist upbringing:
   a. Most men aspire to top positions of income, status, and power in all areas.
   b. Most men who acquire these positions do so as a result of the sexist views of, and discrimination by, the men of the previous generation who held these positions. Those men who win the top positions are not usually from working-class families, but are generally from capitalist families who hold the economic power (though they may sponsor or appoint their agents to some political positions).
   c. Capitalist men use their positions of power to reinforce sexist ideology in the schools, churches, economy, media, politics, and family. Capitalists support sexist ideology both because they believe in it and because it is in their interest (in terms of direct profits and in terms of political power).
4. The next generation repeats process 1.
5. The next generation repeats process 2.
6. The next generation repeats process 3.

This vicious circle—from sexist socialization to sexist power to sexist socialization, and so forth—is sometimes misread from a defeatist point of view. The defeatist view is that the circle has always existed and always will, and that nothing can be done about it. The grain of truth is that it *is* a self-perpetuating circle that *is* difficult to change. Yet there have been societies without sexism. Moreover, the process is not totally automatic, but is aided by overt discrimination and propaganda at each level. Finally, a large-scale socioeconomic change could lay the foundation for reversing the whole process.

SUMMARY

Women face many kinds of discrimination in American society, including social, political, and economic discrimination. The economic discrimination includes lower wages, segregation in employment, and higher rates of unemployment. What causes sex discrimination and sexist prejudice against women? The most conservative and unscientific view is that women are biologically inferior; consequently, women get what they deserve, so there is no discrimination. Thus, lower wages merely reflect the lower economic productivity of women.

Liberal social scientists have shown that women are the equals of men in every way important for virtually any economic position or job. Women are not only equal in intelligence, but in some societies it is women who carry the heaviest physical burdens. If women get lower wages, they argue, it may be partly due to previous discrimination in training, as well as to the irrational sexist attitudes of male employers.

Radical social scientists do not deny previous discrimination or irrational sexist attitudes by employers and some unions. However, they emphasize that the capitalist system also profits from sex discrimination. Capitalists make extra *economic* profit because sexist prejudices divide and weaken unions; because women are paid lower wages in those sectors where they are allowed to work; because women are a handy reserve army of unemployed that can be hired in boom periods; and because various women are hired for such short time periods that they do not qualify for fringe benefits. Capitalists also profit *politically* because most women are socially conditioned to be nonpolitical, and because sexist prejudices divide and weaken liberal, as well as radical, social movements. The capitalist-controlled media of news and entertainment, educational systems, health institutions, and religious institutions all continue to promote sexist stereotypes, which liberal and radical sociologists must, in turn, critically evaluate.

SUGGESTED READINGS

Much of this chapter is based on Barbara Sinclair Deckard's *The Women's Movement*, 3d ed. (New York: Harper & Row, 1983). One very useful article is by Al Szymanski, "The Socialization of Women's Oppression: A Marxist Theory of the Changing Position of Women in Advanced Capitalist Society," *The Insurgent Sociologist* 4 (Winter 1976): 31–61. For a critique of Szymanski by a feminist collective and his reply, see *The Insurgent Sociologist* 4 (Spring 1976): 35–45. For an excellent, strongly argued analysis of the basis of sexism, which is critical of much traditional thinking, see Gail Omvedt, " 'Patriarchy': The Analysis of Women's Oppression," *The Insurgent Sociologist* 13 (Spring, 1986): 30–50. Two important books on a very negative manifestation of sexism and ways to prevent it are Pauline Bart and Patricia H. O'Brien, *Stopping Rape* (New York: Pergamon Press, 1985), and William B. Sanders, *Rape and Woman's Identity* (Beverly Hills, CA: Sage, 1980). The best source of data on women in U.S. industry and the professions is the U.S. government, especially the Women's Bureau of the Department of Labor in *Employment and Earnings*. A good summary with an extensive bibliography is Susanne M. Bianchi and Daphne Spain, *American Women: Three Decades of Change* (U.S. Department of Commerce Special Demographic Analyses CDS-80-8, August 1983). An excellent survey is Barbara Bergmann's *The Economic Emergence of Women* (New York: Basic Books, 1986). For many excellent discussions of sexism and efforts to eliminate it, from 1500 to the modern era, see Marilyn J. Boxer and Jean H. Quataert, eds., *Connecting Spheres: Women in the Western World, 1500 to the Present* (New York: Oxford University Press, 1987).

REFERENCES

Bergmann, Barbara 1973. "Economics of Women's Liberation." *Challenge* 16 (May–June).
——. 1986. *The Economic Emergence of Women*. New York: Basic Books.
Bianchi, Susanne M., and Daphne Spain. 1983. *American Women: Three Decades of Change*. U.S. Department of Commerce Special Demographic Analyses (August).

Boxer, Marilyn J., and Jean H. Quataert, eds. 1987. *Connecting Spheres: Women in the Western World, 1500 to the Present*. New York: Oxford University Press.

Franklin, Ray, and Solomon Resnick. 1973. *The Political Economy of Racism*. New York: Holt, Rinehart and Winston.

Friedman, Milton. 1957. *Capitalism and Freedom*. Chicago: University of Chicago Press.

Institute for Social Research Newsletter. Spring 1978.

McAfee, Kathy, and Myrna Wood. 1972. "Bread and Roses." In Roberta Salper, ed., *Female Liberation*. New York: Knopf.

Morton, Peggy. 1971. "A Woman's Work Is Never Done." In Edith Altback, ed., *From Feminism to Liberation*. Cambridge, MA: Schenkman.

Rytina, Nancy. 1981. "Occupational Segregation and Earnings Differences by Sex." *Monthly Labor Review* 104 (January).

Winnick, Andrew. Forthcoming. "The Changing Distribution of Income and Wealth in the U.S., 1960–1985." In Patricia Voydanoff and Linda Majka, *Families and Economic Distress*. Beverly Hills, CA: Sage.

Women's Bureau, U.S. Department of Labor. 1975. *Handbook on Women Workers*.

chapter *12*

Racism

American sociology has traditionally shown much interest in the study of race and ethnic relations. Years ago the famous "Chicago School" of sociology pioneered various investigations of groups based on skin color, national origin, and religion—that is, racial and ethinic groups (Lal, 1986). Technically speaking, groups based on skin color are racial groups, whereas groups based on national origin or religion are ethnic groups; yet more recently the term ethnicity has been used to cover all three groups (Yinger, 1985; Glazer and Moynihan, 1975, pp. 1–26, 1963, pp. 310–315). Motivated by the racial riots of the 1960s, the recent immigration to the United States, and the politico-economic development of Third World countries (countries in Asia, Africa, the Middle East, and Latin America, whose inhabitants are mostly darker skinned), the study of race and ethnic relations has been invigorated in recent years (Pettigrew, 1985; Olzak, 1983; Massey, 1981; Portes and Canak, 1981).

Radical sociology has been particularly concerned with one aspect of the study of race and ethnic relations: the analysis of *inequality* between such racial and ethnic groups as blacks and whites, Protestants and Jews or Catholics, and Chicanos and Anglos.

Traditional sociology has also been concerned with inequality, but in addition it has focused on various other issues (Hirschman, 1983). Besides its own generally inadequate analysis of inequality, traditional sociology has studied ethnic communities, the personalities and abilities of ethnic group members, the political leanings of ethnic groups, ethnic cultures, ethnic families, and ethnic identity (Glazer and Moyhihan, 1975). In traditional sociology these issues are often studied in isolation from the problem of inequality—or with insufficient attention to that problem.

We will first look at patterns of inequality between ethnic groups in the United States. Then we will examine a few important traditional explanations of ethnic inequality and indicate specific weaknesses of these theories. Finally, we will turn to a radical analysis of racial and ethnic inequality, focusing on racism and how racism is built into the structure of modern capitalism.

PATTERNS OF INEQUALITY

Black families have much lower incomes than white families. Because of the victories of the militant civil rights movement of the 1960s, however, new laws against discrimination were passed. The median family income of blacks rose from 54 percent of white income in 1964 to 61 percent in 1969 (Sherman, 1987). In the 1970s and 1980s—particularly during the Nixon, Ford, and Reagan administrations—blacks no longer made relative progress. Some factors holding them back were the fact of poor enforcement of the antidiscrimination laws, reduced federal spending in areas vital to blacks, and the severe recessions of 1975 and 1982. For all of these reasons, black family income fell back to 55 percent of white family income in 1982. Looking only at full-time male workers (to leave aside issues of unemployment and sex discrimination that influence family income), black men's earnings were 66 percent of white men's earning in 1960, rose to 77 percent in 1975, and then fell to 70 percent in 1985 (see Winnick, forthcoming).

In 1985, 31 percent of all black families were below the official (understated) poverty level. According to the Census Bureau (1986) the median wealth (assets minus liabilities) of black families was only $3,397, while the median wealth of white families was $39,135.

Black poverty was reflected in deaths of blacks. In 1984, infant mortality among blacks was 19 deaths per thousand live births, but among whites infant mortality was only 10 deaths per thousand. A black male could expect to live 66 years, whereas a white male could expect to live 72 years. Life expectancy was 74 years for black women, compared with 79 years for white women.

One of the reasons for the number of blacks living in poverty is the job discrimination that results in much higher unemployment rates among blacks than among whites. Decade after decade, black unemployment rates are more than double those for whites. In December 1985, for example, black unemployment was 15 percent, compared with 6 percent for whites. Black teenage workers face particularly severe discrimination; in December 1985, their unemployment rate was 42 percent, compared with 16 percent for white teenagers. All of these unemployment figures are official U.S. Labor Department data, but the official data are badly understated for a number of reasons—for example, a person who wants to work full time, but can get a job for only one hour a week, is counted as employed.

Black females are even worse off than black males because they suffer from both racist and sexist discrimination. Whereas the median black two-parent family in 1984 earned $23,418, the median black female-headed family earned only $8,648. Black female adult unemployment in 1983 in a period of economic recovery was still 17 percent, although white female unemployment had fallen to 8 percent. Most of the poverty suffered by black women, however, was because they were earning less than poverty-level wages at full-time jobs. In 1985, full-time black women workers earned only 57 percent as much as white males, a combined effect of racism and sexism (see Winnick, forthcoming).

In the political sphere, although blacks comprise 11 percent of the U.S. population, in 1987 blacks accounted for only 5 percent of the U.S. House of Representatives. Moreover, there are no blacks in the U.S. Senate. Furthermore, blacks made up only 4 percent of state legislators and less than 1 percent of elected city and county officials in the United States—even though blacks have broken through to become mayors of some major U.S. cities.

Another basic area of continuing discrimination is education. In 1984, in the age group 25 to 34, only 14 percent of blacks had graduated from college, whereas 25 percent of whites had done so. Most blacks who dropped out of college were forced out by economic pressures. National data have shown that "blacks have a smaller presence on American campuses than they did six years ago" (*New York Times*, 1987). Even with a college education, blacks face discrimination. The unemployment rate in 1984 for whites with one to three years of college was 6 percent, but it was 13 percent for blacks with the same education. In fact, black college graduates had about the same unemployment rate as white high school graduates. Moreover, in 1985 black male college graduates had only 78 percent of the income of white male college graduates, while black female college graduates had only 64 percent of the income of white male college graduates (see Winnick, forthcoming).

Finally, there is continuing job discrimination against blacks. It is worth examining the data historically to see both progress and continued discrimination. In 1890, 88 percent of blacks were still in agriculture and domestic service; only 6 percent were in manufacturing (Boston, 1985, p. 53). In 1940, on the eve of World War II, 20 percent of blacks were in manufacturing, but three-quarters of all blacks still lived in the South and most were rural. Then World War II necessitated that millions of blacks take manufacturing jobs in the cities. By 1960, over 40 percent of blacks were in the North and 73 percent of all blacks were urban dwellers. Nevertheless, black men and women in 1987 were still overrepresented among poorly paid unskilled factory workers (20 percent) and domestic servants (53 percent). Blacks represent only a very small percentage of highly paid managers (3 percent) and professional and technical workers (5 percent).

Trends

Trend data show the situation worsening rather than improving in several aspects. Black income was 55 percent of white income in 1945, then rose to 61 percent in 1970, but declined back to 55 percent in 1984. The difference between black and white unemployment rates was *increasing* in the past decade. Moreover, blacks constitute a growing percentage of workers in "declining job categories"— that is, unskilled jobs and industries with no employment growth. Black also constitute an increasing percentage (now over 25 percent) of all the long-term, or permanently, unemployed. A considerable amount of racial discrimination in housing has been documented for the 1980s (Yinger, 1986).

A comparison of the 1970s and 1980s points to three important trends in the pattern of racial inequality: economic improvement for some blacks in the 1970s, economic decline for many other blacks in the 1970s, and decline in economic and educational improvement for most blacks in the 1980s.

Supported by affirmative action programs that encouraged the hiring of minority group members, well-educated blacks had increased opportunities to achieve middle- or upper-middle-class status during the 1970s. Affirmative action policies enabled blacks to have their education more directly translated into income and housing achievements. A recent study by the U.S. Conference of Mayors (1986) reported that affirmative action programs "have been extremely successful." They have "eliminated a lot of institutional barriers" and, for example, helped obtain a Los Angeles city work force that is 23.6 percent black, 16.8 percent Latino, 9.2 percent Asian, and 50.1 percent white (Granos, 1986). In comparison, a study of the Los Angeles work force before affirmative action showed minority groups to be significantly less represented (Greer, 1960). The U.S. Conference of Mayors (1986) noted that affirmative action programs have led to "improved efficiency and productivity, more job satisfaction, better labor-management relations . . . , and improved public perception of the quality of services the cities deliver."

The achievements for blacks in the 1970s are reflected in a black suburbanization trend during the decade. "From 1970 to 1980, there was a 70 percent increase in the number of black people finding the wherewithal, the impetus, the access to live outside central cities" (Blonston, 1986, p. C–1). This meant that the suburban portion of the U.S. black population increased from 16.1 percent to 23.3 percent during the 1970s (ibid.).

Although blacks had more opportunities to obtain suburban housing in the 1970s, they earned considerably less money than their white suburban counterparts—$20,063 versus $30,421 in 1980 (U.S. Census, 1980). However, just as significantly, the black suburbanites earned considerably more money than blacks in the central cities—$20,063 versus $13,362 in 1980 (U.S. Census, 1980). Thus, several million urban blacks remained confined to poverty status—36 percent of black families in 1982. Indeed, Blonston (1986) and others have argued that the suburbanization of blacks, and the related mobility to middle-class status for them, split the black community along class lines during the 1970s and correspondingly weakened black ethnic identity for some mobile blacks. While the suburban blacks were increasingly able to realize the benefits of their education, many urban blacks continued to suffer from racial discrimination and related financial problems (Wilson, 1980).

Reaganomics in the 1980s has been difficult in general for the black community. The black poor were among those seriously effected by the Reagan budget cuts in the early 1980s. In addition, the Census Bureau (1986) found that "the net worth of the typical white American household in 1984 was [almost] 12 times as great as the figure for the typical black household and [almost] eight times as great as the typical net worth of Latinos." The net worth, or wealth, of a household refers to its total assets (such as ownership of cars, houses, stocks, saving accounts, and so forth) minus its total debts. Overall, the median net worth for white households in 1984 was $39,135 versus $3,397 for black households and $4,913 for Latino households (Census Bureau, 1986) These are enormous disparities between ethnic groups and indicate, more than yearly income figures, the extent to which scarce resources are still differentially allocated by race and ethnic background in the United States. To further indicate the difficulties that persist in the 1980s for various minority groups, "nearly one-third of all black households and one-quarter of Latinos had no assets or were in debt." In contrast, "fewer than one in 10 whites had no assets at all" (Census Bureau, 1986).

An important aspect of the 1980s decline in economic improvement for minority groups is their declining numbers in graduate schools. This has significant implications for the future since technically trained professionals come from graduate schools. Thus, any decline in graduate school enrollment for minority groups will mean fewer well-trained professionals for that group in the future.

Buttressed by affirmative action guidelines, the 1970s showed an increase in minority graduate students. This trend was reversed by the mid-1980s, partly due to the Reagan administration's opposition to affirmative action programs. According to American Council on Education official Reginald Wilson (1986), "Black [and Latino] enrollments in graduate school and professional schools are actually declining after increases in the 1960s and 1970s." The positive contributions of affirmative action hiring programs noted by the U.S. Conference of Mayors (1986) will surely be lessened by a political attack on affirmative action educational and employment programs. Ethnic minorities have benefited from these programs, as well as the larger society.

It is not possible to detail the comparative facts for other minorities in America because of lack of space; however, the facts are often quite similar. The degree of inequality is particularly accentuated for two other important minority groups, Americans of Mexican descent and Americans of Puerto Rican descent. Actually, although there might be some controversy over recent trends, most writers on the subject, conservative and liberal as well as radical, seem largely to agree on the present extent of inequality. The argument comes over the causes and the solutions.

TRADITIONAL EXPLANATIONS OF INEQUALITY*

Biological Determinism

The most conservative view is—now as always—that there are inherited biological differences, making the blacks (or Mexicans, Native Americans, Jews, Catholics, ad infinitum) intellectually and physically inferior. This so-called biological inferiority is seen as the cause of lower income, less educational achievement, poor housing, and so forth. Moreover, these groups are seen as lazy and liking to live in squalor. These arguments are not backed by any scientific evidence. Races are, of course,

*We are indebted to Robert Blauner's very useful discussion of the major theories of race and ethnic relations in America. See Robert Blauner, *Racial Oppression in America* (New York: Harper & Row, 1972), Introduction, pp. 2–18.

defined by their superficial physical differences, but there are no important biological differences among the races of humankind, much less any inherited intellectual differences. As various researchers have noted, there are greater biological variations within racial and ethnic groups than between these groups.

Racists have often used the theory of biological inferiority to the detriment of oppressed groups. For example, slave owners in the American South before the Civil War claimed that all blacks were biologically inferior. According to the stereotype, all blacks were stupid and lazy, shuffled their feet when they walked, but liked to sing and dance (to celebrate their happy lives as slaves). The stereotype also claimed that blacks were oversexed. This stereotype provided an excuse for white men to rape black women, while lynching black men for unsubstantiated rapes of white women.

There are still those who claim that all blacks are mentally inferior. For example, in 1973 Dr. William Shockley, a white physicist, claimed that data "from Negro populations with average IQs of 80 in Georgia and 90 in California [shows] that each 1 percent of Caucasian ancestry raises average IQ by one point for these low IQ populations" (United Press, 1973). So the blood of the "master race" raises intelligence! Yet, over and over again, anthropologists and psychologists have demonstrated that so-called IQ scores are related to socioeconomic status and cultural background (because of the way the tests are designed), but are not related to race, religion, national origin, or sex. For example, if an IQ test were constructed where all the references and terminology came from life in the black ghetto, the average score for whites would be lower than the average score for blacks—but that would not mean that the average white is inherently less intelligent than the average black. Here the test would simply favor blacks instead of whites, who are typically favored on such IQ tests.

Numerous sociological studies have found people from all racial and ethnic groups to have equal potential for any job or any kind of social behavior. It is social conditioning that gives each group different cultural behavior. There is a wide range of cultures, but none result from inferior or superior racial abilities. The differences are due to social influences:

> Englishmen reared in China can learn to speak flawless Chinese; American Negroes who attend conservatories write symphonies in the classical European tradition; the Japanese display not the slightest hereditary disability in acquiring a knowledge of Western electronics; Jews brought up in Germany have German food preferences, while those brought up in Yemen acquire Yemenite tates. (Harris, 1963, p. 132)

"Deficient" Ethnic Cultures

Most sociologists are sufficiently liberal to acknowledge that blacks are not biologically inferior to whites. Still some traditional sociologists wish to point to some group deficiency to account for inequality. Instead of emphasizing deficient biological makeup, one important school of traditional sociology has emphasized the presumed deficiencies of ethnic culture and social organization (Glazer and Moynihan, 1963; Sowell, 1981). Blacks are said to have "a set of beliefs that favor a social dependency role for the Negro rather than one of independence; . . . and low aspiration patterns that set limited achievement goals" (Ferman et al., 1968, p. 108). This is one statement of the "culture of poverty" argument. Blacks are seen as having low incomes, poor housing, and bad jobs because their cultural beliefs do not sufficiently emphasize upward mobility, self-confidence, the necessity of a college education, and delayed gratification of needs in order to study and save money. These cultural beliefs are thus supposed to account for inequality of income, jobs, housing, and the like.

This theory of inequality is weak on several grounds. There are studies indicating that blacks of a similar social strata and social class background have occupational aspirations similar to whites (Willie, 1975, pp. 406–417). In Chapter 3, we found much behavior affected by class position: working class, capitalist class, or middle class (small farmers, small-business people). That chapter also stressed differences within the working class among different strata. *Strata*—or levels of distinction—are defined by various characteristics such as manual or mental labor, or lower-, middle-, or upper-income levels within the working class. Black students from the middle- and upper-income levels of the working class do have a forward-looking value system with regard to educational and occupational mobility. They are quite willing—as the Protestant ethic dictates—to work hard, delay gratification, and be independent in order to achieve material benefits. Even black students from the lower-income levels of the working class have moderately high educational and occupational aspirations. Blauner has also shown that many blacks have a strong adherence to both mobility values and to black culture and the black ethnic group. Furthermore, he argues—quite contrary to traditional sociology—that for various black students, adherence to black culture can function *in favor* of upward social mobility (Blauner, 1972, chap. 4, especially p. 150).

It is only in the very lowest income levels (the strata of the working class below the poverty level) that blacks do show a divergence from Protestant ethic, mobility-oriented aspirations. For this group, there is much greater concern with basic survival than with upward mobility. "Hustling" for basic needs—and acceptance of low-paid jobs—often takes precedence over concerns of achieving middle-class status.

The difference in aspirations between the lowest income level of black workers and the middle-income level of white workers represents a basically rational response to a racist society. In addition to rational response, however, both blacks and whites are also influenced by continued use of stereotypes in television, newspapers, movies, and school textbooks. Still, racism—and unfavorable class position—are real disadvantages to lower-income level blacks; while the reverse is true for middle-income level whites. These favored white students ought to have relatively high aspirations because there are many more opportunities awaiting them than is the case for lower-income level blacks. In fact, it would often be quite unrealistic for lower-income level blacks to aspire to be head of a big company, graduate from a prestigious medical school, or become a physicist. The society has "loaded the dice" against lower-income level blacks through hundreds of years of subservient position in society, antiblack propaganda by the media, church, and educational system, and institutionalized racist practices in school and work. Thus, lesser aspirations reflect lower-income level blacks' awareness of this situation.

With the same kind of realistic understanding of discrimination, Chicanos have been even less likely than blacks to feel that their chances of success are good in a racist society. Nevertheless, they, too, have upward mobility aspirations, contrary to many incorrect stereotypes of Mexican-Americans. Ironically one interesting study of the mass media finds that minorities, such as blacks and Chicanos, are partly conditioned by television—with all the pictures of affluent families and tales of fantastic success stories—to have success and mobility aspirations, even though most of the successful families portrayed are white (Wright et al., 1973, pp. 43–60; also see Gerson, 1966, pp. 40–50).

With regard to self-confidence and presumed low self-esteem among blacks, recent studies indicate that this may be largely a false myth (Porter and Washington, 1979). Even before the slogan and ideology of "Black is Beautiful," a sociological survey noted little difference between black students' self-esteem and that of other groups (Rosenberg, 1965). An earlier survey had noted that black southern youngsters, who were exposed to daily racism, seemed to have a surprisingly high level of confidence, self-respect, and self-esteem (Coles, 1965, pp. 1121–1132). The "Black is Beautiful" ideology has undoubtedly accentuated these trends.

In sum, the culture and self-esteem patterns of black and other minority communities are not generally averse to occupational and educational upward mobility. Available evidence indicates that blacks and other minorities would welcome it. It is also true that many of the lowest-income level blacks—like the lowest-income level whites and other groups—do not adhere to Protestant ethic values (Lewis, 1959). But the real problem that faces minority groups is not lack of adherence to these values. Rather, the problem that faces them, as we will see, is the existence of artificial barriers set up by the white community that impede minority group progress.

"Deficient" Social Organization

Traditional sociology has also attempted to explain ethnic inequality by pointing to presumed deficiencies in the social organization of oppressed groups. The classic attempt to do this is the government-sponsored Moynihan Report (U.S. Department of Labor, 1965; reprinted in Rainwater and Yancey, 1967, pp. 41–124). Authored by Daniel P. Moynihan, Harvard professor and later holder of high government offices including U.S. senator, the Moynihan Report was much criticized from the start (Rainwater and Yancey, 1967). In it, Moynihan tried to argue that many problems blacks suffer—such as bad jobs, juvenile delinquency, low education, and poor housing—could be explained by the allegedly disorganized black family. For Moynihan, a disorganized family meant one with no father present, which anthropologists call a "matrifocal" (or mother-centered) family. By this argument, families with no father are unable to provide the moral and material resources to elevate their children's status with regard to education, occupation, housing, desire for middle-class respectability, and the like. At the end of his essay, Moynihan concludes with a policy-oriented summary that focuses on the black family structure as the primary source of black inequality. He says that this family structure should thus be the focus of "national effort." Moynihan states:

> The policy of the United States is to bring the Negro American to full and equal sharing in the responsibilities and rewards of citizenship. To this end, the programs of the Federal government bearing on this objective shall be designed to have the effect, directly or indirectly, of enhancing the stability and resources of the Negro American family. (Rainwater and Yancey, 1967, p. 94)

To indicate that this is not only an historical issue, the Moynihan Report was the subject of a Bill Moyers television documentary in the mid-1980s (Sharbutt, 1986). However, Moyers acknowledged that black leader Jesse Jackson would think "it's probably racist in its premise" (Sharbutt, 1986, p. 4).

Moynihan's terminology is not clear and reflects some myths and prejudices about family life. There are two-parent families, with both mother and father—but the fathers are not always the dominant head of the household, as Moynihan implies. Either mother or father may be dominant or they may both play an equal role—though this equality is still unusual in our society, as we have seen in previous chapters. There are also one-parent families as a result of divorce or death of one parent, but not all of these are headed by mothers, as some are headed by fathers.

One problem with Moynihan's kind of analysis concerns the arguable assumptions that one-parent, mother-headed families are disorganized, and that they prepare a person less for upward mobility. A fatherless family is organized on a different basis from one with both parents present, but a family organized around a mother does not indicate instability. Family instability would be better indicated by the existence of high levels of family tensions, conflicts, and anxieties, which Moynihan nowhere documents.

In addition, the link between the one-parent, mother-headed family and upward mobility is not documented by Moynihan. Why should it be the case that mothers are less able to convey mobility aspirations to their children than fathers? On the contrary, some studies have shown that lower-income level black women are more tied into the occupational system than lower-income level black men (Glazer and Moynihan, 1963, pp. 38–40). Thus, these women may be more able than men to instill the ethics of hard work in their children.

On the other hand, one-parent, mother-headed families may be less financially capable of providing their children with excellent educational or occupational opportunities. In other chapters, we show that sexist practices diminish single women's chances of getting high-paying jobs that can support expensive college educations for their children. Similarly, single women—due to sexist discrimination—often do not have the occupational contacts that are useful to young people once they finish their education.

However, it is unlikely that many lower-income level black men—the fathers of these families—have the financial resources or occupational connections that would greatly help their children secure a good education and obtain a good job. Moynihan does not show to what extent the lower-income level black males are able to assist in getting their children good educations and good jobs. The low incomes of these black males would likely prevent them from offering as much assistance to their children as they would like. Thus, inequality for black children is more an issue of poor black families being unable to help their children, as do white middle-income level families (Sussman, 1953, p. 27). It is not primarily a psychological issue of one-parent, mother-centered families.

A major analytical criticism of this family theory of black inequality is that it directs attention away from other key variables that are stronger determinants of inequality. Although Moynihan is not totally unaware of these other factors, his approach does minimize them. In particular, his family approach draws attention away from the fact that black inequality—such as high unemployment or low-wage jobs—is best explained by analyzing the racist character of most American institutions, which we will do below. A proper analysis, from our point of view, would switch the focus from the social organization of the black ethnic group (here, the black family) and would point to the social organization of the larger society (here, the political and economic organization as it pertains to race).

A central problem with the thesis that family disorganization leads to black inequality is that Moynihan did not systematically take social strata or social class into account (Rainwater and Yancey, 1967, p. 57). We know—as does Moynihan—that families in the middle and capitalist classes are more likely to have a father present than families in the lower income levels of the working class. Moynihan should have consistently taken social strata into account when examining the presumed impact of the mother-headed family on black inequality.

One analysis that did take social strata, as measured by family income, into account was done by Lee Rainwater (1966, esp. table 1, p. 181). Rainwater used the same census data as Moynihan did when he attempted to show that more black families are one-parent, female-headed than white families. Rainwater showed that 18 percent of rural black families making less than $3000 were one-parent, female-headed. It was also true, however, that 12 percent of rural white families with incomes under $3000 were one-parent, female-headed. Furthermore, only 8 percent of urban black families making $3000 and over were one-parent, female-headed, whereas 4 percent of urban white families making over $3000 were one-parent, female-headed. Thus, *the differences between different strata or income-levels of the working class are much greater than the differences by race* (see the excellent article by Darity, 1987).

But the issue is families under the poverty level, Moynihan would say. For urban black families earning *less* than $3000, we do find that a large 47 percent were one-parent, female-headed (Rainwater, 1966, esp. table 1, p. 181). However, a similarly large 38 percent of urban white families making less than $3000 also had one parent and were female-headed.

Thus, no matter what the comparison, it is clear that the position in social structure, measured by family income level, has a decisive impact on family behavior. Poorer families—*white or black*—will much more likely be one-parent, female-headed than better-off families regardless of race. Part of the reason is that it is simply harder to keep a poor family together. Poverty brings many anxieties and additional impediments to smooth family cooperaion. It is true that race plays some independent role in predicting one-parent, female-headed families. That is, we do find some smaller differences between blacks and whites even when income level is taken into account. This probably indicates that poverty is harder on the black family than on the white family. For example, it is harder for blacks than whites to get other employment once a job has been lost. When blacks are poor, they face poverty and racism. In contrast, poor whites "only" face problems associated with poverty (for example, difficulties paying rent). But income level has a much stronger effect on the likelihood of one-parent, female-headed families than does race by itself. Even Moynihan appears to recognize this when he acknowledges the harsh impact of unemployment on the black family, and when he says, "higher family incomes are unmistakably associated with greater family stability . . ." (Rainwater and Yancey, 1967, p. 67).

As a result, it is more reasonable to argue that low incomes cause one-parent, female-headed families among blacks, rather than one-parent, female-headed families cause low incomes and other forms of inequality. Black families that have higher incomes have relatively few one-parent, female-headed households, similar to better-off white families. Also, low-income black families have many more one-parent, female-headed households, as do poor white families. Hence it appears that the social strata of blacks affects the likelihood of one-parent, mother-headed families, as well as the likelihood of unequal share of such resources as education, food, recreation, housing, power, and status. It is much less obvious that a one-parent, female-headed family, by itself, has a significant impact on inequality. Thus, to reduce the level of black inequality it is necessary to break down racist barriers facing blacks, and for the general social position of blacks to significantly improve. These goals—not black family goals—should be the proper focus for "national effort."

Assimilation and Equality

A prominent theory of racial and ethnic inequality argues that inequality is only temporary. It is said that various ethnic groups, such as the Irish, Jews, and Italians, began at the bottom of American society, but that after a few generations of urban experience, many group members were assimilated into the larger society and attained middle-class status or higher. Oscar Handlin (1957, pp. 42–43) has noted that each racial or ethnic minority was greeted with bigotry and discrimination by the larger society. However, Handlin and others argue that nevertheless all groups, in time and with increased urban experience, would overcome the initial negative response by the White Anglo-Saxon Protestant (WASP) majority. Thus eventually all racial and ethnic groups would assimilate into the "melting pot" of the larger society and attain some measure of equality.

This overly optimistic view of race and ethnic relations has been formulated in sociological terms by Robert Park (1950). In his theory of the "race relations cycle," Park saw two or more ethnic groups coming into *contact,* as when blacks, Jews, or Irish came to the White Anglo-Saxon-Protestant–dominated United

States. After a period of contact, Park felt that these new groups would then enter a period of *conflict* over material goods, such as jobs and housing, or over cultural values, such as different religions (for example, part of the conflict between Protestants and Catholics in Northen Ireland is religious in nature). Although he is not explicit about how the conflicts get resolved, he says the groups then move to a period of *accommodation* where they learn to live together more peacefully. The black slaves, for example, initially struggled against capture in Africa, only to be "accommodated" to the slave society in the southern United States. A less one-sided example of accommodation would be the Irish and Jews who eventually settled for working-class jobs with the possibility of upward mobility for their children.

After accommodation, the next stage in Park's cycle is *assimilation*. Here the minority group is seen to take over the culture of the dominant society, in particular, to accept its "core values." To varying extents, Jews, Italians, Irish, blacks, and other ethnic groups have absorbed such WASP values as upward mobility, economic and social competitiveness, individual rather than group loyalty, political democracy, secularized religion, delayed gratification of needs, and focus on the nuclear rather than the extended family.

The recent Asian immigration to the United States is instructive in this regard. Migrants like the "boat people" from the Vietnam War and other Southeast Asians such as Cambodians and Laotians, along with immigrants from Hong Kong, Japan, and the Philippines, have introduced a new dynamic element in American society since the mid-1970s. Observers have pointed to the rapid assimilation and upward mobility of numerous members of this group. Parallels have been drawn to the Jewish immigrants and their children in the late nineteenth and early twentieth centuries, and to the Cuban immigrants in the early 1960s.

The Asian proportion of student bodies at some prestigious American universities has significantly increased during the last decade or so. For example, the Asian proportion of the student body at the University of California, Berkeley, has significantly increased during this period and now constitutes about one-quarter of the enrollment. By historical comparison, Asians only constituted a few percent of this student body in the 1950s and 1960s. A recent issue of the University of California at Berkeley alumni magazine, *The California Monthly* (1986), devoted considerable attention to this topic, citing relevant data and interesting interviews with students.

Though the educational and economic mobility of these recent immigrants has been impressive, difficult problems—including language, cultural, and financial problems—similarly exist for many members of this group. A study of one of the most successful Asian groups, Japanese Americans, shows that upward mobility and above-average incomes do characterize the group as a whole (Woodrum, 1981). However, the same study also shows that discrimination against this group persists and that they receive somewhat less income, relative to their qualifications, than whites do. Other Asian groups would likely receive even less income for their qualifications. Some Vietnamese students in the United States, for example, stated they have been called "gooks"—a racial slur for supporters of Vietnamese communists—even though in Vietnam they and their families were anticommunist. So, the benefits of mobility are often tempered by persisting discrimination against these new immigrants.

As Milton Gordon (1964) has shown, cultural assimilation is not the only type of assimilation. Just as important is *structural* assimilation, which is admittance into the dominant group's social institutions of work, family, social clubs, schools and universities, and residences. Gordon's book shows that there has been much less structural assimilation than cultural assimilation because of discrimination against these minorities by the WASP majority.

Although he is not clear how it comes about, Park sees the stage of assimilation leading to the final stage of *amalgamation,* or the biological unification of different groups through marriage and family. Park viewed Hawaii as an excellent example of amalgamation, since groups such as whites and Asians did marry and have children. However, upon looking at U.S. data, Gordon did not find too much amalgamation between the various American ethnic and racial groups.

Park's theory states that when different groups come into contact, they will go through this cycle. There are important implications for equality here. Even though a group may start out at the bottom of American society, in time, with urban experience, and by passing through stages of Park's cycle, the group should eventually be like other groups in the society through assimilation and attain full equality by the almalgamation process.

How do the facts of American ethnic experience support or disprove Park's theory? Clearly, a straightforward progression from contact to amalgamation has not occurred in American society (Hirschman, 1983). It is easier to argue that different parts of Park's theory continue to occur in American society. After initial contact, conflict has broken out between blacks and whites, Chicanos and blacks, Chicanos and whites, Protestants and Catholics, and so on—and these conflicts periodically still occur. For example, the riots by blacks in the 1960s were clearly aimed at a racially segregated society dominated by whites (Blauner, 1972, chap. 3, esp. p. 89). In a backlash against minorities, the Ku Klux Klan has been quite active, as in its antiblack organizing at the Camp Pendleton Marine Base in California. Finally, in areas such as Los Angeles and New York, periodic conflict occurs between members of different ethnic minorities, such as gang wars between blacks and Puerto Ricans and between Asians and Chicanos. These latter conflicts can be viewed as misplaced aggression, because ethnic minorities often take frustrations out against each other when the source of many frustrations is the white establishment.

In spite of these persisting conflicts, accommodation has also taken place. This is often the negative sort of accommodation that means subordination of one group relative to another, as our data have shown. Blacks, Puerto Ricans, Chicanos, and Native Americans are particularly subject to this kind of accommodation, as the white majority remains higher in terms of wealth, education, power, jobs, housing, and prestige. Asians have fared better than other minorities (Light, 1972). But they originally faced severe racism, are still excluded from the top positions of power and prestige, and have been heavily exploited (Ima, 1976, pp. 254–296; Li, 1976, pp. 297–324).

There has been a fair amount of cultural assimilation of minority ethnic groups, but much less structural assimilation (as shown in Gordon's study). The traditional sociological argument has been that if minorities accepted basic "American" (that is, WASP) values, then they would be admitted into the WASP-dominated institutions. This has not occurred on a large scale, especially not for Third World (that is, darker-skinned) American minorities such as blacks and Chicanos. Similarly, without structural assimilation into jobs and neighborhoods, intermarriage and amalgamation are not likely to widely occur and, in fact, have not to a large extent in America.

Thus we do not see any linear progression from one stage of Park's theory to the next, in spite of decades of urban experience for various ethnic minorities, including blacks, a now heavily urban group. Instead, ethnic relations in American continue to be characterized by most of Park's concepts, especially contact and conflict, as well as instances of cultural assimilation. The two categories in Park's theory that do not apply are structural assimilation and amalgamation—which indicates the persistence of racial and ethnic discrimination and the perpetuation of inequality (Feagin and Eckberg, 1980). In sum, Park, Handlin, and others who focus on a linear progression to equality have overlooked the recurring racist barriers that block equality for ethnic minorities. Finally, traditional sociology has not carefully inquired into why these racist barriers persist. This will be our primary focus in the last section of this chapter.

Prejudice

Another traditional theory that emerged in the 1940s was the focus on prejudice as an explanation for discrimination and inequality. Prejudices refer to incorrect, negative beliefs about a group, such as "all Chicanos are lazy," "all Jews are stingy," or "all blacks are ignorant." Various theories have used the concept of prejudice as a main explanation of inequality. The argument usually is as follows: When a dominant group holds these negative views about subordinate groups, the dominant group will discriminate against the subordinate groups. Moreover, this discrimination will produce various inequalities for the subordinate groups, which in turn will reinforce the stereotyped prejudices (Myrdal, 1944).

This type of approach has an intrinsic appeal and fits in well with an American propensity to explain things on the basis of beliefs people hold. There are, in fact, enough historical instances where this type of approach would seem to fit quite neatly.

For example, each succeeding wave of white migrants was met by *nationalist* prejudice, which was directed at them by those who were already here. Thus all Eastern Europeans were held to be backward in culture; Italians were all lazy; Irish were all loud and uncouth. Against Chinese and Japanese immigrants there was a combination of nationalist and racist prejudice. During World War II, all Americans of Japanese ancestry on the West Coast were confined to internment camps. (German Americans never were.) Finally, nationalist and racist prejudice also combine to support discrimination against Americans of Mexican and Puerto Rican origin. Both groups were incorporated into the United States through imperialist expansion—one group in the war against Mexico and the other in the war against Spain—and negative stereotypes have been used against each to justify their subordinate position in America.

Religious bigotry is closely related to nationalist and racial prejudice; indeed, all are similar both in cause and in effect. In Europe, Protestants and Catholics killed each other for centuries over differing beliefs, and in the United States, the Catholic minority is still subjected to a certain amount of prejudice and discrimination. Much worse, of course, was the many-centuries-long oppression of the Jews, forcibly converted, limited to certain occupations, often taxed to bankruptcy, and periodically massacred. Yet in the late nineteenth and early twentieth centuries, it appeared that anti-Jewish sentiment was dying away (it has never been as severe in America as in some other countries, although it certainly exists). But just as the Jews began to feel secure, Hitler's Nazism unleashed the worst racist atrocity in the history of the world. More than 6 million Jewish men, women, and children were tortured, gassed, and burned to death.

Another racist atrocity, supported by false beliefs, was the enslavement of black Africans throughout three centuries and their shipment under horrifying, inhuman conditions to various places of prison and work, especially the American South. It is important to note the considerable evidence (Williams, 1944) that slavery preceded racism; racist ideas do not *create* exploitation of one group by another, but racism does *support* slavery as well as current discrimination and exploitation. This enslavement was not done in the name of Aryan domination, as was Hitler's killing of the Jews and other "inferior" peoples, but in the gentle name of Christianity, it being the white man's burden to bring civilization and the true faith to the black man. One result of this enslavement is that blacks today constitute the largest single minority in the United States, and one of the most oppressed.

When blacks were slaves doing simple agricultural work in the South, racist beliefs played their usual function of explaining that blacks were inferior to whites, that slavery was their natural condition, that such simple labor was all they could do, and that they were very happy in this condition. Some surveys have found that as a result of the civil rights movement, increased education for whites and blacks, the fact that blacks make up a large part of the population of many American cities, and that blacks are now employed in all the complex tasks required to run American industry and urban life, the cruder, more stereotyped prejudices have been reduced (Sheatsley, 1966, pp. 217–238). Yet racial discrimination persists.

It is possible, of course, that increased education for whites might allow them to give more sophisticated, less obviously bigoted answers to survey questions. Yet the basic prejudices may remain. This suggests that sociologists should measure changes in the level of prejudice by other methods in addition to survey questionnaires. Nevertheless, questionnaires, based on random samples, are probably still the best single method of getting at changes in prejudices in large populations. On the other hand, it is wise to be skeptical of the results of any one survey and to look at other evidence of continuing prejudice and discrimination.

Harmful Stereotypes

A key aspect of racist beliefs is that minority groups are held to be biologically inferior. Racist beliefs are called racial *ideologies* because they are systematic sets of beliefs claiming the superiority of one group to others. These beliefs are *prejudices,* in that no amount of evidence can shake them—and even inconsistent beliefs do not bother the "true believers."

Adolf Hitler and his Nazis carried racist beliefs to their ultimate conclusion in the 1930s, when he proclaimed that "Aryans"—white, male, non-Jewish Germans—were a master race, superior to all other groups. He created a stereotype, or ideal picture, of all Aryans as big, strong, blond, and superintelligent—even though Hitler himself was none of these. Jews were portrayed as small, greedy, and cowardly. All other non-Aryans were physically weak and mentally inferior. According to Hitler, all women were unintelligent and useful for nothing but sex and childbearing. (Aryan women were also unintelligent sex objects, but were beautiful as well.) On the basis of these stereotypes, Hitler killed millions of Jews, non-German Europeans, and Russians and enslaved hundreds of millions of people. The conditions of women under fascism were even worse than the conditions of non-German men.

Such unscientific stereotypes are common—though much less extreme—in everyday American thinking and negatively affect blacks and other minorities in occupational and professional roles. The following incident illustrates the power of prejudiced stereotypes:

> A young Negro lawyer recently recalled his first case, in which he was called upon to defend a burglar. The thief, white, appeared before the judge dressed as he had been when apprehended by the police, in dirty work clothes, his hair mussed, an unshaven face. The lawyer . . . was neatly dressed in a business suit, was well-shaven, and was carrying a briefcase. The judge looked at both men and asked, unjokingly, "Which man is the lawyer?" (Quoted in Epstein, 1971, p. 190 n.)

Can you imagine how much attention the judge paid to the black lawyer's arguments?

Radicals agree that often prejudice is the immediate (or proximate) source of discrimination and inequality. But, unlike the traditional view, they then ask what is the source of these racist prejudices? In addition, radical sociologists ask why discrimination has persisted even though there has been some decline in the level of prejudice? Traditional sociology usually does not go beyond the most obvious causes of prejudice, such as children learning prejudices from their families, peer groups, and in their neighborhoods. Why these prejudices exist in families, peer groups, and neighborhoods is usually not explained by traditional sociology. In contrast we will show why racist prejudices have tended to persist in the face of overwhelming contrary evidence.

As noted, cruder prejudices have actually been decreasing over the years. One study shows that white support for integrated schooling increased from 30 percent in 1942 to 49 percent in 1956 and to 63 percent in 1963. Also, for the same dates, the white support for increasing residential integration rose from 35 percent to 51 percent to 64 percent. As for the statement that blacks are as intelligent as whites, in 1942 half of northern whites agreed and about 20 percent of southern whites agreed. By 1963 about 80 percent of northern whites and 57 percent of southern whites felt that blacks were as intelligent as whites. The same study goes on to document many more aspects of lessening prejudice in the white population over time, and it predicted a continuing drop in prejudiced beliefs (Sheatsley, 1966; see also Hirschman, 1983).

But did the reduction in racial prejudice significantly reduce discrimination and racial inequality? The answer is no, indicating that the barriers to ethnic and racial equality go much deeper than the persistence of some irrational prejudices. Our data indicated persisting levels of inequality with regard to jobs, education, housing, and the like. Why is this the case if prejudice has declined?

RADICAL EXPLANATION OF INEQUALITY

Institutional Racism

The reason inequality can persist even though prejudice has declined is that racism, as a system of racial *practices,* is built into the major institutions of our society. These practices can be consciously instituted to exclude racial and ethnic minorities, or they can be instituted for other purposes (even subjectively "noble" purposes), yet have deleterious effects on minority groups.

Conscious racial practices instituted against minorities are the most obvious to any observer. These include practices by real estate agents to exclude minorities from buying houses in white neighborhoods. Before they were declared unconstitutional, for example, restrictive covenants were widely used. *Restrictive covenants* were clauses inserted into housing bills of sale stating that the new owner could not legally sell to blacks, Jews, Chinese, and other excluded minorities. Various real estate agents may not have been personally prejudiced, but went along with such agreements to make a profit. This is a good example of how the social structure of real estate dealings "required" discrimination regardless of the personal views of the people involved.

As an example of conscious racism, the United States government's Federal Housing Administration (FHA) at one time *favored* racial discrimination as an official policy. The official policy stated: "If a neighborhood is to retain stability, it is necessary that properties shall continue to be occupied by the same society and race group" (quoted in Knowles and Prewitt, 1969, p. 27). This official, consciously racist policy had to be dropped after the Supreme Court struck down restrictive covenants in housing codes in 1948.

The FHA, however, may still be guilty of unconscious institutionalized racism in housing by setting income levels to obtain a housing loan that are above the income of many blacks (ibid., p. 28). This pattern is repeated by other financial institutions such as banks and savings and loan companies. The bank practice of "redlining"—refusing loans in specific parts of the city—was common. Thus the FHA and the banks have practiced policies that created racial housing segregation—*not* because of any conscious racist policy—but because of (1) the racial structure of income inequality in the United States and (2) the motivation of private profit that is at the basis of our economic institutions.

One might argue that urban renewal benefits black families by eliminating slums. This has occurred in some instances, but a more typical outcome is for urban renewal to degenerate into "Negro removal." Many urban renewal projects tear down older housing without providing adequate low-cost housing for poorer blacks. Furthermore, provision of federal housing, with *no* guarantee of jobs and income for poor blacks, can easily lead to a federally financed slum (Rainwater, 1970). Thus, again, the housing segregation in this case results *not* from consciously racist policies, but from the structure of income inequality between blacks (many in the lowest strata of the working class) and whites in the American economy.

Conscious racist exclusionary policies exist in many businesses, which still try to "get around" affirmative action demands to hire ethnic minorities. Policies of racial discrimination in business are well known, and they are reflected in the paucity of blacks in high-level business positions. These policies have been interestingly documented in a study of black managers in white-dominated companies (Fernandez, 1975). In the corporations that were studied, there was also widespread discrimination against Jews at the managerial level. Only one percent of the managers in these white Protestant-dominated firms were Jews.

Less well known are the institutional difficulties faced by blacks when they set up their own businesses. For example, in 1963 blacks owned only 13 banks, 50 life insurance companies, and less than 1 percent of the total assets of financial institutions in the United States (Knowles and Prewitt, 1969, p. 16). Various institutional practices make for this bleak situation, among which are the difficulties blacks face in getting credit, high premiums charged by insurance companies for ghetto property, and the negative impact of white-dominated monopolies on small businesses in general and on black small businesses in particular (Knowles and Prewitt, 1969, pp. 16–18). None of these difficulties—credit restrictions, high premiums, and monopoly practices—are consciously aimed against blacks or other minorities. On the contrary, they are all business-as-usual policies aimed at maximizing profit. For example, banks do not consciously refuse credit to poor blacks because they are black, but because they are poor. Yet the negative impact on blacks still occurs.

The individual black job applicant similarly faces institutional racism. In the past, overt conscious discrimination on the basis of color or ethnicity pervaded American business. This persists to some extent, but is combined with other mechanisms to eliminate minority applicants.

The job market for unskilled laborers is less beneficial to current minorities than to the European immigrants around the turn of the century. Capitalism was expanding rapidly and many low-skilled jobs were available to ethnic minorities, such as Irish, Jews, and Italians. Capitalism has now moved to a technologically advanced, monopoly stage. The result is a slower rate of expansion and more formal educational requirements for jobs, thus creating proportionally fewer low-skilled jobs for current minorities (Braverman, 1975). Many businesses cannot as easily absorb low-skilled minority applicants as in the past.

But what about minorities with skills? Here, other kinds of unconscious, institutionalized racism exist. Various companies insist on applicants taking "employment tests," which are used to screen applicants. The tests for better jobs are often geared to those with a cultural background similar to that of the intellectual-professional strata family, and to an education at elite universities; thus the tests discriminate against minorities without this background. Similarly, job interviews are aimed at seeing who will fit in well with the business—which usually means who is the "whitest." Thus many businesses adhere to the "letter" but not the "spirit" of affirmative action decrees. They do interview minority applicants and given them tests, but the structure of business institutions is set up against minorities. Hence businesses can report that they "tried"—but failed—to hire minority applicants (Knowles and Prewitt, 1969, pp. 15–24). Businesses are usually *not* consciously aware of how their policies perpetuate discrimination; they are "merely" trying to maximize profits by hiring on their usual (culturally biased) criteria.

The modern university has also been accused of consciously failing to hire ethnic minorities. Some universities, like some businesses, have had outright bigots formulate their policies, but most are *not* consciously prejudiced. They simply believe that the university will run better if its faculty and administrators have similar educational backgrounds, have compatible personalities, and are similar types of people (read white Protestant males). For example, when Woodrow Wilson was president of Princeton University, he said that faculty recruiting depended upon the selection of men who were "companionable and clubable. . . . If their qualities as gentlemen and as scholars conflict, the former will win them the place" (quoted in Baltzell, 1966, p. 14). Needless to say, white males (with upper class, gentlemanly manners) were "companionable and clubable," not ethnic minorities, however bright. To some extent, these policies, which are now illegal, continue even today as a result of institutionalized, traditional criteria for hiring.

The less conscious racial practices, which nevertheless exclude minorities from privileges of the larger society, are harder to document as racist. Yet they are racist in their consequence, no matter how liberal and well meaning the administrators who enforce the practices are, nor how unprejudiced they may be personally.

Universities can get caught up in this situation. Academic administrators who adhere to such regulations as "high admissions standards" to elite universities perpetuate racial (as well as class) inequality, irrepective of their lesser degree of personal prejudice. Recent policies that rely more heavily on college entrance test scores may hurt the chances of minority groups. The problem is that the content of such tests is oriented toward the background and viewpoint of white, middle- and upper-income level families (*Los Angeles Times,* June 3, 1977). The declared purpose of the added importance of these tests was to combat grade inflation in high schools, but the unplanned result would be to increase institutionalized racism in the universities.

Consider a liberal white person who would condemn the racist bombing of a black church (which occurred in the 1960s in retaliation against the civil rights movement). The same liberal white person might refuse blacks admission to a university or deny them a job on grounds of (culturally biased) qualifications, and thereby help perpetuate institutional racism (Carmichael and Hamilton, 1967, pp. 4–5). Similarly, Blauner (1972, p. 23) notes that "racial privilege pervades all institutions . . ."; however, "it is expressed most strategically in the labor market and the structure of occupations. In industrial capitalism economic institutions are central and occupational role is the major determinant of social status and lifestyle."

If racism is built into the major American institutions—in terms of racial and ethnic practices as well as prejudices—we should ask: Why does the establishment permit or encourage the perpetuation of racism? Looked at differently, we can also ask: who benefits from racism? It is the contention of radicals that racism plays an important role in supporting the status quo and that the capitalist establishment benefits from it directly and indirectly.

WHO BENEFITS FROM RACISM?

Conservatives claim that no one benefits from discrimination; that it is merely a matter of irrational and inexplicable tastes or preferences. Thus Gary Becker (1957, p. 5) says:

> Discrimination and prejudice are not usually said to occur when someone prefers looking at a glamorous Hollywood actress rather than at some other woman; yet they are said to occur when he prefers living next to whites rather than next to Negroes. At best calling just one of these actions "discrimination" requires making subtle and rather secondary distinctions.

Becker seems to think that discrimination against blacks is as trivial as preferring apples to oranges. (Notice that he also has a sexist prejudice in assuming that a "glamorous Hollywood actress" is attractive on an absolute basis, when this simply reflects a stereotyped standard.)

Radicals such as Reich (1981) point out that Becker is wrong to consider discrimination trivial, "just" a preference. First, most employers, union leaders, and military and government leaders are white males who have *power* to discriminate. Second, many employers choose by a double standard—they *assume* that whites are good, qualified workers while blacks and other minorities are not; and the burden of proof is on blacks and other minorities to show themselves to be qualified. Even where there are laws against discrimination, white control of the power structure means (1) the laws are often not enforced; (2) prejudiced propaganda is channeled through the media, church, and schools; (3) blacks and other minorities continue to receive inferior training; and (4) as a result, blacks and other minorities usually have the most undesirable jobs and low wages.

Conservatives emphasize that discrimination by business is irrational because (so they claim) businesses lose profits as a result (Friedman, 1962, pp. 108–118). Conservatives argue, for example, that if there is discrimination in other areas of the economy, then each capitalist is presented with a supply of qualified blacks willing to work for wages *below* the going wages. Since the capitalist can purchase these workers at lower wages, he could make more profit by doing so. Therefore, capitalists who are willing to hire blacks (below the going wage) will make more profits, while those who refuse to hire blacks at any wage will pay higher wages and lose profits.

The conservatives conclude that those capitalists who discriminate do so for irrational reasons and lose money because of the discrimination. They further argue that under pure competition, capitalists who discriminate will eventually be put out of business because of their higher costs per unit. Thus competition will tend to end discrimination and push black wages even closer to white wage levels.

Many liberals agree that capitalists may lose money by discrimination. Some argue, however, that the American economy is characterized by a high degree of monopoly rather than by pure competition. By the exercise of their monopoly power in the labor market, capitalists can hold down all wages; they may also use monopoly power to pass on to consumers some of the cost of discrimination. In other words, the liberals agree with the conservatives that racism is an inexplicable attitude, but they contend that it costs the capitalist only a little to indulge his "strange" preference. Therefore, they believe it might be a long time, if ever, before capitalism automatically ends discrimination. From this perspective, liberals urge the government to pass reform laws to end discrimination.

Capitalism Profits from Race Prejudice

Radicals like Reich (1981), on the other hand, do not believe that capitalists lose money from discrimination or that their attitudes are inexplicable. How could discrimination continue for such a long time if capitalists suffer losses from it? Capitalists *gain* in many ways from racist discrimination and hence have an interest in continuing it. They gain because *racist prejudice divides workers,* making unions weaker and resulting in lower wages for all workers. In the political sphere the same division of workers by race makes capitalist politicians safer from attacks by labor. For example, instead of uniting politically to fight for full-employment legislation, black and white voters may be divided over busing for integration. Racist discrimination also makes it easy to keep blacks as an unemployed reservoir of cheap labor for boom times. Also racism provides white politicians with a scapegoat for many social problems—for example, the untruth that all crime is caused by minorities. Racism helps inspire soldiers, as when they were supposed to kill Asians in Vietnam. As a result, white capitalists as a whole benefit from racism. In contrast, white workers as a whole lose from racism.

In the pre-Civil War South racism was a useful apologia for slavery. It meant that the slave owners would have no guilty consciences, the slaves might accept their lot more easily, and the northerners would not interfere. Racism declared that slavery was divinely ordained by God as a benefit to the inferior black. Thus the first function of racism was to justify economic exploitation.

This function of racism continues today, when apologists contend that black and Chicano workers are poorly paid only because they are inferior workers. More important, to the extent that white workers believe the racist ideology, unions are weakened by excluding black workers—or accepting them reluctantly and keeping them from equal power in unions. White and black workers have frequently broken each other's strikes in the past, though they are now learning to work together. In the areas of strongest racism and weakest unions, such as the South, black workers' wages are very low, but white workers' wages are almost as low. For this reason, one economic investigation concluded: "Far from being indifferent to the existence of discriminatory attitudes on the part of workers, the capitalist gains from them and may find it profitable to invest in their creation" (Silver, quoted in Franklin and Resnick, 1973, p. 23).

Another reason that racism is profitable to capitalists is the provision of a handy, but disposable, labor force. As noted in Chapter 11, if an employer has 10 black and 10 white workers, and must fire half for a couple of months, "he will lay off his ten black workers on the assumption that they will be unlikely to get permanent or better jobs elsewhere because of the disciminatory practices of other employers" (ibid., p. 20). Thus the capitalist can (and does) fire black workers in each recession and easily hire them back in times of expansion. He also gains by not paying the fringe benefits due workers who stay on the job for a longer time. Notice that capitalists may follow these practices even if they have *no* conscious prejudices and are simply following the institutionalized necessity to compete for maximum profits.

Blacks are exploited within the United States, both as workers in a segregated ghetto and as workers in the larger community. Blacks today constitute about one-third of the entire industrial labor force and an even larger percentage of the unskilled manual laborers. Racial discrimination keeps them "in their place" as a large pool of unskilled and/or often unemployed workers to be used to hold down wages in times of high demand for labor; racial prejudice justifies that place. Thus racism is in this respect only one more added apologia for considerable extra profits extracted at the expense of the lowest-paid part of the American working class.

Because that exploitation is at the heart of the system, legal reforms can give only limited help to most blacks. Radicals claim that

the system has two poles: wealth, privilege, power at one; poverty, deprivation, powerlessness at the other. It has always been that way, but in earlier times whole groups could rise because expansion made room above, and there were others ready to take their place at the bottom. Today, Negroes are at the bottom, and there is neither room above nor anyone ready to take their place. Thus only individuals can move up, not the group as such: reforms help the few, not the many. For the many, nothing short of a complete change in the system—the abolition of both poles and the substitution of a society in which wealth and power are shared by all—can transform their condition. (Baran and Sweezy, 1966, p. 327)

In addition, an important political function of racism is to find a scapegoat for social problems. For example, whites are told that the dirt and violence of the modern city are due to blacks. Similarly, Hitler told German workers that unemployment was due to Jewish bankers, and the middle class was told that political agitation was due to Jewish communists.

The second political function of racism is to divide the oppressed so the elite can rule. For example, no one is more oppressed or poverty-stricken than the white southern sharecropper. But poor whites have often fought against their natural allies, the blacks. Instead, poor whites have given political support to the wealthy white southerners who not only monopolize southern state and local politics, but also wield disproportionate influence in Congress because they succeed in holding key committee chairmanships and leadership positions by virtue of seniority. The same kind of divide-and-rule tactic is used in northern cities.

Finally, racism is a particularly handy tool of imperialism. England traditionally used the strategy of divide and rule: Hindu against Moslem, Jew against Arab, Protestant against Catholic in Ireland, and black against Hindu in Guyana. The American ruling elite has been quite willing to use the same tactic: Vietnamese against Cambodian, Thai against Laotian. Moreover, "inferiority" (inherited or acquired) is still being given as a reason for lack of development in many countries—where imperialism is the real reason. Finally, nationalist prejudice, or exaggerated "patriotism," always asserts that aggression comes from the other, evil people, and that the pure motives of our race or nation should not be questioned.

RACISM AND SOCIAL STATUS

Closely related to direct economic sources of racism, there is also the element of social honor and prestige—that is, social status. As long as a separate black "caste" exists—that is, a group that cannot freely participate in the social life of the dominant group—then the dominant group (white people) "know where the bottom is, a fixed point in the system to which they could not sink" (Blauner, 1972, p. 27). Although race helps maintain the class system, racial groups are closer to what Max Weber called status groups, which are "collectivities based on an attempt to monopolize social honor as well as economic advantage" (ibid.). Thus:

The relevance of race to status illuminates the particular aggressiveness with which whites have defended segregated residential communities and, today, the schools that are rooted in them. . . . The sense of community integrity among both white suburbanites and white ethnic groups in the cities is threatened by the presence of non-white people. The other status concern of middle America, the upward mobility of its children, appears endangered by integrated schools. (p. 27)

Such concerns with status assume a racist society. Without blacks—or other minorities—sterotyped as inferior, it would be impossible for whites to fear living next to minorities or having their children go to school together. Furthermore, these prejudices can be used to weaken working class solidarity. If whites *do* lose prestige by having minorities move next door, this creates tension between the white and black portions of the working class and thus reduces working class strength vis-à-vis capitalists. Hence, capitalists often encourage white workers to feel superior to blacks (Cox, 1970). This is using status strains to the benefit of the capitalist class.

Finally, the development of the urban ghettos is particularly useful to keep minorities "in their place." Ghettos not only help maintain segregated neighborhoods, but they effectively keep minorities primarily interacting with other minorities. The dominant group does not have to confront oppressed groups on a daily basis except in a most superficial manner or as a supervisor on the job. Furthermore, the ghettos are largely controlled politically and economically by outside white forces, who also send in police to "maintain order" in the ethnic ghettos (Clark, 1965).

The ethnic ghettos in the United States are *not* the same as classic colonial countries (Fanon, 1968). For one thing, the classic colonial country struggles for political and economic independence from its imperialist masters, whereas the black ghetto strives for equality, some control of its own political life, and at least partial integration into the American economy. American minorities can and do own houses and land; some move to other kinds of neighborhoods; and they are not legally trapped inside ghetto walls (Harris, 1972). Nevertheless, ghettos persist and amount to a primary mechanism—along with other methods of institutional racism previously discussed—to oppress minorities economically, politically, and socially (Wilson, 1973).

SUMMARY

American society is characterized by various inequalities between racial and ethnic groups. Groups such as blacks, Chicanos, and Native Americans are especially subject to inequalities of income, jobs, education, housing, power, and prestige. There are some differences between these groups; but each has been subjected to racist discrimination. In addition, other groups such as Catholics, Jews, Italians, and Irish have also suffered difficulties relative to the White Anglo-Saxon Protestant majority. The recent Asian immigrants have experienced both mobility and discrimination.

Various theories in traditional sociology have been developed to account for these racial and ethnic inequalities. There have been theories emphasizing racial or ethnic deficiencies in biology, culture, or social organization. Also, one tradition in sociology has focused on prejudiced beliefs as an explanation for discrimination and inequality. Still others have argued that inequality is only temporary, and will end with the assimilation and eventual amalgamation of ethnic groups.

Each of these traditional explanations has serious weaknesses. Thus, radical sociologists have felt it necessary to develop their own explanation of ethnic inequality. It was argued that racist practices are consciously or unconsciously incorporated into the major institutions of American society, such as the economy, government, and education.

Racism helps perpetuate inequality by providing a pool of low-wage workers and by splitting and weakening working-class movements. In addition, institutionalized racism also serves the status needs of the larger white population—needs that can be manipulated by the capitalist class. The development of racially segregated internal colonial ghettos in urban areas is an important instrument to keep minorities "in their place" and, therefore, also helps perpetuate inequality.

In light of our discussions, any serious attack on racial and ethnic inequality must focus on changing institutionalized racism and the capitalist and racial social orders that benefit from it. It is necessary to attack every level of prejudice and discrimination, as liberals have often argued. But the level of institutional racism—not the level of prejudiced beliefs—is the most important place to confront inequality.

SUGGESTED READINGS

Radicals have written so much on racism that a full list of books and articles would take many pages. A few of the very best on the sociology of racism are Robert Blauner, *Racial Oppression in America;* Stokely Carmichael and Charles V. Hamilton, *Black Power;* and Oliver Cox, *Caste, Class and Race.* An excellent history of racism in politics and law is C. Vann Woodward, *The Strange Career of Jim Crow* (New York: Oxford University Press, 1957). For an analysis of international race relations, see John Stone, *Racial Conflict in Contemporary Society* (London: Fontana Press/Collins, 1985). Two excellent articles by radical sociologists are Edna Bonacich, "A Theory of Ethnic Antagonism: The Split Labor Market," *American Sociological Review* 37 (October 1972):547–559, and Al Szymanski, "Trends in Economic Discrimination Against Blacks in the U.S. Working Class," *Review of Radical Political Economics* 7 (Fall 1975): 1–21. A large number of excellent articles are found in "The Political Economy of Race and Class," a special issue of the *Review of Radical Political Economics* 17 (Fall 1985). Some outstanding articles on racism have been published by William A. Darity, Jr. (1984, 1986, 1987). The best book on the economics of racism is by Michael Reich, *Racial Inequality: A Political-Economic Analysis* (1981); while the best book on racism against Chicanos is by Mario Barera (1980). For insights on the relation of class to race, see Eric Olin Wright, *Class Structure and Income Distribution* (1979). There have been essays concerning race and ethnic relations discussing traditional, and occasionally radical, themes in several volumes of the *Annual Review of Sociology* during the 1980s. For an excellent analysis of how the "Chicago School" of symbolic interactionism significantly contributed to our understanding of race and ethnic relations, see Barbara Ballis Lal, "The 'Chicago School' of American Sociology, Symbolic Interactionism, and Race Relations Theory" (1986). An important, prize-winning book on the impact of slavery is Orlando Patterson's *Slavery and Social Death* (Cambridge, Massachusetts: Harvard University Press, 1982).

REFERENCES

Baltzell, E. Digby. 1966. *The Protestant Establishment*. New York: Random House (Vintage).

Baran, Paul, and Paul, Sweezy. 1966. *Monopoly Capital*. New York: Monthly Review Press.

Barera, Mario. 1980. *Race and Class in the Southwest*. Notre Dame, IN: Notre Dame University Press.

Becker, Gary. 1957. *The Economics of Discrimination*. Chicago: University of Chicago Press.

Blauner, Robert. 1972. *Racial Oppression in America*. New York: Harper & Row.

Blonston, Gary. 1986. "Suburbanizing of Blacks Takes Ethnic Toll." *San Diego Union*, Sunday, August 10: C–1,5,7.

Boston, Thomas D. 1985. "Racial Inequality and Class Stratification." *Review of Radical Political Economics* 17 (Fall):10–33.

Braverman, Harry. 1975. *Labor and Monopoly Capital*. New York: Monthly Review Press.

The California Monthly (September 1986).

Carmichael, Stokely, and Charles V. Hamilton. 1967. *Black Power*. New York: Random House (Vintage).

Census Bureau. 1986. Reported in *Los Angeles Times* July 19, Pt. I:1, 25.

Clark, Kenneth B. 1965. *Dark Ghetto*. New York: Harper & Row.

Coles, Robert. 1965. "It's the Same, But It's Different." *Daedalus* 94(4):1121–1132.

Cox, Oliver C. 1970. *Caste, Class and Race*. New York: Monthly Review Press.

Darity, William A., Jr. 1984. "Public Policy and the Condition of Black Family Life." *Review of Black Political Economy* 13 (1–2):165–187.

———. 1986. "Losing Ground—Myths and Realities." *Review of Black Political Economy* 14 (2–3):167–177.

———. 1987. "Do Transfer Payments Keep the Poor in Poverty?" *American Economic Review* 77 (May):426–437.

Epstein, Cynthia. 1971. *Woman's Place*. Berkeley: University of California Press.

Fanon, Frantz. 1968. *The Wretched of the Earth*. Trans. Constance Farrington. New York: Grove Press (Evergreen Black Cat). Originally published in French in 1961.

Feagin, Joe R., and Douglas Lee Eckberg. 1980. "Discrimination: Motivation, Action, Effects, and Context." *Annual Review of Sociology* 6:1–20.

Ferman, Louis; Joyce Kornbluh; and J. Miller. 1968. *Negroes and Jobs*. Ann Arbor: University of Michigan Press.

Fernandez, John P. 1975. *Black Managers in White Corporations*. New York: Wiley.

Franklin, Ray, and Solomon Resnick. 1973. *The Political Economy of Racism*. New York: Holt, Rinehart and Winston.

Friedman, Milton. 1962. *Capitalism and Freedom*. Chicago: University of Chicago Press.

Gerson, Walter M. 1966. "Mass Media Socialization Behavior: Negro-White Differences." *Social Forces* 45 (Sept.):40–50.

Glazer, Nathan, and Daniel Patrick Moynihan. 1963. *Beyond the Melting Pot*. Cambridge, MA: MIT Press.

———, eds. 1975. *Ethnicity*. Cambridge, MA: Harvard University Press.

Gordon, Milton. 1964. *Assimilation in American Life: The Role of Race, Religion and National Origin*. New York: Oxford University Press.

Greer, Scott. 1960. *Last Man In*. New York: Free Press.

Gronos, Stanley J. 1986. Cited in Lee May, "Affirmative Action Successful in 100 Cities, Report Says." *Los Angeles Times*, September 18, Part I:1, 31.

Handlin, Oscar. 1957. *Race and Nationality in American Life*. Garden City, NY: Doubleday. Originally published in 1950.

Harris, Donald J. 1972. "The Black Ghetto as Colony: A Theoretical Critique and Alternative Formulation." *Review of Black Political Economy* 2:1–21.

Harris, Marvin. 1968. *The Rise of Anthropological Theory*. New York: Crowell.

Hirschman, Charles. 1983. "America's Melting Pot Reconsidered." *Annual Review of Sociology* 9:397–423.

Ima, Kenji. 1976. "Japanese Americans: The Making of 'Good' People." In Anthony Gary

Dworkin and Rosalind J. Dworkin, eds., *The Minority Report*, pp. 254–296. New York: Praeger.

Knowles, Louis L., and Kenneth Prewitt, eds. 1969. *Institutional Racism in America.* Englewood Cliffs, NJ: Prentice-Hall (Spectrum).

Lal, Barbara Ballis. 1986. "The 'Chicago School' of American Sociology, Symbolic Interactionism, and Race Relations Theory." In John Rex and David Mason, eds., *Theories of Race and Ethnic Relations,* Chapter 13, pp. 280–298. New York: Cambridge University Press.

Lewis, Oscar. 1959. *Five Families.* New York: Basic Books.

Li, Wen Lang. 1976. "Chinese Americans: Exclusion from the Melting Pot." In Anthony Gary Dworkin and Rosalind J. Dworkin, eds., *The Minority Report,* pp. 297–324. New York: Praeger.

Light, Ivan. 1972. *Ethnic Enterprise in America.* Berkeley: University of California Press.

Los Angeles Times. June 3, 1977.

Massey, Douglas S. 1981. "Dimensions of the New Immigration to the United States and the Prospects for Assimilation." *Annual Review of Sociology* 7:57–85.

Myrdal, Gunnar. 1944. *An American Dilemma.* New York: Harper & Row.

New York Times. 1987. "Minority Enrollment Effort Lags at Colleges." Reported in *The San Diego Union,* Sunday, April 19: A–21.

Olzak, Susan. 1983. "Contemporary Ethnic Mobilization." *Annual Review of Sociology* 9:355–374.

Park, Robert. 1950. *Race and Culture.* New York: Free Press.

Pettigrew, Thomas F. 1985. "New Black-White Patterns: How Best to Conceptualize Them?" *Annual Review of Sociology* 11:329–346.

Portes, Alejandro, and William Canak. 1981. "Latin America: Social Structures and Sociology." *Annual Review of Sociology* 7:225–248.

Rainwater, Lee. 1966. "Crucible of Identity: The Negro Lower-Class Family." *Daedalus* 95 (1):172–216.

———. 1970. *Behind Ghetto Walls: Black Families in a Federal Slum.* Chicago: Aldine.

———, and William L. Yancey. 1967. *The Moynihan Report and the Politics of Controversy.* Cambridge, MA: M.I.T. Press.

Reich, Michael. 1981. *Racial Inequality: A Political-Economic Analysis.* Princeton, NJ: Princeton University Press.

Rosenberg, Morris. 1965. *Society and Adolescent Self-Image.* Princeton, NJ: Princeton University Press.

Sharbutt, Jay. 1986. "Moyers Tackles 'Taboo': Black Ghetto Family." *Los Angeles Times,* Monday, January 20, Part VI, pp. 1, 4.

Sheatsley, Paul B. 1966. "White Attitudes Toward the Negro." *Daedalus* 95(1):217–238.

Sherman, Howard. 1987. *Foundations of Radical Political Economy.* Armonk, NY: Sharpe.

Silver, Morris. 1973. Quoted in Ray Franklin and Solomon Resnick, *The Political Economy of Racism.* New York: Holt, Rinehart and Winston.

Sowell, Thomas. 1981. *Ethnic America: A History.* New York: Basic Books.

Sussman, Marvin B. 1953. "The Help Pattern in the Middle Class Family." *American Sociological Review* 18 (Feb.):22–28.

United Press. 1973. Reported in *Riverside Daily Enterprise* (October 23): A–2.

U.S. Census. 1980. Cited in Gary Blonston, "Suburbanizing of Blacks Takes Ethnic Toll," *The San Diego Union,* Sunday, August 10, 1986, p. C–1.

U.S. Conference of Mayors. 1986. Discussed in Lee May, "Affirmative Action Successful in 100 Cities, Report Says." *Los Angeles Times,* September 18, Part I:1, 31.

U.S. Department of Labor. March 1965. *The Negro Family: The Case for National Action.*

Washington, DC: Government Printing Office. This monograph was popularly called "The Moynihan Report," after its author, Daniel P. Moynihan. It is reprinted in Lee Rainwater and William L. Yancey, *The Moynihan Report and the Politics of Controversy,* pp. 41–124. Cambridge, MA: M.I.T. Press, 1967.

Williams, Eric. 1944. *Capitalism and Slavery.* Chapel Hill: University of North Carolina Press.

Willie, Charles. 1975. "Life Styles of Black Families: Variations by Social Class." In Saul D. Feldman and Gerald W. Thielbar, *Life Styles in American Society,* pp. 406–417. Boston: Little, Brown.

Wilson, Reginald. 1986. Cited in Henry Cisneros, "Grad Schools Need More Blacks, Latinos." *Los Angeles Times,* Monday, August 11, Part II:7.

Wilson, William J. 1980. *The Declining Significance of Race,* 2d ed. Chicago: University of Chicago Press.

Wilson, William J. 1973. *Power, Racism, and Privilege.* New York: Free Press.

Winnick, Andrew. Forthcoming. "The Changing Distribution of Income and Wealth in the U.S., 1960–1985." In Patricia Voydanoff and Linda Majka, *Families and Economic Distress.* Beverly Hills, CA: Sage.

Woodrum, Eric. 1981. "An Assessment of Japanese American Assimilation, Pluralism, and Subordination." *American Journal of Sociology* 87 (July):157–169.

Wright, David E.; Esteban Salinas; and William Kuvlesky. 1973. "Opportunities for Social Mobility for Mexican-American Youth." In Rudolph O. de la Garza, Z. Anthony Kruszewski, and Thomas A. Arciniega, *Chicanos and Native Americans,* pp. 43–60. Englewood Cliffs, NJ: Prentice-Hall.

Wright, Eric Olin. 1979. *Class Structure and Income Distribution.* New York: Academic Press.

Yinger, J. Milton. 1985. "Ethnicity." *Annual Review of Sociology* 11:151–180.

Yinger, John. 1986. "Measuring Racial Discrimination with Fair Housing Audits: Caught in the Act." *American Economic Review* 76 (December):881–893.

chapter *13*

Ageism

The United States has experienced a steady growth in its older population since the 1930s. The 1980 census revealed that 11.3 percent of Americans are aged 65 or over; this translates into a figure of over 25 million (a little more than the population of California or Canada). It has been estimated that men and women aged 65 and over will be one-sixth of the whole population in another 50 years. Table 13.1 summarizes the composition and growth of this segment of the population from 1930 to 1980.

Two clear trends emerge from these data: the absolute and relative growth in numbers of persons 65 and over, and the increasing proportion of women in this category until 1970, when it stabilized at 60 percent of the aged through 1980. The first two of these phenomena can be explained by decreases in both mortality and fertility rates (plus a reduction in young immigrants). The growth of the female component is related to the trend of women experiencing greater life expectancy than do men. This latter development gains in importance when we consider the fact that aged women are more likely to be poor than aged men. One reason for the poverty of older women is that they become poor on the death of their spouse and the cessation of that portion of family income that had sufficed to keep the couple above the poverty line.

Many older people face serious barriers because of their age. The now-abolished policy of forced retirement at age 65 or 70 was on obvious barrier that older persons faced. Current restrictions occur with regard to housing, insurance, driving privileges, and the like. In each case, a person's age is formally or informally held against him or her. This discrimination against the aged is accentuated when ageism—the barriers related to age—is combined with barriers of race and poverty.

Table 13.1   POPULATION OF UNITED STATES AGED 65 AND OVER BY YEAR AND SEX (IN THOUSANDS)

Year	Number 65 and over	Aged as percent of total population	Men 65 and over	Men as percent of aged	Women 65 and over	Women as percent of aged
1930	6,634	5.4	3,326	50	3,308	50
1940	9,020	6.9	4,406	49	4,614	51
1950	12,270	8.1	5,798	47	6,472	53
1960	16,560	9.2	7,479	45	9,091	55
1970	20,050	9.9	8,240	40	11,810	60
1980	25,549	11.3	10,305	40	15,244	60

Source: U.S. Bureau of the Census.

The combined impact of older age, poverty, and race in capitalist society will be apparent in this chapter.

Aging has become a topic of public concern. The elderly have demanded legislation to improve their lot (for example, by increasing social security benefits). On the other side, there were threats that the social security system of retirement benefits might go broke. Aging has become a heated public and political issue with the result that the topic of aging has become increasingly important in the sociological literature.

Two extreme views of aging have emerged. On the one hand is the pleasant picture of the aged that is carefully nurtured by Norman Rockwell magazine covers, countless TV situation comedies, and oceans of popular journalism. This picture portrays "senior citizens" (a classic euphemism) as rosy-cheeked, well-dressed, physically fit, enjoying rest from years of productive labor, surrounded by loving families and friends, and residing in a tidy city dwelling or a luxurious minihacienda in a sun-drenched retirement community. On the other hand is the picture of the aged suffering from extreme poverty, terrible housing, chronic ill health, isolation and loneliness, undernourished diet, demeaning bureaucracy, and the unique form of despair engendered by the specter of approaching death.

For the majority of older people in America the actual reality of aging is somewhere in between these two extreme views. To be sure, various older persons do fit the extreme views closely. The life of some elderly millionaires is filled with every possible convenience. The life of an elderly, poverty-stricken, black widow in Mississippi may be terrible.

Yet life for most older persons is neither as harsh nor as easy, as the extreme views imply. We will discuss a number of studies that deal with the positive and negative aspects of aging in America, as well as some studies that state circumstances, such as good versus poor health, that can increase or decrease happiness for the elderly (Riley, Johnson, and Foner, 1972). This traditional literature, though improving in quality in recent years, has one central problem: It often neglects the impact of social class (including poverty and wealth), sex discrimination, and racism in analyzing difficulties of aging. We will show the very important role of these factors in aging, and indicate that capitalist society produces many elderly victims of poverty, sexism, and racism, who are plagued with a disproportionate number of problems.

NEGATIVE APPRAISALS OF AGING

Problems associated with aging in the United States include poverty, isolation and loneliness, physical illness, anxiety, widowhood, generalized unhappiness, and senility. A comparative examination of aging in many societies found that some of these problems, such as widowhood, occur in other societies as well (de Beauvoir, 1972). Our focus here, however, is the present American social structure, which tends to accentuate various problems such as poverty and isolation of the aged. We will discuss numerous studies that have pointed to older people excessively suffering these problems in our society.

One study, for example, pointed to a general pattern of restriction "relating to income, family size, participation in organizations. . . . and in . . . social life space . . ." as a person ages (Kuhlen, 1968). In addition, drawing on statistical data this study finds that "as people get older, at least beyond middle age, their reported happiness decreases. . . ." One aspect of this unhappiness is due to a lowered self-concept in old age. Furthermore, increased anxiety occurs among older persons. In sum, "the evidence seems particularly clear that anxiety and susceptibility to threat increase with the passage of time. . . ."

These and similar themes have been repeated in other research on aging. One study reports that contributions to science decline among older scientists (Lehman, 1968). Depending upon the subject, various scientists made significant contributions beginning at age 25. Yet this contribution began to decline by middle age and was quite low by age 60. The conclusion was that scientists "become progressively less productive" in older age. This conclusion has been echoed in more general terms for various professions (Dennis, 1968). A 1963 study found: "the dominant theme (in the aging literature) had been upon *decline*" (Butler, 1968, p. 235). This decline, in fact, was not just personal, but interpersonal. Thus, another study found that over the years there is less marital satisfaction (Pineo, 1968).

INCOME OF THE AGED

The data on income of the elderly reflect the difficulties of aging especially for certain categories of the elderly. Moreover, as we will see, poverty for many older persons is a main source of other difficulties, such as poor housing, poor medical care and ill health, isolation and loneliness, inadequate diet, and demeaning bureaucracy. Most of these are not problems for the wealthy. The elderly poor, however, are often forgotten and ignored because they are isolated and poor and also perhaps because, as we shall see, so many of them are women and/or black.

Sources of income for the aged include Social Security and other government pensions, earnings from employment (a small amount, mostly from self-employment), welfare payments, interest on accumulated capital, rents and annuities, business and union pensions, personal insurance plans, and capital gains. Other sources include unreported funds from relatives and charitable organizations and the liquidation of previously accumulated capital and savings. There is little data available on the magnitude and distribution of such income; what studies that have been done suggest that the amount involved is relatively small and concentrated in the higher-income segments of the aged population (Steiner and Dorfman, 1957).

Data from the Census Bureau indicate that the percent (and even absolute numbers) of aged poor has actually decreased since 1959. The official poverty line in 1984 for single persons 65 and over was $4979 and for couples it was $6282. Table 13.2 reports on the aged poor for the years 1959, 1970, 1979, 1983, and 1984. The percent of aged poor in these years was 35.2, 24.6, 15.2, 14.2, and 12.4, which is a clear decrease over time. The Social Security payments to the aged in recent years have often been increased proportionally to the rate of inflation. This cost of living adjustment for the aged population has been one of the most important factors explaining why the number of aged poor has decreased. Indeed, these statistics show the general benefits that cost of living adjustments can have for other groups, such as union members, salaried professionals, and unskilled workers.

Even though the number of aged poor has been decreasing, there remain large differentials between groups in the United States. Aged women in households are over twice as likely to be poor than aged men in households (6 percent of men and 13 percent of women). These figures are even more ominous for single people—20.8 percent of the aged men and 25.2 percent of the aged women are poor! The fact that it was previously even worse for them—59 percent of the men and 63.3 percent of the women in 1959—does not negate the reality that almost a quarter (24.2 percent) of aged single people are currently poor.

Table 13.2   PERSONS 65 YEARS OLD AND OVER BELOW POVERTY LEVEL, BY SELECTED CHARACTERISTICS, 1959 TO 1984

Characteristic	Number below poverty level (in thousands)					Percent below poverty level				
	1959	1970	1979	1983	1984	1959	1970	1979	1983	1984
Persons, 65 yr. and over	5,481	4,793	3,682	3,730	3,330	35.2	24.6	15.2	14.2	12.4
White	4,744	4,011	2,911	2,875	2,579	33.1	22.6	13.3	12.1	10.7
Black	711	735	740	796	710	62.5	47.7	36.3	36.2	31.7
Spanish origin	(NA)	(NA)	154	178	176	(NA)	(NA)	26.8	22.7	21.5
In families	3,187	2,013	1,380	1,439	1,205	26.9	14.8	8.4	8.1	6.7
Householder	1,787	1,188	822	844	713	29.1	16.5	9.1	8.7	7.3
Male	1,507	980	629	581	489	29.1	15.9	8.4	7.3	6.0
Female	280	209	193	263	224	28.8	20.1	13.0	15.5	13.0
Other members	1,400	825	559	595	493	24.6	13.0	7.6	7.4	6.0
Unrelated individuals	2,294	2,779	2,299	2,279	2,123	61.9	47.2	29.4	26.6	24.2
Male	703	549	428	426	401	59.0	38.9	25.3	22.6	20.8
Female	1,591	2,230	1,871	1,853	1,722	63.3	49.8	30.5	27.7	25.2

Source: U.S. Bureau of the Census, Current Population Reports, series P-60, No. 149 and unpublished data. Reported in Statistical Abstract of the United States: 1986.

Aged blacks and Latinos are significantly more likely to be poor than aged whites. In 1984, 10.4 percent of aged whites were poor, whereas 31.7 percent of aged blacks and 21.5 percent of aged Latinos were poor. Thus, Latino or black ethnic minority status in 1984 increased two or three times the likelihood of being poor in old age.

Some of the aged poor have lived all of their lives in poverty or close to it. Yet *most* only became poor after they became aged; this is especially the case for aged women. While specific data do not seem to exist on this subject, an examination of what statistics are available suggests that the majority of the aged poor became impoverished *after* reaching 65. A number of causes have been responsible for this: enforced retirement of workers at 65 and even earlier, ill health and crippling medical expenses, inadequate or nonexistent employee pension plans, and persistent inflation, especially in food, housing and medical costs (Harrington, 1963, p. 105).

A Senate Committee Report of 1969 (reprinted in Ginsburg, 1972) points out that two trends have created a "retirement revolution" in the United States: "At one end an increase in the number of the very old aged; at the other, earlier departure from the labor force." Furthermore, the report adds, "the economic position of persons now old will deteriorate markedly in the years ahead," citing the drop in already limited earning opportunities with advancing age, the exhaustion of assets, rising medical needs and costs, and the erosion by inflation of "already inadequate incomes over longer retirement periods." If, as the report states, "an annual [price] rise of only 2 percent will reduce the purchasing power of fixed incomes by 18 percent after one decade and by 33 percent after two decades," imagine the catastrophic effects of much higher rates in inflation on the incomes of the aged.

The Senate report also suggests that the problem of inadequate retirement income should be of direct concern not only to our population of aged and aging Americans, but also to those in middle age or younger, because few families are able to save much, if anything, for retirement, especially workers in the less skilled occupations. The report asks: "How realistic is it to expect today's workers voluntarily to forego consumption in order to save for the years ahead when this requires that they significantly reduce their standard of living to provide adequately for an uncertain and 'distant' old age?" (Ginsburg, 1972, p. 229).

Additionally, the report finds that social security, private pensions, and other forms of retirement income are *not* improving fast enough to reverse these economic trends. An examination of U.S. data indicates that from 1975 to 1980 prices did increase faster than pensions, with an 8.8 percent increase versus a 7.3 percent increase; however, from 1980 to 1983, pensions finally outstripped prices with a 10.9 percent increase versus a 6.5 percent increase (U.S. Social Security Administration, unpublished data). It would clearly benefit the older population if this recent trend continued, especially those Americans (still less than half) who are covered by pensions. Those without pensions are still the ones with the greatest need, as the report states.

If one measure of the success of a society is the treatment of its aged citizens, then America could improve. Some less highly developed countries than the

United States do much better by their aged. Canada, for example, has long out-stripped the United States in the field of old-age pensions. In 1973 the newly elected socialist government of the Province of British Columbia passed an act establishing Mincome, a program guaranteeing every resident of the province aged 65 or over a minimum income (*Ramparts*, 1974, pp. 21–26). The United States—a much wealthier nation—could do at least as much, and preferably a great deal more.

POSITIVE APPRAISALS OF AGING

Some of the recent literature on aging has a more positive appraisal of aging. For example, one study reported that many elderly are not isolated (Townsend, 1968, pp. 255–257). Instead this study found the development of a four-generation family in the United States, Denmark, and Britain. It was noted that as many as 40 percent of the elderly in the United States have great-grandchildren. Although older people without families are seen to face increasing seclusion, those with families are "pushed toward the pinnacle of pyramidal family structure of four generations which may include several children and their spouses and 20 or 30 grandchildren and great-grandchildren" (p. 256). This is an interesting finding and hypothesis about possible relations between different generations of the same family. But the data do not tell us how often the generations actually come into social contact, nor the depth of relations between the generations. In a geograph-ically mobile society like the United States, it is likely that the older persons live significant distances from many of their kinfolk, which reduces interaction with them (Litwak, 1960, p. 15).

Many commentators on middle and old age have pointed to the difficulties of the "empty nest syndrome." That is, married women typically have their last child leave home when they are in middle age. Since women, on the average, live well into their seventies, this means a period of 20 years or more when they are childless. For those mothers who devoted most of their energies to raising children—often at the expense of their own career ambitions—the "empty nest" period is presumably a traumatic time of life (Bart, 1970).

Not necessarily so, says at least one study. This study paints a rosier picture than the empty nest image. Though the sample is small, it shows that only 3 of 49 households studied reported that the postparental phase is worse than the preceding phases of life. In contrast, it shows that 22 of the 49 households reported the postparental phase as better than previous phases (Deutscher, 1968, p. 264, Table 1). Thus, it concludes, "These data seem to indicate that the postparental phase of the family cycle is not generally defined unfavorably by those involved in it" (p. 268).

Furthermore, another study finds strong satisfactions in the grandparent role. The data indicated that the majority of grandparents expressed only "comfort, satisfaction, and pleasure" in this role (Neugarten and Weinstein, 1968, p. 281).

A presumed affliction of old age is the decreasing participation in the larger society by older persons. This process has been called *disengagement* and a major approach to aging is *disengagement theory*. The classic statement of disengagement theory is *Growing Old: The Process of Disengagement* by Cumming and Henry (1961). Yet they argued that disengagement was good for *both* the individual and the society.

According to them, growing old and retirement means that older people no longer have to carry the responsibilities for work that they did when they were younger. Older people have worked a full adult span of years, and old age means they can retire and take life easy for the remainder of their lives. (Of course, that is mainly true if they have an adequate income.)

On the other hand, society will be able to fill its occupational positions with younger people who have greater skills than the retired. By this argument, in a complex society like the United States, technical skills are demanded for various jobs, and older people have neither the highest level of skills nor the desire to learn new skills at age 65. Younger people have these skills and can thus effectively take over jobs vacated by older persons. Without exactly stating it, Cumming and Henry imply that the technological needs for innovation in capitalist society demand that older people retire to make way for younger people trained in the universities of capitalist society. We would emphasize, however, that mandatory retirement is *not* dictated by the technological conditions, but by the functioning of this technology under capitalist relations, particularly large-scale unemployment. In a socialist society with full employment, older people would be encouraged to stay on the job, with the important contribution of their lengthy experience, as long as they wished. A socialist society would also guarantee a continuing good income when someone did wish to retire.

The disengagement perspective on aging has been influential in American sociology (Parsons, 1961; Hochschild, 1976, p. 53). In our terminology, Cumming and Henry emphasized the positive aspects of aging. Although they acknowledge problems of physical disability and the specter of ensuing death, their theory gives even these grim facts of life a positive twist. By disengaging, the infirm individual is not required to keep up a work pace with which he or she cannot cope. From society's standpoint, it is more economically efficient to have younger, healthier people manning industries, universities, and bureaucracies.

Although *Growing Old* has become a recognized classic, it was criticized shortly after its publication. Interestingly enough, some of the critiques also viewed aging in a positive light, although the positive emphasis was different than the original (Hochschild, 1976, pp. 53–87).

Hochschild (1973), for example, argued that the book overstated the case in important aspects. In particular, it was argued that older people did *not* voluntarily "drop out" of society as they became older. Cumming and Henry had argued that older people became disengaged from the larger society and from social life in general, and that they basically liked doing so. In contrast, this study of a community of older women found that only a few of these women clearly "withdrew to their room" and voluntarily became social isolates. Many others were involved in a very active social life in the retirement community.

Other studies have confirmed the finding that older people do not voluntarily lose contact with social life. One very interesting study reported a high level of social activity in a French retirement home (Ross, 1974). The retirement home was highly political, involving a split between communist and noncommunist retirees. The constant "political struggles" appeared to give these people a meaning in life, and also served as a basis of social solidarity, at least within the political groups. The political struggles themselves were often trivial to an outsider, such as a conflict over collecting money for Christmas decorations, which was opposed by the communists; but the political intrigues had positive social significance for the retirees. Both the study of older women and the French retirement home study are thus challenges to disengagement theory (see also Hochschild, 1976).

Another positive appraisal of aging focuses on a group of older people who seem to have fewer problems than others (Gubrium, 1976). These are people who have always been single and therefore do not have to adjust to the isolation of older age. The study points out that this group had experience in fending for themselves and thus saw old age as no special problem in this way. Instead, it was found that: "The available data on single elders indicate (that) they are not especially lonely in old age, (and) their evaluation of everyday life is similar to that of married elders, in the sense that both have a more positive view than divorced or widowed aged person" (p. 184). In conclusion: "Compared to other marital statuses, being single is a premium in old age in that it avoids the desolating effects of bereavement following the death of the spouse."

A decade later Pat M. Keith (1985) arrived at a similar conclusion for the never-married being at least partially better off psychologically in retirement than other marital statuses.

Finally, there have been several other studies indicating a positive view of aging (Rowe, 1976; Strauss et al., 1976). In contrast to the earlier studies, Rowe shows that scientists often remain active in older age, although the myth is that production drops off. It is shown, for example, that a majority of scientists remain active in scientific research in the retirement age categories of 65–70, 71–75, and 76–94 (the percentage remaining active in these categories are 54 percent, 59 percent, and 58 percent, respectively). A high percent of these retired scientists said that they spent time discussing research and on scientific writing—for example, 65 percent of the 71–75 age group reported scientific writing (Rowe, 1976, table 10–1, p. 212).

Another report finds less perceived "status loss" upon retirement than was previously assumed (Strauss et al., 1976). Status loss here means a perceived decline in prestige and respect for a person after retiring from work. Strauss et al. report that a large percentage of their sample reported *no* status loss at all. For example, only 15 percent of males reported status loss and only 4 percent of women reported any status loss (ibid., table 11–1, p. 226). Thus, aging in these studies does not appear to have as many negative consequences as other research has shown.

CONDITIONAL APPRAISALS OF AGING

A third type of study states the conditions under which older age is or is not an especially difficult time of life. There have been various studies aimed at locating conditions that reduce or increase life satisfaction for older people.

One of the compelling conditions of life satisfaction or dissatisfaction for older persons is health. When people are in their sixties and beyond, health becomes a paramount issue. Often illnesses not earlier experienced, such as cancer and heart attacks, become more frequent in this period. Ultimately, no one "overcomes" the problem of health in a physical sense; our bodies all give way to death eventually. (For excellent discussions of death and dying, see Blauner, 1968; Lieberman, 1968; Glaser and Strauss, 1968; Becker, 1973; and Stephenson, 1985.) But, for the period of years between age 60 and death, health can definitely influence the level of life satisfaction a person attains.

In an interesting longitudinal study—a study covering the same older people over the period 1960–1970—two sociologists found that the healthier a person was, the more likely he or she was to be generally satisfied with life (Bultena and Powers, 1976). Conversely, those with poorer health tended to be unsatisfied with life. Furthermore, they found that objective health status was the most important condition influencing life satisfaction among variables they studied (p. 173). Finally, they asked respondents how they compared their health status with others of their own age group. When his or her health was favorably compared to others, the respondent tended to be satsfied with life; but when his or her health was seen as worse than others, the respondent tended to be unsatisfied with life. Thus, as common sense might suggest, health appears to exert an important influence over a person's general happiness in old age.

One of the problems often associated with old age is social isolation and accompanying loneliness, which are seen to reduce life satisfaction. In an important study, two other researchers showed that the morale of older people clearly improved if they had a *confidant*—a friend with whom the respondent could talk about problems and other intimate aspects of life. For example, 59 percent of those with a confidant were satisfied as compared to 41 percent without a confidant. Also, 58 percent of those who engaged in much social interaction were satisfied, as compared to only 15 percent of those without much interaction (Lowenthal and Haven, 1968, tables 1 and 3, pp. 394–395). In addition, when a person had a confidant, even a lower level of social interaction with other people does not appear to decrease one's level of satisfaction. Finally, "the great majority of those who lost a confidant are depressed, and the great majority of those who maintained one are satisfied" (ibid., p. 396). Thus, interaction with other people, especially with a person close to you, appears to enhance life satisfaction for the elderly, and the lack of this interaction reduces it.

This type of finding is supported by another study (Bultena and Powers, 1976). This research shows that life satisfaction is associated with physical mobility. Thus, older people who can get out to visit friends, neighbors, and relatives, can go shopping, and engage in other such social activities are more likely to be satisfied. In contrast, those whose physical mobility is impaired are more likely to be dissatisfied.

Yet these researchers also report a negative finding in this regard. They used a measure of social interaction indicating "the frequency of face-to-face contacts with siblings, other relatives (not a spouse or children), neighbors, and friends . . ." Social interaction, by this measure, had almost no impact on life satisfaction (ibid., pp. 170, 173). This finding indicates that respondents who engaged in this type of intimate interaction were no more likely to be satisfied with life than those without the interaction. Yet, this finding is doubtful and controversial, both because it is contradicted by other studies and most theory, and because its own research method seems flawed. The flaw is that neither children nor spouses were included in the survey of social interactions of the elderly, but surely these are among the most important contacts of older people.

The same study found less life satisfaction if the elderly person participates in organizations—again, quite contrary to the findings of most other studies. A similarly unusual finding by Bell (1976) says that an elderly person's life satisfaction decreases with more contact with his or her family. This contradicts not only most empirical studies but also the theory that family solidarity increases life satisfaction (Durkheim 1951). Bell himself says that his findings may simply indicate that increased family contact (with the accompanying family tensions) may be unable to replace the loss of interests and friends at work that often occurs at this time. This hypothesis is given support by Bell's finding that life satisfaction is *positively* related to membership in voluntary associations, such as retirement groups, and social interaction in the community (ibid., p. 160).

Finally, other studies present data on connections between isolation and mental illness among the elderly (Lowenthal, 1968). These data suggest at least some mental impairment for older people when they are isolated from other people. Other studies indicate a higher death rate for those who are relocated from their homes (Aldrich and Mendkoff, 1968; see also Lowenthal, 1968). Although the data in neither study indicate strong statistical relations, these studies would be included in the evidence that points to a decrease in life satisfaction when older people are socially isolated.

In sum, there is mixed evidence on the hypothesis that more social interaction leads to more satisfaction. But sufficient evidence exists that when older people are isolated from *meaningful* relations—such as relations with a confidant—they are likely to become dissatisfied with life, and their risk of becoming mentally disorganized and even dying may increase.

Some researchers also apply a "theory of relative deprivation" to the aged. This theory suggests that people will be dissatisfied when they *feel* others are better off than they are, whether they actually are or not (Gurr, 1970). Conversely, a theory of relative privilege suggests that satisfaction will increase when people *feel* they are better off than others, whether they actually are or not. Two psychologists used this type of approach to analyze their aging data (Bultena and Powers, 1976). They show that when the respondents compared their life situations favorably to others in their age bracket, the respondents tended to be satisfied with life. This pattern occurred with regard to health, income, and physical mobility, as well as social interaction and organizational participation. These particular researchers found little impact of *objective* patterns of social interaction or organizational participation on life satisfaction, the latter even being a modest negative impact. Yet the favorable *subjective comparison* of their circumstances to others' circumstances appears to increase life satisfaction. Conversely, when respondents negatively compared their life circumstances to others, they tended to be dissatisfied. These perceived comparisons were thus often as significant as objective conditions in influencing life satisfaction for this group (p. 176).

The final circumstance to be discussed that influences satisfaction is participation in activities by older people. One approach argues that the more activity engaged in by older people, the more satisfied they will be. Yet an opposite approach—the disengagement theory—argues just the reverse, stating that the fewer the activities, the more satisfied older people will be.

The relation between activity or disengagement and satisfaction is complex. Cumming and Henry (1961) imply that older persons are satisfied to give up social roles to live a more relaxed old age. Another, newer study partially challenges this view. It argues that "as activity decreases, the sense of well-being associated with it decreases during the years after 60. Most respondents regret the losses in activity, and increasingly so at the oldest ages" (Havighurst et al., 1968, p. 170). Still, it notes that there is not a large drop in life satisfaction with aging, and that older people can accept role loss. In sum, the conclusion is that older people "regret the loss . . . yet . . . they maintain a positive evaluation of themselves and satisfaction with past and present life. . . ." Thus, it appears that older people regret the loss of activities related to work, family life, and social activities, but— at least according to this study—the regret does not have a large impact on general life satisfaction. Still, it appears that social activity is more positively valued by older persons than inactivity.

FACTORS AFFECTING CONDITIONS OF LIFE SATISFACTION

Up to here we have focused on conditions generally associated with the life satisfaction of older persons. We have reviewed some of the literature on the impact of bad versus good health, social isolation versus social interaction, perceptions of comparative deprivation versus comparative privilege, and disengagement as opposed to activity—all as they influence life satisfaction of older people.

Do these conditions apply equally to all people? It is often charged that some groups of people are more likely to experience the favorable conditions in old age, such as good health, social interaction, perceptions of comparative privilege, and social activity. Other groups, it is said, are likely to experience the unfavorable conditions in old age, including poor health, social isolation, perceptions of comparative deprivation, and social disengagement. Let us investigate this hypothesis.

Poor people clearly face the problems of aging more so than other groups. One investigation shows that income is second only to health in influencing life satisfaction (Bultena and Powers, 1976, table 7–III, p. 173). Poorer people are less likely than wealthier people to be satisfied. This also goes for comparative assessments of income. When the respondent perceived he or she was not better off financially than others, the likelihood of satisfaction decreased. In fact, perceptions of comparative income were the second most important variable, among ten variables, in explaining variations in life satisfaction in this group (ibid., table 7–V, p. 175).

The major national study of aging in America of the 1970s, *The Myth and Reality of Aging in America* by Louis Harris (1975) for the National Council on the Aging, addressed the impact of income on satisfaction. Poorer people were decidedly more likely to experience "very serious" problems. As Table 13.3 shows, 31 percent of the poorest group (under $3,000 income) feared crime as a serious problem, as compared to only 17 percent in the wealthiest category ($15,000 and over). Also, poor health is a serious problem for 36 percent of the poorest group, whereas only 11 percent of the wealthiest group reported poor health. Similarly, 32 percent of the poorest group report that they do not have enough money to live on, whereas this is the case for only 1 percent of the wealthiest group.

In addition, poorer people are more likely than others to report loneliness as a serious problem. Serious loneliness occurs for 23 percent of the poorest group in contrast to only 4 percent of the wealthiest group. Similarly the poor are disadvantaged with regard to medical care, education, the feeling of being needed by others, having enough to keep busy, job opportunities for those who wish to work, having enough friends, housing, and clothing. As Harris (1975, p. 131) concludes: "The elderly poor have a far harder time coping with life than those with higher incomes." And, as the data show, there are millions of elderly poor to whom these generalizations apply.

Unfavorable conditions are also more likely to be faced in old age by blacks and other minorities than whites. As Table 13.4 shows, among people over 65, 44 percent of poor blacks (those with income under $3000) fear crime, as compared to 28 percent of poor whites. Forty-two percent of poor black older people

Table 13.3   "VERY SERIOUS" PROBLEMS FOR PUBLIC 65 AND OVER PERSONALLY (BY INCOME)

		Public 65 and over				
	Total (percent)	Under $3,000 (percent)	$3,000–$6,999 (percent)	$ 7,000–$14,999 (percent)	$15,000 and over (percent)	Number of people in millions
Fear of crime	23	31	20	21	17	4.8
Poor health	21	36	21	9	11	4.4
Not having enough money to live on	15	32	13	5	1	3.1
Loneliness	12	23	11	4	4	2.6
Not enough medical care	10	18	9	5	1	2.0
Not enough education	8	15	7	3	5	1.7
Not feeling needed	7	12	7	4	2	1.5
Not enough to do to keep busy	6	10	6	1	*	1.2
Not enough job opportunities	5	8	6	2	4	1.1
Not enough friends	5	7	4	3	1	.9
Poor housing	4	9	3	1	—	.8
Not enough clothing	3	6	2	1	—	.5

Source: Louis Harris, *The Myth and Reality of Aging in America* (Washington, DC: National Council on the Aging, 1975), p. 130.
*Less than 0.5 percent.

Table 13.4 "VERY SERIOUS" PROBLEMS FOR PUBLIC 65 AND OVER PERSONALLY (BY RACE WITHIN INCOME)

	Under $3,000		$3,000–$6,999	
	White (percent)	Black (percent)	White (percent)	Black (percent)
Fear of crime	28	44	18	33
Poor health	34	42	20	28
Not having enough money to live on	26	51	11	30
Loneliness	22	27	10	18
Not enough medical care	13	33	8	20
Not feeling needed	11	15	6	8
Not enough to do to keep busy	8	18	5	10
Not enough friends	6	9	3	6
Not enough jobs, opportunities	6	17	5	13
Poor housing	6	22	2	13
Not enough clothing	4	13	1	9

Source: Louis Harris, *The Myth and Reality of Aging in America* (Washington, DC: National Council on the Aging, 1975), p. 134.

report poor health, as compared to 34 percent of poor white older people. Furthermore, a staggering 51 percent of poor black older people report not having enough money to live on, as compared to 26 percent of poor white older people. Poor black older people were similarly disadvantaged, as compared to poor white older people (and even more so compared to better-off whites) with regard to loneliness, medical care, feeling needed, having enough to keep busy, having enough friends, job opportunities for those who wish to work, housing, and clothing. Zev Harel (1985) reports that many of these same difficulties persisted in the mid-1980s. Thus, being black and poor generates serious problems with most important aspects of life for the elderly. Here barriers of age—ageism—are combined in an unholy alliance with barriers of class (as measured by income) and race.

These problems are reflected in data shown in Table 13.5 on life satisfactions for four comparison groups: older blacks (65 and over), older whites (65 and over), younger blacks (18–64), and younger whites (18–64) (Jackson and Wood, 1976). In one sense, the data reported indicate more satisfaction among older blacks than might be anticipated, especially if one were looking for extreme unhappiness. Yet the data also indicate systematic disadvantages in life satisfactions for older blacks as compared to other groups.

According to Table 13.5 only about half of older blacks expect an interesting future, as compared to 57 percent of older whites—with much higher rates for younger blacks and younger whites. Less than half of older blacks have plans for the next month or year, as compared to 53 percent of older whites—again, with much higher rates of future planning for younger blacks and younger whites. Only 45 percent of older blacks are as happy as when they were younger, as compared to 58 percent of older whites (and still higher happiness rates for younger blacks and younger whites).

Table 13.5   LIFE SATISFACTION BY AGE AND RACE

	65 and over		18–64	
	White (percent)	Black (percent)	White (percent)	Black (percent)
Positive statements:				
Expect interesting future	57	52	88	79
Satisfied on looking back	88	80	86	79
Good appearance compared to age group	84	78	85	85
Things now as interesting as past	73	61	83	72
Got what expected of life	83	73	82	62
Have plans for month/year	53	46	72	62
As happy as when younger	58	45	69	64
Things seem better with age	64	66	66	66
Had more breaks than most	64	55	60	44
Would not change past	63	54	56	52
These are best years of life	31	41	56	55
Negative statements:				
Life could be happier	43	61	47	65
Lot of average man is getting worse	33	45	35	47
Did not get most of things wanted	30	54	20	47
Feel old and tired	44	58	20	31
Get down in dumps too often	12	20	14	20
Dreariest time of my life	22	34	11	20
Most things done—monotonous	13	22	11	17

Source: Maurice Jackson and James L. Wood, *Aging in America: Implications for The Black Aged* (Washington, DC: National Council on the Aging, 1976), p. 20. Data based on Harris' study cited in Tables 13.3 and 13.4.

Furthermore, a large, 61 percent of older blacks felt life *could* be happier, as compared to only 43 percent of older whites and 47 percent of younger whites (younger blacks shared this glum view, with 65 percent feeling this way). Over half (54 percent) of older blacks felt they did not get most of the things they wanted, whereas only 30 percent of older whites felt similarly deprived—with correspondingly lower rates of deprivation feelings by younger whites and younger blacks. Also, 58 percent of older blacks felt old and tired, as compared to only 44 percent of older whites—with much lower rates of tired feelings for younger blacks and younger whites. Finally, 34 percent of older blacks felt old age was the dreariest time of their life, while only 22 percent of older whites felt this way. Thus, older blacks were disadvantaged in comparison to other groups on many significant indicators of life satisfaction.

The present discussion of black aging elaborates upon, and partly modifies, an earlier black aging study (Jackson and Wood, 1976). In that study, evidence of a "double burden" was found, but less than was predicted. That is, it was found that being old and black generated some special disadvantages, but not as many as presumed. The current data add a third variable—poverty—which was not available to the earlier study. The addition of information on income suggests the strength of a "triple burden" approach to black aging (ibid., p. 1). The current data do imply special disadvantages when a person is old, black, and poor—a triple burden that characterizes about one third of the older black population.

Many of these trends on aging recorded by Harris in the 1970s persisted in the early 1980s, along with new problems, such as a huge 42 percent of older people saying fuel costs were a very serious problem (Harris, 1981, p. 10). Other percentages regarding very serious problems were similar in the early 1980s to those of the 1970s.

In Harris's 1975 study, for example, 15 percent of older Americans felt they did not have enough money to live on; this was 17 percent in Harris's 1981 study. Twenty-three percent feared crime in 1975, as compared to 25 percent in 1981. Similarly, 12 percent said loneliness was a serious problem in 1975, as compared to 13 percent in 1981. Harris (1981) discusses many other aging trends and comparisons with data from 1975 in his *Aging in the Eighties*. Clearly millions of older Americans remain burdened with serious difficulties, and these trends are accentuated for the older poor, women, and ethnic minorities.

WHAT IS TO BE DONE?

We need not dwell at any length on the "solutions" offered by conservatives who, if they will admit there is a problem at all, would urge us to do nothing except encourage private thrift and charity. The conservatives argue that even the aged who wish to work cannot do so because they are not productive enough. One program suggested by conservatives is for some restricted and demeaning "workshops" that sound like something out of Dickens:

> It is unrealistic to suppose that the aged poor can be reinstated in the labor force on a large scale, given present trends in technological change, without reducing the over-all efficiency of the labor force and retarding the growth rate of the economy. This does not mean they can do no work. Some are undoubtedly willing to work and capable of respectable performance on certain types of jobs. Sheltered workshops appear to have been effective with the mentally retarded and those in need of vocational rehabilitation for psychiatric reasons. The workshops contract with private firms to have simple tasks done at whatever pace the sheltered workers can attain. Why not have sheltered workshops for the aged as well? Earnings would certainly be low, but the income of the aged could be supplemented while they retain the dignity of earning income and the mentally healthy environment of "something useful to do." (Brennan et al., 1967, p. 225)

That such an egregious "suggestion" is passed off as serious academic analysis of a problem encompassing so much human misery and waste is almost as appalling as the facts of aged poverty themselves.

Liberals, to their credit, are very aware of the scope of poverty among the aged, and some of their proposals for reforms are far-reaching and substantial. The 1969 Senate Committee report's conclusions and recommendations represent a good example of the more enlightened liberal approach. First of all, the problem is recognized as "*not* a transitional problem that, given present trends, will solve itself" (in Ginsburg, 1972, p. 230). Second, the existing Social Security system is seen essentially as a failure. The report admits that "these past efforts have been aimed primarily at maintaining the economic status of the aged at some minimal standard or subsistence level in the face of rising prices." In its recommendations to Congress, the Senate Committee—in addition to requests for immediate aid to poor widows and attention to health-care needs—logically states that

> a reasonable definition of adequacy demands that the aged population, both now and in the future, be *assured* a share in the growth of the economy. . . . What this requires is a substantial transfer of income from the working to the retired population in order to improve the *relative* economic status of the aged. Such assurance can *best* be provided, or can *only* be provided through governmental programs. . . . (ibid., p. 231; emphasis in the original)

However, lest anyone accuse our senators of being socialists, they add that "Private group pensions and personal savings . . . will continue to be essential social security benefits in the future. The Government should explore and lend support . . . promoting and encouraging such supplementary sources of retirement income" (ibid., p. 232).

Radical sociologists—whose solution to aged poverty is the replacement of the American capitalist system with humanistic socialism—will not fail to spot the senators' desire that the working class, not the capitalists, pay for increased Social Security benefits. And they will note the opportunity offered private insurance corporations to profit even further with the help of government promotion and encouragement. Nevertheless, radicals would be ill advised to reject the liberal program out of hand. The problem of poverty among the aged is simply too enormous and urgent to allow one to oppose efforts to alleviate this appalling human suffering on long-run ideological grounds.

Radicals, too, should recognize the important task of effective organization of the aged. While one heard of "Gray Power" for a few years, little has been forthcoming recently. There was an impression in the press, perhaps erroneous, that this Gray Power movement was largely confined to better-off segments of the aged. It would seem that all of the aged, particularly the poorest segments, need a Gray Power movement.

A final policy issue should be addressed: the recent ending of forced retirement. The ending of forced retirement is clearly advantageous to the aged, many of whom now have the opportunity to remain active in work life. Yet the contradiction being discussed is the impact of this policy on younger workers. Corporate, government, and university spokesmen have pointed to dangers of creating unemployment among younger workers. Also, this might prevent younger workers from being promoted, and from bringing innovative ideas to their work place. This type of talk assumes a competitive economy where profit and "rationality" are goals placed over human concerns. It also assumes as eternal the high unemployment levels that often exist in American capitalism. Instead of new positions being created for younger workers, a competitive economy—operating at less than full employment—states that *either* an older person *or* a younger person can have the job, not both. This, in turn, may well produce a new conflict of generations—a conflict clearly created by the policies of corporate capitalism.

SUMMARY

Growing old has many special hazards. There is a literature that focuses on the extreme problems regarding health, housing, income, poverty, and death facing the elderly. Yet, another recent literature has attempted to moderate earlier findings about the hazards of old age. In addition this newer literature has attempted to show that growing old can be an acceptable time of life. The disengagement theory of Cumming and Henry has this type of flavor, as do other recent studies.

A third literature has focused on conditions that favor or hinder life satisfaction among the elderly. This has shown the positive impact of such conditions as having a confidant, being in good health, and interacting with friends often. In addition, we pointed out that *income* and *race* are two factors that help determine the extent to which people have good health, have friends, and have good housing. Poorer people—especially the black poor—are often denied the things that make old age easier. Moreover, older women face special problems because of sex discrimination. Furthermore, we are talking not about small groups of people but millions of people.

As a result we can say that at least a significant minority of older people (over a third) suffer serious problems with regard to health, fear of crime, having money to live on, medical care, and the like, and that the life satisfaction for these people is considerably reduced. Since income clearly affects the likelihood of avoiding these problems and increasing life satisfactions, we recommend significantly increasing and guaranteeing a livable yearly income for older people. This should be a high priority of the federal government. Finally, the older worker who wishes to continue working needs full employment, which can best be provided in peacetime by a democratic socialist society.

SUGGESTED READINGS

The major comprehensive treatment of aging is Simone de Beauvoir's *The Coming of Age* (New York: Putnam, 1970, 1972). She examines aging in many societies, compares aging across these societies, and reaches various general conclusions about aging. Her data are mainly illustrative, drawn from diverse sources of information. The main theoretical study of aging in the United States, sparking much comment and research, is Elaine Cumming and William E. Henry, *Growing Old: The Process of Disengagement* (New York: Basic Books, 1961). Although not as encyclopedic as de Beauvoir's book, nor as theoretical in orientation as Cumming and Henry's book, a number of empirical investigations have been carried out in recent years. The most elaborate is a national random sample of the United States by Louis Harris, *The Myth and Reality of Aging in America* (Washington, DC: National Council on the Aging, 1975). This study contains much useful data for any researcher in the area of aging. In fact, various other monographs have been developed on the basis of Harris's study, such as Maurice Jackson and James L. Wood's *Aging in America: Implications for the Black Aged* (Washington, DC: National Council on the Aging, 1976). Harris's study was repeated for the early 1980s in his *Aging in the Eighties* (Washington, DC: National Council on the Aging, 1981). In addition, a number of readers (collections of articles) have been published. Some of the most important of these books are Bernice L. Neugarten, ed., *Middle Age and Aging* (Chicago: University of Chicago Press, 1968); Jaber F. Gubrium, ed., *Time, Roles and Self in Old Age* (New York: Human Sciences Press, 1976); and Jaber F. Gubrium, ed., *Late Life* (Springfield, IL: Thomas, 1974). An interesting article on comparative problems of aging in the mid-1980s is Zev Harel's "Nutrition Site Service Users: Does Racial Background Make a Difference?" in *The Gerontologist* 25 (June 1985):286–291.

REFERENCES

Aldrich, C. Knight, and Ethel Mendkoff. 1968. "Relocation of the Aged and Disabled: A Mortality Study." In Neugarten, ed., pp. 401–408.

Bart, Pauline. 1970. "Mother Portnoy's Complaints." *Transaction* 8 (1–2):69–74.

Becker, Ernest. 1973. *Denial of Death*. New York: Free Press.

Bell, Bill D. 1976. "Role Set Orientations and Life Satisfactions: A New Look at an Old Theory." In Jaber F. Gubrium, ed., *Time, Roles, and Self in Old Age*, pp. 148–164. New York: Human Sciences Press.

Blauner, Robert. 1968. "Death and Social Structure." In Neugarten, ed., pp. 531–540.

Brennan, Michael J.; Philip Taft; and Mark B. Schupack. 1967. *The Economics of Age*. New York: Norton.

Bultena, Gordon L., and Edward Powers. 1976. "Effects of Age-Grade Comparisons on Adjustment in Later Life." In Gubrium, ed., pp. 165–178.

Butler, Robert N. 1968. "The Façade of Chronological Age: An Interpretative Summary." In Neugarten, ed., pp. 235–242.

Cumming, Elaine, and William E. Henry. 1961. *Growing Old: The Process of Disengagement*. New York: Basic Books.

de Beauvoir, Simone. 1972. *The Coming of Age*. New York: Putnam.

Dennis, Wayne. 1968. "Creative Productivity Between the Ages of 20 and 80 years." In Neugarten, ed., pp. 106–114.

Deutscher, Irwin. 1968. "The Quality of Life." In Neugarten, ed., pp. 263–268.

Durkheim, Emile. 1951. *Suicide*. Translated by John A. Spaulding and George Simpson; ed. George Simpson. New York: Free Press.

Ginsburg, Helen, ed. 1972. *Poverty, Economics and Society*. Boston: Little, Brown. Reprints *Hearings Before the Special Committee on Aging*, U.S. Senate, 91st Congress 1st Session, Part 1, Survey Hearings, April 1969, appendix 1, pp. 155–158. Washington, DC: U.S. Government Printing Office.

Glaser, Barney G., and Anselm L. Strauss. 1968. "Temporal Aspects of Dying as a Non-Scheduled Status Passage." In Neugarten, ed., pp. 520–530.

Gubrium, Jaber F., ed. 1974 *Late Life*. Springfield, IL: Thomas.

Gubrium, Jaber F. 1976. "Being Single in Old Age." In Gubrium, ed., pp. 179–195.

Gubrium, Jaber F., ed. 1976. *Time, Roles and Self in Old Age*. New York: Human Sciences Press.

Gurr, Ted Robert. 1970. *Why Men Rebel*. Princeton, NJ: Princeton University Press.

Harel, Zev. 1985. "Nutrition Site Service Users: Does Racial Background Make a Difference?" *The Gerontologist* 25 (June):286–91.

Harrington, Michael. 1963. *The Other America*. Baltimore: Penguin Books.

Harris, Louis. 1981. *Aging in the Eighties*. Washington, DC: National Council on the Aging.

Harris, Louis. 1975. *The Myth and Reality of Aging in America*. Washington, DC: National Council on the Aging.

Havighurst, Robert J.; Bernice L. Neugarten; and Sheldon S. Tobin. 1968. "Disengagement and Patterns of Aging." In Neugarten, ed., pp. 161–172.

Hochschild, Arlie Russell. 1976. "Disengagement Theory: A Logical, Empirical, and Phenomenological Critique." In Gubrium, ed., pp. 53–87.

Hochschild, Arlie Russell. 1973. *The Unexpected Community*. Englewood Cliffs, NJ: Prentice-Hall.

Jackson, Maurice, and James L. Wood. 1976. *Aging in America: Implications for the Black Aged*. Washington, DC: National Council on the Aging. This study is based on the data in Harris, *The Myth and Reality of Aging in America*.

Keith, Pat M. 1985. "Work, Retirement, and Well-Being Among Unmarried Men and Women." *The Gerontologist* 25 (August):410–416.

Kuhlen, Raymond G. 1968. "Developmental Changes in Motivation During the Adult Years." In Neugarten, ed., 115–136.

Lehman, Harvey C. 1968. "The Creative Production Rates of Present Versus Past Generations of Scientists." In Neugarten, ed., pp. 99–105.

Lieberman, Morton A. 1968. "Psychological Correlates of Impending Death: Some Preliminary Observations." In Neugarten, ed., pp. 509–519.

Litwak, Eugene. 1960. "Occupational Mobility and Extended Family Cohesion." *American Sociological Review* 25 (February):9–21.

Lowenthal, Marjorie Fiske. 1968. "Social Isolation and Mental Illness in Old Age." In Neugarten, ed., 220–234.

Lowenthal, Marjorie Fiske, and Clayton Haven. 1968. "Interaction and Adaptation: Intimacy as a Critical Variable." In Neugarten, ed., pp. 390–400.

Neugarten, Bernice L., ed. 1968. *Middle Age and Aging*. Chicago: University of Chicago Press.

Neugarten, Bernice L., and Karol K. Weinstein. 1968. "The Changing American Grandparent." In Neugarten, ed., pp. 280–285.

Parsons, Talcott. 1961. Foreword to Elaine Cumming and William E. Henry, *Growing Old: The Process of Disengagement*. New York: Basic Books.

Pineo, Peter C. 1968. "Disenchantment in Later Years of Marriage." In Neugarten, ed., pp. 258–262.

Ramparts 1974. (Feb.): 21–26.

Riley, Matilda White; Marilyn Johnson; and Anne Foner, eds. 1972. *Aging and Society*. Vol. 3: *A Sociology of Age Stratification*. New York: Russell Sage Foundation.

Ross, Jennie-Keith. 1974. "Life Goes On: Social Organization in a French Retirement Residence." In Gubrium, pp. 99–120.

Rowe, Alan R. 1976. "The Retired Scientist: The Myth of the Aging Individual." In Gubrium, ed., pp. 209–219.

Steiner, Peter, and Robert Dorfman. 1957. *The Economic Status of the Aged*. Berkeley and Los Angeles: University of California Press.

Stephenson, John S. 1985. *Death, Grief, and Mourning: Individual and Social Realities*. New York: Free Press.

Strauss, Harold; Bruce W. Aldrich; and Aaron Lipman. 1976. "Retirement and Perceived Status Loss: An Inquiry into Some Objective and Subjective Problems Produced by Aging." In Gubrium, ed., pp. 220–234.

Townsend, Peter. 1968. "The Emergence of the Four-Generation Family in Industrial Society." In Neugarten, ed., pp. 255–257.

U.S. Social Security Administration. 1986. Unpublished data reported on p. 367 of U.S. Bureau of the Census, *Statistical Abstract of the United States: 1986*. Washington, DC: U.S. Government Printing Office.

chapter *14*

Exploitation

This chapter covers several controversial subjects. First: Why are some people rich while others live in poverty? Second: What causes economic monopoly and what are its consequences? Third: What causes large-scale unemployment and a cyclical pattern of business depression? Fourth: Have the economic policies of President Reagan—often called Reaganomics—increased or decreased inequality and unemployment? Fifth, in the world economic system: What were the effects of some countries colonizing others? What causes imperialist tendencies? Why are some countries dependent on others? Why are some countries underdeveloped and how can they develop?

THE CONSERVATIVE THEORY OF INCOME DISTRIBUTION

Sociologists have long been interested in why income is unevenly distributed among different groups. They have asked why capitalists get such high incomes and why most workers have much lower incomes. Conservative economic sociology justifies the unequal status quo. In various forms, conservative theory has maintained that each individual is rewarded in the system according to his or her productivity and his or her sacrifices. If capitalists make much profit, it is because they deserve many rewards. The conservative theorists of the early nineteenth century argued that provision of capital for production is a subjective cost, or "disutility." The capitalist practices *abstinence* from consumption in order to invest capital. Therefore, the capitalist is morally justified in making a profit from his or her investment. Similarly, wages result from another disutility, the subjective unpleasantness of work, in providing labor.

The modern conservative theory of marginal productivity was first written in full detail by John Bates Clark in 1899. It is dedicated to the proposition that workers and capitalists each receive in income exactly what they contribute as their addition to the product, and that this is an ethically just system. In other words, a worker's wage will just equal the additional (or marginal) amount that he or she adds to output. Likewise, the capitalist's profit will just equal the additional (or marginal) output that is added by the amount of capital he or she adds to the productive process. This theory is still espoused in conservative textbooks.

Critique of Conservative Theory

In recent years there have been many severe criticisms of the conservative theory of marginal productivity. Conservative theory claims that everyone, including capitalists, merely receives a reward according to his or her productivity under capitalism. In conservative theory, capitalists make profits because they are highly productive. Moreover, the poor make low wages because they are not productive due to lack of intelligence or to laziness. The earliest criticism of this conservative theory came from George Bernard Shaw. Shaw pointed out that even if we accept the whole conservative argument, it proves only that physical capital or equipment is productive when workers use it. But, he said, a machine is not a capitalist. The fact that a machine is productive does not mean that a capitalist is productive, much less that he deserves a profit. Radicals admit that a machine may increase production, that workers need machines, and that they increase the worker's productivity. In that sense, it is correct to say that capital is productive, but it is the physical capital that is productive (jointly with the worker), *not* the capitalist. The capitalist owns the machine, but the capitalist is not the machine. The machine does the work (with the worker); yet the capitalist gets the profit.

Radicals agree that machines are a necessary part of the physical productive process; many would even agree to the importance of managerial labor. Radicals argue, however, that the productivity of physical capital goods (which were themselves created by the labor process) is significantly different from the capitalist owner's ability to capture a certain portion of the product as profit. In other words:

> Under capitalism "the productiveness of labor is made to ripen, as in a hothouse." Whether we choose to say that capital is productive or that capital is necessary to make labor productive, is not a matter of much importance. . . . What is important is to say that owning capital is not a productive activity. (Robinson, 1960, p. 18)

This is clear in the case of a mere coupon clipper, a person who simply receives financial payments from investments with no work, as some stockholders do today. Even when capitalists also perform productive labor through their own managerial work, this does not contradict the fact that, in addition, they make money through mere ownership of capital.

THE THEORY OF EXPLOITATION

Karl Marx argues that *human labor power,* operating on physical nature, is the ultimate source of all wealth. Marx emphasizes the sociological fact that *the capitalist class owns all of the productive facilities and resources, while the working class owns only its own labor power.* Assuming these institutional conditions, the capitalists *must* be paid a profit or they will not invest their capital. Because the capitalists own the resources and productive facilities, they receive a large share of national income while not engaging in productive activity (though some capitalists also do productive managerial labor). As Marx phrased it, by owning the means of production, capitalists are able to extract, or "exploit," this profit from the workers' productive activities.

The theory of exploitation is primarily a statement about the sociological relationships of capitalism, especially the unequal power of different classes. Marx's argument begins with the observation that commodities are *valuable* because the production of commodities requires human effort or labor. If anyone could manufacture an automobile by just wishing for it—with no work—it would have no market value. Thus, air normally has no market value. But if air must be bottled or put in tanks for use underwater, then it will have a market value because labor is required to produce the tanks and put air in them under pressure. All valuable commodities share the quality of being produced by human labor.

What determines the ratio at which one commodity exchanges for another commodity (that is, what determines the price of each commodity in terms of gold or some other money measure)? According to Marx, the exchange value of every commodity is determined by the average number of labor hours required for its production with the available technology. This is the *labor theory of value.* In a precapitalist setting suppose one primitive tribe produces rubber taken from trees, while another tribe produces deer meat by killing deer. Suppose that, on the average, it took 1 hour of labor to produce a pound of rubber and 3 hours of labor to produce a pound of deer meat. Then they would exchange 3 pounds of rubber for a pound of deer meat. If it happens that 1 hour's labor equals $2 in the market (an arbitrary figure, which does not affect the exchange ratio), then a pound of deer meat is worth $6, while a pound of rubber is worth $2. These relationships are summarized in Table 14.1.

Why must rubber and deer meat exchange at these ratios? Suppose the tribe producing rubber tried to sell it at a higher price (that is, get more deer meat in exchange). Then the other tribe would start to produce their own rubber. They would switch to rubber production because they could produce it in fewer hours than they could produce deer meat to exchange for it at the new exchange

Table 14.1   EXCHANGE RATIOS IN A PRIMITIVE SOCIETY

	Number of hours of labor	Exchange ratio	Price of commodity (if one hour is valued at $2)
One pound rubber	1	3	$2
One pound deer meat	3	1	$6

rate. Thus the rubber producers would be left with an excess supply of rubber that nobody would buy at their higher price. Marx here emphasizes that a commodity is valueless if there is no demand for it. In that case, the rubber producers would be forced to lower their price (that is, give more rubber in exchange for deer meat). When they lower their price to the 3:1 ratio determined by the respective labor times of production, then the demand will just equal the supply. That is how the long-run price, or exchange value, of the commodities is determined.

Marx also notes that we must count the labor embodied in tools of production as well as the current labor expended. Thus the price or exchange ratio of a pound of deer meat will reflect not only the current labor of hunting but also the previous labor expended to make the bow and arrows used up in the hunt. So the 3 hours may equal 1 hour expended on bow and arrows (used up in this hunt) plus 2 hours of hunting time. Similarly, the hour of labor required to produce a pound of rubber will include not only present labor but also the labor expended previously in producing the tools used in such work.

EXPLOITATION UNDER CAPITALISM

A capitalist produces commodities by combining various inputs in a production process. The capitalist hires workers to perform labor. The capitalist also buys raw materials and equipment from other capitalists. He must use these human and material inputs to produce a product that will sell *above the cost* of these inputs. How does the capitalist achieve this "magical" result of profits above all costs? If the capitalist pays for labor, machinery, and materials at their long-run market price (that is, the labor required to produce each of them), how does he make a profit by putting these inputs together and selling the product?

Suppose that a producer of rubber tires buys the labor power of rubber workers, a quantity of rubber, and some machinery to produce rubber tires. Suppose also that in a day an average worker uses up rubber that required 3 hours to produce. Assuming that the product of one hour of labor is arbitrarily priced at $2, then the price of the rubber used up is $6. So the cost of rubber used up per worker in a day is 3 hours, or $6, to this capitalist, which influences the price of the product.

The same argument applies to machinery. Suppose that in a day the average worker uses up or wears out machinery requiring 2 hours of previous labor to produce. Then the cost of this machinery to the capitalist is 2 hours, or $4. The cost of the machinery to the capitalist just equals the labor put into it, and this cost is included in the price of the product.

Under capitalism, competition enforces the same rule in the long run as in exchanges among precapitalist tribes (or individuals): The exchange rate of every item sold on the market must be in approximate relation to the number of hours of labor expended on it—including the hours required to produce the materials and machinery used up in its production. Thus the rubber-tire makers must buy rubber at a price determined by the labor that went into producing the rubber. Also, they must buy machinery priced according to the labor that went into it.

Therefore, a capitalist cannot make a profit in the long run merely from buying and using machinery and rubber because their cost is the same as what they add to the price.

Finally, the capitalists making rubber tires must hire workers to expend their labor power. Suppose the average worker works an 8-hour day. These 8 hours then go into creating the value of the commodity. The value of the commodity for 8 hours of labor is $16, according to our assumption that the product of an hour's labor is $2. The total value of the rubber tires produced by one worker in one day is shown in Table 14.2A.

On the cost side, we have already noted that the rubber used costs the capitalist the value of 3 hours' labor time, or $6, while the machinery worn out costs the capitalist the value of 2 hours' labor time, or $4. What is the cost to the capitalist of eight hours of present labor power by one worker? This cost is determined *not* by the value or price of what the worker produces *but* by the value of the worker's labor power in the marketplace—that is, the going *wage rate*. The wage rate of workers, like the value of any commodity, depends on how much labor time is required to produce it.

What constitutes the production of a worker? The answer is the labor time required to produce the worker's own food, clothing, shelter, training, and education—that is, all the things required to get the worker ready to work in the factory. This is why workers with higher training or education cost more than unskilled workers. Furthermore, since a wage is a culturally defined amount, not merely a physical minimum, the wage may rise over time. At any given time, the average wage will vary within a range given by minimum cultural needs and the maximum of the worker's output.

The average wage is also strongly influenced by the degree of unemployment or full employment, so that it rises above its long-run average in a boom and falls below it in every depression. Moreover, the average wage will be influenced by the struggle of workers versus capitalists and of unions versus monopolies. In

Table 14.2A   VALUE (PRICE) OF OUTPUT OF RUBBER TIRES PRODUCED IN ONE DAY BY ONE WORKER

Rubber used up	3 hours of labor time	=	$6
Machinery worn out	2 hours of labor time	=	4
Labor power expended	8 hours of labor time	=	16
Total Price	13	=	$26

Table 14.2B   VALUE (COST) OF INPUTS INTO RUBBER TIRES

Rubber used up	3 hours of labor time	=	$6
Machinery worn out	2 hours of labor time	=	4
Wages of labor	4 hours of labor time	=	8
Total Cost	9	=	$18

Profit = price − cost = $26 − $18 = $8

other words, between the minimum set by culturally given needs and the maximum set by the workers' whole product, the actual wage is determined by the organized power of workers versus the organized power of business, with high unemployment reducing workers' bargaining power.

Suppose the average wage now amounts to the value of 4 hours of labor a day expended in producing the necessities to get the worker ready to work. This 4 hours of labor time is then priced, according to our assumption, at $8. Thus the total *cost* to the capitalist for the production of one day's commodity by one worker is as shown in Table 14.2B.

The mysterious source of profit is now located; the riddle of capitalism is now solved. In terms used by conservative economists:

$$\text{Profit} = \text{price} - \text{cost} = \$26 - \$18 = \$8$$

Marx's observation is that none of this profit came from buying and using rubber and machinery; all of it came from the labor of workers beyond the value (wages) paid to them. The worker expended labor to produce 8 hours' value, but was paid a wage equal to only 4 hours' value. The difference, $8 for another 4 hours, is the *surplus value,* or profit, going to the capitalist. Surplus value is defined as the worth of the worker's product (8 hours of labor power expended) minus the worth of the worker (4 hours of labor power expended). Therefore, the surplus value equals 8 hours minus 4 hours—that is, 4 hours—with a profit of $8 per day per worker.

According to Marx, this surplus product, or surplus value, is the source of all property income. Thus, all property income comes from exploitation of workers. *Exploitation* is defined as those hours of labor expended by workers above and beyond the the hours necessary to produce their wages. It includes the profits of the capitalist manufacturing corporation, as well as profits in the form of interest that the corporation pays to banks or other moneylenders, and rent paid for land to the landlord. All of this surplus value—or profit—derives from the exploitation of human labor.

MONOPOLY

We have now seen how businesses and corporations make profit in the normal routine of competitive capitalism. They make *more* profit, however, through the exercise of monopoly power. The image of prices and profits determined by the competition of millions of small businesses is clearly false in modern America. The size of business was very small before the Civil War but grew rapidly in the late nineteenth century. Then in the 1890s and 1900s there was a vast merger movement. Out of it were formed corporate giants like United States Steel, which owned 60 percent of all steel-producing capacity. Mergers and other types of economic concentration of small firms into giant firms have continued ever since then. These giants now set industry prices.

To appreciate the size of these giants, consider just one of them:

General Motors' yearly operating revenues exceed those of all but a dozen or so countries. Its sales receipts are greater than the combined general revenues of New

York, New Jersey, Pennsylvania, Ohio, Delaware, and the six New England states
. . . G.M. employees number well over 700,000 and work in 127 plants in the United
States and 45 countries spanning Europe, South Africa, North America, and Australia.
The total cash wages are more than twice the personal income of Ireland. (Barber,
1970, p. 20)

In most industries, just three or four giant monopolistic firms control most
of the production—and most of these top firms, as you will see, are part of the
100 largest super-giant conglomerates. Many small firms also exist in most industries, but together they produce only a small percentage of the total output.
U.S. government data for 1963 showed that 39.6 percent of all industries were
highly concentrated—that is, 50 percent or more of their product was sold by
four companies (see Blair, 1972, pp. 53–53). Another 32.1 percent of all industries
were moderately concentrated—that is, 25 percent to 49 percent of their product
was sold by four companies. Only 28.3 percent of all industries were somewhat
competitive—that is, less than 25 percent of their product was sold by four companies.

Moreover, among the top companies, there are many interlocking directorates
(Domhoff, 1983). In 1965, the 250 largest corporations had a total of 4007 directorships, but these were held by just 3165 directors (Blair, 1972, p. 76). Among
these directors, 562 held two or more directorships and 5 held six each. Other studies
have traced control to eight main groups: Rockefellers, Mellons, and duPonts each
hold large blocs of stock in several corporations; Morgan–First National and Kuhn-
Loeb exercise indirect financial control over several corporations; and three other
groups are known for their local control in Boston, Chicago, and Cleveland.

The size and power of the largest firms keep increasing, even as a *percentage*
of the immense and increasing total capital of the United States. The share of
the top 100 manufacturing corporations rose from 23 percent in 1947 to 33 percent
in 1977. This enormous increase was caused largely by conglomerate mergers—
that is, mergers of firms in unrelated industries. For that reason, the previous
data given on concentration by industry far understates the true degree of monopoly power, since one conglomerate—for example, International Telephone and
Telegraph (ITT)—controls the leading firms in several different industries.

Since 1950, one out of every five of the thousand largest manufacturing
companies has been swallowed by an even larger giant. Since 1959, big business
has been absorbing other business firms with $10 million or more in assets at a
rate exceeding 60 a year. Obviously, the business giants are far from satisfied
with the immense size and power they already have, so these industrial empires
are continuing to expand by merger and other means.

There is a high concentration of *all* types of corporate assets in a compar-
atively few firms. By 1969, at the bottom of the pyramid, many small corporations
(890,000, or 58 percent of the total) held a minuscule portion of total corporate
assets ($30 billion, or 1 percent). At the top, a relatively few giant corporations
(1041, or just 0.27 percent) held a majority of all assets ($1218 trillion, or 55
percent). That some thousand American corporations hold more than $1 trillion
in assets is remarkable; that amount was more than the assets of the entire European Economic Community.

The reasons for monopoly include not only the increasing minimum size for an efficient plant but also the desire to control or eliminate competition. The giant monopoly corporations are able to raise their margins of price over cost much higher than competitive firms. The monopolies increase their profit by selling products at higher prices, thus lowering the real purchasing power of workers' wages. In addition, because of their bargaining strength, monopolists can obtain labor power from workers at lower wages. Some profits are also taken by the giants directly from other businesses. They sell their products to small businesses and farmers at high prices, while they buy products at low prices from farmers and small businesses. The monopolies also make extra profit by selling commodities, such as military hardware, well above the competitive price to governments. Finally, the monopolies make extra profit abroad by buying cheap labor power and cheap raw materials from the less developed countries because these countries are too weak to resist monopoly power. The profit rate rises with the financial size of corporations and the degree of economic concentration. All of these facts show how monopolies gain profits at the expense of smaller businesses and workers (see Sherman, 1968).

UNEMPLOYMENT

During the Great Depression, according to official data, unemployment was 25 percent in 1933 and was still 20 percent in 1938. After a long period of lower unemployment, the unemployment rate rose again to 9 percent in 1975 and 12 percent in 1982. Yet official data seriously understate the amount of unemployment. For one thing, the official data count all part-time workers as employed, whereas many of these are people trying unsuccessfully to get full-time jobs. Moreover, the official data do not count former workers who are so discouraged with the failure to find a job that they give up looking. If we add the part-time unemployed workers and the discouraged workers, then the true unemployment rate rises by 50 percent.

It is a common but increasingly incorrect assumption that unemployment mainly affects the uneducated and lower levels of blue-collar workers. In the 1950s and 1960s, college-educated white-collar workers had experienced relatively low levels of unemployment, but this is no longer the case. If anything, employment trends in the 1970s and 1980s created more anxiety for the college-educated, while-collar aspirant group than for other groups. In the 1980s many of the employment expectations of college graduates were not being met.

In a study surveying lack of solid employment among the college educated, some unemployment and a good deal of underemployment were found (see Steiger, 1977, pp. 6–7). Various groups of professionals, such as teachers, engineers, and scientists, have found employment problems that were almost unheard of in the 1950s and 1960s. While outright unemployment for the college educated can still often be avoided, this group has recently faced serious problems of underemployment—working at jobs clearly below one's skill level (for example, the chemist working as a house painter). Therefore, both the college educated and those without this level of education have suffered in the financial crises of capitalism in the 1980s.

What causes the misery of unemployment for millions of people periodically under capitalism? Capitalism is a system in which capitalists hire workers only if they expect to make a profit from their work. If there is no expected profit, there is no employment. The capitalist faces two problems in making a profit. First, the capitalist must successfully exploit the worker—that is, some of the worker's product must be expropriated as surplus value. But that is not the end of the capitalist's problems. The second task is to sell the product. Under capitalism, a product is useless if no one has the desire *and* the money to buy it. In a depression, millions of people desire more food, clothing, and shelter, but they have no money to buy these products. Therefore, the capitalist cannot realize the surplus value he has expropriated because he cannot sell the product. Therefore, he reduces production and fires workers, thereby increasing unemployment.

Consider the first problem—that of producing surplus value or profits. In every economic expansion, costs begin to rise, eventually rising faster than prices. All costs may be divided into labor costs and material costs. As full employment is approached, the wage for an hour's labor does begin to rise. Because workers' productivity rises even faster, however, the direct labor cost of producing a single unit of product tends to fall during most of the expansion.

On the other hand, there is an accelerating demand for machinery and raw materials. As a result, the prices of machinery and raw materials rise much faster than the prices of finished goods in every expansion, especially when bottlenecks arise near the peak of expansion. Thus the total cost per unit may fall somewhat in initial recovery—because of rising workers' productivity—but near the peak of expansion the rising costs of materials drive up the total cost per unit very rapidly. Therefore, the capitalist's margin of production of surplus value is menaced from the cost side.

On the income side, in every expansion the increasing productivity of workers goes unrewarded in large part, so that for most of the expansion the ratio of profits to wages—Marx's rate of exploitation—rises rapidly. This means, however, that more income is going to the people in upper brackets, who spend a smaller percentage of it for consumption. Less income is going to workers (with lower income levels), who spend most of their income for consumption. As a result the percentage of national income spent for consumption falls in every expansion. This causes a lack of demand for the capitalist's products.

Thus, at the peak of every expansion, profit is squeezed from two sides. Costs are rising: wage costs slowly and raw materials costs very rapidly. Demand is limited, however, so it rises more and more slowly. Demand is limited because the income of the masses of workers does not rise as rapidly as profits. Thus, the two-sided squeeze lowers present profits and lowers capitalists' expectation of profits. With lower expected profits, capitalists cut back on present production and also cut back on investment in new factories. The result is unemployment.

Spreading unemployment makes the problem worse because unemployed workers have even less income and less demand for goods in money terms (though their *desire* for goods is unchanged). So for a while the depression or recession gets worse and worse, with more unemployment leading to less demand, and less demand leading to more unemployment. Eventually, however, the process reverses itself. Demand declines more and more slowly because workers still must eat. People maintain their consumption so that it falls less than income. They do this by begging, borrowing (a lot of new debt), stealing (an increase in crime), and government charity (unemployment compensation). At the same time, costs fall rapidly, as worker wage rates decline and raw materials prices fall sharply. Thus the profit squeeze eases, and capitalist expectations improve so that they increase production and invest in new factories. The recovery has begun. The cycle repeats itself. Unfortunately for workers, unemployment is built into the business cycle.

THE ORIGINS OF REAGANOMICS

What is the sociological background of Reaganomics? In the 1950s and 1960s, the United States had a very affluent economy, partly due to a unique set of circumstances. First, at the end of World War II, the U.S. economy was totally dominant in the world, as the economies of both Japan and Western Europe were largely destroyed. Second, U.S. military spending continued at a high rate, stimulating the economy. Third, the economy continued at a high level, with no major depression. Fourth, the United States attracted the top intellects in the world, so there was a high rate of scientific advance.

In this period, such presidents as Truman and Kennedy practiced a liberal, optimistic form of Keynesian economics. They fought unemployment with spending on public works and cuts in the taxes of the poor and middle class.

In the 1970s the situation changed. First, the U.S. economy faced strong competition from Japan and Western Europe. Second, after the Vietnam War, military spending declined somewhat as a percent of gross national product (GNP). Third, the recovery of Europe meant that the United States stopped attracting all the best scientific minds. Fourth, the economy underwent severe recessions in 1975 and in 1982. Fifth, the recessions and stagnation meant reduced investment, leading to less growth in productivity. Sixth, there was a high rate of inflation.

As a result of all of these problems, Presidents Ford (Republican) and Carter (Democrat) found themselves unable to manage the economy, their policies were wavering, and the economic results were poor. In these circumstances, in 1980 candidate Ronald Reagan proposed what Vice President Bush had previously called "voodoo economics"—that is, Reagan proposed to cut everyone's taxes and, as a result, cure both unemployment and inflation, build a strong military, and reduce the deficit.

This policy is called *supply-side economics*. The supply-siders argue that there is no problem of overall demand—that the only problem is a lack of capital. If the taxes of the rich are cut, then they will save more money. Those new savings will provide more capital for investment, the new investment will create new businesses, thus unemployment will diminish, money will be available to build up the military, and more money will be available to reduce the deficit.

The critics of supply-side economics point out that if there is insufficient demand for (or lack of money to buy) their products, then the corporations will not expand their production—no matter how much savings they have available.

THE IMPACT OF REAGANOMICS

What did the Reagan administration actually do? In the dramatic actions of 1981 (its first year) the Reagan administration pushed through Congress a budget that did two things. First, it cut taxes for the rich but not for the poor (when all types of taxes are added together). Second, it significantly cut social services, while drastically increasing military spending.

On the spending side, Reagan cut one-third of all government spending for children, reduced school funds for disadvantaged children, decreased funds for mothers' and infants' nutrition, reduced day care, cut school breakfasts and school lunches, decreased education for the handicapped, cut youth employment funds, reduced Medicaid funds for children in poverty, reduced food stamps (50 percent of which go to children), and made cuts in aid to dependent children (800,000 children were dropped from the rolls in 1981). There are now 11 million children living in poverty.

In contrast, the Reagan administration has *doubled* the level of military spending. This, in turn, has helped produce the largest budget deficits in U.S. history (about a quarter of a trillion dollars a year)—the exact opposite of his pledge to reduce federal deficits. The Reagan administration also eliminated the Youth Conservation Corps and made large cuts in all of the following areas: public-service job programs, education programs, health care, Medicaid, Medicare for the elderly, Social Security benefits, public housing, the Economic Development Administration, the Appalachian Regional Administration, urban development, Consumer Product Safety Commission, mass transit, water cleanup projects, parks, arts and humanities, postal service, public broadcasting, community action programs, and legal services for the poor. All of this reduced income, thereby diminishing consumer demand and employment. There were no cuts in subsidies to big business.

On the tax side, the income taxes of the rich and large corporations were reduced by lower tax rates and by more tax loopholes. The average worker gained a little in less income tax but lost more in extra Social Security taxes. The summary by the United Press International (August 1981, p. 1), the leading U.S. wire service, said: "Although the bill contains massive tax cuts for business and a host of tax breaks for special interests, there were only a handful of changes to help the average worker." Most Americans (60 percent in a poll) perceived that "Reagan represents the interests of business rather than the average American" (Stacks, 1981, p. 23).

The result of this massive transfer of income from the poor and middle class to the rich was that the savings of the rich and the large corporations increased vastly. Yet it did *not* increase investment. Business had plenty of money that it *could* invest. But the mass demand for their products by consumers declined because they had less disposable income to spend. Thus there was a severe recession in 1981 and 1982, with a rapid decline in investment—in spite of the much lower taxes and greater savings of the rich. In 1987, the stock market declined an enormous 508 points in one day, October 19, by far a record decline.

To sum up, Reagan cut the taxes of the wealthy and reduced inflation in part by his many budget cuts. He greatly increased military spending, which helped reignite the cold war tensions and helped produce huge budget deficits. The unemployment rate initially skyrocketed under Reagan to depression levels exceeding 10 percent; by 1985, unemployment levels declined back to the level at which they stood when Reagan took office. Instead of solving social problems, Reaganomics significantly increased them because of large cuts in many social services and created a homeless population not seen since the Great Depression of the 1930s. The stock market decline could have created a serious recession or a depression.

IMPERIALISM

From the fifteenth century onward, the developing capitalist economies of Europe grew economically and militarily at a rate then unparalleled in human history. From the fifteenth to the nineteenth centuries, they eventually came to dominate much of the rest of the world. They plundered, enslaved, and ruled so as to extract the maximum gains from their subjects.

Such havoc was created that ancient and culturally advanced civilizations disappeared, as in Peru and West Africa. At the same time, progress in dominated countries, such as India, was set back hundreds of years by the destruction of native industries. On the other side, the plunder was so great that it constituted the main element in the formation of European capital and provided the foundation for prosperous trade and eventual European industrialization.

By the end of the nineteenth century almost all of the presently less developed countries were under the colonial rule of the more advanced countries. The imperialist countries invested in the colonized countries at astoundingly high profit rates, primarily because of a cheap labor supply and an enforced lack of competition. The capital was invested mainly in extractive industries that exported raw materials to the imperial countries—for example, rubber from Southeast Asia and gold and silver from South America. In the imperial countries, the cheap raw materials were profitably turned into manufactured goods for sale there. In addition, part of the manufactured goods were exported back (tariff free) to the colonized country to be sold there for large profits.

The tariff-free imported goods generally completed the destruction of the colonized country's manufacturing industries. An example of this may be seen in colonial India, especially in its textile industry:

> India, still an exporter of manufactured products at the end of the eighteenth century, becomes an importer. From 1815 to 1832, India's cotton exports dropped by 92 percent. In 1850, India was buying one quarter of Britain's cotton exports. All industrial products shared this fate. The ruin of the traditional trades and crafts was the result of British commercial policy. (Bettleheim, 1968, p. 47)

The economic development of the colonial areas was thus held back by the imperialist countries, while the development of the imperialist countries was greatly speeded by the flow of profits from the colonies. The exception that proves the rule is Japan. Because Japan escaped colonialism, it was able to independently industrialize and develop its own advanced capitalist economy. Japan alone achieved this among the countries of Asia, Africa, and Latin America because the others had all been reduced to colonies, thus preventing their further development.

The half-century from 1890 to World War II was the peak period of colonialism, when most of the world was divided among the Western European and North American powers. In the late 1940s and 1950s, a new era began, with formal independence being achieved by hundreds of millions of people throughout Asia and Africa as a result of struggles fomented by the impact of two world wars, the Russian and Chinese revolutions, and the long pent-up pressures for liberation. The day of open colonialism is over, but the pattern still holds by which the ex-colonies export food or raw materials. In fact, the less developed countries are often dependent mainly on exports of just one product—for example, bananas from Guatemala and copper from Chile. Moreover, the less developed countries still *import* most of their finished goods from the United States, Western Europe, or Japan. Foreign investment still dominates their industries. Because of the continuance of the underlying colonial economic pattern, this situation is often referred to as *neocolonialism,* in spite of formal political independence.

In fact, formal independence has changed the essential economic relationships very little. On the one side are all the less developed, newly independent countries, still under foreign economic domination and still facing all the old obstacles to development. On the other side are the advanced capitalist countries, still extracting large profits from the dependent Third World. Pope John Paul II stated in 1984 that ". . . the poor people and the poor nations, poor in different ways—not only lacking in food, but also deprived of freedom and other human rights—will judge those people who take these goods away from them, amassing to themselves the imperialistic monopoly of economic and political supremacy at the expense of others" (quoted in Dionne, 1984, p. 1).

The giant multinational firms, those that operate worldwide, are the present instrument whereby enormous profits are extracted from the neocolonial countries and sent back to the imperialist countries. American firms' profits from abroad were only 7 percent of total American corporate profits in 1960, but rose to 30 percent by 1974 (see Muller, 1975, p. 183). The top 298 American-based, multinational corporations earn 40 percent of their entire net profits overseas, and their *rate* of profit abroad is much higher than their domestic profit rate (see Barnett and Muller, 1974, pp. 16–17). Moreover, most of these corporate investments are not made from American funds at all, but are provided by local capitalists. In all of the Latin American manufacturing operations of American-based multinational corporations from 1960 to 1970, about 78 percent of the investments were financed by local funds. Yet, the same corporations in that period sent 52 percent of all their profits back to the United States (see Mandell, 1970, pp. 22–23).

As a result of the use of local funds for investment, plus high profit rates, plus the sending of most profits to the United States, the neocolonial, or Third World, countries actually have a net *outflow* of capital to the United States. In the period 1950–1965 in Latin America, American corporations invested $3.8 billion but extracted $11.3 billion, *for a net flow of $7.5 billion from that area* *to the United States.* Yet, at the same time, profit rates were so high that the value of American direct investments in Latin America *rose* from $4.5 billion to $10.3 billion.

Similarly, in Africa and Asia in the period 1950–1965, American corporations invested only $5.2 billion but transferred to the United States $14.3 billion in profits, *for a net flow of $9.1 billion to the United States.* Yet enough profit remained for reinvestment that direct American investments in Africa and Asia rose from $1.3 billion to $4.7 billion.

Two facts are clearly obvious from these data: (1) the rate of profit in American investments abroad is several times higher in the less developed than in the advanced capitalist countries; and (2) the less developed neocolonial countries generously make a good-sized contribution to American capital accumulation.

Although U.S. corporations still obtain these huge profits from abroad, the U.S. economy is now facing its own very difficult international problems. In the 1950s U.S. firms totally dominated international trade. Slowly, however, Japanese and European competitors obtained larger and larger parts of the market. U.S. firms, with strong monopoly positions in the 1950s, saw no need to innovate, so they slowly fell behind technologically in many fields. Now U.S. corporations are unable to find export markets for many products, while U.S. consumers use many Japanese and European products. The result is a very large and increasing deficit in the balance of trade. This means that more money is flowing out of than into the United States for trade, so the net demand for U.S. goods is reduced and U.S. workers lose jobs.

THE WORLD SYSTEM

Some sociologists have begun to look at the whole world as a single socioeconomic system. They tend to see it composed of a core of more developed, industrialized countries and a periphery of poorer countries dominated by the more developed core countries (Wallerstein, 1982, p. 15). The worldwide economic system is portrayed as a capitalist system. This international capitalist system includes the socialist countries, which are said to be integrated into the international trade network.

Capitalism is seen as having contradictory mechanisms striving toward different goals. First, capitalist entrepreneurs keep trying to expand production as rapidly as possible, but demand is restricted by holding down wages and by government actions to cut spending. The result is economic crisis. Second, as the rich countries get richer, the gap between the rich and poor countries has grown. Third, every capitalist country strives to dominate the whole world, but coalitions form against the strongest to try to preserve the present system of nation states.

These contradictions lead to two types of antisystem movements. These movements include protest movements by the working class in the core countries as well as liberation movements against external control in the peripheral countries. Revolutions have succeeded in Russia, China, Cuba, and other countries. There have been cycles of despair and revolution. From 1914 to 1945, there were World War I, the Russian Revolution, the Great Depression of the 1930s, and

World War II. Then, from 1945 to about 1967 there was worldwide optimism and growth under U.S. leadership. From 1967 to the present, the scene has been bleaker, with more adverse economic developments and the end of complete U.S. domination, more chaos in the Third World, and increasing pessimism.

These analysts see a steady drift in the world toward socialism in the sense of government ownership. But they foresee a long struggle over many decades to decide what "socialism" is to mean. Will it be democratic or dictatorial? Will a new elite evolve—as in the Soviet Union—that will create a class-dominated society, even though this new elite will be a new class? Will the road to socialism be peaceful or violent? In subsequent chapters we attempt to provide some answers to these important questions.

SUMMARY

In the conservative view, workers are paid according to their productivity. In the radical view, modern capitalism has devised various techniques to extract profit for the capitalist class. The most basic source of profit is the exploitation of human labor power. Workers produce valuable goods that capitalists sell for profit. Although laborers get some financial return for their work, usually there is a surplus value, which is profit beyond the costs of making products. This surplus value goes to the capitalist class.

Capitalism no longer is carried out in small businesses, as it was over a hundred years ago. Now, monopolies and multinational corporations dominate American enterprise, as well as much of the rest of the world. In the radical view, the results have been greater profits for the capitalist class, but also the perpetuation of poverty and unemployment for millions of people in the United States and many millions more in other countries. Trends such as these point, according to analysts of world systems, to the long-run instability of the capitalist system.

SUGGESTED READINGS

The classic discussion of the theory of exploitation is found in Karl Marx's *Capital* (New York: Random House [Modern Library], 1906; first published, 1867). For a modern explanation, see E. K. Hunt and Howard Sherman, *Economics: Introduction to Traditional and Radical Views*, 5th ed. (New York: Harper & Row, 1986). For current articles on the economic aspect of sociology, the best source is the *Review of Radical Political Economics* (41 Union Square West, Room 901, New York, NY 10003).

REFERENCES

Barber, Richard. 1970. *The American Corporation*. New York: Dutton.
Barnett, Richard, and Ronald Muller. 1974. *Global Research*. New York: Simon & Schuster.
Bettleheim, Charles. 1968. *India Independent*. New York: Monthly Review Press.
Blair, John. 1972. *Economic Concentration*. New York: Harcourt Brace Jovanovich.
Clark, John Bates. 1903. *The Distribution of Wealth*. Clifton, NJ: Augustus M. Kelly (First published, 1889).

Dionne, E. J., Jr. 1984. "Pope John Paul Assails 'Imperialistic Monopoly.' " *New York Times* (September 17).

Domhoff, G. William. 1983. *Who Rules America Now? A view for the '80s.* Englewood Cliffs, NJ: Prentice-Hall.

Mandell, Ernest. 1978. *Europe vs. America: Contradictions of Imperialism.* New York: Monthly Review Press.

Muller, Ronald. 1975. "Global Corporations and National Stabilization Policy." *Journal of Economic Issues* 9(2).

Robinson, John. 1960. *An Essay of Marxian Economics.* New York: St. Martin's.

Scheer, Robert. 1974. *America After Nixon: The Age of the Multinationals.* New York: McGraw-Hill.

Sherman, Howard. 1968. *Profit Rates in the United States.* Ithaca, NY: Cornell University Press.

Stacks, John. 1981. "America's Fretful Mood." *Time* (December 28).

United Press International. 1981. "Tax Cut Seen Having Small Initial Impact." *The Honolulu Advertiser* (August 5).

Wallerstein, Immanuel. 1982. "Crisis as Transition." In Samir Amin, Giovanni Arrighi, Andre Gunder Frank, and Immanuel Wallerstein, *Dynamics of Global Crisis.* New York: Monthly Review Press.

four

POLITICAL INSTITUTIONS AND MOVEMENTS

chapter 15

Political Sociology: The Impact of Society on Politics

In this chapter and in Chapter 16 we focus on the political structure of advanced capitalism. We will answer two questions, emphasizing one in each chapter. First: How does the socioeconomic base affect the political structure and the related distribution of power? Second: How do political institutions affect social and economic behavior?

CAPITALIST GOVERNMENTS: TWO CONFLICTING VIEWS

The United States has a capitalist economy plus a formally democratic political structure. Two extremely different views of capitalist democracy have been popularized. In Fourth of July speeches, the United States is said to be a pure democracy—everyone is equal in influence, everyone has one vote, and the majority wins (while the minority retains rights, such as freedom of speech).

On the other hand, Marx oversimplified for propaganda purposes when he said, "The executive power of the modern state is simply a committee for managing the common affairs of the entire bourgeois class" (Marx and Engels, 1948, p. 11). Just as strongly, while he was president of the United States, Woodrow Wilson wrote:

Suppose you go to Washington and try to get at your Government. You will always find that while you are politely listened to, the men really consulted are the men who have the biggest stake—the big bankers, the big manufacturers, the big masters of commerce, the heads of railroad corporations and of steamship corporations. . . . The masters of the Government of the United States are the combined capitalists and manufacturers of the United States. (Wilson, 1914, pp. 57–58)

Any serious sociological study of the facts will find a large grain of truth in these popular statements of Marx and Wilson, but no one would claim that our complex political structure can be characterized in any simple statement. In reality, the United States is *not* a 100-percent pure democracy, *nor* is it zero percent democratic (a pure dictatorship of the capitalist class). The truth lies somewhere in between, and only empirical research can tell us where. Empirical facts, however, must be selected, analyzed, and interpreted in some theoretical framework—so there continues to be serious disagreement about the power of the capitalist class (Kourvetaris and Dobratz, 1982).

THE PLURALIST VIEW

The dominant school in American political sociology has been the pluralist school. The pluralists assert that the American government is not dominated by a ruling class but is, instead, a democracy reflecting many different interest groups, and that power is held not by one group but plurally by many groups. They assert that the

> power structure of the United States is highly complex and diversified (rather than unitary and monolithic), that the political system is more or less democratic . . . , that in political processes the political elite is ascendant over and not subordinate to the economic elite. . . . (Rose, 1967, p. 492)

A newer, more qualified version of this pluralist conception has been expressed by Dye (1983), as well as by Orum (1978) and Knoke (1982). Pluralists now often argue that "America is ruled by various competing elites" (Kourvetaris and Dobratz, 1982, p. 290).

Notice that in arguing for the proposition that America is democratic in nature, the pluralists find it necessary to emphasize that political power is *to a large degree* independent of and superior to economic power. The reason, of course, is that economic power is so unequally distributed. If the distribution of political power exactly followed that of economic power, the degree of inequality would leave little to call democracy.

The pluralists thus reject the radical view that unequal political power fully reflects the unequal economic power of the capitalist class. Yet the pluralists also reject the simplistic conservative notion that every citizen has equal political power. They admit some inequality, but still see a resulting political democracy that roughly reflects and arbitrates the desires of many conflicting groups. There is not a single ruling class and there are no fundamental class conflicts according to the pluralists. Rather, there are a plural number of groups, and the functional result is a democracy that reconciles the conflicting claims.

The pluralists do not emphasize socioeconomic classes, but define their groups quite differently. In the early 1960s the pluralist David Truman (1964, p. 37) affirmed that if any "shared-attitude group . . . makes its claims through or upon . . . government, it becomes a political interest group." In this broad definition he includes an immense and random collection of groups: American Legion, Parents-Teachers Association, American Medical Association, Farm Bureau, blacks, Jews, Catholics, American Automobile Association, philatelists, and so on. The pluralists discuss all these "interest groups" in the abstract, with no relation to any structured relationship of groups or classes. Yet they are each of very different power. How can one compare the power of philatelists (stamp collectors) to that of all Catholics? Moreover, on basic political issues one cannot state the vested interests of philatelists in the same way as one can calculate the vested interests of the capitalist class. Finally, his main reason for discussing so many groups seems to be a preoccupation with the notion that the overlapping membership in many of these groups will preserve social harmony and prevent conflict. Truman says, "It is . . . multiple memberships in potential groups based on widely held and accepted interests that serve as a balance wheel in a going political system like that of the United States" (ibid., p. 514).

Following this pluralist notion of government as a balance wheel, traditional sociologists visualize the U.S. government as a neutral entity above the class struggle. For example, one traditional text shows the picture of a dejected woman, poor and black, whose claims apparently have been rejected by a government agency. The authors comment, "Government's attempt to adjudicate the interests of various publics and interests inevitably dissatisfy many" (Leslie et al., 1976, p. 438). But the issue is: Does the government adjudicate as a neutral? Or did the government reject the interests of this poor, black woman because it is ruled by and for a class that is mainly rich, white, and male?

Similarly, two liberal writers on pollution problems see plural and conflicting interests being adjudicated by governmental agencies that are above the battle. These two liberals, D'Arge and Wilen, write: "The combatant parties include the manufacturer responsible for the emissions . . . and the affected parties; . . . the neutral party is the federal government" (1974, p. 362). They emphasize the need in pollution cases for "a reasoned noncommittal or neutral review of the evidence by a public official or member of the scientific community community" (p. 364). But is the government neutral in pollution cases if it is strongly influenced by the capitalist class? Are public officials—like former Vice-President Spiro Agnew, who had to resign his vice-presidency over accusations of accepting payments from businesses, or officials in the Reagan administration with ties to Wedtech Corp. (*San Diego Union*, October 1, 1987)—really neutral if they are connected to the corporations? Are even members of the scientific community, many of whom do research that is subsidized by large grants from the federal government, really neutral?

THE RADICAL CRITIQUE BY MILLS AND DOMHOFF

Probably the most systematic and devastating attack on the pluralist theory of power distribution is that of the late C. Wright Mills in *The Power Elite* (1956). Never one to accept conclusions of the liberal academic establishment, Mills singles out the pluralists for special criticism in this book. In fact, he brands this school of thought "romantic pluralism" (Mills, 1956, chap. 11, esp. p. 244).

Mills dramatically begins his book as follows:

> The powers of ordinary men are circumscribed by the everyday worlds in which they live, yet even in these rounds of job, family, and neighborhood they often seem driven by forces they can neither understand nor govern. "Great changes" are beyond their control, but affect their conduct and outlook none the less. The very framework of modern society confines them to projects not their own, but from every side, such changes now press upon the men and women of the mass society, who accordingly feel that they are without purpose in an epoch in which they are without power. (p. 3)

Instead of power being rather evenly distributed between numerous interest groups, Mills argues that the major decisions in America—decisions of national consequence—are made by a power elite comprised of those in the highest echelons of business, government, and the military. The power elite thus consists of the president of the United States and his close associates (this is the political directorate); the heads of major American corporations, such as General Motors, ITT, and General Electric; and the top-ranking generals and admirals in the armed services.

This group, for Mills, combines to make decisions that affect all Americans—decisions related to inflating or deflating the dollar, setting oil prices, going to war, making peace, signing treaties with foreign governments, and the like. These decisions of national consequence are certainly vital to all Americans, so that in a democracy all Americans should share equally in the decision-making process. But this is Mills's point: The masses of Americans—even those who hold upper-middle-class positions—are excluded from making these big decisions that are reserved for the power elite. The Iran-*contra* Congressional hearings in 1987, for example, pointed to a small and very secretive group of high government, military, and business officials combining to carry out foreign policy for the United States in Iran and Nicaragua. Thus the power elite is seen as highly removed from the masses of everyday citizens and groups, which points to a very undemocratic political structure in the United States. That is, American society cannot be called democratic when a small elite makes the major decisions of national consequence.

Mills suggests a diagram of American society that looks like Figure 15.1. The diagram points to one other level of power besides the power elite and the dispossessed masses. This is the middle level of power in American society, comprised of such groups as trade unions, churches, schools and universities, and—most important—Congress.

As with other analyses, Mills and the pluralists seriously differ with regard to this middle level of power. On the one hand, Mills concedes that the middle level has some power, particularly with regard to special interests such as higher wages for workers, more money for education, and medical care for the elderly. Special interest groups help pass national legislation benefiting their constituencies, which may even number several millions. But these are still limited constituencies, affecting the lives of only a smaller proportion of the American population of about 240 million people. Mills does *not* argue that the power elite decides everything regarding the goals of interest groups, such as organized

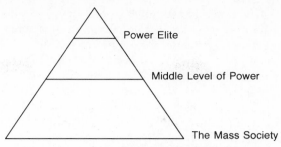

Figure 15.1   Mills's concept of American society.

workers, organizations for the aged, and organizations of the retired. Groups at the middle level of power have some influence over these special interest types of decisions. But middle-level groups, for Mills, do not make the decisions of national consequence that affect all Americans (and, often, many people in other countries). These momentous decisions are made by the power elite.

Even if some pluralists admit that universities, for example, are not on a par with giant corporations in making decisions of national consequence, the pluralists adamantly reject the idea of Congress being located *below* the power elite (Rose, 1967). Congress presumably represents the American people in general because members of Congress are elected from geographic areas throughout the United States. According to the pluralists, this should guarantee democratic input by citizens throughout the United States with regard to any national decisions.

This should be especially the case for the House of Representatives. The two senators per state can be somewhat removed from their constituency because senators are not responsible to smaller geographic districts. However, members of the House of Representatives are elected by—and are thus supposed to be responsible to—smaller geographic areas nationwide. Thus, according to the pluralists, even local interests have some input into national decisions.

If, in fact, members of the Senate and House of Representatives did control national decisions, Mills would have a difficult task arguing that a small, elite group really ran the show. But Mills argues that Congress is only at the middle level of power and thus does not regularly participate in decisions of national consequence. Congress is often the place where numerous interest groups vie to gain special favors for their smaller constituencies. But lobbying for favors is quite different from making decisions of national consequence. Indeed, what especially bothered Congress about the Iran-*contra* activities of using money from arms deals with Iran to support the *contras* fighting the Nicaragua regime was the total exclusion of Congress from these decisions of national consequence.

Some other writers are in the Millsian tradition without exactly duplicating his own analysis (it might be noted that Mills was probably the first and last "pure" Millsian). Most notable among analysts following Mills's tradition is G. William Domhoff. In such books as *Who Rules America?* (1967) and its sequel (1983), Domhoff has followed up on various ideas about power originally stated by Mills. However, Domhoff emphasizes more the role of the upper class as a major political force than Mills did. Domhoff (1968, 1971, 1972, 1975a, 1975b,

1979–80, 1983) has shown upper-class influence in American political life in a number of his studies. The political prominence of the late millionnaire Nelson Rockefeller (contender for the presidency and a vice-president) is only one example of the upper economic class making direct political decisions. As we will see, the upper class often influences politics in a less direct and less public manner than Rockefeller (Block, 1977).

One methodology used by the pluralists to demonstrate democracy in America is to examine voting statistics (Campbell et al., 1960; Berelson et al., 1954; Almond and Verba, 1963). Voting studies occupied a prominent place in political sociology until recently (and still do in traditional political sociology). The general approach is to determine which groups are likely to vote Republican or Democrat, on the underlying assumption that the ability to vote makes America a democracy. Many of the voting studies showed that the probusiness Republican party tended to attract people who were wealthier, more educated, owned property, and generally occupied higher-status positions in the community. In contrast, the Democratic party tended to attract poorer people, the working class, ethnic and religious minorities, and various easterners and southerners (Lipset, 1985). Any change from these voting habits would be of interest to the student of voting behavior. (For example, workers who voted for Nixon in 1972 and Reagan in 1980 and 1984 were of interest to voting analysts.) Whether stability or change in voting habits is the issue, those who meticulously charted voting behavior over the last 40 years or so assumed the vote was crucial to making America democratic. But does the ability to vote—especially in the face of many other inequalities—really mean that a society is democratic? In particular, does voting (which is often restricted to two main candidates) counterbalance patterns of undemocratic decision making at the top of our society, as is suggested by Mills, Domhoff, and others? This is a question we hope to resolve in the remainder of this chapter by showing the great influence of the economic and political elite over the American system.

An attempt to give the American voters an option to mainstream policies was Jesse Jackson's bids for the Democratic party nomination for president in 1984 and 1988. What were these alternative policies and what happened? Jackson's was more or less a populist campaign, focusing on improvements for the poor and middle classes and a change in direction of U.S. foreign policy. In policies presented to the Democratic party's platform committee in 1988, for example, Jackson wanted to raise taxes of the rich, freeze defense spending, renounce first use of nuclear weapons, and call for Middle East peace initiatives stressing self-determination for all parties involved (*Los Angeles Times*, 1988). Raising taxes on the rich and freezing defense spending would generate billions of dollars that could then be used for improved education, health care, day-care centers, drug-abuse programs, and job-training programs. Ruling out first use of nuclear weapons and basing Middle East peace on self-determination would be significant departures from current U.S. policies. How did the elite of the Democratic party respond? The Michael Dukakis forces on the committee completely rejected these alternative proposals.

Another of the methodologies used by pluralists is the community study. Community studies proliferated before, and especially after, the publication of

Mills's *The Power Elite*. Some community studies showed a clearly unequal distribution of power at the city level (Hunter, 1953; Lynd and Lynd, 1929; Vidich and Bensman, 1958). In particular, the local upper economic classes were seen to make a disproportionate number of community decisions. However, a number of community studies beginning in the early 1960s have pointed to a more pluralistic—and therefore allegedly more democratic—distribution of power on the local level (Clark, 1975).

The most famous of these pluralist community studies is probably Robert Dahl's *Who Governs?* (1961). In this book, Dahl argues that although there is an inequality of resources in New Haven, Connecticut, democracy thrives there nevertheless. For example, he tries to show that different groups only exercise power over issues of specific concern to them. Thus, business leaders in New Haven were influential in the urban redevelopment of the downtown business district, since this was of clear concern to them. Dahl argues, however, that business leaders did not control education, hold a large number of political offices, or greatly influence political nominations in New Haven. Even in urban redevelopment, business leaders were not seen as a "ruling class," since others, including a strong mayor, also had a say in these decisions.

The difficulty with Dahl's argument is not so much that he incorrectly depicts democracy in New Haven—though Domhoff (1977) has challenged Dahl on these grounds and other studies (Tabb and Sawers, 1978, 1984; Lyon et al., 1981) support this critique. The biggest problem is that Dahl's study—and all the other local community studies—cannot be used to examine democracy at the national level, which is Mills's focus. Thus, even if New Haven is relatively democratic, this does not refute the existence of a national power elite.

One study that does attempt to indicate pluralism on a national level is Arnold Rose's *The Power Structure* (1967). Rose's position is pluralist, like Dahl's, and his reasoning is similar, taking into account various differences between national and local politics. Rose tries to refute Mills's theory by attempting to show that various groups make national decisions and that Congress is very much involved in these decisions. Thus, two very different views on power distribution in the United States have emerged over the years: one view pointing to a rather plural distribution of power, and the other to power concentrated at the top of American society, either in the hands of a power elite, à la C. Wright Mills, or in the hands of an economic upper class.

THE MARXIST VIEW

Many contemporary radicals, such as Domhoff, are strongly influenced by the view of political sociology first enunciated by Karl Marx. Marx himself had a very sophisticated and complex view of political sociology, as is shown by Miliband (1969), Draper (1977), and Avineri (1968). Marx's view is quite different from some of the vulgarized versions that often pass for Marxism. Whereas vulgar Marxists usually speak of only two classes fighting for political power, every one of Marx's own analyses—including detailed political studies of France, England, Germany, and the United States—specified numerous classes, subclasses, remnants of classes, in-between or middle classes, and strife by factions of a single class. Whereas vulgar Marxists assume that capitalist governments bear a one-to-one relation to the economic interests of the capitalist class, Marx shows that governments do have a certain limited autonomy from the dominant class and that politics represent a tangled skein of long-run and short-run interests of a wide variety of different classes and different factions within classes.

To begin with, Marx argues that there are two sides to the origin and functioning of the state. Marx uses the term "the state" to mean all of the power structure of government—everything from making laws to police functions to propaganda functions of government public relations personnel. Marx states that one source of the origin of state power was the need for control of some common functions in the interest of the whole community. For example, in ancient Egypt it was necessary to control the Nile River and irrigation. A second source of the origin of state power was the need by the ruling class, as in ancient Egypt, to hold down the oppressed classes, such as the slave class in Egypt, in order to exploit the slaves' labor. American government functions today still have these two aspects: common functions for the community and class functions for the ruling class. For example, the building of highways serves the whole community, but which highways and how many highways are built is largely determined by the profit goals of the automobile industry and the construction industry, both of which maintain huge lobbies at the federal and state levels.

Marx was also very critical of theorists who insist that there always has been and always will be an elite of rulers and an oppressed mass of the ruled. Marx and Engels were among the first political theorists to take seriously the findings of some anthropologists that many primitive societies are built around the extended family or clan, have no government in the modern sense, and certainly no police or other repressive forces. Marx said that this absence of a repressive state was due to the fact that there was no class division. People were elected for temporary leadership of community functions, but there was no need for repression because there was no exploited class.

The goal of Marxists is a communist society in which there will again be no classes, no ruling elite, voluntary cooperation by all, and no repressive state machinery. As the first step in this direction, Marx advocated socialism as the only consistent form of democracy. Marx pointed out that in various capitalist states the forms of democracy function in the political sphere; however, the continued domination of a small number of capitalists in the economic sphere extends their power in substance to the political sphere as well. Socialism means a society of democracy in substance as well as form. In a socialist society, the democratically elected government, and local workers' councils own and control the economy. Thus power over the lives of the majority is taken away from a few capitalists and exercised by all of the people at the local and the national levels.

Vulgar Marxists argue as if the capitalist class directly runs the government of capitalist countries. Marx, on the contrary, emphasized that the actual day-to-day running of the government is usually left to a specialized group and that capitalist control is often indirect. (Politicians are employed by capitalists the same way engineers are employed by capitalists.) The control is exercised not by a conspiracy but by the built-in features of the whole system and its institutions.

In his writings Marx emphasized a long list of means by which capitalists and the capitalist state exercise control over the masses of the working class, mostly indirectly and mostly by peaceful propaganda and economic means.

According to Marx, some of the ways the capitalist class controls society are by influencing:

1. Religious organizations
2. Media, which in modern society means radio, television, newspapers, and all forms of advertising
3. Educational system
4. Political system, legal system, and the courts
5. Control of jobs and cooptation of many potentially dissident workers into top positions to pressure and condition people into a probusiness frame of mind
6. Family, as the institution that transmits the need for "discipline" and "respect" in order to get ahead in the work world

Through all these channels ideologies are encouraged that divide and weaken the working class. Those ideologies include racism, sexism, nationalism, and a more general ideology that individualism is a good thing and that elitism is necessary and inevitable in any society. The capitalist institutions, particularly the media, also push apolitical events such as sports spectaculars (for example, baseball and football) and Roman circuses of violence (for example, enormous coverage of terrorist activities, murders, fires, and earthquakes).

According to Marx, the capitalist class, through its government apparatus, also sometimes grants reforms as a necessary concession to workers—for example, the many reforms of Roosevelt's New Deal, which were certainly prolabor, but clearly designed to save capitalism. Only the most vulgar Marxists think that no reforms can be wrested from the capitalist state. On the contrary, Marx emphasized that reforms may be won by working-class pressure, or by one faction of the capitalist class to gain popular support, or by the government acting somewhat autonomously. Marx also shows that the capitalist government is sometimes farsighted enough to pass reforms in the interest of the whole capitalist class in the long run, even though many capitalists vociferously oppose the reforms from the viewpoint of their immediate interests. A modern example might be the ending of the Vietnam War against the immediate interests of the capitalists who were supplying military commodities. Yet ending the war helped defuse large-scale protests against the entire capitalist system in the United States.

Another means of capitalist influence mentioned by Marx is the direct use of corruption and bribery by the capitalist class. For example, in the United States, big business routinely gives millions of dollars to the Republicans and Democrats in elections in order to assure election of their candidates. Big business also routinely spends millions of dollars on lobbying. The Watergate scandal exposed many kinds of links and illegal payoffs between business and the president. Yet, Marx notes that such illegal means are always quite secondary compared with the systematic institutionalized modes of control exercised by the capitalist class over the working masses.

Finally, only infrequently does the capitalist state resort to outright repression—another means of controlling society—as in the period of Senator Joseph McCarthy and the House Un-American Activities Committee. Similarly, the capitalist state only occasionally turns to the last resort of force and violence. Government violence includes using police against protesting students or strikers; armies against national liberation movements; protecting property by sending the poor, who are often minorities, to prison; or suppressing radicals through the Federal Bureau of Investigation (FBI) or the Central Intelligence Agency (CIA). Such means are inconvenient, expensive, and sure to stimulate reactions against them. Therefore, wise capitalist politicians try to avoid these means of control wherever possible. Violent repression, fascism, or military dictatorships usually emerge only when the capitalist system is in an extreme economic and political crisis, as in Germany in 1931.

A great deal of new radical research on the state in the last decade or so has produced three sophisticated theories, discussed in the appendix to this chapter. Indeed, a recent review points to the decline of pluralism and to the rise of the "political economy" approach, which emphasizes the relation of the economy to the state and includes these three theories (Kourvetaris and Dobratz, 1982).

CLASS AND POLITICAL PARTICIPATION

Most radical or Marxist sociologists usually do not make dogmatic assertions about politics. Instead, they study empirical evidence of the various mechanisms in capitalist society whereby economic inequality in fact leads to political inequality. The institutions of the United States are democratic in form but not in content because of differences in economic power. Thus, a millionaire owning a newspaper chain has only the same formal political rights as an unemployed poor worker, but surely their actual political influence is very different. An empirical study discovers the following:

> The existence of a national upperclass that meets generally accepted definitions of social class . . . that this upperclass owns a disproportionate amount of the country's wealth and receives a disproportionate amount of its yearly income, and that (its) members . . . control the major banks and corporations, which . . . dominate the American economy . . . that (its) members . . . and their high-level corporation executives control the foundations, the elite universities, the largest of the mass media, . . . the Executive branch of the federal government . . . regulatory agencies, the federal judiciary, the military, the CIA, and the FBI. (Domhoff, 1967, pp. 10–11; see also Domhoff, 1983)

Among the mechanisms of economic control over the American political process are limitations on political participation, use of the news media and advertising, money flow to political candidates and parties, class ties of government officials, and use of open and secret police. Each of these will be discussed in turn. In order to avoid the imputation of a radical bias, almost all the data in these sections are taken from traditional texts, such as Irish and Prothro (1965), which also refers to well-known conventional political sociologists.

We begin by noting that consciousness of class background can significantly affect political behavior (Useem, 1984; Hamilton, 1972; Curtis and Jackson, 1977). The sociological study conducted by Irish and Prothro found, contrary to the myth of an all-middle-class America, that 56 percent of all Americans said they thought of themselves as working class. Some 39 percent considered themselves middle class. (It is true, though, that 35 percent of all those questioned said that they had never thought of their class identification before that moment.) One percent said they were upper class, and only 2 percent rejected the whole idea of class (Irish and Prothro, 1965, p. 38; see also Lopreto and Hazelrigg, 1972).

Since an individual's political behavior can be influenced by class background, this leads to a puzzle. A majority of Americans are in the working class (according to our definition in Chapter 2). If everyone has one vote, why do parties favorable to the working class not win every election? Why do government policies usually further, not working-class interests, but (as Woodrow Wilson asserted) those of the wealthy capitalist class? More precisely, given formal democracy and capitalism, exactly how does American economic inequality tend to be translated into inequality of political power?

In the first place, there is the simple fact that the degree of political participation tends to vary with class background (Kourvetaris and Dobratz, 1982; Orum, 1978). "The average citizen has little interest in public affairs, and he expends his energy on the daily round of life—eating, working, family talk, looking at the comics [today, TV], sex, sleeping" (Irish and Prothro, 1965, p. 165). Indeed, since this was written, there has been a steady decline in the percentage of Americans voting in presidential elections, with only 54 percent voting for president in 1980 as compared to 62 percent in 1964 (Lipset, 1983, p. 340).

A 1964 study showed that 86 percent of those identified as middle class voted, but only 72 percent of the working class did. Similarly, 40 percent of the middle class had talked to others about voting for a party or candidate, but only 24 percent in the working class had done so. Among the middle-class people interviewed, 16 percent gave money to a political cause, 14 percent attended political meetings, and 8 percent worked for a party or candidate; in the working class, figures for the same activities were only 3 percent, 5 percent, and 3 percent, respectively (Irish and Prothro, 1965, p. 38). Although the percentage of voters has declined, many of these class tendencies persist (Orum, 1978).

Thus, even though traditional researchers have argued for a declining role of social class for political participation (Ladd and Hadley, 1975, 1978), nevertheless political participation of all kinds increases with income (Kourvetaris and Dobratz, 1982; Orum, 1978). Some of the reasons are obvious. Lower-income workers have less leisure, less money above minimum needs, and more exhausting jobs. Furthermore, detailed studies show that because lower-income workers have less education and less access to information, they have less knowledge of the importance of various issues—which accounts, in part, for their lower participation. The same studies show more cross-pressures on lower-income workers—for example, the racial antagonisms that conveniently divide and weaken their working-class outlook (Irish and Prothro, 1965, p. 193). Finally, at the other extreme, Useem's investigations indicate: "Compared with the internal cohesion of other

classes within America . . . that of the U.S. corporate elite appears unrivaled";
and that "major business policy associations . . . [such as] the Business Council,
Business Roundtable, Committee for Economic Development, and Council on
Foreign Relations, [are] the crucible of political cohesion" (1980, pp. 56–58; 1984).

CONTROL OF NEWS AND ADVERTISING

Unequal political power is also achieved through control of the news media (Gitlin,
1980). Even if the average worker "had an interest in politics, he would have
great difficulty getting accurate information; since the events of politics unfold
at a great distance, he cannot observe them directly, and the press offers a partial
and distorted picture" (Irish and Prothro, 1965, p. 165). Even the quantity of
news is limited. Although 80 percent of Americans read newspapers and 88 percent have television sets, only 2.8 percent of total newspaper space and even less
television time is devoted to political news (p. 183).

If political news is found wanting in quantity, its quality is worse. The first
problem is that only one view is available to most people because of the increasing
concentration of newspaper ownership. In 1910 some 57 percent of American
cities had competing daily papers, whereas in 1960 only 4 percent had competing
dailies. Furthermore, news media tend to have a conservative bias. One reason
is that they do not want to offend any powerful interests. They especially do not
want to offend major advertisers, most of which are big businesses. And perhaps
most important: "Since the media of communication are big businesses, too, the
men who control them quite naturally share the convictions of other businessmen"
(Irish and Prothro, 1965, p. 184).

Economic power also affects the amount of political power available to different pressure groups. Thus a standard political science textbook points to status
as the most important factor in determining the influence of a pressure group.
After listing other sources of status, it concludes: "Finally, since status is so closely
tied to money in the United States, the group with greater status will almost
automatically be able to command greater financial resources. And it costs money
to engage in pressure politics. . . ." (ibid., p. 245).

The fact of economic power weighs all the more heavily because advertising
is now a vital component of politics.

> Pressure groups . . . are now spending millions of dollars every year on mass pro-
> paganda. Not only broad groups like the National Association of Manufacturers, but
> even individual companies maintain elaborate bureaucracies to sell "correct" ideas
> on general policy questions along with favorable attitudes to the company. (Ibid., p.
> 249)

The vast amount of business advertising reinforces the general ethos of capitalism. What is its message? Ours is a lovely country; material luxuries represent
the only important goal; and everyone can have these material luxuries. A certain
percentage of business advertising is devoted to specifically political issues. Yet
business advertising has been counted as a cost that can be deducted from income

when taxes are computed. Labor unions, in contrast, are not allowed this tax deduction for political advertising.

ECONOMIC POWER AND THE PRESIDENT

There is no great mystery about how economic power gains dominance over the president. Money, big money, is required for presidential campaigns. For example, just in the few months of primary campaigns in 1972, Edmund Muskie spent about $2 million. In 1976 President Ford spent $13 million in the primary campaigns. It is estimated that President Nixon spent $29 million in the whole 1968 campaign and about $55 million in the 1972 campaign. The traditional political scientists admit that "because campaigns are exceedingly costly, the wealthier a person is, the more strategic his position for bringing pressure to bear on politicians" (Dahl and Lindbloom, 1953, p. 313). Regarding the more recent fundraising Political Action Committees (PACs), corporate and other upper-status PACs provide more money to conservative candidates than union or liberal PACs provide to liberal candidates (Domhoff, 1983, pp. 123–126).

In return for the money showered on him, Nixon appointed conservative businessmen to most cabinet and subcabinet positions, to almost all committees and agencies, to most high posts in the Republican party, and to many ambassadorships (including 16 of the 19 in Western Europe). President Reagan's support from business likely influenced his appointment of a large number of businessmen to his cabinet—for example, Defense Secretary Caspar Weinberger from Bechtel and Treasury Secretary/Chief of Staff Donald Regan from Merrill Lynch (Useem, 1984, p. 79).

Those government positions were desired and used in furthering the interests of the individual business appointees and of business in general. An example was the business favors carried out by Nixon's friend John Mitchell, who became attorney general. Thus, the process by which the president is elected by economic power and then appoints economically powerful people to positions from which they can further extend and defend economic power may be called a *feedback mechanism*. In general, a feedback mechanism is a means by which one part of a process (for example, economic power) influences another part (for example, political power), which then has a positive feedback, or reinforcement, on the first part (for example, economic power is increased by additional political power). Later, we shall look at how the political feedback mechanism operates on education, farm subsidies, tax loopholes, military spending, and so forth.

More direct mechanisms to influence the political process itself include business requests for use of police to stop demonstrations. There is also the well-documented use of the CIA and FBI to disrupt and attack "radicals," which can mean anyone opposed to the business establishment or the administration (Gary T. Marx, 1982). There is also the use of the president's prestige in TV and press announcements to promote policies favoring large businesses.

Last, but not least, there was the Watergate scandal, in which the president's men bugged the telephone of the opposition party and used many other "dirty tricks" to win elections, including the use of confidential information from the

CIA, FBI, and Internal Revenue Service. This scandal exposed the joint use of economic power and the president's political power to conduct political espionage, a combined power possibly so extensive as to prevent the opposition party from winning an election. If it could be used to such an astounding degree against liberal Democrats, how much could it be used against socialist radicals? The Socialist Workers Party has contended in court that they were spied upon by the government for years. Notice that Watergate involved economic power in several ways. On the one hand, at least $2 million was required for the actual conspiracy, of which about $800,000 apparently came from Texas oil men anxious to be given presidential favors. On the other hand, the fact that Nixon was in power reflected the large amount of money that went into electing him.

One more word on Watergate: It points to the fact that when conservatives talk about "law and order," they mean primarily the protection of private property here and abroad—by any means available. Thus, police use of violence against unemployed black or Hispanic workers for petty theft is an example of law and order. Breaking into and bugging the Watergate Democratic headquarters (or breaking into and robbing a psychiatrist's office in the Pentagon Papers case) was also law and order because it aided an administration that was protecting private property. When Cambodia was secretly bombed by Nixon—even though it was unconstitutional because Congress had not authorized it—this was law and order because it protected the friends of capitalism abroad. Thus the conservative view of law and order is to protect property but not people. *This function of law and order (or protection of private property) is the main function of the U.S. government.*

CONGRESS AND ECONOMIC POWER

Whether Congress should be placed at the middle level of power or the highest level, Congress does vote on issues that affect millions of Americans. We would therefore expect members of Congress to be influenced by capitalist economic power. In fact, this is the case.

Congressmen need money to get elected and reelected: They need it for paid time on TV and other advertising, for airfare and for many other basic necessities of political life. Lincoln is said to have spent only 26 cents on his congressional campaign, whereas in the 1950s congressional candidates spent about $15,000 to $25,000, and in the 1970s many were spending over $100,000 on each campaign. In the 1970 Senate race in New York alone, Goodell spent $1.3 million, Buckley $2 million, and Ottinger $4 million. In 1980 corporate organizations alone donated $19 million to congressional candidates (Domhoff, 1983, p. 125).

The Republican and Democratic parties together spent about $140 million in 1952, $155 million in 1956, $175 million in 1960, $200 million in 1964, $300 million in 1968, and $425 million in 1972. One investigation found that about 55 percent of the Democratic party's money comes from corporations, 20 percent from labor unions, 15 percent from racketeers and gangsters, and 10 percent in small contributions from middle-class Americans. The Republicans usually raise about twice as much, mostly from big business. Conservative Senator Russell Long guessed that "about 95 percent of congressional funds are derived from businessmen" (Cummings and Wise, 1971, pp. 304–305).

Members of Congress are also indirectly affected by economic power through the strong influence of the president. Furthermore, big business can threaten to open or close plants in a particular congressional district. Business can give a member of Congress free time on radio or TV or a free plane ride. In addition, there are about 5000 full-time lobbyists in Washington, about 10 for each member of Congress, and many lobbyists are former members of Congress or good personal or business friends of congressional leaders. Except in emergencies, lobbyists do not directly buy votes. They merely serve as the main channel for the largest campaign contributions; for example, they buy lunches and dinners, and supply petty cash, credit cards, profitable investment opportunities, legal retainers to members of Congress (most of whom are lawyers), provide lecture fees, poker winnings (members of Congress usually win), vacations, and fringe benefits ranging from theater tickets to French perfume.

Two of the largest lobbies are the oil interests (which have made billions from special tax loopholes) and the military armaments industry. All of this economic power is so strong—and so necessary for election—that even liberals like Senators Fulbright, Mansfield, and Pastore have voted consistently for the direct needs of business interests and related jobs in their districts, no matter how they may have voted on broader issues. Thus one friendly senator, Boies Penrose, said to a meeting of business leaders (back in 1900, when such things were said more frankly):

> I believe in a division of labor. You send us to Congress; we pass laws under . . . which you make money; . . . and out of your profits you further contribute to our campaign funds to send us back again to pass more laws to enable you to make more money. (Quoted in Green et al., 1972, pp. 7–8)

This is a feedback mechanism!

One rather obvious lobby is the maritime industry, including maritime businesses and maritime unions, which receives huge subsidies for ship building and ship operation. Consider a bill forcing more oil imports to be carried by American ships, which would cost—according to the Government Accounting Office—at least $240 million a year in unnecessary charges to consumers. A congressional committee voted 31–5 for this amazing bill—26 of the committee members had received campaign contributions from the maritime industry. President Carter received $100,000 from the maritime industry in his primary campaign and endorsed the bill. Altogether the maritime industry gave $1.1 million in contributions to Carter and selected members of Congress in the 1976 elections (*Washington Post*, 1977, p. A–22).

Even more pervasive is the fact that the *structure* of capitalism forces even the most liberal members of Congress (and the president) to follow the dictates of capital *in the interest of economic growth and jobs for their constituents.* For example, the congressional delegation from Hawaii is probably the most liberal in Congress on most issues. Yet in 1977 it pushed for and obtained a subsidy on Hawaiian sugar that would force taxpayers to give about $100 million a year to the 14 oligopolistic corporations that control Hawaiian sugar (Fogle, 1977, p. A–3). If these corporations cut down on investment and production, then thousands of Hawaiians would lose their jobs—so the congressional delegates had no choice.

In like manner, the very liberal Democratic members of Congress from Michigan consistently vote against the Clean Air Act for automobiles because thousands of auto workers might lose their jobs, even though they know that millions of Americans will suffer health problems from polluted air (including many in Michigan). In each of these situations, as long as unemployment exists under capitalism, and as long as capitalists control investments, any government—no matter how liberal or pro-working class—must bow to their dictates in many economic policy questions.

ECONOMIC BACKGROUND OF POLITICAL LEADERS

Most members of Congress need no pressure to get them to vote as the economic powers desire because they are already selected so that this is their natural inclination. Most are white, male, and affluent. Upper-income members of the capitalist class hold a disproportionate percentage of the top political positions. From 1789 to 1932, 38 percent of the fathers of American presidents and vice-presidents were professionals, 20 percent were proprietors and officials, 38 percent were farm owners, and only 4 percent were wage earners or salaried workers. Similarly, from 1947 to 1951, 22 percent of the fathers of American senators were professionals, 33 percent proprietors and officials, 40 percent farm owners, and only 4 percent wage earners or salaried workers. Finally, from 1941 to 1943, 31 percent of the fathers of American representatives were professionals, 31 percent proprietors and officials, 29 percent farm owners, and only 9 percent wage earners or salaried workers (Cummings and Wise, 1971, p. 39).

Data for 1970 show that 266 of the 435 members of the House of Representatives had outside financial interests providing over $5000 in income per year beyond their congressional salaries. This figure may be an underestimation because the income of wives and children was not listed (nor was income under $5000 listed). To make $5000 a year from stocks and bonds requires at least $70,000 or $80,000 in holdings. Members of Congress were not required to reveal the extent of their holdings. Some voluntarily disclosed this information. Very wealthy men, with fortunes ranging from many tens of thousands of dollars up to the $3 million of Congressman Pierre du Pont, sit in Congress (House Committee on Standards of Official Conduct, 1971). In 1978, 19 members of the Senate were millionaires, as were possibly 13 or 14 others (Domhoff, 1983, p. 127).

What are the sources of their wealth? A total of 102 members of Congress in 1970 held stock or well-paying executive positions in banks or other financial institutions, and 81 received regular income from law firms that generally represented big businesses. Sixty-three got their income from stock in the firms of top defense contractors; 45 in the giant (federally regulated) oil and gas industries;

22 in radio and television companies; 11 in commercial airlines; and 9 in railroads. Ninety-eight members of Congress were involved in numerous capital gains transactions, from which each netted a profit of over $5,000 to as high as $35,000. In 1978, 95 out of 100 senators had income from stocks or real estate investments, and some held directorships or other business positions (ibid., p. 127).

In the executive branch, upper-income, business-oriented individuals have held a majority of all the important positions throughout U.S. history. This includes members of the cabinet, their assistants and department heads, and heads of most regulatory agencies. They quite naturally, with no conspiracy, tend to consult leaders of big business and business groups as experts for such committees as the Committee for Economic Development or the Council on Foreign Relations. Wealthy families have also contributed a majority of federal judges, top military men, and top leaders of intelligence agencies. Finally, it should be noted that there is much crossing over at the top, with ex-generals becoming corporate executives and corporate executives becoming cabinet members.

Few radicals would state the thesis of big-business control of government as strongly as President Wilson did in anger at the moment he wrote his attack against big-business control. There are many qualifications to the thesis of big-business control of government. For example, although there are many people of means in Congress, the influence of wealth in Congress is much less than in the cabinet and other executive offices. Similarly, in state and local governments the influence of the wealthy is very strong, but certainly they do not have exclusive control. Moreover, even among the members of the capitalist class in high positions, there are many differences of opinion, mistakes in perceiving their own interests, and conflicts of interest between different business groups. Thus the rule of the capitalist class is by no means monolithic; it rules through the forms of shifting coalitions and liberal or conservative styles, as reflected in the Democratic and Republican parties. Finally, the working class (including farmers, industrial workers, intellectual and professional workers, the poor and unemployed, and workers from minority groups) can sometimes organize sufficiently to overcome the power of money by sheer weight of numbers. The working class may exert pressure, elect representatives, and sometimes even prevail on particular issues. Nevertheless, big business's influence is usually felt in most important national decisions.

SUMMARY

In this chapter we have seen the influence of society—particularly the capitalist economy—on politics. We began by looking at two differing views of power distribution in the United States. One position argues that the United States is basically democratic because power is dispersed among various groups in society. The other position sees the United States as an essentially undemocratic society because major decisions of national consequence are determined by the power of a small elite. In C. Wright Mills's formulation, the elite is a combination of those in the "command posts" (that is, at the highest levels) of business, government, and the military. In G. William Domhoff's formulation, the elite is mainly composed of the upper economic class. In the view of many Marxist sociologists, the capitalist class is the ruling class, though it rules indirectly as much as directly.

The preponderance of evidence presented in this chapter points to the strength of the Mills-Domhoff-Marxist analysis of power distribution in America, particularly when contrasted with the pluralist position. Those in high positions—and certainly those who control a large amount of wealth—appear to predominate in terms of major national political decisions affecting foreign policy, war and peace, taxes, military spending, inflation, education, mass media, protection of private property, and the like. Congress is involved, but we have shown that Congress itself is clearly influenced by wealth. Moreover, the whole structure of capitalist society is such that the capitalist class exercises indirect control of political decisions through its control of the news media, educational system, location of industries, and jobs.

To sum up, American democracy is not extinct, but democracy in the United States amounts to a government whose actions reflect the power of the elite—primarily the capitalist class—in our society.

APPENDIX: THREE RADICAL THEORIES OF THE STATE

Some of the most interesting debates in political sociology in the last decade or so concern the necessity for radicals to take a flexible approach to the state in capitalist society. In a synthesizing article, Esping-Andersen, Friedland, and Wright (1976) distinguish between *instrumentalist, structuralist,* and *political class struggle* perspectives on the state in capitalist society. The instrumentalist view sees the state as an instrument of the ruling economic class in society. The ruling class is seen to utilize rather directly the government for its own benefit. This is possible because the key positions in the capitalist state are often held by members of the capitalist class.

At first glance, the instrumentalist position appears deterministic instead of flexible in its approach to the state in capitalist society. That is exactly how one author categorized as an instrumentalist felt. In a reply to Esping-Andersen, Friedland, and Wright (1976), and others, entitled "I am not an 'Instrumentalist,' " Domhoff (1976) stated that instead of focusing solely on the political power of the capitalist class, he made class struggle basic to his analysis. He argued that the Wagner Act—often looked at as the great emancipator of labor—was a means of institutionalizing class conflict. Organized labor was seen to gain in terms of improved hours, wages, and working conditions; but the capitalist class was seen to gain in terms of more productivity from labor, less personnel turnover, greater disciplining of the workers by the union, greater predictability of labor costs over a period of time, and a reduction of radical labor viewpoints (ibid., 1976, p. 222). Thus, even though Domhoff sees the capitalist class influencing the government, his analysis also shows the involved relations between capitalist industry, organized labor, and the government—which is clearly more complex than focusing on a one-way determinism of complete capitalist control over the government.

A structuralist approach "views state structure as determined by the systemic constraints and contradictions of capitalism" (Esping-Andersen et al., 1976, p. 188). Two of its most well-known formulators are Nicos Poulantzas (1973, 1974, 1975) and Louis Althusser (1971). The emphasis is on the state existing in an objective capitalist environment and solving problems that emanate from this environment. In a possible reversal of expected relations, Poulantzas argues that the capitalist class cannot by itself attain domination of a society and thus must use state power to assist in becoming sufficiently organized as a class to attain this domination (Esping-Andersen, Friedland, and Wright, 1976, p. 188).

Along these lines, Baran and Sweezy argue that the state must solve the contradictions and temporary crises of capitalism, such as helping guarantee effective demand for its economic products (ibid.). Although the government may be influenced by capitalism in the structuralist perspective, the influence is again complex and dialectical, and does not imply a straightforward, direct control over the government by the capitalist class.

The final perspective considered here is the approach of political class struggle, often thought to be the most flexible of all these perspectives. This perspective "focuses on state structures as an object of class struggle" (ibid., p. 190). The government is seen as an important arena in which class struggle takes place and where partial solutions are evolved. This viewpoint sees the capitalist class attempting to "create state structures which channel working-class political activity in ways that do not threaten capitalist political dominance and objective interests" (ibid.). However, working-class challenges are seen to make the achievement of this goal problematical and set in motion dialectical relations between the capitalist and working classes—with the state as a focus of the conflict between the classes.

The political class struggle approach spells out various ways in which the internal structure of the state tries to solve the contradictions of capitalism. Thus, capitalism is seen as generating many unmet social needs, such as unemployment and lack of adequate health care for many citizens. The rise of the welfare state, which provides some financial benefits for the unemployed and some health care for the poor, is seen as a way the modern state tries, however inadequately, to solve the problems systematically generated by the economic system. In this regard, Claus Offe (1972) argues that the state acts with a degree of "relative autonomy" from direct domination of the capitalist class. The notion of relative autonomy from such economic control points to the flexibility of this approach to the relation between the state and capitalist society.

Other variations of the political class struggle approach—or similarly flexible approaches—are James O'Connor's analysis *The Fiscal Crisis of the State* (1973), which focuses on the relationship between decline in corporate profitability and state bankruptcy; Fred Block's "The Ruling Class Does Not Rule" (1977), showing instead that the ruling class often uses "state managers," such as President Lyndon Johnson; and Paul Joseph's (1981) intriguing analysis of the Vietnam War, in which he demonstrates much inconsistency in policymaking about the war among those representing the upper economic classes. In addition to the discussion of Esping-Andersen et al. (1976), Gold, Lo, and Wright (1975) similarly provide an excellent critical synthesis of this literature, which has usefully demonstrated the necessity of examining the many complicated functions of the state in capitalist society.

SUGGESTED READINGS

The pioneering radical effort in political sociology in the 1950s was C. Wright Mills, *The Power Elite* (New York: Oxford University Press, 1956). His most influential successor has been G. William Domhoff, whose best-known book is *Who Rules America?* (Englewood Cliffs, NJ: Prentice-Hall, 1967). The excellent sequel to this work is the same author's *Who Rules America Now? A View for the '80s* (Englewood Cliffs, NJ: Prentice-Hall, 1983). In addition, Domhoff has also written several very extensive empirical studies. A good radical textbook, covering all aspects of American politics—and very readable—is Michael Parenti, *Democracy for the Few*, 2d ed. (New York: St. Martin's, 1977). For up-to-date articles, an excellent source is the radical journal *Politics and Society* (subscriptions: Geron-X, Publishers, Box 1108, Los Altos, California, 94022). By far the best single statement of the facts and theory of radical political sociology is Albert Szymanski, *The Capitalist State and the Politics of Class* (Cambridge, MA: Winthrop Publishers, 1978). For a very good overview of the complexities of the relationship between the state and capitalist society, focusing on important recent analyses and debates, see Martin Carnoy, *The State and Political Theory* (Princeton, NJ: Princeton University Press, 1984).

In 1981, the expanded edition of Seymour Martin Lipset, *Political Man* (Baltimore: Johns Hopkins University Press) was published. *Political Man* was probably the most cited work in political sociology when it originally came out in 1960. It was quite influential in helping to delineate the entire field of modern political sociology. The 1981 edition includes updated analyses of many important issues initially considered. An excellent overview of much recent research in political sociology is George A. Kourvetaris and Betty A. Dobratz, "Political Power and Conventional Political Participation," *Annual Review of Sociology* 8 (1982):289–317.

There have been several other excellent analyses in political sociology. Theda Skocpol produced a major work in comparative political sociology in her multiple award-winning *States and Social Revolutions* (Cambridge, UK: Cambridge University Press, 1979). This was followed by her collaborative effort to emphasize the relative importance of the state in society, *Bringing the State Back In* (Cambridge, UK: Cambridge University Press, 1985), edited by Peter B. Evans, Dietrich Rueschemeyer, and Theda Skocpol. Other discussions have focused on the complex political relations in capitalist society: Michael Useem, *The Inner Circle: Large Corporations and the Rise of Business Political Activity in the U.S. and U.K.* (New York: Oxford University Press, 1984), cowinner of the 1985 C. Wright Mills Award; Alan Wolfe, *The Limits of Legitimacy: Political Contradictions of Contemporary Capitalism* (New York: Free Press, 1977); Maurice Zeitlin, *Classes, Class Conflict, and the State* (Cambridge, MA: Winthrop Publishers, 1980); Robert R. Alford and Roger Friedland, *Powers of Theory: Capitalism, the State and Democracy* (Cambridge and New York: Cambridge University Press, 1985); and Samuel Bowles and Herbert Gintis, *Democracy and Capitalism* (New York: Basic Books, 1986).

REFERENCES

Almond, Gabriel, and Sidney Verba. 1963. *The Civic Culture*. Princeton, NJ: Princeton University Press.

Althusser, Louis. 1971. "Ideology and Ideological State Apparatuses." In his *Lenin and Philosophy and Other Essays*, pp. 127–186. New York: Monthly Review Press.

Avineri, Shlomo. 1968. *The Social and Political Thought of Karl Marx*. Cambridge, UK: Cambridge University Press.

Berelson, B. R.; P. F. Lazarsfeld; and W. N. McPhee. 1954. *Voting*. Chicago: University of Chicago Press.

Block, Fred. 1977. "The Ruling Class Does Not Rule: Notes on the Marxist Theory of the State." *Socialist Revolution* 7:6–28.

Campbell, Angus; W. E. Miller; and D. E. Stokes. 1960. *The American Voter*. New York: Wiley.

Clark, Terry Nichols. 1975. "Community Power." *Annual Review of Sociology* 1:271–295.

Cummings, M., and D. Wise. 1971. *Democracy Under Pressure*. New York: Harcourt Brace Jovanovich.

Curtis, R., and E. Jackson. 1977. *Inequality in American Communities*. New York: Academic Press.

Dahl, Robert. 1961. *Who Governs?* New Haven, CT: Yale University Press.

——, and Charles Lindbloom. 1953. *Politics, Economics, and Welfare*. New York: Harper & Row.

D'Arge, Ralph, and James Wilen. 1974. "Government Control of Externalities." *Journal of Economic Issues* 8 (June).

Domhoff, G. William. 1967. *Who Rules America?* Englewood Cliffs, NJ: Prentice-Hall.

——. 1971. *The Higher Circles: The Governing Class in America*. New York: Random House.

——. 1972. *Fat Cats and Democrats: The Role of the Big Rich in the Party of the Common Man*. Englewood Cliffs, NJ: Prentice-Hall.

——. 1975a. *The Bohemian Grove and Other Retreats: A Study in Ruling-Class Cohesiveness*. New York: Harper & Row.

——, ed. 1975b. *The Insurgent Sociologist* 5 no. (3). Issue title: "*New Directions in Power Structure Research*."

——. 1976. "I Am Not An 'Instrumentalist': A Reply to 'Modes of Class Struggle and the Capitalist State' and Other *Kapitalistate* Critics." *Kapitalistate* 4–5:221–224.

——. 1977. *Who Really Rules? New Haven and Community Power Re-examined*. New Brunswick, NJ: Transaction Books.

——, ed. 1979–80. *The Insurgent Sociologist* 9(2–3). The title of this issue was "Power Structure Research II."

——. 1983. *Who Rules America Now? A View for the '80s*. Englewood Cliffs, NJ: Prentice-Hall.

——, and Hoyt B. Ballard, eds. 1968. *C. Wright Mills and the Power Elite*. Boston: Beacon Press.

Draper, Hal. 1977. *Karl Marx's Theory of Revolution*. New York: Monthly Review Press.

Dye, Thomas R. 1983. *Who's Running America?* 3d ed. Englewood Cliffs, NJ: Prentice-Hall.

Esping-Andersen, Gosta; Roger Friedland; and Erik Olin Wright. 1976. "Modes of Class Struggle and the Capitalist State." *Kapitalistate* 4–5 (Summer): 186–220.

Fogle, Jon. 1977. "House Votes 13 1/2 Cent Sugar Support." *Honolulu Advertiser*, July 26, A–3.

Gitlin, Todd. 1980. *The Whole World Is Watching: Mass Media in the Making and Unmaking of the New Left*. Berkeley: University of California Press.

Gold, David A.; Clarence Y. H. Lo; and Erik Olin Wright. 1975. "Recent Developments in Marxist Theories of the Capitalist State." *Monthly Review* 27 (5):29–43; 27 (6):36–51.

Green, Mark; James Fallows; and David Zwick. 1972. *Who Runs Congress?* New York: Bantam (Ralph Nader Congress Project).

Hamilton, R. 1972. *Class and Politics in the United States*. New York: Wiley.

House Committee on Standards of Official Conduct. April 1971. Discussed in an article in the *Los Angeles Times* (May 24, 1971): pt. 1:12.

Hunter, Floyd. 1953. *Community Power Structure*. Chapel Hill: University of North Carolina Press.

Irish, Marian, and James Prothro. 1965. *The Politics of American Democracy*. Englewood Cliffs, NJ: Prentice-Hall.

Joseph, Paul. 1981. *Cracks in the Empire: State Politics in the Vietnam War*. Boston: South End Press.

Knoke, David. 1982. "Power Structures." In S. Long, ed., *The Handbook of Political Behavior*. New York: Plenum.

Kourvetaris, George A., and Betty A. Dobratz. 1982. "Political Power and Conventional Political Participation." *Annual Review of Sociology* 8:289–317.

Ladd, E., and C. Hadley. 1975, 1978. *Transformations of the American Party System.* New York: Norton.

Leslie, Gerald; Richard Larson; and Ben Gorman. 1976. *Introductory Sociology.* New York: Oxford University Press.

Lipset, Seymour Martin. 1985. *Consensus and Conflict: Essays in Political Sociology.* New Brunswick, NJ: Transaction Books.

———, and William Schneider. 1983. *The Confidence Gap: Business, Labor, and Government in the Public Mind.* New York: Free Press.

Lopreato, J., and L. E. Hazelrigg. 1972. *Class, Conflict, and Mobility.* San Francisco: Chandler.

Los Angeles Times. 1988. "Dukakis Forces Reject Key Jackson Platform Issues." Sunday, June 26: 1, 36.

Lynd, Robert S., and Helen Lynd. 1929. *Middletown.* New York: Harcourt Brace Jovanovich.

Lyon, L.; L. Felice; M. Perryman; and E. Parker. 1981. "Community Power and Population: An Empirical Test of the Growth Machine Model." *American Journal of Sociology* 86:1387–1400.

Marx, Gary T. 1982. "External Efforts to Damage or Facilitate Social Movements: Some Patterns, Explanations, Outcomes, and Complications." Chapter Twelve, pp. 181–200. In James L. Wood and Maurice Jackson, *Social Movements: Development, Participation, and Dynamics.* Belmont, CA: Wadsworth.

Marx, Karl, and Frederick Engels. 1948. *The Communist Manifesto.* Originally published in 1848. New York: International Publishers.

Miliband, Ralph. 1969. *The State in Capitalist Society.* New York: Basic Books.

Mills, C. Wright. 1956. *The Power Elite.* New York: Oxford University Press. Paperback edition, 1959.

Offe, Claus. 1972. "Advanced Capitalism and the Welfare State." *Politics and Society* 2(4).

O'Connor, James. 1973. *The Fiscal Crisis of the State.* New York: St. Martin's.

Orum, Anthony. 1978. *Introduction to Political Sociology.* Englewood Cliffs, NJ: Prentice-Hall.

Poulantzas, Nicos. 1973. *Political Power and Social Classes.* London: New Left Books.

———. 1974. *Fascism and Dictatorship.* London: New Left Books.

———. 1975. *Classes in Contemporary Capitalism.* London: New Left Books.

Rose, Arnold. 1967. *The Power Structure.* New York: Oxford University Press.

San Diego Union. 1987. "Meese role in Non-Bid Contracts for Wedtech Alleged." Thursday, October 1: A–2.

Tabb, W., and L. Sawers, eds. 1978, 1984. *Marxism and Metropolis.* New York: Oxford University Press.

Truman, David. 1965. *The Government Process.* New York: Knopf.

Useem, Michael. 1984. *The Inner Circle: Large Corporations and the Rise of Business Political Activity in the U.S. and U.K.* New York: Oxford University Press.

———. 1980. "Corporations and the Corporate Elite." *Annual Review of Sociology* 6:41–77.

Vidich, Arthur J., and Joseph Bensman. 1958. *Small Town in Mass Society.* Garden City, NY: Doubleday.

Washington Post. 1977. "How to Buy a Bill." Editorial. September 1: A–22.

Wilson, Woodrow. 1914. *The New Freedom.* Garden City, NY: Doubleday.

chapter *16*

Political Sociology: The Impact of Politics on Society

This chapter continues the discussion of American government and society. Here we focus on the ways that political institutions affect social and economic behavior. We will be especially interested to see if the government regulates business, as many pluralists assert, or if it actually aids business, as many radicals contend. The role of Reaganomics is discussed at the end of the chapter.

EFFECTS OF GOVERNMENT ON ECONOMIC INEQUALITY

Although large-scale inequality in the United States is acknowledged, liberals argue that the inequality is much reduced by higher tax rates on the rich, welfare payments to low-income workers, subsidies to low-income farmers, universal public education, and antitrust laws, all of which are supposed to decrease the concentration of income and power. Thus the famous economist Paul Samuelson (1973, p. 804) asserts that the U.S. government has at least somewhat reduced income inequality: "The welfare state, through redistributive taxation and through educational opportunity . . . has moved the system a bit toward greater equality." Radicals object to this conclusion on several grounds.

First, the facts on the history of American income distribution show that (1) there was very little overall change in income distribution between 1910 and 1985; (2) the share of the poorest 20 percent of the population has actually declined; and (3) the share of the richest 20 percent was the highest on record in 1985. Therefore, in spite of many promises by several liberal U.S. government administrations (such as those of Wilson, Roosevelt, and Kennedy), there has been virtually no reduction of income inequality since 1910 (Kolko, 1962, chap.

2). Indeed, as was shown in chapter 3, when overall wealth is considered, the Reagan administration increased the share going to the wealthiest group.

Second, the main function of the capitalist governmental system is the preservation of "law and order," which means that police, armies, courts, and prisons all protect the private ownership of vast fortunes for the rich. Government thus preserves capitalist control of land and factories. With the help of local government in breaking strikes, the rich can continue to pay low enough wages to farm and industrial workers to continue to make the high profits by which they grow richer.

Third, radicals have shown that the administration of every program, from taxation to welfare, has been such that the rich have benefited more and the poor less than the law would seem to indicate at first glance. Some of these programs are discussed in the following paragraphs.

Taxation

It is certainly true that income tax rates rise as income rises, so that in theory individuals in the higher income brackets not only must pay more taxes but also must pay a higher percentage of their income in taxes. In practice, however, rich taxpayers find many loopholes that allow them to pay much lower tax rates. Thus, in 1969 the official rate on income over $1 million was an apparently confiscatory 91 percent; yet that category of taxpayers actually paid only 34 percent to the government (Gurley, 1967).

Loopholes, such as lower taxes on capital gains from property and stock sales, mean that some of the rich income receivers pay little in taxes and some pay nothing. A 1986 study, reported on television, revealed that several major corporations paid *no* taxes the previous year. In 1974 some 3302 people earning more than $50,000 paid *no* federal taxes—and that included 244 people with incomes over $200,000 and 5 people with incomes over $1 million (Internal Revenue Service, 1976). *It has been estimated that the total loss of government revenue from all loopholes in the income tax laws has been about $77 billion a year* (Lechman and Okner, 1972, pp. 13–40).

Whereas the rich, with their income from property, can find many tax loopholes, there are few loopholes for the average worker with wage income. Consequently, there is actually only a slight redistribution of income as a result of the federal income tax. Even more important is the fact that the federal income tax amounts to only 40 percent of all taxes. The other 60 percent of taxes are mainly regressive, in that they fall more heavily on the lower-income groups. When all kinds of taxes (federal, state, and local) are added together, the proportionate burden on the poor is actually heavier than on the rich. In 1967, families with incomes under $3,000 paid 34 percent in total taxes, but families with over $25,000 income paid only 28 percent in total taxes (Lekachman, 1972, p. 94). As a result, in 1967 the richest 5 percent of taxpayers had 15 percent of all income *before* taxes, but they had 17 percent of all income *after* all federal, state, and local taxes were paid (Pechman, 1969). These tendencies are even stronger when the total wealth of the "super rich" is considered. The Joint Economic Committee of Congress found that the top one-half percent of the U.S. population held 35.1 percent of the nation's wealth in 1983, an increase of 10 percent from 20 years earlier (*San Diego Union,* 1986).

In the last 30 years, the tax burden has been shifting further away from rich capitalists toward all workers and toward the poor. In 1944, corporate income taxes were 34 percent of all federal income taxes, but corporate taxes fell to only 15 percent of federal taxes by 1974. At the same time, Social Security taxes (paid mostly by workers) rose from 4 percent of federal taxes in 1944 to 29 percent in 1974 (Nader, 1974). Similarly, among individual taxpayers, the share paid by the lowest 20 percent of income recipients rose from 4 percent in 1950 to 11 percent in 1970—while the share of taxes paid by the top 4 percent of income recipients fell from 43 percent to just 27 percent (U.S. Department of Commerce, 1960, 1974). In the coming years it will be important to analyze the actual effects of the Reagan administration's mid-1980s policy of tax reform in terms of who benefits from it. A recent detailed analysis indicates that the well-to-do have especially benefited (Rothschild, 1988).

Welfare

Many of the rich cry that the poor are getting vast amounts of welfare payments. Actually, the total of all federal, state and local welfare expenditures is still fairly small. Moreover, it has been declining as a percentage of personal income. All welfare payments—including unemployment payments, workmen's compensation, health, education, medical, and housing programs—as a percentage of personal income were only 6.7 percent in 1938, 3.9 percent in 1950, 3.3 percent in 1960, and 3.8 percent in 1968 (Edwards, 1972, p. 244). Furthermore, there are many kinds of welfare payments to the rich—such as business subsidies and loan guarantees. No wonder, then, that our tax and welfare systems have not resulted in a significant redistribution of income.

Farm Subsidies

The rural poor have suffered the most pathetic poverty. For most of the twentieth century the incomes of small-farm owners and farm workers have lagged far behind other American incomes. For that reason, liberals have persuaded Congress to pass various bills to aid farmers with subsidies. What has been the practical effect of these subsidies?

First, economic concentration among the business firms engaged in farming has increased. By 1963, the richest 20 percent of farm owners received 51 percent of all farm income, while the poorest 20 percent received only 3 percent of farm income. Second, the farm support programs benefit mainly the richest farmers and give very little support to the poorest ones. In the period 1963–1965, the richest 20 percent of all farms (with the highest incomes before subsidies) received 83 percent of the farm subsidies for sugarcane, 69 percent of those for cotton, 65 percent of those for rice, 62 percent of those for wheat, 56 percent of those for feed grains, 57 percent of those for peanuts, 53 percent of those for tobacco, and 51 percent of those for sugar beets (Bonnen, 1972, pp. 235–243). In the face of such facts as these, the rock and country music communities in the mid-1980s organized the popular Farm Aid benefit concerts to raise money for poorer farmers who were losing their farms because they could not pay their mortgages and loans, and who were not helped by the Reagan administration.

Education and Inequality

Government-subsidized education is often thought to decrease the inequality of incomes. It has been argued that the government gives free education to all. Therefore, it is said, anyone can improve his or her station in life by going to school for a longer period.

It is a fact, however, that individuals from high-income families are able to get more schooling in the United States than individuals from lower-class families. This may be seen in the following data from a survey that classified students graduating from high school in 1966 according to family income in 1965. Of those in the under-$3,000 group, only 20 percent started college by February 1967; in the same year, fully 87 percent of those with family incomes over $15,000 started college (Ackerman, 1972, pp. 25–26; see also Bowles and Gintis, 1976, pp. 31–33). Thus the higher one's family income, the greater was one's chance of going to college. Moreover, many students drop out of college simply because they have no money on which to live while in school.

GOVERNMENT WELFARE PAYMENTS TO BUSINESS

The United States government today pays far larger amounts of welfare in subsidies to business than all payments to individuals. There are farm subsidies. There are subsidies to the merchant marine. Billions are given for research to military firms with no return to the taxpayer, even though any actual military product is also paid for excessively. There are also guarantees on enormous loans to save the inefficient Lockheed corporation. None of this is new in American history.

The railroad magnates were among the most important entrepreneurs in the American Industrial Revolution. The federal government responded by generously giving federal lands to the railroads. Between 1850 and 1871, the railroads were handed 130 million acres of land, an area as large as all the New England states plus Pennsylvania and New York. During the same period, state governments gave the railroads another 49 million acres. All this—and yet some economic historians still refer to the second half of the nineteenth century as an age in which government stayed out of business affairs. Toward the end of the nineteenth century, the relationship between the federal government and big business became a symbiosis in which the government governed in ways big business wanted it to govern, while big business furnished the money, organization, and power structure through which politicians could come to power in the federal government.

REGULATORY AGENCIES

Since late in the nineteenth century the U.S. government has established many regulatory agencies, such as the Interstate Commerce Commission, supposedly designed to protect consumer and environmental interests. Thus telephone and electric companies have been given monopolies, but public agencies are placed above them to regulate their profits. These commissions are commonly thought to be the watchdogs of the public interests—especially by pluralist thinkers—but they often turn out to be merely a legal way to give monopoly powers to a few large corporations. The commissions are generally dominated by those interests they are supposed to regulate, and neglect the public interest. For example, when the public does not give them careful attention, the public utilities commissions normally grant most price increases desired by the "regulated" companies.

The Federal Power Commission (FPC), for example, almost always grants the rate increases asked by the gas and electric companies it regulates. One of the reasons is that its members are usually former executives, lawyers, or lobbyists for these firms—and most of them expect to go back to these firms when they leave the FPC.

This cozy relationship between the firms and the regulatory agency appears in almost every industry, but it is perhaps best documented by the radio and television industry and the Federal Communications Commission (FCC) (Scheer, 1977, p. 1). The industry is represented by the National Association of Broadcasters, which has a big, modern building in Washington full of lobbyists and statistics of every sort to prove their case. On the other hand, a reporter visiting the FCC building describes it as old, full of an "aura of failure," and with little available data at hand. The reporter was told that the data he wanted was in the annual report, but the annual report was three years late. Moreover, even the annual reports do *not* say how much money the broadcasters make with their publicly granted licenses. The FCC is supposed to protect the consumer, but actually has protected the three major networks against investigations and excessive controls over their policies and, until recently, against the possibility of a fourth national network and of widespread competing cable television. The situation becomes quite clear when one learns that:

A Brookings Institute study of the 25-year period from 1945 to 1970 found that, of 33 commissioners who held office during that period, 21 of them went on to "employment by a firm regulated by the FCC" . . . (Ibid., p. 10).

Furthermore, most of those who did not join these businesses simply retired. The exact same symbiotic relation betwen business and regulatory agencies has been found in studies of the U.S. Maritime Commission, the Department of Defense, the Civil Aeronautics Board, the Interstate Commerce Commission, many state electric and gas utility commissions, and various telephone regulatory commissions (Nader, 1973). Thus, a study showed that "more often than not, regulatory agencies are 'captured' by those they are supposed to regulate" (Domhoff, 1983, p. 131).

FISCAL POLICY

The economic role of government that most directly influences the levels of manufacturing output, income, and employment is its taxing and spending of money—its *fiscal policy*. The prevailing economic philosophy until the 1930s was that taxes should be used only to finance necessary government expenditures. It was thought to be an unsound financial practice for governments to borrow money. However, the experiences of the Great Depression and World War II forced a change in this policy. The trend since that time has been for government spending to rise much more rapidly than taxes.

Federal government spending in the United States in 1921–1929 was only 1 percent of the Gross National Product (GNP). In 1930–1940, as the New Deal responded to the depression, it had increased to 4 percent of GNP. During World War II, government spending rose to the incredible height of 41 percent of GNP in 1943 and 1944. After the war it fell, but it increased again in the Korean War, so that federal spending averaged 11 percent of GNP in 1945–1959. In 1960–1970, partly owing to the Vietnam War, federal spending averaged 13 percent of GNP—about two-thirds or more being military (Cypher, 1973, chap. 6). Total government spending—state and local as well as federal—rose to 31 percent of GNP in 1970.

Since World War II, the American economy has entered a new stage, in which government has become an intimate partner of business. Since the 1890s, the economy has been dominated by the giant monopoly corporations, with some help from the government. Now the economy is dominated by these same corporations working intimately with a government that strongly affects the economy and is itself highly influenced by the economy.

There are three different policy views of what government fiscal policy ought to be. The most conservative economists, such as Adam Smith or the contemporary American economist Milton Friedman, argue that no discretionary fiscal measures are needed. The government should stay out of the economy. Friedman agrees with Adam Smith that the less government, the better. He attributes many of our economic problems to too much government interference with private enterprise, which would otherwise automatically adjust to all situations in a supposedly near perfect manner. To the extent that conservatives admit any need for government policy, they say that only monetary measures are necessary. Conservatives view an adequate money supply merely as one of the prerequisites for a private enterprise economy. Other prerequisites, which they believe government should provide, include police and armies to maintain "law and order," primarily to protect private property from its domestic and foreign enemies.

The second view, the liberal position, is that of such economists as John M. Keynes and the contemporary American scholar Paul Samuelson. Liberals admit that capitalism has serious problems, such as general unemployment and inflation. Liberal Keynesians argue that if there is unemployment—because of deficient demand—then the government can add to demand in one of two ways. It can directly increase government spending, which is a component of demand; and/or it can lower taxes, which increases the income available for consumer or investor demand. On the other hand, if there is inflation because demand is at too high a level (perhaps because of large government military spending), then the government can reduce demand in one of two ways. First, it may lower the level of government spending. Second, it may raise taxes, which reduces the amount people have left over for consumer or investor spending.

The liberal Keynesians used to maintain that such measures can *always* successfully bring about full employment with stable prices. Now, many of them, including Samuelson, simply admit that ending inflation *and* getting full employment at the same time is one "little thing" not yet solved by establishment economists: "Experts do not yet know . . . an incomes policy that will permit us to have *simultaneously* . . . full employment and price stability" (Samuelson, 1973, p. 823).

The radical view, first expressed by Karl Marx, argues that problems like periodic unemployment are deeply rooted in the capitalist system and cannot be cured by any amount of monetary or fiscal measures. Radicals contend that the American economy has reached full employment *only* during major wars. In normal peacetime years, it appears that unemployment and/or inflation is the usual state of capitalism. Radicals argue that the necessary drastic fiscal measures cannot be taken by capitalist governments because powerful vested interests oppose each such step, apart from military spending.

Granted that the government can cure unemployment by enough spending, the problem remains one of finding suitable ways of spending the amounts of money necessary to maintain full employment. Many outlets that would be socially beneficial conflict with the vested interests of large corporations or wealthy individuals. Larger welfare payments tend to raise the wage level. Government investment in industrial ventures or public utilities (such as the Tennessee Valley Authority) tends to erode monopolistic privileges and profits.

There might be other welfare spending—for example, on hospitals and schools. The rich, however, see these as subsidies to the poor for things that the rich can buy for themselves out of their own pockets. Proposals to increase unemployment compensation or lower taxes paid by the poor often encounter even greater resistance because they would transfer income from the rich to the poor. If any of these measures are to some extent allowed, it is only after a long political fight, certainly not promptly enough to head off a developing depression or recession.

In every area of possible constructive government spending, powerful vested interests stand in opposition to the satisfaction of some of the nation's most basic social needs. These conservative interests will not tolerate government competition with private enterprise, measures that undermine the privileges of the wealthy, or policies that significantly alter the relative distribution of income. They therefore oppose government spending *except* (1) subsidies to business, (2) highway building (pushed by oil and auto producers), and (3) military spending. This is not to deny that certain "progressive" business leaders and corporations favor some reforms for the needy. These reforms include increased welfare benefits, hot lunches for poor children, and Medicare for the elderly. In fact, support of, rather than opposition to, these moderate social reform measures usually characterizes the liberal versus the conservative wing of the upper class. The important point, however, is that these moderate reform measures do not significantly affect the wealth and power of the capitalist class in America.

One liberal Keynesian cure for depression is reduction of taxes to allow more money to flow into private spending. Given the composition of the United States government, however, tax cuts end up benefiting mainly the rich and the corporations. Even in the liberal Kennedy administration, the taxes of the poor were reduced very little and those of the rich very much, resulting in a redistribution of income that benefited members of the wealthy class. Especially in a depression, however, the wealthy will not spend their increased income. The consumption of the wealthy remains at adequate levels even in a depression, and they have no desire to invest in the face of probable losses. Hence the political restriction as to who gets the tax cuts makes this policy of tax reduction economically ineffective as regards depressions.

MILITARY SPENDING

In the years immediately after World War II, the goal of full employment required spending an additional $15–$20 billion annually. This might have been a very agonizing social and political issue except for the advent of the Cold War. Dollars for purchasing Cold War armaments did not violate any vested interests. Big business has been shown to be a part of the "Iron Triangle" of weapons development and procurement, which includes the Pentagon, key congressional committees on military expenditures, and private industry (Caldicott, 1986, pp. 32–33).

Big business considers military spending an ideal antidepression policy for three reasons. First, such expenditures have the same positive short-run effect on employment and profits as would expenditures on more socially useful projects. Second, military spending means big and stable profits, whereas welfare spending may shift income from rich taxpayers to poor recipients. Third, the long-run effect is even more favorable because no new consumer goods or producer goods are created, so there is no competition with nonmilitary producers. During the past 35 years, the main change has been that the necessary addition to the income stream—if high employment is to be maintained—has risen over $100 billion a year. If it were politically possible, the whole amount could be spent on public commodities, such as housing, health, or education, rather than on military waste. But such useful spending is not *politically* possible as long as the United States government is dominated by big business.

The political reality is that vested interests oppose each of the possible constructive, peaceful programs with negative rhetoric and successful political pressure. It is a fact that the U.S. economy prospered in the late 1960s by spending immense sums of money to kill the people of Vietnam; and it continues to spend vast amounts of money on unnecessary military hardware. President Nixon, who was elected with big-business support, vetoed bills and impounded money intended to clean up the rivers. President Ford vetoed hosts of bills for more health, education, or welfare benefits, including a bill for school lunches for poor children. President Reagan declared that catsup was to be considered a vegetable to avoid spending the appropriate amount of money on actual vegetables in the school lunch program. The Department of Defense has estimated President Reagan's "Star Wars" project, involving missiles in outer space, could cost $1 trillion (Caldicott, 1986, p. 46).

Moreover, the liberal Democratic administrations have been just as militaristic as the conservative Republican administrations. The Kennedy administration greatly increased military spending, invaded Cuba at the Bay of Pigs, and expanded the Vietnam War. The Johnson administration invaded the Dominican Republic and further expanded the Vietnam War on a vast scale. The Carter administration promised to reduce military spending by $5 to $7 billion, but instead increased it in his first two years in office.

To measure the full extent of the military impact on the economy, we must recall that the U.S. Department of Defense is the largest "planned economy" in the world today outside the Soviet Union. It spends more than the net income of all American corporations. By 1969 it had 470 major and 6,000 lesser installations, owned 39 million acres of land, spent over $80 billion a year, and used 200,000 primary contractors and 100,000 subcontractors—thus directly employing in the armed forces and military production about 10 percent of the United States labor force (Melman, 1970). Even though the United States was involved in the costly war in Vietnam in 1969, the military budget nevertheless increased even after the war was over. In 1984, the United States spent $264 billion on the military, which was 55 percent of all federal general funds. The amount spent increased to $293 billion just one year later in 1985. From 1985 to 1989 the Reagan administration planned to spend at least $1.8 trillion on defense (Caldicott, 1986, pp. 31–32).

Some key areas of the economy are especially affected. As early as 1963, before large-scale American entry into the Vietnam War, studies show that 36 percent of the output of producers' durable goods was purchased directly or indirectly by the federal government, mostly for military use. In the entire period from 1947 through 1971, the military spent $1.7 trillion, enough to buy the entire GNP of the United States for 1969 and 1970 (Cypher, 1973). In the same 1947–1971 period, direct military spending averaged 13 percent of GNP. In the peacetime economy of the mid-to-late 1980s it has been about 7 percent of GNP. There is also a very large indirect or secondary effect on (1) additional consumer goods from the spending of those who receive military dollars and (2) additional investment in factories and equipment by military industries. The indirect effect is estimated at another 12 or 13 percent, so the total effect of military spending is in the neighborhood of 20 percent of GNP. However, many Americans are alarmed by the recent argument that these huge military expenditures could ruin the economy (Caldicott, 1986, pp. 32–34). Japan and West Germany, which spend much less on their military than does the United States (1 percent and 3.5 percent of GNP, respectively), are more financially able to modernize their economies and scientifically develop products, such as cars and computers, that millions of people can buy for nonmilitary purposes (ibid.).

Speaking of the serious international consequences of the arms race, former President Dwight Eisenhower said: "Every gun that is made, every warship

launched, every rocket fired signifies, in the final sense, a theft from those who
hunger and are not fed, those who are cold and are not clothed. This world in
arms is not spending money alone. It is spending the sweat of its laborers, the
genius of its scientists, the hopes of its children . . ." (quoted by Caldicott, 1986).
This waste of resources needed to meet basic needs throughout the world can
be partly solved by arms reduction by the superpowers. Treaties for reducing
arms by the United States and the Soviet Union are under way. However, to be
effective, arms reductions should transpire without huge new arms buildups,
which could occur.

How did the U.S. economy come to have such an enormous military sector?
Of course, in World War II, the United States had a huge military production.
Yet it was assumed by almost all policy makers, including economists, business
leaders, and politicians that the United States would mostly disarm after the war.
It was also assumed that this would lead to a depression; therefore, every possible
solution was considered, with most analyses leading to the sole suggestion of
renewed military spending. It was in this atmosphere that the Cold War was
born; it provided an excuse for every possible increase in military spending. In
fact, since the United States had a monopoly of atomic bombs, the Soviet Union
was very unlikely to be aggressive. Moreover, Soviet foreign policy was mostly
very cautious and conservative, so much so that revolutionaries in other countries
accused them of betrayal for *not* supplying arms. In reality, the Soviet Union had
its sphere of influence—Eastern Europe—which the United States had not invaded, while the United States had spheres of influence and imperial power in
much of Latin America, Africa, and Asia, which the Soviet Union had not invaded.
Thus, despite the Cold War rhetoric, the two major powers have never clashed
militarily, except indirectly by supporting others (for example, Soviet support of
Cubans in Angola and U.S. support of the *contras* in Nicaragua).

Therefore the armaments spending justified by the Cold War rhetoric was
probably not militarily necessary. It was utilized, as in Southeast Asia, to protect
American investments abroad, but also in large part to support the U.S. economy
at home. Thus we find in both world wars that the industrialists instructed the
government exactly how the procurement process should be run, dominated the
Department of Defense, and made enormous rates of profit. This condition has
continued ever since.

The huge military profits are best revealed in a study by the U.S. General
Accounting Office (GAO). The GAO asked 81 large military contractors by questionnaire what their profit rates were for 1966 through 1969. The replies admitted
an average profit rate of 24.8 percent—much higher than nonmilitary profits in
the same industries. But spot checks showed that these profit rates were still
very much underreported. So the GAO did its own audit of the books of 146 main
military contractors. The study found that the profit rate of these military merchants was a fantastic 56.1 percent rate of return on invested capital.

Yet, the GAO said that these data still underestimated profit rates because
the military firms hide profits in numerous ways. These firms allocate costs of
other parts of their business to military contracts and add in many other unrelated
costs. Some have even included the costs of call girls to influence government
inspectors (called "entertainment" in their accounts). They also make hidden

profits through the use of complex subcontracting procedures to subsidiaries, unauthorized use of government-owned property, and getting patents on research done for the government.

Not only are the profit rates on military spending extraordinary, but these profits mostly go to relatively few firms. Almost all military contracts go to just 205 of the top 500 corporations. Just 100 of these firms get 85 percent of all military contracts.

It is worth noting how military spending has affected the U.S. economy at various times. As late as 1939, it had very little effect, being only 2.6 percent of GNP. In World War II, it rose to about 40 percent of GNP, which brought full employment (and even a shortage of labor). After World War II, there were several times when the drop in military spending seems to have been the main catalyst setting off a recession. Thus it fell in 1948, 1954, and 1970—all years in which recessions began. On the other hand, military spending has been used by government to stimulate the economy. Thus military spending rose in 1949, 1955, 1958, and 1971—all years in which the economy needed a boost to begin a recovery.

The automatic and inherent pattern of American business cycles has now been overlaid with a more politically motivated business cycle. When there is an all-out boom, business influence gets government to reduce military spending. This reduction is desired to avoid inflation as well as to avoid full employment, which would mean "uppity" workers and higher wages. Since, however, it is hard to time the military spending reductions exactly when desired and very hard to estimate exactly how much is needed, this always seems to do more than just limit the boom; it almost always seems to turn into a full-scale recession.

Indeed, the capitalist economy never stands still since cumulative forces are always pushing it rapidly up or down once it gets going. Thus when vested interests reduce military spending a bit—in order to limit the boom—this action sets off a recession. On the other hand, as the recession gets worse and profits decline, the same politico-economic power is used to start increasing military spending again, thus setting off another boom. Of course, this oversimplifies a complex situation. The government does not cause the business cycle; that is caused by the capitalist system. The government does help cut off the expansion at the peak and does help the recovery from the bottom of the depression, which is one more aspect of the intimate relationship between government and business.

WAGE-PRICE CONTROLS

In recent years, the U.S. economy has experienced a "first" in the nation's history: simultaneous unemployment and inflation. We previously showed that this is mainly caused by the increasing monopoly power of the giant corporations. President Nixon discovered that he could not cure the inflation by cutting government spending because that would vastly increase unemployment; and he could not cure the unemployment simply by more military spending because that would increase inflation. So, against all his conservative principles, Nixon was forced to use direct intervention in the economy by wage-price controls.

Nixon began the intervention in 1971 in order to make the economy look better for the 1972 elections. Controls lasted from August 1971 till April 1974, but they were made much looser by January 1973 when the election was safely won. During the entire period of controls, Nixon's Pay Board severely limited wage increases, but prices rose by 4 percent in 1972, 8 percent in 1973, and 12 percent in 1974. Therefore, real wages (the actual purchasing power of wages) fell rapidly. In 1973, real wages fell 4 percent, the only time they had ever fallen in a peacetime expansion. In the same period, there were no controls on profits, so profit rates kept rising. Profit rates even continued to rise in 1974, the first year of the 1974–1975 depression, another unprecedented occurrence.

In fact, Nixon boasted that he intended to raise corporate profits while holding down wages. He subscribed to the famous "trickle-down" theory, which claims that the government can best help the poor by giving to the rich. The rich will stimulate the economy, so some money will trickle down to the poor. In his speech announcing the wage-price controls, Nixon said:

> All Americans will benefit from more profits. More profits fuel the expansion. . . . More profits mean more investment. . . . That's why higher profits in the American economy would be good for every person in America. (Nixon, 1971)

Vice-President Agnew (1971) repeated the theory: "Rising corporate profits are needed more than ever by the poor." Can you think of some things the poor might need more than rising corporate profits?

Nixon and Agnew succeeded extraordinarily well in their objectives of reducing real wages and raising profit rates. Profit rates were "only" 16.5 percent on investment (before taxes) in 1971 but rose to 23.4 percent in 1974, the first full year of the depression—a strange depression.

One way Nixon achieved these results was by appointing a probusiness Pay Board to make wage decisions. The big unions first joined it, hoping to salvage some crumbs, but then withdrew when they found that they were to be allowed nothing. The American Federation of Labor-Congress of Industrial Organizations (AFL-CIO) said:

> We joined the Pay Board in good faith, desiring—despite our misgivings—to give it a fair chance. . . . The so-called public members are neither neutral nor independent. They are tools of the Administration, and imbued with its viewpoint that all of the nation's economic ills are caused by high wages. As a result, the Pay Board has been completely dominated and run, from the very start, by a coalition of the business and so-called public members. . . . The trade union movement's representatives on the board have been treated as outsiders—merely as a facade to maintain the pretense of a tri-partite body. . . . (AFL-CIO Executive Committee, 1974, p. 7)

We conclude that wage-price controls under capitalism normally redistribute income away from wages and toward profits. The meaning of the political business cycle is also clarified. At the peak of expansion, when workers are pushing for higher wages, the U.S. government talks about inflation, and it uses restrictive monetary, fiscal, or direct controls to lower wages and even promote a little unemployment. At the bottom of the depression, the U.S. government is moved by corporate pleas to stimulate the economy. The capitalist system would generate boom and bust cycles without government interference, but the government does reinforce them and may often serve as the catalyst, setting off the downswing as well as the upswing. The important point is to realize how deeply involved the government and business are in each other's affairs, which can have negative consequences for the rest of society.

REAGANOMICS (1980–1988)

The Reagan administration argued—contrary to the earlier Keynesian view—that there is no lack of demand, that the unemployed can always get jobs if they really want them, and that the real problems are on the supply side of economics. Supply-side economics contends that capitalists do not invest enough of their money mainly because taxes are outrageously high (they also worry about wages being too high). The argument is that, if the taxes of the wealthy and the big corporations are reduced, then there will be more savings. If there are more savings, the increased savings will be used to invest in expansion of production, which will result in more employment.

There are several problems with supply-side economics. First, the increase in income after taxes may be used for more luxury consumption rather than savings, or for corporate mergers that do not result in more employment. Second, even if more money is saved, it will not be invested if there is no demand. For example, in 1981 and 1982 the Reagan administration reduced taxes for the wealthy and the large corporations. Investment in new plant and equipment continued to drop, however, because there was no demand even for current factory output. In spite of the tax cuts, factory utilization dropped to 68 percent of capacity in 1982.

Furthermore, the tax cuts to the wealthy were paid for by reducing services to the unemployed, to women and children, and to the elderly. In the 1981 budget, for example, there were major spending cuts in public service job programs, education programs, aid to disadvantaged children, health programs, medical care for the elderly, social security, public housing, food stamps, mothers' and infants' nutrition, school lunches, day care for children, aid to mass transit, safety inspections, parks, and postal service. "In 1983, a total of $30 billion was withdrawn from [these] programs to help people . . ." (Caldicott, 1986, p. 31). Subsidies to big business remained the same, while military spending grew by leaps and bounds. The huge tax cuts plus the enormous increase in military spending resulted in the record deficits of the Reagan administration.

SUMMARY

This chapter asked if government regulated business or actually aided the profits and power of business. The preponderance of the evidence suggests that the government has become a close ally of business instead of a stern regulator of business. The position of pluralists like Arnold Rose argues that, especially since the Roosevelt administration in the 1930s, government has increasingly controlled big business. The data presented in this chapter suggest an opposite conclusion.

In general, this chapter and the previous one have indicated a closer and closer relationship between big business and government. When vast military spending is also included in the discussion, we begin to see a picture of the American government and economy similar to the one painted by C. Wright Mills, G. William Domhoff, and various Marxists who were discussed in the previous chapter. Thus, instead of a plural distribution of power with government regulating business, the data point to a concentration of power at the top of American society with the government directly and indirectly aiding the wealthy corporations. Reaaganomics has accentuated these tendencies.

SUGGESTED READINGS

The reader is referred to the suggested readings in the previous chapter for important analyses of political sociology. An excellent compilation of various points of view can be found in Richard G. Braungart, ed., *Society and Politics: Readings in Political Sociology* (Englewood Cliffs, NJ: Prentice-Hall, 1976). Richard Braungart also has been the editor of a very sophisticated journal, *Research in Political Sociology,* which contains many outstanding articles addressing issues of concern here. A fascinating exposé of business influence in various regulatory agencies has been done by the Ralph Nader group in Mark Green, ed., *The Monopoly Markers* (New York: Grossman, 1973). A very careful and intensive investigation of the subservience of the Federal Trade Commission to big business is found in Alan Stone, *Economic Regulation and the Public Interest: The Federal Trade Commission in Theory and Practice* (Ithaca, NY: Cornell University Press, 1977). Finally, a very important, well-documented, contribution to our understanding of how politics and economics affect the arms race and the possibility of nuclear war is Dr. Helen Caldicott's *Missile Envy,* Rev. Ed. (Toronto and New York: Bantam Books, 1986).

REFERENCES

Ackerman, F., et al. 1972. "Income Distribution in the United States." In R. Edwards, M. Reich, and T. Weisskopf, eds., *The Capitalist System.* Englewood Cliffs, NJ: Prentice-Hall.

AFL-CIO Executive Committee. 1974. *The National Economy, 1973.* Washington, DC: AFL-CIO.

Agnew, Spiro. September 1971. Speech at National Governors Conference.

Bonnen, James. 1972. "The Effect of Taxes and Government Spending on Inequality." In R. Edwards, M. Reich, and T. Weisskopf, eds., *The Capitalist System.* Englewood Cliffs, NJ: Prentice-Hall.

Bowles, Samuel, and Herbert Gintis. 1976. *Schooling in Capitalist America.* New York: Basic Books.

Caldicott, Dr. Helen. 1986. *Missile Envy.* Rev. ed. Toronto, New York: Bantam Books.

Cypher, James. 1973. *Military Expenditures and the Performance of the Post-War Economy.* Ph.D. diss., University of California, Riverside.

Domhoff, G. William. 1983. *Who Rules America Now? A View for the '80s.* Englewood Cliffs, NJ: Prentice-Hall.

Edwards, Richard. 1972. "Who Fares Well in the Welfare State?" In R. Edwards, M. Reich, and T. Weisskopf, eds., *The Capitalist System.* Englewood Cliffs, NJ: Prentice-Hall.

Gurley, John. 1967. "Federal Tax Policy." *National Tax Journal* (September).

Internal Revenue Service. 1976. "Vote Would Close Loopholes for Rich." Reported by Associated Press, in *Riverside Daily Enterprise,* May 13: A–3.

Kolko, Gabriel. 1962. *Wealth and Power in America.* New York: Praeger.

Lechman, J., and B. Okner. 1972. "Individual Income Tax Erosion by Income Classes." In U.S. Congress Joint Economic Committee, *Economics of Federal Subsidy Programs*, pt. 1. Washington, DC: Government Printing Office.

Lekachman, Robert. 1972. *National Income and the Public Welfare*. New York: Random House.

Melman, Seymour. 1970. *Pentagon Capitalism*. New York: McGraw-Hill.

Nader, Ralph. 1973. Mark Green, ed. *The Monopoly Makers*. New York: Grossman.

———. 1974. *People and Taxes* (October). Discussed in Labor Research Association, *Economic Notes*, April 1975: 3–4.

Nixon, Richard. 1971. TV speech, August 15.

Pechman, Joseph. 1969. "The Rich, the Poor, and the Taxes They Pay." *The Public Interest* 17 (Fall).

Rothschild, Emma. 1988. "The Real Reagan Economy." *The New York Review of Books* 35 (11): 46–53.

Samuelson, Paul. 1973. *Economics*, 9th ed. New York: McGraw-Hill.

Scheer, Robert. 1977. "Aura of Failure Grips FCC in Overseeing TV." *Los Angeles Times*, August 15: 1.

U.S. Department of Commerce. 1960, 1974. *Statistical Abstract of the United States*. Discussed in Labor Research Association, *Economic Notes*, April 1975: 4.

chapter 17

Sociology of Protest Movements

Two questions that are significant for sociologists, as well as for politicians and the general public, are: (1) When will oppressed groups protest their circumstances? (See Smelser, 1963; Useem, 1975; Piven, 1976; Braungart, 1979; McAdam, 1982; and Klandermans and Oegema, 1987.) (2) What happens when they do protest? (See Turner and Killian, 1987; Wood and Jackson, 1982; Zald and McCarthy, 1979; and Freeman, 1979.) In this chapter we will answer these questions by examining the conditions under which protest occurs and by illustrating these conditions primarily by reference to a century of black protest in the United States. Then we will examine some consequences of protests.

THE SINGLE-FACTOR APPROACH TO PROTEST

Until the 1960s, sociology tended to explain the occurrence of protests—that is, challenges to the existing social order—in terms of one or a few factors, or conditions, that led to the protests. These single factors were discussed in the literature on collective behavior. Collective behavior refers to various types of unconventional group behavior, such as protests, including riots, reform movements, and radical movements, as well as crazes, panics, and group hysteria. Our focus will be on protests, especially radical and reformist social movements.

Among the factors seen to explain protests were economic hardships, sophisticated leaders or "agitators" who could organize the masses, and ideologies such as communism, socialism, and fascism. Usually a given study would emphasize the importance of one of these factors or possibly a few of them in combination. Thus, one or a few factors would presumably explain why a protest such as a strike, riot, or revolution occurred.

For example, revolutions in France have been analyzed in terms of the underlying *beliefs* of the French population. The French author Belin-Milleron (1957, pp. 353–359) argued that in the revolutions of 1789 and 1848, "the public mind . . . linked together juridical and political ideas—'civil liberty,' 'constitution,' 'democracy,'—[and] moral and social notions—'public good,' 'civic virtue,' 'solidarity'. . . ." Furthermore, these ideas were synthesized into the revolutionary slogan, "liberty, equality, and fraternity," which was seen to underlie revolutionary agitation. Such cultural determinist views of historical change are criticized in Chapter 2 of this book.

Similarly, the French syndicalist Georges Sorel (1957) argued that a belief in the "general strike" should underlie socialist political activity. He states that syndicalists must concentrate "the whole of socialism in the drama of the general strike," which would paralyze capitalist society. Even if one large general strike did not bring down capitalism, Sorel (1957, p. 360) argues that the mere *idea* of this is crucial in revolutionary organizing. As he says, *"It is the myth [of the general strike] . . . which is alone important."*

In addition to ideologies, strong leaders were often singled out in the collective behavior literature as determinants of protest. Hertzler (1957), in an interesting historical study, examines the role of dictators in mobilizing the masses. He shows that in times of social-economic crisis, when people are in an insecure situation, dictators have arisen to offer sweeping solutions to the problems at hand. In times of crisis, such as a losing war, political turbulence, depression or famine, "problems present themselves which are insoluble by the old or existing social machinery . . ." (1957, p. 365). Here, Hertzler argues, the would-be dictator is able to mobilize the masses into his or her political movement over which he or she has firm control. Among examples cited are Cromwell's dictatorship in England in 1649, Napoleon Bonaparte's and Louis Napoleon's in nineteenth-century France, and Hitler's in twentieth-century Germany.

Finally, various forms of material and social deprivation have been seen as circumstances leading to protest. Deprivation refers to people being denied by others things, such as money, land, prestige, food, or freedom to live as they please, *and* to the subjective awareness of being so deprived. For example, the takeover of the lands of Native Americans by white settlers—and the great disruption of Indian culture and material livelihood—has been seen to underlie "Ghost Dance" protests among the Indians. In a classic discussion of "Nativistic Movements," Ralph Linton (1957, pp. 388–389) notes that the Ghost Dance "laid great stress on the revival of . . . distinctive elements of Indian culture" that whites had destroyed or greatly weakened. Although the Native Americans were unable to mount a fully successful protest against white settlers, the Ghost Dance assured its adherents that "when the dead [ancestors] returned and the whites were swept away . . .," the Native Americans would have their land and property returned to them.

Many other studies have shown protests and social movements associated with economic deprivation in the 1930s depression in the United States, with political oppression of minority groups, with lower social status of religious sects, with exploitation of the working class in capitalist countries, and with colonialism in the Third World (Turner and Killian, 1957). All of these studies, and many others (see Gurr, 1970), point to the central role of some kind of social or material deprivation underlying the protests and social movements.

THE MULTIPLE-VARIABLE APPROACH TO PROTEST

Each of the studies above focuses on one or a few specific conditions underlying protests. Taken separately, studies such as these often provide many insights into the groups under investigation. Yet, when one tries to correlate each of these single factors with a variety of protests, usually a low correlation is found (Smelser, 1963, pp. 12–18, 82–84, 345–347). For example, if we looked at groups that were economically deprived or exploited, we would probably find some protest activity, but we would also find periods of *inactivity*. Similarly, if we studied groups that were attached to left-wing ideologies, we would find various attempts at protest, but we would also find periods devoid of protest activity. Furthermore, if we studied leaders who tried to organize the masses, we would find examples of where they were successful, but also many instances in which the leaders did not organize the masses.

Why do such single variable approaches to protest often result in low ability to understand or predict protests? The reason is that many factors—not just a few—must combine in order to motivate a group to collectively challenge the existing arrangements of society. Thus Neil Smelser (1963) argues—and much data support him—that a multiple variable approach to protest, and to collective behavior in general, is required (Marx and Wood, 1975).

There are numerous factors from which to choose when selecting an appropriate multiple variable approach to protest. In fact, the earlier literature had an *ad hoc*, or random, character to it because numerous factors do influence protests, but different authors would select different factors to explain different protests. We have already seen that ideologies, leaders, and social or material deprivations were central determinants in different studies. The problem with this ad hoc approach to protest is that the reader may be convinced by the analysis of a single protest but still be left without a more comprehensive theory to apply to various protests.

What would be the factors to include in developing a more comprehensive approach to protests? Smelser (1963), Oberschall (1973), McAdam (1982), and various Marxists (Marx, in Smelser, ed., 1973; Fanon, 1968) have tried to answer this question. Some of the factors that appear to be required before a major protest movement occurs would be:

1. *Social structural conditions* must lead to certain stresses and strains between classes or other groups in a society.
2. Objective economic, political, or social *deprivation*, resulting from the structural conditions, must occur.
3. These objective deprivations must lead to conscious feelings of deprivation, which will crystallize into an ideology.
4. This ideology must lead to the organization and *mobilization* of the discontented group.

5. The structural conditions must also include *weakened social control* by the ruling class.

6. Given these five conditions, many kinds of *precipitating events* will lead to a protest movement.*

The full meaning of each of these conditons is spelled out in detail in the following sections.

A RELATIONAL AND HISTORICALLY SPECIFIC ANALYSIS: A CENTURY OF BLACK PROTEST

The multifactor approach, stating these several conditions, is a major advance over the old approach of single factors, each used in an ad hoc manner, without a clear theoretical base. Yet some traditional sociologists still treat each of the conditions mentioned above as distinct and unrelated to one another. Radicals, on the contrary, stress—as we showed in Part I—that society must be treated as a totality, an organic whole with different aspects, in which each aspect is internally related to the others as part of one whole.

So the list of six conditions for protest is *not* arbitrary, but flows from the social structure we revealed in Part I. We showed that society is built on a certain economic base—including both technical forces of production and human relations within the productive process. On each particular economic base arises a different kind of social and political superstructure—including both particular institutions, such as the family, schools, the government, and religious institutions, as well as ideologies, such as racism or sexism. These institutions and ideologies play a vital role in supporting and justifying the present economic arrangements. Thus the question of protest movements might be phrased to ask: How and why do new ideologies arise which do not support but will attack the present economic, social, and political relations?

To answer that question, we will examine approximately a century of protest by black Americans, using our six-condition model of protest. The first condition states that social structural conditions must lead to strains and contradictions in society. For example, the existing forces of production may no longer be harmonious or congruent with the existing human economic relations (or their social and political reflections). Thus, in the American South before the Civil War, the productive relations were those of slavery, the laws and governing institutions supported slavery, and the ideology justifying slavery was spread by the newspapers, the schools, and the church. Yet slavery was totally unfitted for applying the new industrial technological forces that were evolving in the North. Slavery was therefore a barrier to industrialization, and this created growing structural tensions both in the South and between the South and the North.

The second condition—objective deprivations—certainly existed under

---

*This list contains our own summary of the literature. Our conditions are similar, but not identical, in meaning and interpretation to Smelser's (1963) six necessary and sufficient conditions of collective behavior. In his *Theory of Collective Behavior,* Smelser synthesizes a large literature, ranging from traditional sociology to Marxist analysis.

slavery from the moment that blacks were captured in Africa and brought to the South to be exploited. Furthermore, it should be noted that economic exploitation and social oppression actually *increased* in the early 1800s when the invention of the cotton gin made slavery more profitable, and revived a dying institution.

The third condition—feelings of deprivation and formation of ideology—certainly also existed among the slaves. The slaves had no school system because teaching slaves to read and write was a crime punishable by death. And they certainly were not allowed to publish any newspapers nor elect any official spokespersons. But the slaves did have their own religious institutions. Although the black church was sometimes prohibited or declared illegal, it survived underground and rapidly established a counter-ideology. While the white churches preached the divine will to maintain slavery, the blacks preached the equality of human beings under God. To this day, the black church has remained a center of protest ideology, especially because other avenues have often been closed.

The fourth condition—mobilization of the discontented group—was very difficult for black slaves to achieve. Slaves forming protest organizations or protesting or campaigning in any conceivable way was punishable by death or torture. Therefore, slaves never openly organized nor openly campaigned for reforms. Instead, they formed underground organizations (usually with a brief life span) and attempted to launch revolutions. The slave revolt led by Spartacus in ancient Rome is famous, but slaves in the American South also launched hundreds of armed revolts, all put down with great bloodshed and the execution of the slaves involved.

Mobilization can occur with regard to a reform or revolutionary movement. The authorities in society are usually more tolerant of reform movements that do not aim to bring large changes in the social order represented by these authorities. In contrast, the authorities often try to suppress revolutionary movements. In the South, slave protests were clearly viewed as potentially revolutionary because the slaves were correctly seen as wanting to abolish the institution of slavery. Hence punishments against slave mobilization were severe and any such mobilization among slaves was underground.

There was a protest movement—the abolitionist movement—but it existed in the North. There, blacks and whites could and did organize, both for reforms and for revolutionary change, the abolition of slavery. But this was possible in the North because it was a capitalist economy with democratic political forms (although blacks and women were excluded from voting). Still, the northern authorities did not view the abolitionist movement as a threat against the northern social structure. Whatever changes it might produce would be in the South. This mobilization for the abolition of slavery was "above ground" and did enlist scores of whites and blacks into the protest.

The fifth condition—weakened social control by the ruling class—did exist to some extent before the Civil War. The northern ruling class, the capitalists, came into increasing conflict with the southern ruling class, the slave owners. As a result, social control was weakened in the North to the extent that the abolitionists could propagandize and organize (though not without battles for civil liberties both in the courts and in the streets). Even in the South, support from the North allowed for a slight spread of abolitionist propaganda in mild forms, as well as increased slave escapes and revolts.

When these five preconditions of protest existed, a great many events precipitated actual protests, organization, and finally, war. On the legal level, the *Dred Scott* decision, recognizing the rights of slave owners all over the United States, sparked much protest. In the border state of Kansas, the free settlers and the slave owners fought for control mostly by bullets, though with some use of ballots. Similar were the actions of John Brown and his black and white followers in Kansas and, later, at Harper's Ferry in the South. On the political level, the final precipitating event of the Civil War to end slavery was the election of Abraham Lincoln. But all of these precipitating events only crystallized a violent struggle that had already become inevitable. The underlying causes were the structural conditions and contradictions, the exploitation and deprivation of the slaves, the rise of the abolitionist ideology in conflict with the ideology of slavery, the weakened social control over dissidents due to the conflict between the southern ruling class and the northern ruling class, and the resulting mobilization on both sides of the conflict in political as well as military terms.

STRUCTURAL CONDITIONS FROM THE 1870s TO THE 1940s

After the Civil War, the South had undergone a revolution (though limited) giving it a new economic base with new human relationships in production. The old slave owners still owned most of the land, but no longer had a slave labor force. The blacks were free men and women, but had no land and no other assets of any sort, except their labor power. The former slaves were therefore forced to beg for land from the former slave owners, who gave the blacks land, but with an enormous burden of rent to be paid in kind as a share of the crop each year. The burden was so heavy that few sharecroppers ever got out of debt or ever had any actual cash. At harvest time, they would give a large share of the crop to the landowner. At first, they could sell the rest (usually to the owner), but this amounted to very little money. In a short time after the harvest, the sharecropper would be penniless. Then he or she would have to live on credit at the local store, which would also be owned by the landowner. By the next harvest, the whole crop would be needed to give the landowner his share *plus* more to pay back the accumulated debt. So blacks began the new agricultural year with no money, going ever deeper into debt. This system lasted from the 1870s right down to the 1940s. The rural, southern blacks were, in a large majority, sharecroppers. These blacks—as well as some whites—remained heavily in debt, mostly illiterate because few schools were built in their areas, and even unable *legally* to leave the farm. Leaving the farm without paying the accumulated debt was a crime punishable by an indefinite prison term in most southern states.

The white landowning class (a small minority even among whites) continued to own the newspapers and other media and to control most culture and ideology in the South. Also, except for a short period of occupation by federal troops after the Civil War, the large landowners and some commercial capitalist allies continued to dominate southern politics. Blacks mostly were able to vote for some years after the Civil War, but were not able to hold any political power because they lacked any economic strength. When federal troops left the South in 1876, state governments were changed by force and violence, often led by the terrorists of the Ku Klux Klan. In theory, blacks continued to vote, but their votes were counted in a bloc for whatever candidate the ruling class wanted to win.

In the 1890s, some poor white farmers were joined by many blacks in the Populist movement, trying to challenge the political control by the big landowners and the growing number of southern capitalists (usually tied to northern banks). Because of the Populist threat, an all-out campaign was launched by the ruling class on two fronts. One effort was a huge media campaign to stimulate racist prejudice in the poor whites, and it was largely successful in getting them to desert their black allies. The other effort was to pass Jim Crow laws, partly to separate the races, but mostly aimed at depriving blacks of the right to vote by various devices. These devices—such as the poll tax or the test of ability to understand the Constitution (as *interpreted* by the voting registrars)—not only eliminated almost all black voters, but also eliminated most poor white voters.

DEPRIVATION AND DISCRIMINATION

After the Populists were defeated by these means, there was no major protest movement in the South until the 1950s. Of course, there remained much objective exploitation and deprivation of all kinds. As we have shown in previous chapters, there were low incomes, a burden of debt on the sharecroppers, unemployment and undesirable jobs in the cities, inadequate medical care—the list could go on and on. As Martin Luther King (1958, pp. 27–28) noted, the median income for blacks in Montgomery, Alabama in 1950 was $970 a year. There is obviously enough evidence of objective deprivation for blacks in America to motivate strong protests.

Why, then, was there little or no organized protest for so many years? In the first place, the structural conditions (our first condition) were not appropriate. The forces of production in the South were still mainly land and unskilled farm labor, with very little capital. Sharecropping was a very likely and easy to maintain system of human relations of production under these conditions. It was convenient and profitable for the landowner-merchant, and impossible to break out of for the sharecropper. As we have seen, it gave rise to overwhelming political power and cultural control by the white racist ruling class.

Blacks not only suffered objective exploitation and deprivation, but they also felt subjectively deprived. Thus the second condition did exist. Nevertheless, in these structural circumstances there were many obstacles to organization of a protest movement. The white racist ruling class's control of the South was very strong and not weakened in any way. The control was by propaganda in all the media, by use of economic power, and by violence—numerous lynchings continued into the early 1950s. The northern ruling class had reached a compromise in 1876 giving them national control in return for not interfering in the South. Thus the fifth condition, weakened social control, was missing.

Not only did the white rulers control the press, but most blacks were too illiterate and too poor to have any press of their own—both results of existing economic and educational deprivations. In this situation, it was hard to formulate and spread a militant ideology. The black church was against the white establishment, but due to *the objective conditions of oppression,* it tended to spread an ideology of resignation among blacks (with salvation after death). The result, then, was pessimism rather than militancy among generations of blacks, so that the third condition, ideology, was also missing.

In addition, rural sharecroppers were scattered over the countryside and isolated. There has seldom been an organized movement of sharecroppers, white or black. Where people are physically isolated, it is hard to mobilize. Thus the fourth condition, mobilization, was missing. In no era have isolated peasants been able to organize nationwide, but have usually led brief and bloody local revolts. Even today, with modern communications, it is almost impossible to organize farm workers in the South because they are so scattered. It is somewhat easier, but still difficult, in California because the farm sizes are much larger, with less isolation of farm workers.

CHANGING STRUCTURAL CONDITIONS IN THE 1940s AND 1950s

All of these conditions—from social structure to ideology—changed in the 1940s and 1950s, thereby setting the stage for the emergence of the civil rights movement as a major force. One should not think there was *no* movement for civil rights before the mid-1950s. There were protests against all forms of racial discrimination ever since the Civil War and even before. For example, in 1947 one of the authors of this book was in a black and white delegation of students in a bus going from Chicago to Washington to lobby Congress. We stopped in a small Ohio town for lunch and the restaurant refused to serve our black members. We all marched out and picketed the restaurant for three hours. There were hundreds—perhaps thousands—of such isolated and unsung protests by small groups (and a few nationwide campaigns) in the decades before the 1950s. Only in the late 1950s and early 1960s, however, did the civil rights movement gain nationwide strength, with the active involvement of large numbers of blacks, plus a certain strata of whites. Only then did it achieve great visibility in the news media, and achieve success in at least some of its goals. It was this qualitatively new and greater outpouring of protest that is usually called the Civil Rights Movement, comprised of many organizations and individuals.

What began the change in conditions was World War II (1941–1945). There had always been some black migration from the rural South to urban areas of the South and the North, but it was relatively small. In the war years, black migration greatly increased. The defense industries had an almost unlimited capacity for more workers. Millions of blacks moved from agriculture and sharecropping productive relations to jobs as workers in urban industries, often acquiring impressive skills in a short time (the same was true for millions of women, as we showed in earlier chapters). After the war, not only did these workers remain in the cities, but—because of the promise of a better life—more and more blacks joined them, till the black population is now more urbanized than the white population.

This change in the location and productive relations of blacks had an enormous impact on degree of deprivation, on ideology, on ability to mobilize, and on social control. The change in actual and perceived levels of deprivation is most interesting and important, but not so simple. The average standard of living for blacks *rose* greatly in this period. Although blacks had the lowest wages and became the most exploited of industrial workers, this was still a big step upward from the income levels of sharecroppers. Furthermore, the big cities had some amenities of culture and public sanitation that were totally lacking in the rural areas.

Yet this improvement in the absolute level of deprivation was more than offset by an increase in *feelings* of deprivation *relative* to the affluence of surrounding whites. This *relative deprivation* was based on the objective facts that blacks lived in segregated ghettoes with poor housing conditions and poor public utilities—yet they went to work with whites and saw much better white housing surrounding them. Blacks were also more directly confronted with discrimination every day; that is, whites got better jobs at work, better schools in their areas, and better service in restaurants and stores (where blacks often received *no* service). So the relative comparisons were far clearer in urban areas than in the isolated rural areas, which often had no schools or restaurants.

Some of the traditional sociological literature even argued that *better-off* blacks, with higher educations, were more likely to participate in the civil rights movement than poorer, less educated blacks (Pettigrew, 1964, 1971; Matthews and Prothro, 1966). This would point to an approach emphasizing the relative *instead* of absolute deprivation underlying these protests. For example, middle-class blacks would presumably compare themselves to middle- and upper-class whites, who were better off still.

This perception of deprivation relative to whites was seen by some traditional sociologists as a prime mover of black civil rights protest. Surely, this is an overstatement since the rock on which the civil rights movement was built is the very real objective discrimination, exploitation, and deprivation of the average black person. It is true, though, that subjective and relative deprivation played a role, particularly at that time when blacks were moving into the midst of white dominated cities.

Furthermore, the theory of relative deprivation of the small black middle class is stronger when recruitment patterns for civil rights activities (that is, who joined them) are compared to recruitment patterns for more radical groups like the Black Panther Party in the 1960s. The Black Panthers had a mass base comprised largely of working-class and unemployed blacks (Seale, 1970). These decidedly poorer and less educated blacks were drawn to the revolutionary Black Panther Party because it challenged the entire racist and capitalist system that oppressed them (Newton, 1969). Thus relative deprivation was *one* of the underlying conditions for many of the civil rights movement protests, whereas more extreme deprivations underlay more radical black protests. Nevertheless, we have seen that the ultimate bases for all of these protests were the changes in structural conditions of blacks and the continued objective deprivation of black people in America.

So far we have explained the civil rights movement of the 1950s and 1960s by the first condition, basic structural tensions and *changes* in the structural productive forces and relations. We also found in existence the second condition—continuing objective exploitation, discrimination, and deprivation of blacks—as well as *increases* in the level of relative deprivation. These first two conditions were the basis for the rise in black militant ideology (condition three) in the late 1950s and 1960s. In addition, this rise of a more militant ideology was initially greatly helped by the impact of World War II in several ways. For one thing, hundreds of thousands of blacks served in the United States armed forces, in which they learned to handle weapons and to shoot back at an enemy. They refused to go back to a life of kowtowing to all whites in the United States without a struggle. Blacks also heard all of the ideals of equality in American propaganda against fascism. They compared that propaganda to existing discrimination at home, as well as to the complete segregation of white and black units (with all white officers) in the U.S. army. Black soldiers also saw the lesser discrimination and lesser racism in England and France—and the reversal of discrimination patterns by the Japanese in the Pacific.

So the ideology of the civil rights movement did not emerge from nowhere, but rather from the impact of World War II, as well as from the change to urban living in continued poor conditions in close proximity to more affluent whites. This same set of conditions also helped to reduce the social control over the protesters (condition five). The white government of the United States had projected an image of democracy and equality in the war and needed to continue that image to achieve world leadership in the 1950s. Yet talk of equality and human rights in the United States was discredited by most people in the world so long as we practiced overt discrimination against blacks, including almost complete segregation in the South, massive denial of the right to vote, and a continued stream of lynchings year after year with no arrests. There were even numerous cases where diplomats and United Nations officials were refused housing or food service in Washington, D.C., because of race.

Furthermore, when blacks moved to the big cities of the North, they began to exert significant political force for the first time since the 1870s. Even a few black congressmen could easily embarrass the U.S. government by pointing to injustices. And more and more white politicians needed black votes to get elected. So the U.S. government was pressured both by the civil rights movement and by many white politicians (also by the U.S. State Department) to help end the legal segregation and voting denials in the South, as well as to stop some of the repression and lynchings.

Above all, these changed needs of the northern ruling class and the changes in the political atmosphere led to dramatic changes in the Supreme Court's interpretations of the Constitution. The court is definitely susceptible to the political winds and to the views dominant in the ruling class and in the media. The justices are, after all, raised in and living in this society, mostly in upper-income circles of society. As we saw in the 1850s, the court voiced the view of the politically dominant slave owners in the Dred Scott case. In 1896, when northern capital lived in an easygoing compromise with the southern rulers, the Supreme Court stated in *Plessy* v. *Ferguson* that separate is equal in public conveyances (and the doctrine also applied to schools).

Under the new political conditions (and new needs of the northern ruling class), in May of 1954, the Supreme Court of the United States made a historic decision that would affect the South and the rest of the country. In the case of *Brown* v. *Board of Education*, the Supreme Court, headed by Earl Warren, decided that "separate but equal" schools in the South were not equal and were therefore unconstitutional. As a result the schools in the South were ordered to desegregate. This was a momentous decision in that an elite institution, the Supreme Court, declared that another institution, the southern school system, was essentially racist. This Supreme Court decision proved to be a major spark that ignited the civil rights movement.

To sum up, we can see that the Supreme Court decision was a result of weakened social control (condition five), which in turn was the result of ideological changes (condition three) caused by structural changes in production forces and relations, as well as relocation of the black population (condition one), combined with continued absolute deprivation and rising relative deprivation (condition two). In turn, this decision became a major precipitating cause of the civil rights movement.

Other precipitating causes are related to the circumstances that allowed mobilization (condition four) of blacks and some whites into an organized movement. Again, we begin with the fact that blacks moved in the 1940s and 1950s from isolated rural areas into compact areas of cities. Now blacks could easily communicate with each other. Not only did they live close together, but many hundreds and thousands would work together in the same factory. Blacks could then organize in many ways, including trade unions. They also began to publish community newspapers. Moreover, when circumstances were ripe and precipitating events occurred, the black church immediately reacted. As we have seen, for a long time the black church was the *only* organization of blacks, and it was their main center of resistance to slavery. It remained their main community organization, as much social as religious, while its militant political tradition, which had been dormant but not forgotten, was to be revived as a focus of civil rights agitation.

A young minister, Dr. Martin Luther King, Jr., joined the Dexter Avenue Baptist Church in Montgomery, Alabama in September of 1954. With his appointment as minister of the church came the traditional *political* responsibilities of the black minister. As was shown earlier, blacks in Montgomery—as well as elsewhere in the South—faced serious discrimination in employment, politics, housing, and schools, and were segregated in public facilities such as restaurants, hotels, and buses. Since his church was also a political institution for blacks, King decided to develop strategies to help solve the problems of racial discrimination and segregation in Montgomery.

It was thus quite traditional that black ministers, like King, would lead the civil rights movement, and that the movement would be mobilized within the framework of the black churches. The leadership offered by King and others was outstanding, especially in our day of rather dull political "leaders." Of course, these black leaders—like their ideology and like the Supreme Court decision—did not spring from nowhere or by accident. Given the underlying changes in structure and deprivation, the times were ripe for the movement and its leaders to emerge. The same brilliant leaders, if they had preached the same ideas fifty years earlier around the rural South, would have been largely unheard or greeted with passivity. In fact, other leaders of the earlier period, such as Booker T. Washington, were forced into much more conformist activities rather than protests. King and others received the recognition they deserved because all the other conditions, including the possibility of mobilizing a movement among masses of people, were already there.

THE UNFOLDING OF THE CIVIL RIGHTS MOVEMENT

The basic goal of the civil rights movement was to generate reforms for blacks *within* the existing political-economic system. The main formulator of civil rights ideology was Martin Luther King (1958, 1967), who spelled out his ideas in numerous speeches and books. He argued that Negroes should wrest social, political, and economic reforms from society in a nonviolent fashion.

At first, the civil rights movement was faced with changing some of the most elementary forms of social interaction between blacks and whites. All public facilities were segregated in the South, and King and his followers decided to challenge this. A black woman, and civil rights advocate, Mrs. Rosa Parks, refused to go to the back of the bus in Montgomery, Alabama on December 1, 1955. For this act she was arrested. Her arrest ignited a massive bus boycott by blacks in Montgomery. This was a major event in the civil rights movement, and influenced other protests for nearly two decades. Ultimately, public transportation and various other public facilities were desegregated in the South as a result of these efforts.

The civil rights movement also attempted to gain reforms in education, employment, and politics. The vote was a major issue in the South because various Jim Crow laws prevented most blacks from voting. Civil rights workers carried on massive voter registration drives among southern blacks that, with the aid of the federal government, eventually gave southern blacks the vote.

The placement of blacks in higher political positions has been less successful. Baron (1971) discussed the underrepresentation of blacks in higher offices in one city, and similar studies still could be repeated for many other cities and the federal government. One opposite trend—the election of black mayors in various cities—does not negate the larger fact of political underrepresentation. Nor does the placement of some blacks in visible positions of power, such as President Reagan's appointment of a black ambassador to South Africa, negate the larger trend. Nevertheless, getting southern blacks the vote, the election of various black mayors, and the placement of a limited number of blacks in positions of power were probably the main *political* accomplishments of the civil rights movement.

The civil rights movement also attempted to desegregate southern education.

James Meredith enrolled at the University of Mississippi in 1963 amid great controversy. This was a continuation of the struggle to desegregate southern (and northern) education beginning in 1954 with the *Brown* v. *Board of Education* decision. Partial victories have been won to desegregate American schools, but the battle—exacerbated by the busing controversy—continues to this day.

As for employment, the civil rights movement probably aided careers of various middle-class blacks. Affirmative action programs have aided some especially qualified blacks to secure employment they otherwise would not have obtained. Yet our data on racial inequality clearly show that many blacks still suffer serious employment and financial difficulties. As much as the civil rights movement tried to generate major changes in employment for blacks, more still remains to be done. Nevertheless, the civil rights movement attempted to generate significant reforms in many aspects of American society.

PRECIPITATING EVENTS IN THE MOVEMENT

Social movements usually require the occurrence of actual events that dramatize the problems of oppressed groups. There were many precipitating factors in the civil rights movement, but none as significant as the 1954 Supreme Court decision, and the Rosa Parks arrest and subsequent bus boycott. With regard to Rosa Parks, the news media throughout the country—and even in other countries—became aware that a challenge to segregated transportation had occurred. News of the arrest was soon broadcast over national television as well as in all major newspapers and magazines in the country. This incident focused attention on the basic injustices blacks suffered in the South, and pointed to one solution: massive resistance against segregated institutions.

Rosa Parks engaged in nonviolent civil disobedience. This tactic was to be used often throughout the rest of the 1950s, into the 1960s and part of the 1970s. Sit-ins, lie-ins, and swim-ins were used to desegregate lunch counters, swimming pools and beaches, restaurants, movie theaters, as well as some schools and businesses. In a sense, each publicized action of civil disobedience served as a precipitant of other such actions.

Of particular note was a sit-in by black southern college students on February 1, 1960. These well-dressed, mannerly college students wished to be served at a segregated Woolworth's lunch counter in Greensboro, North Carolina. When they were denied eating privileges, they refused to leave—and were arrested. This sit-in amounted to the first distinctive, nontraditional political activity by *students* in the 1960s, which, of course, would be repeated many times thereafter. The New Left student movement is usually associated with white middle-class students from the North. Yet the first distinctively student protest was by these southern black college students at Greensboro.

A final type of precipitant for the civil rights movement was the action by southern policemen against blacks and whites in the movement. Television undoubtedly gave a big impetus to the civil rights movement by showing national films of police unnecessarily beating peaceful demonstrators, and generally acting in an intimidating manner. Probably the most extreme version of this was the unleashing of vicious dogs against these demonstrators. It was actions such as these that sent many northern white students down South to aid the civil rights cause (Pinkney, 1968).

MOBILIZATION OF THE MOVEMENT

Protest movements come into being by a process of mobilization. Even though there are structural conditions, discontented people, and ideologies, a protest movement does not arise until the affected group is actually organized to challenge the existing social arrangements.

Leaders and formal organizations are important in mobilizing discontented people into protest movements. King was the central leader in the civil rights movement. He was a charismatic leader who possessed a brilliant ability to verbally communicate with large audiences. His obvious commitment to democratic values and human dignity inspired millions of blacks and whites throughout the United States and the rest of the world (King was eventually given the Nobel Peace Prize). When King was assassinated in 1968, the civil rights movement lost an important leader. The grief and rage at his assassination showed how many millions of people really did view him as their leader.

King's organizaton was the Southern Christian Leadership Conference (SCLC). This group was quite influential in organizing thousands of blacks and whites into the civil rights movement. SCLC—and the rest of the civil rights movement—staged numerous demonstrations against segregation and discrimination throughout the 1950s and 1960s. The famous March on Washington in 1963 was the most publicized of these demonstrations, but it was only one of many. Although the protests began in the South, by the 1960s they had spread to the North.

SCLC was not the only organization that enlisted mass support to challenge segregation. Other important groups were Student Nonviolent Coordinating Committee (SNCC), Congress of Racial Equality (CORE), and Students for a Democratic Society (SDS). As the names imply, student political activists were highly involved in some of these civil rights organizations, especially in the earlier part of the 1960s. The Vietnam War and internal organizational conflicts moved SDS, SNCC, and CORE in other directions in the latter part of the 1960s, but they (and civil rights leaders like King, Stokely Carmichael and Bayard Rustin) were crucial in sustaining civil rights protests for well over a decade.

The *resource mobilization* perspective has significantly contributed to our knowledge about how social movements get organized, secure needed resources, and obtain goals (Zald and McCarthy, 1979; Freeman, 1983; Wood and Jackson, 1982, pt. 3; and *Research in Social Movements, Conflicts and Change*, 1984–1986). This perspective focuses attention on issues of importance to movement organizers, such as how to develop and sustain movement organizations, get people motivated to join, raise money and obtain other resources such as mailing lists and media attention, deal with efforts at social control aimed at them, and create strategies to attain goals. Jo Freeman (1983) has assembled an excellent set of case studies that show how various movements have dealt with these issues. The movements that Freeman includes range in diversity from the black and brown lung movements of coal miners and textile workers, to movements of the disabled, draft resisters, students, Native Americans, farm workers, and tenants. Although the resource mobilization perspective is not characterized by numerous well-documented principles or generalizations, the case studies show how social movements have dealt with many problems, such as raising money and control efforts, in attempting to accomplish their goals.

WEAKENED SOCIAL CONTROL

Protest movements always face the possibility of being greatly diminished or eliminated by forces of social control such as the police, national guard, or army. Whenever there is a challenge to the existing social order, the established society usually takes some stand regarding the protests. The action taken by the government and police forces often significantly influences the outcome of protest movements.

When protest movements are basically reformist instead of radical, the state is usually less repressive. That is, if the protesters only want to make more limited changes *within* the existing social arrangements instead of advocating a large-scale change *of* the social arrangements, then authorities tend to be more tolerant of the protests.

The civil rights movement was basically a reformist movement. It primarily wanted to improve the social, political, and economic positions of blacks within the existing framework of American society. It is true that the civil rights movement engaged in various illegal protests, such as sit-ins and lie-ins, that resulted in thousands of arrests. But this civil disobedience was not aimed at overthrowing capitalism or basically altering the political system. It was to generate needed reforms.

As a result of its reformist nature, authorities, at least in the North, were able to tolerate various civil rights activities. That is, there was little outright attempt to crush the civil rights movement in the North. In contrast, the Federal Bureau of Investigation (FBI) and other government agencies did try to crush the more radical Black Panther Party (Seale, 1970; Marx and Wood, 1975, p. 399).

However, authorities in the South viewed the civil rights movement as a much more radical threat to the established southern society. Racism was a more "official" part of southern social structure in the 1950s and 1960s than it was in the North. To be sure, there was racism in the North, but in a somewhat more subtle form; for example, segregation of neighborhood schools was practiced, but was not legally sanctioned. Since southern authorities openly wanted to maintain racist practices, they were often brutal to civil rights protesters, beating them, jailing them, unleashing vicious dogs on them, and, infrequently, participating in their murder.

Social control—even harsh social control—can have varied effects. It can crush or greatly weaken a movement. Yet, if a movement is strong enough and operates under favorable socioeconomic conditions, then harshness of control can generate great indignation and eventually recruit people to a movement who might not otherwise have joined. Southern brutality to civil rights workers tended to have the latter effect. The movement did not collapse due to harsh reprisals by southern sheriffs. Instead, publicity of "horror stories" seemed to enlarge the movement. Of course, the South was never able to be as violent toward demonstrators as some elements in it wished. The federal government (for reasons stated earlier), issued warnings against extreme violence, investigated the Ku Klux Klan murder of three civil rights workers, and even came out in favor of basic civil rights goals. As a result, social control over the civil rights movement was never fully complete, and the harshness employed often enlisted new members. Thus the civil rights movement had less than a fully repressive network of social control in which to operate.

To sum up, we have a situation where all six determinants of protest were present: favorable structural conditions, strain such as absolute and relative deprivations, ideology, precipitating events, mobilization, and weakened social control. As a result, the civil rights movement arose and gathered enough momentum to become one of the major protest movements of our time.

Space limitation does not allow us to discuss other protest movements—such as the New Left student movement or the women's liberation movement. For detailed discussions of those and other such movements, we refer the reader to the suggested readings for this chapter.

CONSEQUENCES OF PROTESTS

The final question we shall address is: What consequences do these protest movements have? First, it is essential to distinguish between radical (including revolutionary) movements, and reformist movements. Revolutionary movements aim at making a large-scale, basic change in society. This is especially the case when a revolutionary movement not only takes over state power from an existing government, but when it attempts to make large-scale socioeconomic changes in the rest of the society. When successful, a revolutionary movement can make huge changes in the basic arrangements of society. This has happened in the French and Russian revolutions, as well as in the more recent revolutions of Cuba and China. As Sorokin (1925) notes, in this type of revolution, everything changes, from property ownership and poverty or wealth distributions, to patterns of speech, work, crime rates, religious activity, sexual activity, family life, and the nature of ideology.

In reformist movements, the goals are more limited. Above, we discussed some of the reform goals and the accomplishments of the civil rights movement. In addition, Greer (1949) studied a series of reform movements in America, indicating that various successful reforms have come about, at least eventually. For example, he shows that in 1867 the farmers' movement, represented by the National Grange, demanded railway regulation, a federal department of agriculture, and cooperative farm marketing associations. By 1887, railway regulation was enacted, by 1889 the U.S. Department of Agriculture was created, and by 1922 cooperatives became exempt from antitrust laws (p. 282).

Of course, not all revolutionary or reform movements are successful. They may fail to mobilize mass support and other significant resources; they may meet stiff resistance from the state; or they may become disillusioned with their original goals. Yet the few available studies of the consequences of social movements do indicate the success of various important radical and reformist movements.

SUMMARY

We have shown that single factor explanations of protests tend to be inadequate. Often there are people who are discontented, or who are attached to some political ideology, or who might risk arrest to fight for a cause. Yet protests only occur at infrequent intervals. Thus it is necessary to use a multiple variable approach, treating the entire society as an organic whole, in analyzing protests. Protest movements depend upon structural conditions that produce conflicts, absolute or relative deprivations, development of an ideology, mobilization of the discontented group, weakened social control, and the occurrence of precipitating events. When all these conditions exist, we can predict that a group will challenge the existing social arrangements.

We also examined a few consequences of protest movements. Here it is necessary to distinguish between radical or revolutionary movements that attempt broad-scale changes, and reform movements that aim at more limited changes. Additional study is needed in this important area of sociology. Yet studies exist that point to the large-scale changes made by some successful revolutionary movements, and to the achievement of social reforms made by at least some reform movements.

SUGGESTED READINGS

A review of the literature in collective behavior, social movements, and protests can be found in: Gary T. Marx and James L. Wood, "Strands of Theory and Research in Collective Behavior," *Annual Review of Sociology* 1 (1975): 363–428. Detailed discussions of recent movements include: Barbara Sinclair Deckard, *The Women's Movement,* 3d ed. (New York: Harper & Row, 1983); Martin Luther King, Jr., *Stride Toward Freedom: The Montgomery Story* (New York: Harper & Row, 1958); and James L. Wood, *The Sources of American Student Activism* (Lexington, MA: Lexington Books, Heath, 1974).

Some of the books used in our discussion of the Civil War against slavery and the development of black protest movements from then until now are listed in the suggested readings to Chapter 21 on history (especially Eugene Genovese's two books) and in the suggested readings to Chapter 12 on racism (including the books by Robert Blauner, Stokely Carmichael and Charles Hamilton, Oliver Cox, Victor Perlo, and C. Vann Woodward). An excellent socioeconomic investigation of black life in the sharecropping situation of the late nineteenth century is Roger Ransom and Richard Sutch, *One Kind of Freedom: The Economic Consequences of Emancipation* (New York: Cambridge University Press, 1977).

An excellent synthesis of the literature on protest movements is Michael Useem's *Protest Movements in America* (Indianapolis, IN: Bobbs-Merrill, 1975). A very interesting book by William A. Gamson, *The Strategy of Social Protest* (Homewood, IL: Dorsey Press, 1975), studies American reformist movements from 1800 to 1945, with the finding that various reformist movements have been violent and that those movements were at least partially successful (contrary to the dictum that "violence never pays"). For an historically oriented sociological account of the June 1848 insurrection in Paris, see Mark Traugott, *Armies of the Poor* (Princeton, NJ: Princeton University Press, 1985).

The main book discussing the collective behavior literature through the 1950s is Ralph H. Turner and Lewis M. Killian, *Collective Behavior* (Englewood Cliffs, NJ: Prentice-Hall, 1957). In 1963, Neil J. Smelser wrote the major theoretical synthesis of the field, *Theory of Collective Behavior* (New York: Free Press), which has stimulated much research since then. Two other synthesizing discussions are Anthony Oberschall, *Social Conflict and Social Movements* (Englewood Cliffs, NJ: Prentice-Hall, 1973), a complex and dialectical approach to protests, and Ted Robert Gurr, *Why Men Rebel* (Princeton, NJ: Princeton University Press, 1970), an analysis of protest focusing on the condition of relative deprivation.

Marxists have contributed enormously to the protest literature. One good collection of some of Marx's own discussions of protests is Neil J. Smelser, ed., *Karl Marx on Society and Social Change* (Chicago: University of Chicago Press, 1973). The classic discussion of revolutionary protest in Third World countries is Frantz Fanon, *The Wretched of the Earth,* trans. Constance Farrington (New York: Grove Press, 1961, 1968). Some outstanding studies of the French Revolution have been done by George Rudé in such books as *The Crowd in the French Revolution* (Oxford: Clarendon Press, 1960). The most famous Marxist historian of the French revolution is Albert Soboul, *The Sans-culottes: The Popular Movement and Revolutionary Government, 1793–1794* (Garden City, NY: Doubleday [Anchor Books], 1972). The many Marxist studies of the Russian revolution are listed in the suggested readings to Chapter 19.

Two excellent new books on late-nineteenth-century protest movements in America are Lawrence Goodwyn, *Democratic Promise, The Populist Movement in America* (New York: Oxford University Press, 1976), and Michael Schwartz, *Radical Protest and Social Structure: The Farmers' Alliance and Cotton Tenancy, 1880–1890* (New York: Academic Press, 1976). Books on the American socialist movement are cited in Chapter 18.

The resource mobilization perspective has added to our knowledge of problems faced by social movement organizers and how they have addressed such practical problems as setting up movement organizations and securing finances to sustain the movement. A major contribution to this literature is Meyer N. Zald and John D. McCarthy, eds., *The Dynamics of Social Movements* (Cambridge, MA: Winthrop, 1979). This book outlines resource mobilization theory and presents several case studies in the approach. Case studies related to resource mobilization theory are also presented in Jo Freeman, ed., *Social Movements of the Sixties and Seventies* (New York: Longman, 1983); James L. Wood and Maurice Jackson, *Social Movements: Development, Participation, and Dynamics* (Belmont, CA: Wadsworth, 1982), pt. 3; and *Research in Social Movements, Conflicts and Change* (1984–1986). Doug McAdam, *Political Process and the Development of Black Insurgency 1930–1970* (Chicago: University of Chicago Press, 1982), criticizes both traditional social movement theory and resource mobilization theory. His detailed and important, but at times overstated, analysis is evaluated by James L. Wood in the *Journal of Political and Military Sociology* 12(Fall 1984):350–352.

REFERENCES

Baron, Harold M., et al. 1971. "Black Powerlessness in Chicago," pp. 74–80. In Gary T. Marx, ed., *Racial Conflict.* Boston: Little, Brown.

Belin-Milleron, Jean. 1957. "Symbolic Expressions in the Collective Psychology of Political Crises." In Ralph H. Turner and Lewis M. Killian, *Collective Behavior,* pp. 353–359. Englewood Cliffs, NJ: Prentice-Hall.

Braungart, Richard G. 1979. *Family Status, Socialization and Student Politics.* Ann Arbor, MI: University Microfilms International.

Fanon, Frantz. 1968. *The Wretched of the Earth.* Translated by Constance Farrington. New York: Grove Press. Originally published in 1961.

Freeman, Jo, ed. 1983. *Social Movements of the Sixties and Seventies.* New York: Longman.

Greer, T. H. 1949. *American Social Reform Movements: Their Pattern since 1865.* New York: Prentice-Hall.

Gurr, Ted Robert. 1970. *Why Men Rebel.* Princeton, NJ: Princeton University Press.

Hertzler, J. O. 1957. "Crises and Dictatorships." In Turner and Killian, pp. 364–372.

King, Martin Luther, Jr. 1967. *Where Do We Go From Here: Chaos or Community?* New York: Harper & Row.

———. 1958. *Stride Toward Freedom: The Montgomery Story.* New York: Harper & Row.

Klandermans, Bert, and Dirk Oegema. 1987. "Potentials, Networks, Motivations, and Barriers: Steps Towards Participation in Social Movements." *American Sociological Review* 52(August):519–531.

Linton, Ralph. 1957. "Nativistic Movements." In Turner and Killian, pp. 387–395.

McAdam, Doug. 1982. *Political Process and the Development of Black Insurgency 1930–1970.* Chicago: University of Chicago Press.

Marx, Gary T., and James L. Wood. 1975. "Strands of Theory and Research in Collective Behavior." *Annual Review of Sociology* 1:363–428.

Matthews, D. R., and J. W. Prothro. 1966. *Negroes and the New Southern Politics.* New York: Harcourt Brace Jovanovich.

Newton, Huey. 1969. "A Prison Interview." In Carl Oglesby, ed., *The New Left Reader,* pp. 223–240. New York: Grove Press.

Oberschall, Anthony. 1973. *Social Conflict and Social Movements.* Englewood Cliffs, NJ: Prentice-Hall.

Pettigrew, Thomas F. 1964. *A Profile of the Negro American.* New York: Van Nostrand.

———. 1971. *Racially Separate or Together?* New York: McGraw-Hill.

Pinkney, Alphonso. 1968. *The Committed: White Activists in the Civil Rights Movement.* New Haven, CT: College University Press.

Piven, Frances Fox. 1976. "The Social Structuring of Political Protest." *Politics and Society* 6(3):297–326.

Seale, Bobby. 1970. *Seize the Time: The Story of the Black Panther Party and Huey P. Newton.* New York: Random House.

Smelser, Neil J. 1963. *Theory of Collective Behavior.* New York: Free Press.

———, ed. 1973. *Karl Marx on Society and Social Change.* Chicago: University of Chicago Press.

Sorel, Georges. 1957. "The Myth of The General Strike." In Turner and Killian, pp. 359–360.

Sorokin, Pitirim A. 1925. *The Sociology of Revolution.* Philadelphia: Lippincott.

Turner, Ralph H., and Lewis M. Killian. 1957, 1987. *Collective Behavior.* Englewood Cliffs, NJ: Prentice-Hall.

Useem, Michael. 1975. *Protest Movements in America.* Indianapolis, IN: Bobbs-Merrill.

Wood, James L., and Maurice Jackson. 1982. *Social Movements: Development, Participation, and Dynamics.* Belmont, CA: Wadsworth.

Zald, Meyer N., and John D. McCarthy, eds. 1979. *The Dynamics of Social Movements.* Cambridge, MA: Winthrop.

chapter *18*

History and Sociology of Socialist Movements

Socialism arose as a protest movement in the early nineteenth century. It reflected the very difficult conditions of the British and French workers in the early stages of industrialization. Not only were the early factories unsafe and filled with exhausted children working as many as 14 hours a day, but the urban environment consisted of slum housing, open sewers in the streets, and enormous amounts of smoke and noise.

In France, one of the earliest socialists was Henri Saint-Simon, who was also a founder of sociology. He had absorbed the ideals of liberty and equality of the French and American revolutions, but he thought that the capitalist system perverted these ideals. He evolved many utopian schemes for a better, collectivist, cooperative, socialist society. The election and reelection, in 1988, of François Mitterand as president of France indicates the contemporary relevance of socialism to France.

THE SOCIALIST VISION

For the last 150 years, millions of people have committed their lives to the fight for socialism. In this struggle many have lost their jobs, or gone to jail, and many have been killed (for example, thousands of socialists were killed in Hitler's Germany). Why were all these people willing to give so much for the goal of socialism? Socialists have a vision. It is a vision of a world without poverty, without unemployment, without discrimination, and without war. To achieve such a world they believe it is necessary to end private capitalist ownership of the economy and to make the economy owned collectively by all the people. Socialism is seen

323

as a world with jobs for all at decent wages under pleasant working conditions, with equality and freedom for all, and with peace in a unified world community. It is a world in which there is no economic competition for survival of the alienated dog-eat-dog variety. It is a world in which all people will cooperate and will run the economy in a democratic manner. There will be no more rich employers and poor workers. Socialists believe that this can be achieved with a socialist economy.

Socialism means the democratic control of the economy by the entire working class. The working class now comprises over 84 percent of the American people. Under socialism, the capitalists would be deprived of their monopolistic private ownership of industry, and the working class would eventually become 100 percent of all Americans. So socialism in the long run means ownership and control of the economy by all the people and for all the people. It means an economy no longer operated for profit, but run according to the goal of maximum social well-being for everyone, black or white, male or female, young or old. This goal of people's ownership and control of the economy is shared by all socialists, though there are significant controversies between socialists about the details of the organization of a socialist society and about the strategies of how to achieve such a society.

Karl Marx

Radical critiques and visions of socialist utopias have existed for several centuries, but the first serious attempt to produce a comprehensive radical social science was made by Karl Marx. Marx was born in 1818 in Trier, Germany. Although his family wished him to be educated as a lawyer, he chose to obtain his doctorate in philosophy, concentrating mainly on the philosophy of G. W. F. Hegel. Because Marx's views were already "too liberal," the German government prevented the young Marx from obtaining a job in a German university. Perhaps if the witch hunters of that day had not been so diligent, Marx would have settled down to become a brilliant but eventually forgotten German professor; instead, Marx developed an elaborate critique of capitalist society. He based this critique on his knowledge of the harsh circumstances of workers in early capitalist industrialization. He felt that capitalism would eventually be replaced by a socialist and then a communist society.

Marx turned to journalism and ran a liberal newspaper for a time, until he was exiled by Germany for his antimonarchist ideas. Subsequently, in Paris, Marx learned the views of the French socialists and the tradition of the French Revolution. His conversion to socialism was also aided by his friend Frederick Engels, who had reached a socialist viewpoint before Marx. Eventually the French government—and several other European governments—also decided that Marx was too radical, and therefore he had to be deported. Marx eventually emigrated to England, where he spent most of his life—from 1849 until his death in 1883.

In London, Marx spent several decades studying classical political economy, especially the works of Adam Smith and of David Ricardo. In addition, he read the reports of the factory inspectors and carefully studied the official parliamentary investigations of the terrible conditions in British factories—which he brought to public attention in his writings. Thus the intellectual heritage of Marxism was derived from three main sources: German Hegelian philosophy, French revolutionary socialism, and English classical economics. Marx fused these divergent views into one unified social science. His analysis has been discussed throughout this book.

1848 to the Paris Commune

In 1848 there were revolutions in France, Germany, Austria, Hungary, and Italy in favor of democratic rights and against monarchy. Marx participated in that revolutionary drive for democracy. After the failure of the 1848 revolution, Marx led the politically inactive life of a political exile for many years while he continued his investigations into capitalism. Then in 1864 he joined with British, French, and Belgian trade unionists, as well as certain groups of socialists and anarchists, to form the International Workingmen's Association. Marx was the head of this first international association devoted to workers' rights. The International succeeded in coordinating the efforts of trade unionists in several countries, in preventing strike-breaking by workers of adjoining countries, and in giving support to the revolutionary nationalist movements of Poland and Italy. The International also supported the North in the American Civil War against the slaveholders. In this action it succeeded in rallying large numbers of British workers against the views of the British government and the conservative ruling class, who might otherwise have intervened on the side of the South.

The most important event during the first International was the dramatic takeover of Paris by its working class at the end of the Franco-Prussian War of 1870–1871. In 1871 when the French armies had been defeated by the Germans, Napoleon III was dethroned and a republican government came into being. The republican government, however, was quite reactionary and also was unpopular because of its forced concessions to the Germans. The Parisian populace then took matters into its own hands and elected its own government, called the Paris Commune. An overwhelming majority of the delegates were socialists, though not members of the Marxist International. The Commune lasted only a few months, but it did raise hope for the future by showing that workers could run their own government. Then it was violently overthrown by the French government.

During its brief time in power, all of the European establishment was aghast at the revolutionary Commune of Paris. Just as horrified were the respectable British unionists who had constituted the base of the International in England. When Marx wrote a flaming defense of the Commune, the International was doomed because of the repression by the European establishment as well as the withdrawal of the British unions. The International was formally dissolved in 1876.

The Paris Commune to the Russian Revolution

Marx continued working and writing until his death in 1883. The early 1880s witnessed at the same time the beginnings of strong socialist parties in France, Germany, and much of Western Europe. In spite of initial persecution, the German

Social Democratic party eventually came to be very large and highly respectable. The various socialist parties together formed the Second International in 1889.

Although the Second International continued to use revolutionary Marxist language, the content of its actions grew less and less revolutionary as its member parties grew more and more respectable. The various socialist parties of Europe and the United States drew large numbers of votes, ran their own newspapers, controlled most of the trade union apparatus, and acquired many vested interests in the continued operation of capitalist society. The socialist parties grew in numbers year after year until they were the largest single party in several European countries and very important even in the United States. Most socialists believed that a slow but steady and peaceful victory of socialism in the whole world was inevitable. It would be followed by a united, democratic world government based on socialism, ushering in an unprecedented era of peace and prosperity, with an end to alienation and discrimination.

As the official socialist parties became less and less radical, there arose a left, or radical, opposition, which became ever more vocal and important. It was led by such striking personalities as V. I. Lenin and the fiery Rosa Luxemburg, whose powerful oratory moved thousands of workers. Although they disagreed on other issues, Lenin and Luxemburg agreed that imperialism was leading to war and that the socialist parties must take united revolutionary action as a result.

In 1914, when World War I broke out, the Second International was put to the test. It was uncertain whether the socialists of all countries would stand together against the war, or whether the socialists of each country would support their own ruling class against the other countries. To the dismay of many socialists, the Second International flunked its test. Workers from various countries butchered each other in the war, and the Second International was thereafter terminated in all but name. Officially it has continued to this day, but in practice most of its constituent "socialist" parties have given up the goals of socialism, and are content with more limited reforms and welfare programs within capitalism.

In 1917 the Russian Revolution broke out. Its first phase was a democratic revolution in February 1917, which put the liberals and moderate socialists into power. In October 1917 there was a radical socialist revolution led by the Bolsheviks. The Bolsheviks had constituted the left faction of the socialists in Russia; they were later to be called the Communist party. Under the leadership of Lenin, the Bolsheviks attempted to transform Russia into a socialist country. Their attempt was opposed not only by the forces of the tsar in Russia, but also by the right wing of the old socialist parties. Yet the left wing of the socialist parties in every country were enthusiastic about the Russian socialist revolution, hailing it as the wave of the future. These "left" socialists then formed communist parties. In 1919, Lenin gathered the communist parties of the world into the new Third International, or Communist International.

POPULISM AND SOCIALISM IN THE UNITED STATES

Let us examine in some detail the history of the socialist movement in the United States. Socialism in Europe began with the industrial revolution and the creation of a large, urban, industrial working class. In the United States, for most of the nineteenth century, much of the population was rural and agrarian. The existence of a frontier with cheap land prevented the formation of a permanent, urban working class with a strong socialist ideology. Many of the best, most active and frustrated workers simply left the cities to try to settle their own farms on the frontier.

There were some beginnings of trade unions and some very small socialist parties in the nineteenth century, but American radicalism had its major thrust among the farmers. In the 1880s, farmers created a very strong and remarkably radical organization, beginning in Texas and spreading throughout the South and the West. Farmers perceived that the railroads, who charged them exorbitant fees for transport, and the bankers, who charged them high interest rates and sometimes refused any credit, were their main enemies.

In the 1890s, these radical farm organizations created the Populist party of America, joined by some labor unions and some black organizations. The Populists were very successful in the early 1890s, electing several congressmen and senators and winning a majority in the legislatures of some southern and western states. In states dominated by the Populists, laws were passed to regulate the railroads and banks, but many of these laws were held unconstitutional by a conservative U.S. Supreme Court. All of their party organizations tried to integrate black and white farmers with varying degrees of success. The national platform of the Populists called for nationalization of railroads and other monopolies, laws to protect labor unions from police interference, and cheap credit for farmers (the most famous plank).

What happened to the Populists? In the election of 1896, at the height of their power, the right wing of the Populist party bargained away the party to the Democratic party. The Democrats did adopt a fairly radical program, but their candidate—William Jennings Bryan—ignored the platform and spoke only about adding silver to the existing gold coinage. His famous speech began: "Thou shall not crucify mankind upon a cross of gold." The additional silver money would have meant a cheaper supply of money and credit to farmers, and it frightened many eastern capitalists. But Bryan's position tended to bury the other radical and prolabor measures. Therefore, urban workers voted against Bryan. So the national Populist party disappeared forever into the complex mixture forming the Democratic party, though a few populist parties persisted in local areas for a while.

In the South, where Populists had threatened to take over from the Democrats, they were weakened by racism. A large, well-planned and financed campaign for "white supremacy" managed to split white and black farmers to the benefit of their common enemies. Furthermore, blacks, who had voted since the Civil War, were now prohibited from voting by a series of laws, such as the poll tax laws, which excluded poor whites and blacks from voting. Moreover, there were literacy requirements (such as reading and understanding the Constitution), which were unfairly applied mostly to blacks. As a result of this successful racist attack, not only were the populists defeated in the South, but socialists were never able to get a foothold in the South.

As noted in Chapter 15, the Jesse Jackson campaigns for the Democratic nomination for president in 1984 and 1988 had a populist flavor, supporting the poor and middle class and critical of the rich and powerful. While key parts of his platform were rejected by the Democratic party in 1988, Jackson nevertheless was considerably more successful than many anticipated. He attracted over 1000 Democratic convention delegates and gave Michael Dukakis a realistic contest. As former President Nixon said, Jackson tapped existing radical sentiments in the U.S. population and was an expert campaigner (lest this seem uncharacteristic of Nixon, he also said Jackson could not win). The fact that Dukakis got approximately twice as many delegates as Jackson shows that, in general, American political sentiment in 1988 was more mainstream than Jackson's populism. However, the fact that Jackson received so many delegates demonstrates the existence of a desire for change from Reagan conservatism by a significant part of the U.S. population by the end of the 1980s.

The Rise of the Socialist Party

In 1900, the Socialist party of the United States was formed from several existing socialist groups, some populist groups, and some trade unions. It began with fewer than 10,000 members and only about 95,000 votes in 1900. It grew very rapidly, however. By 1912, the Socialist party had over 150,000 dues-paying members and received over 900,000 votes. In the whole period it elected over 2,000 of its members to elective offices, including one congressman, and over 60 members of state legislatures. It elected 56 mayors in 1911 alone, and—at various times—elected socialist mayors in Milwaukee, Wisconsin; Berkeley, California; Butte, Montana; and Schenectady, New York—with a narrow miss in Los Angeles. There was a widespread network of socialist newspapers, some with very large circulations. And last, but not least, socialist strength grew in the American Federation of Labor (AFL) so that their candidates and resolutions obtained over one-third of the votes in many contests.

What were the sociological reasons for this rapid growth of the socialist movement? First, the rise of monopoly capitalism meant further oppression and frustrations for farmers. The farmers had led the populist movement for reform in the 1890s. In the early 1900s some of them were angry enough at big business to join the socialists. This may be seen in the fact that the early centers of socialist strength were in some of the old populist strongholds—Texas, Kansas, and other western states. In fact, for some time the highest percentage of socialist members, voters, and newspaper readers was among the farmers of Oklahoma.

More important in the long run was the contrast of wealth and poverty in the United States. The wealth of capitalists was growing rapidly and ostentatiously around 1900. At the same time, the working class suffered from continued long hours (with 12-hour work days not uncommon), difficult working conditions, low wages, and court injunctions against strikes. The result was an increasing spread and militancy of the labor unions, including the American Federation of Labor. This period also witnessed the formation and swift rise of the radical Industrial Workers of the World (IWW), which was important during this period. So the working class began to support the Socialist party, as seen by its increasing party members, increasing votes, and local election victories by 1912 in places like Ohio and Pennsylvania. The Socialist party was also helped by the growth of a militant women's movement for the right to vote. By the time the right to vote was won in 1920, about 2 million women were formally part of the women's movement—and some of them also became socialists.

Decline of the Socialist Party of the United States

Yet the powerful Socialist party declined and fell between 1921 and 1929. What caused this failure to establish a firm and lasting socialist movement in the United States, as had been accomplished in Europe? Many reasons have been given, including:

1. Divisions within the American working class by nationality, race, occupational background, income, and sex
2. A high degree of geographical mobility
3. The swift decline in farm population, but an exceptionally slow formation of a permanent working class
4. Rising living standards
5. Antisocialist myths of the eternal prosperity and individualism of American capitalism
6. Domination of unions by nonsocialist forces
7. Impact of the Russian revolution, which resulted in splits within the Socialist party
8. Incorporation of various labor and welfare demands into the Democratic party platform
9. Repression by the U.S. govenment

There are disagreements about the importance of these different factors, not only between radical and traditional sociologists, but also within each group. It will be worthwhile to examine each factor in some detail because that examination will reveal many issues of sociological analysis.

1. Divisions Within the Working Class. The working class in most Western European countries has been relatively homogeneous as regards race and ethnic background. Religion divided workers in some earlier periods and in Hitler's time by the use of anti-Semitism. Yet, even religion had not been an extremely divisive factor in the nineteenth and twentieth centuries in most of Western Europe (except in Hitler's Germany and Ireland). This relative homogeneity of the working class in each Western European country was conducive to solidarity and a rapid growth of socialist consciousness.

On the contrary, the American working class has been strongly divided by race, nationality, and religion, as well as by the other divisions (also present in Europe) of sex, income, and occupation. We have pointed out in Chapter 3 that there are very real splits by income and occupation in the U.S. working class. A very low-paid unskilled laborer has a wholly different political outlook from a high-paid aerospace engineer, even though both are workers by our definition.

What most differentiates the United States from Western Europe, however, are our long-lasting hatreds and prejudices by race, nationality, and religion. As we have seen previously, the United States is a "melting pot" that has never melted certain differences, resulting in a working class that is divided by many kinds of prejudice. In the first place there has always been white prejudice against blacks. This prejudice originated in the slave economy. We noted that this prejudice helped destroy the Populist party in the South, and it has ever since prevented the emergence of strong trade unions in the South—so that both white and black workers in the South are subject to much lower wages and cannot get together politically to elect candidates and parties favorable to the working class. The Socialist party did have some branches in the South, but they were mostly— to its detriment—segregated. Thus the socialists were never able to direct much of the anger of black Americans into a socialist movement.

In addition to racism, however, antiforeign, nationalist prejudices played a much bigger role in this period than one might now think. As late as 1920, about 40 percent of urban workers were foreign-born immigrants, who faced strong prejudice from native-born Americans. At first, the Socialist party was based on white, native-born farmers and did not recruit foreign-born workers. Later, after 1912, when they began to lose their strength among farmers, the socialists gained considerably among the foreign-born workers. This fact was then used against the socialists since they were pictured as foreign agitators. Moreover, most of these foreign-born Americans could not vote in elections.

Similarly, there were prejudices in the early 1900s against any political participation by women. The socialists did make an effort to integrate women into the party, even as leaders, but prejudices among some male socialists still operated to keep many women out of the Socialist party. For example, many socialist clubs met in male-dominated bars. Finally, even when many women were won over to socialism, they could not vote until 1920.

2. Geographical Mobility.   Even after the end of the frontier, millions of Americans continued to move to the West. There have also been major migrations from the South to the North and, recently, from the North to the South. Every year, millions of Americans change jobs and homes. Western Europe, on the other hand, has not had new frontiers for centuries (though there has been a steady drift from farm to city). Many Europeans have had the same job in the same city all their life, and some Europeans hold the same job that their parent or even grandparent held. Thus European working-class communities have maintained much greater continuity and class solidarity.

3. Slow Formation of Working Class.   Since the 1890s the number of farmers in the United States has continued to decline rapidly until less than 5 percent of our population is now in agriculture. The widespread farmers' protest movements therefore lost their base, and present-day farmer protests often have a relatively small political impact, even being unable to prevent the recent loss of many family farms. Yet, we have noted that the working class in the cities was divided by race, religion, national origin, income, occupation, sex, and even how recent was their farm background. The working class also moved rapidly from one geographical area to another. So, in the 1920s there was still no large, homogeneous working class—and little consciousness of being a permanent working class. Thus the decline of socialist strength among farmers was hard to replace by strength among urban workers.

4. Rising Living Standards. The 1920s were a period of increasing prosperity for the United States. Hence all protest movements were weakened in a great flood of optimism, reflected in the attitude that any individual could "make it" and get rich. Such opportunities for riches were never a reality for the vast majority of Americans, but most did have some increase in their standard of living in the 1920s, after the American victory in World War I.

5. Antisocialist, Procapitalist American Mythology. The United States never had a rigid feudal society, as Europe did. On the contrary, America was seen as a land of promise where anyone could get rich. The myth was one of eternal prosperity with everyone having the chance to be a capitalist. We have seen that this myth is often inaccurate, but it has persisted (with the aid of the media) for a remarkably long time. The fact that living standards have usually risen, except in our periodic recessions and depressions, helps feed the myth. The philosophy of rugged individualism has also been celebrated in America by the media and the educational system—with the myth that any individual can rise to be president of a corporation or president of the United States. Because of the early frontier conditions and long periods of rising living standards, the ideology of rugged individualism is also deeply rooted. This ideology helps prevent the increase of class consciousness, which is a prerequisite for the rise of socialist consciousness.

6. Nonsocialist Domination of Unions. Another difference from Europe lay in the fact that most European unions were started by socialists and almost automatically supported socialist parties. In the United States few unions began as explicitly socialist, though the early American Federation of Labor (AFL) constitution did pledge the union to fight a class war against the capitalists. The AFL was close to being won by the socialists in the 1910–1912 period, but they never quite attained dominance so as to get the formal support of the AFL. Moreover, ideological sectarians among the socialists resisted any idea of a broader labor party—to be led by the AFL—in which the socialists might be swallowed.

7. The Russian Revolution and Socialist Splits. The American Socialist party was always divided into warring factions. The left wing of the party wanted more revolutionary rhetoric and actions. The right wing of the party wanted a more typically American party that would concentrate on getting votes, with little emphasis on principles. Sometimes, they spent more time fighting each other than fighting the capitalist Republicans and Democrats. Then, in 1917 the Russian Revolution occurred, bringing to power a party that called itself a socialist party (later a communist party). At first, all socialists greeted the Russian Revolution with enthusiasm. Later, when reports of strife and oppression within the Soviet Union became widespread, the Socialist party split wide open on its relation to the Russian Revolution. The factions within the party split off in 1919 and 1920 to become socialist sects or parties of their own. One became the Communist Party, always favorable to the Soviet Union, which also split in the 1930s to form smaller Trotskyite parties, favoring Leon Trotsky and opposing Joseph Stalin, and in the 1960s Maoist parties favoring China and opposing Russia. All of these sects spent large amounts of time fighting each other, as well as fighting capitalist interests.

8. Incorporation of Various Labor and Welfare Demands by Democrats.   The Democratic party saw the need to include progressive and labor issues in its platform to attract the working class. The left wing of the Democratic party began to emphasize reforms sufficient to attract would-be socialists. The Democrats' emphasis on reform measures—especially in the New Deal of the 1930s—did reduce the membership and voting strength of the socialist movement in the United States.

9. Repression by the Government.   Finally, the capitalist class in the United States has a long record of getting the federal and state governments, as well as the FBI and CIA, to attack and harass radical and socialist groups. Such repression would not have been successful if the socialist movement had otherwise been strong and united. Yet government repression and infiltration has weakened the socialist movement at various crucial times.

In World War I, the Socialist party of the United States was one of the few socialist parties in the world that stuck by its principles, declared that the war was a conflict among groups of imperialist nations, and refused to support the war. As a result, Eugene Debs, its highly charismatic leader, was put in prison, as were many other leaders. Perhaps more important, the very large number of socialist newspapers (with a circulation of about 2 million households) were prevented by arbitrary government orders from using the U.S. mails. In places like Kansas and Oklahoma, where socialist farmers lived many miles away from each other, the prohibition of their newspapers had a devastating effect on their local socialist movements.

In the 1920s there was a period of highly intense anticommunism and a widespread disregard of civil liberties. Hysteria was created by the capitalist-owned press, which claimed that the United States was about to be taken over by Russian Bolshevik agents. There were numerous measures taken against socialist and communist parties. There was also a reign of terror against the foreign-born suspected of radicalism. In the Palmer raids—so called because they were directed by U.S. Attorney General Palmer—thousands of foreign-born socialists were arrested for deportation in one night. It turned out that many were not socialists, some were not even foreign-born, and no evidence of any subversive action was ever proved in any of the hundreds of cases tried. Almost all were eventually released, but fear of further government action against radicals was widespread.

In a period when civil liberties are fairly well preserved (as at present), it is hard to imagine how pervasive and hysterical repressive campaigns have been in the United States. Such repression has included loss of jobs, as well as jailing and deportation of many effective labor and socialist leaders. In the late 1920s it even included the famous frameup and execution of two poor anarchists, Sacco and Vanzetti. It also included the formation of so-called Red Squads in the police departments of many U.S. cities, whose sole duty from then to now has been to infiltrate, gain information, provoke incidents, and otherwise harass radical organizations. The police have had a very broad definition of "Red"—including at times many militant black organizations such as the Black Panthers in the 1960s.

Why was there so much repression in the 1920s? First, the American ruling class was afraid that the Russian Revolution—which had inspired strong socialist movements in Western Europe—would also result in a major increase in American socialist strength. Second, labor unions had gained strength during World War I, a development that worried the ruling class. Third, the Socialist party still appeared to be quite strong. For example, its presidential candidate was the popular Eugene Debs, who received 1 million votes for president in 1920, even though he was in jail for the whole campaign (for his opposition to World War I). So the ruling class felt that any measures were justified to preserve the capitalist system of the United States by crushing the labor and socialist movements.

Why was the antisocialist repression successful in the 1920s? On the one hand, there have been many cases where repression was not successful when an attempt was made to stop a popular mass movement. For example, in the late 1950s and early 1960s, the more that violence and legal barriers were used in the South against the civil rights movement, the angrier people got and the stronger the movement became. On the other hand, in the 1920s, as we have seen, the Socialist party was split by various sexist, national, and racist prejudices. Furthermore, it was badly split by ideological differences; it had lost its base among farmers, but had not yet gained a strong working-class base; there were rising living standards; and there was the myth of everlasting American prosperity with unlimited opportunity. Thus, the socialist movement was already in such a weak situation that government repression could succeed in crushing it.

AMERICAN SOCIALISM FROM 1930 TO THE PRESENT

In the 1930s the massive unemployment caused by the Great Depression rapidly radicalized millions of Americans. The Socialist party grew considerably, and the Communist party rapidly developed into a significant force on the left. The communists had very good ties with the newly formed, more militant trade union federation known as the Congress of Industrial Organizations (CIO). In the CIO unions it was well known that many organizers were communists, since the CIO was willing to take help from any quarter. Many communist organizers were beaten up (and a few killed) for their trade union activity in company-controlled towns. Yet the CIO expanded to 5 million workers in a short time, and about one-third or more of the CIO unions were led by the left, with strong communist ties. If the communists had not uncritically praised every aspect of Soviet domestic life and foreign policy, but had had an independent vision of democratic socialism in the United States, they might have emerged as a long-term significant party in permanent alliance with labor.

In the late 1940s and early 1950s, however, the Communists—and all radicals in the labor movement—came under extremely heavy attack from Senator Joseph McCarthy, the House Un-American Activities Committee, and other conservative government agencies. The repression of the 1950s had many points in common with that of the 1920s. Once again, the American ruling class saw that socialist ideas had spread anew to a large part of the world in the late 1940s (the Chinese communists came to power in 1949). Once again, the labor unions had gained strength in World War II and threatened to become a powerful political factor. There were also some indications of a new upsurge of women and blacks who had gained better jobs during the war and did not want to lose them. The repressive campaign was therefore launched to try to stop these and other radical movements (such as the Progressive party of 1948, which supported many labor and socialist goals).

As a result of this wave of repression, and to a much lesser extent their own mistakes, the left-wing unions were isolated and expelled from the CIO. The remainder of the CIO was very weak, since the left-wing unions had amounted to about one-third of the whole organization. The CIO then merged with the AFL to form one, less militant union federation. Since that time, the left in the United States has not managed to form many alliances, much less any permanent base, in the labor movement.

In addition to the labor unions, the anticommunist hysteria of the Cold War was used to attack liberals and radicals in many other walks of life. Many U.S. government employees were fired for their political opinions. Many news commentators, college professors, teachers at all levels, and Hollywood actors and writers lost their jobs. Many people went to jail for contempt of the House Un-American Activities Committee. A large number of alleged Communists were sent to jail solely for that reason under the Smith Act of 1940, which prohibited advocacy of revolution. Two Jewish radicals, Ethel and Julius Rosenberg, were executed for giving information on the atomic bomb to the Russians, though much of the evidence has since been denounced as fabricated.

Thus, repression was successful in eliminating the left from union leadership, in silencing students and faculty at universities, and in suppressing the political opinions of many other people. It was also successful in electing candidates like Richard Nixon. Most important, it was effective in largely destroying the American left and the American Communist party. Once again, however, the left, and especially the Communists, succumbed to repression partly because of much more general factors in the 1950s (the world situation—especially the Korean War and the Cold War—and the rapid growth of the United States economy) and partly because of their own mistakes—such as their dogmatic devotion to the Soviet Union.

As a result, the protest movements of the 1960s were not explicitly socialist and had only a weak socialist movement to draw upon. These protest movements—such as the civil rights movement, the antiwar movement, and the women's movement—did involve millions of people, but they had no broad socialist consciousness to start with. They had a major impact on the Democrats in 1968 and 1972, and helped end the Vietnam War, but they did not create a socialist party.

Moreover, because the left had been destroyed in the labor movement in the 1950s, the protest movements of the 1960s got little support and some hostility from the labor unions.

From the mid-1970s on, however, there have been attempts to create progressive or socialist movements in the United States, drawing in part on New Left experiences of the 1960s. The Democratic Socialists of America (DSA), Tom Hayden's Campaign for Economic Democracy (CED), the Institute for Labor and Mental Health in Oakland, California, the Jackson campaigns themselves, as well as nationally distributed publications, such as *In These Times* and *Mother Jones*, have all tried to build on the economic critiques and programs for democratic political participation arising in the 1960s. The results of these efforts have been mixed in that no large-scale, European-style socialist party has emerged in the United States; but progressive ideas have been disseminated by these groups and publications, and 1960s activist Tom Hayden has been quite successful in electoral politics in the 1980s. Thus the progressive legacy from the 1960s persists in the late 1980s and could be built upon in the 1990s.

THE WORLD SOCIALIST MOVEMENT, 1917–1953

The year 1917 was the year of the Russian Revolution, while Joseph Stalin died in 1953. During most of those years the Soviet Union and Stalin dominated much of the international socialist movement. At first, the example of an existing socialist government, even if it was in an underdeveloped country, was an inspiration to socialists all over the world. The Socialist party in Japan rapidly gained adherents, the Chinese Communist party began to grow, and both socialist and communist parties grew very rapidly in Western Europe.

The German Social Democratic Party headed the German government for most of the 1920s. When all the capitalist economies plunged into a great depression in 1929, however, the socialists were unable to cope. Germany polarized to the left toward the communists and to the right toward the Nazis. When the Nazis took power in the early 1930s, they outlawed the socialist and communist parties, jailing hundreds of thousands of party members along with millions of Jews.

In France and Spain, the socialist, communist and other leftist parties formed united fronts against fascism—and the left came to power in both countries in 1936. A military uprising under General Franco ended the Spanish republican socialist government. France went through various political changes until the Nazis invaded and occupied France in 1940. Hitler soon controlled all of Europe except England and the Soviet Union. During World War II, the communists were the most determined resistance fighters against the Nazis all over Europe.

When the war was over, many millions of voters turned to the communists in Western Europe because of their wartime heroism. Combined communist-socialist-liberal governments were formed in many West European countries. But a cold war of words, economic power, and limited violence began between the Soviet Union and the United States. Western Europe was forced to choose, and so the communists were eliminated from all the Western European governments.

Communists continued, however, to maintain their leadership of the working class and the trade unions and to remain very large parties in France and Italy.

In Asia, Africa, and Latin America, those countries that were under formal colonial rule struggled against colonialism. Eventually, in the 1940s, 1950s, and 1960s, most of the colonial empires decided it was too expensive to maintain outright colonies against the will of the people in them. So colonies were given political independence; however most remained economically dependent on the imperialist countries. During these struggles for independence, the socialists and communists in these countries led the fight. Socialist parties, therefore, came to power in many of these countries, while communist parties also became very important. Because the French refused to give up their colony in Vietnam, the struggle there became a liberation war, led by the Vietnamese communists.

Perhaps the most important single event of the period just after World War II occurred in China. The government of the Chinese nationalists was weak and corrupt. It had been unable or unwilling to fight when Japan invaded China. Most of the fight against Japanese imperialism was led by the Chinese communists. Therefore, after the war the Chinese communists had the most popular support, especially among the peasants, who were promised land reform. In spite of enormous American aid to the nationalists, the communists won the civil war in 1949.

Thus, by 1953 socialist and communist parties were spread out all over the world. However, the communists often accused the socialists of advocating only mild reform, and of selling out the greater socialist goals. In turn, the socialists often accused the communists of being in favor of one-party dictatorships if they ever came to power. The further spread and evolution of the socialist movement after Stalin's death will be examined in the next chapter.

SUMMARY

This chapter discussed the growth of the socialist movement from its early beginnings in the industrial revolution in Europe to the Russian Revolution of 1917. The question was then asked: What makes the spread of socialist ideology so prevalent in Europe (and later Asia and Africa), while there is only a minscule socialist movement in the United States? There was a significant and growing socialist party in the United States in the period from 1900 to World War I, including a remarkable number of members, voters, socialist newspaper readers, and elected officials at state and local levels.

The American Socialist party disintegrated by the 1920s for the following reasons:

1. Division among American workers by race, religion, nationality, sex, income, and status
2. Factionalism in the Socialist party, exacerbated by the Russian Revolution
3. Incorporation of various progressive and labor demands into the Democratic party platform
4. A large amount of repression by the U.S. government

5. Domination of American unions by nonsocialists
6. Swift decline of farmers and slow formation of a permanent American working class
7. High degree of geographic mobility
8. Rising living standards, except in depressions and recessions
9. Antisocialist and procapitalist myths of unlimited opportunities and individualist competition.

In Europe, on the contrary, there have been more homogeneous working classes, with less rapidly rising living standards, fewer myths about individualism and more working-class consciousness, and continued socialist and communist domination of trade unions. In Asia and Africa, socialists and communists have been successful because the struggles for national liberation from colonialism merged in many cases with the struggles against capitalism and for socialism. Whereas the United States does not have a large socialist party, there is a progressive legacy from the 1960s that could be built upon in the 1990s.

SUGGESTED READINGS

An exciting history of the rise of the early American socialist movement is Ira Kipnis's *The American Socialist Movement, 1897–1912* (New York: Columbia University Press, 1952). For a careful analysis of its downfall, see James Weinstein, *The Decline of Socialism in America, 1912–1925* (New York: Monthly Review Press, 1967). A useful collection of arguments by historians and sociologists is found in John Laslett and Seymour M. Lipset, eds., *Failure of a Dream? Essays in the History of American Socialism* (Garden City, NY: Doubleday [Anchor Books], 1974). There is no single book clearly presenting the whole history of world socialism, but one readable, interesting history of the period from 1917 to the 1960s is Fernando Claudin's *The Communist Movement* (New York: Monthly Review Press, 1975), in two parts.

The best history of the populists is Laurence Goodwyn's *Democratic Promise: The Populist Movement in America* (New York: Oxford University Press, 1976). There is also a brilliant analysis of populism versus McCarthyism in Michael P. Rogin, *The Intellectuals and McCarthy* (Cambridge, MA: MIT Press, 1967). Some details of the Jesse Jackson and Michael Dukakis campaigns for Democratic party nominee for president in 1988 can be found in: *Los Angeles Times*, "Dukakis Forces Reject Key Jackson Platform Issues" (Sunday, June 26, 1988): 1, 36. An interesting attempt to tie everyday (often problematical) experiences into progressive politics is Michael Lerner's *Surplus Powerlessness* (Oakland, CA: Institute for Labor and Mental Health, 1986). For a detailed, informative and personal account of his experiences in the 1960s, with an eye toward the future, see Tom Hayden, *Reunion: A Memoir* (New York: Random House, 1988).

chapter **19**

Sociology of Socialist Countries

This chapter begins with a discussion of the Soviet Union, its planned economy and remarkable achievements, its one-party government, and its class structure. We try to explain *why* the Soviet Union has achieved much, but also has suffered from elite control. The rest of the chapter explores the present status of the socialist vision, the development of the socialist movement from 1953 to the present, and the many continuing bitter controversies over the details of socialism in the modern world.

Some who call themselves socialists say it is only necessary to have large welfare payments while retaining private capitalist ownership—that is the Swedish situation. Others who call themselves socialists advocate government ownership of the economy but are not democratic in that they also advocate a one-party government—that is the Soviet situation. There are also arguments among socialists as to whether socialism means national control of the economy by the entire working class or local control by workers in each firm, or a mixture of the two. Another argument rages over the degree of equality in socialism. Should all wages be equal? What goods and services should be free? All of these issues are discussed in the latter part of this chapter, as are the issues of *perestroika* and *glasnost*.

ACHIEVEMENTS OF THE SOVIET UNION

In 1917 the Soviets set up the first government completely devoted to the goal of a socialist society. Their first success was survival. The Soviets faced civil war by the old ruling class of tsarist officials, merchants, landlords, and generals. They faced invasion in 1918 to 1921 by 14 capitalist powers, including the United

States, which invaded Siberia. Later, in 1941, the entire might of the Nazi German army, which had conquered most of Europe, invaded the Soviet Union. The Soviets not only survived but pushed the Nazi armies back to Germany (though 20 *million* Soviet people perished in the war).

From 1928 to the present, all Soviet industry has been owned and managed by the Soviet government. Workers are paid wages by government enterprises with bonuses and extra pay for extra production. It is a crime in the Soviet Union to hire anyone for a private profit, but cooperatives have now been legalized. Profits of public enterprises all go to the government. The government uses those profits to expand the economy, to pay for welfare services, including free health and education, and to finance the military. Beginning in 1928, Soviet industry has been directed by a series of five-year plans formulated by the government according to what it believes are the needs of the country. The country runs its industry without any private capitalists (with the exception of cooperatives).

In a period of about 10 years from 1928 to 1938, the Soviets put all their resources into economic expansion, which changed the Soviet Union from an economically backward, less developed country to one of the most advanced industrial countries in the world. In the 1920s, the Soviet Union had little industry. At present, it is the second largest industrial producer in the world, ranking just after the United States. In 1928 the Soviet Union was mainly agricultural and most people lived in rural areas; today it is mainly industrial and most people live in cities.

In tsarist Russia, only about 15 percent of its people were educated and the rest were illiterate. At present, over 99 percent of the Soviet people are educated, with illiteracy less than 1 percent. All education in the Soviet Union is free, and college students receive hefty stipends so long as they maintain good grades. The stipends are enough to live on without doing other work.

Tsarist Russia had few doctors, and most peasants never saw a doctor. The present Soviet Union has more doctors per capita than the United States, though not as many specialists. All health services in the Soviet Union are free, and a great deal of preventive medicine is practiced to keep the population healthy. Any tourist can see that Soviet cities are kept quite clean, even the subways. This cleanliness is true even of the cities of Soviet central Asia, in contrast to the filth that may be seen in some other large cities throughout the world.

In the purely economic sphere, Soviet industry has grown much faster than American industry in every peaceful decade since 1928. Soviet planning ensures that there is *never any unemployment* other than people changing from one job to another. Since private profit is not the motive, Soviet planners can always find some kind of useful jobs for workers to do. On the contrary, the Soviet planners often err in the direction of trying to produce too much, so that there is often a shortage of labor. In the period of most rapid industrialization and in World War II, this shortage of labor resulted in drastic inflation. Since about 1950, however, there has been little or no inflation in the Soviet Union; the planners simply reduced the pace of growth a little—though the Soviet economy still grew much faster than the American economy from 1950 to the present. Recent problems and reforms in the Soviet Union are discussed later in this chapter.

THE STALINIST DICTATORSHIP

While all of the above points are strongly favorable to the Soviet Union, it must also be said that the Soviet people have suffered from dictatorship that has deprived them of democratic rights. After a struggle lasting from 1924 to 1928, Stalin won undivided power. His main opponent, Leon Trotsky, was exiled in 1928 and finally murdered in Mexico in 1940. The other old Bolshevik leaders continued to work under Stalin's direction until most were killed in the purge trials of 1936 to 1938. During the Stalin era, many hundreds of thousands of possible (or even rumored) opponents were jailed and thousands were killed. In the meantime, the Soviet Union was rapidly industrializing. The industrialization was carried out on the basis of restricted consumption enforced by extreme repression.

After 1928, Stalin ruled alone until his death in 1953. He ruled not only the Soviet Union but also the other communist parties of the world, including the new rulers of Eastern Europe. In theory, the Communist International was dissolved in 1943; however, in practice Stalin continued to direct the other parties. Only Tito of Yugoslavia dared to defect in 1948.

Soon after he took power, Stalin transformed Marxism-Leninism into a rigid doctrine. Only Stalin could make new interpretations, which he did to suit his needs, with little regard for theoretical niceties. Dissent met with imprisonment or death, and silence descended on the Marxist theoretical stage. Through his hold on foreign communist parties, and through their position in each country, Stalin dominated international Marxist thought from about 1926 till his death in 1953. This was a period of sterility, with few major contributions, in Soviet Marxist thought. No serious attention was paid to western social science, except to criticize it. Ironically, many of Stalin's successors in the Soviet leadership not only continued to use Stalin's version of Marxism, but also imported Talcott Parsons's functionalist sociology as a prop for *their* status quo.

Even when Stalin was laid to rest in 1953, he was still venerated in Red Square with Lenin. The communist leaders, always with the exception of Tito, continued to act in accordance with Stalin's image toward the outer world. In 1956, however, Nikita Khrushchev, then the leader of the Soviet Union, dug up the old bones of Stalin along with the old ghosts of Stalinism. He stunned the communist world, but achieved popularity at the Twentieth Congress of the Communist Party of the Soviet Union by denouncing the repression and murders of Stalin's day and promising a new era of freedom.

WHY THE STALINIST DICTATORSHIP?

Radicals have argued that government under capitalism is dominated by the capitalist class to an extent that diminishes democratic political forms. On the other hand, conservative sociologists have argued that central planning and bureaucracy under socialism must inevitably lead to a dictatorship by a few people at the top. Their favorite case in point has been the dictatorship of the Soviet Union that grew up under Stalin. There is no question that the Soviet Union under Stalin was highly centralized (and that it is now less centralized with some elements of democracy). The sociological question is why. We contend that Soviet dictatorship was established *in spite* of public ownership and planning, not because of them. Other factors seem to bear the primary responsibility. These factors are:

1. The antidemocratic tradition of tsarist Russia
2. The underground training of the Bolshevik leaders
3. The effect of the Russian civil war
4. The effect of foreign intervention
5. The overwhelming realities of economic backwardness and illiteracy, combined with the industrialization drive to end backwardness

Tsarist Russia

Prerevolutionary Russia, headed by the tsar, was an absolute autocracy for most of its history; it was strongly militarist and imperialist, and it was supported by a feudal landowning nobility. Ideas of political democracy came very late in Russia, and for some time after the French Revolution they influenced only the few intelligentsia. After the abortive revolution of 1905, there was a modest degree of parliamentary political democracy practiced from 1906 to 1917. But even then the Russian Duma (parliament) was neither very popular nor very effective. There was thus very little consciousness of democracy or practical experience with democracy among the Russian people.

The Underground Viewpoint

The Russian Marxists were forced to pursue an illegal conspiracy by the repressive laws of the tsarist government. Therefore, they instituted a very strict discipline within the party, did not always hold elections for top officers, and enforced orders from the top down. In theory, Lenin argued for "democratic centralism," which meant democratic election of central officers plus strict obedience to orders from elected officers. Tsarist repression made fully democratic elections impossible, but the communist leaders still demanded obedience to orders. The tradition by which the party led the masses, and the top leaders directed the party, was probably necessary for political and military action and was not too detrimental before the Revolution of 1917. Since anyone could leave the party without harm, the party could ask only for voluntary self-discipline. Few revolutionaries thought about what might happen if the party became the all-powerful ruler of the nation. They could not foresee persuasion giving way to censorship and coercion, while voluntary discipline was replaced by external compulsion.

Civil War

The Revolution of October 1917 resulted in a government of *soviets*—that is, councils of workers, peasants, and soldiers, led by the Communist party (Bolsheviks). Within a month after the Revolution, the first step against Western-style political democracy was taken when all the parties (and all the newspapers) advocating capitalism or monarchism were banned. This was partly explained as a temporary measure during the violence of the revolution and attempts at counterrevolution. But it was also given a more ominous meaning as a "natural act of proletarian dictatorship."

Nevertheless, there were free elections to a Constituent Assembly (which was to write a constitution), in which the biggest winner was the Socialist Revolutionary party and the Bolsheviks ran a poor second. Then, two months later the Constituent Assembly was dispersed because, it was said, the attitude of the people had greatly changed and the Socialist Revolutionary party had split. Thus elections to the assembly were now outdated. This was a reasonably democratic argument, except that new elections to the assembly were not called then or ever. A further argument was that the soviets (meaning councils) were more democratic than a parliamentary assembly because the soviets represented soldiers, industrial workers, and farmers. Since the owning classes were to be dispossessed, they would eventually also be part of the working classes, so eventually everyone could vote in elections to the soviets. Furthermore, in 1917–1918 all of the various socialist parties still participated in the soviets. Therefore, except for the exclusion of the capitalist and monarchist parties, the soviets, it was said, would eventually turn out to be a more democratic instrument than the assembly.

Within a few more months, however, as the civil war grew in intensity and bitterness, the other socialist parties were also prohibited to a large extent from political participation. Even this further measure of political restriction might be defended in view of the terrible conditions of the time—a single, poor and exhausted workers' state standing alone against formidable domestic enemies and massive foreign intervention. The problem is that this temporary emergency measure became a permanent policy that rigidified under Stalin.

Many democratic forms tend to fall by the wayside during any violent and rapidly changing civil war. After the bitterness of civil war, it is not easy to let the opposition immediately reenter politics. The long and bloody civil war in the Soviet Union, worsened by foreign intervention, made immediate initiation of widespread political democracy very unlikely. The civil war killed off or dispersed much of the old working class. In fact, the number of workers shrank from a small 2.6 million in 1917 to an even smaller 1.2 million in 1920. Furthermore, the unpopular measures necessary for warfare alienated many former supporters. As a result, the few surviving old Bolsheviks felt as if they were a tiny remnant defending a besieged fortress, but who has ever heard of a besieged fortress being ruled democratically.

Foreign Intervention

A large number of foreign capitalist countries intervened militarily against the Soviet communists in the years 1918–1921 (including the United States, England, France, and Japan). This intervention has been interestingly documented in a British Broadcasting Company film, *The Forgotten War*. Furthermore, the economic blockade of the Soviet Union continued for many years. Foreign threats never ceased until they culminated in the devastating Nazi invasion in 1941. This was followed by the Cold War in the 1950s, the threat of the nuclear bomb, and the renewal of attempts at economic blockade by the United States.

These circumstances *do* partly make political democracy objectively more difficult. They also have been used, however, as a rationale for repression by some of the ruling elements in the Soviet Union, just as Senator Joseph McCarthy used the Korean War as an excuse for repression in America and just as President Nixon used the Vietnam War to justify more repression. Moreover, each side points to repression in the other country as a reason for its own repression.

Economic Backwardness

A great many of the underdeveloped countries, from the Soviet Union to Somalia, have tended toward both socialist state ownership of the means of production *and* one-party control of political life. Why should economic backwardness generate both state ownership and one-party government? These are countries filled mostly with a raging desire for rapid economic growth. Yet they are also largely poor, agrarian countries with little modern industry in buildings, technology, equipment, skilled workers, or experienced managers.

Socialism is viewed as a useful instrument of industrialization in the underdeveloped countries. For one thing, there are few educated and experienced planners; thus the central government can best make use of the ones that exist, whereas many decades might be required for the voluntary emergence of bold, private entrepreneurs. Furthermore, the extreme lack of capital in the underdeveloped countries can most easily be remedied by government control of resources. The government can tax the rich, gather the small savings of the poor, and expropriate foreign profits, in order that the government itself may invest in new factories and equipment.

It is thus clear why socialist state ownership may be chosen as an instrument to overcome backwardness. But why does backwardness also generate one-party governments? The reason lies within exactly the same set of circumstances.

The Soviet people may have been convinced of the desirability of rapid economic growth. Yet the Soviet leadership and their economic planners soon found that there was a conflict between rapid long-run growth and immediate consumption. Concretely, they discovered that to gather the resources required to build up basic industry, it was necessary to take food from the farm population in order to feed the new industrial working class. In addition, food, as well as raw materials, had to be exported in order to raise the capital needed to import the machinery required by basic industry. Aside from foreign investment, there was simply no other source of capital.

Stalin "solved" the resource problem by forcefully putting the peasantry into collective farms from which the entire surplus could be taken. This was at the cost of a long stagnation or drop in living standards, especially among landowning peasants, and was accompanied by strong resistance to the regime among much of the farm population. Stalin succeeded in putting heavy investments for several years into basic industrial capital and education of a whole new working class. Such a sudden transformation, which was unpopular with the peasant majority, probably could not have been accomplished without a dictatorship. The main historical issue is whether Soviet industrial transformation could have taken place somewhat more slowly and with more democratic consent. Though this question cannot be definitively answered for the Soviet Union, such a question is relevant since a significant part of the world is at present underdeveloped but wants to develop economically. Clearly, different political strategies are available to a society undergoing economic development.

Although there have been major setbacks, political freedom in the Soviet Union *has* increased since Stalin's death. This improvement in civil liberties is partly due to the improved economic situation. The Soviet Union has now progressed to the stage where it has a large industrial base capable of generating sufficient surplus within itself to facilitate continued rapid growth of production, as well as increasing satisfaction of consumer needs both in cities and on the farm. Moreover, modern industry requires a high level of education. The intensive education of a large part of the Soviet population has now provided that population not only with scientific knowledge but also with at least a minimum level of liberal arts education. Even with a generous amount of propaganda, this education makes the population capable of using and demanding a wider democratic process.

We conclude that political dictatorship in the Soviet Union resulted from the Russian autocratic and underground political traditions, civil war, foreign wars (and encirclement), and economic backwardness. It was *not* caused by socialism, but arose in spite of socialism. In an advanced economy, like the United States, a socialist system would provide a better environment for political democracy than does capitalism.

CLASS AND STRATIFICATION IN THE SOVIET UNION

Soviet sociologists deny that there is any ruling class in the Soviet Union, although they are quick to speak of an exploitative ruling class in the United States. This is exactly the same stance as that of the traditional American sociologists, who deny that there is any ruling class in the United States, but are quick to find one in the Soviet Union. In Chapter 3, we described the ruling, capitalist class of the United States. Here we examine the ruling class of the Soviet Union, which is quite different from the American ruling class in many ways. Two leading American Marxists conclude that the Soviet Union is still "a stratified society, with a deep chasm between the ruling stratum of political bureaucrats and economic managers on the one side and the mass of working people on the other" (Sweezy and Huberman, 1967, p. 11).

There are four main groups in the Soviet ruling class. The first and most important is the top level of the Communist party apparatus, including 10 or 15 people in the highest body, the Politbureau, and a few hundred more in the next highest body, the Central Committee. Second, there are the top levels of the government bureaucracy, such as the Council of Ministers, though most of these people also hold top positions in the party. Third, there are the top officers of the Soviet military establishment. Fourth, there are the top levels of economic management, including the central planners.

Each of these four groups merge and intertwine at the top, and individuals often move from one hierarchy to another at all levels. This merger at the top is why we can speak of one ruling class in the Soviet Union (again, as in the United States). Yet the party leaders, whose abilities are political and not technical, are still dominant. The government bureaucrats, even the very top ones, are still subordinate to the party, though they have shown somewhat more independence and initiative in recent decades. The power and influence of the economic managers have risen with the increase of technology and industrial complexity, but there has been no technocratic challenge to the clear supremacy of the party apparatus. The military is steadily becoming more professional and independent, for example, pushing for higher levels of military spending. The party, however, exercises its control of the military through several channels: almost all officers are party members, there is intensive indoctrination at all levels, and there is direct interference from party commissars in individual units.

One way in which the Soviet elite differs from the American elite is in relative size. Whereas the very wealthy and powerful of the American ruling class number up to a million or so, the similar group in the Soviet Union is far smaller, less than a hundred thousand. From an economic equalitarian standpoint, this is quite good in the sense that the Soviet rulers take a very much smaller amount of the total national income for their own use than do the American rulers—as we shall see when we compare the income distribution of the two countries. On the other hand, it means that political power is much more concentrated than in the United States.

This difference in the size of the two ruling classes results from the fact that all of the middle-level of the Soviet elite—such as middle-level managers, local party bosses, majors in the army, and middle-level government bureaucrats—actually live on salaries derived from their own labor. They are paid relatively high amounts compared with ordinary workers, but just about all of these salaries represent differences according to actual ability and quality of the labor that they do. Only at the top of the Soviet hierarchy are the salaries of the leadership a complete secret, classified for "security" reasons. This group is not extremely wealthy by U.S. standards, but they can obtain almost anything they want. These top leaders get undeclared salaries and fringe benefits far beyond their own contribution of labor. Thus some large part of their income comes from the value created by the working class of the Soviet Union. So, "their incomes are at least partially derived from the 'surplus value' produced by the workers" (Deutscher, 1969, p. 56).

Yet, unlike the American ruling class, these groups own neither land nor factories, nor can they expand their incomes by investments. The ruling groups have not so far tried to vest their controlling privileges in their children by legal means. They do, however, give their children a head start through an intellectual home atmosphere and, sometimes, through legal and illegal means to get them admitted to college or placed in a job.

Because the Soviet ruling class has no legal ownership of the means of production, as does the capitalist ruling class, their need for direct repressive controls is even greater than that of the capitalists. "The power of property having been destroyed, only the State, that is, the bureaucracy, dominates society; and its domination is based solely on the suppression of the people's liberty to criticize and oppose" (Deutscher, 1969, p. 106). Thus bureaucratic power (and increasing material prosperity) are the mechanisms used by the Soviet leadership to organize society, including the means of production.

Income distribution in the Soviet Union is far more equal than in the United States because the Soviet ruling class is so much smaller than the American ruling class and because it exploits a much smaller share of national income from its working class. This is clear when we compare the official figures on income distribution from both countries (even though both contain several kinds of biases and distortions in them). In the Soviet Union in 1960 the top 10 percent of families had a total income that was 4.8 times as much as that of by the bottom 10 percent of families. Additional evidence indicates that this ratio has dropped in the Soviet Union since that time. In the United States, on the other hand, in 1960 the top 10 percent of families had 30 times the total income of the lowest 10 percent of families. Almost all of the greater inequality in the United States results from the existence of private profits, private rent, and private interest income—most of which goes to the top income group. The Soviets, on the other hand, have only wage and salary income even in the top group.

The most recent available Soviet data shows the decile ratio for all state employees from 1956 to 1976. The *decile ratio* is the ratio of the income of the 90th percentile group of Soviet workers by income compared with the 10th percentile (that is, the 10th percentile from the bottom). The decile ratio was 4.4 in 1956—that is, workers in the 90th percentile earned 4.4 times as much as workers in the 10th percentile. The decile ratio dropped to 2.83 in 1968 (indicating less inequality), then rose to 3.35 in 1976 (McAuley, 1977, p. 228).

It is striking that there is very little difference between the range of inequality of *just* wage and salary income between the United States and the Soviet Union. However, this is very different from *overall income distribution because that includes American profit, rent, and interest incomes.* Immediately after the 1917 revolution, wage and salary income in the Soviet Union was equalized to a very great extent. In the 1930s, however, Stalin decided that the rapid industrialization drive demanded high wage differentials between workers in order to promote incentives. There was little money to pay workers, so wages of unskilled workers were kept very low. At the same time, those who had the skills to produce more or to do important jobs were paid very high wages. Therefore, in the 1930s the ratio of most skilled wage rates to unskilled wage rates stood at 3.5:1 in the officially prescribed wage scales, and piece-rate bonuses undoubtedly increased this ratio in practice. This was a much higher wage differential than prevails currently in the United States. On the other hand, the United States had much higher wage differentials—of just about that magnitude—during our own period of rapid industrialization.

In the late 1950s, when a more relaxed political climate prevailed in the Soviet Union, the leaders came to realize that such wide wage differentials were no longer necessary, and might make the mass of unskilled workers angry at the leadership. Therefore, a number of measures were taken to raise the minimum wages of the unskilled, while holding down the wages of the most skilled. As a result, by 1958 the official differential between the wages of the unskilled and the most skilled had fallen to the ratio of 2.8:1. Since that time, the range of wages has been somewhat further narrowed, so the degree of wage inequality in the Soviet Union is now less than in the United States (and, of course, its *overall* income distribution is far less unequal than in the United States). In 1972, if the average manual worker's pay was 100 in the USSR, then the pay of routine, nonmanual workers (such as clerical and sales workers) was only 85 (a ratio of .85:1), while the pay for intellectual workers (such as engineers and lawyers) was 134 (a ratio of 1.34:1)—but these are not wide differences (Connor, 1979, chap. 1). A comprehensive review of all the research on Soviet inequality by traditional American and West European sociologists concludes: "These studies suggest that the extreme economic inequality of the late Stalinist period has been reduced appreciably in recent years; along with a reduction in interoccupational variation in industrial wages. . . . there has been a general leveling and a rise in per capita income" (Dobson, 1977, p. 302).

Soviet sociologists—like their American counterparts—have presented quite a bit of data on the inequality and stratification within the working class. In addition, one useful book of translated essays of Soviet sociologists shows that they not only discuss inequality but also apologize for it (Yanowitch and Wisher, 1973). In a familiar functionalist manner, they argue that such inequality is necessary for the proper functioning of the Soviet Union. This apologia has the same basic cause as in the United States—namely the dominance of a ruling class ideology, though it parades as Marxism in the Soviet Union. The only difference made by the Marxist approach is that the Soviet authors say that the present inequality is proper only for the present level of development, but that some day, in the distant future under communism, this inequality will disappear.

All of these Soviet essays recognize only two classes in the Soviet Union. These are the nonantagonistic classes of collective farmers and working class. The working class includes manual and mental, rural and urban, male and female, Russian and non-Russian workers. These two classes are distinguished by their different relations to the means of production, but it is pointed out—quite correctly—that neither of these two classes exploit each other.

The most useful essays in the book show the degree of various forms of inequality between strata *within* the working class, as well as some discussion of the difficulties of moving up from lower to higher strata. For example, the essays show concretely that unskilled workers have less education, lower wages, fewer cultural activities, and less political participation than more skilled workers, who in turn have less of all of these characteristics than do the intellectual workers (including engineers) and the supervisors and managers. For example, one excellent study of the machine-building industry in Leningrad finds: "It is typical that almost 60 percent of unskilled workers in manual, hand labor have no more than a six-year education, and their average educational level is 6.5 grades of school" (ibid., 1973, p. 75). The study also found that 26 percent of the unskilled workers do not read books at all; perhaps it is more remarkable that 20 percent did read one or more books a week. A more ominous sign was the finding for three different Soviet cities that participation in "community activities" (political to some extent) was very low among unskilled workers and very high among intellectuals and managerial personnel. Other studies of mobility reveal that families with highly educated parents tend to have the most highly educated children, so that the inequality is reproducing itself in the Soviet as in the American educational system.

In the years of rapid industrialization there was far more upward mobility in the Soviet Union than in the United States. Sons and daughters of poor peasants could and did emigrate to the cities and become workers—often very skilled workers—yet more rarely rose to be technicians and professionals. This vast inflow from the rural areas has been reduced and spectacular upward mobility is less frequent than in the earlier period. It is still probably greater than in the United States, since there is no private ownership of factories and land, and no inheritance of income-producing property. *If* one can get a higher education in the Soviet Union, the doors are open to advancement to the highest levels of the society. On the other hand, as we have noted, it is clear that the children of educated families (technicians, professionals, and managers) more often succeed in getting a higher education than the children of ordinary manual workers.

The competition for a higher education is even greater than in the United States. There is less of an economic barrier, however, because every good student gets free tuition plus a very considerable scholarship (usually equal to the average wage). Nevertheless, the competition for limited places in the universities means that a high proportion of the children of unskilled workers are *not* likely to get a higher education—because of a less intellectually oriented family environment. The widespread facilities for training in skills—plus full employment—does mean, however, that most children of unskilled workers do *rise* up the economic ladder to the level of a skilled worker. Upward socioeconomic mobility is thus greater than in the United States at the present time, but is still far less than could ideally be desired.

WORLD COMMUNISM AFTER STALIN

In 1956, Premier Nikita Khrushchev denounced Stalin's dictatorial methods. His denunciation of terror and dogmatic thinking had a profoundly traumatic—yet liberating—effect on communist intellectuals throughout the world. Most of them escaped from the heavy chains of Stalin's dogmatic orthodoxy. Many proclaimed a renaissance of Marxist thought and began to take seriously Marx's injunction to "doubt everything." The frozen thinking of the Stalinist bureaucrats was challenged from many sides at once.

De-Stalinization, however, went far beyond what Khrushchev had anticipated. Eastern Europe took Khrushchev's teachings to heart and showed a restless independence. In October 1956, Poland ousted its own Stalinists and established a more liberal communist regime, barely avoiding the violence of civil war in the process. Poland, however, has continued to have internal dissension and even revolts from time to time. Other Eastern European countries have had violent uprisings, as in Hungary in 1956 and Czechoslovakia in 1968. China split from the Soviet Union in the 1960s and has continued its own independent road with many twists and turns.

The genie of independent thought, once unleashed, was not easily put back into the bottle. The Italian Communist leader Palmiro Togliatti voiced the thoughts of many when he said that the 1960s and 1970s would be an era of "polycentrism"—that is, of many divergent national paths to socialism.

In 1968, the Czechoslovakian people lifted their heads, ousted the old leadership, and began to build a "socialism with a human face." This was the most important experiment in democratic communism to date. It was led by Alexander Dubcek and the Czechoslovakian Communist party. Yet it was crushed by the Soviet army. This Soviet action was criticized by many on the left throughout the world, including many New Left political activists in America. Communists, themselves, are thus strongly divided at the present time.

The majority of the world today considers itself socialist or communist. To understand the present-day world we must understand the major controversies between socialists and the several varieties of communists. The first issue is the degree of nationalization or government ownership—which divides countries such as Sweden from the Soviet Union. The second issue is the degree of decentralization and workers' control—which divides the traditionalists and reformers throughout Eastern Europe and the Soviet Union. The third issue is the degree of income equality and free public goods. The fourth and final issue is the degree of democratic political processes and freedoms for individuals and for opposition parties—which is causing sharp divisions among communists, even in the Soviet Union. These issues will be considered in turn.

NATIONALIZATION: SWEDEN VERSUS THE SOVIET UNION

Sweden—like most of Scandinavia, England and Germany—has had a so-called socialist government for many years. Sweden, however, has very little government-owned industry and only a small cooperative sector. More than 90 percent of the Swedish economy is still privately owned. Most of the profits still go to the capitalist class; just 1000 individuals own 32 percent of all stock in Swedish corporations. The Swedish capitalists are the rich and socially dominant class. That is *not* socialism according to our definition, because socialism means that the people (particularly the working class) control the economy. The Swedish Socialist party claims that socialism just means government *regulation* of business, government controls to prevent the worst depressions, and considerable welfare payments to the poor. It is more precise to say that Sweden has a capitalist economy with considerable regulation and welfare spending.

By contrast, the Soviet Union and the Eastern European countries certainly have government ownership and control of almost all of their industry. There is no capitalist class because there is no privately owned capital. It is quite clear that the Soviet government both owns and plans its economy—the question a socialist must answer is, Who runs the Soviet government?

DECENTRALIZATION: CENTRAL PLANNING VERSUS PERESTROIKA

One problem of the Soviet economy is the inefficiency that results from trying to plan every detail from a single central planning office. The Soviet Union is three times the geographical size of the United States and produces over two million different products in every possible climatic and topographical zone. Yet, for many years, the Soviet Union attempted to plan an incredibly detailed level of production for every product in every plant in the central planning agency in Moscow. This resulted in some real mistakes in technology, including an imbalance between one product and another. For example, there might not be enough tires for the number of trucks built. Also some things produced for consumers were of poor quality. These problems are now recognized by all economists, even Soviet economists.

In the late 1960s the Soviet Union and Eastern European countries tried to correct these problems by a considerable degree of decentralization. The Soviet Union had previously tried decentralizing decisions to 101 separate geographical regions, but this still left the power in the hands of a few bureaucrats in each region—and raised the additional problem of coordinating the regions. Now the Soviet Union gives additional decision-making power to each manager. Hungary went much further, giving the enterprise manager all decision-making power over technology, what kinds of products to produce, and even what prices to set on products of the enterprise. The manager was instructed simply to maximize profits by increasing revenue and holding down costs.

Workers' Control

Decentralization, however, has another aspect, that of political power, or *who* makes decisions at every level. Yugoslavia is the only socialist country that has not only decentralized most economic decisions to the enterprise level, but has also given this power to elected representatives of the workers in the enterprise. The final authority in the Yugoslav enterprise is the elected workers' council, *not* the manager. The manager runs day-to-day operations, but he may be fired by the workers' council (with the agreement of the local government).

Many East Europeans felt that control of enterprises by local workers' councils was the only true road to democracy, mostly because they despaired of democracy at the national level. When Czechoslovakia went through its brief period of democracy in 1968, it began to allow and encourage local workers' councils, but full implementation was blocked by the Soviet invasion. Moreover, workers' councils are not a democratic panacea. Yugoslavia still has a one-party government at the national level that retains decision-making power over most political and economic questions.

Perestroika

The Russian word *perestroika* roughly means rebuilding or reconstruction. The present Soviet leader, Mikhail Gorbachev (1987), says that overcentralization has led to serious problems of inefficiency and waste in the economy, so he has called for a complete restructuring (perestroika) of the economy. Gorbachev emphasizes that the Soviet growth rate has declined significantly in the last two decades and is now too low. One reason, he stresses, is that the central planners in Moscow have tried to dictate exactly how things should be done all over the Soviet Union. For someone in Moscow to decide the details of building houses in the far north of Siberia, for example, is a clear formula for inefficiency. Moreover, monthly results were demanded of each manager, so managers were afraid to try new technology that might ruin their performance during a transition period.

These and other problems forced the Soviet leadership to realize that their economy was facing a crisis; they decided to reform socialism in order to save it. There are two basic reforms. First, each firm must earn its own profits to exist or to go bankrupt. Second, each manager's performance will be judged basically on the profitability of the firm, not on physical targets set by the planners. So central planning will provide mostly long-run guidelines, not detailed instructions. Of course, the profits still go to the public, not to private owners—so this is reformed socialism, not a return to capitalism. Other important reforms include allowing workers to form cooperatives outside the planning system, more participation by workers in controlling public enterprises (possibly electing the manager), a wholesale market so that firms can buy directly from each other (without government rationing and allocation as is now the case), and some decontrol of prices.

Taken together, these reforms would be a revolutionary change in Soviet society. Many Soviet leaders support them because they feel they are absolutely necessary. But these reforms would remove much power from the bureaucracy—including government planners and middle-level party leaders—giving the initiative to individual firms. So the bureaucracy is strongly resisting these reforms. We cannot tell at this time whether the reforms will be fully implemented or whether they will be sabotaged and reversed, or partially implemented.

EQUAL DISTRIBUTION: EQUALITY VERSUS INCENTIVES

Almost all Marxist socialists agree with the goal of a world having approximately equal distribution of income and wealth, with no super-wealthy and no poor; this is part of the socialist vision of a just society. On the other hand, there is great controversy—even among Marxists—over how fast it is possible to reach this goal.

In the Soviet Union, at the height of Stalin's industrialization drive in the 1930s, there was a conscious effort to increase inequality in order to provide an incentive for very hard work. Managers, engineers, and outstanding workers were paid a lot of money, while millions of people—especially on the farms—hovered on the brink of starvation. At present, the Soviet wage and salary distribution (between highest paid and lowest paid workers) is a little more equal than in the United States. In addition, there are *no* huge private fortunes from private profit, *no* private rental income, and *no* interest from moneylending—all of these types of incomes are illegal. Therefore, as shown above, *overall* Soviet income distribution is far more equal than in the United States—which has very high incomes of private profit, rent, and interest. Moreover, it should be noted that the Soviet Union has a much wider range of free public services, such as health and education, than the United States.

The socialist vision says that eventually all the basic necessities of life could be given away free. Could the U.S. government furnish all the major necessities at no cost? Critics have always argued two main points of "human nature" as sociological constraints that would prevent such a system from working. First, they allege, it is human nature to be lazy, so if all necessities were free, nobody would work. Second, they argue, it is human nature to be greedy, so there would be an infinite, unsatisfiable, demand for all the free goods.

Such arguments could be quite convincing if we think of making such a drastic change overnight. Assume, however, that we had a socialist government democratically elected in the United States, and all major private enterprises—such as the oil and steel companies—were changed over to public ownership. It would be feasible to slowly widen the sphere of free public goods. Suppose we began with a free, national health-care system of the kind that every other major industrialized country now has. People are not going to stop working just because they can get free health care; on the contrary, more people will be able to work if they are healthier. Furthermore, people are not going to demand an infinite amount of health care; they have not done so in any other country, and Americans are not worse hypochondriacs than other people. Who wants to sit in a doctor's office or be operated on if there is any way to avoid it?

Similarly, the United States could provide a minimum of free public transportation in its cities. This would not only reduce smog but also make it easier to administer transportation. It would be cheaper, for example, not to have ticket sellers or ticket collectors on subways. Again, people are not going to stop working just because their transportation to and from work is free, nor are many people going to ride the subways just for fun. Another area in which people must pay is education; our entire higher education system could be free as is most of our elementary to high school education system. People have not stopped working just because elementary and high school education is free, nor have they demanded infinite amounts of it. In the further future, some basic amount of housing and some basic foods could be provided free. Getting minimum food and shelter is not going to stop many people from working hard for other things in life, nor is anybody likely to demand an infinite number of potatoes or any other basic food.

Finally, we have made the point that human psychology is not fixed for all time, but can be changed by new circumstances. It is true that our present culture takes human greed and laziness for granted, but that does not always have to be so. If the ideology coming through the press, television, and advertising were to change from individual acquisitiveness to a commitment to society—and if most basic necessities were free, so that people did not feel an urgency to compete with their fellow man or woman for status or survival—then human nature might slowly begin to change. For example, who would want to steal food or medicine if it were given to everybody? Thus, eventually much crime might slowly disappear—in the same way as full employment would lead to the disappearance of unemployment compensation.

We see the very practical possibility of a limited but growing area of free public goods. From this structural change, many positive sociological changes might occur in government and in human attitudes. Ultimately, many broad social changes are possible—changes that would clearly transcend the existing socio-economic arrangements of the present society.

DEMOCRACY: STALINISM VERSUS GLASNOST

Marx's political goal was democratic rule by the entire working class; under socialism this would be all the people. Marx's example of a socialist democracy was the short-lived Paris Commune of 1871, under which Paris had multiple conflicting parties, elections, freedom of speech, and every other democratic right. Marx wrote that "the commune was formed of the municipal councillors, chosen by universal suffrage in various wards of the town, responsible and revokable at short terms" (Marx, 1871, p. 12). He assumed that socialism meant democratic, public control of the economy; he certainly never condoned dictatorial rule by a small elite over the government and the economy.

Lenin agreed with Marx that the Paris Commune was a good example of socialist democracy. He wrote that under socialism "representative institutions remain. . . . Without representative institutions we cannot imagine democracy, not even proletarian democracy" (Lenin, 1917, p. 41). Lenin supported some restraints on other political parties and factions only as a *temporary*, wartime measure in the midst of a bloody civil war in Russia.

Stalinism

After Stalin consolidated his power in the late 1920s, he launched a massive industrialization drive based on huge sacrifices by that whole generation. He used repression against anyone objecting to the manner of industrialization or any other aspect of Stalin's leadership. He claimed that socialist democracy meant rule by the Communist party, representing the working class. Furthermore, he said that it meant rule by Stalin, representing the Communist party. On this complete distortion of socialist ideology he justified killing or imprisoning thousands of people, including the execution of every other top Communist leader and about three-fourths of the leadership of Stalin's own faction.

Stalin claimed that all the people he killed were subversive foreign agents of capitalist imperialism and a few left-over Russian capitalists. On the other hand, he claimed that all of the working population of the Soviet Union was happy and harmonious, so it had no need to express criticism. One of the faithful Stalinists in the United States, William Z. Foster, echoed Stalin:

The existence of many political parties in capitalist countries . . . merely signifies that the class struggle is raging. In a fully developed socialist country, inasmuch as the

> people's interests are fundamentally harmonious, there is a proper place for only one
> political party, the Communist Party. (Foster, 1953, p. 271)

One wonders, if such perfect harmony prevails, why even one party is needed.

This antidemocratic Stalinist ideology continues to be followed in varying degrees in the Soviet Union, China, Cuba, Vietnam, and Eastern Europe. As we have seen, the historical reason for this antidemocratic ideology is that all of these parties came to power through violent civil wars of national liberation—and most were economically underdeveloped countries with no tradition of political democracy. While some of these countries have moderated their practices, they still exercise some dictatorship and punish deviants, though mostly by imprisonment rather than executions.

Most independent Marxists, however, take a position in favor of the absolute necessity of democratic processes as a component of a socialist society. The Italian Communist party has led in the ideological debate in favor of democracy (for which they have been reviled by the Soviet Communists and other Stalinists). The Italian, French, and Spanish Communists have specifically declared that a multiparty system and full civil liberties must be part of socialism.

For one thing, there is *not* perfect harmony in the early development of a socialist society; many conflicting interests must be represented. Even if all capitalists should disappear, there is still a range of income distribution, differences in training, differences between city and rural areas, and differences between the few political leaders and the millions not in leadership positions. Mao Tse-tung himself emphasized that even in socialism there are conflicts or "contradictions" between farm workers and industrial workers, between manual workers and intellectuals, and between ordinary individuals and government leaders or bureaucrats (see Mao Tse-tung, 1957).

Even in socialism for example, there may be conflicts over locating hospitals in city or rural areas, which may lead to short-run differences of interest between farm workers and industrial workers and, possibly, hospital workers. Each of these segments of the working class needs the right to elect its *own* representatives and voice its *own* views. To do so may require factions within one party or entirely different parties. But each needs some vehicle to exercise free speech in an organized way with or against the majority of other voters.

The antagonisms with which successors to Stalin and to Mao have fought for power indicate the clear need in socialism (as in capitalism) for an orderly, democratic process of choosing leadership. Once leadership is chosen, it remains necessary to criticize its errors and inefficiencies. Both China and the Soviet Union allow and encourage criticism of the opposition but not of the man in power. Thus, Nikita Khrushchev was a near deity while in power, but was reviled for all his mistakes *after* he was dethroned. The brilliant critical Marxist Rosa Luxemburg pointed out the need for a nonviolent process of criticizing *existing* top leadership:

> Freedom only for the supporters of the government, only for the members of one
> party—however numerous they may be—is no freedom at all. Freedom is always

and exclusively freedom for the one who thinks differently. Not because of any fanatical concept of "justice" but because all that is instructive, wholesome and purifying in political freedom depends on this essential characteristic. (Luxemburg, 1918, p. 69)

It is only by the exercise of this freedom of speech that errors can be corrected, a minority become a majority, and a leader be prevented from becoming a dictator. Through repressing free speech and criticism by all means at his disposal, Stalin kept power for almost 30 years.

Glasnost

The Russian word *glasnost* roughly means openness. The present Soviet leader Gorbachev has used it to mean the opening of public discussion to many points of view—that is, a large amount of freedom of speech. He has launched this campaign most likely not from an abstract support of democracy, but because he realizes that his economic reforms cannot succeed without a changed atmosphere, a society open to new ideas. He can only succeed if the ordinary Soviet citizen is free to criticize the bureaucracy. He can only succeed in modernizing Soviet industry if managers and scientists are free to speak in an open society, conducive to innovation.

This openness also refers to a greater openness in relation to the United States and the West. In an era of atomic weaponry, Gorbachev is keenly aware that unbridled conflict between the U.S. and the Soviet Union could lead to a nuclear holocaust. It was in the spirit of decreasing the chances of such a world-wide disaster that Gorbachev entered into the unprecedented agreement in 1988 with President Reagan to remove intermediate-range missiles, such as cruise missiles, from Europe (INF treaty). Only a few years earlier the peace movement in Britain called for the removal of these same missiles, but it seemed unlikely to occur in the near future. The British, American, and other peace movements throughout the world now join Reagan and Gorbachev in hoping for similar agreements on long-range missiles.

Gorbachev has succeeded in getting the Soviet Union to buzz with discussion on many previously prohibited subjects. But he has not changed the basic political institutions, so the Soviet Union could revert to a freeze on discussion. Without democratic institutions there is no guaranteed freedom of speech. He has institutionalized free elections of officials and delegates within the Communist Party; yet this leaves a long road to democratic, multi-party elections.

Two important areas for protection of freedom are the media and job security. Socialists have criticized capitalism because a small number of corporations own most of the media, so unpopular voices may go unheard. Moreover, private capitalists control most U.S. jobs, so people with opinions critical of capitalism may be—and have been—fired.

But the critics of centrally planned socialism in the Soviet Union point out that the Soviet state controls all of the media and most of the jobs. So people with anticommunist opinions cannot be heard in the media and can be fired from their jobs. This does happen to Soviet dissidents even if they are not imprisoned.

Therefore, to be serious about the policy of glasnost, political reforms must be extended from open elections within the Communist Party (which is an historically significant change) to open elections in the government, specific safeguards against job discrimination, and freedom in the media.

There are many ways to institutionalize such safeguards; some important ones are the following. First, there must be regularized, civil service guarantees against arbitrary hiring or firing. Second, there must be a legal right for the opposition to express their views in the government-owned media, as in the British Broadcasting Corporation (BBC) in England. Third, any group of citizens must have the right to launch their own independent media, though it might be restricted to nonprofit organizations to avoid private profiteering.

With such democratic guarantees—including all those in the American Bill of Rights—we can expect a socialist economy to produce a greater degree of political democracy than ever before. Indeed, socialism should be defined as collective ownership of the economy *plus* democratic control of the economic collective, both at the national government level and at the level of local governments and local economic enterprises. That is the vision of most radical sociologists.

SUMMARY

This chapter has discussed the development of socialism in the Soviet Union. (We could have repeated this analysis for other Communist countries, such as Cuba or China, but the sociological factors often would have been similar.) It has been shown that the Stalinist dictatorship resulted from (1) the condition of economic backwardness and illiteracy, combined with the intensive effort needed to overcome this backwardness in a brief time by enormous sacrifices; (2) the legacy of tsarist oppression and underground political activity against tsarism; and (3) the bitterness and difficulty of democratic debate engendered by revolution, civil war, foreign intervention, and the later Nazi German invasion of the Soviet Union.

Against this backdrop of rapid economic progress and one-party government, the present class structure of the Soviet Union was examined. We found that there is a new sort of ruling class emerging, which includes top party officials, government leaders, military generals, and top economic managers and planners. These people clearly have a higher salary, greater prestige, and more power than other workers, and some of their income may derive from exploitation of other workers. Nevertheless, the overall distribution of income is clearly more equal in the Soviet Union than in the United States. And there is more upward mobility than in the United States, though the degree of mobility is perhaps declining to some extent. Within the Soviet working class there are definite strata by income, education, status, and so forth, but there is a good deal of upward mobility within the working class from strata to strata.

Given the very different conditions and background of the United States, we see no reason why an American socialism would not be even more democratic than American capitalism—since there would be no enormous centers of private economic power. While the Soviet Union supports a one-party system in principle, most American radicals favor the fullest possible extension of democracy, with a vast increase of participation in the political process by the millions who are presently not involved in it. Socialists continue to argue over (1) how centralized or decentralized the economy should be under socialism; (2) exactly what sectors should be under public ownership and what kinds of small business left to function privately; and (3) how much wage equality and how many free public goods and services could be introduced immediately in countries such as the United States. These issues are raised because a democratic, socialist, equalitarian, nonracist, nonsexist, and nonmilitaristic society is the goal of radical sociologists.

SUGGESTED READINGS

The best works analyzing the Soviet Union are the many books of Isaac Deutscher. His biographies offer a vivid insight into individual leaders, amounting to historical and sociological analyses of the Soviet Union, and are masterpieces of literature. See Isaac Deutscher's *Stalin* (New York: Oxford University Press, 1966), and *Trotsky*, in three volumes (New York: Random House, Vintage Books, 1965). Two totally opposed versions of what happened in the early Soviet Union, written by two of its main leaders, are Leon Trotsky, *The History of the Russian Revolution* (Ann Arbor: University of Michigan Press, 1967), and, on the other side, Joseph Stalin, *History of the Communist Party of the Soviet Union* (New York: International Publishers, 1939). Also fascinating is the historical summary by Isaac Deutscher in *The Unfinished Revolution, 1917–1967* (New York: Oxford University Press, 1967).

A very thorough and comprehensive survey of all the American and Soviet sociological studies of Soviet class structure (written from a traditional viewpoint) is Richard Dobson, "Mobility and Stratification in the Soviet Union," *Annual Review of Sociology* 3 (1977):297–329. The most interesting and useful single study is Murray Yanowitch, *Social and Economic Inequality in the Soviet Union* (White Plains, NY: M. E. Sharpe, 1977). The issues of central planning and decentralization, wage equality, and free public goods are discussed in Howard Sherman, *Radical Political Economy* (Armonk, NY: M. E. Sharpe, 1987), which also has an extensive bibliography on these subjects.

Soviet functionalist sociology is discussed in J. W. Freiberg, "Sociology and the Ruling Class," *Insurgent Sociologist* 3 (Summer 1971). Also, on this issue, see Alvin Gouldner, *The Coming Crisis of Western Sociology* (New York: Basic Books, 1970). Allied intervention in the Soviet Union in 1918–1921 is documented in a British Broadcasting Company film, *The Forgotten War,* available on videotape. The data in this chapter on the Soviet Union are from Andrew Zimbalist and Howard Sherman, *Comparing Economic Systems* (Orlando, FL: Academic Press, 2d ed., 1988). Anticipated changes in the Soviet Union are discussed by the Soviet leader, Mikhail Gorbachev, in *Perestroika* (New York: Harper & Row, 1987).

REFERENCES

Connor, Walter D. 1979. *Socialism, Politics, and Equality.* New York: Columbia University Press.

Deutscher, Isaac. 1967. *The Unfinished Revolution.* New York: Oxford University Press.
———. 1969. "Roots of Bureaucracy." In R. Miliband and J. Saville, eds., *The Socialist Register, 1969.* New York: Monthly Review Press.

Dobson, Richard. 1977. "Mobility and Stratification in the Soviet Union." In Alex Inkeles, James Coleman, and Neil Smelser, eds., *Annual Review of Sociology* (3): 297–329.

Foster, William Z. 1953. *History of the Three Internationals*. New York: International
    Publishers.
Gorbachev, Mikhail. 1987. *Perestroika*. New York: Harper & Row.
Lenin, V. I. 1917. *State and Revolution*. New York: International Publishers.
Luxemburg, Rosa. 1918. *The Russian Revolution*. Ann Arbor: University of Michigan
    Press. Republished 1961.
Marx, Karl. 1871. *The Civil War in France*. New York: International Publishers. Repub-
    lished 1948.
Mao Tse-tung. 1957. *On the Correct Handling of Contradictions Among the People*. New
    York: New Century Publishers.
McAuley, Alistair. 1977. "The Distribution of Earnings and Incomes in the Soviet Union."
    Soviet Studies 27 (April).
Sweezy, Paul, and Leo Huberman. 1967. "50 Years of Soviet Power." *Monthly Review* 19
    (November).
Yanowitch, Murray, and Wesley Wisher, eds. 1973. *Social Stratification and Mobility in
    the USSR*. White Plains, NY: M. E. Sharpe.

five

SOCIAL EVOLUTION

chapter 20

Social Change

The dominant theoretical perspective in the ancient and medieval periods—when social and technological change was very slow—asserted that no basic changes ever could or should occur. Medieval philosophers believed that they lived in "a fixed world, a realm where changes went on only within immutable limits of rest and permanence, and a world where the fixed and unmoving was . . . higher in quality and authority than the moving and altering" (Dewey, 1957, p. 54). This social viewpoint led to purely static social analyses in praise of present structures, which would exist eternally. It is still reflected in the popular slogan, "There is nothing new under the sun," or in the even more pessimistic ideology, "You can't change human nature."

In the early capitalist period, when the overthrow of European feudalism was still fresh in mind, the leading theorists recognized the reality and desirability of past change, but thought that humanity had now reached the perfect, or "natural," order. Many social scientists of the early nineteenth century "thought of social organization as something that had changed materially in the past, but had reached maturity and would not change materially in the future" (Mitchell, 1937, p. 207).

TRADITIONAL VIEWS OF SOCIAL CHANGE

Contemporary social scientists agree that change does occur in society. Yet there are sharp disagreements over what kinds of change occur. Is there only change in limited aspects of society—or can there also be changes in the most essential and basic relationships of society? Must changes be very slow, incremental, and continuous—or can there also be revolutionary, discontinuous social change? Are changes only improvements in the efficiency and harmony of society benefiting all classes—or are there also changes caused by antagonistic class conflicts, to the benefit of some classes, but to the detriment of others?

The functionalist perspective of Talcott Parsons tends to lead many traditional sociologists toward the view that changes can only be limited, slow and incremental, and to the benefit of all classes. Many functionalists believe that certain functional relations are found universally in all societies. Parsons believed that all societies must solve the functional problems of (1) pattern maintenance and tension management, (2) goal attainment, (3) adaptation, and (4) integration. These very general and abstract functions, supposedly found in every society, lead Parsons and other functionalists to claim that certain very specific institutions are necessary and inevitable in every society—and hence are not subject to change.

For example, Parsons and many other traditional sociologists have found that a woman's function in the family is to be kind, sensitive, and emotionally supportive. A man's function in the family—according to the traditional view— is to be an aggressive leader. According to Parsons, if these activities are disturbed or basically changed, then the family as an institution must work poorly or may even collapse, thus threatening the stability of the whole society. This traditional view does leave room for sociologists to posit smaller reforms in family attitudes or practices, but tends to rule out consideration of basic changes in family relations.

We also saw in Chapter 2 that two functionalists, Kingsley Davis and Wilbert Moore, found that inequalities of wealth and prestige play a necessary and useful function in all societies. These inequalities tempt the "most qualified persons" to take the "most important positions." The substance of that view has often been critized. The important point here, however, is that this traditional, functionalist view not only offers no explanation of change but also tends to prevent consideration of basic change toward equality in the family, the economic system, or other institutions. The reason for this conservative bias is that any basic changes are assumed to be harmful—that is, dysfunctional—for society.

By the end of the 1950s, many sociologists became uncomfortably aware of the conservatively biased restrictions placed on their research questions by this type of functionalist view. For example, the same Kingsley Davis who had defended the universal function of social and economic inequality, became president of the American Sociological Association in 1959 and switched to a new position in his presidential address. He declared: "However strategic it (functional analysis) may have been in the past, it has now become an impediment rather than a prop to scientific progress. . . . The claim that functionalism cannot handle social change because it posits an integrated static society is true by definition . . ." (Davis, 1959).

UNIVERSAL UNCHANGING INSTITUTIONS OR BASIC CHANGES?

Unfortunately, even after Davis and many others had criticized functionalism for its bias against examination of basic change, its main propositions about unchanging, universal social functions and institutions continue to be repeated. For example, in 1974, Harold Hodges wrote a typical introductory textbook of sociology, in which he summed up the traditional view as follows:

> Institutions such as governments, families, and religions are universal because they are functional: they enable society to meet its needs for maintaining social order, reproducing and caring for offspring, etc. If institutions are universal, they vary enormously from society to society in two important respects: in the dominance they exercise in a particular society and in the form they take. (1974, p. 287)

In this view, there can be many changes in the importance and in the forms of these institutions of society, but they will always exist; they cannot be eliminated and replaced with some entirely different institutions.

On the contrary, radical sociologists point out that there have been primitive societies in which there were no government structures to apply force against people—that is, there were no specialized police forces, courts, prisons, or armies. Moreover, there was little inequality and no private ownership of productive forces. Finally, there was no family in the modern sense of the nuclear family. Instead, there were clans or extended families consisting of a large number of people, with collective child care and collective economic functions—not just a mother, a father, and a few children as in modern society. Since these basic changes have occurred in the past, they may also occur in the future. By a basic (radical or revolutionary) change, we mean a total change in an important aspect of human relations. The most basic changes are those in the relations of production—for example, a change from slavery to capitalism. There may also be accompanying basic changes in governmental institutions (for example, creation of police and prisons where there were none) or basic changes in family relations, religious institutions, or any other institution. Thus basic, revolutionary changes occur when entirely new types of human relations are created, not when smaller changes occur within the same institution.

Almost all modern sociologists acknowledge that social changes do occur, but many of them are reluctant to examine basic revolutionary changes, leading most investigators to examine only smaller, limited reforms. A few even deny the possibility of revolutionary change and try to reduce any revolution to nonessential changes in the forms of institutions. For example, Robert Nisbet acknowledges that some revolutions do occur. He then tries to show, however, that elites predominate in revolutions and that not much really changes. Nisbet states:

> Despite a still widespread belief, revolution as we have known it in the West since the eighteenth century is no spontaneous welling up of the masses, no inexorable, deterministic response of large aggregates to conditions of poverty, political deprivation, or social injustice. . . . [The] heart of every revolution, successful or unsuccessful, lies in small minorities—elites. . . . (1973, p. 251)

In Nisbet's pessimistic view, there are no underlying historical forces leading to revolutions, just a switch from one elite to another. There is really no basic, or "revolutionary," change; in fact, there is hardly any real change in the way things are run. Nisbet's view follows the long tradition of conservative sociologists, such as Gaetano Mosca and Vilfredo Pareto, who argued that there must always be a small, ruling elite and a large, ruled class of poor working people—because that is the only way that society can function (see Bachrach, 1971).

The traditional sociologists' deemphasis of the specific class relations of each society allows them to contend that all problems are universal and unchangeable. This universalizing of problems permits many traditional sociologists to ignore the role of specific social institutions in creating social difficulties.

> In short, to base an analysis on the common factors and relationships that permeate any human society is to take the focus of analysis away from the specifics of the given social order, with its particular forms of privilege and oppression and its particular possibilities of development and reconstruction. (Horowitz, 1971, p. 8)

The influential radical sociologist C. Wright Mills insisted that sociological investigation requires historical specificity (1959, chap. 8). Historical specificity means that an investigation of poverty, inequality, or oppression by an elite group should not begin with speculation on universal functions in all societies, but should inquire about the function such an institution plays in this society in the framework of our particular socioeconomic and class relations.

TRADITIONAL MODELS OF SOCIAL CHANGE: VALUES AND ATTITUDES

In the prescientific world, one important source of change was believed to be God. If a society experienced a change for the better or worse, God was seen to be very involved. For example, God might bring favorable changes, such as increased wealth to "good people," but would bring poverty, misery, and natural disasters to "bad people." With the emergence of a scientific approach to the world, God was rejected as a determinant of change in the social world. Instead, the physical sciences suggested that social change occurred because of geological changes in the terrain or climate, or because of physiological evolution in humans. But any of these changes takes tens of thousands or even millions of years to be significant. They are important conditioning factors in the environment, but they usually cannot account for social changes because these occur within a much shorter time.

Traditional social science has developed many sociological theories of change, though many of them focus on more limited types of change. Instead of focusing on physical factors such as climate or terrain, most traditional sociologists argue that social changes occur because of such factors as cultural values, dissatisfactions, certain psychological dispositions, and the activities of liberal politicians. For example, Max Weber, in his studies of the origins of capitalism (to be discussed in detail in Chapter 21), argued that the cultural values of Protestantism—as opposed to Catholicism or other traditional religions—helped promote the change from a feudal to a capitalist economy (Weber, 1958). Weber, however, was criticized by Tawney (as we shall see in Chapter 21) for neglecting the earlier impact of class relations on ethical values (Tawney, 1954).

Neil Smelser argues that many changes in technology and family patterns were initiated by dissatisfactions with previously existing technologies and family structures in England (Smelser, 1959). Smelser posits a seven-stage model of social change that culminates in a more differentiated—that is, more complex—social or technical structure. This more differentiated structure is seen to relieve various tensions and problems within the system, thus making Smelser's approach a functional theory of change. However, some Marxists have criticized Smelser for deemphasizing class conflicts. (See Thompson, 1963; and Young, 1967, p. 27.) Smelser's theory will be further explored in Chapter 21.

Another approach—taken by many political scientists and sociologists, of whom Arnold Rose is a good example—stresses the influence of liberal politicians and established political institutions on generating social change. Sociology and political science have gone to great effort to show how reformist change can be produced through established institutions such as Congress, the Supreme Court, and the presidency. For example, Congress has been singled out by Rose as crucial for passing legislation like Medicare for the elderly, civil rights laws for blacks and other minority groups, and legislation giving organized labor better hourly wages (Rose, 1967). This approach usually assumes that liberal politicians, using existing institutions, are capable of generating significant changes. Rose and others of this school have been severely criticized by William Domhoff and other radicals for neglect of the class conflicts through which these laws came to be enacted (Domhoff, 1969, pp. 35–37). Each of these laws was passed through the pressure of long struggles by the working class, blacks, and other oppressed groups. In most cases, they were aided by liberal politicians only after a section of the capitalist class had already realized that some reforms were necessary to avoid more violent confrontations and prevent the rise of revolutionary movements.

Various traditional sociologists thus see social change originating in changes in individual attitudes and actions. An extreme example of this is seen in the psychological determinist view of student protest and social change taken by Lewis Feuer, which was discussed critically in Chapter 2. Radical sociologists, on the contrary, argue that sociologists cannot understand social change merely by looking at the immediate causes of change coming from new values or new psychological attitudes. Radical sociologists have emphasized the need to probe further to ask: Why do the values and attitudes themselves change? For the answers, we must look at prior changes in the socioeconomic base of society—though this is affected in turn by still earlier values and attitudes, as well as other institutional and economic changes. Only by examining society as an evolving organism, divided by class conflicts, do we reach a really dynamic analysis of social change.

At times, traditional sociologists and traditional political scientists continue to use static psychological or political models even when their subject matter is the process of social development itself. For example, some traditional sociologists and political scientists studying development have produced two static models that are contrasted to each other—such as the "negative" Afro-Asian dictatorship versus the "positive" Western democratic model. They provide little explanation of how development might proceed from one to the other, and few ideas about the historical prerequisites for one or the other.

Many sociologists studying economically "underdeveloped" societies tend to treat a small tribe or small area as a static and isolated society, ignoring its relations to the rest of the country or to the rest of the world. "Recent sociological theories . . . select small 'societies' in Africa and elsewhere for study and analyze them as though they had an isolated existence independent from the imperialist system of which they formed an integral part at the time of the study" (Frank, 1967, p. 34).

Another traditional theory claims that some countries do not develop and are "underdeveloped" because of psychological deficiencies. For example, the traditional economist Everett Hagen claims that oppressed, underdeveloped societies are "so persistent" because the people in these societies have personalities of the sort that find submissiveness satisfying (Hagen, 1966, p. 139). According to Hagen, the reason that Africans and Asians have difficulty in ridding themselves of reactionary ruling classes and dictators, such as the former Shah of Iran, is not the support of imperialism for these dictators; it is, rather, the fact—in his view—that these people are masochists, who like being ground into the dust by their exploiters. He thus avoids a dynamic analysis by relying on static "human nature." One of Hagen's "profound" suggestions for improving economic development is a psychoanalytic discussion called "Comments on Toilet Training" (Hagen, 1962, Appendix).

David McClelland (1961) also argues that economic growth and development derives basically from psychological dispositions. He contends that entrepreneurs—business people willing to take risks and expend much energy to achieve goals—have been largely responsible for economic growth in countries as different as the United States and the Soviet Union. For the Soviet Union, he emphasizes the importance of executives, instead of capitalist business leaders as such. So, for McClelland, it is the personal qualities of gifted individuals that account for broad social changes such as rapid economic development. Many different authors have taken McClelland to task for neglecting the specific historical situations and class relationships in which development (or lack of it) took place.

Using a purely psychological approach to socioeconomic development, McClelland claims that: "it is values, motives, or psychological forces that determine ultimately the rate of economic and social development" (quoted in Frank, 1967, p. 65). Since he is talking about Southeast Asia, one would think he might have at least mentioned the concentration of landholding by the ruling class, the hindrances of foreign imperialism, and other social and group relations. On the contrary, McClelland complains that most sociologists think that man is shaped by his environment; they even have the "incorrect" idea that "he must start by modifying material arrangements in the environment which in turn will gradually reshape institutions and eventually ideas" (ibid., p. 66).

McClelland himself believes that to accelerate economic growth we must concentrate on psychological factors. It is particularly necessary, he says, to decrease father dominance, convert people to the Protestant ethic, and reorganize the fantasy lives of people in the less developed countries. In other words, no socioeconomic revolution, no liberating struggle from imperialism, is needed. We need only preach Western values, tell the children more hero stories about en-

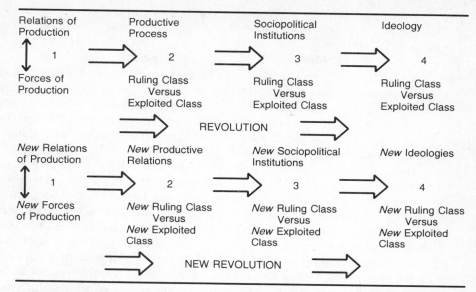

Figure 20.1 A picture of social change. The numbers mark the four levels of contradiction. The process is actually more complex than shown here, with each level of contradiction rebounding on the others. For example, ideological battles and the revolution itself usually appear to be merely a political-level phenomenon. Also, it is possible that someday a revolution will end class divisions, which will end this type of change.

trepreneurs, and gradually bring these "backward" peoples to the Western view of life. All of this psychologizing of change is weak on supporting empirical evidence and does not lead to an understanding of the socioeconomic barriers to social change.

A RADICAL MODEL OF SOCIAL CHANGE

Chapter 4 systematically listed the four most important contradictions, or tensions and conflicts, in the various societies so far recorded in history. In Figure 20.1, the four types of contradictions are shown as part of a simple picture of change. The process shown is continuous, so that the analysis must break in at some arbitrary point in the cycle of events.

The four types of contradictions discussed in Part One may be briefly restated as follows:

1. Frozen class relations versus new productive forces. This contradiction shows up, for example, in mass unemployment and depressions
2. Ruling class versus exploited class in the productive process. This contradiction is manifested, for example, in a strike
3. Ruling class versus exploited class in sociopolitical institutions. This contradiction is reflected, for example, in debates in Congress over health care for the poor

4. Ruling class versus exploited class in ideology. This contradiction is manifested, for example, in arguments between traditional and radical sociologists.

These different social contradictions are related to one another, and usually follow one another in a given order. Suppose we begin with the first contradiction, antiquated class relations holding back new productive forces. For example, in eighteenth-century France there was a considerable spread of new industry and commerce, yet the old feudal class relations imposed many restrictions on industry and commerce. Merchants could only trade in prescribed ways with certain countries, manufacturers were told exactly how they must produce goods (even how many threads per foot of fabric), and most of the labor force still had certain duties of serfdom and could not freely move to the cities.

This basic contradiction led to struggle (the second contradiction) over economic policy between the new bourgeois class, that is, the owners of industry and commerce, and the feudal landlords. This struggle was mainly fought out at the political level (the third contradiction), where it became a fight for control of political power in France. As the bourgeoisie became stronger and stronger—because of the growth of industry and commerce—they showed increasing political power.

The political struggles were reflected in a literary and ideological struggle (the fourth contradiction). In the realm of literature, writers like Voltaire and Rousseau attacked every aspect of the antiquated feudal monarchy; their writings constitute some of the greatest revolutionary prose ever written. As a result of this ideological onslaught (based on the changing socioeconomic conditions), many French people changed their consciousness from an acceptance of the feudal system as eternal to an active hostility to it.

Thousands of French people began to protest and to demand liberty, equality, and fraternity. Ultimately, the bourgeoisie—with the support of many peasants and urban workers—swept away the feudal system in the French Revolution of 1789. They established new class relations, with full economic and political power in the hands of the bourgeoisie, together with new laws and a new dominant ideology.

In terms of these same categories, any revolutionary change may be examined: from the bourgeois democratic revolutions of England and France to the socialist revolutions of Russia, China, and Cuba. It may be more useful, however, to examine in these terms an event closer to home in U.S. history—the American Civil War of the 1860s.

The Civil War resulted in a revolutionary change, the end of slavery in the United States. For the South the abolition of slavery was roughly equivalent to the end of feudalism in France through the French Revolution. The drastic nature of the changes that the South underwent is captured in the popular movie *Gone With the Wind*.

The northern states, of course, forced the revolutionary abolition of slavery through their victory over the South in the war. The interesting question is, What made the North go to war to abolish slavery in the South? One traditional explanation (that still finds great favor in the North) argues that the northern states adhered to a superior moral value system that forbade slavery. It may well be true that more northerners than southerners disagreed with the principle of slavery. But would this disagreement on purely moral grounds be enough to provoke a devastating civil war? We think not. Instead, we suggest it is necessary to examine contradictions in the productive processes that were emerging between the northern and southern states, in order to get a more complete understanding of the conditions that ultimately led to the Civil War.

The forces of production in the South consisted mainly of agricultural implements and slaves. The productive forces in the North included factories, machinery, and free workers. The main productive relations in the South were those between slaves and slaveowners, and in the North between the capitalists and the working classes, though there was also a large class of farmers in both areas. (Notice that a full sociological analysis of this period must include at least five different classes.)

The primary basis of conflict between North and South was the fact that the relations of slavery prevented the spread of the new productive forces of industrialization into the South, since industry requires a supply of free labor. Moreover, the southern slave owners even tried to prevent industrial productive forces from spreading to the West. This conflict was the first contradiction: the frozen class relations of the South versus new productive forces.

While the northen industrialists wished to limit or abolish slavery, there were also attempts by slaves to challenge or abolish it. In the South, even the friendliest observers admitted that a certain number of whippings and other punishments of slaves occurred each year on every plantation. To combat this, the slaves used slowdown tactics. Furthermore, they also launched many violent revolts that were put down with terror and bloodshed by the slave owners. These conflicts were examples of the second contradiction: class conflicts in the productive process.

Both of these contradictions were in turn reflected in struggles within many sociopolitical institutions. In the South, which was dominated by the slave owners, all institutions—the media, the state governments, the educational system, and the religious institutions—were overwhelmingly proslavery. In the North, because of the dominance of the capitalist classes, all institutions—the media, the state governments, the educational system, and the churches—favored the spread of capitalist industry and farming, as well as various degrees of restriction or abolition of slavery. The federal government was the arena of political conflict over the control of basic economic policies, including (1) the fight over whether tariffs should be placed on industrial goods (to help the North) or agricultural goods (to help the South), and (2) the fight over whether new states should be admitted as slave or free. This was the third contradiction: class conflict in sociopolitical institutions.

Finally, the ideology developed by southern preachers, journalists, and politicians was an elaborate defense of slavery, largely on racist grounds put in terms of divine providence. On the other hand, the abolitionist ideology, promoted by most northern preachers, journalists, and politicians on the eve of the Civil War, attacked slavery in the words of the democratic credo of the American Revolution, also phrased in terms of divine providence. This was the fourth contradiction: class conflict in ideology.

This fourth contradiction is the only one that parallels the traditional interpretation of the Civil War. However, even in this case, there is an important difference between our explanation and the traditional explanation. We argue that the southern ruling class developed a proslavery ideology that supported its productive system, whereas the northern ruling class developed an antislavery ideology that supported its productive system. The traditional approach focuses solely on the ideology of the North and the ideology of the South without analyzing the role of the productive systems in encouraging their differing ideologies.

Obviously, these four conflicts were not, in reality, neatly distinct from one another. They are, in fact, four aspects of one social process, a single conflict arbitrarily divided into four separate conflicts for convenience of analysis. We could easily divide the social process into many more specific conflicts. Or we could even speak of it as just one social-political-economic conflict. Moreover, the people of the Civil War period perceived these revolutionary forces not as four separate parallel conflicts but as one big conflict, with the two sides slowly edging toward war.

MUST REVOLUTIONARY SOCIAL CHANGE BE VIOLENT?

We have shown how basic social conflicts lead to revolutionary change, but we have not said that this change must be violent. As the word *revolution* means any basic, thoroughgoing change in society, it may be violent—as in the American Civil War—or it conceivably may be nonviolent. It is true that much revolutionary change in the past has been violent, but it does not have to be, as indicated by the Philippine revolution of 1986.

When Abraham Lincoln was elected, slavery could have been abolished peacefully by action of Congress and the president. That would have been a peaceful revolution. It was thwarted, however, by the force and violence used by the southern slave owners against the legitimately elected government of Lincoln.

Similarly, in 1970, when Chile elected a socialist president, Salvador Allende, that country might have followed a peaceful path to socialism. Instead, the Chilean capitalist class pushed the army—supported by the U.S. Central Intelligence Agency (CIA)—into an armed counterrevolution. They killed the president, jailed thousands of people, tortured many, and thwarted peaceful socialism.

Violence thus seems to arise mainly from the old ruling class's attempts to defend its vested interests against the majority interest. When American radicals call for socialism in the interests of the whole working class, they are speaking of a change that would benefit 80–90 percent of the people. Such a change may yet be voted by a majority. The question, then, is whether the ruling class will resort to violence to attack the legally elected government—as the southern ruling class did in the Civil War in the United States and as the Chilean ruling class did in Chile.

WHEN DOES THE PROCESS END?

Must this same process of change through class struggle continue forever? No, we hope and predict that the process will someday end. Radicals take no glee from class struggle and do not concede that it is eternal. Class struggles did not exist for 90–95 percent of human existence in primitive economies, according to all available anthropological data. In a future classless society, which socialists hope will be the end stage of socialism, there is no possibility of class struggles because there will be no classes. This does not mean that a classless society will be a static society without contradictions or change, but the contradictions will be very different. They will not include class struggle and will lead to change in new directions, mostly unpredictable at the present time.

SOME LESSONS OF DYNAMIC ANALYSIS

A few general lessons for social science may be summarized from the radical analysis of dynamic change. First of all, never assume that a social problem is static and unchanging. Always look to see if it is changing fast enough to be relevant to a dynamic social analysis. Ask the origins of the problem. Ask the direction and rate of present tendencies. "In other words, consider the subject matter in terms of its evolutionary path of development, and try to see it in relation to what it was and what it is likely to become" (Somerville, 1946, p. 209).

There is probably no major social issue in which past evolution could safely be excluded from the explanation. For example, in explaining the Watergate crisis and the impending impeachment of Nixon in the United States in 1974 or the Iran-*contra* scandal of 1987, it is impossible to merely consider the current facts of the crisis, even including the specific context of American politico-economic relations and institutions. A full explanation would have to include the past evolution of American constitutional traditions and laws, as well as the past evolution of its class relations and institutions. On the most obvious political level, one would need to stress the past history of struggles for democratic freedoms, particularly the repressive period of the 1950s and its deeper causes, the recovery of civil liberties in the 1960s and its causes, and the high points of political protest in the middle and late 1960s. All of these historical changes must be considered in order to understand some of the forces that brought down Nixon and that encouraged investigation into the Iran-*contra* scandal.

Most vital to understanding American civil liberties at each stage are our evolving class attitudes and relations as well as class interests in various democratic freedoms. Any historical example—such as Watergate—shows the need to examine not just change and evolution in general but especially the trends in the class conflicts within each social process. What is the relative strength of each class and each of the strata within the classes? Which elements are getting stronger and which are getting weaker? This analysis can aid us in predicting the path and the direction of change of each social process.

In contrast to traditional tendencies, radical sociologists are trying to make sociology more dynamic. Radical sociology studies the historical evolution of the basic institutions of society through past stages of class conflict. Because traditional sociologists are overly impressed by what appears stable and dominant in present society, they seldom dig deeper into new and opposing trends. Thus they usually believe major change to be unlikely, and are often surprised by even smaller social changes such as the wave of protests and new lifestyles of the 1960s, not to speak of more comprehensive revolutions. Of course, any historical vision must be based on consideration of present tendencies. We must identify which current social forces we expect to grow in the future.

SLOW, EVOLUTIONARY CHANGE AND SUDDEN, REVOLUTIONARY CHANGE

Evolutionary change can be viewed as slow, continuous, marginal, and incremental. For example, the rising percentage of women in the U.S. labor force is an evolutionary change. The rising percentage of all American manufacturing output controlled by the 100 largest firms is an evolutionary change. A steadily declining American birthrate is an evolutionary change.

Revolutionary change is not only basic change of the whole system of relations; it is also change that is relatively sudden and discontinuous. The industrial revolution in England changed England from an agricultural country to an industrial country within a few decades—which is sudden relative to the thousands of years of slow progress in agriculture, with only negligible industry. What is "sudden" is always relative to what came before; there is no absolute standard for distinguishing slow from sudden change. But it is clear that this change did lead to an entirely new set of economic and human relations in England. Similarly, the French Revolution was relatively sudden, creating a major discontinuity from the previous regime and leading to an entirely new set of human relations in France. Revolutionary changes in the twentieth century include the Russian, Chinese, and Cuban revolutions.

From our discussion of the model of social change, it should be clear that we recognize the need to study both evolutionary and revolutionary change. In each of the examples of revolutionary change we have discussed, very lengthy historical processes led to the revolutionary change. In each of the examples, there was a very slow evolutionary growth of tensions and conflicts over many decades or even centuries. The French bourgeoisie fought the feudal lords over two or three centuries. The Civil War in America did not come out of nowhere, but emerged as an ultimate end to a long process including slave revolts, growth of northern industry, economic expansion into the western states, slow growth of the abolitionist movement and the Republican party, and so forth. The lesson seems to be that each revolutionary change must be understood in terms of a long period of preceding evolutionary changes. On the other hand, each new process of evolutionary change must be understood on the basis of the fundamental framework established by the previous revolution.

To describe smaller, evolutionary changes, a purely quantitative analysis may be sufficient. A quantitative social analysis numerically measures changes in the level or amount of each social variable. A quantitative analysis furnishes us with a continuous statistical picture of evolutionary changes. To describe a revolution, however, a quantitative analysis is not sufficient, though it may be useful as one part of the analysis. Rather, what is needed is a qualitative analysis—that is, an examination of the change in the whole system of relations in the society. In other words, we must examine whole institutions and sudden changes in them, as well as the long, slow evolution leading to major changes.

To fully understand the French Revolution of 1789, it is not enough to look at immediate events such as the rise of bread prices in 1789. The more basic reasons must be discovered in the slow evolution of society before the precipitating events occurred. Once the social tensions had reached a certain critical level, any further "historical accident" might set it off. So the sociologists should examine the previous evolution quantitatively. Yet the revolutionary change itself can only be described in qualitative terms because it is sudden and discontinuous.

> The Russian Revolution shook the world in ten days, and the U.S. Constitution was hammered out in a few weeks. . . . The reason for the speed is that the change is prepared everywhere at once. Even though individual elements of reform seem weak . . . the older order finds itself overwhelmed. . . . (Platt, 1970, p. 4)

In every sense of social change, the two kinds of analyses are both necessary for a more complete explanation. On the one side, formal quantitative analyses of the slow evolutionary changes in the process are needed to determine precisely what has been and is going on. This analysis usually requires mathematical models and statistical estimation. In addition, however, one also needs qualitative, theoretical, or narrative kinds of analysis to predict the direction of the next jump to a new type and quality of social relations. Without the painstaking quantitative kind of analysis, one has no scientific basis for understanding. Without the qualitative analysis of possible institutional changes, however, the investigator will be lost in the labyrinth of detail and will fail to anticipate major changes.

PROBLEMS OF PREDICTION

Some critics ask: "Exactly what date will a revolution take place?" or "Exactly what point must the quantitative trends in social conflicts reach before there will be a revolution?" No sociologist, traditional or radical, can answer such questions in that detail because reality is much too complex. Radicals merely insist that sociologists should be encouraged to ask certain questions about evolution and revolution; they do not pretend to reach exact answers. There are two kinds of questions. If a revolutionary, qualitative change occurs, the sociologist should ask, What quantitative, evolutionary changes occurred in the previous period to cause the revolutionary change? If qualitative, evolutionary changes are observed over a long period, then one should ask, In what directions are they moving, what tensions are building, and what revolutionary, qualitative changes may result from those tensions?

An exact prediction of the timing of a revolutionary change, even on the basis of detailed research into quantitative evolutionary trends, is not possible for any sociologist at our present level of knowledge. The same problems of prediction exist to a more or less similar degree in many natural sciences. Geologists may find that a volcano is still active and will probably explode some day, but they cannot yet predict exactly when. Similarly, an investigation may reveal social contradictions, but there are so many variables, including many still only partially understood, that we cannot predict exactly when the society will explode. It is, however, a tremendous achievement to explain past explosions and predict the conditions under which future ones will occur, if not exactly when.

Since it is difficult enough to predict a revolutionary change—or the direction of the change or the forms of the transition—it is obviously wishful thinking to expect a prediction of the exact details of a future society before a major, qualitative change actually occurs. Entirely new relationships will engender entirely new quantitative trends, far beyond our ability to predict before the event, even if we have some idea of future patterns.

BACKWARDNESS AND UNEVEN DEVELOPMENT

Progress in social evolution does not mean movement toward some well-defined absolute goal, nor is it predetermined by God or history, nor does it move in a straight line. Evolutionary progress means only an increase in a society's adaptability to the environment, the destruction of the most poorly adapted types of societies, and the survival of the best-adapted social system. This understanding of the process of social destruction and development makes it much easier to understand the rise and fall of civilizations, especially how the "most advanced" may be suddenly overtaken by the "most backward."

In a way that is analogous to biological evolution, a society may evolve very specific and overspecialized institutions until it fits into a given niche in one environment. Just as the polar bear was beautifully adapted to the Arctic environment, so too was Eskimo society adapted to that environment and no other. Neither the polar bear nor the customs of Eskimo society could exist if the climate in their region suddenly became tropical. Obvious examples of frozen social relationships, well adapted to one period but increasingly obsolescent, include the ancient Roman Empire or the modern British Empire, both of which experienced decline and fall.

On the contrary, the less rigid, less specialized, and even backward economies may spurt forward to surpass the previously more advanced economies. The backward frontier society of the early nineteenth-century United States rose with incredible rapidity to the industrial forefront, as did Japan in the 1870s, Germany in the 1880s, and the Soviet Union in the 1930s. In fact, there almost never seems to be straight-line, or linear, evolution in which the most advanced country of one stage becomes the leader in the next stage. On the contrary, history usually produces a zigzag development that surprises many observers.

One sociologist who explored the potential power of "backwardness" was Thorstein Veblen. In his many writings on Germany, he showed how it had an advantage over England in the late nineteenth century because it did *not* have a vast amount of investment sunk in antiquated machinery. It could—and did—

begin from scratch to build, with the latest borrowed technology, a brand new industrial plant that eventually surpassed England's. Similarly, when Japan and Germany were defeated in World War II, with their manufacturing base largely destroyed, they were able to employ the latest technology so as to progress much faster than the victors in that war.

Another example of the process of uneven (zigzag) development came in the late feudal period. Until the sixteenth century, England was among the weakest areas in economic development. At that time, Italy, Belgium, and France were all more developed, but the very strength of their medieval institutions led to collaboration between some feudal lords and merchants. This strengthening of feudalism made further capitalist development most difficult. Thus, by the eighteenth and nineteenth centuries, British capitalism had moved far ahead of these other countries. In all of these cases, the more backward country moved ahead because it was less frozen into a specialized and "comfortable" set of relations.

EXTERNAL AND INTERNAL CONFLICTS

To explore the social process of change in a given phenomenon, such as a prison riot, the investigator should begin by examining its most basic relationships based on its own conflicts or tensions—that is, its internal *contradictions*. Since a prison riot does not materialize out of nowhere, a sociologist must look for the main grievances and conflicts between prisoners and jailers that led to the riot. These internal contradictions, however, only explain the riot as a dynamic process apart from the rest of the world. Yet it cannot be understood in isolation. The investigator must also examine its external surroundings, or environment, which constitute the *conditions* of its existence. A prison riot must be understood not only in terms of its own internal relations but also in terms of its relation to the society around it. A good sociologist will ask, for example, why a disproportionate percentage of prisoners are black and what the economic condition of American blacks is. This type of issue must be considered when understanding the broader picture of prison riots.

Of course, what is internal and external is always relative. What is external to one process is internal to a wider set of relationships. In fact, it is often misleading to speak of any individual unit, because all units, all phenomena, are so interconnected. For each different investigation the sociologist must decide the relevant limits of the phenomenon in order to focus on its main contradictions, but always keep other "external" relations in mind. Thus, where one theory of the economy keeps government action as an *external* factor, a more comprehensive politico-economic theory may put the relations between government and economy at the heart of the society's *internal* development. Government military spending, for example, is in part a result of lobbying by vested economic interests, but it in turn has a powerful impact on the economy.

Radical sociology urges us to try to explain social development at least partly as a result of internal conflict within social processes. Yet radical sociology does not deny that change can also be caused by interaction with other external phenomena within a larger social process. Only human society of the world as a whole has no external social relations, though it does have external relations with nature. Most social change must be viewed in the context of both internal and external causes. Thus, the internal evolution of countries is affected by interaction between them, including such actions as imperialism, invasion, or even friendly help. On the other hand, the internal evolution of each country tends to dictate what kinds of influences it is susceptible to incorporating from another country—including assimilation of new cultural values, economic invasion, or political domination.

It is fruitful to look at all social processes as linked and interacting (Vaillancourt, 1986). But to understand any given process of change, the sociologist must often isolate it, abstract it from its environment, and concentrate on its internal development. Only on the basis of that detailed knowledge of its functioning can we then analytically *reunite* it with its environment to understand its development in the real world of which it is a part. For example, the cultural anthropologist must first understand a particular tribe's own structure and behavior. Then the anthropologist must consider the tribe and its evolution in terms of its interaction with its near neighbors as well as its relations to distant countries.

SUMMARY

We have looked at major processes of social change in this chapter. In contract to traditional sociology, we have emphasized the role of class conflict as a major source of social change. The transition from feudalism to capitalism in France or from a slave society to a slaveless society in the southern United States did not occur without conflict. In fact, conflict—indeed, all-out warfare—was involved in these changes, as it is in many other significant social changes in history.

When one social system gives way to a different type of social system, vested interests in the older system are usually threatened. The threat to vested interests often brings about resistance to broad changes by the ruling class of the older system. This resistance, in turn, often sets the stage for conflicts that can ultimately result in social change.

For the sake of simplicity, we formalized this process into roughly four stages (though four is an arbitrary division). The four stages are:

1. tension between frozen class relations and expanding productive forces, as shown in economic crises of unemployment and inflation, which leads to
2. economic conflict between a ruling and an oppressed class, as shown in strikes, which leads to
3. political conflict between a ruling class and an oppressed class, as shown in protest marches, election struggles, civil wars, or revolutions, which leads to
4. ideological conflict between a ruling class and an oppressed class, as shown in propaganda in the newspapers, television, books, advertising, and other media.

And, of course, each of these levels reacts back upon the earlier, so the time ordering of them is often obscure. Moreover, in any given instance just one of these levels of conflict may be all-important while the others may be of less importance.

Social change can come about in an evolutionary or revolutionary fashion. Radicals point to the importance of examining the role of internal conflicts in generating either revolutionary or evolutionary change. This is not to deny the significance of external factors in producing change. Indeed, the impact of colonialism and imperialism of Western nations created great—and usually detrimental—changes in the social arrangements of countries in Africa, Asia, and Latin America. Nevertheless, it is important to begin an analysis of change by looking at the internal conflicts or contradictions in the "unit" of research interest (for example, an entire society like the United States). Once the main internal contradictions have been specified, it is then important to look at the external conditions of evolution or revolution. In all cases, radical methodology stresses that specific sources of change must be investigated through detailed empirical analysis.

APPENDIX: EVOLUTION AND REVOLUTION IN SCIENTIFIC RESEARCH

Thomas Kuhn has described the process of development of science in history. Kuhn begins by describing how scientists normally work within some general framework, called a *paradigm*, which is taken for granted for a long period. Newtonian physics would be one example in which physicists took Newton's general framework for granted, while working to extend it, to clarify some of the ambiguities left by Newton, to explain some new facts encountered, and to solve scientific puzzles arising from the attempts to fit new facts into the theory. Here we have the routine of smaller evolutionary advances within a given paradigm; the paradigm itself is not questioned. Kuhn puts it this way: "In so far as he is engaged in normal science, the research worker is a solver of puzzles, not a tester of paradigms" (Kuhn, 1962, p. 143). Thus the ordinary Newtonian physicist worked within the Newtonian paradigm, not questioning it, but assuming that his or her job was to amplify the details of that paradigm. Similarly, the traditional sociologist does not question his or her paradigm, but strives only to apply or extend it. He or she looks for new fields to conquer, but always within that framework.

The process of scientific development described by Kuhn is interesting because he discusses not only the slow, evolutionary advances made in scientific knowledge under a given paradigm, but also the major shifts to revolutionary or qualitatively new paradigms that occasionally occur in the history of science. He not only points out that the history of science is continuous and cumulative, but also demonstrates qualitative jumps at the introduction of a new paradigm. The contradiction, or tension, between the old paradigm and the facts of new discoveries—which cannot be explained by the old paradigm—impels the jump to a new paradigm.

Scientific fact and theory are not categorically separable, except perhaps within a single tradition of normal-science practice. That is why the unexpected discovery is

> not simply factual in its import and why the scientist's world is qualitatively transformed as well as quantitatively enriched by fundamental novelties of either fact or theory. (Ibid., p. 7)

He emphasizes the truly qualitative changes that may occur in a scientist's view, since "after a [scientific] revolution, scientists work in a different world" (ibid., p. 134).

Yet, he also emphasizes that the qualitative, revolutionary change in a paradigm does not occur without lengthy preparation and follow-up. The scientific revolution is not all accomplished at one time by one genius apart from the whole process of scientific development. The assimilation of a new paradigm is: "an intrinsically revolutionary process that is seldom completed by a single man and never overnight. No wonder historians have difficulty in dating precisely this extended process that their vocabulary impels them to view as an isolated event" (ibid., p. 7). Thus, on the one side, Kuhn attacks those analysts of the history of scientific thought who see only incremental, evolutionary advances and deny revolutionary leaps. On the other side, he attacks those analysts who see only revolutionary, qualitative leaps, and deny the quantitative process of development leading up to them.

Kuhn himself speaks of the parallelism between scientific and political revolutions:

> Political revolutions are inaugurated by a growing sense, often restricted to a segment of the political community, that existing institutions have ceased adequately to meet the problems posed by an environment that they have in part created. In much the same way, scientific revolutions are inaugurated by a growing sense, again often restricted to a narrow subdivision of the scientific community, that an existing paradigm has ceased to function adequately in the exploration of an aspect of nature to which that paradigm itself had previously led the way. (Ibid., p. 91)

The sense of malfunction—if it is objectively based—leads to a crisis and then to a revolution.

Kuhn's work is immensely useful both in itself as a guide to the dynamics of scientific progress and as an analogy to general social change. The prerevolutionary situation in a science could be described as an increasing contradiction between facts and theory, reflected in increasing tensions between two paradigms. The paradigm shift should be visualized as a revolutionary qualitative jump coming as the result of a long quantitative evolution.

Kuhn also describes the revolutionary conflict in the period just before a qualitative jump in science. He shows that the new interpretation is usually first voiced by a few individuals who have concentrated on those problems most difficult to answer under the old paradigm. "Usually, in addition, they are men so young or so new to the crisis-ridden field that practice has committed them less deeply than most of their contemporaries to the world view and rules determined by the old paradigm" (ibid., p. 143). Furthermore, Kuhn rightly points out that whereas science normally proceeds with little questioning of the validity of methodology, a revolutionary period is usually marked by deep conflicts over the "rules of the game." This follows from the fact that theories and methods are so closely tied together in the ruling paradigm; if the older methodology is challenged, this also can challenge the older theory, and vice versa. It is because of the ingrained strength of the old paradigm among scientists (and their immense intellectual investments in it) that a new paradigm is always preceded by conflict and crisis, and is often first enunciated by "amateur" outsiders and first accepted by younger scientists. All of these features characterize sociology, especially as related to the newer challenge of radical sociology.

Although Kuhn does a magnificent job of pointing out the inner contradictions of a scientific revolution, his sociological approach is very inadequate in that he overlooks the external relations linking science to the rest of society. As we have shown, links obviously exist between the development of social science and the development of society, but links to social development are also present in the history of the natural sciences. For example, Galileo had to contend not merely against a preceding paradigm but also against the overwhelming power of the Church. The Church fought against his subversive notions about the real shape and movements of the earth, not merely because of intellectual commitment to a theological dogma, but because that dogma was considered important to protect the Church's earthly power and vested interests. Moreover, the new paradigm emerged at that time not by accident but because the growth of commerce demanded better ships and navigation, which in turn depended on a greater knowledge of physics and astronomy. Furthermore, the new paradigm did not triumph only because Galileo gave better answers to puzzles. It also triumphed because it fit into the social changes of the entire Renaissance and Reformation, including the rising power of the bourgeoisie, with its concrete needs for better scientific knowledge.

In another period of important scientific advance, it has been shown that in seventeenth-century England socioeconomic needs were somewhat more influential than "pure science" in determining the selection of scientific problems to investigate (Merton, 1949). Similarly, the practical development of atomic power in the twentieth century did not occur out of pure scientific love of difficult puzzles, but out of the U.S. government's desire to develop a more potent weapon to win World War II. Thus the external conditions influencing science include (1) changing technological and economic conditions, and (2) the changing power of various interest groups. These same external conditions may affect the evolution (and revolutions) in sociological theories even more so than in the natural sciences because sociology is more directly associated with ideology and human relationships. As we have shown, ideology and human relationships are shaped by economic conditions and the power of interest groups.

SUGGESTED READINGS

Many of the books suggested in Chapters 2 and 4 contain discussion of social change by sociologists. In addition, a good general statement by an anthropologist is V. Gordon Childe's *Social Evolution* (London: Watts, 1951). A brief but excellent exposition of the Marxist view of social change is given by the historian Eric Hobsbawm in his introduction to Karl Marx, *Pre-Capitalist Economic Formations* (New York: International Publishers, 1964). A quite unique Marxist view of social change, emphasizing ideology and consciousness in political struggles, is Antonio Gramsci's *The Modern Prince and Other Writings* (New York: International Publishers, 1959). A fascinating radical view of the history of science is found in Samuel Lilley, *Men, Machines, and History* (New York: International Publishers, 1965). Also see the very scholarly J. D. Bernal, *Science in History*, 4 vols. (Cambridge, MA: MIT Press, 1971). For an excellent synthesis of Marxist principles of research, see Pauline Marie Vaillancourt, *When Marxists Do Research* (New York: Greenwood, 1986). For analyses of particular historical periods and changes, see the suggested readings for Chapter 21. Ivan Light has written an outstanding, comparative analysis of urban change, *Cities in World Perspective* (New York: Macmillan, 1983).

REFERENCES

Bachrach, Peter. 1971. *Political Elites in A Democracy*. New York: Atherton Press.
Davis, Kingsley. 1959. "The Myth of Functional Analysis as a Special Method in Sociology and Anthropology." *American Sociological Review* 24 (Dec.): 752–772.

Domhoff, G. William. 1969. "Where a Pluralist Goes Wrong." *Berkeley Journal of Sociology* 14:35–57.

Dewey, John. 1957. *Reconstruction in Philosophy*. Boston: Beacon Press.

Frank, Andre Gunder. 1967. "Sociology of Development." *Catalyst*, 2(3).

Hagen, Everett. 1962. *On the Theory of Social Change*. Homewood, IL: Dorsey.

———. 1966. "How Economic Growth Begins." In Jason Finkle and Richard Gable, eds., *Political Development and Social Change*. New York: Wiley.

Hodges, Harold. 1974. *Conflict and Consensus: An Introduction to Sociology*. New York: Harper & Row.

Horowitz, David. 1971. *Radical Sociology*. San Francisco: Harper & Row.

Kuhn, Thomas. 1962. *The Structure of Scientific Revolutions*. Chicago: University of Chicago Press.

McClelland, David. 1961. *The Achieving Society*. New York: Van Nostrand.

Merton, Robert K. 1949. *Social Theory and Social Structure*. London: Free Press.

Mitchell, Wesley. 1937. *Backward Art of Spending Money*. New York: McGraw-Hill.

Mills, C. Wright. 1959. *The Sociological Imagination*. New York: Grove Press.

Nisbet, Robert. 1973. *The Social Philosophers*. New York: Crowell.

Platt, John. 1970. "Hierarchial Growth." *Bulletin of the Atomic Scientists* 9(2).

Rose, Arnold. 1967. *The Power Structure*. New York: Oxford University Press.

Somerville, John. 1946. *Soviet Philosophy*. New York: Philosophical Library.

Smelser, Neil J. 1959. *Social Change in the Industrial Revolution*. Chicago: University of Chicago Press.

Tawney, R. H. 1954. *Religion and the Rise of Capitalism*. New York: New American Library.

Thompson, E. P. 1963. *The Making of the English Working Class*. New York: Pantheon.

Weber, Max. 1958. *The Protestant Ethic and the Spirit of Capitalism*. New York: Scribner.

Young, Nigel. 1967. "Prometheans or Troglodytes? The English Working Class and the Dialectics of Incorporation." *Berkeley Journal of Sociology* 12 (Summer).

Vaillancourt, Pauline Marie. 1986. *When Marxists Do Research*. New York: Greenwood.

chapter *21*

The Sociological Analysis of History

To understand modern American capitalism, it is necessary to have at least a rough understanding of the societies that preceded it. Radical social scientists classify as *primitive societies* those at the lowest technological level of productive forces, where productive relations are classless, with collective ownership and use of most goods. In some areas, primitive societies were followed by slave societies.

Slavery means private ownership of human beings. *Feudalism,* on the contrary, means that land and workers are controlled but not owned by the feudal landlord. The serfs are bound to the land and the king may transfer control of the land from one landlord to another, but the feudal landlord may not sell the serf or the land.

Under *capitalism,* capitalists buy and sell land, factories, equipment, and products, as well as buy workers' labor power. Yet capitalists may not buy and sell workers, as under slavery. Of course, slave owners and capitalists own all the products produced under their direction and may sell them for a profit in the market. Feudal lords owned the product produced on their own land but not that produced on the serf's land (though much of the serf's product might be owed to the landlord as rent).

Most radical and Marxist social scientists view the past history of society as an evolution from primitive societies (by many different paths) to capitalist societies—with the hope of a further evolution to socialism at some time in the future. The term *evolution* is defined here to mean the changes in society that have occurred through a series of roughly defined stages by the mechanisms of internal conflict, competition, and adaptation—which is similar to Darwin's definition of biological evolution.

The economic determinist view (sometimes *wrongly* thought to be Marx's view) is that human society must "inevitably" pass through certain preordained stages: primitive society, slavery, feudalism, capitalism, socialism, and communism. Thus the economic determinist view insists on a simple straight-line road of rigidly similar evolution in all societies. One Soviet writer takes this economic determinist view when he says: "All peoples travel what is basically the same path. . . . The development of society proceeds through the consecutive replacement, according to definite laws, of one socioeconomic formation by another" (Keiusinen, 1961, p. 153).

Many areas of the world, however, have not followed this exact progression. Moreover, the stages of society defined here are never met in pure form, and real societies always contain elements of other systems. Although it is useful insofar as it points to the fact of historical evolution, the economic determinist view of change turns out to be wrong on several grounds. Furthermore, "the general theory of historical materialism requires only that there should be a succession of modes of production, though not necessarily any particular modes, and perhaps not in any particular predetermined order" (Hobsbawm, 1964, p. 19).

The fullest, concrete Marxist study of the socioeconomic stages in early human history concludes from a lengthy study of archaeological and anthropological facts that "it is not in the least surprising that the development of societies observed in different parts of the Old World, to say nothing of the New, should exhibit divergence rather than parallelism. This conclusion does not invalidate the use of the term 'evolution' to describe social development" (Childe, 1951, p. 166). In fact, one can still use the analogy between social and organic evolution because "organic evolution is never represented pictorially by a bundle of parallel lines, but by a tree with branches all up the trunk and each branch bristling with twigs" (ibid.).

Radicals emphasize that there are many alternative evolutionary roads followed by human societies. Furthermore, some very specific *qualifications* to any general schema must be stressed, indicating that it is not continuous and not unilinear. First, evolution is used broadly here to include both slow, incremental change and sudden, revolutionary change, as discussed in the preceding chapter. Second, even similar stages of evolution will be found at very different times in different places. For example, civilization arose independently and by somewhat parallel evolution in China and in Peru, but at quite different times.

Third, there are cases of retrogression from a supposedly later to an earlier stage. The decline of the Roman Empire, for example, brought a real decline in knowledge, communication, and commerce over large areas. That decline was not overcome for several centuries.

Fourth, there are many complex time lags in the process, so changes are seldom uniform or complete. For example, although enormous slave plantations came to dominate ancient Roman agriculture, large numbers of small peasant farmers continued to fight for existence for centuries. Although a few hundred corporations dominate the U.S. economy, millions of small businesspeople and small farmers persist in trying to eke out an independent living.

Fifth, many of the politico-economic transformations in human history took place not only through the internal evolution of one society but through diffusion from a different society. *Diffusion* means that social relations, technologies, or ideas from one society come to another in many different ways, including conquest, colonialism, trade, and religious or political missionary work. The Roman Empire spread its mode of production and ideology over many previously primitive economies. In the medieval period the Europeans learned a great deal of the technology and culture from their trade relations with the Arabs.

Diffusion also opens the possibility for jumps over traditional evolutionary stages. Primitive as well as slave-type economies have jumped straight to capitalism through conquest or other contact, though colonial capitalism is usually a stagnant type of capitalism. Diffusion, however, may lead to backward jumps as well as progressive jumps. The primitive Mongol nomads under Genghis Khan brought destruction to numerous Asiatic civilizations.

Some writers are so impressed with the amount of diffusion that they think it replaces the internal evolutionary mechanism. The anthropologist Alfred Kroeber wrote: "The vast majority of cultural elements have been learned by each nation from *other* peoples past and present" (1923, p. 197). Even if we borrow much from other societies, however, *some* society had to do each thing the *first* time. Therefore, diffusion may be an important part of the evolutionary process, but it can in no way replace it. We must still understand the internal conflicts and contradictions leading to entirely new social structures for the first time—before these structures and institutions can be diffused around the world.

With all these qualifications, one can still speak of a process of social change through stages of evolution. Among *societies* there is a competitive process—like the Darwinian biological one—whereby the obsolete societies are destroyed and the fittest societies survive in the long run. That society will survive whose politico-economic relationships are best adapted to the fullest development of both the inanimate productive forces and the human productive forces. For example, the obsolete slave society of the American South perished, while the young and healthy northern capitalist industry survived and expanded rapidly. Unlike some economic determinists, however, *we* do *not* claim that there is an inevitable march of progress to "better" societies, an idea that originated with eighteenth-century liberalism. Progress though social evolution only means better adaptation or ability to survive under given conditions. For example, the ancient slave civilizations of Egypt, Greece, and Rome replaced earlier primitive economies thereby leading to vast economic expansion, but that certainly does *not* make slavery ethically better than primitive, tribal societies.

It might be thought that such an evolutionary framework, with all its qualifications, would be a truism to any reasonable sociologist. Yet one set of ideological commitments has led some economic determinists to speak of universal and unilinear evolution. A different set of ideological commitments has led some traditional sociologists to deny any validity to the concept of social evolution, believing that the status quo should and will exist indefinitely. In contrast to either position, we hold that a flexible approach to evolution is a useful way to comprehend social change.

The remainder of this chapter provides a brief synopsis of the sociological characteristics of the main social formations in human history. It also attempts to describe how major changes occurred from one society to another.

PRIMITIVE SOCIETIES

Primitive societies in the Old Stone Age, lasting for one or two million years, were very different from ours in basic ways. Not only were family structures different, but in the most primitive societies there was little or no evidence of class division and class repression. The characteristics of most areas of human settlement in our first million years or so may be listed as follows:

1. Very small communities that were quite isolated, self-sufficient, with little or no trade
2. No writing
3. A homogeneous group of people
4. No full-time specialists
5. The economic unit usually consisting of the large extended family of kin
6. Personal relationships and inherited status, rather than economic-based relationships and status
7. Few or no political institutions
8. Food obtained by hunting and fishing or gathering fruits and vegetables

A detailed study describes one contemporary primitive community where even today "there is no private property in productive goods, and whatever the hunting band manages to kill is shared out among the members of the group" (Nash, 1967, p. 3). In general, the most primitive societies have no market exchange, no money, and no economic competition in the modern sense. It is true that even the most primitive peoples known to anthropologists usually own their weapons, tools, and ornaments as individual private property, but the basic means of production at this stage are the hunting grounds, which are owned collectively.

The point cannot be overstressed that in primitive societies people are not hired for jobs, they are not paid money, and purely economic relations do not prevail in any area (nor is force used in most cases to achieve economic goals). Rather, "men work together because they are related to each other, or have social obligations to one another" (Forde and Douglas, 1967, p. 17). Furthermore, work is done collectively and the results shared collectively. One anthropologist writes that "with qualifications such as the special shares locally awarded for special contributions to the group endeavor—the principle remains . . . goods collectively produced are distributed through the collectivity" (Sahlins, 1965, p. 142).

Collective activity in primitive society is necessary because life is very insecure and on the margin of subsistence, so each person knows that his or her own life depends on his or her neighbors' cooperation and generosity. Moreover, the results of a hunt may come in all at once, and there is no way to preserve perishable goods in the primitive situation. Furthermore, any man or woman who is not generous and does not fulfill the traditional "voluntary" social obligations would eventually be left out of the tribe, to face almost certain death through inability to cope with the world alone.

THE TRANSITION TO CLASS SOCIETY

When civilization became established in the Middle East in the Bronze Age, beginning about 5000 years ago, it was marked by

1. Large-size communities
2. Taxes
3. Public works
4. Writing
5. Use of mathematics and astronomy
6. Internal and foreign trade
7. Full-time specialists such as farmers and metallurgists
8. Political organization beyond family or kinship
9. A privileged ruling class
10. An exploited class of workers.

This exploited class may have been slaves, feudal serfs, or peasants paying economic tribute. The key revolution, however, is the earlier transformation from hunting and gathering—which characterizes primitive societies—to animal herding and agriculture. Once this initial agricultural revolution has taken place, it may be argued that the coming of civilization (and class rule) depends merely on further quantitative increases in community size and economic productivity.

How did the agricultural revolution occur, how did it end the primitive classless societies of these areas, and how did it bring about class rule? We know that there was a slow expansion of knowledge and improvement of tools over hundreds of thousands of years. Then, in a few particularly fertile areas—more or less independently in China, the Middle East, Egypt, Mexico, and Peru—men discovered how to tame and breed animals, while women learned how to grow desired plants. This "revolution" did not occur in a momentary flash of insight by some individual; rather, it seems to have been a very gradual process over thousands of years (about 5000–7000 years ago).

Recent work presents a detailed picture of this process, based on the Middle East and the Aztec areas of Mexico. First, communities became more permanently settled, intensively collected food, and hunted in a given smaller area than previously. Second, the New Stone Age saw better tools being produced, including improved bows, drills, digging tools, and even boats and nets. Third, some crop that was already growing in the area—wheat for example—might be moved to different areas as desired. This crop was protected by removing any weeds, and eventually the seeds were selected so as to obtain the desired food characteristics. Similarly, hunters of goats or cows might begin to follow one particular herd, then protect it against its other enemies, and finally feed and shelter it at times. All these changes could take thousands of years.

Once the pastoral-agricultural revolution is well under way, several important changes occur as a direct result. The level of productivity per worker increases. The first consequence of this is a much higher population density. Herding and agriculture can support many people per square mile, whereas hunting and gathering require several square miles per person. At the same time, agriculture means that the population settles in one place rather than moving here and there around the country. Such large, settled agglomerations mean the founding of permanent villages and, eventually, towns and cities in the most favored places.

There is enough economic surplus over immediate needs that the economy may support various specialists, such as carpenters, shoemakers, and the like. Specialization, in turn, calls for exchange of products between individuals and between groups. When exchange becomes too complex for barter to be convenient, then money, the medium of exchange, rears its head. Moreover, the higher productivity makes available large amounts of "money" (commodities like cattle or gold) as well as consumer durables. Then, the specialization and exchange slowly destroy the *collective* use and possession of money and consumer durables, so some *individuals* come to own more wealth than others.

With this increase of private property, plus the larger, more permanently located groups of people, there is a need for a broader and stronger political structure to replace the family unit. At first, both in the possession of private property and in the control of political power, the families or clans retain the semblance of unity and direction. In the economy, however, individuals slowly accumulate more private property and specialists demand more private rewards. At the same time, individuals slowly accumulate more political power as politics grows more complex.

A war chief may be elected from time to time in small tribal conflicts; the post is likely to become permanent for a lifetime or even hereditary as larger armies come into being. The area and intensity of wars increase at this time, because wars for economic motives are used by advanced agricultural societies for the acquisition of cattle or slaves. Most large-scale introductions of slavery seem to follow as the effect of a war of conquest. Yet such wars of conquest and enslavement only occur when the technology is high enough that it is profitable to keep a slave. It is profitable to keep slaves *only* when a slave can produce a surplus above his or her own subsistence needs. Slavery and wars of conquest are thus intertwined as cause and effect at a certain level of economic evolution.

A similar increase of power may accrue to those in charge of public works. A director of irrigation for a small tribe may be appointed for a short time in one season; a director of irrigation for a large agricultural area along the Nile must be given more power for a lengthy period of time. Thus, in ancient Egypt, the government separates from and rises above family or clan for two different kinds of reasons: (1) to carry through public projects including irrigation and warfare, and (2) to guard private property, where property includes slaves, and to prevent slave revolts.

A higher product per worker—due to the first agricultural revolution—meant that a society could for the first time "afford" to have some nonworking individuals, such as slave owners, landlords, priests, and full-time warriors. Until the amount produced per worker passed the point where one worker could just keep himself alive, there could have been no surplus left for the ruling classes. Before then, slavery or serfdom could not pay—hence prisoners were simply killed or, in cannibalistic tribes, eaten. Many writers agree that

> among hunters and fishers the requirements of a nomadic existence render slavery rather unproductive; out of eighty-three hunting and fishing tribes examined by one student, in sixty-five there were no slaves. On the other hand, among agricultural tribes slavery tends to be productive and therefore more widely used. (Dahl and Lindbloom, 1953, p. 281)

We may conclude that most hunting and gathering societies did not hold slaves because their technology was too primitive for a slave to produce a surplus, while most agricultural societies had slaves because a slave could produce a surplus. But there were many exceptions. A few unusually well-off societies had some specialists and some slaves even before the agricultural revolution. Moreover, better agriculture did not immediately and automatically produce slavery; the process usually took centuries and its form depended on the consequences of war and conquest.

Furthermore, it is not so clear at exactly what level of productivity a slave can produce a surplus over basic necessities. Even in terms of food alone, the number of calories necessary to sustain life varies not only according to geographical elements, such as temperature, but also according to the type of activity an individual does. The necessary calorie consumption depends not only on the type of economic work done but also on other activities—such as dancing—which may be considered absolutely necessary for recreation or religion. So there is a marginal area of societies where it is not easy to say if they can produce a surplus or not, but most primitive societies clearly cannot produce a surplus over necessities, while all slave societies clearly do produce a surplus. Thus it is only in the very long run that we can say with certainty that the agricultural revolution leads to an economic surplus, which leads to the possibility of a profitable exploitation of slaves.

Finally, we might note that class rule was a useful or even necessary means to advance the level of technology and general culture far beyond what it had been. Primitive societies create neither pyramids nor vast irrigation projects—neither Plato's philosophy nor Euclid's geometry. It required exploitation of the many to give leisure time to a *few*. A much higher level of technology is required to have leisure time for *everyone* in a classless society. We now have the necessary technology, but we certainly do not have a classless society as yet; this would involve large changes in human relations and institutions, as we have previously indicated.

ALTERNATIVE PATHS OF SOCIAL EVOLUTION

Evidence on transformation from primitive societies to the classic type of slavery is mostly limited to Egypt; elsewhere evolution took different paths. Even Greek and Roman slavery seems to be explained in part by diffusion from Egypt. Going further afield, an independent evolution may be assumed for the Inca, Mayan, and Aztec areas of America. Information on these areas, however, is very limited; yet even that limited information shows great differences from the Middle East pattern, both in institutional and the technological developments.

Furthermore, in India and China and in the Middle East, although slavery does appear at some time after the agricultural revolution, it is *not* the predominant system in most of these areas. In the Middle East, it is true that "at the bottom of the social hierarchy were slaves, individuals who could be bought and sold" (Adams, 1965, p. 102). Still, the rest of the social hierarchy was very complex, including free craftsmen as well as priests, warriors, and several ranks of a nobility that might well be called "feudal." Moreover, it was the priesthood that was mainly in control in early times. The complex interaction of church and government in most of these early societies is a feature sometimes overlooked in the simplest class models.

In India, some researchers have found primitive societies of hunters and gatherers in the earliest remains. In the period following the agricultural revolution, however, there was only a small amount of slavery in India. Not only was the percentage in the total population very low, but almost all the slaves were either domestic servants or held by the royal family. India, from that time until well into the twentieth century, was mainly characterized by the caste system. In this system, each person's rank and occupation in society was fixed by birth as the same as that of their parents. Yet there was no slave caste; even the lowest caste was theoretically free (though with many restrictions) and was paid some pittance for its product or services. In the countryside, during most of Indian history, farmers were "free" men, owning their own product *except* for taxes, rents, and tributes, which left them very little income. Actually, the village commune usually owned or possessed the land rather than the individual farmer. Finally, above the village commune, any conquest by outsiders imposed a ruling hierarchy, which extracted tribute from the village.

In China, slavery existed only as a small part of the whole economy, and only from the Shang (1750–1125 B.C.) to the Ch'in dynasties (250–202 B.C.). The main economic basis for society in these dynasties was the peasant commune, which possessed its land in return for the payment of a tribute to the noble landowners. After the Ch'in dynasty, a very small amount of slavery continued up to the Yuan dynasty (A.D. 1271–1368). In the official history, the dominant system after the Ch'in dynasty is termed feudalism in view of the decentralized power of many provincial warlords. Nevertheless, the peasant commune and its tribute remained the most important economic base for a very long time. Even through the nineteenth century, the important role of the Chinese peasant commune and the large, extended family is reported by all observers.

In the light of the new facts on precapitalist societies revealed by archaeologists, anthropologists, and economic historians, a very heated debate has taken place concerning the classification of societies into the Marxist stages of history. One of the new trends is the revival of interest in what Marx called the *Asiatic mode of production*. Marx defined it as based in large part on the continued existence of communal property, with the entire tribe (or kin group) owing tribute in the form of goods or services to various ruling classes. Logically, the Asiatic mode might be viewed "merely" as a transitional form from primitive societies to slavery or to feudalism. Yet the facts show that this is a surprisingly stable economic model, lasting in some areas for thousands of years. Nevertheless, it also may have been a major source of economic stagnation for societies with a similar mode of production.

SLAVERY TO FEUDALISM IN WESTERN EUROPE

Slavery in the Roman Empire was eventually replaced by feudalism. In many other parts of the world, however, it now appears that an *alternative* path of evolution was followed, in which primitive societies *never* entered a slave phase but evolved directly to feudalism. The term feudalism, in fact, is now probably too loosely applied, since it has been used to cover contemporary northern Nigeria and parts of Latin America, as well as tsarist Russia up to 1867 and China up to 1911.

The discussion of feudalism in this chapter is mainly concerned with the unique case of medieval Europe. It is perhaps the best-known and best-researched case. Feudalism in this form may be defined by the following characteristics. An exploited class, the serfs, do all the agricultural labor. They usually work 200 or more days a year for the lord of the manor. They are bound to the land but may *not* be sold as slaves can be sold. In addition to their economic power, the landlords are also a political ruling class.

One famous historian, Henri Pirenne (1956), contends that medieval European economic development was determined *purely* by the operation of politico-economic forces *external* to that society. On the other hand, a few writers have seen the development of feudalism purely in terms of the *internal* evolution of European society based on conflicts within it. To illustrate the difference that a given approach makes, we can ask whether the Roman Empire fell (making way for the medieval world) because it crumbled away from within or whether it was toppled from the outside? The traditional view used to be that the empire was imply inundated in the fourth and fifth centuries by waves of Germanic barbarian invasions.

Pirenne argues that the Germanic invasions did *not* interrupt the basic socioeconomic continuity of the Roman Empire. He contends that agriculture in Western Europe in the fifth to seventh centuries still followed the Roman pattern. Furthermore, he claims that the Roman peasant, who was already tied to the land, simply became the serf of the medieval period. Pirenne declares that Western European commerce continued to thrive and that trade was brisk with the Byzantine Empire across the Mediterranean. Moreover, the Western Europeans still had a certain amount of industry, professional merchants still exported their products, and they even continued to issue as money the Roman *solidus* with the emperor's picture on it.

Pirenne finds that feudalism, defined as a fragmented political economy based on the independent land estate, did not begin until the end of the eighth century, the period of Charlemagne. In the eighth century, according to Pirenne, the Arabs suddenly burst into the Mediterranean, disrupted its commerce, and limited the Franks to a land empire. Only then, as trade declined, was there a tendency toward economic self-sufficiency on the estate of each feudal lord, followed by political disintegration of the central authority in the face of decentralized landlord power.

Invasions by the Germans and Arabs, as well as the Slavs, Vikings, and Huns, surely were the catalyst that finally ended the Roman politico-economic entity. Marxists maintain, however, that the underlying process of disintegration began in noticeable degree by the second century, long before the Arab invasion. The Roman *latifundia* (great estates) had almost entirely eliminated the independent peasant through competition based on cheap slave labor. The absentee slave owners let techniques stagnate, while the slaves often revolted or destroyed machinery. Because of slavery, only the crudest implements and simple one-crop systems could be used. The result was the exhaustion of the land, and the disappearance of the military reservoir of peasant soldiers. Similarly, slave labor in industry meant that it was unprofitable to use complicated machinery, so the benefits of large-scale enterprise were largely lost to the Romans. Since there was little use of large, specialized machinery, and since transport costs were very high, there developed a strong tendency for industry to decentralize out to the frontiers. Therefore, by the fourth century, except for a few luxury goods, trade had declined from international to regional and finally local commerce.

Feudalism, or serfdom, began to evolve through several paths long before the main barbarian invasions. Whereas the slave was owned in body, the serf was merely bound to a landed estate, to which he owed services or a share of his produce. The slave was often emancipated into a serf in order to obtain more efficient production and more secure military support. Sometimes, the free Roman peasant was "persuaded" to become a serf in order to be protected by a powerful landlord from imperial taxes as well as against barbarian plunderers. On another path, some of the Germanic tribal members were reduced to serfdom through long reliance on their tribal chiefs for protection and leadership.

While Pirenne dates feudalism from the end of the eighth century, most Marxists place its beginning in approximately the fifth century. The fifth century was already characterized by self-sufficient estates run by serf labor, a minimum of industry, a balance of trade unfavorable to Europe, and an absence of the formation of new cities. Contrary to Pirenne, most historians argue that Mediterranean trade was thoroughly disrupted by the fifth century. Moreover, it was the strength of local landlord estates and the self-sufficient, decentralized character of production that—long before the Arab invasions—caused both the decline of international trade and the fall in payment of land taxes to the royal treasury.

In the case of Western Europe we may conclude that the transition from slavery to feudalism resulted from internal evolution in that area plus the impact of external events (such as the Germanic and Arabic invasions). There is a continuing debate on the *quantitative importance* of the internal decline of Rome due to slavery versus the impact of invasions and other external events. At any rate, internal and external factors determined together the beginnings of the feudal system, which lasted over a thousand years in Europe until the rise of capitalism.

THE RISE OF CAPITALISM

Capitalism may be defined as an economic system in which one class of individuals called capitalists own the means of production. These means of production are capital goods, such as factories and machinery. The capitalists hire another class of individuals who own nothing productive but their labor power; this class is called workers. The capitalists engage in production and sales in order to make private profit. A classic definition says that the capitalist economy is an exchange economy

> with private ownership of the means of production, to which the further sociological datum is added that the population is divided into two parts, one of which owns the means of production while the other part, owning no means of production, is compelled to work as wage earners. (Lange, 1935, p. 201)

In *The Protestant Ethic and the Spirit of Capitalism,* written in 1904–1905 and focusing on Europe and America, Max Weber stressed the rise of the Protestant work ethic as an important factor leading to capitalism. The type of capitalism Weber analyzed was of rather recent origin. This was "rational bourgeois capitalism" that developed in the seventeenth to nineteenth centuries. As Parsons says:

> For understandable reasons [Weber], like others, emphasized profit-making business enterprise, but he was careful to point out that it was not orientation to profit alone which was the crucial criterion, but such orientation in the context of careful, systematic rational planning and discipline, which connected profitmaking with "bureaucratic" organization of the economy and with high technology which eventually, for the most part after he wrote, developed a scientific base. (Parsons, 1958)

So this was not simply the profit motive, nor was it even the mercantile capitalism that had existed some centuries before. It was a new type of "rationalistic" profitmaking—which Weber felt was peculiar to the West—that was the focus of his attention in *The Protestant Ethic and the Spirit of Capitalism.*

Weber argued that the new Protestant ethic declared a dedication to hard work and individualism. As such, it helped legitimize profit making and interest income. This new ideology undoubtedly did help create a favorable climate for capitalism. The new ethic replaced the medieval ethics that had been supportive of feudalism. The medieval ethics had emphasized otherwordly goals, prayer and meditation, and had prohibited all interest on loans—which was considered the sin of usury. Nevertheless, a religious explanation of the rise of capitalism is far from complete. Like all such explanations based on changes in ideas, it leaves us asking: Where did the new religious ideas come from? Weber has been criticized on that score by numerous writers, such as R.H. Tawney (1954).

Weber, however, did not exclusively rely on a religious explanation of the origin of capitalism as is sometimes thought. Instead, in books such as *Economy and Society,* he tried to show how Protestant religion, together with other more or less distinctive Western institutions such as the nuclear family, the occidental city, and modern bureaucracy, combined to explain the development of capitalism in the West. His explanation is therefore not incorrect but still needs to be supplemented by a description of the development of the productive forces and class relations of late medieval Europe to explain where the new ethics and new institutions originated.

The upswing in European agriculture and industry beginning in the eleventh century was caused primarily by the cumulative effect of new inventions that made more animal, water, and windpower available. The earliest important innovations were better plows, better yokes on horses, and better systems of crop rotation—and eventually water wheels and other new energy sources. These technological improvements themselves resulted from the insufficient supply of labor, which motivated the landlords to find substitutes for human labor. It also resulted from the fact that Western European feudalism gave the serf far more reason for initiative—both in making and in using inventions—than was allowed the peasant by eastern forms of serfdom and slavery. The remnants of slavery were, in fact, ended about this time because the new methods made it more profitable to use serfs or even free labor.

Local trade was stimulated by the improved agricultural productivity that made available a surplus for the local market of both food and artisan-made goods. It was from this local trade that the cities arose, more money came into use, goods began to be traded at greater distances, and industry started to be concentrated in the towns.

The improvements in power and transportation made it profitable for the first time to concentrate industry and produce on a mass scale for a wide market (as had *not* been profitable even in the Roman Empire). Thus it is the industrial innovation that leads to wider commerce and a growing mercantile class. The new merchants were recruited from the mass of vagabonds, small itinerant merchants, and landless younger sons of peasants. They needed new trading posts as well as permanent commercial centers. They constructed large new residential areas, usually around old feudal centers, that became the towns of the later Middle Ages.

The use of money and the certainty of markets induced the landlords to begin to produce for the market and to collect money rents. Also, the feudal lords wanted more cash in order to buy the manufactured products and luxuries offered by the towns and the trade with the East. To some extent, the greater desire of the feudal lords for money rather than the serfs' services led to the emancipation of serfs and their transformation into rent-paying tenants.

Serfdom, however, did not disappear in simple proportion to the widening market. In the twelfth century there was increased industrial productivity, which created a larger marketable surplus and thereby stimulated commercial activity. This led to the greater use of money, resulting in some switch from the feudal services by serfs to the use of money rents.

In the thirteenth and early fourteenth centuries, however, there was a feudal reaction. The increase in profit from marketing in the growing urban areas caused the greater feudal lords to demand more produce from the serfs. By working the serfs harder, they tried to obtain more output in order to make more profits. The widespread peasant revolts of the thirteenth and fourteenth centuries were not designed to end traditional serf-landlord relationships, but to prevent the imposition of new, *additional* feudal burdens and to prevent the feudal lords' attempts to increase the exploitation of the serfs. Thus, most peasant revolts of this period were attempts to defend traditional rights, not attempts to overthrow feudalism. Feudalism was finally overthrown in France and England in revolutions led by the bourgeoisie and supported by the peasants, when the bourgeoisie found that feudal restrictions got in the way of *their* own growing commercial and industrial power.

TWO ROADS TO CAPITALISM

We have traced the new forces of production, reflected in increasing industrial production and a widening sphere of trade and commerce. Ultimately, capitalism resulted from the interplay of these new forces of production and the older class relations. The capitalist system came into full control, however, in two very different ways in different parts of the world.

In Japan and Prussia (and most of Eastern Europe) the big merchants and the biggest landlords themselves became the owners of industry. The merchants and landlords did *not* try to destroy the feudal system, but sought to bolster the status quo by keeping all industrial growth in their own hands. Moreover, as soon as the merchant accumulated some wealth, he bought land and married into the landowning class. Thus, in these areas there was very little of an independent capitalist class. As a result, monarchist and feudal forms continued right into the twentieth century. There was no clear bourgeois revolution and capitalist forms developed very slowly for a long time.

In Britain and France, on the other hand, a far more revolutionary road was taken in economic and political development. There, the new forces of production came into the hands of small craftsmen, who became capitalist factory owners. There was far less intermarriage and far more conflict between capitalists and landlords, with the merchants favoring now one and now the other according to circumstances. In these areas, we may briefly review the four types of contradictions discussed in Chapter 20 to see how they led to revolutions.

The first contradiction lay in the fact that the new industrial and commercial forces of production did not fit easily with the old feudal class relations. Feudalism included prohibitions on movement of the serfs to the cities and strict regulations of trade and industry. During the sixteenth to eighteenth centuries, the second level of socioeconomic contradiction was apparent in class struggles between serfs and landlords, between capitalists and the newly formed working class, and most of all between the aristocratic landlords and the rising capitalist class of merchants and industrialists. At the third level of contradiction—political struggle—the capitalists also fought against the feudal nobility for a larger share of the economic spoils and the political power.

These class struggles were reflected at another level of social contradiction in ideological battles. The old regimes used the full weight of feudal ideology, especially as put forward by the church, to support their legitimacy and their God-given rights to rule. They claimed that it was natural and divinely ordained that some people should work while others should rule. On the contrary, the growing bourgeoisie—capitalist industrialists, merchants, and master craftsmen—slowly evolved their own ideology of the divine rights of every man to liberty, equality, and fraternity. This ideology of bourgeois democracy was put forth by writers like Locke, Rousseau, and Voltaire and was reflected in the French Rights of Man and the American Declaration of Independence.

After the bourgeoisie gained political power through revolutions, their ideology became dominant. They then swept away the last vestiges of the old feudal relations of production, ending serfdom to create a "free" labor force, ending feudal land possession in favor of enclosed private farms, and ending all restrictions on commerce and industry. As a result of these new class relations (and their legal reflections), the productive forces threw off the feudal chains and bounded ahead in what we call the Industrial Revolution. Eventually, this would lead to new contradictions, new class conflicts, and new revolutionary attempts to overthrow capitalism.

CHANGE IN THE INDUSTRIAL REVOLUTION

Smelser (1959) employs the theoretical framework of Talcott Parsons to help explain changes in technology, the working-class family, and trade unions in industrializing Britain. Using Parsons's scheme of the four functional problems of every social system, Smelser shows that the developing capitalist system in England put pressure on the working-class family to change its social structure. In the mid-eighteenth century—just before the development of modern capitalism around 1760—the typical textile family in England was also an economically productive unit. The mother, father, and children engaged in weaving as an occupation. Even though there was some division of tasks in this family structure (the father usually wove, and the women and children spun cloth), it was a relatively undifferentiated social system in which each member did similar tasks. Thus, the father not only engaged in the production of cloth, but he also helped bring up his children. For example, various fathers helped train their children for the skills of the weaving trade.

All of this began to change under the pressures exerted by early capitalism. Capitalism required that laborers work in factories away from the weaver's household. Between 1770 and 1845, many such families migrated to the cities, where factories were expanding greatly. The ultimate result was the separation of the family from the productive process. The adult male no longer worked at home, but was employed in the factory. After the Factory Acts of the 1840s prohibited certain kinds of child labor and imposed some safety standards, there was less participation of women and children in the factory. Most women and children remained at home, away from production. In short, we see the beginnings of the modern nuclear family as a response to the functional needs of the new capitalist system in England.

The transition from the earlier family working all together to the modern working-class family system, with very different roles for mother and father, was not smooth. In fact, within a functionalist perspective, Smelser explains a series of conflicts that occurred due to these pressures on the family division of labor. In particular, he argues that the working-class family did not easily accept the changes demanded by the capitalist system. The father still wanted to bring up his children and not be separated from them. This was exacerbated by the institution of child labor (and labor by the wife). At certain periods, child and female labor were preferred over male labor. Smelser argues that many of the industrial protests that occurred between 1770 and 1845 could be understood as a rebellion by the family against capitalist demands to change the family structure. Smelser's analysis thus adds a new emphasis on the family to traditional explanations of social change and conflict in industrializing England.

In addition, a Marxist writer, E. P. Thompson (1963), extensively depicts the role of exploitation and class conflicts in analyzing change in Britain. At the heart of Thompson's analysis is the fact that workers labored long hours (often 13 to 14 a day), under difficult conditions and for very low wages, to make a product, much of the value of which was taken by the capitalist in the form of profit. This extraction of profits from the worker is, of course, called *exploitation*, and Thompson shows in dramatic detail how it led to violent conflicts that molded the outlook of workers into a consciousness of their class position. Finally, he shows how the workers' struggles and changing attitudes led them to organize and to begin to grope for more radical solutions. In the twentieth century, similar struggles by the workers' movement have led to revolutions in some countries and electoral battles in other countries to end capitalism and form a new, democratic, socialist society.

SUMMARY

In this chapter we have applied concepts from radical sociology to analyze the development of various broad types of society, such as primitive society, feudalism, and capitalism. A dogmatic Marxist approach sometimes focuses on a few "fixed" stages of social development through which all societies presumably must pass. Recent Marxist analyses, on the contrary, have shown that social development is often more complex than a simple transition from, for example, primitive society to slavery to feudalism to capitalism. Instead, alternative paths of social evolution have been emphasized, with the introduction—or reintroduction—of such concepts as the Asiatic mode of production where appropriate.

Similarly, we have seen the ability of the radical approach to analyze such important historic events as the fall of the Roman Empire and the development of capitalism in Britain. With regard to each of these historical events, as well as the analysis of social development in general, we have shown the utility of a flexible radical, or Marxist, analysis.

SUGGESTED READINGS

In order to get a feel of everyday life in primitive societies, with their very different attitudes and behaviors from our own, it is best to begin with the thought-provoking books of Margaret Mead, such as her *Sex and Temperament in Three Primitive Societies* (New York: Dell,

1935, 1971). Another delightful book by a social anthropologist, which amusingly destroys some traditional theories, is Marvin Harris, *Cows, Pigs, Wars and Witches* (New York: Random House, 1974). A very important book is Rayna Reiter, ed., *Toward An Anthropology of Women* (New York: Monthly Review Press, 1975). For the overall radical approach, see Maurice Bloch, ed., *Marxist Analyses and Social Anthropology* (Berkeley: University of California Press, 1975).

On ancient slavery, see Frank W. Walbank, *The Awful Revolution: The Decline of the Roman Empire in the West* (University of Toronto Press, 1969). On slavery in the American South, see Eugene Genovese, *The Political Economy of Slavery* (New York: Pantheon, 1965). For day-to-day life under southern slavery, read Eugene Genovese, *Roll Jordan Roll* (New York: Pantheon, 1976).

On feudalism, see Marion Gibbs, *Feudal Order* (New York: Abelard-Schuman, 1953), and Marc Bloch, *Feudal Society* (Chicago: University of Chicago Press, 1961). For the lives of ordinary people under feudalism, see Eileen Power, *Medieval People* (New York: Barnes & Noble, 1924, 1963).

The best single book on the rise of capitalism is Maurice Dobb, *Studies in the Development of Capitalism* (London: Routledge, 1946). A fascinating and enlightening debate among Marxists is found in Rodney Hilton, ed., *The Transition from Feudalism to Capitalism* (London: New Left Books, 1975). The lives and attitudes of workers in the industrial revolution are portrayed in E. P. Thompson, *The Making of the English Working Class* (New York: Pantheon, 1963). A major functional analysis of change in Britain is Neil J. Smelser's *Social Change in the Industrial Revolution* (Chicago: University of Chicago Press, 1959). The most charming radical history of the United States is Leo Huberman's *We, The People* (New York: Monthly Review Press, 1970). Of the many other powerful radical books on American history, there is only space to mention Phillip Foner's *History of Labor in the United States,* 4 vols. (New York: International Publishers, 1947–1960). For informative discussions of historical-comparative methodology, see Theda Skocpol, ed., *Vision and Method in Historical Sociology* (Cambridge, UK: Cambridge University Press, 1984), and Neil J. Smelser, *Comparative Methods in the Social Sciences* (Englewood Cliffs, NJ: Prentice-Hall, 1976). A very good example of historical sociology is Perry Anderson's *Passages from Antiquity to Feudalism* (London: New Left Books, 1974).

REFERENCES

Adams, Robert M. 1965. *The Evolution of Urban Society*. Chicago: Aldine.

Childe, V. Gordon. 1951. *Social Evolution*. London: Watts.

Dahl, R. A., and C. E. Lindbloom. 1953. *Politics, Economics, and Welfare*. New York: Harper & Row.

Forde, Daryll, and Mary Douglas. 1967. "Primitive Economics." In George Dalton, ed., *Tribal and Peasant Economies*. Garden City, NY: Natural History Press.

Hobsbawm, Eric. 1964. Introduction to Karl Marx, *Pre-Capitalist Economic Formations*. New York: International Publishers.

Keiusinen, Otto. 1961. *Fundamentals of Marxism-Leninism*. London: Laurence and Wishart.

Kroeber, Alfred. 1923. *Anthropology*. New York: Harcourt Brace Jovanovich.

Lange, Oscar. 1935. "Marxian Economics and Modern Economic Theory." *Review of Economic Studies* 2.

Nash, Manning. 1967. "Organization of Economic Life." In George Dalton, ed., *Tribal and Peasant Economies*. Garden City, NY: Natural History Press.

Parsons, Talcott. 1958. Preface to New Edition, in Max Weber, *The Protestant Ethic and the Spirit of Capitalism*. New York: Scribner.

Pirenne, Henri. 1939. *Mohammed and Charlemagne*. London: Allen & Unwin.

Sahlins, Marshall D. 1965. "On the Sociology of Primitive Exchange." In Michael Bantom, ed., *The Relevance of Models for Social Anthropology*. New York: Praeger.

Smelser, Neil J. 1959. *Social Change in the Industrial Revolution*. Chicago: University of Chicago Press.

Tawney, R. H. 1954. *Religion and the Rise of Capitalism*. New York: New American Library.

Thompson, E. P. 1963. *The Making of the English Working Class*. New York: Pantheon.

Weber, Max. 1958. *The Protestant Ethic and the Spirit of Capitalism*. New York: Scribner.

Name Index

Subject Index